D0848061

Contemporary Philosophy in Scandinavia

Contemporary Philosophy in Scandinavia

Edited by Raymond E. Olson
and Anthony M. Paul

Introduction by G. H. von Wright

THE JOHNS HOPKINS PRESS
Baltimore and London

The Johns Hopkins Press, Baltimore, Maryland 21218
The Johns Hopkins Press Ltd., London

Library of Congress Catalog Card Number 70-148242
International Standard Book Number 0-8018-1315-8

For Brenda, Cynthia, and Mark

Preface

In the past thirty years there has been a considerable affinity between Anglo-American and Scandinavian philosophy. Scandinavian philosophers often lecture in British and American universities, and a recent collection of philosophical papers in English or volume of an English language philosophical periodical is quite likely to contain papers by Scandinavians. Yet there has heretofore been no book in English that provided a broad representation of the current philosophical activity in Denmark, Finland, Norway, and Sweden (as is usual in the literature, Finnish philosophy is here treated as Scandinavian). Raymond E. Olson, an American philosopher of Swedish and Norwegian descent who taught for many years at Miami University in Ohio, was by background and inclination especially equipped to assemble such a book.

In 1966 Professor Olson conceived the idea of seeking manuscripts from a number of established or promising young philosophers from the Scandinavian countries, and publishing them together with a general introduction to the philosophical traditions surrounding them. In 1967 the Johns Hopkins Press agreed to publish the volume, and by March of 1969 all of the contributors had been invited to participate and all but a few of their manuscripts had been received. Then, tragically, Ray Olson died. He has been well memorialized elsewhere; I would simply record in this, his last academic project, that those who knew him knew him to be the most conscientious of teachers and the kindest of men.

Upon his death, all who were interested in the project—the Press, the contributors, the American Philosophical Association, and his colleagues at Miami University—were concerned that it be seen through to completion. As a friend of Ray's at Miami and a fellow graduate of Johns Hopkins, I was especially interested in the book's progress, and the Press invited me to continue his work. It has been a privilege for me to serve his memory in this way.

In a project of this size and complexity, there are a number of explanations to tender and a number of thanks to express. Certain conventions in format and punctuation (in particular, the use of quotation marks) have been imposed by the editors for the sake of uniformity. I must especially express our regret that more authors could not be included here. In each Scandinavian country there certainly are other philosophers who fully deserve inclusion in this volume. Several of these were asked to contribute, but declined. Others have not been included simply because space limitations have required us to confine the book, somewhat arbitrarily, to Professor Olson's original list of candidates.

The contributors have been admirably forbearing. Since 1969 they have patiently endured the delays occasioned by Olson's death and by my own academic schedule. We originally intended to present only previously unpublished papers, but that plan has now proven unfeasible. We are grateful to the publishers of the five previously published papers for permitting us to include them here.

Moral support and editorial advice have come from several sources. Ray's widow, Brenda, graciously provided materials, information, and her blessing. Other friends from Miami, especially Robert and Peggy Harris, have helped in every way possible. Maurice Mandelbaum, Chairman of the Board of Officers of the American Philosophical Association, and Lewis White Beck have supported the project from the very beginning, and the Association itself, through its Committee on Publications, aided and encouraged publication by means of a generous grant which defrayed some of the editorial expenses and enabled us to offer each contributor an honorarium. Without this help the project could not have been successfully undertaken.

I am especially grateful to Jaakko Hintikka. After Professor Olson's death he agreed to act as a consultant, and he has unstintingly provided a great deal of indispensable advice. He is not responsible for the selection of contributors or, of course, for any infelicities that may have escaped me despite his help. I also wish to thank G. H. von Wright who, responding promptly to my somewhat belated request, has considerably enhanced the book with his compact but comprehensive introductory survey of recent Scandinavian philosophy.

Finally, members of the staff of The Johns Hopkins Press have been most helpful, especially Carol Lee Zimmerman. From a collection of manuscripts that were exceedingly diverse in style and condition, her care and patience have produced what we hope will be found a readable and worthwhile book.

A. M. P.

Contents

Contemporary Philosophy in Scandinavia

G. H. von Wright

Introduction

1

It is not without trepidation that I have yielded to the editor's kind request that I write an introduction to this anthology of contemporary philosophy in Scandinavia. I have tried to survey the present situation in philosophy in Denmark, Finland, Norway, and Sweden against the background of its evolution from roughly the time of the Napoleonic wars. Although the field is neither very broad nor very rich, it is doubtful whether one man can claim to master it completely. The Danish contributors to this volume are most probably better qualified than I to evaluate the situation, past and present, in Danish philosophy. The same, *mutatis mutandis*, holds true for the contributors from Norway and Sweden. Perhaps some other contributor from Finland would have presented developments in that country rather differently. By its very nature an evaluation is subjective, and a survey, since it must be selective, will be evaluative. So the reader must be warned not to attach undue authority to *my* introduction to this book.

2

For obvious historical and geographical reasons the Nordic countries have not been a fountainhead of new developments in philosophy. Their role has largely been that of recipients of ideas and currents of thought that have originated elsewhere. Denmark, geographically a part of middle Europe, has probably been most alert in registering what was going on in the major centers of culture. This country has therefore often been the gateway through which new ideas have

The names of all contributors to this volume are followed by an asterisk (*).

The author is indebted to Mr. Olay Flo of Bergen for various biographical and bibliographical data used in writing this introduction.

penetrated to the North. Sweden, with its shielded position in the heart of Scandinavia, exhibits a more distinctly national profile in philosophy than its three neighbors. This may be considered both a strength and a weakness. Swedish philosophy strikes me as having been in some ways more 'original' but in certain respects also more 'provincial' than philosophy in the rest of Scandinavia. Finally, the history of thought in Norway and Finland is marked by the political past of these countries. For several hundred years, Norway was a part of Denmark, but in the nineteenth century it came to be politically united with Sweden. Finland became an autonomous grand duchy under Russia in the nineteenth century after having been a part of the kingdom of Sweden for some six hundred years. The full political independence of Norway and Finland dates from this century. They are the 'new' countries in Scandinavia, and are rather heavily dependent upon their cultural inheritance from the Scandinavian neighbors with whom they were formerly united. For some reason, perhaps accidental, they also appear to be the two countries in Scandinavia that are most avant-garde in philosophy at present.

3

Throughout the nineteenth century, philosophy in Scandinavia was dominated by a strong German influence. Kant had followers in all of the four countries and was much studied during the whole period. Schelling and other romantic philosophers also made an impact on literature and natural science (*'Naturphilosophie'*) during the first two or three decades of the century. By far the greatest influence, however, was that of Hegel.

In Denmark the philosophy of Hegel was first championed by J. L. Heiberg, famed also as a writer and literary critic. After the mid-century Hans Brøchner was an influential representative of the neo-Hegelian movement of the 'left' and of a philosophy of religion in the spirit of Feuerbach and Strauss. A pupil of Brøchner's was the brilliant literary critic and historian of ideas, Georg Brandes, whose 'radicalism' became a major cultural influence in all the Nordic countries in the last three decades of the nineteenth century.

By far the most interesting reaction in Denmark to Hegel and to 'system philosophy' generally was that of Søren Kierkegaard (1813–55). He is one of the most original minds Scandinavia has produced and his impact on world literature is probably deeper than that of any other Scandinavian. His influence, however, has been stronger in theology than in philosophy proper. Kierkegaard scholarship has become an established tradition among Danish philosophers, but Kierkegaard as a forerunner of Nietzsche or of contemporary existentialism has not much influenced philosophy as an academic subject in Denmark or the other Scandinavian countries.[1]

---

[1] See also the paper by Johannes Sløk in this volume.

In Norway the supremacy of Hegelianism was more thorough and longer lasting than in any other Scandinavian country. Here, too, as in Denmark, Hegelianism was first introduced by a poet and author, Poul Møller. The figure who looms over Norwegian philosophy in the second half of the century is Marcus Jacob Monrad, whose university career lasted from 1845 to his death in 1897. Monrad combated the positivist and naturalist tendencies of the era, thus making Hegelianism into a bulwark of conservatism against reformist movements in Norwegian society. The reformist ideas found their best expressions in literature, particularly in the works of Henrik Ibsen (1828–1906), the greatest of the many authors of world renown from the golden age of Norwegian literature.

Philosophy in Finland in the middle of the last century was dominated by the powerful figure of Johan Vilhelm Snellman (1806–81), an independent thinker of the Hegelian 'moderate left.' He is remembered chiefly, however, as the founder and instigator of the national movement that eventually secured for the Finnish language its proper place in education and public affairs in Finland. Snellman is a rare example of the successful combination of a first-rate philosopher and a great statesman. Finland's growth to national self-identity and political independence owes more to him than to any other single individual.

Fichte, Schelling, and Hegel were introduced to Sweden by Benjamin Höijer, who was the leading philosopher of the early romantic period in Sweden. The influence of Hegel was never as strong in Sweden as elsewhere in Scandinavia (particularly in Norway and Finland, where Hegelianism eventually came to thwart other developments). Instead, Swedish philosophy was long dominated by an indigenous thinker of great stature, Christopher Jacob Boström (1797–1866), a professor at Uppsala. Boström has been called the Plato of Sweden. In certain respects he may more appropriately be considered an independent Swedish parallel to Hegel. His philosophy is a kind of idealism for which he himself used the epithet "rational." He regarded ideas as 'persons' endowed with a higher or lower degree of self-consciousness. Boström's contributions to social and political philosophy and the philosophy of religion hold a central place in his work. His influence was confined to Sweden, but there it was indeed profound, and made itself felt even into this century.

4

The reaction to idealist and speculative philosophy and the turn to an empiricist and naturalist orientation was heralded in Denmark by Harald Høffding (1843–1931). His writings, like those of his compatriot Georg Brandes, became widely read and influential in all the Scandinavian countries. Thanks to Høffding, the dominance of German philosophy in the North was lessened and French and British philosophy gained influence. Høffding wrote on Mill and Darwin and Spencer, and on scientist-philosophers such as Maxwell, Hertz, and Mach. He made important contributions to ethics and value theory and to the philosophy of religion.² Perhaps the best known of all his works is *Outlines of Psychology* (in Danish, 1882),³ an outstanding synopsis of the then young science of psychology. Two other prominent Danes, Carl Lange and Alfred Lehmann, influenced psychology in the Nordic countries. The latter was the first to introduce experimental psychology to Scandinavia. The former, who was a professor of medicine, shares with William James the distinction of having advanced the well-known theory of the physiological basis of emotions. The close alliance between philosophy and psychology became a long-lasting tradition in Denmark (Copenhagen), and was also characteristic of the situation in Norway and Finland, though not so much, it seems, in Sweden.

The influence of Høffding and the Danish psychologists was a main force behind the reaction against Hegelianism and the turn to empiricism in Finland. The men of the breakthrough were Hjalmar Neiglick (1860–89), Edward Westermarck (1862–1939), and the somewhat younger Rolf Lagerborg (1874–1958). Neiglick and Lagerborg were oriented toward French philosophy, psychology, and sociology. Westermarck was the first in Finland, perhaps in all of Scandinavia, to effectively champion an Anglo-Saxon orientation. His scholarly work is divided between moral philosophy and social anthropology; his academic life was divided between England, where he held a chair in sociology in London, and Finland, where he was professor of philosophy first in Helsinki and later at Turku (Åbo). His major philosophical works, *The Origin and Development of the Moral Ideas* and *Ethical Relativity*, also made an impact on the general 'cultural climate' in Finland, particularly among the Swedish-speaking group of which he was himself a member. On the whole, however, Westermarck's influence was stronger in social anthropology, in which he had a number of distinguished pupils, than in philosophy proper. Lagerborg is, among other things, memorable for having introduced behaviorism, Freudian psychology, and Machian empirio-criticism to the educated public in Finland. This occurred chiefly in the two decades before and after World War I.

As already noted, Norway was slower to emancipate itself from the Hegelian inheritance than the other Nordic countries, and the tide of new ideas was there felt more strongly in literature than in academic philosophy. J. M. Vold and A. Løchen, professors at Oslo around the turn of the century, represented the combination of philosopher-psychologist characteristic of their day; Løchen also wrote a book on John Stuart Mill's logic. But a definitive break with the speculative tradition was not achieved until Anathon Aall's professorship at Oslo, which lasted from 1908 until 1937. Aall was a distinguished combination of philosopher, classical scholar, and psychologist. His best known work deals with the idea of *logos* and its place in Greek philosophy and Christian literature. Thanks to Aall, the study of philosophy and the study of the history of ideas came to be more

² See the essay by Mogens Blegvad in this volume.
³ The titles of all works written in Scandinavian languages will be given in English translation here, with the original language specified parenthetically in the text.

closely allied in Norway than in the other Nordic countries. A modern representative of this double tradition is Egil Wyller* (b. 1925), a leading Platonic scholar in present-day Scandinavia.

In Sweden, too, the breakaway from idealist metaphysics was less intimately connected with general changes in the climate of opinion than in Denmark or in Finland. A new era in Swedish philosophy was inaugurated by Axel Hägerström[4] (1868–1939) and Adolf Phalén (1884–1931), two men of great acumen and depth. They are the founders of the so-called Uppsala School in philosophy, which can be regarded as a noteworthy forerunner of what is currently known as analytic philosophy. Phalén in particular explicitly stated that the task of philosophy was conceptual analysis. He thought that a great many concepts that puzzle philosophers are what he called "dialectical," i.e., involve contradictions. To expose these internal contradictions is a characteristic method of problem solving in philosophy. The general position of Phalén and Hägerström is perhaps best expressed in the expositions of it that they wrote themselves for the German series *Philosophie der Gegenwart in Selbstdarstellungen*.

Hägerström's criticism of idealism and subjectivism and his defense of epistemological realism were first propounded in *Prinzip der Wissenschaft* (1908). His position has affinities with the Anglo-Saxon neorealism of the period and particularly with the analytic approach of G. E. Moore. In ethics and value theory, Hägerström, like Moore, was a forceful critic of various forms of naturalism, including emotivist and subjectivist theories like Westermarck's ethical relativism.[5] But, unlike Moore, Hägerström denied cognitive meaning and truth to all practical discourse. Hägerström's views of norms and values are known as "value nihilism." They have made a strong impact, especially on legal philosophy and juristic thinking in Sweden and Scandinavia. The work of Alf Ross* (b. 1899) in Denmark (from *Kritik der sogenannten praktischen Erkenntnis* [1933] to *Directives and Norms* [1968]) and of Karl Olivecrona (*Law as Fact* [1939]) and Manfred Moritz* (b. 1909) in Sweden testifies to the continuing creative influence of Hägerström's thought. Hägerström was a versatile philosopher of unusual circumspection and also a first-rate scholar on legal thought in ancient Rome, as documented in his monumental work *Der römische Obligationsbegriff*, the second volume of which was published posthumously in 1941.

5

The origin of the current philosophic climate of opinion in Scandinavia goes back to the early 1930's and is largely attributable to the work and influence of

---

[4] See the essay by Konrad Marc-Wogau in this volume.
[5] It was the appearance of Westermarck's *Origin and Development* (1906–8) that stirred Moore to his criticism of subjectivism in *Ethics* (1911); and it was largely against the same target that Hägerström directed his critical acumen in the famous inaugural lecture at Uppsala in 1911, "On the Truth of Moral Ideas."

three men. They are Jörgen Jörgensen (1894–1969) in Denmark, Eino Kaila (1890–1958) in Finland, and Arne Naess* (b. 1912) in Norway. Thanks to them, analytic philosophy, in the first instance of the neopositivist and logical empiricist blend, was introduced into these three countries. The Swede Åke Petzäll (1891–1957) should also be mentioned here, although the situation in Sweden, because of the existence of the Uppsala School, was somewhat different from that in the other Nordic countries.

Jörgensen's three-volume *Treatise of Formal Logic* (1931) is the first major attempt in Scandinavia to assess the importance to philosophy of the developments in logic since Boole. Jörgensen and Kaila made mathematical logic an integral part of the teaching of philosophy in their countries. Yet neither of them was a 'logician' in the more demanding, technical sense. The first mathematical logician of great stature in Scandinavia—indeed one of the modern classics of the entire discipline—was Thoralf Skolem (1887–1963), professor of mathematics at Oslo.

Jörgensen and Kaila were the last distinguished examples in the Nordic countries of the philosopher-psychologist combination. *Psychology Based on Biology* (in Danish, 1941–46) may be regarded as Jörgensen's chief work. In its emphasis on consciousness as the highest form of organic life, it shows kinship to the phenomenological, as opposed to behavioristic, trend that has been characteristic of Danish psychology (Rubin, Tranekjaer-Rasmussen). Kaila, who had also done important experimental work in psychology, wrote a synoptic exposition called *Personality* (in Finnish, 1934) that was widely read and became influential in all of the Scandinavian countries. As a psychologist, Kaila was strongly oriented toward the *Gestalt* and related forms of a 'holistic' theory of mental and behavioral phenomena.

Another trait common to Jörgensen and Kaila was their concern for the philosophy of the natural sciences. Toward the end of his life Kaila wrote several works on the foundations of physics. His last publication, *Terminalkausalität in der Atomdynamik* (1956), was planned as the first of three volumes, the second and third of which were to deal with the foundations of biology and neurophysiology. The whole was regarded by its author as constituting a modern *Naturphilosophie* rather than a contribution to analytic philosophy of science.

Arne Naess was appointed to the chair of philosophy in Oslo in 1939, at the age of 27. His first major work, *Erkenntnis und wissenschaftliches Verhalten* (1936), testifies to the influence of the physicalism and logical behaviorism of the later years of the Vienna Circle on him. Naess acquired his characteristic intellectual profile as the creator and theoretician of a type of study of linguistic contexts and usages by empirical means in order to ascertain meaning, synonymity, the analytic-synthetic distinction, etc. Characteristic of this inquiry, also called "empirical semantics," is the extensive use of questionnaires. Naess used his method to investigate the 'ordinary' meaning of truth; his results were presented in *Truth as Conceived by Those Who Are Not Professional Philosophers* (1938). His major work on the theory of the method is *Interpretation and Preciseness* (1953).

In a stronger sense than Jörgensen or Kaila, who introduced a new type of philosophy to their countries, Naess became the creator of a distinctive trend in contemporary analytic philosophy, often called the Oslo School. A singular intellectual vitality and an undogmatic attitude are characteristic of Naess as philosopher. In recent years his interests have moved in new directions, as shown for example by his studies on Gandhi, by his interest in existentialism, and by his philosophy of scepticism. The change in the philosophical climate that has been noticeable in Norway in the last few years owes much, at least implicitly, to Naess's open-mindedness and the encouragement he has given to new ventures in philosophy.

Kaila, and later Naess, did research in Vienna; Kaila was for rather long periods a 'member' of the circle around Moritz Schlick. Another Scandinavian visitor to this center of philosophy was Åke Petzäll, who later became professor at Lund. Kaila and Petzäll published the first studies of the new movement. Kaila's, published in 1930, was called *Der logistische Neupositivismus*, and Petzäll's, which appeared one year later, *Logistischer Positivismus*. These titles, as far as I know, are the ancestors of the term "logical positivism."

Petzäll took a somewhat critical and detached attitude toward the movement, and his contact with Vienna did not effect a change in the philosophic atmosphere in Sweden. The more orthodox members of the Uppsala School remained alien or hostile to analytic philosophy of the positivist type. Gradually, however, the indigenous logico-analytic tradition in Sweden began to merge with influences from Vienna and, to an even higher degree, from Cambridge (Moore, Russell, Broad). The breakthrough of modern analytic philosophy in Sweden is above all due to three men, all of whom studied at Uppsala under Hägerström or Phalén. They are Konrad Marc-Wogau* (b. 1902), Ingemar Hedenius* (b. 1908), and Anders Wedberg* (b. 1913).

Marc-Wogau's scholarship ranges over a very broad field. In his early studies on Kant's theory of space and critique of judgment he applies Phalén's 'dialectic' method of analysis. His most important work, *Die Theorie der Sinnesdaten* (1945), is not only a thorough examination of existing theories of sense data (in British philosophy) but also a defense of the author's own 'realistic' view of the relation between sensory experience and the physical world. Marc-Wogau has been a prolific author of textbooks and editor of anthologies and classical texts in Swedish. His younger colleague at Uppsala, Ingemar Hedenius, wrote his early works on Berkeley and Hume in the vein of Phalén's dialectics. Hedenius has made distinguished contributions to ethics and the philosophy of law, defending what could perhaps be termed an unorthodox Hägerströmian position. The work of his that has had the strongest influence on philosophic discussion in Scandinavia is *On Law and Morals* (in Swedish, 1941). Wedberg paid tribute to the methods of the Uppsala School in his doctoral thesis, which was an examination of the logical structure of Boström's philosophy. His historical studies, *Plato's Philosophy of Mathematics* (1955) and the highly original *History of Philosophy* in three volumes (in Swedish, 1958–66), show the influence of the semantic methods of Naess and the Oslo group in the way philosophic arguments are presented and dissected. His contribution to the present anthology has acquired something of the status of a classic in modern Scandinavian legal philosophy.

6

Since World War II there have been two philosophic centers of rather different general character in Denmark: Copenhagen and Aarhus. (Since 1966 there has also been a chair in philosophy at Odense; its holder, D. Favrholdt, wrote a dissertation on Wittgenstein's *Tractatus*.) In Copenhagen, work in the analytic tradition has been continued by Mogens Blegvad* (b. 1919), Johannes Witt-Hansen* (b. 1908), and Alf Ross.* Ross was, until his retirement, professor of jurisprudence. He was originally strongly influenced by Hägerström and the Uppsala School. His work in legal philosophy and the general logico-philosophical theory of norms has been influential and widely noted even outside of Scandinavia. Blegvad, Jörgensen's successor in one of the chairs of philosophy, has done work chiefly in ethics and value theory. Witt-Hansen is primarily a philosopher of science. His dissertation (1958) was an exposition and critique of Arthur Eddington's philosophy of physics. He has also written on the concept of matter in Newton, Kant, and Einstein, on generalization in the mathematical and the historical sciences, and on historical materialism and other aspects of Marxist philosophy. A major influence on modern Danish philosophy has emanated from the country's great physicist Niels Bohr, particularly from his ideas on correspondence and complementarity. An account of this aspect of Danish philosophic thought is given in Witt-Hansen's contribution to the present work.

Philosophy at the new University of Aarhus acquired a distinctive character thanks to Justus Hartnack* (b. 1912). He is the first and major representative in Scandinavia of the type of analytic philosophy that is associated immediately with the 'linguistic movement' of the Oxford School and indirectly with the later philosophy of Wittgenstein. Hartnack is the author of one of the best known books on Wittgenstein (*Wittgenstein and Modern Philosophy* [1960], translated into many languages), of several publications on problems of epistemology and mental philosophy, and of a number of monographs on subjects in the history of philosophy.

Despite Kierkegaard, phenomenology and existentialism have not much influenced academic philosophy in Denmark. A Danish representative of these trends in modern philosophy is Johannes Sløk* (b. 1916), originally a theologian and now professor of the history of ideas at Aarhus.

7

Arne Naess was a highly successful teacher who had the good fortune to attract a number of gifted people to become his pupils. (In this respect his position in Norwegian philosophy is very similar to that of Eino Kaila in Finland.) At least three of the contributors to this anthology besides Naess came from the Oslo group of 'empirical semanticists' (Gullvåg,* Ofstad, Tennessen). Harald Ofstad* (b. 1920) was prepared to assume a chair at Bergen, when he was appointed to his present position as professor in Stockholm. His major work, *An Inquiry into the Freedom of Decision* (1961), though 'unorthodox,' is still probably the most important illustration of the relevance of the theoretical apparatus developed within the Oslo School for the treatment of a classical problem of philosophy. Herman Tennessen has been active in the speech department at Berkeley and is now professor at the University of Alberta, Canada; he and Ofstad have taken the traditions of the Oslo group outside the borders of Norway.

A Norwegian philosopher with a looser affiliation to the group is Anfinn Stigen.* He is the author of a work called *The Structure of Aristotle's Thought* (1966). Dagfinn Føllesdal* (b. 1932), professor at Oslo, and Knut Erik Tranöy (b. 1918), professor at Bergen, are not pupils or followers of Naess. Both may be considered 'analytical' philosophers, though (like Naess) they have considerable sympathy for and knowledge of other types of philosophy. Tranöy is the author of an excellent book on Saint Thomas Aquinas's moral philosophy, *Thomas av Aquino som moralfilosof* (1957). Føllesdal's achievements in philosophical logic rank very high; this, in combination with his long association with Harvard and Stanford Universities, has established him as one of the leading figures in the borderline area between logic and philosophy. In these respects he resembles his Finnish colleague Jaakko Hintikka.* Føllesdal is also in the process of working out an interpretation of Husserl's phenomenology which brings out the affinities between Husserl and certain traditions within analytical philosophy. A glimpse of this work is provided by Føllesdal's contribution to the present volume.

There is in Norway a strong undercurrent of phenomenology and related trends in philosophy (existentialism, hermeneutics, neo-Marxism). Egil Wyller* is not only a Platonist scholar but also an expert on Heidegger. A further testimony to the current interest in Heidegger's philosophy is the essay by Guttorm Fløistad* in this collection and a recent doctoral dissertation by Gunnar Skirbekk. The latter may be regarded as the protagonist of a 'radical' or leftist political and social philosophy influenced by the Frankfurt School and by Marxist 'socialist humanism.' A representative in Norway of hermeneutic philosophy of science is Hans Skjervheim, whose *Objectivity and the Study of Man* (1959) is the first noteworthy contribution in Scandinavia to the current debate on understanding versus explanation in historiography and social science.

8

Aside from his contributions to psychology, Kaila's work was done chiefly in epistemology and philosophy of science. His influence, however, tended more toward mathematical and philosophical logic. Many of those who became his pupils and whom he attracted to philosophy—for example, Oiva Ketonen (b. 1913), Erik Stenius* (b. 1911), and Veli Valpola (b. 1922)—were originally mathematicians. All three wrote dissertations in logic: Ketonen (1944) on proofs in the predicate calculus, Stenius (1949) on the logical antinomies, and Valpola (1955) on the logic of negation. Ketonen eventually succeeded Kaila as the professor of 'theoretical philosophy' in Helsinki when Kaila was appointed to the Academy of Finland.

It was also under Kaila's guidance and influence that von Wright* (b. 1916) began his career with research in inductive logic. Later von Wright's interests extended to logic generally and to modal logic and its applications (deontic and epistemic logic). In all these fields he found a highly successful follower in Jaakko Hintikka* (b. 1929), who, like so many other Finns, came to philosophy from mathematics. Hintikka has contributed important ideas to practically all branches of philosophical logic and is also well known for his historical research. Two of his pupils, Risto Hilpinen* (inductive and modal logic) and R. Tuomela (methodology and philosophy of science) have already won professorships.

Linguistic philosophy and the Oxford School have not had much influence in Finland. But interest in the philosophy of Wittgenstein has been and continues to be strong. Stenius is the author of a well-known commentary called *Wittgenstein's "Tractatus"* (1960); it is remarkable also as a forceful defense of the 'picture theory' of language.

A lively interest in ancient philosophy shared by philosophers and classical scholars (H. Thesleff, R. Westman) may be regarded as another offshoot of the inspiration stemming from Kaila. Stenius has written on the pre-Socratics; J. Tenkku, professor at Turku, on hedonism in Plato; Hintikka is known for work on Aristotle's logic; and, recently, L. Routila has published a thesis on Aristotle's metaphysics.

There has also been a phenomenological current in Finnish philosophy, not influenced by Kaila and partly in opposition to the philosophic climate of opinion for which he was responsible. Its center in recent decades has been at Turku, and its chief exponent is Sven Krohn (b. 1903). Krohn's major work is a two-volume critical examination of logical positivism, *Der logische Empirismus* (1949, 1950). The aforementioned Routila is a pupil of Krohn's. Interest in hermeneutic philosophy is now prominent in Turku. A similar trend is also noticeable in Helsinki, where it has particularly been stimulated by the writings of Reijo Wilenius (b. 1930) on Marx and on social and political philosophy generally. Wilenius's dissertation was an examination of Francisco Suárez's thought.

9

After the breakthrough of modern analytical philosophy in Sweden, at about the time of World War II, interest in logic—mathematical and philosophical—has been the most conspicuous feature of philosophy in that country. The situation has in this respect been similar to that in Finland, though, I would say, with a stronger 'formalist' emphasis.

Eminent representatives of philosophical logic are Sören Halldén* (b. 1923) and Stig Kanger* (b. 1924), professors of theoretical philosophy at Lund and Uppsala, respectively. Both have contributed to modal logic and to its applications. Halldén's *The Logic of "Better"* (1957) is a pioneer work in the field usually called preference logic and an important contribution to the formal theory of value concepts. The lively interest in the logical study of practical discourse generally and deontic logic in particular is a characteristic feature of philosophy in Sweden today. Perhaps there is a connection here with an older tradition in moral and legal philosophy that goes back to Hägerström. In addition to Halldén and Kanger, interesting results in deontic and pro-hairetic logic have been achieved by Lennart Åqvist* (also erotetic logic), Sven Danielsson, Bengt Hansson, and Lars Bergström* (logical theory of action).

Kanger, with Marc-Wogau and Wedberg, has inspired an impressive number of gifted younger people to research in pure logic. Among contemporary Swedish logicians, Jan Berg* (*Bolzano's Logic* [1962]), Dag Prawitz* (*Natural Deduction* [1965] and other proof-theoretical studies), Rolf Schock, Krister Segerberg (modal logic), and Lars Svenonius (model theory) should be mentioned. Prawitz was recently appointed professor of philosophy at Oslo (after Naess).

A couple of years ago a chair in 'theory of science' was instituted at Göteborg. Håkan Törnebohm* (b. 1919), then professor at Khartoum (Sudan), was invited to be its first occupant. Törnebohm has distinguished himself through a number of studies on the theory of relativity (*A Logical Analysis of the Theory of Relativity* [1952]), on the philosophy of physics generally, and on confirmation and information theory. Younger members of the institution that he has built up at Göteborg have also taken an interest in hermeneutic philosophy of the human sciences (for example, G. Radnitzky, *Contemporary Schools of Metascience* I–II [1968]). In the new university at Umeå, a second chair in theory of science was recently founded. Its occupant is Göran Hermerén,* whose chief work to date is in philosophical aesthetics.

The only distinctive representative in Sweden of the Oxford type of analytic philosophy and of serious interest in the thoughts of the later Wittgenstein is Mats Furberg,* docent at Göteborg. His thesis, *Locutionary and Illocutionary Acts* (1963) is a study in J. L. Austin's philosophy of language. Ivar Segelberg (b. 1914), the professor of philosophy at Göteborg, wrote his dissertation on Zeno's paradoxes (1945). In later publications he analyzed the concepts of a property, the self, and consciousness. His orientation in philosophy shows influences from Husserl. Unlike Norway and Finland, on the whole, philosophy in Sweden has remained but little affected by phenomenology and related currents of contemporary thought. The major Hegel scholar in Scandinavia, however, is the Swedish philosopher and historian of ideas Gunnar Aspelin* (b. 1898); he is also author of a recent work on Marx (1969).

10

There seems to be no survey available in non-Scandinavian languages of the history of thought in the Scandinavian countries. Anathon Aall was the author of a valuable work in Norwegian on *Philosophy in the Nordic Countries* (1917). The theologian-philosopher Søren Holm has written a two-volume work in Danish bearing the same title; it is due to be published in German as a part of the fourteenth edition of Ueberweg's well-known *Grundriss*.

Ake Petzäll founded the periodical *Theoria* with consulting editors in the other Northern countries. *Theoria* also issues a series of monographs, the Library of Theoria, in which many distinguished contributions to Swedish philosophy have been published over the years. Arne Naess is editor in chief of the philosophical and interdisciplinary journal *Inquiry*, which is published in Oslo. The Danish Society for Philosophy and Psychology issues the *Danish Yearbook of Philosophy* (beginning in 1964). The Philosophical Society of Finland also publishes a yearbook called *Ajatus* ("Thought" in Finnish) (beginning in 1926) and a series of monographs, *Acta Philosophica Fennica*. Today, most contributions to the above publications by Scandinavian authors are written in English. They are thus accessible to Anglo-Saxon readers who want to keep themselves informed about events and trends in philosophy in the Scandinavian countries.

I

Logic
Philosophy of Language
Epistemology
Philosophy of Science

A

Logic
Philosophy of Language
Semiotics

G. H. von Wright

Some Observations on Modal Logic and Philosophical Systems

1

Modal logic has turned out to possess a surprising wealth of fruitful applications to traditional fields of philosophic inquiry. We could mention its applications to the study of normative ideas (deontic logic), or to the concepts of knowledge and belief (epistemic logic), or to the notion of time (tense logic). Recently, Hintikka has shown that conceptual problems of perception (sensation), may also be profitably treated using the tools of modal logic.[1]

I shall in this paper suggest another use of modal logic. Some philosophers, e.g., Aristotle and Leibniz, have held specific views on the modal concepts themselves. Others may not have speculated deeply about the nature of modalities, but may still have made important use of the notions of necessity or possibility or contingency in the building of their systems. Spinoza, Kant, and Hegel are perhaps cases in point. My suggestion is that one should try to investigate *which* modal logic those systems can be said implicitly to embody. Is it a 'non-committal' logic like M; is it a stronger logic such as S 4 or S 5; is it a logic of 'Diodorean modalities'; or is it perhaps a logic which so far no modal logician at all has studied? To answer such questions can be interesting because it illuminates the conceptual structures of various philosophical views (systems) or *types*

Professor von Wright, of the Academy of Finland, is a native of Finland.

The inspiration to write this article came from a conversation in Warsaw in January, 1967, with Dr. Boguslav Wolniewicz. I am particularly grateful to Dr. Wolniewicz for urging me to try to 'formalize' in modal logic the *Tractatus* notion of a significant proposition.

A preliminary version of the present paper was mimeographed for a volume of essays in honor of Professor Konrad Marc-Wogau (Uppsala, 1968).

[1] Jaakko Hintikka, "On the Logic of Perception," in *Perception and Personal Identity*, edited by N. S. Care and R. Grimm (Cleveland: The Press of Case Western Reserve University, 1969), pp. 140-75.

of views. But it can also be suggestive of new ideas for the formal logical study of the modalities.

No systematic attempt will be made here to put the above suggestion into effect. I shall confine myself to some remarks about the formal tools themselves and to some scattered observations on their applicability for the suggested purpose.

2

A convenient point of departure for formal considerations on modal logic is provided by the so-called system M. The axiomatics of this system consist of a substructure which is identical with (classical, two-valued) propositional logic (*PL*) and a superstructure with the following three axioms:

A 1. $M(p \vee q) \leftrightarrow Mp \vee Mq$
A 2. $p \rightarrow Mp \ldots$
A 3. $\sim M \sim t \ (= Nt)$

The rules of inference are:

R 1.   Substitution (of well-formed formulas for variables).
R 2.   Detachment (*modus ponens*).
R 3.   Rule of extensionality: formulas which are, in the system, provably equivalent, are interchangeable *salva veritate*.

I shall assume that my use of symbols here and my bracketing conventions are self-explanatory. The letter *t* is used as an abbeviation for an arbitrary tautology of *PL*.

There is another more elegant and simple axiomatics known as system T (after Feys). The two systems, M and T, are easily shown to be deductively equivalent. For reasons of perspicuity I prefer the exposition employed in M.

From A 2 (and *PL*) we immediately prove *Mt*. If we replace A 2 by *Mt* as an axiom, we obtain a modal logic slightly weaker than M.

From A 1 and A 2 we derive $Np \rightarrow Mp$. From A 1 (and *PL* and R 3) we obtain $M(p \ \& \ q) \rightarrow Mp \ \& \ Mq$. In M, the relation of entailment expressed by these two theorems does not also hold in the reverse direction.

3

We now consider a modal logic with the substructure *PL*, the rules of inference R 1–R 3, and the following additional axioms:

B 1.   = A 1
B 2.   *Mt*
B 3.   = A 3
B 4. $Mp \ \& \ Mq \rightarrow M(p \ \& \ q)$

This modal logic is isomorphic with a tense logic which assumes that time is discrete and which uses as its only (tense logical) primitive a binary connective T meaning "and next." The two logics may be formally linked through the equation $Mp =_{\text{df}} tTp$—i.e., through the interpretation of the phrase "it is possible that p" as formally equivalent to the phrase "it is true of the next moment that p."[2] (This interpretation, of course, makes no claim on the meaning of these phrases in ordinary language.)

We substitute $\sim p$ for q in B 4. This gives us the formula $Mp \,\&\, M \sim p \rightarrow M(p \,\&\, \sim p)$. For $p \,\&\, \sim p$ we can write $\sim t$. By contraposition we then obtain $\sim M \sim t \rightarrow \sim (Mp \,\&\, M \sim p)$, and from this by virtue of B 3 (and R 2), $\sim (Mp \,\&\, M \sim p)$.

$Mp \,\&\, M \sim p$ says that it is contingent (contingently true or false) that p. We shall introduce a special symbol C for the modal status of contingency. The theorem which we just proved can thus be written simply: $\sim Cp$.

Since the variable represents an arbitrary proposition, the theorem says in effect that no proposition is contingent. It says, in other words, that every proposition is either necessarily true or necessarily false (i.e., impossible).

It is easily shown that if we replace B 4 by the simpler formula $\sim Cp$, we get a system that is deductively equivalent to the original one. If, again, we replace B 2 by the stronger A 2, the system 'collapses' into *PL*.

A philosophic position according to which everything that is, is a necessity, and everything that is not, is an impossibility, is an extreme version of *rationalism*. The axiomatic system *PL* + B 1–B 4 + R 1–R 3 can thus be called the modal logic of a (certain type of) rationalist view of reality. It might be of interest to inquire whether philosophers such as, e.g., Spinoza, Leibniz, or Hegel, have professed a rationalism of this type.

4

According to Wittgenstein's view in the *Tractatus Logico-philosophicus*, every significant (meaningful, *sinnvoll*) proposition has a characteristic *bipolarity* in relation to truth and falsehood.[3] A significant proposition *can* be true and it *can* be false (see *Tractatus*, 2.21, 3, 4). Whether it is the one or the other has to be determined on the basis of a confrontation between the proposition and reality (2.223, 4.05). There are no significant propositions that are true (or false) *a priori* (2.225). Tautologies and contradictions, Wittgenstein says (4.461, 4.4611) are meaningless (*sinnlos*) though not nonsensical (*unsinnig*).

It is clear that Wittgenstein's conception in the *Tractatus* of a meaningful proposition is essentially related to the modal idea of contingency, although this

---

[2] The tense logic in question is described in my paper "And Next" in *Acta Philosophica Fennica*, vol. 18 (1965). Cf. also the paper by Krister Segerberg, "On the Logic of 'Tomorrow'" in *Theoria*, vol. 33 (1967).

[3] The term "bipolarity" is used by Wittgenstein himself only in the 1913 "Notes on Logic." See Wittgenstein, *Notebooks 1914–1916* (Oxford: Basil Blackwell, 1961), appendix 1.

technical term is nowhere used. The 'logic' of the *Tractatus* notion of propositional significance is also a logic of the notion of contingency.

It is possible to construct a modal logic with C as the only (modal) primitive.[4] Such a logic will, however, in a characteristic sense be void of 'independent
interest.' This is so because of the following facts:

Not only can one define the concept of contingency in terms of possibility, one
can also define the notion of possibility (impossibility, necessity) in terms of
contingency and truth. A proposition is possible if and only if it is either true *or*
contingent. It is necessary if and only if it is true *and* non-contingent. And it is
impossible if and only if it is false and non-contingent. Thus we have, in addi-
tion to the defining identity $Cp = Mp \& M{\sim}p$, the defining identities $Mp = p \text{ v } Cp$ and $Np = p \& {\sim}Cp$.

Assume now that a formal system contains truth-functional notions and the
modal primitive C (and no other primitives). Assume also that the rules of
formation of the system allow truth-functional compounds of expressions of *PL*
and expressions involving C—as, for example, the formula $p \text{ v } Cp$. On these
assumptions, we can express everything in our calculus that can be expressed in
a modal logic with truth-functional notions and M (or N) as sole modal primitive. All truths, or purported truths, about necessity and possibility will be
formulable in this logic too. If the calculus with C is semantically incomplete
with regard to a residue class of theorems about M, it is also incomplete with
regard to a corresponding class of theorems involving C. And if it is complete
with regard to all theorems involving C, it is also complete as a modal logic. This
is so independently of how we choose our criterion of completeness.

For a modal logic which is deductively equivalent to the system M but uses
C as its only modal primitive we can give, e.g., the following axiomatic basis:

C 1. $p \text{ v } q \text{ v } C(p \text{ v } q) \leftrightarrow p \text{ v } q \text{ v } Cp \text{ v } Cq$

C 2. $Cp \rightarrow C{\sim}p$

C 3. ${\sim}C{\sim}t$

(The rules of inference are R 1–R 3.) From C 2 we obtain, through substitution and cancellation of double negation, the formula $C{\sim}p \rightarrow Cp$. This formula
and C 2 are jointly equivalent to $Cp \leftrightarrow C{\sim}p$. We shall call this last formula
the Bipolarity Theorem.

5

We shall consider, in passing, a modal calculus whose well-formed formulas
are defined as follows:

An *atomic* formula of degree 1 is a formula of *PL*. A *formula of degree 1* is
either an atomic formula of degree 1 or a truth-functional compound of formulas of
degree 1.

[4] Cf. the paper by H. Montgomery and R. Routley, "Contingency and Non-contingency
Bases for Normal Modal Logics," *Logique et Analyse*, vol. 9 (1966).

An *atomic* formula of degree n is of the form $C(-)$, where the place of "$-$" is taken by a formula of degree $n - 1$. A formula of degree n, finally, is either an atomic formula of degree n or a truth-functional compound of atomic formulas of degree n.

The well-formed formulas of the modal calculus now under consideration are the formulas of any degree n. I shall conjecture that all well-formed formulas of this calculus which are also theorems of the system M can be derived from the following two axioms (and *PL*).

D 1. $Cp \leftrightarrow C(p \ \& \ q) \ \& \ C(\sim p \ \& \ q) \ v \ C(p \ \& \ q) \ \& \ C(\sim p \ \& \ \sim q) \ v$
$C(p \ \& \ \sim q) \ \& \ C(\sim p \ \& \ q) \ v \ C(p \ \& \ \sim q) \ \& \ C(\sim p \ \& \ \sim q)$
D 2. $= C3$

In support of this conjecture I offer the following argument: We consider a partitioning into two non-empty subclasses of the class of 2^n state-descriptions ('possible worlds') in terms of some n propositional variables. Take the statement that the disjunction of the members of one subclass is a contingent proposition. This statement entails that *no* member of the first class, or disjunction of some members of the first class, is a necessary proposition. Otherwise the disjunction in question would itself be necessary. The statement under examination also entails that not *all* of the members of the first class are impossible propositions, since otherwise the disjunction of all of the members would be an impossible proposition, too. Hence, *some* (at least one) member of the class must be contingent. But then it follows that *some* (at least one) member of the second class of state-descriptions must also be contingent. For, since at least one member of the first class is contingent, no member or disjunction of members of the second class can be necessary; and if all members of the second class were impossible, some member or disjunction of members of the first class would have to be necessary.

Take next the statement that some member of the first class of state-descriptions *and* some member of the second class are contingent. This statement entails that the disjunction of the members of the first class of state-descriptions, and also the disjunction of the members of the second class, must be contingent. These disjunctions cannot be impossible, since they contain at least one contingent disjunct each; nor can one of them be necessary, since the other disjunction could not then contain a contingent disjunct.

Through the above considerations we have found a sufficient and necessary condition for the contingent character of a disjunction of state-descriptions. The criterion of contingency is that at least one state-description which is a member of the disjunction and at least one which is not a member of it should be contingent. Since any truth-functional compound of n propositional variables has a disjunctive normal form, it follows that we have in fact obtained a sufficient and necessary condition for the contingent character of any such compound. The condition, moreover, is such that no tautologous or contradictory truth-functional compound can satisfy it.

It is the content of this condition of contingency that the two axioms D 1 and D 2 propose to capture.

We substitute p for q in D 1. The right member of the equivalence then becomes Cp & $C(p$ & $\sim p)$ v Cp & $C\sim p$ v $C(p$ & $\sim p)$ & $C(\sim p$ & $p)$ v $C(p$ & $\sim p)$ & $C\sim p$. By virtue of D 2, this reduces to Cp & $C\sim p$. We have thus proved the equivalence $Cp \leftrightarrow Cp$ & $C\sim p$. By substitution, we get the equivalence $C\sim p \leftrightarrow Cp$ & $C\sim p$. By transitivity, the two equivalences jointly yield $Cp \leftrightarrow C\sim p$ or the Bipolarity Theorem.

6

It seems feasible to equate the *Tractatus* notion of meaningfulness or propositional significance with the modal concept C. But it would certainly not be correct to maintain that the calculi for the concept that we have outlined in the two preceding sections capture the modal logic of the *Tractatus*. If this were the case, that modal logic would be 'uninteresting.' It would be 'uninteresting' in the sense that it embodies only non-committal, more or less universally held principles of modal logic.

The philosophically interesting aspects of the modal logic of the *Tractatus* have to do with the distinction that Wittgenstein makes between that which can be *said*, i.e., expressed in meaningful propositions, and that which cannot be said but only shown. The latter category of things is very heterogeneous. It includes, i.e., all 'logical facts' about language—for example, the fact that a certain proposition is significant (contingent) or non-significant, or the fact that a thing can or cannot occur in a state of affairs of a certain structure. Such facts are not contingent, and therefore—in the *Tractatus* sense—not 'facts.' They are grounded in the 'nature of things' (2.0123). Nothing logical, Wittgenstein says (2.0121), can be merely possible (*nur-möglich*). That this or that should be a logical possibility is, if true, a necessity; and, if false, an impossibility, one could also say.

Thus, according to the *Tractatus* view, any proposition to the effect that a proposition is significant (meaningful), is not itself a significant proposition. The same holds true for any proposition about the modal status of a proposition. If meaningfulness is equated with contingency, it too is a 'modal status.' We can then summarize an important aspect of the modal logic characteristic of the *Tractatus* in the thesis that propositions about the modal status of propositions are never contingently true or false.

The thesis just mentioned can be formalized with the aid of C (and truth-functional symbols) and divided into a number of sub-theses:

(a) $\sim CCp$ which says that it is not contingent whether a given proposition is contingent.

(b) $\sim C(p$ v $Cp)$ which says that it is not contingent whether a given proposition is possible.

(c) $\sim C(p \mathbin{\&} \sim Cp)$ which says that it not contingent whether a given proposition is necessary.

(d) $\sim C(\sim p \mathbin{\&} \sim C \sim p)$ which says that it is not contingent whether a given proposition is impossible.

7

How are these four subtheses mutually related? In particular: If we add an arbitrary one of them as an axiom to the modal logic with the axiomatic basis $PL + \mathrm{C}\,1\text{--}\mathrm{C}\,3 + \mathrm{R}\,1\text{--}\mathrm{R}\,3$ (= system M), can we derive the rest of them as theorems?

Subtheses (c) and (d) are, of course, equivalent. We obtain the one from the other through a simple process of substitution (and application of R 3 for cancelling double negations).

Subtheses (b) and (d) (and, *a fortiori*, (b) and (c) as well) are equivalent if we accept the Bipolarity Theorem (and R 3). By virtue of this theorem we have the equivalences $\sim C(p \vee Cp) \leftrightarrow \sim C(\sim p \mathbin{\&} \sim Cp)$ and $\sim Cp \leftrightarrow \sim C \sim p$. By virtue of R 3 we obtain from them the equivalence $\sim C(p \vee Cp) \leftrightarrow \sim C(\sim p \mathbin{\&} \sim C \sim p)$.

In order to clarify the mutual relation of (a) and (b) it will be helpful first to 'unpack' their content in terms of the notions of possibility (M) and necessity (N).

If we translate (a) into terms of M, we obtain in the first place the expression $\sim[M(Mp \mathbin{\&} M \sim p) \mathbin{\&} M(\sim Mp \vee \sim M \sim p)]$. We thereupon transform this expression, using successively the following principles: de Morgan's Law, the distribution axiom for M (A 1), the definition of N in terms of M and the distribution principle for N (the 'dual' of A 1), and the principle that a disjunction $\sim f \vee g$ can also be written in the form of an implication $f \rightarrow g$. The transformations yield the formula $M(Mp \mathbin{\&} M \sim p) \rightarrow N(Mp \mathbin{\&} M \sim p)$. By partly reverting to C, we can write this in the simpler form $MCp \rightarrow NCp$. The thesis $\sim CCp$ which says that the proposition to the effect that a given proposition is contingent is not itself a contingent proposition is thus tantamount (accepting the laws of PL and M) to a thesis that if it is possible that a proposition is contingent, then it is also necessary that it is contingent. Since necessity entails possibility, we can strengthen the implication into an equivalence: $MCp \leftrightarrow NCp$. But since (in M) necessity entails truth ($NCp \rightarrow Cp$) and truth entails possibility ($Cp \rightarrow MCp$), we also have the equivalence $MCp \leftrightarrow Cp$. Herewith it has been shown that subthesis (a) is tantamount to the idea that contingency by itself is equivalent to possible contingency, and also equivalent to necessary contingency.

Next we perform a similar 'unpacking' of the content of (b). First we get $\sim[M(p \vee Mp \mathbin{\&} M \sim p) \mathbin{\&} M \sim (p \vee Mp \mathbin{\&} M \sim p)]$. The first conjunct under the principal negation sign can also be written $Mp \vee M(Mp \mathbin{\&} M \sim p)$, by virtue of A 1. The second conjunct can be written $M(\sim p \mathbin{\&} (\sim Mp \vee \sim M \sim p))$. The last expression, after distribution, becomes $M(\sim p \,\&\, \sim Mp) \,\text{v}\, M(\sim p \,\&\, \sim M \sim p)$. But $\sim p \,\&\, \sim M \sim p$, which says of a certain proposition that it is both false and necessarily true, is refutable. Hence, by virtue of A 3 and R 3, $M(\sim p \,\&\, \sim M \sim p)$ also is refutable. The disjunction, consequently, reduces to $M(\sim p \,\&\, \sim Mp)$. But $\sim p \,\&\, \sim Mp$ is equivalent to $\sim Mp$ alone (by virtue of A 2). Hence we can simplify $M(\sim p \,\&\, \sim Mp)$ to $M \sim Mp$.

Subthesis (b) has now assumed the form $\sim\{[Mp \,\text{v}\, M(Mp \,\&\, M \sim p)] \,\&\, M \sim Mp\}$. Applying de Morgan's Law to this, we get $\sim[Mp \,\text{v}\, M(Mp \,\&\, M \sim p)] \,\text{v}\, \sim M \sim Mp$, which can be further transformed into $Mp \,\text{v}\, M(Mp \,\&\, M \sim P) \rightarrow NMp$. The last may be dissolved into the conjunction $(Mp \rightarrow NMp) \,\&\, [M(Mp \,\&\, M \sim p) \rightarrow NMp]$.

If in the second conjunct we substitute $\sim p$ for p, the antecedent remains the same (the order of conjuncts being irrelevant) and the consequent becomes $NM \sim p$. The conjunction NMp and $Nm \sim p$ can be contracted into $N(Mp \,\&\, M \sim p)$. Hence $M(Mp \,\&\, M \sim p) \rightarrow NMp$ is equivalent to $MCp \rightarrow NCp$. But this, as we already know, is just another form of the subthesis (a) or $\sim CCp$ (accepting the laws of the system M).

Consider now the first conjunct in the formula above, $Mp \rightarrow NMp$. The antecedent can also be written $Np \,\text{v}\, Mp \,\&\, M \sim p$. That a proposition is possible means that it is either necessary or contingent. We can thus dissolve $Mp \rightarrow NMp$ into the conjunction $(Np \rightarrow NMp) \,\&\, (Mp \,\&\, M \sim p \rightarrow NMp)$. The first conjunct is a theorem of M (by virtue of A 2 and R 3). The second conjunct may first be amplified to $Mp \,\&\, M \sim p \rightarrow NMp \,\&\, NM \sim p$, then contracted to $Mp \,\&\, M \sim p \rightarrow N(Mp \,\&\, M \sim p)$, and finally abbreviated to $Cp \rightarrow NCp$. But this formula too, as we know, is but another version of (a) (accepting the laws of the system M).

Herewith it has been shown that, within the frame of the system M, subtheses (a) and (b) are equivalent and hence that all four subtheses into which we divided the characteristic thesis of the modal logic of the *Tractatus* are equivalent. The simplest form of the thesis is

C 4. $\sim CCp.$

If we add this as a new axiom to system M, we obtain a system of modal logic which is that of Wittgenstein's *Tractatus*. But this system is deductively equivalent to the system of modal logic known as S 5. Hence it seems right to say that the modal logic embodied in Wittgenstein's theory of propositional significance is S 5.

The formula $Mp \rightarrow NMp$ is the characteristic axiom of S 5. It is of some interest to notice that this formula can be given the form of a conjunction, whose one conjunct is a theorem of M and whose other conjunct is in M deductively equivalent to $\sim CCp$. What the characteristic axiom of S 5 says, over and above the things already contained in the system M, is thus simply that (possible) contingency entails necessary contingency.

8

By an *atomic* modal expression, we shall understand an expression consisting of the letter M or N or C followed by a well-formed formula of any of our modal calculi. And by a *modal expression*, generally we understand either an atomic modal expression or a truth-functional compound of atomic modal expressions. Hence, in S 5 and therewith in the modal logic of the *Tractatus*, only expressions (propositions) that are *not* modal can be contingent, whereas all modal expressions (propositions) are either necessary or impossible. Thus the modal logic of modal expressions, according to the *Tractatus* view, is the modal logic which we earlier (in section 3) called that of a *rationalist* conception of the world. The modal logic of non-modal expressions, according to this view, is system M.

I should like to insert here, as a personal comment, that the idea that the modal logic of modal propositions is, in the sense defined, 'rationalist' seems to me philosophically sound. But the view that the modal logic of all propositions whatsoever are of this nature seems to me philosophically eccentric.

9

An alternative to the 'rationalist' view of the modal logic of modal propositions would be the view that all modal propositions are *contingent*. In defense of this latter view one may advance an argument such as the following one:

The modal status of a proposition depends upon contingent facts about the use of language. What is the source of the necessity in the proposition that, for example, it is raining or not raining? An answer might be that the necessity in question flows from the *meaning* of the logical constants "or" and "not." What words mean depends upon linguistic convention, and conventions are 'arbitrary' in the sense of being contingent. This is sometimes called a *conventionalist* view of necessity and of modal status generally.

The idea that modal status is contingent can be expressed by negating each one of the subtheses (a) to (d) above. The four negated subtheses, however, will no longer be deductively equivalent. This is a consequence of the following fact:

If we add to the system M as an axiom the thesis CCp which says that the proposition that a given proposition is contingent is itself a contingent proposition, we have a contradiction. In M we can derive the inference rule usually called the rule of necessitation. It says that, if f is a theorem of M, then Nf is a theorem too. But Nf, by definition, is equivalent to f & $\sim Cf$. Therefore, if CCp were (an axiom or) a theorem of a modal logic including M, then $CCCp$ would be a theorem (by substitution of Cp for p), but so would $\sim CCCp$ (by virtue of the rule of necessitation). Thus we have a contradiction.

The above does not mean that the conventionalist view of modal status is, in itself, self-contradictory. The root of the inconsistency is easily detectable and can be removed. We have to omit from the system M the axiom A 3 which says that the contradiction $(\sim t)$ is an impossibility or, alternatively, the axiom C 3 which says that the contradiction is non-contingent. This done, the rule of necessitation is no longer derivable. The truth of the tautology and the false-hood of the contradiction are still provable in the system. But these truth values are not at this point necessities.

If A 3 (C 3) is dropped from M, (a) is no longer equivalent to (b), (c), or (d). But the last three are still equivalent to one another. The modal logic of a philosophy which professes a conventionalist view of modal status ought, in addi-tion to the negation of (a), also to adopt as an axiom the negation of one of the subtheses (b), (c), or (d). It could, for example, be a system with the following axiomatic basis (in addition to *PL*):

E 1.   = C 1
E 2.   = C 2
E 3.   *CCp*
E 4. $C(p \ \& \ \sim Cp)$

and the rules of inference R 1–R 3.

Lennart Åqvist

On the Analysis and Logic of Questions

1. A Suggestion

Let us consider the following questions (interrogatives):

(1) Is linguistic philosophy still alive?

(2) What is the smallest prime greater than 873?

What do (1) and (2), respectively, 'mean'? The idea that I am going to defend and expound can be briefly stated as follows. We focus our attention on certain 'standard' situations in which questions (1) and (2) may be asked. The situations I have in mind satisfy the following conditions: (a) The questioner does not know whether or not linguistic philosophy is still alive; also, he does not know with respect to any entity that *it* is the smallest prime greater than 873 (whereas he is likely to know that *something* is the smallest prime greater than 873). (b) The questioner tries to remove his ignorance in these respects by addressing to an appropriate respondent (possibly himself) sentences that are synonymous with the following imperative or optative formulations:

(1a) Let it (turn out to) be the case that [I know that linguistic philosophy is still alive or I know that linguistic philosophy is not alive any longer].

(2a) Let it (turn out to) be the case that [there is an object with respect to which I know that it is the smallest prime greater than 873].

The sentences at stake are of course (1) and (2), respectively, and my suggestion is to equate them with (1a) and (2a), respectively. In other words, questions may be interpreted as kinds of *epistemic imperatives* (or *optatives*), the

Dr. Åqvist, of the University of Uppsala in Sweden, is a native of Sweden.

This paper derives from a talk that the author gave at a Scandinavian Philosophy Meeting in Lillehammer, Norway, in June, 1965. A more complete and systematic exposition of the present theory of questions was given in his book *A New Approach to the Logical Theory of Interrogatives*, Part 1: *Analysis* (Uppsala: The Philosophical Society Series, 1965).

primary use and function of which is to serve as a means of increasing the questioner's knowledge.

In this paper, I shall assume the correctness of the hypothesis just presented, and attempt to show how it can be elaborated and developed into a theory concerning the analysis and logic of questions that turns out to be surprisingly powerful and far-reaching.

2. OUTLINES OF A LOGICAL THEORY OF QUESTIONS

No doubt the most salient features of translations (1a) and (2a) of questions (1) and (2), respectively, is the following: Both mobilize an *imperative operator*, "Let it (turn out to) be the case that," as well as an *epistemic operator*, "I know that." It is well known that promising attempts have been made, especially in recent years, to characterize the formal behavior of both of these operators within the framework of systematic logical or semantical theories. I refer the reader in particular to Stig Kanger's *New Foundations for Ethical Theory* for the imperative operator, and to Jaakko Hintikka's *Knowledge and Belief* for the epistemic one.[1] We now envisage a program that embodies two steps. First, we combine in some reasonable way an imperative logic in the Kanger style with an epistemic logic in the Hintikka style (step 1). Consider then the formalized language of such a combined imperative-epistemic logic. We introduce into this language various types of question-forming (interrogative) operators by explicit definitions or definitional schemata in such a way that every formalized question (formed by means of some interrogative operator) abbreviates some sentence containing imperative and epistemic operators (step 2).

The result of implementing the above program will apparently constitute a reduction of interrogative logic to imperative-epistemic logic, which is in certain respects analogous to the reduction of deontic logic to alethic modal logic made by Alan R. Anderson in his "Formal Analysis of Normative Systems."[2] To be sure, we may later, if we wish, 'relax' the reduction somewhat by introducing the interrogative operators as *primitive* in our system, our expectation being that formalized questions are to be provably equivalent to those imperative-epistemic sentences that they were formerly taken to abbreviate definitionally.

The following feature of an interrogative logic construed as just indicated seems to me to be particularly attractive. We are able to apply ordinary truth-functional sentence composition to questions, that is, to speak of the negation of a question, of the conditional of two questions, and so forth. A prerequisite for doing so is of course that the same thing can be justified in the case of imperatives; here, I can only observe that an excellent justification has in fact been pro-

---

[1] Stig Kanger, *New Foundations for Ethical Theory* (Stockholm, 1957); Jaakko Hintikka, *Knowledge and Belief* (Ithaca, N.Y., 1962).

[2] Alan R. Anderson, "The Formal Analysis of Normative Systems," in *The Logic of Decision and Action*, edited by Nicholas Rescher (Pittsburgh, 1968).

vided by Kanger.[3] In my opinion, we then obtain a corollary of utmost import-ance: logical relations among questions such as implication, equivalence, and the like can be studied without our having to specify in advance the so-called ques-tion-answer relationship. This is probably one of the crucial points of difference between our theory and others that have been proposed in the literature. Accord-ing to a widespread view, perhaps shared by every author on the subject except myself, any interrogative logic *must* be based on a specification of the question-answer relationship.[4] For one thing, this amounts to a claim that logical relations among questions have to be defined in terms of logical relations among the answers to the questions under consideration. For instance, the following type of definition is a good case in point: Question Q_1 'interrogatively' implies question Q_2 iff, every (direct) answer to Q_1 logically implies some (direct) answer to Q_2. However, I take the fact that our approach does not commit us to basing inter-rogative logic on the question-answer relationship to be a definite advantage, because it turns out that in quite a few cases this relationship simply lacks the clarity and determinacy so often attributed to it. Now, this does not of course exclude, for example, the above definition of interrogative implication's being adequate after all; the point is just that alternative and more traditional explica-tions of the notion of interrogative implication are available for us as well.

Let us now quickly consider what is basically involved in carrying out my two-step program.

3. A Semantical System of Imperative-Epistemic Logic

By and large, we adopt the formal machinery of Hintikka's epistemic logic, as it is given in *Knowledge and Belief*. "K" and "P" (without subscripts) are read as "I know that" and "It is compatible with everything I know that." Iteration of these operators is allowed, and so is quantification into contexts of the form $Kp(a_1, \ldots, a_n)$, where the a_i are individual variables occurring freely in p. The expressions "$(Ex)(x = a)$," "$(Ex)K(x = a)$," "$(Ex)KFx$," "$(Ux)KFx$," and "$(Ux)(Ey)(y = x \ \& \ KFy)$" are taken to be formal counter-parts of the everyday locutions "*a* exists," "I know who [what] *a* is," "I know who [what] *F*'s," "Of each *x known to me*, I know that *x* is *F*," and "Of each *x*, I know that *x* is *F*," respectively, provided, of course, that the latter locutions are understood in an appropriate sense. (Please observe the distinction between the last two; further elucidation is to be found in chap. 6 of Hintikka's book.)

We then enrich this vocabulary with two imperative operators "!" and "*i*" (to be read as "Let it be the case that" and "It is permissible that"). There is no reason for us to allow either iteration of these operators or quantification into contexts governed by them. Nor do we allow our imperative operators to occur within the scope of "K" or "P."

---

[3] Kanger, *New Foundations for Ethical Theory* (the concluding dialogue).

[4] See, e.g., Nuel D. Belnap, Jr., *An Analysis of Questions* (Santa Monica, Calif., 1963), p. 13.

The logic that we are now going to describe is a first-order predicate-calculus with identity as well as imperative and epistemic operators. It is called "*QIE*." We define a *QIE model set* as any set μ of *QIE* formulas satisfying Hintikka's conditions $(C.-)$, $(C.\&)$, $(C.v)$, $(C.--)$, $(C.-\&)$, $(C.-v)$, $(C.U_o)$, $(C.E_o)$, (108), (109), $(C.-U)$, $(C.-E)$, $(C.=)$, $(C.self\neq)$, $(C.EK=)$, $(C.K)$, $(C.-K)$, $(C.-P)$, as well as the following conditions pertaining to imperative operators:

$(C.-!)$ If $-!\mathrm{p}\varepsilon\mu$, then $i-\mathrm{p}\varepsilon\mu$.

$(C.-i)$ If $-i\mathrm{p}\varepsilon\mu$, then $!-\varepsilon\mu$.

Define further a *QIE model system* as any set Ω of *QIE* model sets that is ordered both by a (binary) relation of *epistemic alternativeness* satisfying Hintikka's conditions $(C.KK^*)$, $(C.P^*)$, and $(C.EK = EK = *)$, *and* by a (binary) relation of *imperative alternativeness* meeting the requirements:

$(C.i^+)$ If $i\mathrm{p}\varepsilon\mu$ and $\mu\varepsilon\Omega$, then there is in Ω at least one imperative alternative μ^+ to μ such that $\mathrm{p}\varepsilon\mu^+$.

$(C.!^+)$ If $!\mathrm{p}\varepsilon\mu$ and μ^+ is an imperative alternative to μ in Ω, then $\mathrm{p}\varepsilon\mu^+$.

$(C.!^+\text{min})$ If $!\mathrm{p}\varepsilon\mu$ and $\mu\varepsilon\Omega$, then there is in Ω at least one imperative alternative μ^+ to μ such that $\mathrm{p}\varepsilon\mu^+$.

Furthermore, a set of *QIE* formulas is said to be *satisfiable* (in *QIE*) iff it can be imbedded in a member of some *QIE* model system; otherwise it is said to be *contradictory*. A *formula* (of *QIE*) is satisfiable iff its unit set is, and *valid* iff its negation is contradictory.

This 'semantical' system has an intuitive interpretation in terms of 'worlds that are possible relative to the actual world,' for which I have again to refer the reader to Hintikka.[5]

It is useful to introduce a special label, for instance "*PIE*," for the *propositional logic fragment* of *QIE*. Such notions as *PIE* model set (system), *PIE* satisfiability, and the like, are easily obtained by deleting those conditions that pertain to quantification and identity in the definition of the corresponding *QIE* notions.

4. MODIFICATIONS OF *QIE*

Is *QIE* an intuitively acceptable system of imperative-epistemic logic? Hardly so, I think. Let us briefly discuss two difficulties that affect the interpretation of the epistemic operators and the imperative ones, respectively, and consider some ways to eliminate them.

---

[5] As far as the imperative or 'quasi-deontic' alternativeness relation is concerned, Hintikka ("Quantifiers in Deontic Logic," *Societas Scientiarum Fennica* [Helsinki, 1957], pp. 3–23) and Kanger (*New Foundations for Ethical Theory*) should be sufficiently clarifying.

(i) It is readily seen that the following formulas are already valid in *PIE*:

(1) $-$KP $\supset$ P$-$p
(2) $-$Pp $\supset$ K$-$p

as is the rule

(R) If $p \supset q$ is valid, so is K$p \supset$ Kq (where no imperative operators occur in p or q).

In our reading of "K" and "P," none of these should turn out to be valid, in view of the existence of clear-cut counterexamples to each one of them. The conditions in Hintikka that appear to be the 'offenders' here are obviously $(C.-K)$ and $(C.-P)$. Hintikka is reluctant to weaken his system by giving them up, however, and prefers to reinterpret the *metalogical* notions of satisfiability, validity, etc., in terms of what he calls defensibility, self-sustenance, etc. In short, this reinterpretation amounts to a claim that his epistemic logic (including (1), (2), and (R)) fits nicely into what 'sufficiently rational' people could be said to know (implicitly or 'virtually,' if not 'actively'). Thus, Hintikka's theory seems to a certain extent to be concerned with some logical fiction of ideal knowledge; in this respect it resembles the theory of games, as he himself points out.[6]

I believe that we are able to represent this idea fairly adequately if we adopt a simple modification of the system *PIE* (*QIE*). The essential use of our imperative operator "!" is evidently that of picturing certain states of affairs as ideal in some sense, to indicate that they *are to be* realized and the imperative alternatives μ^+ to a model set μ in a model system Ω are supposed to describe ideal worlds where everything that is to be realized in the actual world is in fact realized (with an important restriction to be discussed below). The move that then suggests itself is to restrict the applicability of the problematic conditions $(C.-K)$ and $(C.-P)$ by appending this proviso to them: provided that μ is an imperative alternative to some member of Ω.

This restriction necessitates certain other alterations in the definition of *QIE* model system, which may be disregarded here. The essential effect of adopting it is that none of (1), (2), or (R) remain valid, while variants such as

(1') !($-$Kp $\supset$ P$-$p)
(2') !($-$Pp $\supset$ K$-$p)

and

(R') If $p \supset$ q is valid, then !(K$p \supset$ Kq) is valid

will still hold in the restricted, weaker system. In this system, for example, the following conception turns out to be a natural and useful one: *p normatively implies q*, iff, !($p \supset q$) is valid. We may then say that (1), (2), and the conse-

---

[6] Hintikka, *Knowledge and Belief*, p. 38.

quent of (R) express valid normative implications by virtue of the validity of (1′), (2′), and (R′), in spite of the fact that they fail to be valid *simpliciter*.[7]

(ii) An upsetting difficulty that pinpoints our interpretation of the imperative operators is this. Both

(3) $Kp \supset p$ (where p does not contain any epistemic or imperative operators)

and the rule

(S) If $p \supset q$ is valid, so is $!p \supset !q$ (where p and q don't contain any imperative operators)

are valid. Take (3) as $p \supset q$ in (S), and we obtain

(4) $!Kp \supset !p$

as a valid result. Now, if we think of "!" as a kind of deontic ought-operator, (4) will assert that if I ought to know that p, then it ought to be that p. To see that this is absurd, we just have to substitute for "p"—e.g., "6,000,000 Jews were killed by the Nazis" or any true statement that describes a real matter of fact which ought not to be real but is such that I ought to know that it (alas!) obtains.

An interesting way out of the present difficulty was indicated to me by Hintikka. It consists in treating "!" as a genuine imperative operator only when it operates on epistemic sentences containing "K" or "P." When "!" operates on ordinary sentences (not containing "K" or "P"), it is vacuous, so to speak, so that $p \equiv !p$ will be valid whenever p does not contain "K" or "P." To put the solution in terms of imperative alternatives and possible worlds, we might say that the former describe such possible worlds as differ from the actual one *only* with respect to my state of knowledge, namely, as far as the realization of my epistemic obligations is concerned. The only change in the definition of a *QIE* model system required by these considerations will then be the addition of a condition

(C.+) If p does not contain imperative or epistemic operators, and if $p\varepsilon\mu\varepsilon\Omega$ and μ^+ is an imperative alternative to μ in Ω, then $p\varepsilon\mu^+$.

Under this reinterpretation of the imperative operator "!," (4) becomes equivalent to

(4′) $!Kp \supset p$

[7] Here are some further possible modifications of *QIE* that deserve serious discussion. (1) Drop (C.KK*) and (C.EK=EK=*) altogether and replace them by (C.K*) and (C.EK=*). (2) Make the same replacement, but retain the former pair of conditions *with the proviso* just considered in connection with (C.—K) and (C.—P). Hintikka has argued that the knowledge requested in my paraphrase of questions is normally just true information which need not amount to 'philosophers' strong' sense of knowledge; and furthermore that such conditions as (C.KK*) distinguish 'strong' knowledge from 'mere' true opinion. Since my feelings about this particular issue are not (yet?) very definite, I shall not try to decide here whether (1) and/or (2) should be adopted.

which expresses the plausible principle that I ought to know that p only if p is actually the case, where p describes an 'ordinary,' 'non-epistemic' state of affairs.

In my opinion, Hintikka's suggested reinterpretation has not only the virtue of providing a satisfactory solution to the 'paradox' under discussion; it also leads, within our theory, to an interesting explication of the notion of the *presuppositions* of a question. For it turns out that in the reinterpreted system we are able to say that Q *presupposes* p (where Q is a question and p an ordinary statement) iff Q logically implies p, that is, $Q \supset p$ being valid in QIE, and that such a definition yields acceptable results.

5. Analysis and Formalization of Different Kinds of Questions

Let us now try to carry through the second step in the program outlined in section 2 above. First of all, I want to suggest that questions of ordinary discourse be divided into two main groups: (I) those that are adequately formalizable within the imperative-epistemic *propositional* logic *PIE*, and (II) those that require formalization within the wider imperative-epistemic *quantificational* logic *QIE*. The distinction between *whether*-questions and *which*-questions, as given for instance by Prior, Harrah, and Belnap, coincides to a large extent with this division of ours.[8] The following comment would seem to be appropriate, though. All whether-questions appear capable of being formulated as which-questions, e.g.,

(1) Will the next crisis affect Cuba, Greece, Berlin, or Israel?

can be rendered as a which-question

(1a) Which of the following applies: The next crisis will affect Cuba, . . . Greece, . . . Berlin, . . . Israel?

Moreover, I think it is correct that all whether-questions can be formalized within *PIE*; hence, there are which-questions (given in ordinary discourse) that can be formalized with *PIE*, and that do not *require* formalization within *QIE* (let alone that this be always *possible* in the case of the latter).

Another two, somewhat troublesome comments: several authors seem to take for granted that the division of ordinary discourse-given questions into yes-no ones (whether or not questions) and so-called fill-in-the-blank ones (which-questions) is exhaustive. If so, how should (1) above be classified? Clearly, (1) must be carefully distinguished from the yes-no question

(1b) Is it the case that the next crisis will affect either Cuba, Greece, Berlin, or Israel?

---

[8] M. Prior and A. N. Prior, "Erotetic Logic," *Philosophical Review* 64: 43–59 (1955); D. Harrah, *Communication: A Logical Model* (Cambridge, Mass., 1963); Belnap, *An Analysis of Questions.*

but, on the other hand, (1) also differs from fill-in-the-blank questions in important respects in which yes-no questions differ from the latter as well. The reasonable view is to conceive of yes-no questions as a mere special case of the wider category of whether-questions, as we learn from Prior *et al.*[9]

Is the division into whether-questions and which-questions an exhaustive one? Hardly so. Prior has drawn attention to the fact that there is a group of *conditional* questions that seems to cut across whether- as well as which-ones, and that this group certainly cannot be reduced to any of the other two. He submits, however, that something like the Kantian trichotomy of 'judgement' could possibly fit questions, so that the latter should be classified as either categorical, disjunctive, or conditional (where which-questions are taken to be categorical). If we do not worry too much about anomalous cases, I think Prior's suggestion will be seen to be basically sound.

A number of definitional schemata will now be presented, which introduce interrogative operators en masse into the language of *QIE* (*PIE*). I shall then proceed to illustrate their application in translating (formalizing) questions given in ordinary discourse.

A. *Operators Applicable to Group I (PIE-Formalizable Questions)*

(Def $?_n$) $?_n(p_1, \ldots, p_n) = df$ $!(Kp_1 \lor \ldots \lor Kp_n)$

where $n = 1,2,3, \ldots$, and p_i are ordinary statements (not containing imperative or epistemic operators). A unary yes-no operator can be introduced by

(Def ?) $?p = df$ $?_2(p, -p)$

The operators $?_n$ are sufficient to handle 'genuine' whether-questions as opposed to conditional ones. For the sake of the latter we introduce

(Def $?_{n/m}$) $?_{n/m}(p_1, \ldots, p_n/q_1, \ldots, q_m) = df$ $![q_1 \& \ldots \& q_m \supset$
$(Kp_1 \lor \ldots \lor Kp_n)]$

where $m,n = 1,2,3,\ldots$, and p_i, q_j are ordinary statements.

B. *Operators, or Quantifiers, Applicable to Group II (Questions Requiring Formalization Within QIE)*

(Def $?_B^m$) $(?_B^m a_1, \ldots, a_m)p = df\,!\,(Ux_1) \ldots (Ux_m)\{p(x_1/a_1, \ldots, x_m/a_m) \supset$
$(Ey_1) \ldots (Ey_m)[y_1 = x_1 \& \ldots \& y_m = x_m \& KP(y_1/a_1, \ldots, y_m/a_m)]\}$

where p is a *QIE*-formula lacking occurrences of imperative and epistemic operators and containing exactly m free distinct variables $a_1, \ldots, a_m$, and where $x_1, \ldots, x_m, y_1, \ldots, y_m$ are the alphabetically earliest distinct variables that are not bound to any quantifier in p.[10] Also, $m = 1,2,3, \ldots$.

---

[9] *Ibid.*

[10] If x and a are variables such that a is free in p, $p(x/a)$ is the result of replacing every free occurrence of a in p by one of x.

The interrogative quantifiers ($?_B^m$) are intended as tools for formalizing what Harrah and Belnap call "complete-list which-questions." It is advisable, though, to consider the following variants of the form ($?_B^m a_1, \ldots, a_m$)p: ($?_{KB}^m a_1, \ldots, a_m$)p, the definition of which is obtained by insertion of "K" immediately after "!" in (Def $?_B^m$); ($?_{EB}^m a_1, \ldots, a_m$)p, the definition of which results from insertion of a clause "$(Ex_1) \ldots (Ex_m) Kp\ (x_1/a_1, \ldots, x_m/a_m)\ \&$" immediately after "!" in (Def $?_B^m$); and ($?_{EKB}^m a_1, \ldots, a_m$)p, the definition of which is obtained by inserting that very same clause in between "!" and "K" in the definition of ($?_{KB}^m a_1, \ldots, a_m$)p. The purpose of these variations will be briefly discussed below.

Belnap was undoubtedly the first to call attention to what I shall label "at-least-which-questions" and "exactly-which-questions." We confine ourselves to the following simple cases here:

(Def $?_{C_1}^1$)   ($?_{C_1}^1 a$)p $= df$ $!(Ex)Kp(x/a)$

(Def $?_{D_1}^1$)   ($?_{D_1}^1 a$)p $= df$ $!(Ex)K[p(x/a) \& (Uy)[p(y/a \supset y = x)]$

where *p, a, x, y* are as in (Def$?_B^m$) with requisite alterations. To be sure, we also define the general forms ($?_{C_n}^m a_1, \ldots, a_m$)p and ($?_{D_n}^m a_1, \ldots, a_m$)p, but we refrain from doing so here for reasons of limited space.

Conditional varieties of the quantifiers thus far introduced may be formed in analogy with $?_{n/m}$ above.

The application of our interrogative operators to some examples is illustrated in Table 1 (page 36).

Comments. (i) In the table we use "*H*," "*S*," and "*W*" as formal counterparts to the sentences "You have a wife whom you have beaten," "You have stopped beating her," and the predicate "is a member of the Vienna Philharmonic Orchestra," respectively. Moreover, I assume that the reader understands the reading of the imperative-epistemic formulas (otherwise, Hintikka is helpful).[11]

(ii) Consider (1)–(4), and the corresponding formalized questions. Appealing to the translations (1b)–(4b), we verify in *PIE* that (2a) is stronger than the remaining three, and that (4a) is stronger than both (1a) and (3a). According to the suggested definition of the presuppositions of a question (at the end) of section 4, it is also the case that (2a) is the only one among the four that presupposes that the respondent has a wife whom he has beaten ($?_2(H \& S, H \& -S) \supset H$ being valid), whereas the remaining three questions only presuppose *logically true* ordinary statements. Let us define a *correction* to a question as the negation of any presupposition of the question. Then, $-H$ is a consistent correction of (2a), while all corrections to (1a), (3a), and (4a) are inconsistent. Using the Harrah-Belnap terminology, we may say that a question is *risky* iff it has a consistent correction (possibly false presupposition), and that it is *safe* otherwise. The riskiness means, roughly speaking, that if some consistent correction to the question were to turn out true (some possibly

[11] Hintikka, *Knowledge and Belief.*

Table 1

Question Given in Ordinary Discourse	Corresponding Formalized Question	Imperative-Epistemic Translation
(1) Is it the case that you have a wife whom you have beaten and have stopped beating?	(1a) $?(H \& S)$	(1b) $![K(H \& S) \vee K-(H \& S)]$
(2) Have you stopped beating your wife?	(2a) $?_2(H \& S, H \& -S)$	(2b) $![K(H \& S) \vee K(H \& -S)]$
(3) Given that you have a wife whom you have beaten, have you stopped beating her?	(3a) $?_{2/1}(H \& S, H \& -S/H)$	(3b) $!\{H \supset [K(H \& S) \vee K(H \& -S)]\}$
(4) Have you stopped beating your wife, or don't you have any wife whom you have beaten?	(4a) $?_3(H \& S, H \& -S, -H)$	(4b) $![K(H \& S) \vee K(H \& -S) \vee K(-H)]$
(5) Which are (all) the members of the Vienna Philharmonic Orchestra (VPO)?	(5a₁) $(?^1_B x)Wx$	(5b₁) $!(Ux)[Wx \supset (Ey)(y = x \& KWy)]$
	(5a₂) $(?^1_{KB} x)Wx$	(5b₂) $!K(Ux)[Wx \supset (Ey)(y = x \& KWy)]$
	(5a₃) $(?^1_{EB} x)Wx$	(5b₃) $!\{(Ex)KWx \& (Ux)[Wx \supset (Ey)(y = x \& KWy)]\}$
	(5a₄) $(?^1_{EKB} x)Wx$	(5b₄) $!\{(Ex)KWx \& K(Ux)[Wx \supset (Ey)(y = x \& KWy)]\}$
(6) At least who is a member of the VPO?	(6a) $(?^1_{O_1} x)Wx$	(6b) $!(Ex)KWx$
(7) At least which two (persons) are members of the VPO?	(7a) $(?^1_{O_2} x)Wx$	(7b) $!(Ex)(Ey)K(Wx \& Wy \& x \neq y)$
(8) Who is the (only) member of the VPO?	(8a) $(?^1_{D_1} x)Wx$	(8b) $!(Ex)K[Wx \& (Uy)(Wy \supset y = x)]$
(9) Exactly which two (persons) are members of the VPO?	(9a) $(?^1_{D_2} x)Wx$	(9b) $!(Ex)(Ey)K\{Wx \& Wy \& x \neq y \& (Uz)[Wz \supset (z = x \vee z = y)]\}$

false presupposition to turn out false), then there is no way of satisfying the request made by the question. For instance, if $-H$ is in fact true, then there is no way of satisfying the command expressed by the imperative (2b). What could be done in such a situation, however, is to replace the risky question by a safe one, which is such that the command expressed by it can always be obeyed somehow ('in principle,' if not in practice). The safe questions (1a), (3a), and (4a) can then be viewed as the results of 'guarding' the risky (2a) in different ways. Still another method of guarding it is suggested by Prior (and also, for that matter, by Richard Whately);[12] according to this method we are to replace (2a) by the *conjunction* of (3a) and the following yes-no question:

(1') ?*H* ("Is it the case that you have a wife whom you have beaten?")

We readily show in *PIE*, however, that this method yields a result that is equivalent to (4a).

(iii) Let us consider $(5a_1)$–$(5a_4)$ from the point of view of their presuppositions. We find that $(5a_{1,2})$ are safe, whereas $(5a_{3,4})$ are risky in that they both presuppose $(Ex)Wx$ (i.e., the existence of at least one member of the VPO), the negation of which is consistent. Furthermore, $(5a_{2,4})$ differs in an interesting way from the remaining two questions. On a closer comparison of the translations $(5b_1)$ and $(5b_2)$ with one another, we find that while $(5b_1)$ makes a request that the questioner know about each member of the VPO that he is one, $(5b_2)$ makes the stronger request that, in addition, the questioner *know* that he has this knowledge about each member of the VPO; in other words, that he really know himself to have *exhausted* the class of members of the VPO.[13] Such a completeness request is likely to be quite often involved in 'complete list' which-questions, as the label suggests, which in turn supports the conjecture that the quantifiers ($?^m_{KB}$) and ($?^m_{EKB}$) have a wider range of applicability than ($?^m_B$) and ($?^m_{EB}$) when formalization is at stake.

(iv) As far as (6)–(9) or (6a)–(9a) are concerned, we simply note that they presuppose, respectively, the existence of at least one, at least two, exactly one, and exactly two members of the VPO.

(v) Finally, I ought to remind the reader that my speaking of the which-question-forming operators as *quantifiers* seems to be supported by a venerable tradition in the literature on our subject. Ajdukiewicz, Hiż, Carnap, Reichenbach, and Kubiński, among others, have submitted that which-question-forming operators resemble quantifiers in that they *bind* free variables and thus transform conditions (open sentences) into complete (closed) sentences, namely, interrogatives.[14] (The literal reading of (9a), for instance, is then: "For exactly which two *x*'s does it hold that *x* is a member of the VPO.") Now, I take this idea to be a perfectly sound one; what I miss in my venerable predecessors, however, is a rigorous semantical interpretation of interrogative quantification.

---

[12] Prior, "Eroetic Logic," pp. 43–59; R. Whately, cited by Prior.

[13] Hintikka, *Knowledge and Belief*, pp. 165–66.

[14] H. Hiż, "Questions and Answers," *Journal of Philosophy* 59: 253–65 (1962); R. Carnap, *Logical Syntax of Language* (London, 1937), p. 296; H. Reichenbach, *Elements of Symbolic Logic* (New York, 1947), pp. 340–41; T. Kubiński, "An Essay in Logic of Questions," *Atti del XII Internazionale Congresso di Filosofia* (Venice, 1958), pp. 315–22; K. Ajdukiewicz, cited by Kubiński.

6. Additional Topics

Having now drawn the main outlines of a systematic logical theory of questions (in an admittedly rough way), I should perhaps wish you a very good night and a better day tomorrow—however, I feel that something has to be said about the rich variety of topics that remain to be dealt with on our approach.

The quantifiers ($?_\text{B}^\text{m}$) and their variants, as well as ($?_{\text{C}_\text{n}}^\text{m}$) and ($?_{\text{D}_\text{n}}^\text{m}$) are useful for the purpose of analyzing what I call *pure* relational questions of the type, "Which [at least which n, exactly which n] ordered m-tuples are elements of the relation R^m?" But there are also *mixed* relational questions such as

(1) Exactly which two French emperors, together with at least which three generals, defeated which Russian emperors during the nineteenth century in exactly which four battles?

It goes without saying that the analysis of this kind of question becomes extremely complicated. We should be able to enunciate certain general principles guiding formalization, however.

Our interrogative quantifiers may be refined in an important way if, in the spirit of Belnap, we start playing with so-called *categorical qualifications*. A simple example:

(2) When did you arrive in Boston?

may be translated ("Tx" for "x is a time," "Sx" for "you arrived in Boston at x") either as

(2a) $!(Ex)\text{K}(Tx \, \& \, Sx)$

or as

(2b) $!(Ex)(Tx \, \& \, \text{K}Sx)$

where (2b) is obviously weaker than (2a). If QIE were construed as a *many-sorted* predicate-logic with, for instance, special temporal variables $t, t_1, t_2, \ldots$, we could certainly render (2) as

(2c) $!(Et)\text{K}St$

the counterpart of which in a one-sorted theory would be (2b) rather than (2a).

With reference to the analysis of different forms of questions, let me finally point out that if we enrich the vocabulary of QIE with some set-theoretical machinery, we can expect an impressive increase in the number of then definable interrogative forms.

We have already touched upon the notion of interrogative *presupposition*, but a lot more can be done here; for one thing, it turns out that this notion admits of three or four different but equivalent explications (within proper limits, at least) on our approach. One of these explications connects the notion of presupposition with that of *direct answer* in the following way: Q presupposes p, iff, every direct answer to Q logically implies p. This takes us over to the question-(direct)-answer relationship, the explication of which is of course an utterly urgent task even for us, in spite of the fact that, as was pointed out in section 2, we do not have to base interrogative logic on it. Now, a very natural principle guiding explication is one to the effect that the request expressed by a question is satisfied when some direct answer is known by the questioner to be true; another equally important one is the Harrah-Belnap requirement that the question-direct answer relationship must be effectively decidable on the syntactical level.[15] Also, I want to stress here the importance of Harrah's and Belnap's outstanding contributions to the theory of answers in general. Many of their results can be more or less directly mapped into our theory.

The logic of questions itself has already been elaborated upon sufficiently in section 2, but perhaps a few additional words on truth and falsity as applied to questions and imperatives would not be amiss. The idea, due to Kanger, is to use a Tarskian semantical definition of truth that is extended to cover imperatives and interrogatives as well. Since we seem to be able to lay down plausible conditions for the truth (or 'correctness') of the latter, a justification is thus obtained for adopting such a procedure. Let us just note, with Kanger, that our view does not have to conflict with the traditional one to the effect that imperatives and interrogatives are neither true nor false.[16]

[15] Belnap, *An Analysis of Questions*, p. 58 ff.

[16] Again, reference is due to the concluding dialogue of Kanger, *New Foundations for Ethical Theory*.

Ingemund Gullvåg

Reference and the Object Theory

We speak to each other and sometimes understand each other, and we often speak *of* singular things, persons, events, places. Prima facie, we may distinguish between different aspects in this simple conception of a certain way of using language: reference and intersubjective communication. I utter something, mean something by the utterance, and am perhaps understood. Part of the meaning of the utterance is perhaps a reference to some particular thing, and, if so, understanding the meaning involves grasping this reference.

We assume that it is possible to use language in this way; perhaps we want to say that it *must* be possible so to use language if there is to be language at all. But *how* is it possible? For reference as well as intersubjectivity raises old and familiar questions: How can we understand each other, and what is involved in intersubjective understanding and all that presupposes communication? And how can we *refer* to something? What is involved in this? How can language bridge the gap between the given and the non-given; and how can it be a bridge for communication between different persons? Can this occur—can words 'stand for' things, and can they have the same meaning for different persons? Can we know whether they do or not? Is not meaning, insofar as there is any such thing, private? Are we not imprisoned each in his own sphere of experiences and thoughts? We conceive of language as a wonderful bridge from the given experiences to other things—to non-given objects and to others' experiences. But is not this merely a fantasy? How could such a bridge be erected? How can we know that it can? We seem to presuppose such knowledge when we assume that we have common knowledge that concerns reality; but do we have such knowledge, and can we acquire it at all?

The possibility of reference, of identifying and speaking about something real, perhaps distant in space or time, has long seemed puzzling. "Consider . . .

Dosent Gullvåg, of the University of Trondheim in Norway, is a native of Norway.

how the absent is securely present to mind . . . ," said Parmenides. And Wittgenstein asked, "Isn't it queer that in Europe we should be able to mean someone
who is in America?"[1] For convenience, I use the expression "the problem of
reference," although I do not think that there is one very clear problem which can
reasonably be said to be *the* problem of reference, one which is always or usually
intended in this connection. Rather, it seems that we have to do with a notion
that has given rise to a cluster of interrelated puzzles. A search for 'answers' to
puzzling questions may not lead to 'solutions' as much as to awareness of the
underlying notion or notions.

What is it that occurs when we refer to persons, things, events, places, or
understand others' references? An obvious response here is to seek a kind of
answer by considering an elementary, everyday form of reference. We seem to
have this in the situation where someone points or nods toward someone else and
says to me, "His name is Smith." I see the gesture or nod; I follow the direction
with my glance and see the person indicated. The pointing (or nod) is an
action, an action which makes me direct my attention to that which is indicated;
and all reference, one might say, is based upon this elementary pattern. Verbal
means of referring are merely secondary substitutes for pointing. Since we know
what pointing is, we thereby know what reference in general is.

One problem about this is that in order to understand the gesture as pointing I must already understand what it means to point toward something; hence
I must have the notion of pointing, but the idea of *reference* is already involved
in this. So it appears that the attempt to account for reference in terms of pointing will beg the question. Let us disregard this for the sake of argument and
assume that reference to something *present* can be reduced to visible pointing in
this way. But what if the reference is to an absent person or to a place far away
or an event long ago? Then, apparently, it can no more be a question of pointing
or of seeing what is indicated and talked about. What is involved in referring to
something in such cases, and understanding others' references?

One obvious answer is that I simply think of it, mean it, intend it. This
mental act gives the expression its meaning. But how can thoughts refer to
things, to something in reality? What is involved in this? How can we *mean*
something definite by a thought or an utterance? How can we 'point to' some
particular thing by means of an expression in an utterance? How can I indicate
something that is not present, something that I do not see, even something whose
whereabouts I do not know? Must there not be a kind of vision of the soul that
resembles ordinary vision but is mysterious and supernatural? Must there not be
a kind of aiming of the mind that in a peculiar manner aims at the thing even
when it is not here, even when I do not know where it is, even when I do not
know whether it can be said to be in any definite place at all? But what kind of
vision or aiming is this? What is such a mental act of meaning or intending? Do

---

[1] Ludwig Wittgenstein, *Preliminary Studies for the "Philosophical Investigations"* (Oxford, 1960), p. 39 (generally known as the *Blue and Brown Books*).

I tie a kind of connector between the name and the thing (or place, etc.), e.g., between "Piccadilly Circus" and the place itself, perhaps 1000 miles away? What kind of supernatural string could this be?

The relationship between thought of something, and its presence or absence for more direct cognition, e.g., sensation or intuition, has long been felt to be puzzling. Often there has been an assumption that thought, memory, understanding of symbols, and the like, in the absence of that which is thought about, remembered, or is the designatum of the symbol, can be reduced to direct 'presentation' via *representation*. Of this view, it is not the place itself that we connect with the name "Piccadilly Circus" but a representation, a conception, an image of the place.[2] Here an attempt is made to analyze *reference* to an object on the basis of *representation* of the object. If one surveys traditional epistemology one finds that this kind of representational theory has been quite widespread. Plato's doctrine of reminiscence can be so classified; likewise some of Hobbes', Locke's, Berkeley's, and Hume's theories,[3] Mill's, Pierce's, and Russell's in a certain period,[4] and Marxist doctrines of knowledge as something 'mirroring' the world.[5] We find representation theories in various versions in connection with so-called conceptual realism (as in Plato), conceptualism (as in Locke's doctrine of 'abstract ideas in the mind'), and nominalism (as in Berkeley). In all cases, some kind of mental representation is assumed to account for singular reference, whether to abstract or concrete entities. However, such 'accounts' again beg the question insofar as the notion of reference is involved in the notion of representation: something represents something else by virtue of an (intended or understood) reference to the latter. Like all attempts to explain something prior in terms of something posterior this leads to a circle or a regress. I suspect that the same applies to attempts at accounting for reference in terms of verbal significations and how we have learned them, and for *uses* of language in terms of its features as a system (attempts at reducing pragmatic questions to syntactic and semantic questions).

The problem of reference seems to stem from a feeling that understanding is understandable and unproblematic only in connection with references to things here and now, to what is *present*. What is this curious business of *thinking of* something in its absence, *intending* something, *being conscious* of something that is not here, "the mystery of the presence of the absent," as Lovejoy says,[6] echoing the words of Parmenides that "the absent is securely present to the mind?" We

---

[2] A clear statement of the view is one by Suzanne Langer: "In talking *about* things, we have conceptions of them, not the things themselves; and *it is the conceptions, not the things, that symbols directly mean*" (*Philosophy in a New Key* [London: Pelican Books, 1948], p. 49).

[3] See, e.g., L. J. Cohen, *The Diversity of Meaning* (London, 1962); and E. J. Furlong, "Berkeley's Theory of Meaning," *Mind*, vol. 73 (1964).

[4] Bertrand Russell, *The Analysis of Mind* (London, 1921).

[5] See, e.g., A. Schaff, *Zu einigen Problemen der marxistischen Theorie der Wahrheit* (Berlin, 1954).

[6] A. O. Lovejoy, *The Revolt Against Dualism* (LaSalle, Ill., 1955), p. 18.

are hardly concerned with a psychological problem. Nevertheless, perhaps it may be enlightening to consider psychological motivation for the question. A question (when posed and experienced as a problem) can sometimes suggest an underlying motive. Is there not some doubt or insecurity in the problem of reference, not merely a doubt whether we or words can refer to reality but perhaps even whether there *is* any non-present reality to which to refer? This kind of question and doubt may be a reminiscence of the leap we all once took into communication and the conception of an objective world, from what Piaget calls the "egocentric stage," where there is no such consciousness of an enduring common world that stretches beyond the immediate present. (Hence, obviously, there is no notion of the present as the present.)

The question may be posed quite generally, not merely as a problem of remoteness in time and space but of all assumptions that given symbols, signs, words, conceptions, images, or sensations stand for, refer to, or represent *objects* which are not present, or at least are not entirely given here and now. This is the general problem of the relationship of connection between the given and that which is not given, and of *object assumptions*. But here the 'object model' or 'object theory' is presupposed: in perception, thinking, and the use of language we are concerned with objects; that experiences, thoughts, or utterances 'have objective reference' is interpreted as meaning that they have reference to objects.

The object theory applied to *thinking* and the use of language is the doctrine which Price called the "classical theory" of thinking and meaning:[7] thinking involves apprehension or inspection of objects, and the same applies to understanding of language. In the case of *perception*, the object theory has often been combined with epistemological dualism—the doctrine that in perception there is a distinction between a content or datum that is immediately presented to the subject and the real object perceived. Epistemological dualism may be analyzed as the conjunction of two doctrines which we may call the "thesis of transcendence" (i.e., the notion that the object itself is not content or datum immediately present to the subject) and the thesis of an 'immanent' content or datum given to the knowing subject. However, the object theory—the assumption that knowledge, thoughts, messages, etc., 'have objects'—does not *have* to be combined with such dualism. One may assume that there are objects but that object and content are the same, or that there are no 'contents' or 'data' of perception but merely objects. Hence, we may regard epistemological dualism and the classical theory of meaning as results of applications, in different contexts, of a general model which we called the *object theory*.

Thoughts—mental acts—have objects. We inspect, aim at, or grasp objects. Subjects apprehend objects and communicate about objects with each other. This theory is connected with the notion of truth as a relationship between thought and object, and it seems to have an early precursor in a more naive idea that

[7] H. H. Price, *Thinking and Experience*, chap. 10 (London, 1953).

may be discerned in the first glimmering of Greek epistemology, in philosophers as different as Parmenides and Protagoras.[8] They may not have distinguished between the question of what a proposition *is about* or *refers to* (if anything), and whether it is *true*. Answers to both questions were sought rather indiscriminately in terms of the idea of 'grasping an object.'[9] Parmenides and Protagoras may have had a common problem that arose from this idea: if thinking is the 'grasping of objects,' if there is no thought without an object, and if every thought that 'grasps' its object is true, then how are error and falsehood at all possible? A false thought cannot be one without an object, for there is no thought without an object. Nor can a false thought be one that grasps another object than its own, for this would simply be *another* (true) thought. Therefore, according to this view, every thought must be true. The difference between Parmenides and Protagoras may have been in the application of this conception. Parmenides applied it only to thinking in accordance with the Way of Truth, i.e., thinking regulated by the laws of thought, and not to 'opinion' or sense experience; whereas Protagoras may have applied it to thinking and experience generally, which he may have regarded indiscriminately as 'perception' or grasping of objects and, therefore, true. This difference is connected with the difference in conception of the relationship between the object of knowledge or thought and the manifold of perceptions. Parmenides and other Eleatics represented a kind of 'neither-nor' position in their view of the relationship between the object (Being) and varying perceptions. As changing things, two contrary or conflicting sensations cannot, either one or the other, give an adequate impression of the object itself. Sense impressions are all illusory. Only *thinking* (logical thought) provides true knowledge of the object. On the other hand, according to one interpretation, Protagoras represented a 'both-and' position; contrary impres-

[8] According to Parmenides, thinking that is to lead to true knowledge—the Way of Truth—must be subject to the laws of thought, e.g., the principle of identity. ("Subject to" here means that thinking which conflicts with the laws of thought is *impossible*, i.e., would not be thinking. It is tempting to interpret this in modern terminology and say that the laws of thought are constitutive rules of reasoning. See Rawls' and Searle's distinction between regulative and constitutive rules in John Rawls, "Two Concepts of Rules," *Philosophical Review*, vol. 64 (1955), and John Searle, "How to Derive 'Ought' from 'Is,'" *Philosophical Review*, vol. 73 (1964), and "What is a Speech Act?" in *Philosophy in America*, ed. M. Black (Ithaca, N.Y.: Cornell University Press, 1965). That which thought is to grasp and give true knowledge of must *be* in the sense of being identical and unchangeable. That is, it is, was, and remains the same in every respect. There can be no thought without an object (a thought that does not grasp something identically being, is impossible); and all thoughts have the *same* identically being object. Protagoras, according to Plato's perhaps not entirely reliable account in *Theaetetus*, maintained that "it is not possible to think the thing that is not, nor to think anything other than what one perceives, and all perceptions are true" (Plato, *Theaetetus*, trans. in F. M. Cornford, *Plato's Theory of Knowledge* (London, 1935).

[9] Cf. Cornford, *Plato's Theory of Knowledge*, p. 116. Morton White mentions grasping as a traditional analogy to understanding in *Toward Reunion in Philosophy* (Cambridge: Harvard University Press, 1956), p. 5 ff. Wittgenstein suggests the object theory in Parmenides' version in *Philosophische Untersuchungen/Philosophical Investigations*, 2nd ed., section 518 (Oxford, 1958).

sions of the object are all true, the object *has* contrary properties, and varying perceptions involve different selections of such contrary properties.[10]

Attempts have been made to overcome the difficulties involved in these early versions of the object theory of knowledge by replacing them with more refined and more clearly dualistic versions in which thinking was conceived of as vision of or 'stretching towards' objects rather than 'grasping' of them. Plato's epistemology is an example of such a more clearly dualistic version of the object theory; and the modern act-object theories are descendants of such dualistic conceptions.

The object theory was developed in one version as a substance theory, in another as a Platonism. The notions of substance were gradually connected with a dualistic theory of perception in which impressions or perceptions are assumed to be distinct from the real substance itself, which, however, is a *cause* of sensations. Reality (substance) may be assumed to differ from what human experiences seem to indicate, or to be similar to it in essential respects (e.g., with regard to movement, geometric form, and the like). Plato's version of the object theory differs from substance theories in regarding the 'being things' which are the objects of thoughts—the ideas or forms—as ideal types in relation to perceptions rather than as causes of them.

The object theory of thinking and knowledge was, in different versions, dominant in philosophy up to the beginning of this century. It structured the medieval discussions: the struggle concerning universals was precisely a conflict over how extensive an application the object model was to be given—whether universals were to be regarded as objects or 'substances' to which abstract words ("redness," "human nature," etc.) refer.[11] The object theory has also marked modern philosophy—e.g., Descartes, Locke, and Kant. Through Brentano's works it influenced epistemological and logical discussions at the end of the last and the beginning of the present century—the various versions of act-object theories of 'psychologists' as well as 'logists.' In the writings of Brentano's pupil Meinong, one of the logists, we encounter a conception of objects neither as ideal types in relation to perceptions nor as substantial causes of them, but simply as intention-possibilities. Object is whatever can be intended, thought of—and

[10] In this connection we may distinguish between two interpretations of claims that the object is 'transcendent' in relation to immediate experiences, sensations, phenomena: (1) that it is something entirely apart from, distinct from, phenomena, in the sense that no part of the object can be a member of the class of immediate phenomena; (2) that it is something *more than*, exceeding, additional to certain given experiences or phenomena (at one instant, or in a single subject). Parmenides' Being was supposed to be transcendent in sense (1); Protagoras may, according to certain interpretations, have meant that the object or reality was transcendent in the sense of (2), but not in the sense of (1).

[11] Discussed (*passim*) in Porphyry's introduction to Aristotle's *Categories* (Porphyrius, "Einleitung in die Kategorien," in *Aristoteles Kategorien/Lehre vom Satz* [*Organon I-II*], Philosophische Bibliotek, vol. 8–9 [Hamburg, 1962]). Cf. W. V. O. Quine's chapter, "On What There Is," in his *From a Logical Point of View* (Cambridge: Harvard University Press, 1953).

Meinong placed no such limitations on what he would accept as 'thinking of something' as Parmenides might have done.[12] Qua possibilities, Meinong's objects were 'being' in Parmenides's sense—self-identical, unchanging.

In the versions of Brentano and his pupils the object theory became the doctrine of mental, subjective acts and objects. This scheme was applied quite generally to empirical, logical, and mathematical knowledge, evaluation, and even to emotions or emotive attitudes. At one time (e.g., for Meinong) it constituted the basis for distinguishing among philosophy, mathematics and logic, natural science, and psychology. It was used for attacking 'psychologism,' defined as a conflation of the study of mental acts or processes with the study of intentional objects as such.[13] The scheme was also a part of the basis for attacking subjectivism and idealism in early analytic philosophy.[14] As modified by Husserl, the act-object scheme influenced phenomenological and, to some extent, existentialist views.

Another version of the object theory fixes not so much on the idea of mental acts' intending objects, but rather on the idea of words or utterances referring to objects. The object theory is here attached to the notion of verbal references to things (reality). We assume that *words* often denote (or 'stand for') real things,[15] and we assume that utterances or propositions refer to reality. By virtue of making an assertion about something with a claim to saying something factually

[12] For Meinong, even contradictions were 'objects,' in addition to real objects and ideal ones (relations, numbers, universals, propositions, etc.) Every object is given, as intention-possibility, prior to our determination of whether it subsists or exists or not. It is given in a way which does *not* prevent it from being non-real or non-subsisting. See A. Meinong, "Über Gegenstandstheorie," in *Abhandlungen zur Erkenntnistheorie und Gegenstandstheorie*, Gesammelte Abhandlungen, vol. 2 (Leipzig, 1913), pp. 486–87, 489–90, 491.

[13] Cf. also Husserl in *Logische Untersuchungen*, vol. I (Halle, 1928).

[14] See, for example, G. E. Moore's "Refutation of Idealism," *Mind*, vol. 12 (1903); reprinted in Moore's *Philosophical Studies* (London, 1922). Russell too at one time accepted the act-object theory as a basis for rejecting subjectivism and idealism, but gave it up in *The Analysis of Mind* (London, 1961). Cf. also A. Phalén, "Kritik af subjektivismen i olika former med särskild hansyn till transscendentalfilosofien" [Criticism of various versions of subjectivism with particular regard to the transcendental philosophy], in *Festskrift till E. O. Burman på hans 65 års dag* (Uppsala, 1910).

[15] Precursors of such views may be found in distinctions in traditional logic, e.g., among "things, conceptions, and names" or between "sign and designatum." Frege distinguished among objects, conceptions, and words but claimed that conceptions (*Vorstellungen*) must be distinguished from the word's sense (*Sinn*), so that we here pass from the psychologistic trichotomy to the logical or semantic one—word-sense-designated object. Analogous semantic distinctions have been drawn by R. Carnap (see *Introduction to Semantics* [Cambridge: Harvard University Press, 1946], pp. 8–9), and Quine. Certain versions of the object theory of meaning have influenced discussions on the foundations of mathematics and logic (Quine, "On What There Is," and A. Church, "The Need for Abstract Entities in Semantic Analysis" *Proceedings of the American Academy of Arts and Sciences*, vol. 80, no. 1 [1951]). The object model has also been used in linguistics. In all of these cases it is said that signs refer to or stand for 'things' (*Gegenstande*, objects). Plainly, the notion of a common, objective reality or world of 'things' is associated with this. The sign is assumed to 'indicate' or stand for something in this common reality; sometimes it is assumed that the sign has or acquires its meaning or signification by virtue of its being used to refer to reality.

true we mean to *refer* to it; thereby we *presuppose* the existence of that which we mean to assert something about. The possibility of the reference is not a function of whether the proposition is true or false[16] but of whether the *presupposition* is true, i.e., of whether there is something to which the referring expression refers.[17]

That a statement or assertion *presupposes* something which it is about has been maintained by many in different camps, for example, by Frege (with respect to singular statements).[18] Far from being a *new* theory, one might indeed call this the classical theory. Urban mentions "the Platonic axiom, that for an assertion to be significant at all, it must always be, directly or indirectly, an assertion about what is,"[19] and he remarks that this view has been held by many earlier logicians and philosophers, e.g., Ueberweg, who thought that statements like "God is just," "The soul is immortal," "True friends are to be valued," "must involve the statement that there are such things as God, a soul, true friends."[20] It is not my purpose here to criticize details in the application of the object theory or to trace the limits of its justified application, if any, but rather to indicate its prevalence. According to the object theory as applied to the use of language, we use words *inter alia* for the purpose of referring to objects in reality (including persons) which are there, and are what they are, regardless of whether we think or speak of them or not.[21]

Object or act-object theories may be seen to have a connection of sorts with various kinds of familiar phenomena which perhaps were their natural roots or points of departure. The theories make us think of the grasping (manipulation) of concrete things, of perceiving them, and of naming them in connection with pointing. In the pointing situation there is a distinction between the person who speaks and points, the person who understands him, and *that* which is pointed out and mentioned (the 'object'). This elementary pattern might seem applicable to communication and thinking in general—the pointing becomes an 'act' that is 'directed toward' an 'object.' The distinctions which are clear enough in the concrete situation become more problematic in their abstract application, however. Controversies arise about purported 'abstract objects' such as Meinong's

---

[16] Cf. P. T. Geach, *Reference and Generality* (Ithaca, N.Y.: Cornell University Press, 1962), p. 52.

[17] Cf. P. F. Strawson, "On Referring," *Mind*, vol. 59 (1950); reprinted in A. Flew, ed., *Essays in Conceptual Analysis* (London, 1960).

[18] G. Frege, "Über Sinn und Bedeutung" [On sense and reference], *Translations from the Philosophical Writings of Gottlob Frege*, ed. P. Geach and M. Black (Oxford, 1960).

[19] W. M. Urban, *Language and Reality* (London, 1961), p. 302.

[20] *Ibid.*, p. 303.

[21] Strawson expresses this presupposition of reality thus: "We think of the world as containing particular things some of which are independent of ourselves; we think of the world's history as made up of particular episodes in which we may or may not have a part; and we think of these particular things and events as included in the topics of our common discourse, as things about which we can talk to each other" (P. F. Strawson, *Individuals: An Essay in Descriptive Metaphysics* [London, 1961], p. 15).

"Gegenstände höherer Ordnung" and Brentano's *"Objekt (worunter . . . nicht eine Realität zu verstehen ist),"* and about the *"immanente Gegenständlichkeit"* (immanent object-relatedness) of thinking and understanding.[22] The 'object of intention' is now something immaterial or not publicly observable and has probably often been identified variously with *connotation, meaning, concept,* or *universal,* as well as with *proposition.* Such notions of abstract objects of reference or intention may arise, for instance, in attempts at applying the schema in discussions of logic and mathematics (e.g., in discussions of "what numbers are"). A need for them was also felt in connection with religious statements or problems (e.g., "How can God be one and yet three?" The medieval solution was, as follows: He is an 'abstract object,' a universal or essence pervading the three personifications); and there might conceivably be a need for them in connection with discussions of value statements. For some types of communications there may arise questions of what the 'object' is; for others, what the nature of the 'indication' of it is. In connection with locutions, conflicts between conceptual realism and nominalism may rage; mentalism-physicalism conflicts, or controversies about whether God or goodness or the past exist may be connected with other types of communications. More or less profound disagreements of these kinds might perhaps be taken as symptoms that a scheme has extended too far beyond its natural application.

According to various versions of the object theory, we can perceive, think of, have knowledge about, and refer to and speak about objects of various kinds— material things, persons, events, places, numbers, concepts, properties, relations, classes, etc. And we presuppose that we sometimes think of, speak of, and perceive the same things as others do. If in fact we do one or all sometimes, it must be *possible* for us to do it; this is an aspect both of the traditional and common notions of reality, and of the idea of the 'object': the object is something *public* which different persons can perceive, think of, speak about. It is 'objective' in three senses: (1) *transcendent* in relation to the perception, thought, or intention and the consciousness of the person concerned, not just 'mental content' of some mind; (2) *independent* of the perception, thought, or intention and consciousness, not something which exists only by virtue of and dependent upon that perception, thought, or intention, or on a personal mind; (3) *intersubjective,* i.e., something that can be perceived, thought of, and referred to by *different* persons. The 'problem' or puzzles traditionally felt in this connection derive from the presuppositions of the object's 'objectivity' in these three senses. Among the questions asked are the following: What is the meaning of, or what is involved in, thinking of or knowing the object when it is not immediately and directly *given* in its entirety (which it is not, according to the presupposition of 'transcendence')? How is such thinking or intending or knowing of something beyond the immediately given possible? How can changing conceptions and thoughts

---

[22] Cf. F. Brentano, *Psychologie vom empirischen Standpunkt* (Leipzig, 1874).

'grasp' or be in agreement with something that is in itself independent of those conceptions and thoughts (as the object is, according to the presupposition of independence)? How can we know about this correspondence? How can different persons think of, know, and communicate about the *same* object (which should be possible, according to the presupposition of intersubjectivity)? How can they *know* that they are concerned with the same object (which, apparently, it is necessary to presuppose is possible if we are to assume that we do have intersubjective knowledge of things, are able to describe and measure the same objects, and so on)?

These presuppositions of what characterizes the object as such were elements of so-called realistic epistemology, as applied to concrete objects (substance theories) as well as abstract objects (conceptual realism). But in reaction to the puzzles of reference and scepticism, deviant epistemologies arose through negations of one or more of the presuppositions: relativism (the object is 'dependent' upon perception or thought); idealism (the object is 'immanent in' and 'dependent upon' the subject); neutral monism or phenomenalism (the object is 'immanent' content in mind, when known, but exists independently of being known); pluralism (objects are not intersubjective, i.e., identical for different persons, but personal, or culturally determined, or the like, and each person or group lives in his [its] own world). It may be true to say that there is no *one* concept 'object' involved in all of these different types of epistemological doctrines, since the different theories are distinguished precisely through different conceptions of 'object.' But these different conceptions may be said to be related and to show family resemblances in accordance with this concept as discussed by Wittgenstein. It is not merely a matter of the same *word* being used, without any similarity between the uses in different theories.

As the problem of reference was posed in the beginning, there was presupposed a distinction between what is *immediately given* and *known* and that which is *not* immediately given but to which one refers. The origin of this distinction was the discrimination between what is *present* for me here and now, and what is not present. This point of departure, however, does not involve the thought of the possibility of something that is *in principle* precluded from being present. The point of departure is the actual, contingent dichotomy between my present situation and other things which I can think of, remember, etc., which are absent, but which may have been present for me before, or may come to be so.

Traditionally, the problem of reference arose as a question that presupposed a *necessary, essential* distinction between the given and the non-given, the 'immanent' and the absolutely 'transcendent.' Kant and others assumed that 'immanent' sensations, conceptions, thoughts, etc., 'stand for' or 'indicate' something 'transcendent to knowing,' i.e., in principle unknowable. Kant assumed that *'Erscheinungen'* or phenomena have objects which are non-empirical, transcendent entities. Others, in the same vein, have presupposed an 'absolute reality' which cannot itself be known, but which signs, etc., 'indicate' or 'refer to.' Such a development may occur naturally if the question of the connection between that which is in fact present and that which is in fact absent makes one wonder whether so-called present objects really *are present*, or whether they too involve some kind of 'transcendence' beyond that which is given in sensation. Then all kinds of 'object references' or object presuppositions may be felt as going beyond *the given*, but thereby also as problematic. But the 'given' and the 'not given' things are then so determined that the distinction is one of the principle of necessity rather than contingency. Whereas before only the purported ability of thought to bridge the gap between that which is actually present and that which is actually absent was felt to be peculiar, now the conception or presupposition of reality in general becomes problematic.

Now pointing may appear puzzling too, for other reasons than before. It is not merely a question of what is involved in understanding the gesture as a reference to or indication of something, but also the question of what is this *something* referred to, and how can another person lead *my* look and *my* attention toward something that *he* intends and sees? His experiences in the situation are presumably not the same as mine. I do not see the same that he sees, if "see the same" means having identical or completely similar given sense impressions (sense data). We presuppose that we are aware of the same object; but what is this 'awareness of an object?' If we are both aware of the same object but have more or less different sense impressions, the object cannot be *identical* with the given sense impressions of the one or the other; for, when I am aware of *the object*, it is obviously not the other person's sense impressions I am aware of; and the same applies to him with regard to my sense impressions. But what then is involved in this awareness of 'the object,' which is apparently something *different* from the sense impressions of the one or the other? Is 'the object' a kind of ideal conjunction or construction of sense impressions of several persons? But of *which* impressions? Obviously not all, for then this 'object' would comprise everything ever sensed.

In order to know which impressions were to enter into the constituting of a certain object we should first have to know that they were impressions of that object (and the same object). Is the object a common *cause* of our several and differing sense impressions? But when we speak of the object we do not necessarily mean, presumably, to refer to any cause of perceptions. "That is a beautiful vase." Do I mean to say that the cause of our sense impressions is beautiful? Hardly. But what then is the object? Is it simply nothing but a *something* that we can refer to and speak about, a kind of projection from our system of communication? Some epistemologists, such as Kant, have apparently conceived of a kind of causal relation between the object and the mental content or conception representing it.[23] However, the assumption of a causal relation here is epistemologically irrelevant or secondary.

---

[23] The famous objection of the 'transcendental philosophers' on this point was that Kant applied the category of causality beyond the limits of applicability drawn by himself. This objection seems less fundamental than the one mentioned in the text.

The problem is not to explain the impression or conception as the result of an external influence, but to indicate the meaning of claims that the impression or conception or sign, etc., 'represent,' 'indicate,' 'refer to,' or 'stand for' an 'object' that may perhaps be presupposed to be 'absolutely transcendent' and 'unknowable.' In the latter case it seems to become impossible by presupposition to say what could be meant by "referring to the object." To say that a conception or impression 'stands for' or 'represents' or 'refers to an object'—a mere something of which we cannot say or know anything whatever—seems equivalent to saying that we cannot indicate rules or criteria for the application of these expressions in this context.

Analogous objections may be made against traditional doctrines of knowledge of objects which are in themselves unknowable—reality itself—via signs or symbols. If the signification of certain referring signs is supposed to consist in their referring to objects, and we can have *no* knowledge of the 'objects,' then we do not know anything about what the signs stand for; i.e., the signs have no signification for us and are thus not signs for us. In other words, assumptions of this kind can be reduced *ad absurdum*. We could not even conceive of ourselves as having the same relationship to such 'signs' as to Arabic or Chinese characters of which we have no understanding whatever. For somehow we have been told, in a language that we do understand, that these signs symbolize things, situations, ideas, and the like; and examples may be given which suggest approximately how the signs function, perhaps what they 'stand for.' But this could not happen with 'signs' that are claimed to 'stand for,' 'refer to,' or 'indicate' something that no one can know or say anything about.

Hence, the transition from conceiving of the distinction between the given and the non-given as a contingent distinction to construing it as necessary, so that the non-given becomes *in principle* and *necessarily* non-given and unknown, seems to lead to assumptions reducible to absurdity. This, however, applies not only when the distinction is made the basis for the problem of reference in connection with the object theory, but even more generally.

For the problem of reference may be regarded as a particular version of the general epistemological 'problem' of 'explaining' or 'accounting for' the 'non-given' in terms of the 'given.'[24] A related, historically well-known version is 'the problem of knowing,' i.e., of how the subject (presupposed as given, unproblematically known) can *know* the object (which is supposed not to be given in the

[24] This general epistemological problem, if it deserves this title, may be regarded as one version of a still more general problem, the traditional philosophical 'problem' par excellence: the question of finding a 'fixed point,' an 'absolute,' and of 'accounting' for everything else— all 'relative' things—in terms of this absolute. It seems clear that what we encounter here is a *form* of question, a *scheme*, rather than any determinate problem. As Phalén once noted, the ancient 'metaphysicacosmological problem' of natural philosophy (about the primeval stuff or the elements and the constitution of the world) may be seen as one kind of completion of this general scheme, while the general epistemological problem may be regarded as another. (See Phalén, "Kritik af subjektivismen"; cf. G. Oxenstierna, *Vad är Uppsalafilosofien?* Verdandis Småskrifter, no. 400 (Stockholm, 1938).

same manner as the subject). The epistemological problem may be phrased as a general problem of accounting for all purported knowledge in terms of something epistemologically primary, given, absolutely fundamental, regardless of whether this is conceived as sense data or other mental contents, or subject, mind, pure consciousness, etc. In all of these cases something is supposed to be unproblematically known, given, whereas something else is problematic; and the question asks for some kind of transition to the latter from the former, some 'account,' perhaps a justification or reduction. But it holds in general that if the distinction between the problematic and the unproblematic—that which is to be 'accounted for' and that which may be taken for granted as a basis of the account—is turned into something *necessary* so that the non-given is necessarily non-given, then the 'problem' will assume a form that renders it in principle unsolvable.

If the object is construed as *absolutely* 'transcendent' and unknowable in relation to an absolute basis of 'immanent' knowledge, then no account can be given of what could be meant by 'referring to' the object, not to mention 'knowing' it. The 'problem,' thus posed, proves to rest upon conflicting presuppositions. The very notion of a necessary distinction, a limit, between the 'given' and the 'non-given,' the 'immanent' and the 'transcendent,' the epistemologically unproblematic and the problematic, seems absurd. If one *can* meaningfully draw a distinction, without getting involved in absurdity, then one can indeed pose the 'problem' of 'crossing' the boundary or limit. But then one has already crossed it, as a presupposition of posing the problem. The two sides of the borderline then do not have fundamentally different epistemological statuses. They presuppose each other mutually. Otherwise the attempt at drawing a limit involves a more or less hidden absurdity—'statements' about the 'limit' can be reduced *ad absurdum*. But in that case there is no problem of 'crossing' any 'border' either. The 'problem' is my own confusion. The idea of a limit which we can indicate, and which is absolutely 'impassable for cognition,' is absurd. If a 'limit' were 'absolutely impassable for cognition,' we could not draw it or perceive it.

It is tempting to reject all such traditional questions and puzzles simply as '*Scheinprobleme*,' and one form of such rejection is implied in the claim that the query rests on presuppositions which are reducible to absurdity. However, in the case of the problem of reference it is not clear that *all* plausible versions or interpretations of it must involve contradictory presuppositions. And other types of *Scheinproblem*—charges with a point of departure in logical empiricism and the discussion of the criterion of meaning—have lead back to a discussion of object presuppositions and suppositions of 'singular existence' in connection with terminological frameworks or conceptual schemes.

One may say that within analytic philosophy sceptical questions about 'explaining' or 'justifying' or 'accounting for' something problematic (knowledge of 'transcendent' objects) on an unproblematic basis became questions of 'reconstruction' of the problematic (object-)assumptions on an epistemologically primary basis. But the problems of choice of basis and justification of the choice ultimately lead back to questions about object reference and existence, the status of objects, and object presuppositions. In this discussion within analytic philosophy, one may distinguish between a 'conventionalist-pragmatic' and an 'absolutistic-descriptive' tendency. Both may be distinguished from linguistic relativist views of the kind maintained by B. L. Whorf. The former tendency, represented, for example, by Carnap and Quine (in spite of their divergences), involves an assumption that we can *choose* terminological frameworks or conceptual schemes and ontologies (object presuppositions); choices may be evaluated in terms of theoretical utility, fruitfulness, and simplicity.

Carnap as well as Quine would say that questions of whether a certain framework or scheme is true or adequate in relation to reality do not express real problems. For we can only compare frameworks or schemes with each other, not with any reality independent of languages or conceptual schemes. Carnap claimed that such 'external' questions about existence or reality, questions 'external' in relation to a certain framework, have no theoretical, cognitive meaning; only 'internal' questions of existence do. External questions about existence may perhaps be reinterpreted as questions of the utility or fruitfulness of a certain framework.[25] Quine thought that assumptions about objects, e.g., assumptions that physical things exist, or that numbers, concepts, properties, classes, or propositions do, may be regarded as *myths* analogous to beliefs in gods, although more theoretically useful or fruitful than mythologies.

On the other hand there is what we might call an 'absolutistic-descriptive' tendency, represented, for example, by Strawson (*Individuals*) and Hampshire (*Thought and Action*), which holds that there is one *fundamental* conceptual scheme which is not a matter of convention, arbitrary choice, or utility, but which is the conceptual scheme that we must all presuppose by virtue of our *use of language*, in science as in ordinary discourse. The conceptual schemes and systems developed in formal and empirical sciences may perhaps be regarded as conventions or myths which are more or less fruitful; but the *basis* of all human intellectual activity is a certain conceptual scheme that is the one we all presuppose and must presuppose (or, to which we cannot imagine any radical alternative). This we can simply investigate and describe in descriptive metaphysics. But Strawson and Hampshire also seem inclined to think that it is a question of a *conceptual scheme*; it is the *scheme* that is investigated, and there can be no question of comparing the scheme with an independent reality. Hampshire remarks that in the case of the relationship between thinking or knowledge and reality, we are concerned with *one* question not several (of knowledge, and reality, and the relationship between them). This one question is: What are the necessary conditions for making statements and for distinguishing between truth

    [25] R. Carnap, "Empiricism, Semantics and Ontology," *Revue Internationale de Philosophie*, vol. 4, no. 11 (1950); reprinted in R. Carnap, *Meaning and Necessity*, 2nd ed. (Chicago, 1956) in slightly changed form, and in R. Rorty, ed., *The Linguistic Turn* (Chicago, 1967).

and falsehood when we refer to reality?[26] Among other things, it is a matter of investigating presuppositions of singular existence, and these presuppositions are attached to our conceptual scheme. A third kind of view is the Whorfian one, i.e., that there are different conceptual schemes in different linguistic communities, and that no essential and indispensable common features of such different conceptual schemes can be indicated.[27]

However, outside of analytic philosophy, the older versions of the problems of reference and presuppositions of existence may still be encountered. In Marxist theory of knowledge, one finds a good old-fashioned doctrine that human perceptions and beliefs are more or less adequate reflections (representations) of an objective reality that is in itself independent of human perceptions, languages, conceptual schemes, etc. It is not only meaningful and permissible to say that human perceptions and conceptual schemes are confronted with an independent, objective reality with which they can be compared; but such comparison (practice) is precisely the basis for determining *truth*.

In phenomenology, as mentioned before, we find an act-object theory (Husserl's scheme *Noesis-Noema-Gegenstand*). However, the object (*Gegenstand*) is disregarded (by 'phenomenological reduction'). At first, this is as a methodological principle, but gradually it seems to aquire metaphysical consequences in the direction of subjectivism or idealism. These metaphysical consequences may be traced into existentialism as represented by Sartre's and Heidegger's early writings. Employing a few slogans, we may say that within recent analytic philosophy there is a tendency to regard the existence of objects as something that is presupposed by virtue of the acceptance or use of a certain *system*, language, or conceptual scheme, and not actually as something independent of system. We may speak of an underlying assumption of objects as being *system-dependent*.[28] In phenomenology and existentialism there are underlying assumptions that 'objects' are dependent upon intention or consciousness. These assumptions emerge in, for example, Sartre's suggestions that consciousness "spontaneously creates" its objects.[29] In Marxist philosophy there is an explicit doctrine that 'objects' (or reality) are *independent* of consciousness or intentionality and systems.[30]

---

[26] S. Hampshire, *Thought and Action* (London, 1960), p. 13.

[27] See, e.g., E. A. Burtt, "Descriptive Metaphysics," *Mind*, vol. 72 (1963); and G. Iseminger, "Our Conceptual Scheme," *Mind*, vol. 75 (1966).

[28] See, e.g., Carnap's rejection, in *Der logische Aufbau der Welt/Scheinproblem in der Philosophie*, 2nd ed. (Hamburg, 1961), of the distinction between concept or conception and object as inessential; and his rejection of 'external' questions of existence, in connection with frameworks, in "Empiricism, Semantics and Ontology." Cf. Quine's remarks that we cannot compare our conceptual scheme with an independent reality, and Hampshire's observations in a similar vein; and Quine's "Ontological Relativity," *Journal of Philosophy*, vol. 65, no. 7 (1968).

[29] See M. Farber, "Pervasive Subjectivism," *Philosophy and Phenomenological Research*, vol. 25 (1965), and E. Fink, "'l' Analyse intentionelle et la problème de la pensée speculative," in *Problèmes actuels de la phénoménologie*, ed. H. L. van Breda (Paris, 1952).

[30] See, e.g., Schaff, *Zu einigen Problemen der marxistischen Theorie der Wahrheit* (Berlin, 1954).

In analytic philosophy the notion of the system, the framework, the conceptual scheme, has in a sense taken over the role of the notion of *subject* in traditional epistemology. Instead of problems of how the subject can refer to or grasp the object, we now find problems of the relationship between the system and the world or reality, in other words, existence presuppositions. Instead of theses of the object's dependence or independence of the subject, we may now speak of implicit theses of dependence or independence of *system* or framework. (A good case in point is Quine's paper "Ontological Relativity.") Instead of problems of intersubjectivity, we may now speak of problems of relationships between systems. Whether this transition from anthropocentric or subject-centered to system-centered philosophy involves a real liberation from or dissolution of the traditional epistemological problems is quite doubtful. I suspect that essentially the same general type of fallacy that was involved in traditional epistemological idealisms may be rediscovered in more recent explicit or implicit notions of objects (or existence) as something dependent upon system. Instead of "to be is to be perceived (or thought)" the underlying motif is now "to be is to be presupposed by (in) an accepted system," or "to be is to be an element in the domain (universe of discourse) of an interpreted system"; but in both cases it seems implicit that "to be," "to exist," "to be real," etc., are terms or notions capable of definition or analysis in other terms. I suspect that this is a fundamental mistake, but I shall not try to defend this suspicion here.[31]

[31] I do so in another context, *Filosofiske Problemer*, vol. 34: *Referanse, mening og eksistens* (Oslo, 1967) (forthcoming in English translation).

Erik Stenius

The Concepts 'Analytic' and 'Synthetic'

1. THE PROBLEM OF HOW TO MAKE THE KANTIAN DISTINCTION BETWEEN "ANALYTIC" AND "SYNTHETIC" MORE PRECISE

In the third section of the *Prolegomena*, Kant remarks that the division of judgments into 'analytic' and 'synthetic' is indispensable for the critique of human reason and thus deserves to be considered classical within that discipline. Kant's appraisal has endured. If by "critique of reason" we understand what today is called "epistemology," his division has indeed become classical, and it has been considered of fundamental philosophical importance by almost all later philosophers, including the logical empiricists.

In recent times, however, the tenability of this division has been assailed. The idea that a dichotomy can be made between 'analytic' and 'synthetic' statements has been declared an untenable dogma which leads to bad philosophy. The main leaders of this attack are the Harvard professors W. V. O. Quine and Morton G. White.[1] For my part, I think the attack is partly founded on an insufficient understanding of what the question is about, and that it applies the pragmatistic doctrine that there are no sharp distinctions, but only differences in degree, to an area in which it leads to intellectual incapacity rather than clarity. But this does not mean that I regard the criticisms of the distinction between 'analytic' and 'synthetic' as wholly unjustified. It is remarkable that a distinction that has been considered to be of such philosophical importance has never, so far

Professor Stenius, of the University of Helsinki, is a native of Finland.

[1] W. V. O. Quine, "Truth by Convention" (1936), reprinted in *Readings in Philosophical Analysis*, ed. H. Feigl and W. Sellars (New York: Appleton-Century-Crofts, 1949), pp. 250–73; "Two Dogmas of Empiricism," *Philosophical Review*, vol. 60 (1951); *From a Logical Point of View*, ed. 2 (Cambridge, Mass.: Harvard University Press, 1961) (contains a revised version of "Two Dogmas of Empiricism"). Morton G. White, *The Analytic and the Synthetic: An Untenable Dualism* (1950), reprinted in *Semantics and the Philosophy of Language* (Urbana, Ill.: University of Illinois Press, 1952), pp. 272–86.

as I know, been given an even moderately adequate definition, and that such an abundance of what could be called logical misconceptions has developed around these concepts.

We must thus state that the question of how the concepts 'analytic' and 'synthetic' should be defined has not been satisfactorily clarified. I want to add that a clarification of this question involves us in a tangle of other questions of semantic and epistemological theory, at which I can only hint in this paper.

One of the main tasks of philosophical analysis, I think, is to make clear the difference between questions about linguistic convention and questions about the subject matter of discourse, that is, to make clear the difference between linguistic conventions and such questions as concern matters of fact, values, moral norms, and so on. It is as a step in the clarification of this difference that the distinction between 'analytic' and 'synthetic' is important. Thus I think that this distinction is important not only in epistemology but also in other branches of philosophy. However, in the following I shall dwell only upon epistemology, or rather on the application of our distinction to language as used to make statements about facts.

2. The Distinction Is Semantic, Not Epistemological

How then are the concepts 'analytic' and 'synthetic' to be defined? In *Prolegomena*, section 2, Kant characterizes them in this way:

(A) Metaphysical knowledge must contain nothing but judgments *a priori*; this is required by what is peculiar to their [*or* its] sources. But whatever be the origin of judgments and whatever be the kind of their logical form, there is a difference between them as to their content, according to which they are either *explanatory* and add nothing to the content of knowledge, or *enlarging* in that they increase the given knowledge; the former can be called *analytic* judgments, the latter *synthetic* judgments.[2]

To this characterization Kant adds the following remark:

(B) Analytic judgments say nothing in the predicate that was not already thought in the concept of the subject, though not so clearly and with equal consciousness.

According to the *Critique of Pure Reason*, this means that we arrive at the concept of the predicate by an analysis of the concept of the subject into its component concepts.

Formulation (A) does not appear in the *Critique of Pure Reason*; there the definition of our terms is rather of the form (B). This has led later philosophers to accuse Kant of thinking of the whole division as one of subject-predicate

---

[2] The italics are Kant's. Kant's pronoun can be translated either as "their" or "its" because of the fact that its reference is ambiguous; it may refer either to the "judgments" or to "the metaphysical knowledge" spoken of earlier. If the sentence is read in isolation, the latter alternative sounds grammatically and rhetorically more natural, but the next sentence suggests rather the former alternative. See also n. 3.

sentences only. I do not think that Kant should be so interpreted even in the *Critique of Pure Reason*, but however one interprets what he says in this work, it is to be noted that definition (A) can be applied to any kind of assertion, and that the phrase "whatever be the kind of their logical form" could be taken as an express hint that this is so. As the characterization is worded, it immediately stresses an important difference between, on the one hand, the distinction between *'a priori'* and *'a posteriori'* and, on the other hand, the distinction between 'analytic' and 'synthetic.' Metaphysical statements must—if they are true—be *a priori*, because this is required by their 'sources.' "Sources" here obviously means the sources of our *knowledge* of the truth of these statements.[3] The distinction between *'a priori'* and *'a posteriori'* must therefore be characterized as an *epistemological* distinction; it concerns the basis of our knowledge. The distinction between 'analytic' and 'synthetic," however, is of a different kind. It expressly does *not* concern the sources of our knowledge of the truth of a statement but rather the *content* it expresses. We are told of some statements that they do not increase our knowledge, and this can only mean that they are what we currently call "factually empty." But the question of whether a statement is factually empty or not is what today we would call a semantic question. So we must consider the distinction between 'analytic' and 'synthetic' a *semantic* distinction. Using Kant's example, the statement "All bodies are extended" is analytic and does not increase our knowledge, because "being extended" is semantically contained in "being a body"—this statement can therefore be said to be factually empty. The same is not true of the statement "All bodies are heavy," which therefore is synthetic.[4]

3. Kant's View on Logical Truth Foreshadows That of Wittgenstein

In the *Prolegomena* (section 2) we are further told that all analytic judgments rest wholly on the law of contradiction. This presumably means that an analytic judgment is characterized by the fact that its negation is a contradiction. This is not much of an explanation, for what is the criterion for deciding

[3] I have based my analysis on the translation "their" in quotation (A) (see n. 2, above). If we choose the translation "its," the argument becomes simpler. As a matter of fact, I do not think Kant had made up his mind about how this sentence should be analyzed grammatically. The "sources" spoken of are the sources of metaphysical knowledge and, consequently, also the sources of metaphysical judgments (insofar as they express metaphysical knowledge). Hence, in Kant's thought the reference of his pronoun was indeed ambiguous. Grammatical inadvertencies like this occur too often in Kant's writings. It should perhaps be added that there is plenty of other evidence for the view that the distinction between *a priori* and *a posteriori* as applied to statements is in Kant (and most other writers) an epistemological distinction.

[4] The fact that the distinction between 'analytic' and 'synthetic' is a semantic distinction in Kant is concealed to a certain degree by the fact that Kant expresses himself in 'psychological' terms, when he actually wants to make semantic distinctions. The idea 'semantics' was not familiar to him. This had led Ayer to mistakenly regard Kant's argument against the analyticity of arithmetical propositions as a matter of mere psychology (A. J. Ayer, *Language, Truth and Logic*, ed. 2 [London: Victor Gollancz, 1946], p. 78).

whether the negation of a sentence is a contradiction? It is, however, part of Leibnizian terminology to say that all statements of logic and mathematics "rest on the law of contradiction." Kant protests against this with respect to mathematical statements, so that his use of the phrase "rest on the law of contradiction" seems to imply that he regards what can in some sense be called "logical truths" as analytic.

If we agree that Kant regards logical truths as analytic and if we heed the fact that analytic statements are statements empty of factual content, we arrive at the conclusion that, according to Kant, logical truths are factually empty, and some of Kant's ways of expressing himself seem to indicate that this is indeed what he thinks. This is a view that approaches Wittgenstein's in the *Tractatus*, according to which all logical truths are tautological, which means precisely that they are empty. We may thus state that the Wittgensteinian doctrine of logical truths as tautologies is hinted at even by Kant, though of course Kant does not possess the technical conceptual apparatus which for Wittgenstein is the basis of this doctrine—the construction of logic on the basis of truth-value tables.

4. SUMMARY OF THE DIFFERENT FEATURES OF THE KANTIAN CONCEPT OF ANALYTICITY

I shall sum up the modernized formulation of those features of the Kantian view that have been indicated above:

(I)   The distinction between 'analytic' and 'synthetic' statements is a semantic distinction (in contradistinction to the distinction between '*a priori*' and '*a posteriori*' which is epistemological).

(II)   An analytic statement is seen to be true on the basis of an analysis of the concepts it contains (we could say, of the symbols it contains).

(III)   As to their factual content, analytic statements are empty (analytic statements are tautological).

(IV)   All logical truths are analytic.

Thesis (III) implies that we apply the term "analytic" only to true statements. This is how Kant uses the term. Sometimes, however, the term has been applied not only to true statements but also to false, a distinction being made between 'analytically true' statements and 'analytically false' statements (that is, contradictions). In this respect I follow the Kantian usage here.

5. IGNORING THE PROLEGOMENA LEADS TO MISCONCEPTIONS

As was stated above, we can read features (I) and (III) from definition (A) in the *Prolegomena*. Unfortunately, analytic philosophers as a rule have not started from this definition but from the much more obscure and unsatisfactory definition in the *Critique of Pure Reason*. As a consequence of this, many philosophers have failed to notice the difference between the concept pairs 'analytic-synthetic' and '*a priori-a posteriori*' as stated in (I) and have therefore misconceived both distinctions. In this way they have arrived at the most monstrous interpretations of Kant and of other philosophers. I think this kind of confusion is also relevant for Quine's position. It is more reasonable to think that apriority is a matter of degree than to think the same of analyticity.

6. QUINE'S PARAPHRASE AND VON WRIGHT'S DEFINITION

In his criticism of the analytic-synthetic distinction in "Two Dogmas of Empiricism," Quine begins with the Kantian way of making this distinction, which he paraphrases as follows: "A statement is analytic when it is true by virtue of meanings and independently of fact."[5]

Quine repeats this formulation in *From a Logical Point of View*, and he rejects it on grounds (somewhat different in the two works) which I shall not touch upon. His formulation, however, resembles G. H. von Wright's formulation of the definition of "analytic" in *Den logiska empirismen*,[6] which may be translated thus: "A sentence is called analytic when its truth follows from the meanings of the words it contains." To this definition, von Wright immediately adds: "Analytic judgments do not enlarge our knowledge of reality but concern exclusively the sphere of language." Thus, von Wright emphasizes the same features in the character of an analytic statement as does Quine in his paraphrase of Kant. Nevertheless, there is an essential difference between the two formulations. Whereas Quine seems to conceive of features (II) and (III) as mutually independent components of the Kantian concept of analyticity, von Wright seems to think of feature (III) as a consequence of feature (II). That the truth of analytic sentences 'follows from' the meanings of the words they contain implies that those sentences are empty of factual content.

7. LIKE AYER, VON WRIGHT REGARDS FEATURE (III) AS A CONSEQUENCE OF FEATURE (II)

In order to understand what is meant by this, we need to be clear about what is implied by the phrase "follows from" as used here. von Wright's exposition is popular and does not aim at technical precision. Therefore, we must gather his meaning from his examples. The fact that the truth of a sentence 'follows from' the meanings of the words it contains is illustrated in the following way: ". . . The sentence 'iron is a metal' is analytic, for iron is *defined* as a metal with such-and-such characteristics. . . ." He illustrates the thesis that an-

---

[5] Quine, "Two Dogmas of Empiricism," p. 21; Quine, *Logical Point of View*, p. 21.
[6] G. H. von Wright, *Den logiska empirismen* [Logical empiricism] (Helsingfors: Söderström & C:o, 1943), p. 18.

alytic judgments do not enlarge our knowledge of reality with this example: "The proposition that iron is a metal does not teach me anything about iron which I do not know as soon as I understand what is *meant* by iron."[7]

This example indicates that von Wright's definition of "analytic" is much the same as that given by A. J. Ayer in *Language, Truth and Logic*: "A proposition is analytic when its validity depends solely on the definitions of the symbols it contains, and synthetic when its validity is determined by facts of experience."[8] The difference between von Wright's and Ayer's formulations is that Ayer uses the phrase "depends solely on the definitions of the symbols it contains" whereas von Wright says "follows from the meanings of the words it contains."[9] For Ayer, too, the third feature of analyticity is thought to be a consequence of the second, as seems clear from the definition of "synthetic" in which "determined by facts of experience" is given as the opposite alternative to "depends solely on the definitions of the symbols it contains."

8. The Motivation Being that an Analytic Sentence Can Be Transformed into a Tautology in Propositional Logic

Von Wright's book contains an argument which can be conceived of as an explanation of the fact that the third feature of analyticity is a consequence of the second. He argues as follows:[10] Consider how the word "iron" could be defined. The definition would be of the form: "Iron is a metal which . . .," where what follows after "which" is a list of those conditions in addition to being a metal which a substance must fulfill in order to be iron. Assume that the complete definition of "iron" is "a metal the specific gravity of which is 7.9." If we render the expressions "x is iron," "x is a metal," and "the specific gravity of x is 7.9," as "Ix," "Mx," and "Sx," respectively, we could render the sentence "Iron is a metal" as $(x)(Ix \rightarrow Mx)$. However, according to the definition of "iron," the expression "Ix" in this sentence can be replaced by "$Mx \& Sx$," so we get the sentence

(1) $(x)(Mx \& Sx \rightarrow Mx)$.

Now (1) can be regarded as a conjunction of all sentences of the form $Ma \& Sa \rightarrow Ma$, where "a" denotes some object in our universe of discourse. Every member of this conjunction is, however, a tautology of propositional logic, and the same is true of any conjunction of such tautologies. (1) can thus be conceived of as a tautology in propositional logic. Thus we see that the sentence "Iron is a metal" is analytic from its reduction by means of the definition of

---

[7] *Ibid.*; italics are von Wrights.

[8] Ayer, *Language, Truth and Logic*, p. 78.

[9] I disregard here the fact that Ayer's definition (unlike von Wright's) formally applies not only to 'analytic' propositions (in the Kantian sense) but also to contradictions. See above, section 2.

[10] *Den logiska empirismen*, p. 68ff.

"iron" into a tautology in propositional logic. Since this is what is meant by the phrase that the truth of the sentence "follows from" the meaning of the words it contains, the third feature of analyticity is a consequence of the second.

The argument shows that, at least at the time of writing *Den logiska empirismen*, von Wright embraced the Wittgensteinian doctrine that *all* analytic sentences are reducible by means of definitions to tautologies in the sense of the propositional logic. Actually, von Wright finally gives a more precise definition of "analytic," which can be rendered as follows:

(C)   By an analytic sentence we understand a sentence which, by such substitutions as do not change its meaning, can be transformed into a tautology in the sense of propositional logic.

9. Criticisms of This Motivation

Now I think it is entirely in accordance with the Kantian distinction to assume that feature (III) of the concept of analyticity is a consequence of feature (II). But I think there is much to object to in the reasons von Wright gives for this view, and, as a consequence, I regard definition (C) as unsuccessful. A first objection, which von Wright himself notes, concerns the problem of universal sentences.[11] A necessary condition for the possibility of demonstrating that (1) is a tautology in propositional logic is that we conceive of (1) as a conjunction of a *finite* number of members. This certainly is not possible if the universe to which the all-operator refers is infinite. von Wright says, however, that this is "of subordinate import for the 'philosophical' kernel" of his argument.[12] I cannot agree. The problem of the universal sentence shows that there are *other* ways of ascertaining that sentences are analytic than reducing them by means of definitions to tautologies in propositional logic.

Moreover, if this reduction is to be obtained in the manner prescribed in definition (C), it does not, strictly speaking, work, even if our universe is supposed to be finite. For then the reduction presupposes that this universe consists of a *fixed* number of named objects. If the *all*-operator is to be defined explicitly as a conjunction, we will get different definitions, depending on the number of individuals contained in the universe, and this is rather unsatisfactory.

10. Color Incompatibility and Related Problems

Apart from the problem of universal sentences, there is the further difficulty that in order for *all* analytic sentences to be reducible to tautologies of propositional logic, we must think of our world as described in terms of certain 'elementary sentences' that are *mutually logically independent*. This means that

[11] *Ibid.*, p. 69.
[12] *Ibid.*

as the framework of our description of the world we must assume what in connection with Wittgenstein's terminology I have called a logical space with a "yes-and-no structure."[13] But whatever we think about the *possibility* of giving such a conceptual framework for a description of the world, there is no metaphysical necessity for a description of the world to be framed within such a conceptual apparatus.

I shall, however, not go more deeply into the question in this form. I only want to stress that *if* we conceive of the sentence

(2)   No object is both blue (all over) and red (all over)

as analytic, this is *not* because we think the concepts 'blue' and 'red' must be definable in terms of predicates which are logically independent, and because the sentence could in that way be reduced to a tautology in propositional logic. We think rather that its analyticity is seen *immediately* on the basis of the mutual semantic relations between "blue" and "red." The corresponding fact is still more evident in respect to the sentence:

(3)   If A is older than B and B is older than C, then A is older than C.

So analyticity must be understandable in a way which is independent of reducibility into truth-functional tautologies.

11.   Quine's 'Improved' Definition of "Analytic"

Quine avoids the problem of universal sentences by making all the 'logical truths' of the *predicate* logic the basis of his definition of "analytic." He defines a logical truth in the following way. First, he assumes as given a class of what we call "logical particles," including "and," "if . . . then," "all," "no," etc. A logical truth is then a true statement which remains true even though all components of the statement except the logical particles are reinterpreted.[14] This means in essence that the logical truths of the predicate logic and no others are regarded as 'logical truths.' It follows that what Quine takes to be a paraphrase of the Kantian definition should in fact be stated as:

(D)   A sentence is analytic when it either (a) is a logical truth in the predicate logic or (b) can be transformed into such a truth by substituting synonyms for certain of the expressions which it contains.

This definition seems to be the one Quine finds most acceptable. But he thinks that it, too, must be rejected, because we cannot explain the meaning of "synonymity" otherwise than in terms of analyticity.[15]

---

[13] Erik Stenius, *Wittgenstein's "Tractatus": A Critical Exposition* (Ithaca, N.Y.: Cornell University Press, 1960), chap. 4.

[14] Quine, "Two Dogmas of Empiricism," p. 23; Quine, *Logical Point of View*, p. 23.

[15] "Two Dogmas of Empiricism," p. 31; *Logical Point of View*, p. 32.

12. Why Are the Logical Truths of Propositional Logic Called Analytic?

Now I find definition (D) as unsuccessful as definition (C). The error lies in the fact that it does not take the following question into consideration: Why should the truths of predicate logic be regarded as especially 'logical' truths, and why should they be called *analytic* in any sense which resembles that of the Kantian term?

One answer to these questions is that the truths of predicate logic form a natural generalization of those truths which are traditionally called "logical," and that, therefore, the conception of the truths of predicate logic as analytic is in accordance with the fourth feature in the Kantian concept of analyticity. In view of this argument, we may put our question in the following way: What is the connection between this fourth feature and the other features in the concept of analyticity? For example, is feature (IV) a consequence of features (II) and (III)?

This problem raises a question as to what, if any, the capacity is in which tautologies of *propositional* logic are *themselves* to be called "analytic" on von Wright's account. If we examine von Wright's original definition and take into account that, as we have seen, "follows from the meanings" means "transformability through definitions into a tautology of the propositional logic," then it does not, strictly speaking, apply to sentences that are *themselves* of this sort. Since such sentences are seen to be tautologies *without* any recourse to substitutions of a definiens for a definiendum, 'meanings' seem not to come into play with respect to them. We may therefore ask whether such tautologies are analytic at all in von Wright's sense. Well, they are naturally conceived of as analytic according to definition (C). But if this is the reason why they are regarded as analytic, they do not possess feature (II) of the concept of analyticity but only feature (III). So we may say that in this case feature (III) is not valid as a consequence of feature (II) but on its own account; in this case there is not the consequence-relation between features (II) and (III).

13. The Truth-Value Tables as Definitions

Von Wright's book does, however, contain a line of thought which makes feature (III) a consequence of feature (II) with respect to logical truths in propositional logic. Consider how we can satisfy ourselves that such a logical truth is a 'tautology.' Let us take as an example the logical truth *"Ma & Sa → Ma"* considered above, which may be written in the form

(4) $p \mathbin{\&} q \to p.$

How can we establish that this is a logical truth? We can do so by a combined application of the truth-value tables for conjunction and implication, which renders a truth-value table that gives (4) the value *truth* for any combination of truth values of p and q. Since this is so, (4) is true "no matter what is the case."

This means that the sentence is tautological in the sense that it is empty of factual content.

But how do we know that the truth-value tables for conjunction and implication are the *correct* truth-value tables for the signs "&" and "→"? Elsewhere in von Wright's book, he points out that the truth-value tables for "and," etc., can be conceived of as a kind of definitions for these particles: "The conjunction 'and' is defined as that connection between sentences which holds true [if and] only if each of the connected sentences is itself true."[16] He adds that this could be taken as a criterion for testing whether a child understands the conjunction "and" correctly. "If the child is observed to affirm the conjunction of two sentences only in those cases where each of them is true, and never otherwise, we should think that the child knows what 'and' is." This of course is not quite correct for the particle "and" of everyday language, since "and" has different uses. But it is undoubtedly correct for the *and* concept of symbolic logic. The truth-value table for "&" shows how the sign "&" is used in propositional logic; and likewise, for the truth-value table for the sign "→." The truth-value tables form a kind of definition; they show how certain signs are used.

This aspect of the essence of the truth-value tables has, oddly enough, been almost ignored in the logical literature. One reason for this is that logicians tend to regard 'definitions' as 'equations' of a sort, by means of which one expression is explained to have the same meaning as another. Since every such definition allows for an elimination of the expression defined, I shall call them *elimination definitions*. The truth-value tables are evidently not definitions of this kind. If we try to formulate them in words, we are compelled to use the same words in the definiens as occur in the definiendum. But here we have no elimination definitions: the way in which we teach a person how these tables should be understood and used is indifferent. Rather, they resemble a kind of 'ostensive' definition in a broad sense. We 'indicate' the use of the connectives by means of the truth-value tables.

But if the truth-value tables are definitions, in that they indicate the meaning of certain signs, then we can say that the way in which we come to see that 'logically true' sentences of propositional logic are true is by an 'analysis' of the *meanings* of the words they contain. The words whose meanings are analyzed are the connectives of propositional logic. The formation of the truth-value table of (4) is based on an analysis of meanings of the connectives "&" and "→."

14. ANALYSIS OF THE MEANINGS OF A STATEMENT'S SYMBOLS ESTABLISHES, PROPERLY SPEAKING, NOT ITS TRUTH BUT ITS EMPTINESS

We must nevertheless take note of a certain lack of precision in this way of expressing ourselves. Do we really show the *truth* of (4) by analyzing the

---

[16] *Den logiska empirismen*, p. 55.

meanings of the connectives it contains? In a sense, we do not. What we show by the analysis is that (4) is a *tautology*, that it is true no matter what is the case that it will be verified *by any fact whatsoever*. In order to say of *any* statement that what it says is true, we have to perform two steps: (a) analyze it in order to determine its truth conditions, and (b) ascertain that these conditions are fulfilled. What is peculiar to tautologies is that step (b) is *trivial*, and only in *this* sense do we show the truth of a statement by analyzing the symbols it contains. But, properly speaking, what is shown by *analysis* is not the truth of a statement but the fact that it is a tautology. This fact indicates the real connection between the features (II) and (III) of analyticity; if (II) is rightly understood, it trivially has (III) as a consequence. In order to get a clear conception of what analyticity is, we ought therefore to give feature (II) a form which explicitly includes (III), that is, the form:

(II′)   An analytic sentence can be by an analysis of the meanings of the symbols it contains, seen (a) to be true no matter what is the case, and thus (b) to be empty as to its factual content (tautological).

15. Formulations (E) and (F) of the Definition of "Analytic"

This formulation implies a new definition of "analytic." However, some philosophers will find the phrase "analysis of meanings" vague. Thus, as we have seen, Ayer replaces it with the phrase "definitions of the symbols it contains." We might try to move in the same direction by replacing (II′) with the following definition:

(E)   A statement is analytic if and only if as a consequence of the definitions of the symbols it contains it is true no matter what is the case.

However, it is to be noted that we certainly need not know the definitions of *all* the words that a statement contains in order to be able to see that it is analytic. If, for instance, a statement is a truth-functional tautology, we can state its analyticity on the basis of the definitions of its *connectives* only, regardless of how other words in it are defined. Our definition thus becomes clearer if we change it to:

(E′)   A statement is analytic if and only if as a consequence of the definitions of certain of the symbols it contains it is true no matter what is the case.

But, in fact, even this formulation seems to be too narrow. Consider, for example, sentence (2) or (3). One can doubt that we have any definition of the relevant words "red," "blue," or "older than" of which the tautologicality of these sentences is a consequence. And though I think that we in a sense have such definitions in the cases under consideration, there are other cases where we obviously do not—at least if we do not include among definitions so-called implicit definitions.

Then we ought, after all, to avoid the word "definition" in this context. One reason why it leads to greater clarity to speak of "definitions" instead of "analysis of meanings" is the fact that a *definition*—as it is conceived of in modern logic—is an obvious *convention* about the use of certain words. Consequently, we arrive at greater generality and still greater clarity if we drop the word "definition" and speak of "semantic conventions" instead. We then get the definition

(F)   A statement is analytic if and only if, according to the semantic conventions for the use of certain of the symbols it contains, it is true no matter what is the case.

16. THE REASON FOR CALLING THE TRUTHS OF PREDICATE LOGIC ANALYTIC

At the end of the essay this definition will be further clarified. But for the time being we can accept it as it stands. On the basis of it, we can see that not only the logical truths of propositional logic, but also those of predicate logic are really analytic. Indeed, we can go further and maintain that, no matter what logicians say, it is precisely the fact that they are analytic that essentially justifies the honorific name of "logical truths" for these statements.

As mentioned above (section 11), Quine defines a *logical truth* as a statement which is true and remains true if all components of the statement except the logical particles are reinterpreted. Thus (1) is a logical truth, because it is true and remains true even if the predicates "$M\hat{x}$" and "$S\hat{x}$" are given any other interpretation than that given in section 8. But how does Quine *know* that (1) actually *is* true, and how does he know that it remains true after any reinterpretation of the predicates it contains? Is it by some kind of induction, based upon experiments made for different interpretations of "$M\hat{x}$" and "$S\hat{x}$," and the observation that the statements arrived at in this way always are true (or are confirmed)? Evidently not—we could say that Quine's method *must* be of the following kind. He knows that if "a" denotes a fixed individual, then the statement

(7) $Ma \ \& \ Sa \rightarrow Ma$

is a tautology; it is true no matter what is the case. This he knows—as has already been stated—on the basis of the definitions of the connectives "$\&$" and "$\rightarrow$." And since (7) is seen to be a tautology in *this* way, that is, without recourse to the semantic rules governing the use of the predicate symbol "$M\hat{x}$" and "$S\hat{x}$," he also knows that (7) remains a tautology and therefore is true *whatever* interpretation we give to these predicates.

Further, the basis on which (7) is shown to be tautological is independent of the denotation of the symbol "a." We might express this by saying that the complex predicate

(8) $M\hat{x} \ \& \ S\hat{x} \rightarrow M\hat{x}$,

which in (1) is said to apply to 'all' individuals, does not actually attribute anything to any individual. It is what could be called a tautologically predicative ex-

pression, or, briefly, a "tautological predicate." Finally, (1) is seen to be tautological according to a semantic convention for the use of the universal operator,
which could be formulated as follows:

(α_0)   If $F(x)$ is a tautological predicate, then the sentence $(x)F(x)$ is true no
        matter what is the case, that is, tautological.

The ground on which we state that (1) is a logical truth within predicate
logic thus consists of two essential observations: (a) that it is true no matter
what is the case, and (b) that the fact that this is so is a consequence of the
conventions regulating the use of the connectives "&" and "→," and the universal operator "(x)."

Thus (1) is an *analytic* sentence according to our definition; and that this
is so is the reason why it is a logical truth in Quine's sense.

17. The Connection among the Different Features of Analyticity

We can now see the connection among all four features of the Kantian
concept of analyticity. Features (I)–(III) are already united in formulation (F).
The connection between formulation (F) and feature (IV) is as follows: A
'logical truth' is a statement which is true no matter what is the case—we *cannot*
infer that a statement F is true no matter what is the case except by the consideration that this is so according to the conventions for the use of the symbols which
F contains. Thus every logical truth is analytic.

18. The Definitory Character of the Rules of Predicate Logic

The "meanings" of symbols used in a purely descriptive context are indicated
by the different conventions by which the truth conditions of sentences containing
them are determined. Rule (α_0) is one convention of this kind. It is a convention
according to which sentences of a certain shape are to be accepted as true no
matter what is the case. This rule is a semantic convention concerning the use
of the universal operator, which, together with other such conventions, determines its meaning.

A rule of the type (α_0) can thus be considered 'definitory' for some of the
symbols it contains—in this case, the universal operator. Quine has objected
that such a view forms a logical circle. In order to understand rule (α_0), we must
understand that it is to be conceived of as a general rule, one that concerns *all*
tautological predicates. Thus we must already understand "all" in order to understand the rules for the use of the universal operator.[17]

This objection—like corresponding objections to conceiving of truth-value
tables as definitory—is founded on the misconception criticized above, that of
regarding all definitions as elimination definitions. Rule (α_0) as a definitory rule

[17] Quine, "Truth by Convention," pp. 271–72.

is about an object language (in this case, the language of predicate logic) and is formulated in a metalanguage. In the same way, as with respect to ordinary ostensive definitions, we must in such a case use symbols in the metalanguage which have approximately the same meaning as the terms, whose use within the object language is characterized by the rule. But it is not necessary to understand any *linguistic expression* for the rules we follow in order to understand the use of the universal operator; it is sufficient that we are in some way capable of following the rule. In order to be able to follow a rule one need not be able to formulate it in words. *How* we make it clear that, for instance, rule (α_0) is to be followed is entirely irrelevant to understanding the use of the universal operator.

19. The Import of 'Axioms' of a Logical Calculus

In the development of the predicate logic as a calculus, one sometimes lays down not only general rules like (α_0), but also particular 'axioms.' Thus we could introduce as an axiom the sentence

(9) $(x) [P \lor Q(x)] \rightarrow P \lor (x)Q(x)$.

The semantic import of introducing such a formula as a 'logical axiom' is that we introduce the ad hoc principle that (9) is a logical truth and thus a tautology as a rule for the use of the universal operator (in combination with the disjunction sign). The convention we lay down when we introduce (9) as an 'axiom' ought actually to be written:

(10)   The formula "$(x) (P \lor Qx) \rightarrow P \lor (x)Qx$" is a tautology.

(Among our semantic conventions, we assume that a special sentence is to be true no matter what is the case.)

Therefore, there is no obstacle to doing so in other cases, too. As a rule for the use of predicate symbols "Rx" and "Bx" as symbols for the properties "red" and "blue," we could simply prescribe

(11)   The formula "$(x) [\sim (Rx \,\&\, Bx)]$" is a tautology,

as an ad hoc convention; that is, the formula it contains should be accepted as true no matter what is the case. Thus the analyticity of (2) is granted without any alleged 'reducibility' to propositional or predicate logic. We could, moreover, say that (11) belongs to the 'logic' of the symbols "$R\hat{x}$" and "$B\hat{x}$" in the same way that (10) belongs to the logic of the symbols "(x)" and "v," and that the fact that (4) is a tautology belongs to the logic of the symbols "&" and "$\rightarrow$."

20. Every Analytic Statement Can Be Considered a Logical Truth within "The Logic of the Symbols Which It Contains."

The foregoing way of expressing matters could be generalized. We have said that all 'logical truths' are analytic. It is clarifying to convert this statement. Every analytic statement is a tautology because of the 'logic' of some of the symbols it contains. Let us adopt this use of the term "logic." Then we can add to features (I)–(IV) of the concept of analyticity listed above a fifth feature that is the conversion of feature (IV):

(V)   Every analytic statement is a logical truth; that is, its tautological character belongs to the logic of certain of the symbols it contains.

This way of expressing oneself could help to eliminate a confusion that has prevailed ever since the 'logistic' program was introduced. According to the logistic program, all mathematical concepts should be defined in terms of certain fundamental concepts which were regarded as 'logical.' But what is meant by a 'logical' concept? Frege and Russell regarded as fundamental logical concepts the 'meanings' of certain terms chosen on mere intuitive grounds. The same seems to be true of Quine. What is a Quinean 'logical particle'? Quine seems to think the logical particles can be given by a list. But why should precisely the signs listed be called "logical particles," and no others? Why could not the word "red" be counted among the logical signs as well as the word "and"?

Now there *is* certainly a difference. We could in fact characterize the Quinean logical particles as signs whose meanings are *completely* determined by the *logical* relations which obtain in a language. So, for instance, we can fully determine the meaning of the universal operator by giving its logic—that is, the rules that determine what sentences containing it are 'logical truths' or 'logical contradictions,' what 'relations of logical consequence' hold among such sentences, etc. The fact that the meaning of the quantifiers and the logical connectives is completely determined by their 'logic' is a characteristic feature of those symbols, and distinguishes them from such words as, for instance, "red" and "blue." But rules indicating the logic of the symbols "$R\hat{x}$" and "$B\hat{x}$"—as, for instance, in rule (11)—can never completely determine the meaning of these symbols. For this purpose, an assignment of these symbols to definite properties is also required.[18]

This difference between 'logical particles' and other symbols is noteworthy. But it should not lead us to conclude that 'logical truth' is definable in terms of 'logical particles,' for, on the contrary, the definition of a logical particle is founded upon, among other notions, the concept of 'logical truth.' Nor is the difference one that should mislead us into believing that the logical rules for the use of these particles are 'logical' in some more exalted manner than the logical rules for the use of other symbols—such as, for instance, those for the use of predicate symbols, modal operators, and the like. In order to achieve a correct conception of logic we must forego *religious awe* for 'logical constants,' an attitude which inclines us to ascribe to the logical truths of propositional or predicate logic a higher potency than that possessed by other logical truths.

[18] On this question, compare the discussion in Stenius, *Wittgenstein's "Tractatus,"* pp. 197–203.

21. The Best Way of Formulating Rules of Synonymity Is To Give Them the Form of Conventions Stating that Certain Equivalences Are Tautological

Returning to Quine's definition (D) of analyticity (see above, section 11), on the basis of our analysis, we may affirm that Quine is quite right in saying that this definition involves a logical circle. In fact, the best way of explaining synonymity is to state an ad hoc analyticity. To take Quine's examples, the synonymity of the terms "bachelor" and "unmarried man" can be stated by laying down the rule:

(12)   The statement "a is a bachelor $\rightarrow$ a is an unmarried man" is tautological, whatever individual "a" denotes.

This metastatement belongs to the logic of the terms "bachelor," "unmarried," and "man."

22. Is Definition (F) a Contradiction in Terms?

Some philosophers would object to definition (F) that it is a contradiction in terms, since if the truth of a sentence is not dependent on what is the case in any other way it is dependent on the fact that certain semantic conventions and no others are valid in the language in which it is formulated.

It is probably in view of such an objection that Carnap, in *Meaning and Necessity*,[19] explains what is meant by an analytic sentence in essentially this way:

(Cp)   A sentence F is analytic in the semantic system L if and only if F is true in such a way that its truth can be established on the basis of the semantic rules of L alone, without any reference to (extra-linguistic) facts.

Carnap does not regard his formulation as a 'definition' of "analytic," but only as an informal 'convention' which must be replaced by an 'exact formal definition.' However, as Quine rightly points out, the formal definition is entirely unsuccessful.[20] Carnap's mistake could be characterized in the following way. On the one hand, Carnap wants to define the logical signs of a language L. Let us call one of his logical signs c. In the formulation of the definition of c he needs the notion of analyticity. On the other hand, he wants to define this notion. But then he confuses the two definitions, thinking that his definition of c is at the same time a definition of analyticity. The result is that neither c nor analyticity is defined. If we were to look at rule (α_0) in a Carnapian way, we would have to regard this rule as definitory of *both* the universal operator *and* the term "tautological." But this is of course impossible. Rule (α_0) can be definitory of the

---

[19] Rudolf Carnap, *Meaning and Necessity* (Chicago: University of Chicago Press, 1947), p. 10. In his own formulation, Carnap replaces the term "analytic" with the equivalent term "L-true."

[20] "Two Dogmas of Empiricism," p. 32; *Logical Point of View*, p. 33.

universal operator only if the term "tautological" has been defined in advance, and this we have done by giving it the meaning "true no matter what is the case."

Quine maintains, however, not only that Carnap's formal definition is unsuccessful but that this is also true of his informal convention. I think he is right in this, too, although my reasons are different.

23. TRUTH IN THE 'INTENSIONAL' AND THE 'SEMANTIC' SENSE

For one thing (Cp) shares with the Quinean paraphrase of Kant the error of taking features (II) and (III) of analyticity to be two different characteristics instead of two parts of one and the same characteristic. Further, (Cp) is more obviously unsatisfactory than Quine's paraphrase because of the term "extra-linguistic" added within parentheses. If we interpret the explanation literally, we arrive at the conclusion that the sentence

(13)   The word "man" is an English word

is analytic, in spite of the fact that its (linguistic) factual content is obviously not empty.

So if the class of facts to which the expression "without reference to facts" refers in (Cp) is in some way to be restricted, it is in any case of no help to characterize the facts of this class as 'extra-linguistic.'

The difficulty here arises from an ambiguity in Carnap's phrase "establish the truth" of a sentence. Consider the sentence

(14)   The earth is round.

If we know what object "the earth" refers to, and what is meant by being round, we know the state of affairs described by the sentence; I call this state of affairs the descriptive content of the sentence. The descriptive content of (14) is the same regardless of whether the earth is round or not; in the former case I say that the state of affairs described by (14) obtains, in the latter that it does not obtain.

Now, by "establishing the truth" of (14) we could mean investigating whether the descriptive content of (14) obtains or not, and arriving at the result that it does obtain. That is, we establish the truth of (14) simply by establishing the fact that the earth is round. I call this the *primary* sense of establishing the truth of a sentence; here, no reference to linguistic rules or linguistic facts is needed unless the content of the sentence is linguistic.

Another sense of "establishing the truth" of a sentence would be, for example, to establish the fact that (14) is an expression which in the English language describes a fact. In this sense the establishment of the truth of (14) involves

(a) determining what state of affairs (14) describes according to the semantic rules of English (including determining what object the expression "the earth" refers to and what property the word "round" refers to), and

(b) establishing that this state of affairs obtains.

I call this the *secondary* sense of establishing the truth of a sentence. The establishment of the truth of a sentence in the secondary sense thus (always) also contains the establishment of certain linguistic facts.

The primary sense of the establishment of the truth of a sentence could also be called the establishment of its *intensional* truth, the secondary sense the establishment of its *semantic* truth. The establishment of the semantic truth of a sentence thus consists of the semantic determination of what its descriptive content is and the establishment of its intensional truth.

24. The Final Formulation (G) of the Definition of "Analytic"

Carnap operates mainly with the 'semantic' concept of truth (though certain of his formulations seem to indicate that he vacillates between the two concepts of truth as they have been explained here). Therefore he probably uses the phrase "establish the truth of a sentence" in its secondary sense. What is meant by saying that "its truth can be established on the basis of the semantic rules of L only" is obviously that the semantic truth of an analytic sentence can be established by the mere determination of *what* its descriptive content is, because when this has been done, no additional fact remains to be established. The statement, then, is *intensionally* true no matter what the case is.

By the insertion of the phrase "according to the semantic conventions" as an adverbial adjunct to the predicate "is true," and by the use of the word "statement" instead of "sentence" our formulation (F) escapes the Carnapian difficulties. But in order to be certain of avoiding misunderstandings on this point we may reword (F) as follows:

(G)   A statement is analytic if and only if, according to the semantic conventions for the use of certain of the symbols it contains, it is true (in the intensional sense) no matter what is the case.

25. The Corresponding Definition of "Synthetic": The Distinction between "Analytic" and "Synthetic" Concerns Statements, Not Formulations

The definition of "synthetic" corresponding to (G) may then be expressed as follows:

(H)   A statement is synthetic if and only if, according to the semantic conventions for the use of the symbols it contains, its truth value is dependent on what is the case.

As is clear from these two formulations, the question of whether a statement is analytic or synthetic is dependent on the conventions for the use of the symbols it contains. This means, among other things, that that question can be put for a *sentence* only in respect of a *fully determined* interpretation of it. Since sentences may have differing interpretations according to the occasion upon which they are uttered, it is essential that our definitions of "analytic" and "synthetic" refer to *statements*, not to formulations.

Today, we often hear philosophers say that certain scientific principles, such as the inertial law, change their epistemological status in that they are at one stage of the development of science regarded as synthetic and *a posteriori*, at another as analytic and *a priori*. This is a very careless way of expressing oneself. As Schlick pointed out, what really happens is not that the same principle changes its epistemological status, but that a certain *wording* is given a new *interpretation*, so that it passes from the formulation of a synthetic statement into the formulation of an analytic statement.[21] It is our conventions about linguistic usage that change, not what is analytic or synthetic according to these conventions.

Quine concludes his account of the untenability of the distinction between 'analytic' and 'synthetic' by saying, "Any statement can be held true come what may, if we make drastic enough adjustments elsewhere in the system" of scientific statements.[22] What he ought to have said was rather that any *wording* that has been accepted as a formulation of a synthetic principle can be made analytic by a reinterpretation of the terms it contains, if only one is consistent enough to reinterpret other formulations correspondingly. And here it is very important to note a fact which Quine does not mention, that is, that we never can make *every* formulation within a scientific theory analytic without its losing all of its predictive value. Make the inertial law analytic, and *no* prediction about the behavior of bodies can be made by means of it. For any 'predictions' in this area will then be founded on the 'hypothesis' that under certain circumstances no unknown forces will disturb the orbit calculated for a certain body on the basis of the inertial law and existing *known* forces. Indeed, one can ask oneself whether the inertial law as applied to experimental physics has really ever been interpreted as an analytic principle.

26. The Importance of the Distinction as an Instrument for the Analysis of the Foundations of Science

The truth of this reveals a fact that an investigation of the foundations of science must take into consideration. If Quine means that the semantics of scientific terms is not as a rule sufficiently systematic to allow us to decide definitely whether a certain formulation is the formulation of a (true) synthetic or an analytic statement, he is completely right. Definitions (G) and (H) allow for three possibilities with respect to a given *formulation*: either the symbols it contains are sufficiently well determined semantically to enable us to state that it is

---

[21] Moritz Schlick, *Allgemeine Erkenntnistheorie*, ed. 2 (Berlin, 1925), p. 70.
[22] "Two Dogmas of Empiricism," p. 40; *Logical Point of View*, p. 43.

analytic, or they are sufficiently well determined semantically to enable us to state that it is synthetic, or they are not sufficiently well determined semantically to enable us to decide the question. If the last alternative obtains, then there is room for different interpretations of the formulation. And the last alternative does obtain in *most* cases. It is precisely this fact that makes the logical and semantic analysis of scientific terms interesting and fruitful—we can attempt to make the terms more precise in different ways, and then see what happens to the system. Such attempts are by no means irrelevant for the special sciences. Quine's 'undogmatic' position implies that we must be satisfied with being powerless with respect to some extremely important problems within the methodology and epistemology of science—we remain powerless as a result of throwing away one of the most effective instruments for such investigations.

In all this, I do not claim to regard the distinction between 'analytic' and 'synthetic' or my definition of these notions as entirely unproblematic or as applicable to all possible instances without further clarification. I do not know of any concepts that are unproblematic in this way. Our conceptual instruments must ever be sharpened. What I have attempted to point out in this paper is that the distinction can be made in a way that is satisfactory in many respects—and that it is an important philosophical task to increase its precision.

Göran Hermerén

Symbolic and Symptomatic Expression

1. Introduction

The purpose of the present paper is to make explicit one of the senses in which world views or aspects of world views are said to be 'reflected,' 'expressed,' 'symbolized,' 'betrayed,' or 'embodied' in works of art. I do not intend to arrive at a formal definition. But I shall try to isolate what I take to be one interesting relation between works of art and world views by indicating some necessary conditions for a work of art to reflect or express a world view.

The choice of these necessary conditions has been guided by a number of quotations from the writings of such scholars as Jean Seznec, Erwin Panofsky, Charles de Tolnay, William Heckscher, Anthony Blunt, and others. These quotations will be discussed in the next section, and on the basis of that discussion I shall try to make a partial and preliminary explication of statements of this type: "This work of art reflects (expresses, embodies, . . .) a pantheistic or neo-Platonic conception of the world."

The first problem to be discussed here concerns the principles for the selection of examples. Seznec, Panofsky, and the other art historians mentioned above use terms like "express," "reflect," and "symbolize" to refer to the relation I am going to analyze, but these terms are used in many other different ways as well in art historical writings. I shall therefore have to begin by giving examples of sentences in which these terms are used in the way to be analyzed here.

Professor Hermerén, of the University of Umeå, is a native of Sweden.

This is a revised version of a paper presented at a symposium on iconology at the annual meeting of the American Society for Aesthetics, October 12–14, 1967, at Princeton University. It is related to, but not identical with, chapter VI of my book *Representation and Meaning in the Visual Arts: Studies in the Methodology of Iconography and Iconology* (Lund: Läromedelsförlagen/Uniskol, 1969). This paper contains some ideas (mainly in sections 3, 5, 6, and 7) not to be found in the book and the book contains some ideas not developed here.

The following principles have been used to single out examples of the relevant use of "reflect," "express," "symbolize," etc. I have quoted statements of the form "*X* expresses (reflects, embodies, symbolizes, . . .) *Y*," which, negatively, do not satisfy any of the following five conditions:

(1) *X* is a physical part of a work of art, a motif like the lilies in Jan van Eyck's *Annunciation* (National Gallery, Washington, D.C.).

(2) Those for whom *X* expresses or symbolizes something are able to specify what *X* symbolizes or expresses, at least on demand.

(3) There is a tradition for artists to use visual devices like *X* to make beholders think of *Y*.

(4) The fact that *X* makes people think of *Y* depends on the fact that there is such a tradition.

(5) The artist is familiar with this tradition and followed it when he created *X*.

Positively, the statements to be quoted below seem to fall within the description of 'Cassirerian' symbolism given by Panofsky in his introduction to *Studies in Iconology*.[1] However, this description is not quite clear, and I shall try to elaborate the positive criteria of this kind of symbolism or expression in section 3. In the following passage, Panofsky uses Leonardo's famous *Last Supper* to illustrate what he calls "symbols in the Cassirerian sense":

> But when we try to understand it [Leonardo's *Last Supper*] as a document of Leonardo's personality, or of the civilization of the Italian High Renaissance, or of a peculiar religious attitude, we deal with the work of art as a symptom of something else which expresses itself in a countless variety of other symptoms, and we interpret its compositional and iconographical features as more particularized evidence of this 'something else.'[2]

The distinction between 'symbols' or 'symptoms' of this kind and symbols and allegories of other kinds (such as animals, flowers, light rays, the wheel of fortune, or the struggle between virtue and vice) raises a number of interesting and important problems, some of which will be discussed in the following sections. I shall begin by analyzing the relations between works of art and world views or aspects of world views.

2. Examples

In his book *The Survival of the Pagan Gods*, Jean Seznec mentions some pictures in which the figure of a man is enclosed in concentric circles, and in this context he also calls attention to a miniature in a Copenhagen manuscript,

---

[1] Erwin Panofsky, *Studies in Iconology: Humanistic Themes in the Art of the Renaissance* (New York: Harper & Row, Harper Torchbooks, 1962), p. 7 ff. This book was originally published in 1939 by Oxford University Press. All page references in the present paper are to the Harper edition.
[2] *Ibid.*

where "the body is covered with disks, each bearing the image of a planet."[3] He continues as follows:

These small images have much to tell us on attentive examination. They *betray* the conviction which had begun to assert itself in the fourteenth century that man is the prisoner of the heavenly bodies, entirely at their mercy.... But resistance to this tyranny is sometimes *expressed* as well. In one case we have the figure of a happy child, unconcernedly plucking flowers and paying no attention to the nine spheres which gravitate around him charged with their dread symbols. In their own way, these naive images raise the whole problem of necessity versus freedom of the will....[4]

Here Seznec compares a number of images with a (reconstructed) conviction about the place of the individual in the world. The relation between these images and this conviction does not satisfy the five conditions mentioned in the previous section. Moreover, it seems to fall under the description of 'Cassircrian' symbolism given by Panofsky in his introduction to *Studies in Iconology*. The verb "betray" suggests that according to Seznec the images can be used as evidence of the artist's conception of the relation between man and the planets.

Erwin Panofsky's interpretation of Dürer's well-known engraving *Melencolia I* is an instructive example of iconological and iconographical approaches to the study of art. In his book on Dürer, Panofsky summarizes part of his results in the following way: "It is this [Ficino's] new and most humanistic conception of the melancholy and 'saturnine' genius that *found expression* in Dürer's engraving."[5]

Ficino's conception of melancholy is a part or an aspect of the neo-Platonic vision of the world and of the influence of different planets on human beings. I suggest that it is no accident that the author uses the phrase "found expression" rather than "the artist expressed." There is a causal relation of some kind between this neo-Platonic world view and Dürer's engraving; the picture according to Panofsky is a symptom of Dürer's neo-Platonic conception of melancholy.

In a paper on Flemish paintings in the National Gallery, Charles de Tolnay proposes the following iconological interpretation of Jan van Eyck's *Annunciation*:

If one studies this composition—the dimly lit church interior, the motionless figures with their stiff gestures and doll-like faces, the few gleaming objects that bear no signs of use and wear, the lilies, eternally blooming—it seems to be a world on which neither the past nor the future have any hold, where the flow of time is indeed suspended. This is a reality freed from time. We are witnessing the 'perfect peace' spoken of by the mystics. It was in Holland, the native land of van Eyck, that the Brothers of the Common Life preached, from the end of fourteenth century, the contemplative ideal which van Eyck seems to *embody* in the picture.... His new style seemed to

---

[3] Jean Seznec, *The Survival of the Pagan Gods* (New York: Harper & Row, 1961), p. 66.

[4] *Ibid.*, pp. 66–67, my italics.

[5] Erwin Panofsky, *Albrecht Dürer*, ed. 3 (Princeton: Princeton University Press, 1948), 1: 167, my italics.

have been created by him as the most adequate *expression* of his pantheistic conception of the world.[6]

In comparing van Eyck's painting with his world view, de Tolnay is not primarily concerned with the painter's choice of motifs but rather with the style of the picture. The quotation suggests that there is some kind of similarity between the expressive and physiognomic qualities of the work of art and the contemplative ideal embodied in the picture.

In his iconological study of the works of Odilon Redon, Sven Sandström points out that Darwin's writings were the point of departure for the series *The Origins*. But he stresses that it would be a mistake to interpret them as didactic. He adds:

Redon's personal involvement in the ideas which forced the intellectuals of his day to revise their conceptions of the world, his fight to keep a spiritualistic world view, and his belief in the hegemony and eternal character of the spiritual life as opposed to a positivistic materialism, are *mirrored* above all here.[7]

Thus, Sandström argues that the pictures reflect Redon's spiritualistic conception of the world. This, of course, is compatible with the statement that the artist did not have any didactic ambitions in creating this series of engravings. It should also be noted that in comparing Redon's pictures with his world view, Sandström is concerned mainly with the artist's choice of motifs rather than with his style.

The following quotations are taken from William S. Heckscher's iconological study of Rembrandt's painting *The Anatomy of Dr. Nicolaas Tulp*. In the beginning of his book Heckscher makes the following programmatic remark:

My study of Rembrandt's *Anatomy* was undertaken in the belief that every great work of art, apart from its forever changing aesthetic appeal to posterity, is an unchanging *mirror* of its cultural ambient.[8]

Toward the end of the book, he writes as follows:

I believe that the preoccupation with anatomy as an art and as a science can be taken as one of the most impressive *symbols* that the Renaissance had been able to create in token of this new interest in man and in his fate under the sway of death.[9]

Finally, in his recent book on Poussin, Walter Friedlaender stresses Poussin's Stoic interests, pointing out that Poussin painted many works with Stoic subjects in the 1640's.[10] This is further developed in Anthony Blunt's magnum opus on

[6] Charles de Tolnay, "Flemish Paintings in the National Gallery of Art," *Magazine of Art* 34: 178–79 (1941), my italics.
[7] Sven Sandström, "Darwinistisk symbolism" [Darwinistic symbolism], *Tidskrift för Konstvetenskap* 32: 67–68 (1957), my translation. Cf. Standström, *Le monde imaginaire d'Odilon Redon* (Lund, 1955), pp. 77–78.
[8] William S. Heckscher, *Rembrandt's Anatomy of Dr. Nicolaas Tulp* (New York: New York University Press, 1958), p. 3, my italics.
[9] *Ibid.*, p. 107, my italics.
[10] Walter Friedlaender, *Nicolas Poussin: A New Approach* (New York: Harry N. Abrams, 1964), pp. 68–71.

Poussin, written before Friedlaender's work was published. He devotes a separate chapter to Poussin's Stoicism. In the beginning of this chapter Blunt remarks:

> It has often been pointed out that Poussin's works of the 1640's reveal very clearly the influence of Stoic ideas and that his letters contain phrases which are Stoic in flavor; but the influence of this philosophy goes deeper and has more far-reaching effects than is generally stated.[11]

Having shown that in many paintings from this period Poussin represented events which embodied Stoic ideals of life, Blunt continues:

> It might be argued that the choice of these moral subjects was due to Poussin's patrons and does not prove that the artist himself sympathized with the ideas which his paintings *embodied*. This would not be in accordance with Poussin's character, or with his conception of his art, but fortunately there is ample evidence from his letters and from the early biographies to show that he thought in terms of Stoicism and lived in accordance with its precepts.
>
> The evidence, scattered and fragmentary though it is, makes up a surprisingly complete picture of Poussin's *philosophy of life*. He is not, it need hardly be said, concerned with problems of metaphysics, but his views on ethics are set forth with clarity and vigor in his letters, and it is even possible to deduce, if the letters are read in conjunction with the allegories implied in the paintings, that the artist was also influenced by Stoic ideas on the organization and beauty of the cosmos and the position of man in it.[12]

I take it, then, that Anthony Blunt (and probably also Walter Friedlaender) would argue that some of Poussin's paintings reflect a Stoic outlook or embody some aspect of a Stoic world view. It would not be difficult to find other examples, but the ones discussed above will be sufficient for the present paper.[13]

3. A Terminological Problem

I have elsewhere used the expressions "iconological symbol" and "iconological significance" as technical terms for the kinds of symbols and meanings illustrated by the examples above.[14] The relationship between Michelangelo's neo-Platonic world view and his works is obviously in many respects quite *different* from the relationship between the United States and the flag of the United States, and some people may hesitate to use the term "symbol" about both of these relationships.

But I think that my proposal to introduce the term "iconological symbol" in this context can be defended in several ways. It is a fact that Panofsky himself

[11] Anthony Blunt, *Nicolas Poussin*, Bollingen Series XXXV.7 (New York: Pantheon Books, 1967), p. 160. (For a different approach to the art of Poussin than that of Friedlaender and Blunt, see Kurt Badt, *Die Kunst des Nicolas Poussin* [Cologne: DuMont Schauberg, 1969].)

[12] *Ibid.*, p. 167.

[13] For example, Panofsky and de Tolnay have tried to show that Michelangelo's works reflect a neo-Platonic world view. For quotations and references, see my *Representation and Meaning*, pp. 128–29.

[14] *Ibid.*, pp. 130–31.

distinguishes between two kinds of symbols, which he calls "symbols in the ordinary sense" and "symbols in the Cassirerian sense."[15] I referred to the latter as "iconological symbols," since it is the main task of iconology in the modern sense (defined by Panofsky in the introduction to *Studies in Iconology*) to interpret the meaning of such symbols.

Moreover, there is a tradition in German philosophy for using the term "symbol" to mean roughly what I have called "iconological symbol." Ernst Cassirer, for example, is a prominent representative of this tradition,[16] which also has had some influence on American philosophers like Susanne Langer and art historians like William S. Heckscher (see the quotation from Heckscher above); and in conversations Erwin Panofsky has indicated that in his opinion "iconological symbol" would be a good technical term in this context. Further, at the time I could not find a better term; other possible candidates such as "expression" seemed to be even more unclear and ambiguous than "symbol."

Nevertheless, I do not want my terminology to give the impression that there are two kinds of symbols, iconographical and iconological, and that iconographical and iconological symbols have something in common by virtue of which they both are symbols and thus belong to the same class of phenomena. On the contrary, this is precisely what I want to question. The purpose of the present paper is to call attention to the difference between what Panofsky calls "symbols in the ordinary sense" and "symbols in the Cassirerian sense." What is important to me in the present context is the conceptual distinction between these two notions and not the terms "iconographical symbol" and "iconological symbol," but it is of course desirable to have adequate terminology.

I do not know whether there is any really satisfactory solution to this terminological problem. Whatever term one choses to use, it is likely to have some misleading connotations. It is therefore important to remember that the terms to be introduced are technical terms that are explained by the examples and the partial definitions offered in this paper. Keeping all these reservations in mind, I shall here propose to introduce the terms "iconological expression" or "symptomatic expression" for the kinds of relations between works of art and world views illustrated in the previous section.

I realize that some of the objections to the term "iconological symbol" might also be raised against the term "iconological expression." Moreover, "symptomatic expression" is somewhat too general and it covers several kinds of expression in art which fall outside the scope of the present paper.[17] But these terms are per-

[15] *Studies in Iconology*, p. 6, n. 1.

[16] See Ernest Cassirer, *The Philosophy of Symbolic Forms* (New Haven: Yale University Press, 1965), 1: 73 ff., particularly pp. 75, 87, 89, 107. Cf. Susanne Langer on presentational (non-discursive) symbols in *Philosophy in a New Key* (New York: New American Library, 1954), p. 75 ff.

[17] For example, statements like "van Gogh's madness is clearly expressed in his last paintings." I have discussed statements of this kind in my "Uttryck i konsten" [Expression in art], *Insikt och handling* 7: 24–55 (1970).

haps less likely to cause misunderstanding than "iconological symbol," and I shall therefore use them for the time being.

4. Conditions

In this section I would like to raise the following questions: What conditions do art historians themselves consider necessary for X to be an iconological or a symptomatic expression of Y? What criteria is one supposed to use if one wants to decide whether or not X is an iconological or a symptomatic expression of Y? One way of answering such questions is to study the arguments offered *pro et contra* the kind of interpretations exemplified in section 2.[18]

The result of such studies suggests that the following four conditions are necessary: if X is an iconological or symptomatic expression of Y, then

(1) X is a work of art,
(2) Y is a world view,
(3) X and Y are similar,
(4) Y influenced the creation of X.

Condition (4) entails that there is a causal relationship between X and Y; for example, Blunt states explicitly that Poussin was influenced by Stoic ideas on the "organization and beauty of the cosmos." The field of this causal relation is divided; the relation is therefore obviously irreflexive and asymmetric. Each of these four conditions raises various kinds of problems. No doubt the most problematic of them is condition (3), and it will be examined in section 5. In the present section I shall briefly discuss the other three conditions.

With reference to the first condition, there is a considerable amount of literature exploring the vague boundaries and emotive import of the term "work of art" and its cognates. Waismann's ideas about open texture have been applied to the concept of art, and so has Wittgenstein's notion of family resemblance. Some writers have argued against (and others have argued for) the thesis that there is a non-trivial property common to all works of art, and only to works of art. It has been said (and denied) that there are only family resemblances between particular works of art.[19]

But these problems need not be discussed here. For the purposes of the present paper, a broad historical approach seems to be quite sufficient: man-made objects discussed in art historical books or journals are to be considered as works of art. This approach does not eliminate unclear borderline cases, but it

---

[18] See my *Representation and Meaning*, pp. 131–32.

[19] See Paul Ziff, "The Task of Defining a Work of Art," *Philosophical Review* 62: 58–78 (1953); Morris Weitz, "The Role of Theory in Aesthetics," *Journal of Aesthetics and Art Criticism* 15: 22–35 (1956); Charles Stevenson, "On 'What Is a Poem?'" *Philosophical Review* 66: 329–62 (1957); and Maurice Mandelbaum, "Family Resemblances and Generalization concerning the Arts," *American Philosophical Quarterly* 2: 1–10 (1965).

gives an impressive number of clear examples of works of art, seen and described in many different ways; and that is what is needed in the present context.

Thus, if *X* is an iconological expression of *Y*, then *X* is a work of art, a physical object with many properties and features of different kinds that can be described in a variety of ways. It represents, expresses, and symbolizes something in a particular way; and art historians describe, analyze, and interpret its motifs, composition, perspective, and style. All of these features may more or less clearly indicate the world view of the artist. It happens, as is shown by the examples in section 2—that art historians concentrate on some of these features, like the style or the choice of motifs or the perspective, and write that these features reflect or embody a conception of the world.

It seems, then, that it would be possible to define a series of related and partly overlapping concepts of iconological expression, depending on precisely which of the features mentioned above are matched with some aspect of a world view. These distinctions may have important consequences for how the relevant concept of similarity in condition (4) is to be defined and measured or estimated.

But, even so, it is important to see that if *X* is an iconological expression of a particular conception of the world, then *X* is never merely a motif in a work of art, like an apple or a goldfinch, which can appear in many different pictorial contexts, sometimes having symbolic significance and other times lacking it.

With regard to the second condition, it should be noted that the term "world view" can be used in several senses, and it is important to make the following distinction from the very beginning. Among other things, this term can be used to denote a disposition to act (think, write, . . .) in certain ways, but it can also be used to denote the manifestations of such dispositions (that is, particular actions, thoughts, writings, etc.). Here, I shall be using "world view" in the first sense.

Moreover, it should be noted that many writers have stressed the difference between rational inquiries and world views; I would like to recall Dilthey's famous remark that "world views are not produced by thinking."[20] Meyer Schapiro has argued that world views are "abstracted by the historian from the philosophical systems and metaphysics of a period or from theology and literature and even from science,"[21] implying that world views cannot be identified with philosophical systems, metaphysics, or the like.

But the term "world view" is still unclear, both in the sense that it is not quite obvious exactly what conditions are necessary and sufficient for correct application of this term, and in the sense that some of the key terms in these conditions have no fixed denotation. Consider, for example, the following tentative list of characteristic features of world views:

[20] Wilhelm Dilthey, "Die Typen der Weltanschauungen und ihre Ausbildung in den metaphysischen Systemen," in *Gesammelte Schriften* (Berlin: Teubner, 1931), p. 86.

[21] Meyer Schapiro, "Style," in *Aesthetics Today*, edited by M. Philipson (New York: World Publishing Company, 1966), p. 105.

(1) They are general pictures or visions of the world or universe as a whole, and of the place of the individual in it.

(2) The manifestations of a world view imply or suggest a number of basic beliefs about what is ultimately desirable in life.

(3) They are not only or primarily founded on theoretical considerations but on all kinds of experience, including emotional experience.

(4) A person is only dimly aware of his world view—if at all; he has neither stated it precisely nor defended it rationally.

Perhaps the conjunction of these statements can be regarded as a sufficient condition for correct application of the term "world view." At any rate, I maintain that if something has all of the features described in these four statements, it could properly be called a world view.

But is each of these four conditions necessary? Or can the conjunction of these conditions be regarded as a necessary condition? There does not seem to be an obvious answer to these questions; some people may be inclined to answer in the affirmative, others in the negative. It should also be acknowledged that there probably are considerable differences between the world views concerning their degree of articulation. Finally, the four statements above contain many vague and incomplete expressions such as "whole," "desirable," "experience," "theoretical," "emotional," "dimly," "aware," and "rational," which could be made more precise in a number of different ways.

One further point has to be clarified at this moment. To what extent is the iconological or symptomatic expression of a work of art intended by the artist? Since some of the examples discussed in section 2 may be interpreted in several ways, I shall suggest some conceptual alternatives, depending on whether the statement that X is the iconological or symptomatic expression of Y is taken to imply:

(1) It is always the case that the artist who created X intended to express Y in or by X, or

(2) It is sometimes the case that the artist who created X intended to express Y in or by X, or

(3) It is never the case that the artist who created X intended to express Y in or by X.

It is then possible to obtain six alternatives by distinguishing between material and strict implication. "X is an iconological expression of Y," may imply (1) materially but not strictly, etc. Thus, here, too, it is possible to define a series of related and partly overlapping concepts of iconological expression. There is some reason to believe that Panofsky would favor the third strict alternative, i.e., that "*X* is an iconological symbol of *Y*," strictly implies (3),[22] although his position is not quite clear.

There is obviously a great deal more to be said about the relations between particular philosophical systems and world views. But to explore the many ways in which terms like "thinking," "world view," and their cognates are used in different contexts would carry us beyond the limits of the present paper. In concluding this discussion of the concept of a world view, I propose to illustrate the relations between works of art, philosophical doctrines, and world views with the following diagram:

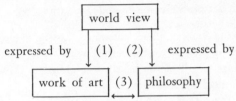

Thus works of art and philosophical doctrines, as well as poetry and other cultural achievements, are parallel products of a world view. The vertical relation (1) is what I have here called "iconological" or "symptomatic" expression. The horizontal double arrow (3) in this diagram stands for similarities and analogies between works of art and specific doctrines. Panofsky and other art historians study such similarities in order to be able to reconstruct the underlying world view.[23]

The diagram above is well illustrated by the following quotation, which concludes Anthony Blunt's discussion of the relations between Poussin and Stoicism:

> This parallel between the order of nature and the nobility of man, which seems to be the theme of Poussin's landscapes such as those embodying the stories of Phocion of Diogenes, has an exact parallel in an idea of the Stoics expressed by Seneca: "Wherever we stir, the two resources which are the fairest of all attend us: nature, which is universal, and virtue, which is our own. . . ."
>
> This belief in the beauty and order of nature, which was common to almost all Stoic philosophers, seems to be the inspiration of all Poussin's great landscape paintings of the 1640's and early 1650's. In them, nature is treated as a direct manifestation of the divine and is seen as organized on principles in accordance with human reason, which is its other great manifestation.[24]

Finally, the last condition for *X* to be an iconological expression of *Y* is as follows: if *X* is an iconological or a symptomatic expression of *Y*, then *Y* influenced the creation of *X*. This requirement is an important part of the notion of iconological expression; similarity between *X* and *Y* is not enough. It has been argued that Michelangelo's works reflect a neo-Platonic world view, and this may

---

[22] See my *Representation and Meaning*, p. 139, and particularly p. 174, n. 40.

[23] See *ibid*., p. 134 ff., particularly p. 138.

[24] Blunt, *Nicolas Poussin*, p. 176.

well be true. But it is logically impossible that they reflect a neo-Kantian world view, or the world view of Picasso or any other contemporary person.

To clarify the relevant concept of influence, one would apparently have to solve a long series of well-known difficult problems concerning the analysis of counterfactual conditionals and causal statements. This cannot, of course, be done here. I shall only indicate tentatively and in a schematic manner an analysis of the requirement of influence. To say that a work of art X was influenced by something else Y in a particular respect a (such as design, choice of motifs, colors, composition, etc.) is to say or imply that if the artist who created X had not come into contact with Y before the creation of X, then X would not have had the properties it has with respect to a.

Obviously, this is only a first step toward a clarification of the notion of influence; I hope to discuss these problems more extensively elsewhere. Art historians are sometimes suspicious of analyses of the kind suggested above, because they think that counterfactual conditionals open the gates to loose speculations of the type: "If he had invaded England in 1941, Hitler would have won the war." But this is a mistake. Some counterfactuals are speculative, but others are strongly supported by the available evidence.

Moreover, I would like to point out that the analysis proposed above seems to fit rather well with what Panofsky once wrote in discussing the relations between Dürer's engraving *Melencolia I* and neo-Platonism:

> If, despite these negative conclusions we can still assert that Dürer's elaborately prepared engraving *owes a debt* to the notion of of melancholy propagated by Ficino, and *would, in fact, have been quite impossible but for his influence*, the proof of this assertion can be based only on internal evidence from the engraving itself.[25]

It should be noted that the statement that influence occurred is here explicitly formulated as a counterfactual conditional. As Panofsky offers internal evidence of the kind mentioned in the quotation, it appears reasonable to conclude that he would accept the statement expressed by the sentence, "Dürer's engraving would, in fact, have been quite impossible but for the influence of Ficino"—that is to say, the influence of Ficino was a necessary condition for the creation of the engraving.

5. SIMILARITY

If X is an iconological or a symptomatic expression of Y, then X and Y are similar. This is an important requirement; there must be an affinity or a similarity between X and Y that is directly discernible (or 'legible') at least by those who are familiar with the artistic traditions and the cultural environment at the time and place of creation of the work that is being discussed.

[25] Erwin Panofsky, Fritz Saxl, and Raymond Klibansky, *Saturn and Melancholy: Studies in the History of Natural Philosophy, Religion and Art* (London: Thomas Nelson & Sons, 1964), p. 284, my italics.

I shall use examples from iconological writings here in order to elucidate the relevant notion of similarity. Many kinds of similarities are discussed in these writings. In this section I shall illustrate and examine one type of similarity, which for several reasons appears to be especially important in the present context: structural similarity.

As a point of departure I will use a map of the east coast of the United States. This map contains latitudes, longitudes, and names, but it also contains dots and squares of various sizes, lines of different thickness and shape, etc. There is a one-to-one correspondence between the latter kinds of elements and towns, cities, rivers, roads, highways, turnpikes, etc., in the eastern part of the United States. Moreover, if a relation holds between some of these elements on the map, then a corresponding relation also holds between the corresponding elements of the country.

There are, for example, three spots on the map of the eastern part of the United States called "New York," "Philadelphia," and "Washington." The spots appear on the map together with these names. There is a one-to-one correspondence between these three spots and three large eastern cities: New York, Philadelphia, and Washington. Moreover, certain relationships hold between the spots on the map and similar or analogous relationships hold between the three cities: the spots are situated on a fairly straight line, and so are the cities; the spot "Philadelphia" is between the two other spots, and Philadelphia is between Washington and New York; and so forth.

To see what is involved in this example, it may be worthwhile to digress and try to spell out the relevant notion of structural similarity in some detail. Let us define a simple relational structure as an ordered couple, $<A, R>$, where A is a set and R, a relation. In the example several structures of this kind are compared with each other; among others:

S_1 $<\{$Philadelphia, Washington, New York$\}$, to be situated between$>$
S_2 $<\{$"Philadelphia," "Washington," "New York"$\}$, to be situated between$>$

For the sake of brevity, I shall introduce the following abbreviations:

S_1 $<A, R>$
S_2 $<A', R'>$

where A is the set of cities and A' the set of spots on the map.

These two structures satisfy the usual technical requirements for two simple relation structures to be isomorphic. There is a function f such that

    (1) The domain of $f = A$
    (2) The range (counterdomain) of $f = A'$
    (3) f is a one-to-one function
    (4) If $x, y \in A$, then $xRy <=> f(x)R'f(y)$

This concept of structural similarity has many attractive features; in particular, it can be defined in a fairly exact way.[26] I shall now try to determine whether this concept, or something like it, is an important part of the notion of iconological or symptomatic expression.

Consider, for example, the following description and interpretation of Michelangelo's tomb of Julius II by Panofsky:

> In the Tomb of Julius, however, heaven and earth are no longer separated from each other. The four gigantic figures on the platform, placed as they are between the lower zone with the Slaves and Victories and the crowning group of the two Angels carrying the *bara* with the Pope, serve as an intermediary between the terrestrial and the celestial spheres. Thanks to them, the apotheosis of the Pope *appears*, not as a sudden and miraculous transformation, but as a gradual and almost natural rise; in other words, not as resurrection in the sense of the orthodox Christian dogma, but as an ascension in the sense of the Neoplatonic philosophy.[27]

The word "appears" italicized above refers to a natural way of seeing the work of art, or to the way it is seen by informed beholders. It is, of course, of considerable importance whether the pope appears to move from the higher to the lower zone, or from the lower to the higher zone; whether the angels carrying the *bara* with the pope appear to pull him up or to push him down, etc. Keeping this point in mind, there seems to be a structural similarity between the arrangement of the figures in the tomb and a neo-Platonic ascension in the following sense.

First, there are certain basic elements in the composition (the terrestrial and celestial spheres and the intermediary elements), and there is a one-to-one correspondence between these elements and certain elements in the ascension of the pope according to neo-Platonic views. Second, there are a number of relations between the basic elements of the composition (e.g., the celestial sphere is above the terrestrial; the pope is between them; there is a gradual rise from the terrestrial to the celestial sphere; and so forth) that correspond to analogous relations between the elements of a proper neo-Platonic ascension as opposed to a resurrection in the orthodox Christian sense.

However, the structural similarity in this example seems to be much looser than the structural similarity in the case of the map. For one thing, it is not quite clear what criteria are used to single out the 'basic elements' of the composition. Moreover, expressions like "gradual rise" may be used more or less metaphorically, and they may be used about processes in various types of space-time regions (physical and theological). But there are also other differences between the two cases. One of them could be stated as follows.

There were conventional rules of projection before the map of the east coast of the United States was made. This map and perhaps hundreds of others were made in accordance with these rules. Thus, given the map and the rules,

---

[26] For details, see Patrick Suppes, *Introduction to Logic* (Princeton, N.J.: Van Nostrand Company, 1960), p. 260 ff.

[27] *Studies in Iconology*, p. 192, last italics mine.

it is possible to say with a fair degree of accuracy what the east coast of the United States in certain respects looks like. And given the coast and the rules, it is possible to predict with a fair degree of accuracy what a map of the coast will look like. But there do not seem to be any such conventional projection rules in Panofsky's example.

The concept of isomorphism provides us with a well-defined conceptual model. Moreover, it can call attention to unclear points in the relevant notion of structural similarity. We have seen that there are a number of differences between isomorphism (as defined above) and the relevant sort of similarity between a work of art and some aspect of a world view, and these differences are important.

In the first place, it is not clear how the 'basic elements' are selected. If the two sets A and A' are not well defined, then the domain as well as the range of the function f is obscure. Nor is it clear exactly how the relations R and R' are defined. The languages of set theory and art history are obviously very different, and attempts to translate one into the other can easily lead to paradoxical results. Nevertheless I hope that the comparison between the structural similarity involved in the case of the map and in the quotation from Panofsky can serve as a useful starting point for a new analysis.

6. A New Analysis

So far I have proceeded in a fairly intuitive manner. I shall now make a fresh start and attempt a somewhat more systematic analysis of the relevant kind of similarity. Let X be a work of art, and let Y be (some aspect of) a world view. If X is an iconological or a symptomatic expression of Y, then X and Y are similar. But which conditions should X and Y satisfy in order to be similar in the relevant sense?

Perhaps no general answer is possible, but an examination of the example discussed above suggests the following tentative list of requirements:

(1) Some structures S of the work or art X (hereafter: S_x) and some structures S of the world view Y (hereafter: S_y) are isomorphic.

(2) An arbitrary one-to-one correspondence between the relations of S_x and of S_y is not sufficient; there must be a qualitative connection or analogy between these relations.

(3) The structures S_x and S_y represent 'natural' ways of seeing or organizing X and Y. What this means could be spelled out in some detail in terms of Gestalt psychology.

(4) S_x is (or could be) directly seen or grasped by informed beholders as a projection or product of the world view or habit of thought Y.

(5) The aspects or structures of a world view S_y to which an art historian calls our attention 'illuminates,' 'clarifies,' or 'explains' the structure S_x.

Thus I shall say that a work of art X and a world view Y are similar in the relevant sense, if there are structures S_x and S_y

(a) each of which has certain properties, both structures satisfying requirements (3) and (4);

(b) which are formally related to each other in such a way that they satisfy requirement (1); and

(c) which are related to each other in certain other ways as well.

Each of these five requirements needs clarification, and I shall now comment briefly on them.

Terms like "structure" and "isomorphic" can be defined rather precisely in set theoretical terms, and I use them here with hesitation. As I have indicated above, the connection between neo-Platonism and the tomb of Julius II is in certain ways looser than the connections between two isomorphic structures. Thus, what I have written about 'isomorphism' between works of art and world views should not be pressed too hard.

The point of the second requirement could be illustrated by the following example. Consider the structures $<A, R>$, where $A =$ {Sigmund Freud, Anna Freud}, $A' =$ {1, 2}, $R =$ father to, and $R' = <$ (less than). Then these two structures are isomorphic in the technical sense outlined in the preceding section. But there is obviously no qualitative connection between R and R' here as there is between (a) the gradual rise from the terrestrial to the celestial sphere in the tomb of Julius II, and (b) the gradual rise of the soul from earth to heaven according to neo-Platonic doctrine. This difference is important in the present context.

As to the third requirement, it should be obvious that it would be possible to construct an extremely large number of structures in a complex work such as Michelangelo's tomb of Julius II or van Eyck's *Annunciation*. The well-known laws of organization described by the Gestalt psychologists help to reduce that number to a manageable size. Moreover, beholders with different background, training, interests, and expectations can perhaps organize X and Y in different ways. What is 'natural' to one beholder need not, of course, be 'natural' to another. The problems raised by this requirement could be studied empirically. If experiments were made with contemporary art historians of the western world, in most cases they would be likely to agree as to what the 'natural' ways of seeing a work of art are.

The most problematic of the requirements above is probably the fourth. The confirmation of particular instances of "X is an iconological or a symptomatic expression of Y" must somehow be related to the ability of informed be-

holders to grasp the proposed similarity between the work of art and the relevant world view, to see the work as a projection of a world view. But who is an
'informed observer'? What is meant by "see as" here? What happens if confirmation is not forthcoming? Whose opinion counts, if some scholars notice the
similarities between X and Y whereas others fail to see them? Clearly, the search
for iconological significance could result in vague but suggestive analogies that
are difficult to confirm or that break down under detailed critical examination.[28]

But, of course, this is not always the case. Sometimes the implicit reasoning
supporting iconological interpretations could be reconstructed and tested along
the lines suggested in E. H. Gombrich's famous game of "ping" and "pong":

> If these [two words "ping" and "pong"] were all we had and we had to name
> an elephant and a cat, which would be ping and which pong? I think the answer is
> clear. Or hot soup and ice cream. To me, at least, ice cream is ping and soup pong. Or
> Rembrandt and Watteau? Surely in that case Rembrandt would be pong and Watteau
> ping.[29]

I shall now digress briefly and try to apply this game in two steps to Panofsky's
interpretation of the tomb of Julius II.

It is true that it may seem arbitrary to assert or deny that there is a sharp
contrast between the three levels in the tomb of Julius II—for what constitutes a
sharp contrast? But the arbitrariness vanishes if we start with a pair of tombs,
for instance, those of Bishop Saltarelli and Julius II,[30] and with the following
pair of statements: (a) there is a sharp contrast between the terrestrial and the
celestial spheres, and (b) there is a gradual rise from the terrestrial to the celestial sphere. If the tombs are matched with the two statements, I think an overwhelming majority of beholders would follow Panofsky in associating the tomb
of Julius with statement (b).

In an analogous way these two statements can be matched with the orthodox
Christian dogma about the resurrection and the neo-Platonic doctrine of the
ascension of the soul. To be sure, both the Christian and the neo-Platonic views
on these matters can be interpreted in several ways. But they are very different,
and here again I should think that an overwhelming majority of informed readers would follow Panofsky in associating statement (b) with the neo-Platonic
doctrines.

It should be stressed that the number of pairs is limited by historical considerations in the examples I have studied. Panofsky compares the tomb of Julius
with tombs made before the beginning of the sixteenth century, and he matches
the two statements above with aspects of doctrines presumably familiar to
Michelangelo.

[28] Cf. the critical remarks by Schapiro, "Style," p. 106.
[29] E. H. Gombrich, *Art and Illusion*, Bollingen Series XXXV.5 (New York: Pantheon
Books, 1960), p. 370.
[30] The tomb of Bishop Saltarelli is reproduced in *Studies in Iconology*, fig. 133. The
tomb of Julius is reproduced in *ibid.*, figs. 135–37, and in my *Representation and Meaning*,
fig. 26.

The fifth requirement is important, since art historians write on the assumption that their readers are familiar with the work of art they discuss or have access to a fairly good reproduction of it. What an art historian writes will have an esthetic point only if it is matched with visual evidence. The comparisons between works of art and *Weltanschauungen* or doctrines may direct the attention of the beholders to certain features of the work of art and may explain them, in that way enhancing the beholders' enjoyment of the work. This pragmatic aspect of giving the spectator a sense of understanding is another important part of iconological interpretations.

I would like to stress the selective character of this section. Structural similarity of the sort discussed above can be combined with various other types of similarity, and I have dealt here only with some relevant kinds of similarities. There are also interesting differences between some of the examples in section 2 which it would be worthwhile to examine in detail, but this cannot be done here.[31]

If a work of art X illustrates a story Y, then there are a large number of fairly conspicuous similarities between X and Y. If, however, X is an iconological expression of a world view Y, then the similarities between X and Y are much more vague and much less obvious. This is the reason why I have spent so much time on various notions of similarity. I do not think it is possible to give a clear and precise definition of the relevant notion of similarity. One has to start with a number of examples and use them as paradigm cases. A vague form of structural similarity is often (and perhaps always) involved, and it is sometimes combined with other kinds of similarity.

7. ICONOLOGICAL EXPRESSION vs. DISGUISED SYMBOLISM

In a paper on the symbolism of light, Millard Meiss interprets some fifteenth-century paintings, including Jan van Eyck's *Annunciation*, and he points out that the "subtle and pervasive symbolism characteristic of the work of both these painters [van Eyck and the Master of Flémalle] shows itself again in the use of precisely seven rays in these representations. . . . Seven undoubtedly refers to the seven gifts of the Holy Ghost . . . ."[32]

The seven rays (like the lilies in the foreground) can be taken as examples of a class of symbols that might be called "established disguised symbols," a subclass of what I elsewhere have called "iconographical symbols."[33] I would like to distinguish between the discovery and interpretation of such symbols (a task that falls within the domain of iconography), and the discovery and interpretation

---

[31] For suggestions, see my *Representation and Meaning*, pp. 148–49.

[32] Millard Meiss, "Light as Form and Symbol in Some Fifteenth-Century Paintings," *Art Bulletin* 27: 178 (1945).

[33] *Representation and Meaning*, chap. 4. The distinction between open and disguised symbolism is discussed in *ibid.*, p. 90 ff.

of the iconological or symptomatic expression of the work of art, which is a task for iconology in the sense defined by Panofsky.

It is of course possible to make an iconographical and an iconological investigation of the same work of art, and this may help to obscure the important differences between these two approaches. Moreover, the results of iconographical investigations are often integrated into and explained by the results of iconological studies, and this can also make it difficult to distinguish between established disguised symbols (like the rays, the lilies, the apple) and the symptomatic or iconological expression of a work. Nevertheless, there are several important differences between these concepts, which I shall try to illustrate now by contrasting the symbolic significance of the light rays (and some other motifs) in Van Eyck's *Annunciation* with the symptomatic or iconological expression of this painting (according to Charles de Tolnay's interpretation quoted in section 2 above).

(1) The light rays are physical parts of the painting, one motif among many others. The painting also depicts a woman, an angel, a stool, a prayer book, several lilies, and a church interior. Some of these motifs are disguised symbols, others are not. But it is not possible to single out one particular motif in this painting and (correctly) say that only this motif is an iconological expression of a world view. On the contrary, the whole painting, including technique, style, choice and arrangement of motifs, expresses van Eyck's conception of the world.[34]

(2) The light rays refer to a concept or an idea, the seven gifts of the Holy Spirit. But, according to de Tolnay, the painting is an iconological or symptomatic expression of van Eyck's 'pantheistic conception of the world.' This world view is abstracted or reconstructed from various (literary, religious, historical) documents, including the teachings of the mystics. Thus there is a difference between disguised symbols and iconological expression, both as to that which symbolizes or expresses and as to that which is symbolized or expressed.

(3) Jan van Eyck's painting contains a number of motifs, symbolizing a diversity of ideas. Some of these motifs have different meanings in different pictorial contexts. They may also be ambiguous and have different meanings at the same time. This multiple meaning of disguised symbols has been stressed by several art historians. But it is not possible to single out two motifs in van Eyck's painting and say (correctly) that they symbolize two different conceptions of the world. Nor is it possible to say (correctly) of the whole painting that it is ambiguous and expresses two different world views at the same time.[35]

(4) We are entitled to infer that Jan van Eyck painted the seven rays with

---

[34] Cf. the programmatic remarks in Panofsky, *Studies in Iconology*, pp. 7–8.

[35] This point is based on the assumption that it is possible to maintain a distinction between the two statements (1) that Mr. X has, at a given moment, an unclear world view that can be described in two or more radically different ways; and (2) that Mr. X has, at a given moment, two or more radically different world views.

the double intention of getting those who looked at the painting (a) to think of a certain concept or idea, the seven gifts of the Holy Spirit, and (b) to recognize that this is what he intended to achieve (wanted them to do). Thus, van Eyck would have been able to specify what the light rays refer to, at least on demand. But we are not entitled to infer that van Eyck created his painting with an analogous double intention of getting those who looked at it to think of a pantheistic conception of the world, etc. He may not even have known that his painting expresses or embodies the world view described by de Tolnay.[36]

(5) If X is an established disguised symbol of Y, it follows by definition (a) that there is a tradition for artists to use devices like X to make informed beholders think of Y, and (b) that the fact that X makes informed beholders think of Y depends on the fact that there is such a tradition. Now a tradition can be more or less strong, and the fact that X rather than X' was chosen as a symbol of Y may at least to some extent depend on the fact that the artist noted similarities between X and Y. This is certainly true of the disguised symbols in van Eyck's painting, but even so there is obviously no tradition for artists to use a visual design like van Eyck's *Annunciation* to make people think of a pantheistic conception of the world.

(6) The idea referred to by a disguised symbol can influence the selection of one motif rather than another as a symbol of that idea, but it does not influence the shape or form of that motif. However, it is evident from the examples in section 2 that the world view expressed in a work of art also influences the shape and form of the work, including the style, choice, and arrangement of pictorial elements. These features are symptomatic of the world view of the artist, and the requirement of influence (discussed in section 4 above) applies to iconological expression but not to disguised symbols. The lilies in van Eyck's painting may well be indistinguishable from lilies in a botanical encyclopedia. The artist has included them because of the supposed similarity between the qualities attributed to lilies and the qualities attributed to Mary.

(7) It is important to distinguish between similarities noticed by the artist and similarities noticed by art historians. If pressed for the basis of the symbolism of the rays, the lilies, the apple, or any other disguised symbol, an art historian would not have to show that there actually are similarities between properties attributed to light rays, lilies, apples, etc., and what they symbolize. Rather, he would have to show that there are good reasons for believing that the artist or his patron found similarities of this kind. However, if pressed for the basis of the iconological expression of a work of art, an art historian would *not* have to show that there are good reasons for believing that the artist or his patron found similarities between properties or structures in the work and some

---

[36] In this context, it should be noted that Panofsky once wrote that what I have here called the iconological expression of a work of art is "generally unknown to the artist himself and may even emphatically differ from what he consciously intended to express" (*Studies in Iconology*, p. 8).

aspect of a world view. He would instead have to show (make his readers see) that there actually are such similarities.

Thus, if *X* is an established disguised symbol of *Y*, then the relation between *X* and *Y* is quite different from the relation I have referred to as "iconological or symptomatic expression" in this paper. However, to avoid misunderstanding, I would like to stress that the distinction between these two relations is not incompatible with the statement that a change in the choice of disguised symbols (of a concept) may indicate—and be explained by—changes in contemporary religious attitudes. On the contrary, this statement is entirely consistent with the point made above under (6).

8. Concluding Remarks

In this paper I have tried to clarify one of the senses in which works of art are said to 'express,' 'reflect,' 'symbolize,' 'betray,' or 'embody' a world view or some aspects of a world view. These terms are used in many different though related senses in art historical writings. For example, works of art are sometimes said to express or reflect social unrest, tensions between classes, or political and economic changes. I hope that some of the suggestions made here will apply to that usage as well. In particular, I think that the problems discussed in section 6 and the analysis proposed there will also be relevant in this context.

B

Epistemology
Philosophy of Mind

Justus Hartnack

Beliefs and Dispositions

It has often been claimed that belief statements are dispositional statements. According to Ryle, for example, the verb "to believe," like the verb "to know," is a dispositional verb, but, unlike the verb "to know," which is a capacity verb, "to believe" is a tendency verb.[1]

Although I think that neither "to know" nor "to believe" is a dispositional verb, I shall in this paper argue only against the dispositional analysis of the verb "to believe."

It is of course quite correct that to believe something implies tendencies to behave in relevant ways. If I believe that it is about to rain I may put on my raincoat, take in my laundry, issue proper warnings, etc. Nevertheless I shall argue that it is a mistake to take this as an analysis of what a belief is. There certainly is a difference between the assertion that if I have a certain belief I have a tendency to say and do an indefinite number of things, and the assertion that if I have a certain belief all that this means is that I have a tendency to say and do an indefinite number of things. According to the first view, the relation between my belief and my tendency to say and do the relevant things is one of implication; but according to the second view, the relation is one of identity. While the former is correct, the latter is mistaken. It may even be the case that the relation is one not only of implication but of equivalence. That is, if I believe that it is going to rain it may be inferred that I have a tendency to say and do certain things; and, furthermore, if I do have such a tendency it may be inferred that I have the corresponding belief. But because two statements are equivalent it does not follow that they have the same meaning.[2]

Professor Hartnack, of the University of Aarhus in Denmark, is a native of Denmark.
[1] *The Concept of Mind* (London: Hutchinson's University Library, 1949), p. 133.

[2] The statement "John is the son of Mary" is equivalent to "Mary is the mother of John." But they do not mean the same thing. The first statement may serve as an answer to (1) "Who is John's mother?" as well as to (2) "Who is Mary's son?" The second state-

It is dangerous to classify "belief" as a motive word since this may lead to neglect of a crucial difference between a belief and a motive.

To elucidate this difference, let us consider a typical motive, vanity. A person who is vain has a tendency to think, speak, and act in certain ways, while a person who has a tendency to think, speak, and act in these ways is of necessity vain. This is necessarily so because by vanity we *mean* a tendency to think, speak and act in these specified ways. "Vanity" is a disposition word, and it describes a state of mind. A person who displays vanity can be characterized as ridiculous, stupid, or childish. His state of mind can be psychologically explained and may be subject to psychoanalytic treatment, but his vanity can be neither true nor false. It is no more true or false than the bursting into flames of a piece of paper when lighted, or the rolling of one billiard ball when hit by another.

Admittedly, belief has some of the same features as do motives. This is due to the fact that belief, unlike knowledge, is a state of mind. Since belief has a psychological status, the word "belief" has some of the same logical characteristics as a motive word like "vanity." It does not make sense to characterize my knowledge as being stupid, ridiculous, or childish. But both my vanity and some of my beliefs may be characterized as stupid, ridiculous, or childish. I may be cured of my vanity by psychiatric treatment as I may of some of my beliefs— beliefs that may be characterized as superstitious or that may border on or be an expression of insanity. My vanity has certain psychological causes; whatever they are, the psychiatrist may be able to reveal them to me and thereby cure me of it.

My vanity has *causes* but it does not have *reasons*. If I talk too much about my own merits the reason may be my vanity, but my vanity itself cannot have a reason. I can explain my talking about myself by saying that I enjoy the idea that people hold me in high esteem. But the existence of my vanity, the fact that I enjoy the idea of being held in high esteem, can be explained by a cause but not by a reason. The same is true of some of my beliefs. If I have a tendency to place my right arm in a special napoleonic way, the reason is my belief that I am Napoleon. And just as my vanity has a cause, so has my belief that I am Napoleon.

Of course, many motives do not require any explanation, namely, motives which fall within the limits of normality. We want an explanation if a person behaves abnormally but not if he behaves normally. Indeed an essential part of what we mean by normality is that which needs no explanation. Beliefs which fall within the limits of normality, i.e., beliefs which naturally can be expected to be held, require no explanation either. They do not require an explanation; they require *evidence*. The fact that a belief requires evidence is due to the dual

---

ment may serve as an answer to (3) "Whom is Mary a mother of?" as well as to (1) "Who is John's mother?" Compare also: (4) "Sixteen divided by two is eight" and (5) "Eight multiplied by two is sixteen." Statements 4 and 5 are equivalent; but they do not mean the same thing.

nature of the concept of belief. Belief is partly a psychological concept and partly an epistemic concept. It is due to its psychological nature that it can be used to explain behavior, and it is due to its epistemic nature that we have to ask for evidence. But to ask for evidence is to ask for evidence of the truth of the belief. Thus, a belief must be something asserted.

As already stated, we do not always ask for the causes or sources of a belief. We do so only if the belief falls outside the limits of normality—a belief for which there is no evidence whatever, or one contrary to all evidence. My belief that I will fall and break my leg tomorrow is of the former kind and my belief that I am Napoleon is of the latter kind (that this belief is contrary to all evidence is, indeed, somewhat of an understatement). Beliefs for which there is no evidence whatsoever, and beliefs contrary to all evidence—that is, beliefs for which one inquires about their causes, and beliefs which are subject to psychiatric treatment —I shall call degenerate beliefs. They are psychological peculiarities which can be called beliefs by courtesy only.

But whether or not there is any evidence for a belief or whether it is a belief expressing insanity, to believe is to believe something. That which is believed—that for which there ought to be evidence—can be expressed in a statement. To believe is necessarily to believe that *p*. Only within the framework of a language, therefore, is it possible to have beliefs. Only language-users can be said to have beliefs.

It may be objected that this excludes that which ought not to be excluded. It excludes the possibility of animals having beliefs. Thus one might argue that a dog may believe that its master is coming into the house, or that it is going to be fed, or it may have beliefs about where it has buried its bones. But a dog cannot have beliefs in the same sense of "belief" as human beings have beliefs. It cannot be a belief of which the animal is conscious. The dog can be aware neither of what it has a belief in nor that it has a belief. It could be conscious or aware of something only if it had a language. A dog could have a belief only in the sense in which a belief is definable in terms of behavior. And since behavior can be neither true nor false, to identify belief with belief-behavior would be to overlook the simple fact that a belief, by conceptual necessity, is either true or false. Behavior, to be sure, may be often characterized as, for instance, goal-directed and, therefore, as either successful or unsuccessful. But in the sense in which a belief must be either true or false, behavior can be neither.

To believe is not to be disposed to assert, but to have evidence for asserting. There is a radical difference between the two concepts 'to be disposed to assert' and 'to have evidence for asserting.' The concept of disposition belongs to the same family of concepts as 'cause' and 'law of nature.' A disposition or a tendency can be expressed as a law-like statement. An occurrence which is a manifestation of a disposition or a tendency presupposes an event functioning as a cause.

The fact that I have a disposition to do certain things is known from my doing these things. The fact that I am vain is something I have discovered by ascertaining how I behave. My behavior is the clue for knowing what dispositions (needs, interests, motives, etc.) I have. If I say that I behave as I do because I am vain I say so because I have discovered that the law-like statement expressing vanity applies to me.

Just as I can explain many acts by means of motives or dispositions, so I can explain many acts by means of my beliefs. However there is a radical difference: while I discover my dispositions from the acts I perform, the acts implied by my beliefs presuppose that my beliefs are known already. I do not discover that I believe it is going to rain from the fact that I put on my raincoat.

This difference is connected with the previously mentioned fact that whereas I define my dispositions by my behavior, I do not define my beliefs this way. By a disposition I *mean* the different things I tend to do. By a belief I do not *mean* this, but imply it.

Some may object to my assertion that I do not discover my beliefs from my acts but that my acts presuppose my already knowing my beliefs. It may be maintained that the true way to discover one's beliefs is to observe one's acts. I may believe that I love my brother, but my acts, my dreams, my slips, and the like, may reveal that my belief is false: I do not love him; really, I hate him.

It is important, however, to notice the following difference. My belief that I love my brother is the belief that I have certain tendencies to act in certain ways. My belief that it is going to rain is a belief, not in certain tendencies to act in certain ways but in the occurrence of a certain state of affairs, an occurrence which, obviously enough, is independent of how I act. My acts can neither verify nor falsify my belief that it is going to rain. To say that I believe that I love my brother is the same as to say that there is evidence for the existence of a tendency to act in certain ways. Quite obviously, I cannot meaningfully say that the evidence I have for the existence of a tendency to act in a certain way is my reason for acting in this particular way. Yet it is different with the belief that it is going to rain. To say that I believe it is going to rain is the same as to say that there is evidence that it is going to rain. The evidence is evidence, not for any tendency or disposition to act in certain ways, but for the existence of certain facts. It is meaningful to say that my reason for acting in a certain way is the evidence for the rainy weather, but it would be meaningless to say that the evidence for the rain is my acts.

Another difference, relevant to those discussed above, should be noticed. The statement "I believe it is going to rain" can be true or false in two ways. (1) It may be accepted as true because, although the belief is false in the sense that it is not going to rain, it is nevertheless the case that I do believe it. It is thus regarded as a statement, not about the weather, but about my psychological state. (2) It may be regarded as false because, although I do in fact have the belief, it is nevertheless false that it is going to rain. It is then regarded as a statement concerning that which I believe.

However, these two aspects of the belief statement cannot be separated. Any belief statement is, at one and the same time, a statement about the existence of my belief and a statement about the existence of that which is believed. The term "belief" is meaningless if it is cut off from its accusative. The analysis of the meaning of a belief statement must involve the truth of that which is believed. If we affirm a belief statement on the sole ground that the belief exists, it is a misleading statement unless we add that the epistemic aspect of the statement is not included.

It seems that the statement "I believe that I love my brother" may also be true or false in two ways. It may be verified or falsified as a statement about my love. Yet in contrast to the statement about the weather, there appears to be no difference between the verification (or falsification) of these two ways of regarding the statement about my love of my brother. A verification of the existence of the belief that I love my brother must be to ascertain the existence of a tendency to think, speak, and act in certain ways. But this is also the verification (or falsification) of the existence of my love of my brother. Hence it may be concluded that belief statements about motives operate as motive statements. This is different from other belief statements. Suppose the statement "I believe it is going to rain" were regarded as a statement exclusively about the existence of my belief, that is, as one whose truth value is independent of the state of the weather. It would be a statement verifiable only by ascertaining the existence of my tendency to think, act, and speak in certain ways. But the statement can never be so conceived, because, as already mentioned, it is never correct to conceive of a belief statement exclusively as a statement about the existence of a belief. A belief statement can never be without its epistemic value. A belief must always be a belief in something. Except for belief statements about motives, belief statements cannot be verified without reference to something independent of my tendency to act in specified ways.

To be disposed to assert, therefore, is to discover the disposition by discovering that one makes certain statements. But this is impossible. It is impossible because to discover that one is making a statement is not to make a statement at all. I cannot *discover* that I assert that *p*. I can discover that, more or less parrot-like, more or less mechanically, or more or less unknowingly, I utter some sentences; but this is not to make an assertion. A parrot which utters that *p* is not asserting that *p* because it is not *using* language. The teacher who uses *p* as an example of a sentence with certain grammatical properties is not using *p* to assert. In order to assert that *p*, it is not enough that the sentence "*p*" is uttered. The sentence must be used with the intention to assert that *p*. And a necessary condition of doing something with intention is precisely that one does not *discover* that one is doing the intended thing. To say that one is discovering what one is doing is the same as to say that one is not doing it intentionally.

If I discover that I am using a sentence "*p*," it then follows that I cannot be asserting *p*. And if I do something from being disposed to do it, it implies that I know of my doing *x* by discovering it. Consequently, I cannot make assertions from being disposed to make them. The concepts of 'doing something from disposition' and 'doing something by intention' are incompatible concepts. The concept of belief consequently is incompatible with the concept of disposition.

Jaakko Hintikka

Different Constructions
in Terms of the Basic Epistemological Terms:
A Survey of Some Problems and Proposals

In studying the conceptual problems connected with any logically or philosophically interesting term, one of the very first questions we encounter concerns
the different grammatical constructions in which it normally occurs (insofar as
there is a non-trivial difference in meaning between them). Some distinctions
between such constructions have figured prominently in recent philosophical
literature. A case in point is Ryle's emphasis on the distinction between *knowing
that* and *knowing how*, to which I shall soon return. However, in most cases
surprisingly little systematic work has been done to clear up the precise relations
between the different constructions and their relative priorities. For instance, even
though there are a great many books and articles on the concept of goodness and
on the meaning of the word "good," it seems to me that the interrelations of the
different grammatical constructions in which it can occur are but imperfectly
understood. Some of the most acute discussions of the meaning of "good," for
example, those by Paul Ziff in *Semantic Analysis* and by Jerrold J. Katz in
Philosophy of Language, concentrate almost exclusively on the use of the word
"good" in the construction "a good X."[1] These authors do not ask whether this
is a basic and irreducible construction for the relevant logical and philosophical
purposes, or whether it can be analyzed in terms of other uses of "good," for
instance, the one exemplified by "It is good that." I suspect that the latter is
more fundamental than the use in the form "a good X."

In the case of the different constructions which involve the verb "know,"
a number of results, some very interesting, are scattered about in the literature.
Several observations that I have made elsewhere (in print or informally) can be

---

Professor Hintikka, of the Academy of Finland, is a native of Finland.

[1] Paul Ziff, *Semantic Analysis* (Ithaca, N.Y.: Cornell University Press, 1960), see especially the last chapter. Jerrold J. Katz, *Philosophy of Language* (New York: Harper & Row,
1966), pp. 287–317.

regarded as answers to questions concerning the relation of these different constructions to each other or can be illustrated in terms of such answers. A survey of these interrelations will therefore amount to a quick survey of a part of my recent work in epistemology. In order to formulate the answers I am trying to give now, however, it is first necessary to develop a way of raising the questions to be addressed.

What different types of constructions are there involving the verb "know"? The following distinctions between different kinds of constructions are found in the literature or are for other reasons relevant to epistemological discussion:

(1) Knowing that versus knowing how
(2) Knowing that versus knowing whether
(3) Knowing that versus such constructions as knowing what, knowing who, knowing when, knowing where, etc.
(4) Knowing that, or some construction which is like the second part of either (2) or (3) in that it involves a subordinate clause, versus knowing plus a (grammatical) direct object (e.g., knowing someone). We might call these the propositional constructions (or *oratio obliqua* constructions) and the direct object construction, respectively.[2]
(5) Knowing that . . . *a* . . . (where "*a*" is a singular term) versus such constructions as knowing of *a* that . . . he (she, it). . . . There is a related contrast between the constructions "it is known that . . ." and "someone is known to . . . ," for instance:

    it is known that . . . *a* . . .

and

    a is known to be such that . . . *x* . . . is true when $x = a$.

Instead of speaking impersonally of what is known we could of course speak here of what some specified person knows.

The last two distinctions, (4) and (5), concern the ways in which singular terms can enter into a construction governed by the verb "know."

It is not claimed that the above list exhausts all of the interesting distinctions or even all of the distinctions to be met with in contemporary philosophical literature.

I have a definite thesis to put forward concerning these different constructions. I suggest that, as far as the basic logical force of the different constructions is concerned, they can all be characterized or 'defined' in terms of the construction *knowing that*, with the exception of one sense of the construction *knowing how*.

Some of the arguments I can give for this thesis have been or will be presented elsewhere. Here I shall first indicate what interest this thesis would

    [2] This contrast has often been commented on by epistemologists. See, e.g., Roderick M. Chisholm, *Perceiving* (Ithaca, N.Y.: Cornell University Press, 1957), p. 142; David Armstrong, *A Materialist Theory of Mind* (London: Routledge & Kegan Paul, 1967), p. 227.

have, supposing that it can be established. One reason why it is interesting is that it would show that knowing is in a very strong sense a *propositional attitude*. This is shown (or at least suggested) by the fact that all of the different constructions in terms of the verb "know" can be reduced (if I am right) to the sense in which the nature of knowledge as a propositional attitude is most explicit, for the "knowing that" construction quite obviously does not involve a relation of a person (the knower) to any individual object (any individual in the general logical sense of the word). Insofar as the concept of knowledge can be conceived of as a relation, it obtains between a person and an entity or set of entities of an entirely different logical type. Philosophers have sometimes spoken of a proposition as the second term of this relation. I have proposed that the semantics of such 'propositional attitudes' as knowledge, belief, memory, and the like be discussed, not in terms of propositions, but in terms of what I have ventured to call "possible worlds" or "possible states of affairs."[3] The basic idea is that every attribution of a 'propositional attitude' such as knowing to a person can be paraphrased by speaking of the totality of possible worlds compatible with the presence of this attitude in the person in question (at the time about which we are talking). For instance, to say that p is known by a to be true is nothing more—or less—than to say that p is true in all of the possible worlds compatible with a's knowing what he in fact knows. The plausibility of this idea is probably much more obvious than is its great usefulness for a satisfactory semantical (model-theoretical) theory of propositional attitudes.

A reduction of the direct object construction to the *knowing that* construction would be especially interesting in connection with the problem of the nature of the objects of knowledge. Such a reduction would reinforce the suggestion that in the last analysis individual objects can figure as objects of knowledge only in the sense of occurring as members of the possible worlds or possible states of affairs specified by the subordinate clause in "a knows that p."

The construction whose reduction to "knowing that" is easiest to explain is the "knowing whether" construction in distinction (2) above.[4] Clearly,

(6) a knows whether p

is equivalent to

(7)   (a knows that p) v (a knows that not-p).

This gives us a clue as to the analysis of the other constructions of the type *knows* + *an 'interrogative' clause* (cf. (3)).[5] In these constructions we are not confronted by a yes-or-no alternative but a choice of the right (and known)

---

[3] See especially my paper, "Semantics for Propositional Attitudes," in *Philosophical Logic*, ed. J. W. Davis *et al.*, Synthese Library (Dordrecht, Holland: D. Reidel Publishing Co., 1968); reprinted in Jaakko Hintikka, *Models for Modalities: Selected Essays*, Synthese Library (Dordrecht, Holland: D. Reidel Publishing Co., 1969), pp. 87–111.

[4] Cf. my *Knowledge and Belief* (Ithaca, N.Y.: Cornell University Press, 1962), p. 12.

[5] Cf. *ibid.*, pp. 131–32.

answer from a wider selection of candidates. For instance, "*a* knowns who *b* is" might from this point of view be thought of as a disjunction comparable to (7):

(8) *a* knows that $(b = x_1)$ v
      a knows that $(b = x_2)$ v

      . . . .

where x_1, x_2, . . . are all the individuals there are. The intended logical force presumably is captured by

(8)* (Ex) *a* knows that $(b = x)$

or perhaps by

(8)** (Ex) *x* is a person & *a* knows that $(b = x)$.

This suggestion is reinforced by other considerations. One trouble with such disjunctions as (8) is that the range of singular terms one can substitute for the x_i's has to be restricted somehow. (For instance, substituting "*b*" for one of the terms "*x*" would spoil the game.)

We have no such trouble in (8)* or (8)** if we insist that one's bound (bindable) variables have to range over genuine individuals. Eloquent reasons for insisting on this have been voiced by Quine, and I have tried to explore some of the implications of such a course.[6] Here they serve to reinforce the merits of (8)* or (8)**. Knowing *of some definite individual* that it is identical with *b* is surely sufficient for knowing who *b* is, however insufficient merely knowing the truth of some identity of the form "*b = c*" may be. (To know of some actual person that he is the author of *Under the Volcano* is to know who this author is, whereas merely to know that this author is identical with the author of *Ultramarine* is not.)

Virtually the only thing that may sometimes fail to be captured by such reductions as (8)** is the implication or presupposition of uniqueness that is sometimes present in the use of constructions of the type *knows + an interrogative*. I am not sure, however, how integral a part of the meaning of these constructions such implications really are, and, in any case, they can be captured by adding suitable extra clauses to the transcription of these constructions in our 'canonical notation.'

Other constructions involving interrogative clauses admit of a parallel treatment. For instance, "*a* knows when *s* occurred" can be paraphrased (roughly) by

6 See W. V. O. Quine, *From a Logical Point of View* (Cambridge: Harvard University Press, 1953), especially essays 7 and 8; Quine, *The Ways of Paradox* (New York: Random House, 1966), especially essays 13–15. An excellent discussion of Quine's views is presented by Dagfinn Føllesdal in "Quine on Modality," *Synthese*, vol. 19, nos. 1–2 (1968). In addition to the works already mentioned, see my essays "'Knowing Oneself' and Other Problems in Epistemic Logic," *Theoria* 32: 1–13 (1966); "Individuals, Possible Worlds, and Epistemic Logic," *Noûs* 1: 33–62 (1967); "Existential Presuppositions and Uniqueness Presuppositions," in Hintikka, *Models for Modalities*.

> (*Ex*) (*x* is a moment [or period] of time & *a* knows that *s* occurred at [or during] *x*).

In all paraphrases of this sort, the verb "knows" occurs only in the construction "knows that," exactly as I have suggested. From these paraphrases it can also be seen that the meaning of the constructions thus reduced to the "knowing that" construction turns on a rather subtle interplay between epistemic notions and quantifiers. It seems to me that such interplay also underlies distinctions (4) and (5).

From the above discussion, one can perhaps dimly gather what the trouble with (8) is. In order to spell it out, the vocabulary and imagery of 'possible worlds' foreshadowed in my earlier remarks is especially useful. (It also has the deeper merit of admitting of a development into an explicit and precise semantical theory.) A free singular term cannot always be used in (8), for it need not specify a unique individual. The reason can perhaps be seen as follows: A free singular term may refer to different individuals in the different possible worlds compatible with *a*'s knowledge. (If *a* does not know who the author of *Ultramarine* is, then in different possible worlds compatible with what he knows, the term "the author of *Ultramarine*" refers to different persons.) But if these possible worlds are (as I have suggested) part and parcel of all talk about what *a* knows or does not know, then in the context of such talk some singular terms will fail to pick out a unique individual, simply because the individual referred to varies from one relevant possible world to another. For this reason, not all free singular terms can be used as substitution instances of bound (bindable) variables (whose function is precisely to range over individuals), for this would make nonsense of the usual laws of quantification theory.[7]

It can be seen, however, that any free singular term can be used to make statements about a definite individual, namely, about the individual to which it as a matter of fact refers (in the 'actual world'). Thus there is highly important ambiguity in many statements made in ordinary language in terms of a free singular term, for example, "*b*," in contexts which, like epistemic contexts, involve implicit consideration of several 'possible worlds.' Such a statement may be taken as being (so to speak) about *b*, 'whoever he is or may be' (i.e., different in different possible worlds of the relevant sort). However, it may also be taken as being about the individual who in fact is *b*. The two interpretations yield logically independent propositions. For instance, someone might know a lot about the author of *Ultramarine* (e.g., about his stylistic and moral peculiarities) without knowing anything about Malcolm Lowry the individual (for he might fail to know who this author is). On the other hand, an acquaintance of Lowry's might

---

[7] The two laws that typically fail are existential generalization and the substitutivity of identity. A somewhat different diagnosis is required in the case of the failure of these two. However, in "Individuals, Possible Worlds, and Epistemic Logic" (see the preceding footnote), I have suggested that the assumptions which suffice to restore the validity of the former also suffice to vindicate the latter.

know a few things about him without knowing that they were true of the author of *Ultramarine*. Precisely this distinction, it seems to me, is what is signaled by such differences in construction as are listed in (5). These constructions do not constitute infallible evidence as to how a statement is intended to be taken, but quite often they give us helpful clues in this respect.

In order to spell out the difference, it is again useful to recall that bindable variables range over genuine individuals. If "$F(b)$" is a statement about b, 'whoever he is or may be,' we can turn it into a statement about the individual who in fact is b by replacing "b" with a bindable variable (e.g., "x") in "$F(b)$" and specifying this individual by saying that he must (actually) satisfy the condition "$x = b$." If we presuppose that such an individual exists, we obtain

(9) $(Ex) [x = b \mathrel{\&} F(x)]$.

If not, that is, if we are merely speaking of such an individual 'should it exist,' we can use formulation

(10) $(x) [x = b \supset F(x)]$.

For instance, such constructions as

"a knows of b that he is rich"

or

"b is known by a to be rich"

will thus be paraphrased either by

$(Ex) (x = b \mathrel{\&} a$ knows that x is rich$)$

or

$(x) (x = b \supset a$ knows that x is rich$)$.

Again, in these paraphrases "knows" occurs solely in the construction "knows that."

Thus we have obtained what seems to me a viable explication of distinction (5).[8] Again, we witness an interesting interplay of propositional attitudes and quantification.

[8] This distinction is extremely useful for many different purposes. One application which I have not mentioned elsewhere is to set straight the misunderstandings which have led Dagfinn Føllesdal to criticize my treatment of epistemic logic. (The most recent version of his criticism is sketched in his paper, "Interpretation of Quantifiers," in *Logic, Methodology, and the Philosophy of Science*, III, *Proceedings of the 1967 International Congress*, eds. B. Van Rootselaar and J. F. Staal, Studies in Logic and the Foundations of Mathematics (Amsterdam: North-Holland Publishing Company, 1968), pp. 435–44. The gist of his criticisms (in their most recent variant) is that my identity relation cannot be construed as a genuine identity between individuals. I had expected it to be obvious, however, that a simple identity $a = b$ was never intended to express such a relation between genuine individuals in the first place. Rather, it might be said that $a = b$ expresses the 'incidence' of the references of "a" and "b" *in the actual world only*.

What Føllesdal has in mind can also be easily expressed in my langauge. A genuine

The distinction is perhaps especially clear in the case of such statements as

"The king believes the impostor to be the prince who disappeared."

Here the king would not express his belief by saying, "I believe that the impostor is the prince who disappeared." Rather, what is intended is that the king believes of the individual who in fact is an impostor that he is the prince. It seems to me that both the need for distinction (5) and the naturalness of our explication of it can be seen especially clearly in this example.

This leaves only distinction (4) to be analyzed. Since this is by far the subtlest of our distinctions, and since its import turns out to be clearest in the case of the analogous constructions in terms of certain other epistemologically interesting verbs, I shall postpone my discussion of it to a later stage of this paper.

At this point I shall offer a number of supplementary remarks and general comments on the different constructions with the verb "know" and their interrelations.

First of all, the actual usage is somewhat variable, and often one construction can be made to do what is easily seen to be the job of another. In some cases this may even be philosophically misleading. J. L. Austin has pointed out that the direct object construction (cf. (4)) is often used to express what also could be expressed by means of the second construction distinguished in (3): "knowing the winner of the Derby" may mean simply "knowing what won the Derby" (i.e., "knowing which horse won the Derby") although there is no grammatical reason why it could not mean being acquainted with the horse in question, by analogy with, for example, "knowing last year's Miss California."[9]

More subtly, Austin points out that even the "knowing what" construction is occasionally taken in different ways:

When . . . Mr. Wisdom speaks generally of "knowing his sensations" he presumably means this to be equivalent to knowing *what* he is seeing, smelling, etc.," just as "knowing the winner of the Derby" means "knowing what won the Derby." But here again, the expression "know what" seems sometimes to be taken, unconsciously and erroneously, to lend support to the practice of putting a direct object after *know*: for "what" is liable to be understood as a relative "that which." This is a grammatical mistake: "what" can of course be a relative, but in "know what you feel" and "know what won" it is an interrogative (Latin *quid*, not *quod*). In this

---

identity between those individuals which are referred to by "*a*" and "*b*" in the actual world could be expressed by, e.g.,

(8) $(Ex)(Ey)\{(x=a)$ & $(y=b)$ & $(x=y)$ & $N[(x=y) \lor (x \neq y)]\}$

where "N" expresses the propositional attitude in question. It can easily be shown, on the assumptions that I am prepared to make, that (8) behaves just in the way Føllesdal wants his genuine identity to behave.

In (8), the only reason for including the clause $N[(x = y) \lor (x \neq y)]$ is to make sure that we are considering the individuals x and y as members of the several possible worlds we are considering, and not just as members of the actual world only. (Depending on circumstances, we might occasionally want to have a combination of propositional attitudes in the place of "N.")

[9] John L. Austin, "Other Minds," originally published in *Proceedings of the Aristotelian Society*, suppl. vol. 20 (1946), pp. 148–87, and reprinted several times.

respect, "I can smell what he is smelling" differs from "I can know what he is smelling." "I know what he is feeling" is not "There is an x which both I know and he is feeling," but "I know the answer to the question 'What is he feeling?'" And similarly with "I know what I am feeling": this does *not* mean that there is something which I am both *feeling* and *knowing*. . . . Uncritical use of the direct object after *know* seems to be one thing that leads to the view that . . . sensa, that is things, colors, noises and the rest, speak or are labelled by nature, so that I can *literally* say what [that which] I see: it pipes up, or I read it off. It is as if sensa were *literally* to "announce themselves" or "identify themselves" . . .

Austin's remarks illustrate the great philosophical interest of many distinctions one can make here. Needless to say, in the remainder of this paper we shall assume that in the construction, "knowing what," "what" is to be taken as an interrogative and not as a relative, unless the contrary is explicitly stated.

Austin's remarks incidentally serve to point out a fact which is important to keep in mind, if only to avoid misunderstanding. It is that the grammatical direct object construction often serves to express what is easily and trivially paraphrased in terms of the other constructions. These might be called the elliptical uses (or senses) of the direct object construction. Cases in point are, e.g., the phrases "knowing the winner of the Derby" and "knowing the Cramér-Rao theorem," which, respectively, mean simply knowing which horse won the Derby and knowing what the Cramér-Rao theorem expresses (i.e., knowing that the variance of an estimate and differential information are related inversely).

The non-elliptical uses of the direct object construction are those which do not obviously reduce to the other constructions, e.g., knowing a person. It is only the relation of these to the "knowing that" construction that is an interesting problem. In what follows, I shall often disregard the elliptical uses of the direct object construction altogether.

There are other facets of the direct object construction that may be philosophically relevant. Certain philosophers, for instance Bertrand Russell, have discussed what is often called *knowledge by acquaintance*.[10] Although this kind of knowledge cannot, without qualification, be identified with the kind of knowledge which is approximately expressed by means of the direct object construction, the two are obviously closely related, and a better understanding of the direct object construction might therefore be expected to throw some light on the idea of 'knowledge by acquaintance.'

In languages other than English, these different kinds of knowledge are sometimes expressed by different verbs. Here, one is reminded of the German distinction between *wissen* and *kennen* and the French distinction between *savoir* and *connaître*, although they do not completely coincide with ours. It is perhaps not irrelevant to point out that for the Greeks the idea of 'knowledge

10 See, e.g., Bertrand Russell, *The Problems of Philosophy* (London: Home University Library, 1912), chap. 5; and my paper "Knowledge by Acquaintance—Individuation by Acquaintance," in *Modern Studies in Philosophy*, ed. David Pears (Garden City, N.Y.: Doubleday, 1971).

by acquaintance' was much more important than it usually is for modern thinkers.[11]

The connection between the direct object construction and "knows" with the notion of acquaintance will be seen to point to the general direction in which an analysis of the direct object construction (in terms of "knowing that") is to be found.[12]

Emphasizing the difference between the direct object construction and the 'propositional' constructions may help us to get rid of a misunderstanding. Whatever the direct object construction serves in the last analysis to express, it is somehow closely connected with such ideas as acquaintance and familiarity. Emphasizing the distinction, therefore, helps to keep in mind the fact that there are kinds (senses) of knowledge which are unlike the direct object construction and in which familiarity does not breed knowledge.

I shall return to the relation of the direct object construction to the propositional constructions later in this paper in discussing perception.

A second case of a construction which can be understood in different ways is the popular locution "knowing how" which was exploited by Ryle in his criticism of what he calls the intellectualistic misinterpretation of intelligence, presented in the famous second chapter of *The Concept of Mind*.[13] Ryle contrasts "knowing that" with "knowing how" and claims that the latter is more fundamental than the former for the purpose of understanding our concept of intelligence and related concepts.

It is not my purpose here to criticize Ryle's criticism of what he calls "the intellectualistic legend," although this criticism seems to me to rest on far too narrow a view of what it means to 'know that.' In any case, there is a great deal of truth in what Ryle says. However, it seems to me most unfortunate that the way in which he explains his point leans rather heavily on the ambiguous and frequently misapplied locution "knows how." Ryle's emphasis on the contrast between "knowing that" and "knowing how" would be justified if the similarity of these two constructions had been operative in misleading philosophers. Ryle does not claim this, however, and such a claim would be very unlikely to be true. For one thing, the sense of "knowing how" is expressed in many other languages without using any counterpart of the verb "know" at all. For instance, in German "know how" would often be *können* (*imstande sein*), whereas "knowing that" would be *wissen*. No real danger of confusion can be said to obtain here.

[11] This point has been made repeatedly in the literature, most frequently in connection with some of the individual philosophers. See, e.g., W. G. Runciman, *Plato's Later Epistemology* (Cambridge: Cambridge University Press, 1962); R. M. Hare, "Plato and the Mathematicians," in *New Essays on Plato and Aristotle*, ed. R. Bambrough (London: Routledge & Kegan Paul, 1965), p. 23.

[12] Cf. my analysis of the direct object construction, briefly sketched toward the end of this paper.

[13] Gilbert Ryle, *The Concept of Mind* (London: Hutchinson's, 1949); cf. also Gilbert Ryle, "Knowing How and Knowing That," *Proceedings of the Aristotelian Society* 46: 1–16 (1945–46).

What is confusing about the locution "knowing how" is its ambiguity. On one hand,

(11)   *a* knows how to do *x*

may mean (and perhaps most often means) that *a* has the skills and capacities required to do *x*, i.e., that he can do *x*. However, it may also mean (and occasionally does mean) that *a* knows the answer to the question: How should one go about it in order to do *x*? In this sense, knowing how to do *x* does not entail being capable of doing it or even ever having been capable of doing it.

We might dub these two different senses of (11) the skill sense and the 'knowing the way' sense.

It seems to me (although I may be wrong) that we are sometimes uncomfortably aware of this ambiguity and that there are contexts in which the skill sense of "knowing how" smacks of a vulgarism. Suppose, for example, someone asks me: "Do you know how to play the piano?" I would be tempted to reply: "Surely everyone *knows how* a piano is played; but nevertheless not everyone *can* play the piano, myself included." Whether this is to be taken as quibbling or not, it is relevant to point out the difference in logical force between such questions as "Do you know how to play the piano?" and "Do you know how to make a call from this extension phone?" Almost anyone *knows how* a piano is played, but not everyone *can* do it. Almost anyone *can* make a phone call, provided that he *knows how* to do it. It may also be suggested that knowing how in the "knowing the way" sense is not always as much as a prerequisite for being able to do it. I *can* touch-type, but I do not *know how* I do it in the sense that I could recall the positions of the different keys (although my fingers find them 'on their own'), and thus, for instance, could not teach anyone to type without access to a typewriter.

In general, it seems to me that it would have been much more useful for Ryle's own purposes to argue that there are elements of skill and capacity imbedded in the concept of 'knowing that' instead of taking the *knowing that/ knowing how* contrast for granted and using it to criticize 'the intellectualistic legend.' For one thing, I believe that 'knowing that,' in the last analysis, involves an element of skill, or at least capacity. But, if so, then the very 'intellectualistic legend' cannot be satisfactorily formulated in terms of "knowing that" in the way that Ryle does. It seems to me that, however refreshing Ryle's criticism of narrow interpretations of intelligence may be, in his own interpretation of the meaning of "knowing that" Ryle himself succumbs to what I cannot help calling a narrowly intellectualistic view. Very briefly expressed, Ryle's mistake seems to be that he associates "knowing that" far too closely with being able to tell, i.e., being able to produce the right information on request. Of course, Ryle would be the first to admit that what counts here cannot be the mere capacity to produce the right noises on appropriate stimuli. Neither a parrot nor a well-trained idiot *knows* what he is saying. What more has to be required is not easy to express briefly, but, in general, some reasonably good understanding of what one's words stand for is obviously required. And this understanding itself can scarcely be a purely verbal capacity. It presupposes some idea of how one's words are related to the reality they are about. Now I have argued elsewhere that in the case of certain very simple logical words, namely, the quantifiers, it is useful to compare the mastery of the concepts they express with the mastery of certain games (in the precise sense of mathematical game theory).[14] Knowing the truth of a statement is, on this simple model, comparable to knowing certain things about what may happen in one's "games of investigating the world," to use a phrase Ryle himself employs elsewhere. But if this model is at all representative, if it is at all like what is essentially involved in 'knowing that,' then the contrast between 'knowing that' and 'knowing how' is useless as the kind of simple dichotomy which Ryle seems to assume it to be, for 'knowing that' will involve a great deal of 'know-how.'

In any case, we do distinguish between, for instance, "knowing how the piano is played" and "knowing how to play the piano," when the latter is taken in the skill sense. This already serves to show that the construction "knowing how" is not always taken to indicate a skill but is sometimes naturally taken in the other ("knowing the way") sense.

The skill sense of "knowing how" cannot be analyzed in terms of "knowing that." However, it may not be much of an exaggeration to say that this sense of "knowing how" has only an accidental linguistic connection with the concept of knowledge in the sense of "knowing that." We shall not discuss this 'skill' sense further in what follows.

The other sense of "knowing how" is comparable to the meaning of such locutions as "knowing who," "knowing when," etc., and can be reduced to the "knowing that" construction in a parallel way. For instance, knowing how a call is made from a given extension phone is knowing some sequence of manipulations (pushing a button, dialing certain numbers first, etc.) by means of which a call can be made.

Again, it may be useful to be shaken from our parochial ways of thinking and speaking by the realization that the Greeks viewed matters in a light different from ours. For them, there is scarcely any difference that corresponds to our distinction between *knowing that* and *knowing how*. As readers of the *Apology* will recall, in Socrates' view the skills of a craftsman constituted real knowledge or *episteme*. The difference between a real *episteme* and a mere blind *empeiria* is not one between factual knowledge and skill, but, roughly, between on the one hand knowledge or skill which is accompanied by conscious insight into its own aims and principles and on the other hand mere blind capacity.[15]

As far as the other terms which are important in epistemology are concerned, they give rise to the same or closely related problems. Among these terms there

[14] See my paper, "Language-Games for Quantifiers," *American Philosophical Quarterly*, Supplementary Monograph no. 2 (1968).

[15] Cf. my paper "Tieto, taito ja päämäärä" [Knowledge, skill, and purpose], *Ajatus* 27: 49–67 (1965).

are the different words connected with belief ("belief," "opinion," "guess," etc.), perception ("perceiving," "seeing," "hearing," etc.), memory, awareness, and so on. All of these terms occur in some constructions analogous to those listed in connection with knowing, and most of them occur in almost all of these constructions. (It is interesting to see that the skill sense of "knowing how" does not have any counterpart in the case of most of these other terms, however.) In addition, new constructions can make their appearance when we examine these other epistemic terms. The construction "believe in" is an obvious case in point. My thesis concerning these terms is, by and large, the same as that concerning knowledge: the logical primacy of the that-construction. In other words, I think that all of these terms express *propositional attitudes* in a rather strong sense. Insofar as these terms are thought of as expressing relations, they hold between the person having this attitude and certain states of affairs or courses of events (propositions, if you want, or certain sets of 'possible worlds,' as I shall refer to them). If we are discussing what *a* knows or does not know, the second term of the relation is (as I suggested above) the set of all possible worlds compatible with *a*'s knowing whatever he does know. In the same way, when we are attributing any (typical) propositional attitude to *a*, we are implicitly considering the set of all states of affairs or courses of events (as the case may be) which are compatible with *a*'s holding the attitude in question.

If propositional attitudes are conceived of as relations, they do not hold between a person and ordinary objects (individuals). In fact, the major implication of the reduction of the direct object construction to the propositional constructions is that these seemingly 'direct objects' can, in the last analysis, enter into a context governed by one of our terms only as members of a 'possible world' (or several such worlds).

This claim is especially interesting in the case of perception. The direct object constructions with perceptual terms appear independent of others, and perhaps even fundamental and irreducible. (Is not perception a physical and physiological relation between the perceiver and the perceived object or objects?) For this reason, the question of the reducibility of the direct object perceptual constructions to propositional constructions has to be argued much more carefully and at much greater length than I can do here.

There are of course differences between different uses (senses) of the direct object constructions. Some such uses admit of easy paraphrasing in terms of the propositional constructions. Cases in point seem to be "believing what (i.e., that which) someone says" and "seeing an accident," which presumably can be paraphrased in terms of believing that things are as the person in question says they are or in terms of seeing that the accident happened (or perhaps seeing how it happened). More generally, we have the locution "believing someone" in the sense "believing what he says."

These uses will be called *elliptical* ones. However, especially in the case of perception, it is obvious that there are other uses which do not reduce in these simple ways to propositional constructions and which clearly have a great deal of intrinsic interest. The most important case in point is undoubtedly a locution such as

$$a \text{ perceives } b$$

or

$$a \text{ sees } b$$

where "b" is a singular term (i.e., a term referring to a person or to some other individual object). I shall call these "non-elliptical" senses of the direct object construction and shall largely restrict my attention to them.

The whole group of questions connected with the behavior of the direct object constructions (in their non-elliptical senses) is extremely interesting, for it is connected with a number of problems involving the nature of the objects of such propositional attitudes as knowledge, belief, memory, perception, and the like. These problems include the questions concerning the so-called intentionality of these attitudes. In this area we have queries such as the following: What precisely is meant by the intentionality of a concept? How does it manifest itself in the behavior of this concept? Are the basic epistemological notions intentional, and are they intentional to the same extent?

The connection I have sought to establish between such notions as knowledge, belief, perception, etc., and the idea of possible world opens a line of attack on these problems of intentionality. Whatever is or may be meant by this term, it seems clear to me that normally the more the possible worlds a modal concept admits may differ from the actual one, the more intentional it is. The more an attitude turns on one's own 'intentional' mental universe, the more the worlds compatible with this attitude are likely to differ from the objectively determined real world. Thus belief is more intentional than knowledge, for whatever is known by a (i.e., whatever is true in all of the possible worlds compatible with a's knowing what he knows) must also be true in the actual world, whereas this kind of similarity between the admissible possible worlds and the actual one does not have to obtain in the case of belief.

More important than such similarities or differences are those comparisons that pertain to the individuals that exist in the different possible worlds. For instance, is there a way of referring to each individual such that one can say that the same individual is picked out by this way of referring to it in every possible world compatible with the attitude in question? Under what conditions can an individual which exists in the 'merely possible world' compatible with a propositional attitude be said to be identical with an actual individual? These questions seem to me to distinguish rather sharply between the different degrees of intentionality of different concepts. By means of such questions, we can, among other things, approach R. M. Chisholm's semiformal criteria of intention-ability with sharper tools than before.[16] Unfortunately, no details can be taken

---

[16] See Roderick M. Chisholm, "On Some Psychological Concepts and the 'Logic' of Intentionality," in *Intentionality, Minds, and Perception*, ed. Hector-Neri Castañeda (Detroit: Wayne State University Press, 1967); Chisholm, "Notes on the Logic of Believing," *Philosophy and Phenomenological Research* 24: 195–201 (1963–64).

up here, apart from pointing out that since the admissible possible worlds can differ from the actual one in many different ways, there does not seem to be just one dimension of intentionality but a multiplicity of different ways in which a propositional attitude or other modal notion can be intentional.

Furthermore, there are questions concerning the way individuals enter into contexts governed by epistemic notions. What happens to the logical laws to which singular terms are normally subject? Difficulties arising here have fostered considerable discussion. As has already been hinted, these problems are especially closely related to the nature of the last two types of constructions we listed in connection with knowledge, and to the counterparts of these constructions for other terms.

The reduction of the direct object construction to the that-construction can be dealt with only briefly here. It is connected with the central problem which we confront almost at once when we try to analyze the interplay of propositional attitudes with quantification in terms of 'possible worlds' along the lines indicated above. This problem is posed by the question: When are individuals figuring in two different worlds identical with one another? By and large, it seems to me fair to say that 'cross-identifications' of this kind turn on criteria not entirely unlike those criteria of reidentification which have been studied by Strawson and others.[17] (Certain continuity properties will loom large in all such identification.) We might label these *physical* or *descriptive* methods of cross-identification. What makes the conceptual situation very complicated here is the fact that we may have a second set of criteria of cross-identification essentially different from the first set. The nature of this other set of methods is especially clear in the case of perception.[18] Here the different 'possible worlds' involved are really all of the different states of affairs compatible with everything a certain specified person perceives at a certain moment in time. When, then, are two individuals which occur in two respective states of affairs identical? Even if we disregard physical (descriptive) methods of cross-identification, we can still cross-identify individuals in terms of the situations in which they are perceived. These constitute frameworks, as it were, into which certain individuals fall and which serve to 'individuate' these individuals. The man I see in front of me (I am tempted to say) is one and the same definite individual even though I do not see who he is and even though in some of the different possible states of affairs compatible with what I see he will therefore be a different person (a different descriptively identified individual).

Since every use of the quantifiers presupposes methods of cross-identification, the quantifiers relying on such *perceptual methods of cross-identification* will differ in meaning from those relying on physical methods of cross-identification.

---

[17] See, e.g., Peter F. Strawson, *Individuals* (London: Methuen, 1959).
[18] Cf. my paper, "On the Logic of Perception," in *Perception and Personal Identity*, ed. N. S. Care and R. Grimm (Cleveland: Press of Case Western Reserve University, 1969), pp. 140–75; reprinted in my *Models for Modalities*.

(In a sense they may nevertheless 'range over' the same individuals, which only goes to show that the "ranging over" idiom is not a very useful one when used in connection with propositional attitudes.)

My suggestion is that direct object constructions like

(12)   *a* sees *b*

have to be explicated in terms of quantifiers that rely on perceptual cross-identification in a fashion similar to the explication of the interrogative construction

(13)   *a* sees who *b* is

in terms of quantifiers that turn on physical cross-identifications. Roughly speaking, in (13) we typically start from a perceptually given individual and place it (as it were) among the physically cross-identified (individuated) ones, whereas in (12) we start from a physically given individual and find room for it (so to speak) among *a*'s visually cross-identified individuals (among his *visual objects*, we are tempted to say, although there is no separate class of 'visual objects' or 'sense data' different from the ordinary kinds of object in any possible state of affairs).

The explicit (but not quite accurate) explications of (12) and (13), respectively, might thus be:

(12)* there is a visually individuated individual (call it *x*) such that *a* sees that $(b = x)$

and

(13)* there is a physically individuated individual (call it *x*) such that *a* sees that $(b = x)$.

The only construction in which the verb "sees" occurs here is the "sees that" construction. Of course it is also true that in (12)* we rely on the fact that we are dealing with visual perception in another, indirect way, in that we use visual methods of cross-identification. This does not diminish the interest of our reduction of the direct object construction to the that-construction in the case of "sees." It does not eliminate the fundamental fact that the only way in which individuals can be handled in a proper logical (semantical) analysis of the situation is as members of the different possible worlds we are considering.

It is less clear what the analogue to perceptual methods of cross-identification might be in the case of such notions as knowledge or memory. But then the truth conditions of the corresponding constructions

a knows *b*

and

a remembers *b*

in terms of knowledge and memory likewise seem to be less clear. The suggestion that ensues from the above remarks is that one can be said to remember someone (e.g., *b*) if and only if one can place him within the framework of one's personally remembered past, and that one knows *b* if and only if one can place him within one's personal acquaintances.

Generally, this suggestion seems to square rather well with the logical behavior of the direct object constructions involving "knows" and "remembers," respectively, although the whole complex of problems that we encounter in this direction badly needs further study and discussion. In any case, we have already seen how questions that seem to pertain to general and abstract logical (and semantical) problems, such as that of cross-identification, naturally—not to say inevitably—lead to a satisfactory analysis of the problematic direct object constructions in terms of the that-construction (plus a suitable kind of quantification, of course).

What I have said may provide an interesting partial explanation for the pre-occupation of the ancient Greeks with the direct object construction. (Such a preoccupation is easy to document.) Elsewhere, I have briefly noted some aspects of the tendency of the Greeks to think of logical, semantical, and epistemological matters from the point of view of some particular personal situation. If the suggestions made in the present paper are correct, then it is just this kind of personal situation that supplies the individuation methods (methods of cross-identification) which are relied upon in the direct object constructions. A preference for the direct object construction and the tendency to regard one's personal situation as a natural epistemological framework are thus two sides of the same coin. Incidentally, we seem to have found here a common denominator of the Greeks' inclination to think of semantical matters from the standpoints of particular speech situations (this tendency is demonstrated especially strikingly by the marked prevalence of temporally indefinite singular sentences in Greek philosophical literature) and their reliance on the model of perception as a paradigm for knowing (knowledge as "a sort of mental seeing or touching").[19] In both cases, an individual's immediate personal context is relied on as an epistemological framework.

Our parallel analyses of the different direct object constructions also illustrate the fact that there often is a great deal of similarity among the different epistemologically important terms. There are also unmistakable differences, both of kind and of degree. Some of these may have genuine philosophical and logical interest, but several of the differences seem to me to be largely accidental.

Among the differences that seem to be relevant there is a difference between the questions one can ask in the cases of the different terms, as noted by Austin.[20] One can ask

---

[19] For the predominance of the temporally indefinite sentences in Greek thinking about semantical matters, see my paper, "Time, Truth and Knowledge in Ancient Greek Thought," *American Philosophical Quarterly* 4: 1–14 (1967).

[20] Austin, "Other Minds."

and

> How do you know?

> Why do you believe?

but not the other way around. I shall not try to spell out this relevance here, however.

Among the largely accidental differences, there is the fact that the verb "believe" lacks several of the constructions which were registered above for knowledge. For instance, we do not seem to have any locutions such as "believes when," "believes where," nor anything like a direct object construction with "believes," except in its elliptical senses. Furthermore, although we can say

(14) He knows whether *p*,

it would probably be taken to be a solecism to say

(15) He believes whether *p*.

This difference, and others like it, seems to me largely accidental, however. It is an interesting and relevant fact that we can easily understand what would be meant (so to speak) by (15) if it were an admissible locution. This locution could then be related to "believes that" in the same way as "knows whether" is related to "knows that." In other words, "*a* believes whether *p*" would then be a more convenient way of saying that *a* has a belief (opinion) as to whether *p*. In fact, it seems to be less queer to say "He opines whether *p*" than to utter (15).

Moreover, the absence of constructions like (15) can be partly understood by means of their relative unimportance in practice. (Knowing that someone has a belief one way or the other is not likely to be nearly as important as knowing that he knows how things are, one way or the other. The former concerns, as it were, the believer's private affairs, whereas the latter involves an objective element.)

In any case, all of the missing propositional constructions do occur in connection with such verbs as "guess," which is often used in contexts where the mere fact of venturing to show an attitude one way or the other is likely to have consequences.

Furthermore, it may be pointed out that the Greeks were much more liberal with their constructions than we are. Several of the missing constructions with words like "believes" have perfectly good (i.e., grammatically impeccable) counterparts in the Greek. For instance, there is in the Greek what amounts to a direct object construction with a verb which otherwise has the force of "believing" or perhaps "opining." (Some features of the general background of this predilection for direct object constructions were noted above.)

The general suggestion of (logical) similarity between the different propositional attitudes has to be qualified, however, by emphasizing a difference between two kinds of propositional attitudes, vague though this difference is. We have, on the one hand, more or less purely cognitive attitudes—attitudes which in some sense essentially turn on the informative (evidential) situation in which one finds oneself. Knowledge, memory, and perception are cases in point. On the other hand, we have attitudes which partly turn on one's non-cognitive decisions or states of mind, or on some similarly non-informational factor. The concepts of 'being sure' and 'faith' are likely to be as clear cases as one is apt to find.

Although this distinction is not easy to explain in general terms, it is important not to confuse the members of the two groups, closely related though they may be. What makes things especially tricky is that there are concepts whose status vis-à-vis this distinction is not clear. The concepts of certainty and belief are cases of this sort. Thus it appears that in the map of our concepts belief lies somewhere between opinion (which is a predominantly 'informational' concept) and faith (which is not). This is also witnessed by the construction "believe in," which has no analogue for knowledge or for opinion and which cannot be reduced (as far as I can see) to the "believes that" construction.

Again, "being certain" may occasionally have the force of "[really] knowing" but it may also be tantamount to "*feeling* certain" or "*feeling* sure."

One further group of problems which can be mentioned but not discussed here concerns the relations of the different epistemologically important notions. Does knowledge imply belief, and perhaps even certainty? Can knowledge be defined as justified true belief? The philosophical interest of these questions is obvious, and they have in fact figured prominently in recent epistemological literature.

Dag Prawitz

The Philosophical Position of
Proof Theory

The purpose of this paper is to draw attention to some aspects of the philosophical position of proof theory. In my opinion, proof theory deserves attention as philosophically one of the most interesting branches of logic. No doubt, to some extent, the neglect of proof theory by philosophers is due to the way proof theoretical results are often presented; frequently, the technical formulations do not exhibit the significance of the results obtained.

1

For the understanding of proof theory, an essential distinction is that between general proof theory and reductive proof theory.

By *reductive proof theory*, I understand the well-known attempt to analyze the proofs of mathematical theories with the intention of reducing them to some more elementary part of mathematics such as finitistic or constructive mathematics. Here, the study of the proofs of mathematical theories provides the tool for attaining this reduction of the theories. Hence, this study must not use principles that go beyond those occurring in the more elementary theories to which the given theories are to be reduced.

In *general proof theory*, on the other hand, proofs are studied in their own right in the hope of understanding their nature. For instance, we may try to characterize the notion of proof and understand the structure of proofs. Since we do not require a reduction here, there is no restriction on the means that may be used in this kind of study.

Professor Prawitz, of the University of Oslo, is a native of Sweden.

I am much indebted to Professor Georg Kreisel for many conversations that have influenced my views on topics discussed in this paper. He also read an earlier draft of the paper and made many valuable suggestions.

123

Needless to say, there are results that belong to both reductive and general proof theory, that is, both accomplish a reduction of mathematical theories and say something essential about their proofs. Although the distinction is not commonly made, it is obviously essential in a discussion of the significance of different proof theoretical results.[1]

I shall first discuss some of the ideas behind reductive proof theory (sections 2–4) and then describe the kind of results that may be expected from general proof theory (section 5), mentioning briefly some results that have actually been obtained (section 6).

2

2.1. To be meaningful, reductive proof theory must be based on some conception of an order among different principles with respect to how elementary they are, or at least on the recognition of certain kinds of principles as especially elementary. Typically, these principles are of a constructive kind, and often they are further specified as, for example, finitistic, predicative, or intuitionistic. One may then speak about *constructive proof theory, finitistic proof theory*, etc. Proof theory as first conceived by Hilbert, for example, was clearly based on the attitude that only certain mathematical principles, namely the finitistic ones, carried complete conviction.

The task of constructive proof theory is thus to analyze or *interpret* theories in constructive terms. The significance of this kind of proof theory for the foundations of mathematics is of course clear. Also, if one does not share Hilbert's attitude that constructive (or, more precisely, finitistic) mathematics is the only part of mathematics that is completely grasped, the *possibility* of understanding mathematics in these elementary terms would clearly be of great interest.

It must be admitted, however, that although proposals have been made concerning what principles are to be counted as finitistic, predicative, etc., there is not yet any general agreement about these questions. Furthermore, one is often ready to expand a previously considered class of principles to include a new one, if this new principle is needed for an analysis of a certain theory and is more elementary than those occuring in that theory. These facts do not diminish the significance of this kind of proof theory in any considerable degree since (or as far as) it is clear that some kind of reduction is obtained. But the term "reductive proof theory" may thus be advantageous as a better description of the aims of this kind of proof theory; it should be remembered, however, that almost all current reductive proof theory is in some vague sense constructive.

2.2. A reductive analysis of mathematical theories can of course also be obtained by means other than the study of proofs, e.g., it may be possible to use

---

[1] However, the distinction has in effect often been made by G. Kreisel, who has argued in particular for the significance of what I have called general proof theory (see in particular his paper in the forthcoming *Proceedings of the Second Nordic Logic Symposium* [Amsterdam: North Holland Publishing Co., 1971]).

model theoretical interpretations. The characteristic features of reductive proof theory are thus partly *methodological*. Proof theory was conceived in a situation where model theoretical interpretations seemed inapplicable, namely, when an analysis of the theory of natural numbers was desired, and no more elementary theory in which that theory could be interpreted seemed possible.

Clearly, *model theory* of the modern kind introduced by Tarski is out of the question in a reductive analysis. Although this model theory also tries to analyze mathematical theories, its characteristic feature is that it presupposes (on the meta-level) the whole theory that is to be analyzed. Model theory may give us information about mathematical theories, but it is clear that it does not attempt to arrive at the sort of deeper understanding of mathematical theories that is sought in reductive proof theory.[2]

3

To bring out some of the philosophically relevant features of reductive proof theory more clearly, we may consider its relation to some schools in the foundations of mathematics.

3.1. *Intuitionism* and (the greater part of) reductive proof theory share the objective of achieving a constructive understanding of mathematics. Mathematical intuitionism seeks this goal directly by developing mathematics within a constructive framework, and what cannot be developed directly in this way is regarded as uninteresting or meaningless. Proof theory, on the other hand, often starts from given classical, non-constructive theories and tries to analyze them in a constructive meta-language. When doing so, proof theory is prepared for the case in which it is impossible to understand *each* sentence of the classical theory constructively, and is then satisfied with an analysis which gives a constructive understanding of the theory as a whole (cf. the distinction between real and ideal sentences under 4.1). Furthermore, in a proof theoretical analysis of intuitionistic theories, it may be possible to use more restrictive means than those employed in intuitionism, and it may then be possible to obtain a more far-reaching reduction than is obtained within the intuitionistic theory (see 4.3).

3.2. In passing, we may also compare proof theory with *logicism*, another reductionistic school in the philosophy of mathematics. Historically, the logistic idea that mathematics can be understood by reducing it to logic has been one of the main motives behind the formalization of mathematics, and has produced a number of formal systems (such as first-order predicate logic and Russell's

---

[2] It seems fair to say that Tarskian model theory is of comparatively little direct interest for the foundations of mathematics. One sometimes encounters the opposite view that model theory, with its study of meaning and truth, is especially well suited for interpreting mathematical theories. But this is clearly a superficial view; it is only in a very technical sense that the interpretations considered in model theory (where, roughly, a formal notion is interpreted as standing for the corresponding notion in the meta-language) can be said to give the meaning of the notion in question.

ramified higher order logic) which were then studied proof theoretically. But from a constructive point of view, the particular logical notions to which the mathematical notions were reduced are often more difficult to understand than the mathematical ones and are thus in greater need of analysis.

3.3. Reductive proof theory is not to be confused with the philosophical position called *formalism*. We may distinguish two variants of formalism: according to one, mathematical activity may (roughly speaking) be understood as the derivation of theorems *in* formal systems; according to the other, mathematical activity may be understood as being *about* formal systems (typically showing that such and such a formula is provable *in* a certain system). It is true that the second variant of formalism has some points in common with an early formulation by Hilbert of a proof theoretical program (see 4.1), but this agreement must be considered as rather incidental in Hilbert's case, and in any case not essential for reductive proof theory as here understood (cf. 4.2).

In formalism, as usually understood, mathematics is considered as sufficiently understood once it is formalized; mathematics is then to be understood simply as the meaningless play in the formal system or as the investigation of this play, respectively. Of course, a mathematician does not usually work actually in or with formal systems. But the contention of formalism is that his mathematics could be understood as if he did; that is, the relevant features are present in such formal activity.

Reductive proof theory, as here described, is in sharp opposition to this kind of formalism, since it is in no way satisfied with having found an adequate formalization of a mathematical theory. On the contrary, it insists on an analysis of the formal systems so that they can be understood constructively or in some other elementary terms.

It is also to be noted (as has been stressed by Kreisel especially) that both variants of formalism must be considered to have been refuted by Gödel's first incompleteness theorem. It is of course true that much mathematical activity can be understood as derivations in formal systems, a fact discovered by Frege and others. Before Gödel's result, it was conceivable that all of mathematics could be formalized within one formal system, and under that assumption the sweeping formalist assertion is rather plausible. But with this assumption refuted, the formalist position seems untenable since it cannot explain how new formal systems are created and why some formal systems are considered but not others. The formalist may distinguish between consistent and inconsistent systems since these are formal notions, but without some radical refinement in the formalistic position, he will have to regard a large number of systems as equally good, which clearly contradicts the actual situation in mathematics.

4

The early history of reductive proof theory illustrates some of the points made above and illuminates other important aspects of the subject as well. I shall consider in turn (1) the origin of proof theory and Hilbert's program, (2) the impact of Gödel's incompleteness results, and (3) Gentzen's revival of proof theory.

4.1. Reductive proof theory belongs to a well-known reductionistic trend in the study of the foundations of mathematics, which began early in the last century. We may distinguish proof theory as the last of the following three phases of this reductionistic research:

(a) the *arithmetization of mathematics*, carried out in the last century, by which mathematical analysis was reduced to intuitive arithmetic, including some set theoretical concepts;

(b) the *formalization of mathematics*, which originated with Frege and culminated with Russell's and Whitehead's great work; and

(c) the *proof theoretical analysis of formal theories*, whose aim is to interpret the formal theories in constructive or other elementary terms.

A formalization is then viewed as a codification of an intuitive theory, a certain process by which an intuitive theory or a part of it is standardized and precisely delimited. Thus, it should not really be called a reduction since it does not explain the meaning of the given intuitive theory. (When it is understood as a step by which the intuitive theory is replaced by a theory about a formal system, as in formalism or when it forms a part of a logistic development, it of course constitutes a reduction, although a problematic one.)

Proof theory began in 1900, when the problem of proving the consistency of a formal system of arithmetic by combinatorial means was stated by Hilbert (as problem number 2 in the famous list of problems that Hilbert presented to the Second International Congress of Mathematics in Paris). By arithmetic, Hilbert then meant a theory of real numbers that was sufficient for classical mathematical analysis. This problem arose very naturally at that time, since the consistency of the then existing mathematics had been reduced to the consistency of arithmetic (by the work mentioned in (a) above), and the idea of a formal system was becoming known (through the work of Frege mentioned in (b) above).

The first more detailed account of how Hilbert intended to solve the consistency problem was given in 1904. His views on the subject were subsequently modified (partly by the influence of critics such as Brouwer), and developed later into a full-fledged proof theoretical program, most forcefully presented in his paper "Über das Unendliche" given as an address in 1925.[3]

There Hilbert formulated his program roughly as follows: The goal of proof theory is to eliminate the infinite from mathematics. As Weierstrass eliminated the infinite in the form of the infinitely small and the infinitely large from calculus, Hilbert maintained (speaking at a meeting to honor the memory of Weierstrass), proof theory is to eliminate the infinite as it still occurs, for example, in the definition of real numbers as infinite sequences or in propositions about *all* natural numbers. But this elimination is not to be achieved at the

[3] *Mathematische Annalen* 95: 161–90 (1926).

expense of losing the fruitful methods that are formulated in terms of the infinite; on the contrary, the inferences that use the infinite are to be replaced by finite processes that give precisely the same results and allow proofs along the same lines as before. This is to be achieved by showing that the use of the infinite is only a *façon de parler*. More precisely, Hilbert makes a distinction between *real* and *ideal* propositions. The *real propositions* are the unproblematic ones that deal only with finite objects (e.g., the assertion made by an equation built up from numerals and operators for primitive recursive functions). But to restrict mathematics to real propositions would be to mutilate it tragically. Therefore, as geometry or algebra includes points at infinity or imaginary numbers as ideal elements, the propositions that deal with the infinite are, in Hilbert's proposal, to be regarded as ideal elements added to complete the theory and to obtain simpler and more fruitful laws; hence, the name *ideal propositions* for those that deal with the infinite.

Addition of the propositions that deal with the infinite as ideal elements is to be done in a finitary way in two steps. The first step is to formalize mathematics, which provides (formal) sentences and formal proofs. To an intuitive proof containing references to the infinite, there now corresponds the finite verification that a certain formal proof, that is, a finitary object, is formed in accordance with certain mechanical rules. The requirement that nothing is to be lost by the reduction to the finite is thus satisfied. (Note here the similarity to the second variant of the formalist position mentioned in 3.3.)

The sentences in the formal systems are to be considered, in the first place, as objects without meaning. But some of the sentences may also be understood as communications of real propositions; they are called *real sentences*, while the other sentences are called *ideal sentences*. However, a real sentence may have a formal proof to which no intuitive proof in finitary mathematics corresponds. This occurs when the formal proof proceeds over ideal sentences. The second step is therefore to show in finitary mathematics that the real proposition that corresponds to a formally provable real sentence is also provable in finitary mathematics; in other words, to show that every provable real sentence expresses a *true* real proposition, or, briefly, that it is (finitarily) true.

This second step entails a consistency proof for the formal system showing that there is no sentence such that both it and its negation are provable (provided the formal system satisfies the condition that every sentence is derivable from a formal contradiction). Under the assumption that all true real sentences are provable, which condition was satisfied in Hilbert's case (by his way of drawing the line between real and ideal sentences), this second step is actually equivalent to proving the consistency of the system. The distinction between the consistency problem and the problem of showing the truth of all provable real sentences is therefore not always made. However, it is in this second formulation that the full significance of the consistency problem is seen, and Hilbert was usually careful to distinguish between the two problems.

The program was certainly grand and, if carried out, it would in a clear sense have achieved a reduction of mathematics to what Hilbert called finitary mathematics; mathematics could be understood constructively as being about real propositions with ideal propositions functioning as tools for deriving results about real propositions. The situation would in many ways be analogous to a familiar one in empirical interpretations of theories where there is a distinction between observational sentences and theoretical sentences, and where the empirical justification or interpretation consists in showing that the theoretical sentences function as tools for deducing empirically true observational sentences. As in the case of empirical theories, where the distinction between observational and theoretical sentences causes certain difficulties, the drawing of a line between the real and ideal propositions (or sentences) may involve certain problems. Although Hilbert never drew such a line explicitly, he discussed several examples, and it seems clear that he in effect wanted to identify finitary mathematics with a very elementary part of the arithmetic for natural numbers.

4.2. As is well known, Gödel's discoveries in 1930–31 had a great impact on reductive proof theory and defeated the proof theoretical program in Hilbert's particular formulation.

According to Gödel's first incompleteness theorem, there is no complete formalization of arithmetic (let alone of mathematics as a whole). Hence, Hilbert's first step cannot be completely carried out and one cannot say that to each intuitive proof there corresponds a formal proof. The most one can hope for is a complete formalization of the principles actually used in mathematics as it exists at a certain time; and, hence, in Hilbert's scheme, there is at most a finitistic reduction of this mathematics.

According to Gödel's second incompleteness theorem, a consistent formal theory of natural numbers cannot be shown to be consistent by means of the principles that are formalized in the theory. Hence, the theory of natural numbers cannot be reduced to *that* finitary mathematics which Hilbert had in mind. As Gödel was careful to point out, however, this did not exclude the possibility that, for instance, a formal system of arithmetic can be proved to be consistent by *other* finitary means that cannot be formalized in the system.

With some modifications, Hilbert's program thus still remained possible. First, the ambition to formalize the whole of mathematics had to be lowered in the way mentioned, and it now became important to find formalizations of significant parts of mathematics. Furthermore, the connection with the formalist position had to be renounced (cf. 3.3). (Note in particular how absurd it would be if a proposition, e.g., Fermat's conjecture, were replaced by the assertion that the corresponding sentence is provable in a certain formal system; the first may be true but the second false. Hilbert does not say that the intuitive propositions are to be replaced in that way, but some of his formulations come rather close to that idea.) Thus, as remarked in the beginning of 4.1, a formalization is better thought of as a codification.

Second, the distinction between real and ideal propositions (or sentences) remained interesting, but since in any case finitary mathematics would have to be extended in order to carry out the demonstration of the truth of the provable real sentences, the possibility of finding a finitary interpretation of a larger class of statements than the prima facie finitary ones considered by Hilbert was now open.[4]

Finally, it became important to find stronger constructive principles than those thought of by Hilbert and to consider more deeply the epistemological character of different principles that could possibly be used to carry out the program. As long as one hoped to carry out the program once and for all by using certain specific principles, it was sufficient to be convinced about the elementary character of those principles. But it now became interesting to find principles, constructive or not, that were significantly more elementary than the principles formalized in a given system but sufficiently strong to allow a reduction of the system in the sense of proving the truth of the provable real sentences.

4.3. The first person to give new life to proof theory after Gödel's discoveries was Gentzen. In 1936, Gentzen showed for a certain first-order system of Peano arithmetic that every provable real sentence is true. In 1938, he modified this by showing that every proof of a real sentence that proceeds over ideal sentences can be replaced by a direct proof that uses only real sentences. Gentzen's proof used induction over an initial segment of the ordinals (up to the so-called first epsilon number), which constituted an extension of the finitary means considered by Hilbert, but used only quantifier-free reasoning. In this respect, the means were thus essentially restricted as compared to those available in arithmetic. The essential point in Hilbert's program (of obtaining a reduction of the classical quantifications over infinite totalities by showing that they were harmless in the sense of not disturbing the real sentences) was thus carried out for this system, provided that the induction used by Gentzen is accepted as sufficiently elementary.

Gentzen's proof is also applicable to a corresponding intuitionistic system. In this application, the essential point is that the proof does not contain iterated intuitionistic implications; it is thus not only quantifier-free but also essentially logic-free. This illustrates the point made in 3.1 that it may be possible to obtain a more thorough reduction by a proof theoretical analysis than by direct intuitionistic methods, again, provided that the induction used by Gentzen is accepted as sufficiently elementary. A reduction of classical first-order arithmetic to intuitionistic first-order arithmetic had already been carried out by Kolmogoroff in 1925 and Gödel, independently, in 1932, who used a rather simple argument that did not utilize any essentially proof theoretical methods.

---

[4] Examples in which all the sentences of first-order arithmetic receive constructive interpretation are Kreisel's 'no counter example interpretation' ("On the Interpretation of Non-Finitist Proofs, 1," *Journal of Symbolic Logic* 16: 241–67 [1951]) and Gödel's 'functional' interpretation ("Über eine bisher noch nicht benützte Erweiterung des finiten Standpunctes," *Dialectica* 12: 280–87 [1958]).

Since all arguments used in Gentzen's proof except the induction up to the first epsilon number can be formalized in first-order Peano arithmetic, it follows by Gödel's second incompleteness theorem that this induction cannot be formalized within the system (which was verified directly by Gentzen in 1943). It was furthermore shown by Bernays in 1939 that induction up to any ordinal below the first epsilon number was formalizable within first-order Peano arithmetic. The first epsilon number thus measures the strength of the system in a natural way.

Gentzen's result was later extended to more comprehensive systems using higher ordinal numbers, and, again, it has been shown that induction over an initial segment of the ordering determined by the ordinal number in question can be formalized within the system. This makes the status of these inductions over initial segments of the constructive ordinal numbers crucial, and their status cannot yet be considered settled. However, work on justifying induction up to the first epsilon number by obviously very elementary methods was undertaken by Kreisel at the International Congress of Mathematics at Edinburgh in 1958 and was recently refined in his paper, "Principles of Proof and Ordinals Implicit in Given Concepts." [5]

Gentzen's result was based on ideas that he had introduced earlier in "Untersuchungen über das logische Schliessen," [6] which allowed a much deeper analysis of first-order proofs than had previously been attempted. This analysis is of interest apart from its successful application in reductive proof theory and belongs to what I have called general proof theory.

5

Both general and reductive proof theory are epistemology of a kind. In reductive proof theory, we try to understand mathematics by reducing it to certain fundamental principles that we find especially evident; in general proof theory, we study not only the theorems of a theory, that is, *what* we know, but also their proofs, that is, *how* we know them.

During the last few decades, logic has been dominated to a considerable extent by model theory. But the picture produced by model theory is incomplete in essential respects. Model theory almost entirely omits the phenomenon of deductive reasoning, or, more precisely, it treats only an extensional aspect of it— logical validity and the logical consequence relation. It does not say anything about the process by which we establish the validity of an argument or obtain the theorems of a theory. This process is then the subject matter of general proof theory.

What one expects from general proof theory is first of all a *definition* of the

[5] *Intuitionism and Proof Theory* (Amsterdam: North Holland Publishing Co., 1970), pp. 489–516.
[6] *Mathematische Zeitschrift* 39: 176–210, 405–31 (1934–35).

notion of proof, a *characterization* of the proofs, and a *representation* of them. This ought to of course include a characterization of different kinds of proofs.

To settle upon a terminology in this connection, we may use the term "proof" to denote the process by which an argument is established and the term "derivation" to denote the syntactic representation of this process. Insofar as proofs can be represented by derivations (and it is not given that the representation must be, or can be, formal and finitary), one inquires about properties of the representability relation. In particular, one may ask when two derivations represent the same proof; in other words, one may seek a synonymity relation between derivations or identity criteria for proofs.

One may further hope for results that reveal something of interest about the *structure* of proofs—both in the intrinsic interest of a better understanding of the phenomena of proofs and in the expectation that this insight will make it possible to solve other problems in logic.

6

It is of course not evident that the questions mentioned in section 5 are capable of a successful treatment. But, as a matter of fact, the work by Gentzen constitutes a promising approach to these problems, some of which Gentzen himself has satisfactorily solved. In this paper, I shall only indicate the general direction of work in this area.[7]

6.1. Some of Frege's work may be regarded as a first extensional characterization of proofs in certain languages, showing that they can be represented by derivations constructed by mechanical rules. But the representation concerns only the theorems proved, that is, the result of the proof, since the formal derivation may be based on quite different ideas or deductive operations than the proof that it is to represent. In this sense we may speak about an 'extentional characterization.' In contrast, Gentzen's work in 1934—more precisely, his construction of the so-called systems of natural deduction—should be considered an attempt at a real (intentional) characterization of (different kinds of) first-order proofs. This work gives an analysis of deductive operations into *atomic steps* by which the deductive roles of different logical constants are separated. It seems reasonable to claim that Gentzen has isolated the essential deductive operations within these languages and has broken them down as far as possible—in other words, that every deductive operation within these languages can be understood as composed of Gentzen's atomic inferences.

6.2. What makes Gentzen's characterization especially interesting is the discovery of a certain symmetry between the atomic inferences expressed by an 'inversion principle.' The atomic inferences are of two kinds: *introductions* of a logical constant by which a conclusion containing this constant as outermost sym-

[7] For a more detailed review, I refer the reader to my paper "Ideas and Results in Proof Theory," forthcoming in *Second Nordic Logic Symposium*.

bol is inferred, and *eliminations* of a logical constant by which an inference is drawn from premises, one of which—the so-called major premise—contains the constant as outermost symbol. These introductions and eliminations of a logical constant stand in a special relation to each other that can be expressed by saying that one is the *inverse* of the other.

The sense in which an elimination, for instance, is the inverse of the corresponding introduction may be indicated by saying that an elimination only restores what is already contained in a proof by introduction of the major premises (together with proofs of the other premises, if any). Thus, nothing new is obtained by an introduction immediately followed by an elimination since the conclusion can be obtained directly from the premis(es) of the introduction without this sequence of inferences. This suggests certain *reductions* by which such a sequence of an introduction followed by an elimination is eliminated.

Gentzen also suggested that these considerations allow an *interpretation* of the logical constants in which the conditions for inferring a formula by introduction (which are formulated in terms of the subformulas of the formula) are taken as the *meaning* of its logical constants. The eliminations are then *justified* in this interpretation, since, in view of the fact that they are only the inverse of the introductions, they use just these meanings of the constants.

6.3. Neither this interpretation nor the reductions mentioned above were worked out by Gentzen, but they constitute a complex of ideas that formed the basis of Gentzen's so-called *Hauptsatz*, which he stated and proved for the calculi of sequents constructed by him. By remaining within the systems of natural deduction, however, one is able to obtain directly from these ideas a certain *normal form* for derivations.[8]

This normal form, the existence of which contains Gentzen's *Hauptsatz*, has very satisfactory properties, and may be indicated roughly by saying that a normal derivation consists of three parts: an *analytical part* in which the assumptions of the derivation are broken down into their components by the use of eliminations; a *minimum part* following immediately upon the analytical part which may contain operations on atomic formulas; and a *synthetical part* in which the final components obtained in the analytical part (possibly modified in the minimum part) are put together by the use of introductions. A normal derivation is thus *direct* in the sense that it makes no detours over formulas not contained essentially in the assumptions or the conclusions of the derivation.

As a special case, we may consider a derivation of an atomic formula in a first-order theory from assumptions that are also atomic. If such a derivation is brought into normal form, it will contain only the operations on atomic formulas that may be allowed in the theory in question. This indicates why Gentzen's ideas were so successful in the reductions of first-order logic mentioned above:

---

[8] See my *Natural Deduction* (Stockholm: Almqvist & Wicksell, 1965) or A. Raggio, "Gentzen's Hauptsatz for the Systems NI and NK," *Logique et Analyse*, no. 30 (1965): 91–100.

when a derivation of a real sentence that proceeds over ideal sentences is put into normal form, it is transformed into a derivation that proceeds directly over only real sentences. But this result is clearly only an application of insights into the structure of first-order proofs.

The reductions suggested by the inversion principle are such that they obviously preserve the identity of the proof represented. In fact, it is possible to use these reductions to define a particular equivalence relation between derivations, and it may be conjectured reasonably that this relation is the synonymity relation mentioned above (section 5); this conjecture is due to Per Martin-Löf.

6.4. In later extensions of Gentzen's ideas, inferences in more comprehensive languages have been analyzed into introductions and eliminations, and it has been shown that the reductions suggested by the corresponding inversion principles allow the transformation of derivations to a normal form of the kind described above. As examples, the following may be mentioned: extensions to some modal systems and to ramified second-order logic,[9] to the theory of iterated inductive definitions,[10] and to (simple) second-order logic. Second-order logic offered special difficulties because of its impredicative character. These were first overcome only by the use of model theoretical methods (Tait, Takahashi, and Prawitz).[11] Quite recently, the result for second-order logic has been essentially improved by a combination of Gentzen's ideas and by other methods introduced in a somewhat different context.[12]

[9] Prawitz, *Natural Deduction.*

[10] P. Martin-Löf, "Hauptsatz for the Intuitionistic Theory of Iterated Inductive Definitions," in *Second Nordic Logic Symposium.*

[11] For a discussion of these methods, see my paper, "On the Proof Theory of Mathematic Analysis," in *Logic and Value: Essays Dedicated to Thorild Dahlquist on His Fiftieth Birthday* (Uppsala: Filosofiska Föreningen och Filosofiska Institutionen vid Uppsala Universitet, 1970).

[12] See forthcoming papers by Girard, Martin-Löf, and Prawitz in *Second Nordic Logic Symposium.*

C

Philosophy of Science

Sören Halldén

Is Probability a Normative Concept?

1. INTRODUCTION

The meaning, or meanings, of the word "probability" still seem elusive. In the unsatisfactory state in which a long discussion has resulted, the basic conditions of the inquiry have to be discussed. What leads are there to follow? Which are the clues that might lead to a satisfactory account?

The investigator has in front of him the majestic structure of the Calculus of Probability. It is obvious that he must take into account the tradition according to which the formal expressions are handled, as well as the complex and subtle informal considerations of expert statisticians. Also, he should not forget the procedures that are employed when the non-numerical probabilities of everyday reasoning are calculated by men of practical affairs.

What other leads are there? Let us bear in mind that when a word is unclear it is often useful to remind oneself of the function it fulfills. Thus, when the lines between health and sickness or between sanity and insanity are being discussed, the ethics of medical interference may enter prominently into the picture. As a step reflecting this, we may say that a state of sickness is one that a doctor has the right to remove, even if the patient has not given his consent. And we may say that a man is insane if, and only if, certain kinds of restrictions on his personal freedom are justified, regardless of his consent. Similarly, when the import of the expression "logical truth" is discussed by epistemologists, it may be useful to start with a preliminary declaration about the connections between the class of logically true statements on one hand and permissible intellectual operations on the other, and say that a statement is logically true if, and only if, it can be defended and applied in certain ways.

In such cases the point of departure is an expression of the form:

Professor Halldén, of the University of Lund in Sweden, is a native of Sweden.

$$R(x_1, \ldots x_n) \equiv S(x_1, \ldots x_n),$$

which is not nakedly analytic and where the concept S is normative. Let us call such an expression a "pragmatic characterization" of the concept R. The reason for putting it on paper is that the normative concept S may give a hint of a concept suitable for the analysis of R—a concept T coextensive with S and such that we can maintain that R and T are the same concept.

It is possible that this type of approach may be utilized in the discussion of the meaning, or meanings, of "probability." In the following pages, I shall make an attempt in this direction.

2. A Pragmatic Characterization of "Probability"

Probability statements are classified in a variety of ways. A common distinction is that between statements concerning the probability of propositions, and statements concerning the probability of events. This distinction is of dubious value. Personally, I would like to identify the probability of an event E with that of the probability of the proposition asserting the occurrence of E. Of more obvious importance is the distinction between qualitative and quantitative probability statements. A statement of the former kind has the following form:

p is more probable than q,

while the corresponding quantitative statement asserts:

p has the probability x,

where x is a number.

Discussions of the meaning of "probability" are usually focused on statements of the quantitative type. This means a loss both in simplicity and in scope. The quantitative statements are reducible to statements of the qualitative type, while it is by no means obvious that a reduction in the opposite direction is feasible.

Of interest also is the distinction between conditional probability statements, in which the reference to previous knowledge is made explicit, and unconditional probability statements, in which this reference is tacit. Attention will here be focused on conditional probability statements of a specific type, statements in which the comparison between the theoretic possibilities is made on a common basis. These will generally have the form:

p is more probable than q, given u,

where "u" represents the knowledge on the basis of which the probability estimate is made. When I speak without further qualification about 'probability,' the reference will be to this relation with three terms.

Having turned our attention to probability statements of a specific form, let us consider the problem of the pragmatic characterization of the relation asserted in them.

What practical significance shall we allot to the estimate that p is more probable than q, given u? What recommendations and what prohibitions does it lead to, and what does it exclude? Now, it seems quite clear that a probability difference does have some sort of significance with respect to theoretical behavior. If p is more probable than q, it does seem more 'sensible' or 'rational' or 'acceptable' to put one's faith in p than to put it in q. Likewise we can say that we 'ought' to assert p rather than q. And we can say quite simply that asserting p is 'better' than asserting q. Whatever normative expression we choose, it should be remembered that the recommendation that is made is conditional. A reference to the basis u must be presupposed.

The niceties of the definition of the concept of assertion will remain outside the scope of the discussion. For "p is asserted," we shall use the shorter expression "Tp." Some other abbreviations will also prove useful: for "p is more probable than q, given u," we write "pP_uq"; for "$\sim(pP_uq \ v \ qP_up)$," we write "pE_uq"; for "p is better than q, given u," we write "pB_uq"; and for "p and q are of equal value, given u," we write "pS_uq." What has just been said can then be given the following compact formulation:

$$pP_uq \supset Tp \ B_u Tq.$$

As it stands, this principle cannot be accepted, however. A father participating in a guessing contest with his four-year-old son may very well accept a recommendation contrary to that expressed above. In order not to hurt the feelings of his son, the father will try to lose the game, and be inclined to try the least probable of possible guesses. As it stands, the principle will not be acceptable to him.

However, the father in our example will have to admit that the principle will become more acceptable if the evaluative clause is given a hypothetical form. The right-hand expression will then set forth the consequence of an ideal, i.e., it will state what follows if one has acknowledged the discovery of truth as the only worthwhile goal of theoretical activity. The valuation expressed becomes fitting if the view is taken that assertion of truth is the one thing of value. Hardly anyone would accept this somewhat extreme view, but nonetheless one may be interested in its consequences.

I shall say that an evaluative standpoint has the property E if it involves a complete knowledge of logic, involves value axioms according to which (a) the assertion of truth is preferable to the assertion of falsity, (b) the assertion of truth and the assertion of falsity are the only things which are of basic evaluative significance, and furthermore involves nothing else. (Certain modifications will be introduced in this definition in the next section.) We presume that a unique standpoint has the property E, which ensures a denotation for the definite description, "the evaluative standpoint which is E." For the latter expression, we introduce the shorthand notation "O."

A suitable conditional formulation of our principle is now easily given:

$$pP_uq \supset O \text{ logically implies } Tp\ B_uTq. \tag{1}$$

The interesting question then arises of whether the implication can be strengthened into an equivalence. It may here be enlightening to pay attention to the practical meaning of an *absence* of probability difference. What follows with respect to theory choice if one has already accepted pE_uq? A principle which is analogous to (1) recommends itself here:

$$pE_uq \supset O \text{ logically implies } Tp\ S_u\ Tq. \tag{2}$$

The following elementary consequence of (1) should then be noted:

$$qP_up \supset O \text{ logically implies } Tq\ B_uTp. \tag{3}$$

We assume that O is self-consistent and, furthermore, that propositions of the types "rB_us," "sB_ur," and "rS_us" are pairwise incompatible. From (2) and (3), the following can be inferred:

$$\sim(pP_uq) \supset \sim(O \text{ logically implies } Tp\ B_uTq). \tag{4}$$

From (1) and (4) the desired equivalence immediately follows:

$$pP_uq \equiv O \text{ logically implies } Tp\ B_uTq. \tag{5}$$

3. Uncertainty Rules

Before we proceed from the pragmatic characterization of probability to the analysis of this concept, certain points with respect to the position O have to be clarified.

A satisfactory explanation of the evaluative content of this position is possible only if the concept of 'uncertainty rule' is first made clear. An uncertainty rule is a normative proposition[1] concerned with choice under ignorance. It recommends a certain type of action or inaction when knowledge is incomplete. An example is the slogan "Safety First."

The recommendation to always follow the safest course is not uncontroversial. It does not seem odd or irrational to question it. It might even be difficult to find a person willing to follow it in all sorts of situations. The man who is cautious in business will find it right to be careless about his love affairs, and the

---

[1] To simplify formulations I use the term "proposition" in a wide sense. This means that a proposition is not automatically something which is true or false. The terms "rule" and "directive" will be used as synonyms for "normative proposition." By "statement" I mean a linguistic expression whose meaning is a proposition.

man who is cautious in his love-making will find it right to be wild in driving an automobile or in writing political pamphlets. By saying "Safety First" one expresses a personal standpoint.

There are, however, some uncertainty rules which in spite of their normative character do have something impersonal about them. An example is Savage's 'sure-thing principle,' which well deserves the interest of philosophers.[2] Somewhat simplified, this says that if p is known to be not worse than q and p is not known to be just as good as q, then p should be chosen rather than q. As can easily be seen, a person who follows this piece of advice will have nothing to lose and a chance to win something: p may be better than q. The sure-thing principle is just as uncontroversial as any simple truth of logic, but it will be taken for granted here that it is not a logical principle. I shall regard it as a normative proposition, a proposition of value.

A normative system involves a set of basic directives, evaluative rules of a primary nature. Other evaluative rules are derivative with respect to these basic directives. Some of these are motivated by considerations of the relationship between ends and means. A doctor may base his conduct on a rule according to which the patient's survival is the thing of primary importance. Considerations of a technical nature, involving causal connections, will force him to adopt secondary rules, ensuring the safety of the patient's life. If the doctor had been omniscient, a moral code containing elements of these two kinds would have been adequate for a regulation of his conduct. But he is not omniscient. In order to cope with choice situations which are forced on him and from which he cannot escape, he will need rules for action under ignorance, the sort of rules I have called "uncertainty rules." Let us suppose that a patient is brought to him. It is evident to him that the situation is precarious and that the patient will die if certain complex and painful measures are not taken. The doctor is not sure that the treatment will lead to recovery. Nonetheless, as he has nothing to lose and something to win, his plan of action will be clear. This is an application of the sure-thing principle.

A second principle should be mentioned which concerns action under ignorance, and which I personally would classify as normative and therefore as an uncertainty rule. This permits the elimination of residual alternatives. Besides the main alternatives which are compared with each other in choice situations, there are often possibilities which, if actualized, would make the choice pointless. While the doctor contemplates therapeutic measures, the patient may die. What appeared to be a choice between the therapeutic possibilities p and q was in reality a choice between the disjunctions $p \lor r$ and $q \lor r$, where "r" stands for the possibility that the patient may die. It seems reasonable to say that the existence of a residual alternative will not affect a choice. The choice between $p \lor r$ and $q \lor r$ is a choice between p and q.

---

[2] Leonard J. Savage, *The Foundations of Statistics* (New York: Wiley, 1954), pp. 21–22.

Certain restrictions, however, are necessary.[3] Let us limit ourselves to choice situations where only such alternatives s and t are considered which fulfill the condition that $s \cdot \sim t$ and $t \cdot \sim s$ are either both possible or both impossible, given the basic knowledge u. Let us also limit ourselves to choice situations in which no probabilities are known. The following rule for the elimination of residual alternatives may then be formulated:

If $p \cdot r \cdot u$ and $q \cdot r \cdot u$ are both logically impossible, then
$(p \vee r) B_u (q \vee r) \equiv p B_u q$.

The sure-thing principle and the rule just formulated are examples of uncertainty rules which it seems natural to accept as 'valid' or 'acceptable.' The meaning of these terms is intended to be normative. In the following discussion it will be presupposed that a statement of the form "p is valid" is a normative statement, and I shall regard this as implying that it is neither logically true, nor logically false, nor empirically true, nor empirically false.

This brings us to the connection between the new category of normative statements and the definition of O. The essential point is that O includes a set of uncertainty rules. By definition, all 'valid' uncertainty rules will be included in O.

What has just been said involves the property E, as employed in the definition of O, and it involves a property F, which I shall introduce in order to simplify the definition of E. A class A of propositions has the property F if, and only if, three conditions are fulfilled by it: (1) the following propositions are elements of it: (a) a basic directive according to which the assertion of a true proposition is always better than the assertion of a false proposition; (b) a commentary on (a), saying that (a) is the only basic directive (nothing else is of basic importance); (c) all valid uncertainty rules; (d) for any r which is logically true the proposition "r is logically true"; (e) for any r which is not logically true the proposition "r is not logically true"; (2) A is closed under logical implication (which means that if a proposition r is logically implied by elements of A, then r is itself an element of A); (3) A contains only those elements which can be deduced from the two conditions formulated earlier. Building on the definition of F, we can then say quite simply that a proposition has the property E if, and only if, the class of all propositions logically implied by the proposition has the property F.

[3] Of these restrictions, one is modal and the other probabilistic. I am indebted to Hector N. Castañeda for some very acute remarks which have made evident the necessity of the modal restriction. The axiom A7 discussed by him in his review of Sören Halldén's "On the Logic of "Better,'" *Philosophy and Phenomenological Research*, vol. 19 (1958) is closely related to the rule for the elimination of residual alternatives. Relevant here also are Roderick M. Chisholm and Ernest Sosa, "On the Logic of 'Intrinsically Better,'" *American Philosophical Quarterly*, 3: 10–11 (1966); and Bengt Hansson, "Fundamental Axioms for Preference Relations," *Synthese* 18: 428–29 (1968). Of interest in connection with the probabilistic restriction are certain observations made by Richard C. Jeffrey in *The Logic of Decision* (New York: McGraw-Hill, 1965).

The earlier suggestions concerning the expression "evaluative standpoint" are readily accommodated by what has just been said about the structure of evaluative standpoints. With a small change in the formulation used in section 2 we now say that "O" is shorthand for "the proposition that is E." The definition of O has then been given its final form.

It is now possible to comment on the philosophical status of statements concerning the consequences of O. First, it should be emphasized that the statement:

$$O \text{ logically implies } p,$$

can be rewritten in the following form.

Some proposition q is such that q is E, and only q is E, and q logically implies p.

If we want to prove or to refute such a statement, we may have to ask ourselves whether an uncertainty rule which the context has made relevant is valid or not. As the notion of 'validity' has been explained here, this is a normative question. In order to check a statement of the type "O logically implies p," we may thus have to enter a dispute about value.

To make this more concrete, let us suppose that a scientist has to make a choice between two hypotheses that differ in logical strength. Hypothesis h_1 is more far-reaching, while hypothesis h_2 has a comparatively narrow scope. The basic knowledge available to the scientist is contained in the proposition u and the logical relationship between h_1 and h_2 can be summarized by the observation that $u \cdot h_1$ logically implies h_2, while $u \cdot h_2$ does not logically imply h_1.

In order to make my ideas applicable I shall also assume that something has killed the instinct of adventure of our scientist, and that his own ambition is to make a correct guess. Using the concept just defined, one can say that the essential problem for this non-Popperian scientist will be whether O logically implies $Th_1 B_u Th_2$ or whether O logically implies $Th_2 B_u Th_1$.

Of course, the person in this example will see in a flash the two main features of the situation. If h_1 is true, h_2 is true also, and the choice of h_2 involves no risk. But the possibility that h_1 is false and h_2 is true has not been excluded, so the choice of h_2 means that there is a chance of winning something. This means that the sure-thing principle in the simplified form stated above is applicable. If our scientist accepts this principle as valid, he has the right to conclude that the choice of h_2 is better than that of h_1, given the basic knowledge u.

As the problem of the scientist is described here, his choice of hypothesis will be dependent upon his acceptance of a rule of conduct. In our terminology, it involves the recognition of an uncertainty rule as 'valid' in an evaluative sense.

If this is right, the proposition "O logically implies $Th_1 B_u Th_2$" has to be classified as normative, as a proposition of value. This conclusion can, as I see it, be contested only if one maintains that the applied uncertainty rule is logically true, in which case clause (d) in the definition of F will guarantee that the rule is logically implied by O. This possibility should not be entirely disregarded, but a good reason must be produced in its favor if it is to be taken seriously.

Let us say that a concept R involving n terms is factual if, and only if, for every $x_1, \ldots x_n$ the proposition $R(x_1, \ldots x_n)$ is either logically true or logically false, or empirically true or empirically false. And let us say that a concept R involving n terms is normative if, and only if, some proposition $R(x_1, \ldots x_n)$ is a normative proposition.

An important question can now be given a simple formulation. Is the relation "O logically implies $Tp\ B_u Tq$" a normative concept? In view of the definition just adopted, this question has to be answered in the affirmative if a set of three propositions p, q, u is to be found such that "O logically implies $Tp\ B_u\ Tq$" is a normative proposition. In view of the above example, it seems exceedingly likely that such a set of propositions exists. There is an alternative view—one may contend that uncertainty rules which are relevant for a theory choice based on the axioms (a) and (b) are all logically true. At the present stage of the discussion such a contention would appear extravagant, however. It seems sensible to regard the relation in question as indeed normative, and in the following section of the paper I shall assume that this point has been granted.

4. A Normative Analysis of Probability

The pragmatic characterization of a concept is intended to facilitate the analysis of it. Ordinarily one would expect a characterization of a concept in normative terms to have a, so-to-speak, factual core, i.e., an empirical or logical concept which could be used for the analysis. From the pragmatic characterization of health suggested in the introduction, one may thus proceed to a definition of this medical concept in empirical terms. In a similar spirit one may try to find a psychological core corresponding to the suggested characterization of insanity.

Now, it is by no means evident that such a factual core is to be found there. It is entirely possible that the seemingly empirical concept of psychiatric sickness has to be regarded as a normative concept in disguise. A satisfactory definition of mental disorder would then have to be couched in evaluative terms. And this reflection brings with it a question with respect to the concept discussed in this paper. May we presume that the characterization of probability given here has a factual core?

This talk about 'factual cores' may seem confusing. Let us go straight to the central point and stress that the question concerns the existence of a factual relation R which is such that the following equivalence holds for every p, q, and u:

$$R(p,\ q,\ u) \equiv O \text{ logically implies } Tp\ B_u Tq.$$

Does such a relation R exist? Certainly it seems tempting to assume without further reflection that it does. But even if the assumption in question should seem quite inescapable to the philosophical mind, we have to ask ourselves what reasons may be produced in its favor.

Now, there is one reason which may make us believe in the existence of a factual relation R fulfilling the stated condition. One may point to the fact that probability estimates in general are uncontroversial, and one may maintain that only propositions which are either logically decidable or empirically decidable have this uncontroversial character.

In view of the consideration of section 3, however, we are forced to regard the second of the two premises of this argument as incorrect. Our examination of the sure-thing principle (or rather a simplified version of it) has shown that an uncertainty rule may be just as uncontroversial as an empirical or logical statement. And the normative character of the principle in question has here been taken for granted.

One aspect of this is that we have to give serious thought to the possibility that R does not exist. The characterization of probability just given may be without a 'factual core.' What does this mean for the analysis of probability? As far as I can see it means either that we have to accept the normative relation "O logically implies $Tp\ B_uTq$" as a satisfactory analysis of "pP_uq," or that we have to consider some other expression essentially involving normative terms as more suitable for this purpose. This means that we have to regard probability as a normative concept.

This brings us to a second aspect of the situation. What are we to say if a factual relation R, fulfilling the stated condition, exists? Personally, I would like to emphasize that this does not necessarily mean that a definition of "pP_uq" by "$R(p,q,u)$" will appear more acceptable than a definition of the probability relation with the aid of a normative concept. Various considerations are relevant here. Thus, we have to consider the scientific fruitfulness of the different candidates. Will the choice of R shed any light on statistical praxis? Will it give us a formal theory of sufficient richness? And the same questions have to be asked with respect to the normative concepts.

In an earlier paper I tried to show that the relation "O logically implies $Tp\ B_uTq$" has formal properties of the type one would expect from a qualitative probability relation like P_u.[4] The technical aspects of this investigation have to be kept out of the discussion here, but I believe that my result to some degree supports the analysis of P_u with the aid of "O logically implies $Tp\ B_uTq$."

An important question is what reasons may be given *against* the analysis in question. I have already dealt with one possible objection. In view of the uncontroversial character of statistical principles, the view that they are rooted in logical or empirical knowledge may seem inescapable. But this argument loses all force when one has been confronted with the sure-thing principle.

A second objection worried me before I had put it on paper. To feel its

---

[4] Sören Halldén, "Preference Logic and Theory Choice," *Synthese*, vol. 16 (1966).

original force, let us return to the rule for the elimination of residual alternatives, presented in section 3. This involves a restriction to choice situations in which no probabilities are known. An uncertainty rule involving the concept of probability, or a *more precise version* of this concept, may be called a "probabilistic uncertainty rule." I am quite willing to admit that among the valid uncertainty rules implied by O, some may be probabilistic.

This means that if P_u is analyzed with the aid of the relation "O logically implies $Tp\ B_uTq$," the analyzing expression will in some indirect way refer to uncertainty rules involving the analysandum P_u, or more precise versions of this concept.

Does this imply that the analysis in question is circular? It should first be pointed out that if a concept A is defined by a concept B and B is a more precise version of A, such a definition is not to be condemned as circular. Secondly, it should be emphasized that the reference to probabilistic uncertainty rules is indirect, being mediated by a quantifier, which makes the objection still weaker.

I am not entirely certain what people mean when they maintain that an analysis or a definition is circular. I would myself apply this adjective only to such explanations of meaning as fail to be clarifying. And the explanation of P_u by "O logically implies $Tp\ B_u\ Tq$" certainly does not have this particular fault.

BIBLIOGRAPHICAL NOTE

Normative theories of probability have been developed within two traditions. On the one hand, Austin's normative analysis of "I know that p" has led other writers to analyze "It is probable that p" in the same spirit. In this tradition I would refer the reader to: J. N. Findlay, "Probability without Nonsense," *Philosophical Quarterly*, vol. 2 (1952); and Stephen E. Toulmin, *The Uses of Argument* (Cambridge: At the University Press, 1958). On the other hand, the theorists within the subjective school have had a tendency to define probability in terms of ideal behavior instead of actual behavior. An exposition of the normative variant of the subjectivist theory can be found in the work by Leonard J. Savage mentioned in footnote 2.

Risto Hilpinen

Decision-Theoretic Approaches to Rules of Acceptance

1. Epistemic Utility

The problem of whether factual hypotheses may be *accepted* on the basis of inductive arguments has recently been subject to a great deal of philosophical discussion.[1] According to Rudolf Carnap, Richard Jeffrey, and many subjectivist statisticians, inductive reasoning concerning a hypothesis *h* should lead, not to its acceptance or rejection, but merely to the assignment of a probability value to *h*.[2] Many other philosophers, for example, Henry E. Kyburg, Wesley C. Salmon, and Isaac Levi, have argued, however, that rules of acceptance are indispensable for the understanding of scientific method.[3] This controversy is related to the opposition between the *behavioralist*[4] and the *cognitivist* interpretation of scientific method and scientific knowledge. According to the behavioralist conception, the task of the scientist qua scientist is merely the assignment of probabilities to hypotheses

Professor Hilpinen, of the University of Jyväskylä in Finland, is a native of Finland.

[1] For this discussion, see the contributions of H. E. Kyburg, Y. Bar-Hillel, P. Suppes, K. R. Popper, W. C. Salmon, J. Hintikka, and R. Carnap to *The Problem of Inductive Logic*, ed. I. Lakatos (Amsterdam: North-Holland, 1968), pp. 98–165.

[2] Rudolf Carnap, "The Aim of Inductive Logic," in *Logic, Methodology, and Philosophy of Science*, ed. E. Nagel, P. Suppes, and A. Tarski (Stanford: Stanford University Press, 1962), pp. 316–17; Carnap, "Replies and Systematic Expositions. V. Probability and Induction," in *The Philosophy of Rudolf Carnap*, ed. P. A. Schilpp (La Salle, Ill.: Open Court, 1963), pp. 972–73; Richard Jeffrey, "Valuation and Acceptance of Scientific Hypothesis," *Philosophy of Science* 23: 237–46 (1956).

[3] Henry E. Kyburg, Jr., "Recent Work on Inductive Logic," *American Philosophical Quarterly* 1: 277–78 (1964); Kyburg, "Probability, Rationality and A Rule of Detachment," in *Proceedings of the 1964 Congress for Logic, Methodology, and Philosophy of Science*, ed. Y. Bar-Hillel (Amsterdam: North-Holland, 1965), pp. 301–10; Kyburg, "The Rule of Detachment in Inductive Logic," in *The Problem of Inductive Logic*, ed. I. Lakatos (Amsterdam: North-Holland, 1968), pp. 98–119; Wesley C. Salmon, "Who Needs Inductive Acceptance Rules?" in *The Problem of Inductive Logic*, ed. I. Lakatos (Amsterdam: North-Holland, 1968); pp. 139–44; Isaac Levi, *Gambling with Truth* (New York: Alfred A. Knopf, 1967); Levi, "Information and Inference," *Synthese* 17: 369–99 (1967).

[4] This term has been used by Leonard J. Savage, *The Foundations of Statistics* (New York: John Wiley, 1954), p. 159; cf. also Isaac Levi, "Decision Theory and Confirmation," *Journal of Philosophy* 58: 615 (1961).

which may then be utilized by the decision-maker,[5] whereas cognitivists have argued that the aim of inquiry is the "improvement of natural knowledge,"[6] and have described scientific knowledge by means of the "accepted-information model" according to which scientific knowledge consists of statements which are accepted as presumably true.[7] Cognitivists have defended the "autonomy" of science[8] and have emphasized the difference between "scientific conclusions" and "practical decisions."[9] Behavioralism stresses statistical decision theory and the theory of utility, whereas many cognitivists have regarded decision theory as unimportant for the understanding of scientific method.[10]

In this paper I shall not argue for one position as opposed to the other but will instead consider the recent attempts to effect a conceptual unification of the two. Recently some philosophers, notably Carl G. Hempel, Isaac Levi, and Jaakko Hintikka and Juhani Pietarinen, have applied the conceptual tools of decision theory and the theory of utility to the cognitivist analysis of inductive inference and scientific method.[11] These endeavors are motivated by certain similarities apparent between decision problems and the problems concerning the acceptance and rejection of hypotheses. Scientific inquiry is a goal-directed activity; although the scientist qua scientist may not be interested in those utilities relevant to most ordinary (i.e., 'practical') decision-makers, presumably he has certain *cognitive* objectives which control the conduct of inquiry. One such cognitive objective is undoubtedly *truth*: "The pursuit of knowledge as exemplified by pure scientific inquiry, by 'basic research' not directly aimed at any practical applications with corresponding utilities, is often said to be concerned with the discovery of truth."[12] Perhaps these cognitive objectives may be construed as a special kind of *utilities* in the sense of utility theory. Hempel has coined the expression "epistemic utility" to refer to such cognitive utilities.[13] Moreover, the acceptance and rejection of hypotheses may perhaps be regarded as representing a special type of *decision* in which the investigator attempts to maximize the relevant epistemic or scientific utilities. These analogies invite an attempt to apply the concepts of decision theory to the cognitivist analysis of scientific method. According to such an analysis, the alleged difference between deci-

[5] Jeffrey, "Valuation and Acceptance of Scientific Hypothesis," pp. 245–46.

[6] R. A. Fisher, *Statistical Methods and Scientific Inference* (Edinburgh: Oliver & Boyd, 1958), p. 103.

[7] Carl G. Hempel, "Deductive-Nomological versus Statistical Explanation," *Scientific Explanation, Space, and Time*, Minnesota Studies in the Philosophy of Science, vol. 3, ed. H. Feigl and G. Maxwell (Minneapolis: University of Minnesota Press, 1962), pp. 149–50.

[8] Levi, *Gambling with Truth*, pp. 16–18.

[9] John W. Tukey, "Conclusions versus Decisions," *Technometrics* 2: 423–33 (1960).

[10] Fisher, *Statistical Methods and Scientific Inference*, pp. 100–104.

[11] Carl G. Hempel, "Inductive Inconsistencies," *Synthese* 12: 439–69 (1960); Hempel, "Deductive-Nomological versus Statistical Explanation," pp. 98–169; Levi, "Decision Theory and Confirmation," pp. 614–25; Levi, *Gambling with Truth*; Levi, "Information and Inference," pp. 369–99; Jaakko Hintikka and Junani Pietarinen, "Semantic Information and Inductive Logic," in *Aspects of Inductive Logic*, ed. J. Hintikka and P. Suppes (Amsterdam: North-Holland, 1966), pp. 96–112.

[12] Hempel, "Deductive-Nomological versus Statistical Explanation," p. 153.

[13] *Ibid.*

sions and conclusions is attributable to the difference between two kinds of utilities: 'practical' utilities and 'epistemic' utilities.

2. The Rule of High Probability

Let us first consider a very simple measure of epistemic utility. Suppose that an investigator X is considering whether a hypothesis h is worthy of acceptance or not. X is interested in truth and nothing but truth: the epistemic utility of accepting h depends solely upon whether h is true or false. Let $u(h, t)$ be the utility of accepting h if h is true and $u(h, f)$ the corresponding utility if h is false. X obviously prefers truth to error, i.e., $u(h, t) >$ $u(h, f)$. The acceptance of $\sim h$ is equivalent to the rejection of h; if X is interested in nothing but truth, it is plausible to assume that $u(\sim h, x) =$ $u(h, x)$, where x is t or f. In addition to the acceptance and rejection of h, X has a third possibility: suspension of judgment. Let the utility of suspending judgment, $u(S, t)$,[14] be equal to s independently of whether h is true or false.

The Bayesian decision rule of *maximizing expected utility* directs X to choose an alternative for which the expected utility is maximal. The application of this rule presupposes that the utilities $u(h, x)$ and s are interval-measurable, i.e., unique up to a linear transformation; the choices of the unit and the zero point of our utility function are a matter of convention. The simplest choice is that of putting $u(h, f) = 0$ and taking $u(h, t) - u(h, f)$ as the unit; hence $u(h, t) = 1$. X obviously prefers suspending judgment to error, but not to accepting a true hypothesis, for, otherwise, no problem of acceptance could arise at all; hence $0 < s \leqq 1$. Let $E(h/e)$ be the expectation of the utility of accepting h on the basis of the evidence e and $E(S/e)$ the expected utility of suspending judgment. Given the present utility assignment, the expected utilities of the three alternative cognitive decisions are:

$$(2.1) \quad E(h/e) = P(h/e); \; E(\sim h/e) = 1 - P(h/e); \; E(S/e) = s.$$

According to the principle of maximizing expected utility, (2.1) leads to the following acceptance rule:

(R 1)   Accept h on the basis of e, if $P(h/e) > s$. If $P(h/e) = s$, h may be accepted or left in suspense. If $1 - s < P(h/e) < s$, suspend judgment.

As I pointed out above, we have to assume that $0 < s \leqq 1$. If s is less than .5, both h and its negation may be acceptable on the basis of e. To avoid this inconsistency, we have to require that $.5 \leqq s \leqq 1$.

The rule (R 1) may be called the *rule of high probability;* it states that a high probability is a necessary and sufficient condition of acceptability.

The rule of high probability leads to the notorious *lottery paradox*.[15] Ac-

---

[14] This notation is plausible since we do not risk error if we suspend judgment.

[15] See, e.g., Henry E. Kyburg, Jr., "A Further Note on Rationality and Consistency," *Journal of Philosophy* 60: 463–65 (1963); Kyburg, "Probability, Rationality and A Rule of Detachment," pp. 249–87; Jaakko Hintikka and Risto Hilpinen, "Knowledge, Acceptance, and Inductive Logic," in *Aspects of Inductive Logic*, ed. J. Hintikka and P. Suppes (Amsterdam: North-Holland, 1966), pp. 4–5.

ceptable sentences are assumed to be acceptable as presumably *true*, but it may happen that all sentences accepted on the basis of the evidence *e* cannot be true if the following conditions are not satisfied:

(C 1)   If h_1 and h_2 are acceptable on the basis ot *e*, all sentences implied by h_1 and h_2 are acceptable on the basis of *e*.

(C 2)   The set of sentences acceptable on the basis of *e* is consistent.

Let A_e be the set of sentences acceptable on the basis of *e*. According to (C 1) and (C 2), A_e is consistent and logically closed. The rule of high probability does not satisfy these requirements. If (C 1) and (C 2) are satisfied, the lottery paradox will not arise.

According to (C 1), the conjunction of two acceptable sentences is also acceptable. Hence A_e contains a sentence h^* which is equivalent to the conjunction of all members of A_e.[16] Following Levi, we call the sentence h^* *acceptable as strongest* on the basis of *e*; all other members of A_e are implied by h^*.[17] Hence it will suffice that our acceptance rule specifies the sentence h^*;[18] the acceptability of all other members of A_e follows by (C 1) from the acceptability of h^*. In addition, if $P(h^*/e) > s$, all other members of A_e will obviously have a probability higher than s, too, and the lottery paradox is avoided. Because of the conditions (C 1) and (C 2), the acceptability of a given hypothesis h cannot be decided without paying attention to the deductive relationships which h bears to other relevant hypotheses. Thus the cognitive decision problem must be reformulated as the problem of choosing the sentence h^* from a given set H of hypotheses which count as *potentially* acceptable as strongest. The set H may consist, for instance, of all sentences of a given language $\mathcal{L}$ or perhaps of all *general* sentences of $\mathcal{L}$.[19] Inductive probability measures are normally defined on languages; if H consists of all general sentences of $\mathcal{L}$ it consists in effect of all such general hypotheses h for which $P(h/e)$ is defined. The relativity of inductive acceptance rules to sets of sentences has recently been emphasized especially by Isaac Levi.[20] Levi has restricted the membership of H to sentences that count as relevant answers to a given problem.[21] Another natural choice of H is to let it consist of such hypotheses as have been proposed in the context of inquiry.[22]

With regard to the definition of epistemic utility, another observation

---

[16] Strictly speaking, A_e includes an equivalence class of sentences h^* which express the strongest proposition acceptable on the basis of *e*. This subtlety is ignored here.

[17] Levi, *Gambling with Truth*, p. 31.

[18] This idea has been put forth by Isaac Levi (see "Deductive Cogency in Inductive Inference," *Journal of Philosophy* 62: 72–73 [1965]).

[19] This choice of H is plausible since, as Hintikka and Hilpinen ("Knowledge, Acceptance, and Inductive Logic," pp. 1–20) have shown, singular sentences are not acceptable unless they are implied by acceptable generalizations (or by the conjunction of acceptable generalizations and the evidence *e*).

[20] Levi, "Deductive Cogency in Inductive Inference," pp. 68–77; Levi, *Gambling with Truth*; and Levi, "Information and Inference."

[21] See, e.g., Levi, "Information and Inference," pp. 370–71; and below, section 5.

[22] Cf., e.g., Hilary Putnam, " 'Degree of Confirmation' and Inductive Logic," in *The Philosophy of Rudolf Carnap*, ed. P. A. Schilpp (La Salle, Ill.: Open Court, 1963), p. 783.

concerning (R 1) is perhaps of greater interest. We have assumed above that X is interested in truth and nothing but truth. However, in case $s < 1$, as it undoubtedly should be if (R 1) purports to be an *inductive* acceptance rule, X is easily seen to be interested in things other than truth. s is the utility of suspending judgment. In the present decision problem, suspension of judgment may, however, be regarded as equivalent to choosing $h \vee \sim h$ as the strongest acceptable sentence from the set $\mathbf{H} = \{h, \sim h, h \vee \sim h\}$. $h \vee \sim h$ is a truth of logic, and hence certainly true; if X accepts $h \vee \sim h$ as strongest, there is no risk of accepting sentences that are false. If X is interested in truth and nothing but truth, without any qualifications, s should obviously be equal to 1. Consequently, X would accept no sentences apart from those implied by e. If $s < 1$, X prefers the truth h to the truth $h \vee \sim h$.

Accordingly, the statement that scientists are interested in truth and nothing but truth must not be taken too literally. We see that rational investigators are not equally interested in all kinds of truths, since, for instance, they will prefer our h to $h \vee \sim h$. The intuitive basis of this preference is obvious. h is a factual truth, and factual truths are preferred to tautologies; scientists are interested in *informative* truths. It thus seems that in addition to truth there is another epistemic utility, namely, information. An adequate explicatum of epistemic utility should take into account both truth and information, but the simple explicatum discussed above fails to do this. The concept of semantic information has been extensively discussed in recent literature on inductive logic,[23] and it has been shown to be intrinsically ambiguous; there are many different senses of "information." It is far from obvious which concept of information would provide an adequate basis for the definition of epistemic utility. In point of fact, it has been suggested that no unique answer to this question is forthcoming; that "scientific inquiry is much less a single-goal enterprise than philosophers have usually realized."[24] Here our main purpose is to consider which concept of acceptability would correspond most adequately to the classificatory expressions "practical certainty," "worthy of belief," "well-confirmed," "established," and "empirical knowledge." The concept of epistemic utility should be so defined that it is suitable for the definition of this concept.

3. MEASURES OF INFORMATION

Two different explicata have been proposed for the concept of amount of information carried by a sentence. One of them is the customary logarithmic concept of information,

---

[23] See, e.g., Rudolf Carnap and Yehoshua Bar-Hillel, "An Outline of the Theory of Semantic Information," in *Language and Information*, ed. Y. Bar-Hillel (New York: Addison-Wesley, 1964), pp. 221–74; Bar-Hillel, "Semantic Information and Its Measures," in *ibid.*, pp. 298–312; Jaakko Hintikka, "The Varieties of Information and Scientific Explanation," in *Proceedings of the Third International Congress for Logic, Methodology, and Philosophy of Science*, ed. B. van Rootselaar and J. F. Staal (Amsterdam: North-Holland, 1968), pp. 311–31.

[24] Hintikka, "Varieties of Information and Scientific Explanation," p. 321.

(3.1) $inf(h) = -\log P(h)$,

in which the logarithm is usually assumed to be to the base 2; this, of course, is a matter of convention. Another inverse relation between information and probability is defined by the even simpler formula

(3.2) $cont(h) = 1 - P(h)$.

These measures have been discussed extensively in recent philosophical literature on information and inductive logic, and it has been suggested that they correspond to different *explicanda:* (3.1) is a measure of the *surprise* value or the *unexpectedness* of the truth of h, whereas $cont(h)$ expresses the amount of *substantive* information or the *content* of h. This interpretation has been supported by numerous examples.[25] It is plausible to assume that insofar as the epistemic utility of accepting h depends on the information carried by h, it should be defined in terms of the measure of substantive information rather than in terms of *inf*. For the investigator is presumably interested in the content of a hypothesis, not in its surprise value. As a matter of fact, all recent attempts to define acceptability in terms of epistemic utilities proceed on the assumption that these utilities have been defined in terms of the *cont*-measure. According to (3.2), *cont* satisfies the following conditions:

(3.3) (a) $0 \leqq cont(h) \leqq 1$,
       (b) If h is logically true, $cont(h) = 0$,
       (c) If $h_1 \vee h_2$ is logically true, $cont(h_1 \& h_2) = cont(h_1) + cont(h_2)$.

The condition (c) may call for some comment. The disjunction $h_1 \vee h_2$ expresses the *common* content of h_1 and h_2. Both h_1 and h_2 convey at least the information provided by their disjunction, and perhaps some additional information as well. If $h_1 \vee h_2$ is a logical truth, h_1 and h_2 have no content in common; in this case the content-measures of the hypotheses are additive. The crucial difference between the measures *cont* and *inf* is one concerning their additivity. The *inf*-measures of h_1 and h_2 are additive if the sentences are probabilistically independent, that is, if $P(h_1 \& h_2) = P(h_1)P(h_2)$.

On the basis of (3.1) and (3.2) we may define several measures of relative information. Here we shall consider only the measures based on *cont*. The amount of *incremental* information,

(3.4) $cont(h|e) = cont(h \& e) - cont(e)$,

expresses how much information h adds to the information supplied by e, i.e., how much information h carries in excess of that provided by e. In addition to (3.4) we may define another concept of relative information, namely, that of the amount of *conditional* information:

(3.5) $cont(h/e) = 1 - P(h/e)$.

[25] See, e.g., *ibid.*; and Risto Hilpinen, "On the Information Provided by Observations," in *Information and Inference*, ed. J. Hintikka and P. Suppes (Dordrecht: D. Reidel, 1970), pp. 97–122.

(3.5) is simply the definition of the *cont*-measure in terms of the conditional probability of h instead of the absolute probability of h.[26]

Another measure of relative information, the amount of *transmitted* information, is defined by

$$(3.6) \quad cont(hTe) = cont(h) - cont(h|e).$$

By virtue of (3.6), $cont(h)$ is equal to the sum of $cont(h|e)$ and $cont(hTe)$. The relationship between these three measures can also be expressed as follows: h is equivalent to $(h \vee e)$ & $(h \vee \sim e)$, where the conjuncts are content-exclusive (their disjunction is a logical truth); hence (3.3. c) implies

$$(3.7) \quad cont(h) = cont(h \vee \sim e) + cont(h \vee e),$$

where

$$(3.8) \quad cont(h \vee \sim e) = cont(h|e)$$

and

$$(3.9) \quad cont(h \vee e) = cont(hTe).$$

Thus $cont(hTe)$ expresses the amount of common content of h and e or the amount of information carried by h concerning the subject matter of e.[27] (3.6) is symmetric with respect to h and e, i.e., $cont(hTe) = cont(eTh)$. In many applications it is expedient to normalize (3.4) and (3.6) by multiplying them by suitable normalizing factors; an interesting normalized measure of transmitted information is

$$(3.10) \quad cont_e(hTe) = cont(hTe)/cont(e).$$

(3.6) is an 'absolute' measure of the common content of h and e, whereas (3.10) measures the content common to h and e 'relatively'; it expresses how much of the content of e is common to h and e. Hempel and Oppenheim have proposed $cont_e(hTe)$ as a measure of the "systematic power" of h with respect to e.[28]

4. HEMPEL'S MEASURE OF EPISTEMIC UTILITY

According to Hempel, the epistemic utility of accepting h on the basis of e depends "not only on whether h is true or false but also on how much of what h asserts is new, i.e., goes beyond the information already contained in e."[29] Hempel thus defines the epistemic utility of accepting h as a function of the *incremental* information or excess content of h with respect to e. This

[26] The expressions "incremental information" and "conditional information" have been used by Hintikka (see "Varieties of Information and Scientific Explanation").

[27] *Ibid.*

[28] Carl G. Hampel and Paul Oppenheim, "Studies in the Logic of Explanation," *Philosophy of Science* 15: 131–75 (1948), especially pp. 167–73. For another application of the normalized measure of common content, see Hilpinen, "Information Provided by Observations."

[29] Hempel, "Deductive-Nomological versus Statistical Explanation," p. 153.

measure is dependent on the evidence e; thus we let $u(h, t, e)$ be the utility of accepting h on the basis of e if h is true, $u(h, f, e)$ if h is false, and let $u(S, t, e)$ be the utility of suspending judgment. Hempel defines these utilities as follows:[30]

$$(4.1) \quad \text{(a)} \quad u(h, t, e) = cont(hIe),$$
$$\qquad\quad \text{(b)} \quad u(h, f, e) = -cont(hIe);$$

suspension of judgment may again be taken as equivalent to accepting $h \lor \sim h$ as strongest; hence (a) implies that $u(S, t, e) = 0$. According to (4.1), the expectation $E(h/e)$ has the following properties:

$$(4.2) \quad \text{If } P(h/e) > .5, \; E(h/e) > E(S/e);$$
$$\qquad\quad E(h/e) = E(S/e), \text{ if } P(h/e) = .5;$$
$$\qquad\quad \text{if } P(h/e) < .5, \; E(h/e) < E(S/e) \text{ for each factual hypothesis } h.$$

On the basis of (4.2), Hempel has formulated the following acceptance rule:[31]

(R 2)   Accept or reject h, given e, according to whether $P(h/e) > .5$ or $< .5$; if $P(h/e) = .5$, h may be accepted, rejected, or left in suspense.

This rule is no more than a new version of the rule of high probability, and leads immediately to the lottery paradox if applied without any restrictions. In another study Hempel has modified the previous definition of epistemic utility.[32] On the basis of the principle of diminishing marginal utility he sets the utility or disutility of accepting h inversely proportional to the content of e; then (4.1.a) and (4.1.b) are replaced by $u(h, t, e) = kcont(hIe)/cont(e)$ and $u(h, f, e) = -kcont(hIe)/cont(e)$, respectively. This is not, however, a real improvement, for the latter assignment also leads to (4.2) and hence to the same acceptance rule as (4.1). In the work referred to, the lottery paradox is avoided by restricting the application of (R 2) to the choice of a hypothesis h from a set of mutually exclusive and jointly exhaustive hypotheses. If **B** is a set which contains v hypotheses of this type, the investigator has, according to Hempel, $v + 1$ alternative 'courses of action': to accept $h_i (i = 1, 2, \ldots, v)$ or none of the hypotheses $h_i \in$ **B**. The lottery paradox is avoided because **B** may contain at most one hypothesis h_i with $P(h_i/e) = .5$. (If there are two hypotheses h_i with $P(h_i/e) = .5$, Hempel's rule recommends accepting either but not both of them.)

According to Hempel, (R 2) is too lenient even if interpreted in the latter way.[33] The 'confidence level' .5 is presumably too low in Hempel's opinion. But in another respect this rule is too stringent: to be in accord with Hempel's interpretation of (R 2),[34] a disjunction of hypotheses is acceptable if and only if one of the members of the disjunction is acceptable. Conversely, if **B** con-

---

[30] *Ibid.*, p. 154.
[31] *Ibid.*, p. 155.
[32] Hempel, "Inductive Inconsistencies," pp. 439–69.
[33] *Ibid.*, p. 467.
[34] *Ibid.*

tains rejectable members, all members of **B** except one are rejectable. Hempel's rule is an 'all-or-nothing-rule'.[35]

However, this is not the most marked difficulty with Hempel's acceptance rule. The basic inadequacy in the rule is that the informativeness of a hypothesis turns out (according to Hempel's definition of epistemic utility) to be irrelevant to its acceptability. The measure of information cancels out, and the acceptability of h depends solely on its *a posteriori* probability. Thus Hempel's rule is purely probabilistic. This result is not restricted to the specific measures of information considered by Hempel. It is always obtained when $u(h, t, e) - s = s - u(h, f, e)$, where s is the utility of suspending judgment. For instance, if $s = 0$ and $u(h, f, e) = -u(h, t, e)$,

$$(4.3) \quad E(h/e) = P(h/e)u(h, t, e) = [1 - P(h/e)]u(h, t, e)$$
$$= u(h, t, e)(2P(h/e) - 1)$$

which yields (4.2). So we see that Hempel's definition of $u(h, f, e)$ as $-u(h, t, e)$ leads to unacceptable consequences.[36] This part of the definition has also been criticized on other grounds. Isaac Levi has pointed out that an investigator who is interested in true and informative answers, but who is constrained to choose among answers which are false, would, according to Hempel, minimize the informativeness of the hypothesis he chooses. This, says Levi, is "counterintuitive enough to warrant revising Hempel's proposal."[37] As has been pointed out also by Hintikka and Pietarinen, it seems unnatural to take the disutility of the wrong guess that h is true to be the (incremental) content of h, for if $\sim h$ is the case there is no true statement that would have this content. If $\sim h$ is the case, the only relevant available utility is the information conveyed by $\sim h$.[38] It would thus seem more natural to define the utility of accepting a false hypothesis h as a function of $cont(\sim h Ie)$ rather than $cont(h Ie)$, for instance as $-cont(\sim h Ie)$. This definition would satisfy Levi's requirement

$$(C\ 3) \quad u(h_1, x, e) \lesseqgtr u(h_2, x, e) \text{ according as } cont'(h_1, e) \lesseqgtr cont'(h_2, e)$$
$$\text{independently of whether } x = t \text{ or } x = f,$$

where $cont'(h_i, e)$ represents the *cont*-measure on the basis of which $u(h_i, x, e)$ is defined. But this definition of $u(h, x, e)$ in terms of $cont(h Ie)$ fails in that the corresponding expectation

$$(4.4) \quad E(h/e) = P(h/e)cont(h Ie) - P(\sim h/e)cont(\sim h Ie)$$
$$= P(h/e)P(\sim h \ \& \ e) - P(\sim h/e)P(h \ \& \ e)$$

is then identically zero for any hypothesis h.[39] Accordingly, it appears that the use of $cont(h Te)$ as a measure of epistemic utility will not yield reasonable acceptance rules.

[35] Levi, *Gambling with Truth*, p. 96.
[36] If Hempel's rule is applied to the choice of the strongest acceptable sentence $h^* \in H$ it yields the following awkward result: accept as strongest a sentence $h \in H$ with $P(h/e) = .75$.
[37] Levi, "Information and Inference," p. 380.
[38] Hintikka and Pietarinen, "Semantic Information and Inductive Logic," p. 108, n. 12.
[39] Hintikka, "Varieties of Information and Scientific Explanation," p. 326.

5. Isaac Levi's Definition of Epistemic Utility

Like Hempel, Levi defines the epistemic utility of accepting h on the basis of e as a function of the relative information carried by h, but Levi's definition is based not on the *incremental* but on the *conditional* content of h with respect to e.[40] The simplest definition of this kind is obtained by letting $u(h, t, e)$ be equal to $cont(h/e) = 1 - P(h/e)$ and $u(h, f, e)$ to $-cont(\sim h/e) = -P(h/e)$. This procedure fails, however, since the corresponding expected utility

$$(5.1) \quad E(h/e) = P(h/e)[1 - P(h/e)] - [1 - P(h/e)]P(h/e) = 0$$

for any hypothesis h. Levi resolves this difficulty by defining the content measure *cont* in terms of a measure function m different from the inductive probability measure P. In other words, he rejects the definitions (3.2) and (3.5).

According to Levi, the aim of an inquiry is for a given question (or problem) to find an answer that is both true and informative.[41] Let H be the set of hypotheses which count as relevant answers to a given question; Levi's acceptance rule is relative to such a set H. The form and the content of the question determine a set $B \subset H$ which Levi calls the (initial) *ultimate partition;* here B is understood as consisting of the strongest (i.e., most informative) potential answers. This set is assumed to contain v mutually exclusive and jointly exhaustive hypotheses b_i. The members of H are assumed to be equivalent to p-termed disjunctions $(1 \leq p \leq v - 1)$ of the hypotheses b_i. In addition, H is assumed to include a contradictory sentence c which is equivalent to the conjunction of all elements of B and a logical truth d which is equivalent to the disjunction of all elements of B. Of course, the sentences c and d do not really count as relevant answers to the question given, but are included in H for the sake of technical convenience.[42]

Now suppose that the investigator has collected evidence and has accepted the sentence e as evidence. Some hypotheses $b_i \in B$ may be incompatible with e; these hypotheses are discarded. Let B_e be the truncated ultimate partition which consists of those elements of B which are compatible with e. Let the number of such elements be w. The set H_e of *a posteriori* relevant hypotheses consists of sentences that are equivalent to p-termed disjunctions $(1 \leq p \leq w - 1)$ of the members of B_e and of the sentences c_e (the conjunction of all elements of B_e) and d_e (the disjunction of all elements of B_e). Given the evidence e, the cognitive decision problem is that of choosing the sentence h^* (i.e., the sentence which is acceptable as strongest on the basis of e) from the set H_e. Acceptance of d_e as strongest amounts to suspending judgment; acceptance of c_e amounts to self-contradiction.

[40] Levi, *Gambling with Truth*; Levi, "Information and Inference," pp. 381–83.
[41] Levi, "Information and Inference," p. 369.
[42] This is not quite accurate. Normally there is, in addition to the 'new evidence' e, 'background information' accepted at the outset of inquiry. The sentence d is implied by the background information and c is incompatible with it. Here the background information is ignored. Cf. below, section 5.

The epistemic utility of accepting h as strongest is assumed to depend on the conditional content of h. $cont(h)$ is defined in terms of a measure function m by

(5.2) $cont(h) = 1 - m(h)$,

and the conditional content by

(5.3) $cont(h/e) = 1 - m(h/e)$.

m satisfies the customary axioms of the calculus of probability, but it is not identical with the inductive probability measure P; it does not define 'fair-betting quotients.' m is not defined on all sentences of the language in which the hypotheses $h \in H$ and the evidential statement e are formulated, but only on the set H of 'relevant answers.' Hence the conditional measure $m(h/e)$ cannot be defined by the customary formula $m(h/e) = m(h \ \& \ e)/m(e)$. Instead, it is defined by

(5.4) $m(h/e) = m(h \ \& \ d_e)/m(d_e)$.

According to Levi, the epistemic utility of accepting h as strongest depends on the degree of 'relief from agnosticism' provided by the answer h. The $cont$-measure is assumed to reflect this 'relief from agnosticism.' By definition, each element of B gives a 'completely satisfactory' answer to the question corresponding to B. Hence all sentences $b \in B$ receive equal $cont$-values, i.e., $cont(b) = (v - 1/v)$ and hence $m(b) = 1/v$ for each $b \in B$. Consequently,

(5.5) (a) $m(b/e) = 1/w$,
　　　　(b) $cont(b/e) = (w - 1)/w$ for each $b \in B_e$.

If $u(h, x, e)$ is defined in terms of the conditional $cont$-measure, then, according to (C 3), it should, for a constant x, be a monotonically increasing function of $cont(h/e)$. It is obviously prima facie plausible to choose the simplest function of this kind, i.e., a linear function. Moreover, we may assume that the utility differences $u(h_1, x, e) - u(h_2, x, e)$ are independent of the value of x. In this case

(C 4) $u(h_1, x, e) - u(h_2, x, e) = q[cont(h_1/e) - cont(h_2/e)]$, where x is constant (t or f) and q is positive.

The choice of the unit and the zero point of the epistemic utility function is a matter of convention. Levi defines the zero point as

(5.6) $u(c_e, f, e) = 0$.

Since all correct answers (including the suspension of judgment, i.e., the choice of d_e as strongest) are to be preferred to errors, $u(d_e, t, e) > u(c_e, f, e)$, i.e.,

(5.7) $u(d_e, t, e) = s$,

where s is positive. Levi chooses $q + s$ as the unit of the utility function, that is to say,

(5.8) $s = 1 - q$.

(C 4) and (5.6)–(5.8) imply[43]

$$(5.9) \quad \text{(i)} \quad u(h, t, e) = 1 = qcont(\sim h/e) = 1 - qm(h/e)$$
$$ \quad \text{(ii)} \quad u(h, f, e) = -qcont(\sim h/e) = -qm(h/e).$$

(5.9) specifies a class of 'essentially distinct' epistemic utility functions (that is, functions that cannot be defined in terms of each other by linear transformations).[44] The choice of a unique function from this class depends on the choice of q. According to (5.7) and (5.8), $0 < q < 1$.

By virtue of (5.9), the epistemic utility of accepting h as strongest is:[45]

$$(5.10) \quad E(h/e) = P(h/e) - qm(h/e).$$

In view of (5.5), (5.10) is equivalent to

$$(5.11) \quad E(h/e) = \sum_i (P(b_i^{(h)}/e) - q/w),$$

where $b_i^{(h)}$ represents an arbitrary member of $\mathbf{B}_e$ which implies h.

According to the principle of maximizing expected utility, it seems we should accept as strongest a sentence h^* which maximizes (5.11). The sentence h^* which is acceptable as strongest ought to be unique. To solve this difficulty, Levi introduces the concept of *strong* maximality.[46] $E(h^*/e)$ is strongly maximal if $E(h^*/e)$ is maximal and $cont(h^*/e) < cont(h/e)$ for every $h \in \mathbf{H}_e$ with the maximal expectation. Levi shows that there is always a unique sentence h^* the expected utility of which is strongly maximal: if $E(h_1/e)$ and $E(h_2/e)$ are maximal, $E(h_1 \lor h_2/e)$ is maximal, too; hence the disjunction of all sentences $h_i \in \mathbf{H}_e$ with $E(h_i/e) = \max$ has the strongly maximal expectation.[47] Now Levi supplements the Bayesian decision rule with the *rule for ties:*

(R 3)   Accept that element of $\mathbf{H}_e$ as strongest on the basis of e whose expected utility is strongly maximal.

It is easily seen from (5.11) that $E(h/e)$ cannot be strongly maximal if h is implied by an element $b_i \in \mathbf{B}_e$ with $P(b_i/e) < q/w$. Hence (R 3) yields the following acceptance rule:[48]

(R 4)   Reject all elements $b_i \in \mathbf{B}_e$ with $P(b_i/e) < q/w$, and accept the disjunction h^* of all unrejected elements as strongest. Accept all deductive consequences of h^* & e, and no other sentences.

By virtue of the rule for ties, $q = 1$ becomes an admissible value of q. If $q = 1$ and the posterior probability distribution on $\mathbf{B}_e$ is completely even, all members of $\mathbf{H}_e$ have an equal expectation $E(h/e)$; but $E(d_e/e)$ is strongly maximal and hence d_e is acceptable as strongest. For instance, if $\mathbf{B}_e$ consists of the hypotheses "ticket i will win" in Kyburg's example of a fair lottery,

[43] Levi, *Gambling with Truth*, pp. 79–81.
[44] *Ibid.*, p. 81.
[45] *Ibid.*
[46] *Ibid.*, pp. 83–84.
[47] *Ibid.*
[48] *Ibid.*, p. 86.

Levi's rule gives the sound advice of suspending judgment for all values of q where $0 < q \leqq 1$. (But if $\mathbf{B}_e$ is {"ticket i will win," "ticket i will not win"}, the latter hypothesis is acceptable as strongest, provided that q is not too small.[49])

q has a plausible interpretation as *degree of caution* (or boldness).[50] The greater q is, the more willing is the investigator to risk error in accepting hypotheses, and the lower is the degree of caution exercised by the investigator. q may also be taken to represent the *confidence* of acceptance and rejection; if a hypothesis is rejectable with a small value of q, it may be rejected with a high degree of confidence, and conversely.[51]

Levi's rule is a probability-based rule, but it is not a *probabilistic* rule in the sense that a fixed high probability is taken to be a necessary condition of acceptability. In fact, sentences which have a very *low* probability may, according to (R 4) be acceptable if q is near 1.[52] In another respect, Levi's rule is, however, similar to a purely probabilistic rule. If we consider the members of $\mathbf{B}_e$ only, the rejectability of hypotheses (for a fixed value q) depends on the posterior probabilities $P(b_i/e)$ only, i.e., on the shape of the distribution $[P(b_1/e), \ldots, P(b_w/e)]$. If the distribution is completely even, no hypothesis is rejectable; otherwise we may reject such hypotheses as are sufficiently improbable in comparison with others. Roughly speaking, Levi's rule recommends rejecting those hypotheses that are improbable in comparison with other equally informative hypotheses.

Although this seems very reasonable, we should not too hastily accept Levi's rule as a reasonable definition of "justified belief," since Levi defines the concept of information in a somewhat special way. As a result of the partition-dependent definition of *cont*, his rule also has many undesirable properties. It is relative to an ultimate partition. This relativity is perfectly natural, if the concept of ultimate partition is understood in a sufficiently general way (see above, section 2). But the partition-dependence of *cont* makes Levi's rule excessively sensitive to the choice of $\mathbf{B}$, and in certain cases it yields strongly counterintuitive results. For instance, it is possible that a hypothesis h is acceptable with respect to a partition $\mathbf{B}'_e$, but rejectable with respect to another partition $\mathbf{B}''_e$ on the basis of the same evidence e.[53] This is very counterintuitive if "acceptable" is thought of as being equivalent to "worthy of belief."[54] Let $\mathbf{B}'$ and $\mathbf{B}''$ be two distinct ultimate parti-

---

[49] *Ibid.*, p. 92.

[50] Levi calls q an index of caution. Jeffrey ("Review of Isaac Levi's *Gambling with Truth*," *Journal of Philosophy* 65: 316 [1968]) has pointed out that it is more natural to call q an index of *boldness*, since q varies inversely with the degree of caution exercised by the investigator. The degree of caution is expressed by $s = 1 - q$.

[51] Levi defines the concept of confidence differently (see *Gambling with Truth*, pp. 134–35).

[52] See *ibid.*, p. 97.

[53] See Ian Hacking, "Review of Isaac Levi's *Gambling with Truth*," *Synthese* 17: 446 (1967); Jeffrey, "Review of Isaac Levi's *Gambling with Truth*," pp. 317–18.

[54] Cf. Jeffrey, "Review of Isaac Levi's *Gambling with Truth*," p. 321. It is not, however, counterintuitive to assume that it is reasonable to reject h (or accept h) with respect to one partition but suspend judgment between h and $\frown h$ with respect to another partition.

tions and let $\mathbf{H}'$ and $\mathbf{H}''$ be the sets of relevant hypotheses corresponding to $\mathbf{B}'$ and $\mathbf{B}''$, respectively. It now seems plausible to lay down the following condition of adequacy for inductive acceptance rules:

(C 5) If $h \in \mathbf{H}'_e$ and $h \in \mathbf{H}''_e$ and if h is acceptable with respect to $\mathbf{B}'_e$, h is not rejectable with respect to $\mathbf{B}''_e$ (on the basis of the same evidence).

(C 5) is not generally satisfied by Levi's rule, although it is satisfied if $q \leq .5$. The number of rejectable elements in any partition $\mathbf{B}_e$ is at most $w - 1$; hence the sum of the probabilities of the rejected elements is at most $q(w - 1)/w$. If $q \leq .5$, this probability is always less than .5; then $P(h^*/e) > .5$, and h is not acceptable unless $P(h/e) > .5$. Thus no sentence can be acceptable with respect to one partition and rejectable with respect to another. These considerations give some support to the requirement of high probability (i.e., probability higher than .5) within Levi's scheme.[55]

There are other difficulties in regard to Levi's acceptance rule which cannot be solved as easily. Suppose that a sentence h is acceptable with a very high degree of confidence, i.e., with q close to zero. In such a case we might assume that to collect further information concerning h would be pointless, and accept h as evidence in further inquiry. Should it now be legitimate to accept a sentence h' on the basis of $e \ \& \ h$, if h' is not acceptable on the basis of the previous evidence e alone? In my view this should not be possible. If e constitutes 'practically conclusive' evidence for h, the increase of the evidential strength for h' possibly obtained by adding h to e is negligible. If h' is not acceptable on the basis of e, it cannot be acceptable on the basis of $e \ \& \ h$ either. Thus we offer the following condition of adequacy for inductive acceptance rules:

(C 6) If h is acceptable on the basis of e whereas h' is not acceptable on the basis of e, h' is not acceptable on the basis of $e \ \& \ h$ either.

Levi's rule does not satisfy (C 6). He is aware of this property of (R 4) and states that there are cases in which "the strength of the conclusion has been increased by mere bookkeeping."[56] He does not offer any independent arguments for the legitimacy of such 'bookkeeping' acceptance procedures, but says that "this consequence seems inescapable not only for the account of evidence offered here but for any account that concedes that a sentence can legitimately be accepted as evidence from other evidence that does not entail it."[57] This assumption, however, is false; there are consistent and intuitively plausible acceptance rules which satisfy (C 6).[58]

[55] According to Levi, "If a high probability is to be required as a necessary condition for acceptance, considerations other than consistency must be introduced" (*Gambling with Truth*, p. 97). The preceding considerations can, however, be regarded as 'consistency considerations.'

[56] *Ibid.*, p. 151.

[57] *Ibid.*

[58] For instance, the rule defined in Hintikka and Hilpinen ("Knowledge, Acceptance, and Inductive Logic," pp. 1–20) satisfies (C 6). Another rule of this kind is defined below, section 6.

There are other objections to Levi's acceptance rule that are of a more fundamental kind. According to Levi, the epistemic utility of accepting *h* (as strongest) depends on the 'relief from agnosticism' provided by *h*.[59] The measure of epistemic utility is conditional on *e*; when new evidence is obtained the investigator's interests will change. In many cases this account of epistemic utility misconstrues the role of evidence in scientific inquiry and in the justification of beliefs. A hypothesis *h* does not, strictly speaking, relieve us from agnosticism, but the knowledge of the truth of *h* does. To attain the position of knowing that *h* is the case, we have to collect evidence for *h*, and it is having *adequate evidence* for the given hypothesis which yields the relief from agnosticism. Such 'relief' cannot, of course, be expressed by a measure of information that is conditional on *e*, but it can be expressed, e.g., by the absolute informative content of *h*. As Levi has emphasized, apart from the 'new' evidence *e*, there is some 'background information' accepted at the outset of inquiry.[60] It seems plausible to regard the measure of epistemic utility as conditional on the background information, but not on the new evidence *e*. If this is conceded the most obvious reason for using partition-dependent *cont*-measures disappears. Moreover, the counterintuitive results yielded by Levi's rule that were pointed out above are easily seen to be attributable to the partition-dependence of *cont*. It consequently appears reasonable to re-examine the definition (3.2).

6. The Total Content of *h* as a Measure of Epistemic Utility

Jaakko Hintikka and Junani Pietarinen have defined the epistemic utility of accepting *h* in terms of the total content of *h*. Now this, *cont*(*h*), is defined by (3.2). According to Hintikka and Pietarinen, $u(h, t) = cont(h)$, $u(h, f) = -cont(\sim h)$, and $u(S, t) = 0$.[61] Suspension of judgment may again be taken as equivalent to accepting nothing but logical truths; hence $u(S, t)$ is obtained as a special case of $u(h, t)$. This measure yields the expectation.[62]

$$(6.1) \quad E(h/e) = P(h/e) - P(h),$$

i.e., the expected utility of accepting *h* on the basis of *e* is equal to the increase in the probability of *h* brought about by the evidence *e*. Hintikka has discussed this measure of acceptability in detail and has shown that it is equivalent or closely related to many measures of 'evidential power' or 'evidential support' that have been proposed in current literature on inductive logic.[63] Let **H** be a set of sentences and let every member of **H** be equivalent to a *p*-termed disjunction of mutually exclusive members of a set **B**. **B** corresponds

---

[59] Levi, *Gambling with Truth*, pp. 62 ff.
[60] *Ibid.*, pp. 59–60.
[61] "Semantic Information and Inductive Logic," pp. 107–8.
[62] *Ibid.*, p. 108.
[63] Hintikka, "Varieties of Information and Scientific Explanation." For these proposals, see, e.g., Kyburg, "Recent Work on Inductive Logic," pp. 255–57.

to the initial ultimate partition in Levi's theory, but we do not assume here that it is relativized to a question. H may consist, for example, of all general sentences of a given first-order language $\mathcal{L}$ whose depth does not exceed t.[64] The members of $\mathbf{B}$ are called *B-constituents*, and the disjunction $b_1{}^{(h)} \vee \ldots \vee b_p{}^{(h)}$ which is equivalent to h is called the *B-normal form* of h. If the expectation formula (6.1) is applied to the choice of the strongest acceptable sentence $h \in H$, a constituent $b_i \in \mathbf{B}$ is seen to be rejectable if e is negatively relevant to b_i.

Hintikka and Pietarinen's utility assignment may be generalized by introducing an index of boldness q which is similar to Levi's index q. We shall ignore the background information here and assume that H contains a contradictory sentence c and a logical truth d. Let

$$(6.2) \quad \text{(a)} \quad u(c, f) = 0$$
$$\qquad\;\; \text{(b)} \quad u(d, t) = s,$$

where $s \geqq 0$, and let

$$(6.3) \quad u(h_1, x) - u(h_2, x) = q[cont(h_1) - cont(h_2)],$$

where x is constant (t or f) and q is non-negative. Following Levi, we let the unit of our utility function be

$$(6.4) \quad q + s = 1;$$

hence $s = 1 - q$. According to (6.2)–(6.4), the expected utility of accepting h as strongest is:

$$(6.5) \quad \text{(a)} \quad u(h, t) = qcont(h) + 1 - q$$
$$\qquad\;\; \text{(b)} \quad u(h, f) = -q[1 - cont(h)];$$

hence, by the definition (3.2):

$$(6.6) \quad \text{(a)} \quad u(h, t) = 1 - qP(h)$$
$$\qquad\;\; \text{(b)} \quad u(h, f) = -qP(h).$$

According to (6.6), the expected utility of accepting h as strongest is:

$$(6.7) \quad \begin{aligned} E(h/e) &= P(h/e)[qcont(h) + 1 - q] - P(\smallfrown h/e)q[1 - cont(h)] \\ &= P(h/e) - qP(h) \\ &= \sum_i [P(b_i{}^{(h)}/e) - qP(b_i{}^{(h)})]. \end{aligned}$$

According to the rule of maximizing expected utility, supplemented with the rule for ties, (6.7) yields the following acceptance rule:

(R 5)   Reject all constituents b_i with $P(b_i/e) < qP(b_i)$, and accept the disjunction of all unrejected members of $\mathbf{B}$ as strongest on the basis of e.

---

[64] For the concept of the depth of a sentence, see Jaakko Hintikka, "Distributive Normal Forms in First-Order Logic," in *Formal Systems and Recursive Functions*, ed. J. M. Crossley and M. A. Dummett (Amsterdam: North Holland, 1965), p. 52.

The index q may again be interpreted as *index of boldness*. If $q = 1$, the epistemic utility of self-contradiction is equal to the utility of suspending judgment, i.e., accepting nothing but logical truths; otherwise suspension of judgment is preferred to the acceptance of contradictions. If epistemic utility is defined by (6.2) and (6.3), it is natural to define the concept of strong maximality in terms of the total content of hypotheses, and the rule for ties must be modified in the corresponding way. If $q = 0$, the modified rule for ties has an interesting consequence. If $q = 0$, the investigator does not care for information at all; all true hypotheses have the utility 1 and all false ones have the utility 0. Let d_e be the most informative member of **H** which is implied by e. If **B** contains elements which are incompatible with e, d_e is not identical with d. Nevertheless $E(d_e/e)$ is always equal to $E(d/e)$, and the modified rule for ties recommends accepting d as strongest. But d_e is *deductively acceptable* on the basis of e.

This curious result is practically harmless, for deductive acceptance rules ensure that all deductive consequences of e will be accepted on the basis of e. The result, in any case, is avoidable by restricting the application of the rule for ties to those sentences which are compatible with e.[65]

According to (R 5), a constituent $b \in \mathbf{B}$ is rejectable if there is sufficiently strong evidence *against* b, i.e., if e is negatively relevant to b to a sufficiently high degree. A constituent b which is not rejectable on the basis of e may be called a *plausible* constituent. A sentence $h \in \mathbf{H}$ is acceptable on the basis of e if and only if its normal form includes all plausible constituents. Since the 'rejection level' $qP(b)$ is independent of the choice of the partition B, the rule (R 5) satisfies the condition of adequacy (C 5) for all values of q; $0 \leq q \leq 1$. It also satisfies (C 6). (C 6) may be formulated in terms of the concept of rejection as follows: if a constituent $b' \in \mathbf{B}$ is not rejectable on the basis of e and if h is acceptable on the basis of e, b' is not rejectable on the basis of $e \& h$ either. Because the rejection level of b' does not change with evidence, b' cannot be rejectable on the basis of $e \& h$ without being rejectable on the basis of e, if $P(b'/e \& h) \geq P(b'/e)$. This is easily seen to be the case if h is accepted on the basis of e:

$$(6.8) \quad P(b'/e \& h) = P(b'/e)P(h/e \& b')/P(h/e).$$

If b' is plausible (i.e., not rejected) on the basis of e, it occurs in the normal form of h^* and hence in the normal form of h too; hence $P(h/e \& b') = 1$, and (6.8) simplifies as

$$(6.9) \quad P(b'/e \& h) = P(b'/e)/P(h/e),$$

which obviously always is at least as great as $P(b'/e)$. Hence (C 6) is satisfied. The present acceptance rule does not imply the existence of 'bookkeeping' acceptance procedures. If we wish to reject or accept sentences other than those rejected or accepted on the basis of e, we have to collect additional evidence.

---

[65] Another intuitively plausible way of avoiding this result is described below; see section 7.

As was mentioned above, (R 5) likewise satisfies the requirement (C 5). In addition, it satisfies another condition which is closely related to (C 4). If every member b' of a partition $\mathbf{B'}$ belongs to the set $\mathbf{H}$ corresponding to another partition $\mathbf{B}$, we say that $\mathbf{B'}$ is *definable* in terms of $\mathbf{B}$. (R 5) is easily seen to satisfy the following principle:

(C 7) If h is acceptable (or rejectable) with respect to $\mathbf{B}$, and $\mathbf{B'}$ is definable in terms of $\mathbf{B}$, h is acceptable (or rejectable) with respect to $\mathbf{B'}$ if $h \in \mathbf{H'}$.

In other words, if a hypothesis is rejected on the basis of a very detailed analysis of the situation at hand, it is rejectable on the basis of a less detailed analysis, provided, of course, that it may be formulated in such an analysis. The converse of (C 7) does not hold: a hypothesis may be rejectable with respect to $\mathbf{B'}$, but a more detailed analysis $\mathbf{B}$ may show that its normal form includes plausible B-constituents b_i, so that h cannot be rejected after all.

7. The Common Content of e and h as a Measure of Epistemic Utility

According to (3.6), the expectation (6.7) can be rewritten as follows:

(7.1)
$$\begin{aligned} E(h/e) &= P(h/e)[qcont(hTe) + qcont(hIe) + 1 - q] \\ &\quad - P(\sim h/e)[qcont(cTe) + qcont(cIe) \\ &\quad - qcont(hTe) - qcont(hIe)] \\ &= P(h/e)[qcont(hTe) + 1 - q] \\ &\quad - P(\sim h/e)[qcont(cTe) - qcont(hTe)] \\ &\quad + P(h/e)qcont(hIe) \\ &\quad - P(\sim h/e)[qcont(cIe) - qcont(hIe)], \end{aligned}$$

where

(7.2)
$$\begin{aligned} &P(h/e)qcont(hIe) - P(\sim h/e)[qcont(cIe) \\ &- qcont(hIe)] = q[P(h/e)\,P(e) - P(h\,\&\,e)] \\ &- [1 - P(h/e)]P(h\,\&\,e) = 0; \end{aligned}$$

hence

(7.3)
$$\begin{aligned} E(h/e) &= P(h/e)[qcont(hTe) + 1 - q] \\ &\quad - P(\sim h/e)[qcont(cTe) - qcont(hTe)]. \end{aligned}$$

This expression for the expected utility of accepting h as strongest may be obtained directly from the epistemic utility assignment

(7.4) (a) $u(c, f) = 0$
  (b) $u(d, t) = s = 1 - q$
  (c) $u(h_1, x) - u(h_2, x) = q[cont(h_1Te) - cont(h_2Te)],$

where $0 \leq q \leq 1$ and x is constant. (7.4) implies

(7.5) (a) $u(h, t) = qcont(hTe) + 1 - q$
  (b) $u(h, f) = -q[cont(cTe) - cont(hTe)]$
     $= -q[cont(e) - cont(hTe)].$

In maximizing the expected value of the total content of h, we are in effect maximizing the expectation of the *common* content of h and e, i.e., the substantial information carried by h concerning the subject-matter of h.[66] Thus we obtain the same acceptance rule independently of whether epistemic utilities are defined in terms of $cont(h)$ or $cont(hTe)$.

We see now that Hempel obviously took the wrong alternative in his choice between the two content-exclusive components of $cont(h)$, namely, $cont(hTe)$ and $cont(hIe)$. Nonetheless, the latter measure has a useful function in the *rule for ties*. If there are several hypotheses $h \in H$ for which $E(h/e) =$ max, the expected utility of their disjunction is maximal also, whereas the excess content $cont(hIe)$ is minimized by the disjunction. Hence the acceptance rule (R 5) is implied by the suggestion that we ought to accept as strongest such a sentence $h \in H$ as (a) will maximize $E(h/e)$, and (b) if there are several sentences $h \in H$ for which $E(h/e)$ is maximal, will minimize the excess content, $cont(hIe)$. This suggestion also works well if $q = 0$, for $cont(hIe)$ is minimized by any sentence logically implied by e. The rule of minimizing excess content is not at variance with deductive acceptance procedures. Intuitively, also, it seems more plausible than the rules for ties discussed earlier.

8. The Importance of Likelihoods

According to (R 5), a sentence $b_i \in B$ is rejectable on the basis of e if and only if $P(b_i/e) < qP(b_i)$. This rejection criterion can also be expressed as:

(8.1) $P(b_i/e)/P(b_i) < q$,

which is equivalent to

(8.2) $P(e/b_i)/P(e) < q$.

According to (R 5), a hypothesis $b_i \in B$ is rejectable if and only if the likelihood of b_i given e is sufficiently small in comparison with the total probability of e. If $P(e/b_i)$ is small in comparison with the prior expectedness of e, b_i evidently fails to explain the observational results described by e. In addition, (8.2) implies that B includes elements which do explain the data to some extent, i.e., that there are elements $b_j \in B$ for which

8.3) $P(e/b_j) > P(e)$.

Consequently, a small likelihood, simply or 'absolutely' speaking, is not sufficient for rejection, but a small likelihood in comparison with other elements of B is. Our acceptance rule is thus in accord with the emphasis laid upon likelihood *comparisons* in current statistical methodology.[67] If the rejectability of the hypotheses $b_i \in B$ is defined in terms of a small likelihood only, *any* hypothesis b_i might be rejectable on the basis of suitable

---

[66] Hintikka, "Varieties of Information and Scientific Explanation."
[67] Ian Hacking, *Logic of Statistical Inference* (Cambridge: Cambridge University Press, 1965), pp. 89 ff.

evidence e.[68] According to (8.2), we may formulate the following *likelihood condition:*

(C 8)   If b_i is rejectable on the basis of e, all hypotheses $b_j \in \mathbf{B}$ with $P(e/b_j) \leq P(e/b_i)$ are rejectable on the basis of e.

It is important to observe that this likelihood condition is concerned solely with the classificatory concept of rejection. According to the present definition of epistemic utility, $E(b/e)$ does not depend only on likelihoods; it is not normally maximized by the maximum likelihood hypothesis.

Likelihood comparisons become much more important if the acceptability of h is defined in terms of the logarithmic concept of transmitted information, instead of $cont(bTe)$. Let

(8.4) $inf(bIe) = inf(b \,\&\, e) - inf(e) = -\log P(b/e)$.

The amount of transmitted information (i.e., the amount of information provided by h concerning the subject matter of e) is defined by

(8.5) $inf(bTe) = inf(b) - inf(bIe)$
$\qquad\qquad = \log [P(e/b)/P(e)]$.

(8.5) expresses how much the hypothesis h reduces (or increases) the unexpectedness of the data e. If the hypotheses $b_i \in \mathbf{B}$ are judged solely in terms of their power to explain the data e, it is natural to employ the following rule of rejection:

(R 6)   Reject all elements $b_i \in \mathbf{B}$ with $inf(b_iTe) < r \,(r \leq 0)$.

If $r = \log q$, (R 6) is equivalent to the rule of rejection included in (R 5). Thus there is a one-to-one correspondence between the rules obtained from (R 5) by the choice of different values for q ($0 \leq q \leq 1$) and the rules (R 6) with corresponding values of r.

In "Varieties of Information and Scientific Explanation," Hintikka has distinguished between two types of scientific theorizing: *local* theorizing or *explanation*, as opposed to *global* theorizing or *generalization*. In local theorizing, our main interest lies in the explanation of particular data, and we want to find a hypothesis h which maximizes the unexpectedness of e given h. This is accomplished by maximizing $inf(bTe)$, that is, by maximizing the likelihood of h given e. In this case, the investigator does not apply the rule (R 6), but simply adopts the maximum likelihood hypothesis as the 'best' explanation. Thus $inf(bTe)$ is an appropriate measure of acceptability in local theorizing, whereas the expected value of the substantive information of h itself is, according to Hintikka, suitable for the purposes of ('global') generalization. Nevertheless, the equivalence of (R 5) and (R 6) demonstrates that these two cases bear a close mutual relation. The rejectability and acceptability of 'global' generalizations can also be defined in terms of $inf(bTe)$; it depends upon how well the alternative hypotheses under consideration explain the evidential data.

---

[68] Cf. *ibid.*, p. 77. This is the 'likelihood version' of the lottery paradox.

9. Concluding Remarks

According to (R 5), a hypothesis $h \in H$ should not be rejected unless there is sufficiently strong empirical evidence against h. The rejectability or acceptability of hypotheses is defined not in terms of firmness, but in terms of the *decrease* or *increase* in firmness.[69] If our acceptance rule purports to be a definition of 'justified belief,' a rule of this kind is very plausible from the intuitive point of view. If we are required to justify our belief that, for instance, a hypothesis $b_i \in B$ is false, it does not suffice to say that it is improbable, since any member of **B** may be very improbable. To justify our claim that b_i is false, we have to present factual evidence *against* b_i, that is to say, such evidence as is negatively relevant to b_i to a sufficiently high degree.

H. E. Kyburg has recently criticized logical and subjective theories of probability and argued that they imply the existence of factual *a priori* knowledge.

If, from an *a priori* logical or subjectivist probability statement based on (essentially) no evidence whatsoever, it followed that a certain empirical statement was overwhelmingly probable . . . I would take this as evidence of *a priorism* of the worst sort, and evidence that there was something seriously wrong with the theory."[70]

According to logical and subjective theories of probability there are, of course, such *a priori* highly probable factual sentences. Kyburg gives an example of such a statement, and concludes: "If we adopt both subjective probabilities and a rule of detachment [i.e., a rule of acceptance], we are committed to *a priori* synthetic knowledge."[71]

This conclusion may be drawn only if high probability is assumed to be a sufficient condition of acceptability. The lottery paradox shows that this assumption is untenable, so Kyburg's argument provides further grounds for rejecting the rule of high probability. Similar criticism may be directed against Levi's rule (R 4): if the prior probability distribution on **B** is not even, some alternatives $b_i \in B$ may be rejectable *a priori*. If we do not wish to accept any factual hypotheses in the absence of empirical evidence, we are committed to a prior even distribution on **B**. The rule (R 5) is free from such difficulties because acceptability for this rule is defined in terms of relevant empirical evidence.

The preceding discussion indicates that the decision-theoretic approach to rules of acceptance yields interesting and intuitively reasonable results, if the concept of epistemic utility is suitably defined. However, it is important to observe that the Bayesian decision rule of maximizing expected utility alone is insufficient in cognitive decision-making. As Levi has pointed out, the rule of maximizing expected utility must be supplemented by an additional rule—the rule for ties; otherwise in some cases the justification of

---

[69] For these concepts, see Rudolf Carnap, *Logical Foundations of Probability*, 2nd ed. (Chicago: University of Chicago Press, 1962), p. xvi.
[70] Henry R. Kyburg, Jr., "Bets and Beliefs," *American Philosophical Quarterly* 5: 60 (1968).
[71] *Ibid.*, p. 62.

scientific conclusions might be a matter of arbitrary decision. The rule for ties implies that we should suspend judgment between equally acceptable hypotheses. This principle seems reasonable, and the rule for ties is introduced ad hoc, to ensure that this requirement is satisfied. In customary Bayesian decision theory such additional principles are not necessary. The utility assignment is assumed to reflect all our relevant preferences, and we are recommended to behave in accord with the expectation of this utility. If several alternative options possess equal expected utility, there is no reason whatsoever for preferring one course of action to another. Thus the difference between conclusions and decisions cannot be explained simply by the difference between two kinds of utilities. There are also important differences in the strategy of decision-making.

Håkan Törnebohm

A Foundational Study of Einstein's Special Space-Time Theory

INTRODUCTION

The physical information that is contained in Einstein's special space-time theory can be packed into three assumptions, which are readily interpretable in terms of experimental procedures.

I hope to establish the following conclusions:

(1) Einstein's velocity theorem and the theorem that simultaneity of separated events is relative can be deduced from one assumption alone in conjunction with plausible definitions of physical concepts.

(2) The doctrines of clock retardation and length contraction depend on conventions and can be replaced by sensible and better alternatives without violating any information carrying parts of Einstein's theory.

(3) Huygens' but not Newton's theory of light is incompatible with Newton's kinematics.

(4) The Michelson-Morley experiment has not refuted the ether hypothesis. The clash between predicted and actual outcome is due to an inconsistency in the set of premises that were used in predicting the outcome of this experiment.

BASIC ASSUMPTIONS*

E 1. The rate of propagation of light in empty space is a local property. It does not depend on the velocity of the source.

E 2. Light propagation in empty space is isotropic.

E 3. The distance between the end-points of a rod is proportional to the length of the rod when both these magnitudes are measured in the rest system of the rod. The proportionality is a universal constant.

Professor Törnebohm, of the University of Göteberg in Sweden, is a native of Sweden.

Reprinted with slight changes from *Scientia*, vol. 63, pp. 375–87, with permission of the author and editor. Copyright 1969 by *Scientia*, Milan, Italy.

* "E" for "Einstein".

Assumption E 1

Figure 1 maps an experimental setup devised to exhibit the content of information that is carried by E 1. *A*, *B*, and *C* are Minkowski lines representing three observation stations in relative uniform motion in the same direction with respect to each other. *A* is an inertial system; *B* and *C* are therefore also inertial. The three systems depart from each other at an instant *O*. *A*, *B*, and *C* carry isochronous clocks synchronized in *O* to read *O*. Devices are attached to *A*, *B*, and *C* enabling light flashes to be emitted and detected.

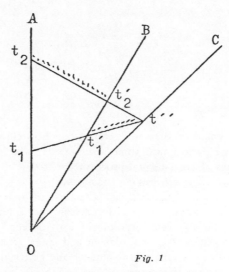

Fig. 1

The following experiment is carried out. When clock *A* reads t_1, a light flash is emitted from *A* towards *B* and *C* which move in the same direction with different speeds. When this flash passes *B* on its path to *C* a flash is emitted from *B* toward *C*. This happens when the *B* clock reads t'_1. It follows from E 1 that both light flashes should be detected simultaneously in the station *C*. When this happens, the *C* clock reads t''. The light flashes are instantaneously reflected in *C* toward *B* and *A*. When they pass *B*, which happens when the *B* clock reads t'_2, another flash is emitted from *B* toward *A*. According to assumption E 1, all three light flashes arrive simultaneously at system *A*. The *A* clock reads t_2 when this happens.

It is convenient to describe these processes in the following way:

$$\left. \begin{aligned} t'_1 &= S_{AB}\, t_1 \\ t'' &= S_{BC}\, t'_1 = S_{AC}\, t_1 \\ t'_2 &= S_{CB}\, t'' \\ t_2 &= S_{BA}\, t'_2 = S_{CA}\, t'' \end{aligned} \right\} \tag{1}$$

The constants *S* will be called "signal connectors." They are defined in (1) by means of measuring conditions.

From (1) we deduce the following relations among the signal connectors

$$S_{AC} = S_{AB}\, S_{BC} \atop S_{CA} = S_{CB}\, S_{BA} \Big\} \qquad (2)$$

(2) expresses the physical content of assumption E 1 in terms of signal connectors.

We will next define three concepts by means of measuring conditions.

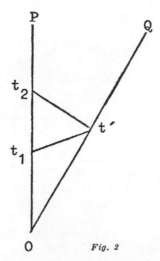

Fig. 2

Figure 2 is a Minkowski diagram depicting a material object Q moving away with uniform velocity from an observation station P which is an inertial frame of reference. Isochronous clocks are attached to P and Q which are synchronized to read zero at the instant O when the two objects depart from each other. A light flash is emitted from P when the P clock reads t_1, is reflected from Q, when the Q clock reads t' and returns to P when the P clock reads t_2.

We define three concepts as follows:

Definition 1. The distance in space from P to the point-event of reflection (t') on Q as measured in system P, is

$$x = \frac{1}{2}(t_2 - t_1).$$

x is also a space coordinate of the event (t') with respect to system P.

Definition 2. The distance in time from O to the instant of reflection (t') as measured in system P is

$$t = \frac{1}{2}(t_2 + t_1).$$

t is also a time coordinate of the event (t') with respect to system A.

Definition 3. *The velocity of the object* Q with respect to P is

$$V_{PQ} = \frac{x}{t} = \frac{t_2 - t_1}{t_2 + t_1}.$$

It follows from definition 3 that $V_{PQ} < 1$. 1 is thus a limiting velocity of material objects which can be reached by light signals.

Combining $V...$ and $S...$ we obtain the relations

$$\left.\begin{aligned} V_{PQ} &= \frac{S_{PQ}\, S_{QP} - 1}{S_{PQ}\, S_{QP} + 1} \\[2mm] S_{PQ}\, S_{QP} &= \frac{1 + V_{PQ}}{1 - V_{PQ}} \end{aligned}\right\} \tag{3}$$

From (2) and (3) we deduce Einstein's velocity theorem as follows:

$$S_{AC}\, S_{CA} = S_{AB}\, S_{BA}\, S_{BC}\, S_{CB} \qquad \longrightarrow$$

$$\frac{1 + V_{AC}}{1 - V_{AC}} = \frac{1 + V_{AB}}{1 - V_{AB}} \cdot \frac{1 + V_{BC}}{1 - V_{BC}} \qquad \longrightarrow$$

$$V_{AC} = \frac{V_{AB} + V_{BC}}{1 + V_{BA}\, V_{BC}} \tag{4}$$

(4) shows that V_{AC} and V_{BC} have the same limiting velocity 1. It is very plausible to assume that this velocity is identical with that of light and to assume that light has the same velocity in all inertial frames of reference. However these assumptions are merely sensible conjectures at this stage, as velocity of light has not yet been defined.

We will next relate the coordinates of a point-event in one inertial frame of reference to those of another in relative, uniform motion.

Let the coordinates of the point-event (t'') on C (see fig. 1) be (t, x) in system A and (t', x') in system B. According to definitions 1 and 2 these coordinates are related to clock readings in the systems A and B, respectively, as follows:

$$\left.\begin{aligned} t &= \frac{1}{2}\,(t_2 + t_1) \\[2mm] x &= \frac{1}{2}\,(t_2 - t_1) \end{aligned}\right\} \quad \text{and} \quad \left.\begin{aligned} t' &= \frac{1}{2}\,(t'_2 + t'_1) \\[2mm] x' &= \frac{1}{2}\,(t'_2 - t'_1) \end{aligned}\right\}$$

These relations can be rearranged as follows:

$$\left.\begin{aligned} t_1 &= t - x \\ t_2 &= t + x \end{aligned}\right\} \quad \text{and} \quad \left.\begin{aligned} t'_1 &= t' - x' \\ t'_2 &= t' + x' \end{aligned}\right\}$$

It follows from (1) and (3) that

$$\left.\begin{aligned} t - x &= S_{AB}^{-1}\,(t' - x') \\[1mm] t + x &= S_{BA}\,(t' + x') \\[2mm] S_{AB}\, S_{BA} &= \frac{1 + V_{AB}}{1 - V_{AB}} \end{aligned}\right\} \tag{5}$$

Let Δt, Δx, $\Delta t'$, and $\Delta x'$ designate coordinate differences between two separated point-events. The following relation between them is obtained from (5):

$$\frac{\Delta t - \Delta x}{\Delta t + \Delta x} = \frac{1 - V_{AB}}{1 + V_{AB}} \cdot \frac{\Delta t' - \Delta x'}{\Delta t' + \Delta x'} \qquad (6)$$

Suppose that the two point-events are simultaneous in both systems A and B so that $\Delta t = \Delta t' = 0$. It follows from (6) that V_{AB} must equal 0.

We conclude that two separated events which are simultaneous (have the same time coordinate) in one inertial frame of reference such as A are not simultaneous (have different time coordinates) in another frame of reference such as B in motion with respect to A (so that $V_{AB} \neq 0$).

The relativity of simultaneity is thus a logical consequence of the assumption E 1 alone.

Assumptions E 1 and E 2, Taken Together

If assumption E 2 is true, then S_{AB} must be independent of directions. We conclude that

$$S_{AB} = S_{BA}. \qquad (7)$$

Combining (5) and (7) we obtain the formulas

$$\left. \begin{array}{l} t - x = \sqrt{\dfrac{1 - v}{1 + v}} \, (t' - x') \\[2mm] t + x = \sqrt{\dfrac{1 + v}{1 - v}} \, (t' + x') \end{array} \right\} \qquad (8)$$

where we have replaced "V_{AB}" by "v" for convenience. (8) may be rearranged into the more familiar form

$$\left. \begin{array}{l} x = \dfrac{1}{\sqrt{1 - v^2}} \, (x' + v \, t') \\[3mm] t = \dfrac{1}{\sqrt{1 - v^2}} \, (t' + v \, x') \end{array} \right\} \qquad (8')$$

Distance in Space-Time

From (8) we deduce the important relation, e.g.:

$$t^2 - x^2 = t'^2 - x'^2 = \Delta s^2. \qquad (9)$$

Δs is thus an invariant. Δs is usually called "space-time interval." I prefer the phrase "distance in space-time between two point-events." This concept is defined as follows:

Definition 4. The distance in space-time between two point-events with coordinates (t_1, x_1) and (t_2, x_2) in a system A is

$$\Delta s = \sqrt{(t_2 - t_1)^2 - (x_2 - x_1)^2}.$$

Δs is an invariant.

APPLICATION OF THE CONCEPT OF SPACE-TIME DISTANCE TO SPECIAL CASES

Distance in space between the end-point of a moving rod. Let B and B' be the end-points of a rod. We want to use the concept of space-time distance to establish a relation between d, the distance in space between B and B' as measured in A and d_o, the distance in space between B and B' as measured in B, in which system the rod is at rest.

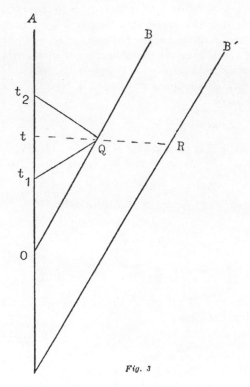

Fig. 3

The coordinate differences between the point-events Q and R (see fig. 3) on B and B', respectively, are

$$(\Delta t, \Delta x) = (0, d) \quad \text{in } A \text{ and}$$
$$(\Delta t', \Delta x') = (\Delta t', d_o) \quad \text{in } B.$$

From the invariance of the distance in space-time between Q and R and the second equation in (8') we establish an important relation between d and d_o as follows:

$$\Delta x^2 - \Delta t^2 = \Delta x'^2 - \Delta t'^2 \longrightarrow$$
$$d^2 = d_o^2 - \Delta t'^2.$$

$$\Delta t = \frac{1}{\sqrt{1 - v^2}} (\Delta t' + v\, \Delta x') = 0 \longrightarrow$$

$$\Delta t'^2 = v^2\, d_o^2.$$

Hence

$$d = \sqrt{1 - v^2}\, d_o. \tag{10}$$

(10) asserts that the distance in space between the end-points of a rod is smaller in a frame of reference in which the rod is moving than it is in a frame of reference in which it is at rest.

Remark. We should *not* infer from (10) that the *length* of a rod is contracted. Indeed, we have not yet introduced this concept.

Distance in time between two point-events. Consider the point-events 0 and Q on B (see fig. 3). The coordinate differences are

$$(\Delta t, \Delta x) = (t, \Delta x) \quad \text{in } A$$
$$(\Delta t', \Delta x') = (t', 0) \quad \text{in } B.$$

From (8') we at once obtain the relation

$$t' = \sqrt{1 - v^2}\, t. \tag{11}$$

Let us apply (11) to the situation that is mapped in figure 4. B represents a system moving away from a system A and then returning to A. We will assume that the acceleration of B is so small that we may ignore it. Let isochronous clocks be attached to the systems A and B, respectively, and let these clocks be synchronized to read 0 in the point-event 0 of departure.

When the clocks meet again in P they ought, according to (11), to read

Clock A: $\displaystyle\int_0^P dt$

Clock B: $\displaystyle\int_0^P \sqrt{1 - v^2}\, dt$

where v is the velocity of the clock B in the system A.

Clock A is thus ahead of clock B in P. (12)

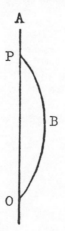

Fig. 4

(12) is usually interpreted as showing that the B clock is slower than the A clock. The B clock is retarded if the clocks measure the same magnitude, the distance in time from O to P. But we need not assume that this is the case. We may instead assume that they measure different magnitudes, the A clock measuring the *duration* of a process from O to P taking place in the system A, and the B clock measuring the *duration* of another process from O to P taking place in the system B. We are then free to assume that both clocks run at the same rate, i.e., would assign the same value to the duration of the same process.

Formula (12) will then be interpreted as asserting that the two clocks A and B measure different durations and that the duration of a process need not have the same value as the distance in time between the beginning and the end of the process.

Duration of a process given by the integral $\int_1^2 ds$ is an invariant, but the distance in time $\int_1^2 dt$ is not invariant.

Remark. What has here been called "duration" is usually called "proper time."

Distance in space-time between points on an optical line that is a line representing the path of a light flash. Consider the line from (t_1) on A to Q on B as representing the path of a light flash emitted from A and received at B (see fig. 3).

The coordinates with respect to system A of these space-time points are

$$(t_1, 0) \text{ and } (t, x) = \left(\frac{1}{2} (t_1 + t_2), \frac{1}{2} (t_2 - t_1) \right)$$

(according to definitions 1 and 2). Hence

$$\Delta s^2 = (t - t_1)^2 - x^2 = 0. \tag{13}$$

What has been shown to hold in a special case is valid in general:

The distance in space-time between two point-events on an optical line is always zero.

Assumptions E 1, E 2, and E 3 Taken Together

Let A and A' in figure 5 be the end-points of a rod and l the length of the rod as measured by means of a meterstick in a frame of reference in which the rod is at rest.

The distance from A to A' with respect to system A is, e.g.:

$$\frac{1}{2} (t_2 - t_1) = d_o.$$

E 3 asserts that

$$d_o = \frac{1}{c_A} l.$$

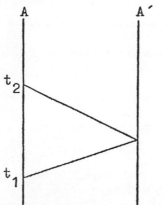

Fig. 5

For another rod BB' in uniform translational motion with respect to the rod AA' the analogous relation $d_o = 1/c_B l$ holds, where this time d_o and l are measured in a frame of reference in which the rod BB' is at rest.

According to E 3 it holds moreover that $c_A = c_B = c$. We may therefore write

$$d_o = 1/cl. \tag{14}$$

The distance in space between the end-points of the rod as measured in the rest system of the rod is equivalent to the length of the rod as measured by a meterstick.

c is a universal constant like the gravitational constant in Newton's theory of gravitation or Planck's constant in quantum mechanics.

c can be regarded as an exchange rate between length units and time units.

c has the dimension of a velocity and can be interpreted as a measure of the velocity of light.

A corollary of E 3 is therefore the following assertion: *The velocity of light is a universal constant*.

To knit E 3 together with the previous assumptions we will express the space coordinates in formulas (8) and (8′) in terms of length units instead of time units. We then obtain the formulas:

$$
\left.
\begin{aligned}
t - x/c &= \sqrt{\frac{1 - v/c}{1 + v/c}}\, (t' - x'/c') \\[2ex]
t + x/c &= \sqrt{\frac{1 + v/c}{1 - v/c}}\, (t' + x'/c')
\end{aligned}
\right\} \tag{8''}
$$

and

$$
\left.
\begin{aligned}
x &= \frac{1}{\sqrt{1 - v^2/c^2}}\, (x' + v t') \\[2ex]
t &= \frac{1}{\sqrt{1 - v^2/c^2}} \left(t' + \frac{v}{c^2} x' \right)
\end{aligned}
\right\} \tag{8'''}
$$

(8''') are the Lorentz formulas, which thus can be deduced from the set of premises E 1, E 2, and E 3.

It is customary to assume that the formula

$$d = 1/c \, l \tag{14'}$$

holds not only in inertial rest systems but also in moving inertial frames of reference.

From (14') and (10) we obtain the relation

$$l = \sqrt{1 - v^2/c^2} \, l_o \tag{14''}$$

(14'') asserts that the length of a rod is shorter for a moving observer than for an observer at rest with respect to the rod.

It is possible to avoid this unpalatable doctrine by means of a definitional shift. Length has so far only been defined in a rest system. The doctrine of length contraction follows if (14') is adopted as a definition of moving length.

If this definition is replaced by the following definition of moving length we avoid the doctrine of length contraction.

Definition 5. The length of a rod moving with a uniform velocity v in an inertial frame of reference is

$$l = \frac{c \, d}{\sqrt{1 - v^2/c^2}} \, .$$

This definition assures that length is an invariant property of a solid body.

Field Causality and the Einstein Special Space-Time Theory

Classical field theories have a type of causality which may be framed in this general way:

F 1. An effect takes place in a region B only if some event has taken place earlier in another region A.

F 2. A process is propagated from A to B.

F 3. The process from A to B has a finite rate of propagation which is dependent only on local properties.

These principles are ingredients in field theories in which the processes referred to above are carried by a material medium such as a solid, a liquid, or a gas.

The principles are also constituents of Huygens' wave theory of light and its successors. This similarity strongly suggested to classical physicists the ontological assumption that the propagation of light is also carried by a medium, the so called ether.

It is evident that assumption E 1 in Einstein's theory and F 3 in application to light have the same truth value. We may therefore conclude that logical consequences of assumption E 1 in conjunction with information free definitions are also logical consequences of the causal principles of field physics in application to light. From this logical fact we may draw conclusions of interest to historians of physics.

Huygens' theory of light is incompatible with Newton's space-time theory, according to which simultaneity is absolute and velocities are added as three vectors. On the other hand, Newton's theory of light according to which light is a swarm of corpuscles, entails a denial of E 1. Indeed, according to that theory the propagation of light should be dependent on the velocity of the source. It was therefore consistent for Newton not to accept Huygens' optics and it was consistent for Huygens not to accept Newton's causal principles.

The dualism between a corpuscular and an undulatory theory of light is thus intimately connected with rival theories of space-time and causality.

It is generally believed that the Michelson-Morley experiment dealt the death blow to the ether hypothesis. This belief is not correct. Indeed, the premises from which the historical prediction of the outcome of this experiment was deduced are incompatible.

One set of premises states that the principles F 1, F 2, and F 3 apply to light. Another premise states that Newton's addition theorem can be applied to the propagation of light.

The clash between the predicted and the actual outcomes of the Michelson-Morley experiment can be accounted for as arising from the incompatibility between field causality, which entails Einstein's velocity theorem and Newton's space-time theory, or kinematics, which includes Newton's velocity theorem. We sum up the situation in scheme 1.

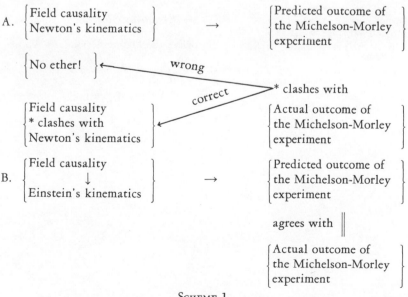

Scheme 1

If Newton's addition theorem is replaced by Einstein's theorem, the clash between prediction and outcome vanishes. The ontological hypothesis that there *exists* an ether in the world is not implicated at all. The experiment is relevant to the ether theory *only* insofar as it shows that the ether cannot combine Newtonian space-time features with the characteristics of a field.

The space-time of Einstein's theory of space-time and gravitation is indeed a successor of the 'classical' ether.

REFERENCES

Aharoni, J. *The Special Theory of Relativity*. Oxford: Clarendon Press, 1959.
Bohm, D. *The Special Theory of Relativity*. Amsterdam and New York: Benjamin, 1965.
Bunge, M. *Foundations of Physics*. New York: Springer, 1968.
Einstein, A., Lorentz, H. A., Weyl, H., and Minkowski, H. *The Principle of Relativity*. New York: Dover, 1923.
Grunbaum, A. *Philosophical Problem of Space and Time*. New York: Knopf, 1963.
————. *Geometry and Chronometry in Philosophical Perspective*. Minneapolis: University of Minnesota Press, 1968.
Milne, E. A. *Kinematic Relativity*. Oxford: Clarendon Press, 1948.
Moller, C. *The Theory of Relativity*. Oxford: Clarendon Press, 1951.
Nevanlinna, R. *Raum, Zeit und Relativitat*. Basel and Stuttgart: Birkhauserverlag, 1964.
Ney, E. P. *Electromagnetism and Relativity*. New York: Harper & Row, 1965.
Papapetrou, A. *Spezielle Relativitatstheorie*. Berlin: DVW, 1955.
Prokhovnik, S. J. *The Logic of Special Relativity*. Cambridge: Cambridge University Press, 1967.
Reichenbach, H. *The Philosophy of Space and Time*. New York: Dover, 1958.
Taylor, E. F., and Wheeler, J. A. *Space-Time Physics*. San Francisco: Freeman and Company, 1966.
Tornebohm, H. *A Logical Analysis of the Theory of Relativity*. Stockholm: Almquist & Wiksell, 1952.
————. *Fysik och filosofi* [Physics and philosophy]. Stockholm: Almquist & Wiksell, 1957.
————. *Concepts and Principles in the Space-Time Theory within Einstein's Special Theory of Relativity*. Stockholm: Almquist & Wiksell, 1963.
————. "Two Studies concerning the Michaelson-Morley Experiment." *Foundations of Physics* 1 (1970): 47–56.

II

Ethics
Political and Legal Philosophy

A

Moral and Legal Logic
and Language

Lars Bergström

Meaning and Morals

1

Moral philosophers are sometimes concerned with *moral* problems. (This might not come as a surprise to anyone.) But they have also displayed a great interest in problems about the *meaning* of those words that are typically used to express answers to moral problems (e.g., "right," "good," "ought," and so on). Problems of the latter kind may doubtless be of some importance, but it is not entirely obvious how they are related to those of the former kind. In particular, it may be wondered whether any moral conclusions can be inferred from a definition of an ethical term. Do such definitions contain or entail moral principles? This is the question that I propose to discuss here. It is not the only question that can be asked about the relation between meaning and morals, but it appears to be a rather fundamental one. Moreover, my own answer to it is different from that which seems to be taken for granted by several prominent moral philosophers.

Let me first mention some typical definitions of ethical terms. It might be suggested, for example, that "good" means "pleasant" or "desired upon reflection"; that "right" means "approved by me (the speaker)" or "commanded by God"; and that "ought to be done" means "has intrinsically better consequences than every alternative." Some definitions of this kind may be more acceptable than others, but this is not something that I want to discuss here. Neither need we bother about the distinction between naturalistic and non-naturalistic definitions. For the purposes of this paper we may concentrate on the following example:

(1)   "Right" means the same as "generally approved."

Other definitions may be treated by implication. The question that I want to

Dr. Bergström, of the University of Stockholm, is a native of Sweden.

discuss, then, is whether it is possible to derive any moral conclusion from (1). In particular, does (1) contain or entail

(2)   If an action is generally approved, then it is right,

or some similar principle? In other words, is (2) a logical consequence of (1)? This may appear to be a rather elementary question. Nevertheless, it seems to me that it needs to be answered.

It should be noticed that we do not have to pay any explicit attention to possible inferences which involve more than one premise but which are otherwise similar to the step from (1) to (2). For example, the inference

(3)   "Right" means the same as "generally approved,"
       This action is generally approved,

       Therefore, this action is right,

presents no special problem. It seems clear that (3) is valid if, and only if, (2) is a consequence of (1). This presumably is not at all controversial. But *is* (2) a logical consequence of (1)? This may seem more doubtful.

2

According to the logical intuitions of many non-philosophers it would presumably be fairly obvious that (2) follows from (1). Many people would probably say that one has to accept (2) if one accepts (1).

On the other hand, some philosophers might object to this by saying that such an inference would violate Hume's thesis that one cannot derive an *ought* from an *is*. But this argument seems to beg the question. Besides, it is not self-evident that the step from (1) to (2) is a step from *is* to *ought*. It does not seem unreasonable to suppose that someone might hold that (2) is factual or that (1) is normative. In particular, it might be argued that (1) is normative if it contains or entails (2); or that (2) is not normative if it follows from (1). So Hume's thesis does not seem to be of much help here.

Some philosophers might wish to say that (2) cannot follow logically from anything at all since it is neither true nor false. By the same token it might be maintained that (3) is a so-called practical inference and that such inferences are never logically valid. However, the thesis that something cannot be logically related to something else unless it is true or false is very far from being generally accepted. Many writers, including myself,[1] have argued that it should be rejected. Moreover, it may be doubted that (2) and the conclusion of (3) are neither true nor false. It might be held, for example, that (2) is analytic and, hence (trivially), true if (1) is true. It might even be argued that (2) follows from (1) for this very reason.

----

[1] See my study *Imperatives and Ethics* (Stockholm: Stockholm University, 1962), pp. 32–42.

The arguments which have been indicated above may be questioned. However, it is surely reasonable to surmise that many philosophers would in fact refuse to agree that (2) follows from (1). On the other hand, it also seems that several prominent philosophers are inclined to take the opposite view. For example, G. E. Moore writes:

It seems sometimes to be vaguely held that when a man judges an action to be right, he is merely judging that he has a particular feeling towards it, but that yet, though he really has this feeling, the action is not necessarily really right. But obviously this is impossible. If the *whole* of what we mean to assert, when we say that an action is right, is merely that we have a particular feeling towards it, then plainly, provided· only we really have this feeling, the action *must* really be right.[2]

A few pages later he says:

No one, I think, would be very much tempted to assert that the mere presence (or absence) of a certain feeling is invariably a sign of rightness, but for the supposition that, in some way or other, the only possible meaning of the word "right," as applied to actions, is that somebody has a certain feeling towards them.[3]

Hence, it seems that Moore would accept the view that if "right" means "approved (by X)," then a given action is right if it is in fact approved (by X). This is perhaps even more obvious from the following passage:

Thus, if, when *I* assert an action to be right, I am merely asserting that it is generally approved in the society to which *I* belong, it follows, of course, that if it *is* generally approved by my society, my assertion is true, and the action really is right.[4]

I conclude, therefore, that it may reasonably be assumed that Moore would regard (2) as a logical consequence of (1).

Now it has been pointed out by C. L. Stevenson[5] that some of Moore's arguments are inconclusive. In particular, Stevenson shows that the definition

(4)   "X is right" has the same meaning as "I approve of X,"

does not entitle one to accept

(5)   If "X is right," said by A, is true, then X is right.[6]

But it should be noticed that Stevenson's criticism applies only to the particular inference of (5) from (4). Stevenson does not question the general assumption, which seems to be implicit in Moore's arguments, that principles like (2) and (5) may follow from definitions. As a matter of fact, he seems to hold that the definition

[2] G. E. Moore, *Ethics* (London: The Home University Library, 1912), pp. 92–93.
[3] *Ibid.*, p. 106.
[4] *Ibid.*, p. 108.
[5] C. L. Stevenson, "Moore's Arguments against Certain Forms of Ethical Naturalism," in *The Philosophy of G. E. Moore*, ed. P. A. Schilpp (Evanston and Chicago: Northwestern University, 1942), pp. 71–90.
[6] *Ibid.*, p. 76.

(6)   "X is right" has the same meaning as "Somebody approves of X,"

does entitle one to accept (5).[7] In other words, it seems that Stevenson would maintain that although

(7)   If someone approves of X, then X is right

is not a logical consequence of (4), it is a logical consequence of (6). Hence, he would presumably also accept the view that (2) is a logical consequence of (1).

A. C. Ewing appears to be another proponent of this view. For example, in criticizing certain naturalistic definitions of ethical terms Ewing claims:

> It is an essential feature of the moral consciousness that I realize that, if I ought to do something, I ought to do it whether others feel approval of it or not.[8]

Now he seems to hold that this moral principle is logically incompatible with a definition according to which "ought to be done" means the same as "is generally approved." For he goes on to say,

> If "what ought to be done" means "what is generally approved," general approval would have to be the only factor which ultimately counted in deciding what we ought to do, and this it certainly is not.[9]

In other words, Ewing seems to hold that the definition in question entails an unacceptable moral conclusion, namely, that something ought to be done if and only if it is generally approved, and that the definition must be rejected in order to avoid this conclusion. A few pages later he seems to argue in a similar way:

> The view that "good" means "what most people desire (or like)" is open to similar objections. Most people desire and like happiness more than great virtue, yet it does not therefore necessarily follow that the former is better.[10]

It appears that Ewing is presupposing that this would follow if "good" meant "what most people desire (or like)" or if "X is better than Y" meant "Most people desire (or like) X more than Y." In general, he seems to hold that (naturalistic) definitions of ethical terms entail (unacceptable) moral principles. Hence, he would probably say that (2) is a logical consequence of (1).

It has often been suggested that, if one accepts a naturalistic definition, then one is also committed to the view that moral or ethical problems can be solved by ordinary empirical methods. For example, R. B. Brandt writes:

> It has been suggested that "is desirable" means just "is desired by somebody." If this proposal is right, then, of course, observation can tell us what is desirable.[11]

[7] *Ibid.*, pp. 76–77.
[8] A. C. Ewing, *The Definition of Good* (London: Routledge & Kegan Paul, 1947), p. 62.
[9] *Ibid.*
[10] *Ibid.*, p. 65.
[11] R. B. Brandt, *Ethical Theory* (Englewood Cliffs, N.J.: Prentice-Hall, 1959), p. 152.

This view seems to involve or presuppose the assumption that naturalistic definitions entail moral principles. If Brandt's argument were expressed more explicitly it would presumably run as follows. From the definition according to which "is desirable" means the same as "is desired by somebody" we may derive the principle that something is desirable if and only if it is desired by somebody. Observation can tell us what is desired by somebody. Hence, if we accept the definition, we are committed to the view that observation can tell us what is desirable. Further support for this interpretation of Brandt's argument can be found in the following passage:

> The reason why all problems of ethics can be solved by the methods of science, if naturalism is true, is that the naturalist's definitions (like every definition) enable him to assert that some fundamental ethical statements are true by definition—statements he can use as the basic premises of his system of normative ethics. For instance, Perry's definitions enable us to say, "Any act is right if and only if it will contribute more to harmonious happiness than anything else the agent could do instead." The Ideal Observer definitions permit us to assert, as true by definition, "Anything is desirable if and only if an informed (and so on) person would want it to occur." In general, a definition will permit us to say something of the form, "Anything is E [ethical term] if and only if it is a PQR." Then, since science presumably can tell us what will contribute most to the harmonious happiness, or what an informed person would want, and so forth, it will carry us to conclusions about what is right or good.[12]

A similar view seems to be held by W. K. Frankena. He writes:

> For example, when Perry tells us that "good" means "being an object of desire," he also tells us that we can test empirically whether X is good simply by determining whether it is desired or not.[13]

And he also says,

> If "We ought to do . . ." means "We are required by society to do . . . ," then from "Society requires that we keep promises" it follows that we ought to keep promises. It will not do to reply, as some have, that no such definitions are possible since we cannot get an Ought out of an Is, for that is to beg the question.[14]

Hence, it is surely reasonable to assume that both Brandt and Frankena would hold that (2) is a logical consequence of (1).

However, Frankena might not accept Brandt's thesis that "all problems of ethics can be solved by the methods of science, if naturalism is true." For it seems to him that naturalistic and metaphysical definitions of ethical terms

> . . . do not suffice to solve the problem of justification. If we accept a certain definition of "good," or "right," then, as we saw, we will know just how to justify judgments about what is good or right. But this means that the whole burden rests on the definition, and we may still ask how the definition is justified or why we should accept it.[15]

---

[12] *Ibid.*, p. 178.
[13] W. K. Frankena, *Ethics* (Englewood Cliffs, N.J.: Prentice-Hall, 1963), p. 81.
[14] *Ibid.*, p. 80.
[15] *Ibid.*, pp. 83–84.

But this does not mean that Frankena questions the assumption that such definitions entail or contain moral principles. On the contrary, his argument seems to rest on just this assumption. This is perhaps even more obvious when he goes on to say,

> When Perry tries to persuade us to accept his definition of "right," he is in effect persuading us to accept, as a basis for action, the ethical principle that what is conducive to harmonious happiness is right. . . . He cannot establish his definition unless he can convince us of the principle. . . . In other words, to advocate the adoption of or continued adherence to a definition of an ethical or value term seems to be tantamount to trying to justify the corresponding moral principle. . . . Such definitions . . . turn out to be disguised ethical principles or value judgments which cannot themselves be deduced logically from the nature of things.[16]

In view of all this I am inclined to believe that many moral philosophers would maintain that definitions of ethical terms entail moral principles. At any rate, this view seems to be held by Moore, Stevenson, Ewing, Brandt, and Frankena, and these writers are all very influential. As far as I can see, however, this view is unjustified. I shall try to show that (2) is not a logical consequence of (1). Similar cases may be treated in the same way. Hence, if I am right about this, one may very well accept a given definition of an ethical term without thereby committing oneself to the acceptance of any moral principle.

My argument is fairly simple, and it does not seem to involve any controversial assumptions. In particular, it will not be based upon Hume's thesis (or upon the thesis that logical relations presuppose truth values). Neither will it be relative to any particular interpretation of (1) and (2).

3

What does it mean to say that X is a logical consequence of Y? In order to answer this question (which is obviously of some importance in the present context) we must distinguish between two different cases, namely: (a) the case where X and Y are *sentences*; and (b) the case where X and Y are *statements*. For our purposes, the distinction between sentences and statements may be explained as follows. A sentence is a linguistic entity, a sequence of words, which belongs to some particular language. A statement is something that may be expressed by a sentence. It is not a linguistic entity; it does not consist of words; it is not a part of any language.[17] A given sentence may be used or interpreted in many different ways. In particular, it may express different statements in different contexts or under different interpretations. Conversely, one and the same statement may be expressed by different sentences.

[16] *Ibid.*, p. 84.

[17] For the distinction between sentences and statements, see, e.g., P. F. Strawson, *Introduction to Logical Theory* (London: Methuen & Co., 1952), pp. 3–4. Notice, however, that I am using "statement" in a fairly wide sense here. In particular, I include moral and normative statements, but I am not presupposing that such statements are true or false.

Let us first consider case (b). The relation which holds between two statements p and q when p is a logical consequence of q may be defined or explained in different ways, depending upon one's choice of primitive concepts and upon the kind of problem which one is trying to answer. In this context, we may presuppose, as a primitive notion, the relation of inconsistency between statements.[18] We may then define logical consequence in the following simple way:

(D1) The statement p is a *logical consequence* of the statement q if, and only if, q is inconsistent with every statement which is inconsistent with p.

However, this definition is not applicable in case (a). It might then be suggested that one sentence is a logical consequence of another when the statement expressed by the former is a logical consequence, in the sense of (D1), of the statement expressed by the latter. But this will not do since a sentence may (usually) be interpreted in more than one way. We might say that (D 1) can be directly applied to sentences if we substitute "sentence" for "statement" throughout in my formulation of (D 1), but we are then faced with the problem of what it means for two sentences to be inconsistent. A reasonable answer to this is that two sentences are inconsistent when every interpretation of them is such that the statements expressed are inconsistent. However, unless we are prepared to maintain that no pair of (distinct) sentences is inconsistent, we must then distinguish between what is and what is not a (permissible) interpretation. This is rather difficult, at least in the case of a natural language, but in the present context we need only give a rough and partial characterization of the distinction in question.

We may conceive of an interpretation as a function which assigns statements to sentences in a certain way. For the sake of simplicity I shall require that the domain of an interpretation contain every sentence (of the language). If P is a sentence and i is an interpretation we may use the expression "$i(P)$" to denote the statement which is expressed by P according to i. Indeed, given (D 1) and the notion of an interpretation, we may then define logical consequence between sentences as follows:

(D 2) The sentence P is a *logical consequence* of the sentence Q if, and only if, $i(P)$ is a logical consequence of $i(Q)$ for every interpretation i.

But this definition would be much too narrow if *any* function from sentences to statements were an interpretation. There are at least two further conditions which must be satisfied. First, an interpretation must not involve any deviation from the standard meaning of purely logical terms like "not," "and," "or," "if . . .,"

---

[18] For a discussion of inconsistency between statements, see, e.g., Strawson, *Introduction to Logical Theory*, p. 2 ff.

then . . .," and so on. Secondly, it must satisfy some consistency requirement of the following kind: it does not imply that one and the same expression has different meanings when it occurs in two different sentences. This particular consistency requirement may be somewhat too strong for natural languages,[19] but we need not go into this problem here. For our purposes it will suffice to say that a given function is an interpretation if it satisfies the conditions mentioned above, but we need not exclude the possibility that some interpretation does not satisfy the last one. (It might be held that an interpretation should also be 'reasonable' from the point of view of common usage. I have no objection to this requirement, but it is usually omitted when one is interested in the purely logical relations between sentences. It seems that (D 2) would be wider or more liberal than usual if we add this requirement. However, for the sake of argument I shall not pay any attention to unreasonable interpretations in the sequel.)

The definitions (D 1) and (D 2) are probably not controversial. As far as I can see they are quite in accordance with the definitions which can be found in modern textbooks. For example, p is a logical consequence of q according to (D 1) if, and only if, q entails p according to P. F. Strawson's definition of entailment.[20] And (D 2) is very similar, in the relevant respects, to the definition of logical consequence which is offered by P. Suppes.[21]

4

Let us now return to our main problem. Is (2) a logical consequence of (1)? It seems that (1) and (2) may be regarded either as statements or as sentences, and I believe that it will be illuminating to distinguish between these two cases. I shall consider both.

Suppose, first, that (1) and (2) are statements. We may then use (D 1). It turns out that (2) is a logical consequence of (1) only if (1) is inconsistent with every statement that is inconsistent with (2). But it seems clear that this condition is *not* satisfied. (It might be objected that (2) is a moral statement and that moral statements are not inconsistent with any statement. If this were correct, then of course the condition would be trivially satisfied. But I shall assume that moral statements can be inconsistent with some statements. This assumption is surely very reasonable.) Consider, for example, the following statement:

(8)   Some actions which are generally approved are not right.

It seems clear that (8) is inconsistent with (2). Almost everyone would presumably agree to this. Moreover, (8) is not inconsistent with (1). In order to see this (which might be less obvious to some people) one should notice two

---

[19] This has been pointed out to me by Mr. Bengt Hansson of the University of Lund.
[20] Strawson, *Introduction to Logical Theory*, p. 20.
[21] P. Suppes, *Introduction to Logic* (Princeton, N.J.: D. Van Nostrand Company, 1957), p. 68; see also pp. 21–22 and 67.

things. First, (1) says something about the expressions "right" and "generally approved," but (8) does not say anything at all about these expressions. Conversely, (8) says something about actions, but (1) does not say anything about actions. The two statements are about wholly different subjects. Second, (1) does not say anything about the expressions which occur in (8). For, by hypothesis, (8) is a statement, and a statement does not contain or consist of any expressions at all. In particular, then, (1) does not say or imply that (8) is self-contradictory. At most, it says or implies that a certain sentence cannot be used to express (8). Neither does (8) say anything about (1). In short, there is no relation between (1) and (8) which prevents us from accepting both. We are therefore entitled to conclude that they are consistent. Hence, if (1) and (2) are statements, then, since at least one statement is inconsistent with (2) but not with (1), (2) is not a logical consequence of (1).

Let us then assume that (1) and (2) are sentences. Then, by (D 2), (2) is a logical consequence of (1) only if every interpretation *i* (of these sentences) is such that the statement expressed by (2) according to *i* is a logical consequence of the statement expressed by (1) according to *i*. But this condition is not satisfied either. For example, consider an interpretation according to which (1) expresses the statement that "right" means the same as "generally approved" and (2) expresses the statement that if an action is generally approved, then it is right. Such an interpretation does not seem unreasonable. But we have already seen that the latter statement is not a logical consequence of the former. Hence, even if (1) and (2) are sentences, (2) is not a logical consequence of (1).

It should be noticed that I do not want to deny that there may be *some* interpretation relative to which the statement expressed by (2) is a logical consequence of the statement expressed by (1). For example, if (1) expresses the statement that an action is right if and only if it is generally approved, and if (2) expresses the statement that an action is right if it is generally approved, then of course, with this particular interpretation, the statement expressed by (2) follows logically from the statement expressed by (1). But (2) does not follow from (1).

5

Has something gone wrong here? Let us consider a possible objection. It might be argued that (2) is analytic given (1), and that (2) must therefore be accepted by anyone who accepts (1). This might then be taken to show that (2) is a logical consequence of (1).

But this argument is surely invalid. Suppose, first, that (1) and (2) are statements. In this case I would be inclined to say that (2) *cannot* be analytic, since analyticity is a property of sentences. (Note, that the usual explanations of analyticity are in terms of synonymy, or the meaning of expressions, or linguistic rules.) However, we may perhaps say that a statement can be analytic in the sense that it is empty or that it follows logically from every statement. *If* (2) were analytic in this sense, then of course (2) would follow quite trivially from (1); but it does not follow from (1) that (2) *is* analytic. What follows from (1) is rather the following statement:

> (9) The sentence "If an action is generally approved, then it is right" is analytic;

but (9) is not equivalent to the statement that (2) is analytic. Neither is (9) equivalent to (2). I conclude that it is not the case that (2) is analytic given (1) when (1) and (2) are statements.

Secondly, suppose that (1) and (2) are sentences. They may then be interpreted in many different ways. On some of these interpretations (1) does indeed express a statement from which it follows that (2) is analytic. See, for example, the first interpretation mentioned in section 4. But on other interpretations (1) does not express such a statement. For example, see the last interpretation mentioned in section 4. Hence, the sentence (1) does not by itself entail or entitle us to conclude that (2) is analytic.

However, it might be held that there is something odd about those interpretations according to which (1) expresses a statement from which it follows that (2) is analytic and (2) expresses a non-empty statement which does not follow from the statement expressed by (1). I have used an interpretation of this kind in order to show that (2) does not follow from (1) if (1) and (2) are sentences; it might now be objected that such interpretations are inconsistent since, roughly speaking, they imply that (2) is both analytic and synthetic. As far as I can see, however, this objection is mistaken. Interpretations of this kind need not violate the consistency requirement indicated above (section 3). In particular, they do not imply that "right" and "generally approved" have one meaning in (1) and another in (2), for these terms do not occur in (1) at all. What occurs in (1) is rather " 'right' " and " 'generally approved.' " (These latter terms may reasonably be taken to denote or refer to "right" and "generally approved," respectively, but that is irrelevant here.) Moreover, it seems clear that we may propose or accept a certain interpretation of a given sentence without accepting the statement which is expressed by the sentence according to this interpretation. In particular, we may very well assign a statement to (1) from which it follows that (2) is analytic, without thereby committing ourselves to the view that (2) is analytic; hence, such an interpretation may consistently assign a non-empty statement to (2) which does not follow from the statement expressed by (1).

As a matter of fact, it seems correct to say that (2) is analytic given (1) only if (1) is a statement and (2) is a sentence. But (2) is apparently not a logical consequence of (1) in this case either—at least not in any ordinary sense. As far as I know, logical consequence is never conceived of as a relation between statements on the one hand and sentences on the other. Neither does it seem reasonable, even in this case, to maintain that one has to accept (2) if one accepts (1). In particular, what does it mean to 'accept' a sentence? Of course, if "to accept (2)" is now taken to mean the same as "to accept the statement that (2) is analytic," then I have no objection, but this is surely a very peculiar use of "accept."

In short, there seems to be no reason for rejecting my earlier conclusion that (2) does not follow from (1). Moreover, since my argument can easily be adapted to similar cases, we may also conclude that no definition of an ethical term entails or contains any moral principle. Some readers may find this trivial, but we have also seen that several moral philosophers appear to hold the opposite view.

Alf Ross

The Rise and Fall of the Doctrine of Performatives

1

The doctrine of performatives is eminently a one-man achievement. J. L. Austin discovered performatives in the late thirties. He delivered lectures on them for many years at Oxford under the title "Woods and Deeds." In his Harvard lectures in 1955, under the new title *"How to Do Things with Words,"* he presented the doctrine in a slightly revised form and actually stated his premises for the conclusion that the doctrine had to be abandoned as a mistake, without, however, drawing this conclusion. But he did draw it in "Performative Utterances," a talk delivered in The Third Programme of the BBC in 1956 and published in *Philosophical Papers* (1961).[1]

Austin is well-known as the author of the doctrine, but less well-known as the man who did away with it. Thus people continue to dispute the definition of "performatives" without discussing (or noticing?) Austin's virtual admission that the concept lacks any *rationale*. Nor does anyone seem to have tried to continue Austin's work where he left it, that is, to develop a general doctrine of speech acts and, in particular, to explain the true nature of the so-called performatives. In this paper I would like to offer a small contribution toward this end.

2

It is no easy task to give a precise account of Austin's definitive ideas about performatives. We have no presentation from his hand intended for publication.

Professor Ross, of the University of Copenhagen, is a native of Denmark.
[1] J. L. Austin, *How to Do Things with Words*, ed. J. O. Urmson (Oxford: Oxford University Press, 1962; hereafter cited as *Words*). The William James Lectures were delivered at Harvard University in 1955. J. L. Austin, "Performative Utterances," in *Philosophical Papers* (Oxford: Clarendon Press, 1961; hereafter cited as "Utterances").

Words is a posthumous editing of his Harvard lectures, based on his written notes; and "Utterances" is a recording of an unscripted broadcast talk. Neither gives a systematic presentation of the author's definitive views. Both present the ideas in dialectic evolution, with the express warning that everything said in the first sections is provisional and subject to revision in the light of later sections (*Words*, p. 4, n. 1; "Utterances," p. 228). This approach gives the reader a very interesting look into Austin's private workshop at the scrupulous and patient way in which he strove to solve the problems. But it does not, of course, facilitate the work of the interpreter. I should add that I find it difficult to grasp and reconstruct the line of reasoning in his lectures. As is commonly acknowledged, Austin had a most wonderful *esprit de finesse*, which made him sensitive to suitable distinctions and slight differences in modes of expression. He was less prone to stating the problems exactly and to giving precise answers. Reading him, I sometimes feel that I am in an exciting labyrinth, but have lost the thread of reasoning that brought me there and should take me out again.

Under these conditions, the only thing to do is to try to follow Austin's ideas in their dialectic evolution, restating or reconstructing the main roads of his thinking, its main problems, and his arguments and answers.

The starting point is the discovery of a type of utterance, of which the following are standard examples:

"I do (namely, take this woman to be my lawful wedded wife)"—as uttered in the course of the marriage ceremony.

"I name this ship the *Queen Elizabeth*"—as uttered when smashing the bottle against the stem.

"I give and bequeath my watch to my brother"—as occurring in a will.

"I bet you sixpence it will rain tomorrow."

"I promise to come."

Although utterances of this type appear grammatically as indicative statements, their logical function is different from that of statements. To say "I promise to come" is not a report of what I am doing (such as, e.g., "I am running")— it *is* to promise (whereas to say "I am running" is not to run). The same is the case in the other examples. There is an asymmetry between "I promise" (which is to make a promise) and "I promised" (which is a report of what I did) that does not exist between "I run" and "I ran."

The discovery of this type of utterance gives rise to the question of how it differs logically from normal statements such as "It is raining," "The cat is on the mat," etc.

Austin proposes that the difference may be stated in the following way:

Utterances of the type under consideration: (1) are the performing of an action (to promise, etc.) in contrast to merely saying something; and (2) cannot consequently be assessed as 'true or false,' but only as 'happy or unhappy.' A promise, e.g., is neither true nor false, but may be void, that is, it may go wrong because of circumstances on the occasion of its being made.

Normal statements, on the other hand: (1) are merely the saying of something, that is, 'describing' or 'reporting' something; and (2) can consequently be assessed as 'true or false' (*Words*, pp. 5–6, 132).

To express this distinction, Austin coined the term "performative" and "constative."

The presentation of the 'performatives' is the subject of his first lecture. In the second, third, and fourth lectures Austin presented his "doctrine of the *Infelicities*"; that is, he explained the various ways in which a performative can go wrong.

In elaborating this doctrine, Austin discovers that the distinction between the 'true/false' dimension and the 'happy/unhappy' dimension is not so clear and precise as it had seemed. On the one hand, the happiness of a performative is somehow dependent on the fulfillment of certain factual conditions (which amounts to the truth of certain statements; *Words*, pp. 45, 53; "Utterances," pp. 235, 238); and, on the other hand, statements, too, may be 'void' rather than false, e.g., "the present king of France is bald" (*Words*, pp. 20, 50–51; "Utterances," p. 235). This leads Austin to wonder whether the difference between performatives and constatives is really so great as his hypothesis implies (*Words*, p. 52). He begins to feel that the distinction is not as clear as it might be ("Utterances," p. 233), and this doubt motivates him to ask whether there were some precise way in which the performative could be definitely distinguished from the constative utterance; and, in particular, whether there were some grammatical (or lexicographical) criterion for distinguishing performative utterances (*Words*, p. 55; "Utterances," p. 228).

This is one point where I find it difficult to understand the drift of Austin's reasoning. I don't see how a grammatical criterion—if any could be found—could help him to meet the difficulty arising from his discovery that there is no clear-cut distinction between the true/false and the happy/unhappy dimensions. Indeed, I believe this to be a case where Austin has been taken in by his characteristic fondness for linguistic subtleties. One would think that when doubts arise as to the soundness of the second part of the hypothesis—concerning the distinction between true/false and happy/unhappy—the next step indicated in the investigation would be to inquire whether the first part of the distinction—the distinction between 'doing' and 'saying'—fares any better.

This in fact is what Austin, more by accident than by logical planning, finds himself doing. Having failed to find a grammatical criterion for performatives, he set out to make a list of performative verbs and in doing so discovered that utterances beginning "I state that . . ." also satisfy the requirements of performativeness insofar as they amount to performances of the action of stating something (*Words*, p. 91; "Utterances," pp. 234, 238).

At this point, Austin understands that something must be wrong with his original distinction between "saying something" and "doing something," and decides that to say something may be to do something. He concludes that it is time to make a fresh start on the problem:

> We want to reconsider more generally the senses in which to say something may be to do something, or in saying something we do something (and perhaps also to consider the different case in which *by* saying something we do something). Perhaps some clarification and definition here may help us out of our tangle (*Words*, p. 91).

Following this plan Austin elaborates his doctrine of the locutionary, illocutionary, and perlocutionary acts, to which I shall return. For the moment the question is what this doctrine implies with regard to his original distinction between performatives and constatives.

The answer should not be difficult, although Austin is reluctant to give it— as is easy to understand psychologically. He has clearly seen and stated that to perform any locutionary act (that is, any speech act, any utterance) is also and *eo ipso* to perform an illocutionary act. And this means that to say something is not merely to *say* something, but at the same time to *do* something in saying something, to perform an act (*Words*, p. 98). It seems inevitably to follow that the initial distinction between merely saying something and doing something is senseless. Austin states the problem frankly in the eleventh lecture:

> When we originally contrasted the performative with the constative utterance we said that
> (1) the performative should be doing something as opposed to just saying something; and
> (2) the performative is happy or unhappy as opposed to true or false.
> Were these distinctions really sound? Our subsequent discussion of doing and saying certainly seems to point to the conclusion that whenever I "say" anything (except perhaps a mere exclamation like "damn" or "ouch") I shall be performing both locutionary and illocutionary acts, and these two kinds of acts seem to be the very things which we tried to use as a means of distinguishing, under the names of "doing" and "saying," performatives from constatives. If we are in general always doing both things, how can our distinction survive? (*Words*, p. 132)

In *Words* his answer to this question is less frank and clear:

> The doctrine of the performative/constative distinction stands to the doctrine of locutionary and illocutionary acts in the total speech act as the *special* theory to the *general* theory (*Words*, p. 147).

It is difficult to understand how the 'special/general' relation can apply in the present case. True, we can isolate constatives by their specific 'force,' which differs from that of a piece of advice, an order, or a promise. We may, therefore, if we wish, classify the last mentioned utterances as 'non-constatives'—but not as 'performatives,' for their distinguishing mark is not to perform an action, but to perform an action of a different kind from the action performed by a constative.

There is, whether we like it or not, only one answer to the question of whether the original distinction can survive, and that answer is, "no." Austin himself gives it in his own the last version:

We see then that stating something is performing an act just as much as is giving an order or giving a warning; and we see, on the other hand, that, when we give an order a warning or a piece of advice, there is a question about how this is related to fact which is not perhaps so very different from the kind of question that arises when we discuss how a statement is related to fact. Well, this seems to mean that in its original form our distinction between the performative and the statement is considerably weakened, and indeed breaks down ("Utterances," p. 238).

3

So much for my interpretation of Austin. For my own part, I agree with his definitive rejection of the distinction between saying and doing something, and, consequently, with the conception of performatives as based on this distinction. What is amazing, in my opinion, is not that Austin ultimately destroyed his own creation, but that a man of his capability could ever have fallen for a distinction that is just as glaringly senseless as that between cows and animals. Austin sometimes states the distinction as that between *doing* something and *reporting* something (*Words*, pp. 13, 25). He might have asked a professional reporter whether, in reporting something, he was really doing nothing! I believe that the idea of regarding saying something as the opposite of doing something could have arisen only in the mind of a man to whom the use of words primarily meant their employment in the discussion of ideas. Such a man would be liable to forget that in a world created by the words of God, words still form a most powerful tool, as it were, in the mouth of man, often more powerful than the sword in his hand—a tool that can be used to create and destroy human relations of all kinds, to fight and rule, to guide and betray.

(Max Black believes that Austin's distinction, if it is to make sense, must be construed as a distinction between "saying something *true or false*" and "doing something other than saying something true or false."[2] I cannot accept this as a true interpretation of Austin's intention because it completely does away with the ideas that justify the use of the term "performative.")

We must clarify what the breakdown of the performative doctrine implies. We still have utterances of the type Austin discovered and labeled "performatives," and the problem of what logical peculiarities utterances of this type have still exists. The negative outcome of the attempt to characterize them as the performance of an action, rather than merely saying something, implies that it is unreasonable to continue to call them "performatives." With the breakdown of the underlying theory there is no more reason to conserve the term "performative."

Austin himself outlined a program for future research into the relation be-

---

[2] Max Black, "Austin on Performatives," *Philosophy* 38: 217 ff., 219 (1963).

tween saying and doing something. When it is understood that saying something and doing something are not exclusive, because any saying is at the same time also doing something, what we need is

> to consider all the ways and senses in which saying anything at all is doing this or that—because, of course, it is always doing a good many different things. And one thing that emerges when we do this, is that, besides the question that has been very much studied in the past as to what a certain utterance *means,* there is a further question distinct from this as to what was the *force,* as we may call it, of the utterance. We may be quite clear what "Shut the door" means, but not yet at all clear on the further point as to whether as uttered at a certain time it was an order, an entreaty or whatnot. What we need besides the old doctrine about meanings is a new doctrine about all the possible forces of utterances" ("Utterances," p. 238).

In his doctrine of the locutionary, the illocutionary, and the perlocutionary act, Austin laid down the foundation for future studies in what we could call the general theory of the speech act. There is no sign that Austin intended, through studies of this kind, to return to his initial problem—the problem of the logical peculiarities of utterances such as "I promise," "I bet," "I name," etc. (wrongly labeled "performatives"). But we might well expect studies of this kind to be able to illuminate the problem.

4

A brief account of the fundamentals of a theory of speech acts is thus called for.[3] In giving such an account, I do not intend to follow Austin. His presentation is couched in a terminology that is not only ponderous and inelegant, but also confusing. He distinguishes between the locutionary, the illocutionary, and the perlocutionary act, and, within the first of these, again between the phonetic, the phatic, and the rhetic act. This manner of speaking may easily mislead one into supposing that the classification is of different acts, although the terms are intended to designate only abstract aspects of one and the same act, the concrete speech act. My views also, to some degree, differ substantially from Austin's.

The subject we are studying is the concrete speech act, e.g., the utterance of the words "Shut the door" or "I shall be there" made by a certain person under certain conditions at a certain time. In studying this phenomenon, we may, however, concentrate on various aspects of it, abstracting from other aspects.

The speech act is essentially a phonetic act, i.e., the production of a sequence of sounds (or symbols for sounds). These sounds are psychophysical phenomena. Phonetics and the general theory of communication attempt to record the sound elements occurring in a particular language and to describe the processes by which the sounds are generated by a speaker, conveyed to another individual, and there received and apprehended. As a physical phenomenon, the phonetic

---

[3] For a more elaborate presentation of my ideas on this subject, see my book *Directives and Norms* (London: Routledge & Kegan Paul, 1968), p. 3 ff.

act may produce effects quite outside the process of communication, e.g., when by shouting, someone causes an avalanche in the Alps.

Not every production of a series of phonetically recognizable sounds is, however, a speech act. The phonetic act must further possess a structure which accords with the syntactical rules of the language concerned, i.e., the rules governing the ways in which the permitted linguistic elements may be combined into compound wholes. Included among these rules are those that govern the structure of sentences or *grammatical syntax*, according to which, for example, the word sequence "That failed of boys yesterday because" does not count as a sentence. Further, there is *syntax of formal logic* that rules out certain combinations of sentences, e.g., "It is raining and it is not raining."

Not every sentence whose structure is syntactically correct, however, can be used in a speech act. A speech act further requires that the sentence possess meaning. The following sentence (borrowed from Carnap), though grammatically correct, does not meet this last requirement: "Five per cent of the prime numbers, having as their father the concept of temperature and as their mother the number five, die, within a period of three years plus five pounds plus seven inches after their birth, of either typhoid fever or the square root of a democratic constitution."[4]

A phonetic sequence of correct syntactic structure with meaning forms the tool with which we operate when speaking; let us call it a locution. The utterance of a locution constitutes a speech act. As this act is not normally a reflex action, but a deliberate and purposive human act, it will normally be performed with the aim of producing certain effects. Of course, these effects will vary with the content of the speech act and, most likely, will depend on other factors as well. If it can be established that speech acts of a certain kind, taken according to content, are normally calculated to produce in a standard recipient under standard conditions effects of a certain kind (e.g., cognitive, emotional, or volitional effects), these effects will be said to be the *function* of that type of speech act.

Austin introduces the term "force" instead of "function." I don't follow him, because in my opinion his term is more obscure than the traditional one.)

I should like to point out, without becoming lost in the intricacies of the concept of 'function,' one very important aspect of that concept. The function of any tool should be determined by its *proper* effect, that is, the immediate effect to the production of which the tool is directly suited. Any further intended effects in the subsequent causal chain are irrelevant. If this qualification is not observed, the peculiar features of the tool and its use may go unmarked, and thus the concept of function may lose its point. The function of an ax is chopping (dependent upon its edge and weight) and hammering (dependent upon its blunt surface and weight). On the other hand, it would be unreasonable to talk about the 'inheritance-acquiring' function of an ax because it may be used to kill

4 Rudolf Carnap, *Einführung in die symbolische Logik* (Vienna: Springer, 1954), p. 76.

a testator. The only connection between this effect and the ax's properties is by way of the immediate function of the ax; as an instrument of murder the ax has to be used either as a chopper or as a 'blunt instrument.' The function of language must likewise be specified in terms of the immediate effects that a linguistic instrument of a certain shape is especially suited to produce. Certain communications, for example, are suited to convey information, that is, to bring about as their immediate effect the recipient's acceptance of a certain proposition. This, then, is their function. It is inexpedient to specify the function of this type of utterance, and hence to classify it, by the further intended effects of the conveyance of information.

(Authors often sin against this principle. Austin did so in giving the sign

This bull is dangerous
(Signed) John Jones

as an example of an illocutionary act whose force is to warn [*Words*, p. 62, cf. pp. 74, 109, 155]. The proper effect of an utterance of this kind is obviously to convey information, and the warning is a further effect to which the information stands in an instrumental relation. *By* informing people of the bull's character, Jones warns them against entering the premises. Under other conditions—for example, if the dangerous specimens in a stock are to be separated out for a special treatment—the same information may produce other reactions.)

The functions of any tool vary with the specific properties of the tool. The functions of an ax, therefore, are different from those of a violin. The tool used in speech is a locution (a meaningful sentence), and the functions for which it is used in a speech act must be supposed to vary with the specific properties of the locution. Pragmatic linguistic studies, therefore, must be based on a classification of various kinds of locutions derived from a description of their specific properties.

It would lead us too far afield to go deeper into the study of linguistic functions. Briefly, it must suffice to mention that I regard indicative speech and directive speech as two fundamental (though not exhaustive) kinds of speech. In indicative speech, the locution expresses a *proposition* (the idea of a topic conceived as part of reality); in directive speech, the locution expresses a *directive* (an action-idea conceived as a pattern of behavior). Each of these instruments may be used with a number of different functions. Thus, for example, to assert a proposition is to use it with an informative function, while to 'pose' it is to use it with what I call a "fabulating function" (as in the case of fictions, hypotheses). Each of these functions may be subdivided into various kinds. The normal use of a directive in communication is to advance it with one or another of a wide range of directive functions, for example, as a coercive command, an authoritative command, a claim, an invitation, a request, a suggestion, a supplication, an entreaty, a piece of advice, a warning, a recommendation, an instruction for use, an exhortation, a legal or conventional rule, a rule of a game, or a moral principle or judgment.

5

I refer the interested reader to another publication of mine for further elaboration of the views hinted at here.[5] The important point to stress is that one and the same locution, according to circumstances, may be used with different functions. If, e.g., *A* utters the locution "I shall be there," it does not appear from the words alone whether they are used with an informative function as a prediction of what will happen; or with a fabulating function as part of an imaginary vision of the future; or with a normative (directive) function as a promise. And if *A* says to *B* "Shut the door," this may be meant as a command, or an invitation, an entreaty, a piece of advice, a warning, a part of the instructions for the use of something, or an exhortation; or the same words may appear in a legal or conventional rule, in a rule of a game, and probably in many other ways.

In most cases the function of a communication appears unambiguously from the situation. When a bankrobber uses the locution "Hand over the money," no further indication is likely to be required to make it clear that this is meant as a coercive command and not as friendly advice. However, the opposite interpretation is obvious in the case of the doctor telling his patient to take his medicine three times a day.

If the situation is not unambiguous, the speaker may use various linguistic and non-linguistic devices to indicate his intention. Tone of voice, cadence, and emphasis are different when the same locution is used as a command, a piece of advice, or an entreaty. The speaker may accompany the utterance of the words with gestures (winks, pointings, shruggings, frowns, etc.), facial expressions, and similar behavior. He may also qualify the locution by means of small additions. "Shut the door, *please*," "Shut the door, *do you hear me*," and "*Well*, shut the door," function in different ways. "I shall *probably* be there" clearly has an informative function, whereas, "I shall, *on my honor*, be there" is a promise.

The speaker may also, in additional remarks, explicitly inform his audience about how his locution is to be taken. We possess in our language names for many of the pragmatic functions, and if no name exists, it is possible by circumscription to explain the intended function. Here are some examples:

"Shut the door—and that is an order."
"Shut the door—that is the best advice I can give you."
"Shut the door—that is my earnest request to you."
"I shall be there—that is a promise."
"I shall be there—I believe so as a matter of fact, although I know my weak character."

Finally, when there is a name for a certain function, there will usually also be a corresponding verb that may be used by the speaker to indicate his inten-

---

[5] *Directives and Norms*, pp. 9–10, 34 ff.

tion. This is of special interest for our investigation. Corresponding to the utterances just mentioned are:

"I *order* you to shut the door."
"I *advise* you to shut the door."
"I *request* you to shut the door."
"I *promise* you that I shall be there."
"I *predict* that I shall be there."

We have found our way back to utterances of that type that Austin labeled "performatives" and are now able to understand their true logical peculiarity. It is true that to say "I order you to . . ." *is* to order you. But this does not mean that such an utterance is more the performance of an action than *any* utterance is the performance of an action—the use of a locution in one of its possible functions. To say "It is raining" is also to perform an action, namely, the action of informing about a fact. The true logical peculiarity is that in utterances of this kind we are using a peculiar linguistic device to indicate the function of a locution. This device consists in the use of a verb that indicates the function of the speech act. The peculiarity is to be found not in the meaning or function of the utterance, but exclusively in the linguistic device used to indicate its function. The utterance "I order you to shut the door" has the same meaning and function as the utterance "Shut the door" said under circumstances indicating that it is intended as an order. The peculiar trait of the first utterance is the occurrence of a *phrase* of the type "I order." The notion that we need to name this peculiar trait is the notion of *function-indicating verbs and phrases*.

Austin was well aware of this linguistic device. He spoke of "verbs which make explicit, as we shall now say, the illocutionary force of an utterance," (*Words*, p. 149) and wrote a list of almost 200 such verbs. He calculated that a complete list would comprise between 1,000 and 10,000 items. But his ideas remained confused as long as he conflated the force-determining function with his original theory of performatives. Austin seemingly continued to regard the illocutionary verbs as performatives (*Words*, pp. 42, 81, 85).

In spite of the great number of function-indicating verbs, appropriate classificatory names are in some cases lacking. There is, for example, no name or verb generally suited to indicate that propositions are used with what I have called a "fabulating function." In some cases such verbs as "to suppose," "to assume," or "to imagine" may be used. The fictitious character of a literary work is usually (if necessary) indicated by a title ("a novel," "Now I am going to tell you a story").

It is commonly accepted that utterances using function-indicating phrases are not reports about what the speaker is doing and therefore not true or false *as reports*. (Utterances beginning "I assert," "I state as a fact," "I maintain," etc., can be true or false as assertions, statements, etc.) Austin asserted this as obvious and would not argue it (*Words*, p. 6). However, some writers do maintain that 'performatives' (as they misleadingly continue to call utterances of this kind) are true or false according to whether the 'performative' effect is realized or not.[6] For example, it is said that a promise-'performative' expresses a true proposition if and only if a promise has come about through the speaker's utterance of the promise-'performative' to the hearer. The utterance "I promise to come" expresses a true proposition if and only if by so saying a promise has come into existence. This is an empirically verifiable state of affairs. In law the conditions under which a promise comes into existence are defined rather precisely. But even outside the area of law, whether or not a person has made a promise by saying certain words under certain conditions is—at least in principle—empirically verifiable.[7]

Although I agree with Max Black that, "This way of looking at the speech episode looks wilfully perverse," and that "It would require a perverse attachment to what Austin used to call the 'descriptive fallacy' to insist that the promise-maker is primarily making a truth-claim," it may be appropriate to plead some arguments in favor of the commonly accepted view.[8]

(a) The true/false doctrine presupposes that the utterance "I promise . . ." is a *report* of what the speaker is doing. This interpretation is obviously contrary to the intention of the speaker. He intends to make a promise, to bind himself to a certain performance, not to inform his audience about anything.

(b) A report is different from the reported subject: the report that a war is going on is different from the war; the report that I am writing a letter, different from the writing of the letter. In the same way, the report that I am making a promise must be different from the making of the promise. But how, then, is the promise made? It is made by uttering the words "I promise." Hence, these words both constitute the act of promising and express a report about this act. However, that is an absurdity. If the act of uttering the words "I promise . . ." is the making of a promise, the *meaning* of the utterance cannot be to state as a fact that the speaker is making a promise, that is, that he is uttering the words "I promise." You could just as well say that to deal a man a blow on the nose is to inform him that he has received a blow on the nose.

(c) The report-interpretation is contrary to the grammatical fact that a report of what is going on in English is expressed in the so-called continuous present tense: "I am writing," "I am promising," etc. If "I promise" is to be taken as a report, it is as the so-called *habitual* indicative ("I promise every New Year to lead a better life").

(d) I suspect that the report-interpretation will lead us into all the intricacies connected with self-referring propositions, but, at present, I am not inclined to go further into this matter.[9]

[6] E. J. Lemmon, "On Sentences Verifiable by Their Use," *Analysis* 22: 86–89 (1961–62); Ingemar Hedenius, "Performatives," *Theoria* 29: 115 ff. (1963).
[7] Hedenius, "Performatives," pp. 117–18.
[8] Black, "Austin on Performatives," pp. 214, 218; cf. Erik Ryding, "The Truth Value of Promises," *Theoria* 33: 148 ff. (1967), published after this paper was written.
[9] Compare my paper "On Self-Reference and a Puzzle in Constitional Law," *Mind* 88:1ff. (1969).

6

We are now in a position to understand better how it was possible for Austin to be lured into the 'performative' fallacy. Almost all speech acts may be performed with or without explicit function-indicating phrases. The use of such phrases is called for whenever situation and context do not make the speaker's intention sufficiently clear. On the other hand, if the intention otherwise is sufficiently indicated, it is redundant to use explicit function-indicating phrases.

This explains why phrases indicating the informative use of locutions are used rather rarely. It is a fundamental norm of communication—more exactly, the norm that makes informative communication possible at all—that, whenever indicatives (propositions) are used in a speech act, they shall be taken as having an informative function, unless a fabulating or any other function is indicated, either expressly by the speaker or by the situation, according to special conventions.[10] This means that when someone utters the locution "It is raining," it is assumed to be an assertion with an informative function and not a fabulation (unless occurring in a novel, or as part of a theoretical hypothesis), a question (unless indicated by tone of voice), or what not. For this reason, explicit phrases indicating an informative function—such as "I assert that . . .," "I state as a fact that . . . ," "I maintain that . . ." are not commonly used in the communication of information, but only when special circumstances demand them. For example:

A. £10 are missing from my wallet.
B. (indignant) I haven't touched it!
A. I simply state as a fact that £10 are missing.

Because *B* has taken *A*'s first utterance as implying the suspicion that *B* has taken the money, there is good reason for *A* explicitly to indicate that his intention is purely informative. But it would be odd if the housemaid, instead of simply saying that dinner was ready, announced: "I state it as a fact that dinner is ready."

It is understandable, therefore, that Austin thought of constatives as being in the form of simple locutions without function-indicating phrases ("It is raining," "The cat is on the mat"); and that, comparing them with utterances such as "I promise . . .," "I bet . . .," "I name . . .," it occurred to him that there is a fundamental, logical difference between the two types of utterances, a difference he expressed in the 'performative' doctrine. It is easy now to see that the difference really stems from a difference between the linguistic means of expression used in the two locutions. The logical confrontation should be either between two explicitly formulated locutions or between two locutions without explicit function-indicating phrases. "I promise . . ." should be compared with "I state . . .," and "I shall, on my honor, be there" with "It is raining." If the comparison had been carried out in this way, it would not have given rise to the fallacy that to produce

[10] See *Directives and Norms*, pp. 19 ff.

the one type of utterance—the 'performative'—is to do something and to produce the other type is merely to say something.

7

Austin classified the illocutionary verbs (i.e., the verbs which make explicit the illocutionary force of an utterance) into five groups:

Verdictives, as the name implies, typified by the giving of a verdict by a
  jury, arbitrator, or umpire; examples are to acquit, to convict, to find;
Exercitives, which indicate the exercising of powers, rights, or influence such
  as appointing, bequeathing, granting, repealing;
Commissives, typified by promising or otherwise undertaking;
Behavitives, which have to do with attitudes and social behavior; examples
  are apologizing, congratulating, condoling, challenging; and
Expositives, which make plain how our utterances fit into the course of an
  argument or conversation; examples are "I reply," "I concede," "I
  postulate," "I assume" (*Words*, pp. 150 ff.).

It will easily be seen that the verbs of the first three categories are primarily used in legal language or in language concerned with conventional rules and human relations derived from them, whereas this is not the case with regard to the two last classes. This fact reflects a fundamental distinction within the function verbs, a distinction that has been blurred in Austin's fivefold division.

The special group of function verbs to which I refer consists of those which are names of *normative acts*. To explain what this means I shall say something about the more special concept of a *legal act*.[11]

In legal rules, legal consequences are attached to conditioning facts. These we shall call the *operative facts*.[12] They may be of many kinds, including *human acts*. The act of killing another man is an example of a human act which is an operative fact; in legal rules a number of legal consequences are attached to the performance of this act. Among the operative human acts are also *verbal acts*, for example, the issuing of libelous utterances. Among these verbal operative human acts is a special group, consisting of linguistic communications whose legal effect is determined by the content of the communication itself, and which are thus suitable instruments of conscious human activity directed precisely toward the creation of legal rules and relations. Operative acts of this kind are called *legal acts*, e.g., statutes, judicial decisions, administrative resolutions, promises, wills, and contracts.

Any legal act presupposes a legal norm determining the necessary and sufficient conditions under which the legal act comes into existence. Such a norm is

---

[11] I propose the use of this term instead of the more ponderous *"acte juridique"* and "act-in-the-law" commonly used in the English literature.

[12] See my book *On Law and Justice*, chap. 9 (London: Stevens & Sons, 1958).

called a norm of competence, and the power it creates for some person (or body of persons) to perform a certain legal act is called a competence.

The conditions defining a competence usually fall into three groups: (1) those that prescribe what person (or persons) is qualified to perform the act that creates the norm (*personal competence*); (2) those that prescribe the procedure to be followed (*procedural competence*); and (3) conditions that prescribe the possible scope of the created norm with regard to its subject, situation, and theme (*substantial competence*).

Since a norm of competence prescribes the conditions for the creation of a norm, it is a tautology to say that if an attempt is made to exercise competence *ultra vires* (outside the scope of the competence) no legal norm is created. This is expressed by saying that the intended legal act (act-in-the-law) is invalid or that non-compliance with a norm of competence results in invalidity.

It is a conspicuous feature of the law of modern societies that the norms of competence in force can be divided into two distinct categories, different in their content and in the purposes they serve in the life of the community.

On the one hand, there are those rules of competence that create the power we call *private autonomy*. They are characterized by the following features. In the personal sphere they create a power for every normal adult individual. This power is in all important respects limited to the individual's ability to incur liabilities and to dispose of matters concerning his own rights. When the dispositions of two or more individuals are coordinated, these individuals are enabled to 'legislate' by contract as far as their mutual relations are concerned. This power is not bound up with a duty to exercise it, or to exercise it only in a certain way. The individual is free to decide whether, and how, he will make use of his autonomy. The social function of private autonomy is to enable the individual to shape his own legal relationships, in accordance with his own interests, within the framework of the legal order. The power itself in relation to a certain object is not a 'right' but is part of a transferable right. With the transference of the right, the power is lost to the successor. The power that we are here considering may therefore be said to be *unqualified* (everyone has it), *autonomous* (it is used to bind the competent person himself), *discretionary* (it is exercised freely), and *transferable* (it can, in certain relations, be transferred to a successor).

On the other hand, there are the rules of competence that create what we call a *public authority*. They have the following features. They create a power only for certain qualified persons. The required qualification consists in a designation in accordance with certain rules of law: in Denmark, Ministers have their power because of their nomination according to Article 14 of the Constitution, members of Parliament because of their election according to the Polling Act, and the King because of his hereditary right to the throne according to the Act of Succession. The substance of this power is a capacity to create rules that bind others (statutory enactments, judgments, administrative acts). The power is not granted with a view to its being used by the competent person freely and at his convenience. Its exercise is a duty, a public office in the widest sense, and when a person exercises it, it is his duty to use the power in an unprejudiced and impartial manner, for the furtherance of certain social purposes. These duties are more than merely moral duties: they are constrained by sanctions and controls of various kinds. The social function of the power is to serve the interests of the community—what is called the 'commonweal.' Public authority is never part of a right and is therefore never transferable. At most, the exercise of power may be delegated to other persons, with the holder's own power left untouched. The competence that we are here considering may therefore be characterized as *qualified, heteronomous, in the public interest,* and *non-transferable.*

The distinction between private autonomy and public authority constitutes the basis of the traditional distinction between private and public law. Public law may be defined as the law which concerns the legal status of the public authorities.

Legal acts play a prominent role in the life of the individual and the society, whether undertaken by the private citizen in the exercise of his autonomy and for the purpose of regulating his relations to other citizens, or by the public authorities in the exercise of their office and with the purpose of coordinating the lives of the citizens under the government.

In performing a legal act the speaker (or writer) indeed "does things with words" in a special sense. The specific effects of his act are different as well from the effects depending solely upon *linguistic* conventions and norms of communication (e.g., the informative effect), as from the further psychological and behavioristic effects evoked through the impact of the locution on the mind of his audience (e.g., by giving a man some information you may motivate him to commit suicide, sell his house, divorce his wife, or what not). The specific effects of the legal act are dependent on the existence of a legal order as a social institution working through a legal machinery comprising legislative, administrative, and judicial organs. This is a most complicated affair which we cannot try to explain in this connection. Here the important thing is to emphasize that because the legal order empowers the competent person or body of persons to release by their words the forces that move the legal machinery, the performance of a legal act comes to look like magic: the words create the effect they name.

We may now shape the notion of a *conventional act* by analogy with that of a legal act. It comprises utterances that are operative according to the intention of their author and the words used, and whose force derives not from a legal order but from normative orders of a different kind, e.g., conventional morality or the rules of a game. To promise, for example, may as well be a conventional act as a legal act. Most everyday promises are not legally binding and enforceable. The conventional norms of competence that define the conditions under which a promissory utterance is conventionally binding, however, are much less precise than the corresponding legal rules. Whereas to name (christen) a child or to name a ship by registering it in a ship's register are legal acts with definite legal consequences, to name a dog or a horse (or a ship in a [christening] ceremony) is a conventional act calling forth expectations and reactions of a less definite and precise character. However, if the family has decided that the name of their pet dog is to be "Caesar," it will be out of order if some visitor insists on calling it "Brutus." The verdict given by the referee in a football game is similar to a judicial decision, and the bylaws of a choral society similar to state legislation.

We may generalize the notions of a legal act and a conventional act in the concept of a *normative act*. It is worth noting that most of Austin's 'performatives'—the verdictives, exercitives, commissives, and some of the behavitives—are normative acts, or, as we could say, to continue the jargon, *normatives*. His standard examples in the first lectures were all of this kind. It is true that to utter a normative is, in a special sense, to perform an action. This is a second circumstance suited to explain how Austin came upon his performative thesis. If any kind of utterance is entitled to the name "performative," it must be the normatives. I believe, however, that the term "performative" is fraught with so many fallacies that it is better to get rid of it and choose other, more adequate terminology, e.g., the term "normative."

We have now discovered the logical peculiarities of that kind of utterances which Austin labeled "performatives": linguistically, they are characterized by the occurrence of a function-indicating phrase; functionally, some of them are operatives.

Stig Kanger and Helle Kanger

Rights and Parliamentarism

Introduction

It is almost a truism that the idea of having a right is vague and ambiguous, and that it can be approached from many angles. It is also clear that good explications of this idea are needed in many fields, but one can hardly say that the attempts to provide them have been very successful. The best attempts, so far, at an explication or analysis of the notion of a right are found in jurisprudence. Hohfeld's contribution should especially be mentioned in this connection. The object of the first part of this essay is to give an analysis of the concept of a right which, in certain respects, is a further development of Hohfeld's distinctions.[1]

The analysis of the notion of a right appears to have some applications in political science. The object of the second part of the essay is to provide an example of such an application. First, the notion of a position structure in government is introduced. Roughly speaking, the position structure is the system of rights to appoint and to dismiss members of the government and to dissolve the parliament which parties like the head of state, the parliament, and the government have towards each other. There is a large number of logically possible position structures, but only a few of them are politically feasible. These are characterized by certain political axioms. Among the feasible position structures, we shall finally distinguish those that are characteristic for parliamentarism.

Professor and Mrs. Stig Kanger, of the University of Uppsala, are natives of Sweden.

Reprinted, with changes, from *Theoria*, vol. 32, pp. 85–115 (1966), with permission of the authors and editor.

[1] The first part is a translation (with minor changes) of the essay "Rättighetsbegreppet" by Stig Kanger, which is contained in *Sju filosofiska studier tillägnade Anders Wedberg* (Stockholm, 1963).

213

PART I. THE CONCEPT OF A RIGHT

1. *The Simple Types of Rights*

Consider the following two examples:

X has a right to have back what he has lent to Y.
X has a right to publish in Sweden a manuscript he has written.

The concept of right which appears in these two examples can be made precise in at least two ways:

(1) One generally regards a right as a relation which a party X has versus a party Y, and which concerns a given state of affairs between X and Y. The examples can be made more precise so that the relational character of the right appears more distinctly. Thereby, they get a somewhat schematic and artificial formulation:

X has versus Y a right to the effect that X receive from Y what X has lent to Y.
X has versus the Swedish state a right that a manuscript written by X be published in Sweden.

(2) Rights can be of different types. X's right versus Y appears to be of the type 'claim,' and X's right versus the state can perhaps be said to be of the type 'power.' The examples can be made more precise so that the types of rights under consideration are indicated:

X has versus Y a claim to the effect that X receive from Y what X has lent to Y.
X has versus the Swedish state a power to the effect that a manuscript written by X be published in Sweden.

We shall now distinguish eight types of rights, which we shall call the *simple types* of rights:

(a)   claim
(b)   freedom
(c)   power
(d)   immunity
(a′)   counterclaim
(b′)   counterfreedom
(c′)   counterpower
(d′)   counterimmunity

The types (a′) to (d′) have a close connection with the types (a) to (d), respectively. To say, e.g., that X has versus Y a counterclaim which concerns a state of affairs S between X and Y is (by definition) the same as to say that X has versus Y a claim which concerns the opposite to S between X and Y. We have thus the following four synonym pairs (where S(X, Y) stands for the state of affairs S between X and Y):

$\begin{cases} \text{X has versus Y a counterclaim to the effect that } S(X, Y) \\ \text{X has versus Y a claim to the effect that not-}S(X, Y) \end{cases}$

$\begin{cases} \text{X has versus Y a counterfreedom to the effect that } S(X, Y) \\ \text{X has versus Y a freedom to the effect that not-}S(X, Y) \end{cases}$

$\begin{cases} \text{X has versus Y a counterpower to the effect that } S(X, Y) \\ \text{X has versus Y a power to the effect that not-}S(X, Y) \end{cases}$

$\begin{cases} \text{X has versus Y a counterimmunity to the effect that } S(X, Y) \\ \text{X has versus Y an immunity to the effect that not-}S(X, Y) \end{cases}$

2. An Explication of the Simple Types of Rights

We shall now give an interpretation of the following four rights-propositions:

(1a)   X has versus Y a claim to the effect that S(X, Y)
(1b)   X has versus Y a freedom to the effect that S(X, Y)
(1c)   X has versus Y a power to the effect that S(X, Y)
(1d)   X has versus Y an immunity to the effect that S(X, Y)

The interpretation we intend to set forth yields an explication of the simple types (a) to (d) of rights, and thereby also of the types (a') to (d'). It will be formulated in a semiformalized language and it has the advantage that the differences between the simple types of rights are carried over into logical differences which can be expressed by the positions of the symbol, "not," of negation and the variables X and Y. The interpretation of (1a) through (1d) is as follows:

(2a)   It shall be that Y sees to it that S(X, Y)
(2b)   Not: it shall be that X sees to it that not-S(X, Y)
(2c)   Not: it shall be that not: X sees to it that S(X, Y)
(2b)   It shall be that not: Y sees to it that not-S(X, Y)[2]

Instead of the expression:

Not: it shall be that not: . . .

we may use the synonymous expression:

It may be that . . .

With this interpretation, the examples of § 1 become:

---

[2] The interpretation is, in all essential respects, identical with that which was given in S. Kanger, *New Foundations for Ethical Theory* (Stockholm, 1957).

It shall be that Y sees to it that X receive from Y what X has lent to Y. It may be that X sees to it that a manuscript written by X be published in Sweden.

The concepts 'shall' and 'seeing to it,' which are used in the interpretation, are vague and admit different specifications in different contexts. The question of how they are to be made precise, however, we may leave open here. We shall assume only that they are interpreted in a reasonable way, and that they satisfy certain logical principles.

Let F and G be arbitrary propositions or conditions. Let us write shall-F in place of the longer expression: it shall be that F. Let X be an arbitrarily chosen party. Let the arrow $\longrightarrow$ denote the relation of logical consequence.[3] Among the logical principles which the concepts 'shall' and 'seeing to it' are assumed to satisfy, we then have the following five:

   I.   If F$\longrightarrow$G, then shall-F$\longrightarrow$shall-G
  II.   (Shall-F and shall-G)$\longrightarrow$shall-(F and G)
 III.   Shall-F$\longrightarrow$not shall-(not-F)
  IV.   If F$\longrightarrow$G and G$\longrightarrow$F, then X sees to it that F$\longrightarrow$X sees to it that G
   V.   X sees to it that F$\longrightarrow$F

Finally, our notion of a state of affairs needs some comment. By a state of affairs we shall, in this essay, always mean a relation between parties. If X and Y are parties, S(X, Y) means that the party X stands in the relation S to the party Y. S may, for instance, be specified as the relation between any two parties P_1 and P_2 such that P_1 receives from P_2 what P_1 has lent to P_2. Then, of course, S(X, Y) means: X receives from Y what X has lent to Y. We shall note that X or Y need not always occur in S(X, Y) when S is specified. Thus—to allude to a specification with which we shall be concerned subsequently—S(X, Y) may become: X resigns as prime minister. Here Y does not occur.

3. *Some Relations among the Simple Types of Rights*

As a direct consequence of the logical principles I–V and the explication of the simple types of rights, we get the synonymity of certain rights-propositions. Thus we get the following four pairs of synonyms:

$\Big\{$ X has versus Y a claim to the effect that S(X, Y)
  Not: Y has versus X a freedom to the effect that not-S(X, Y)

$\Big\{$ X has versus Y a freedom to the effect that S(X, Y)
  Not: Y has versus X a claim to the effect that not-S(X, Y)

---

[3] Thus F$\rightarrow$G if G follows from F by ordinary logic extended in a suitable way with logical principles for the concepts shall and seeing to it. Note that the relation $\rightarrow$ is assumed to fulfill principles like:
(i) if F and if F$\longrightarrow$G, then G;
(ii) if F$\longrightarrow$G, then not-G$\longrightarrow$not-F;
(iii) if F$\longrightarrow$G and G$\longrightarrow$H, then F$\longrightarrow$H.

$$\begin{cases} \quad\quad \text{X has versus Y a power to the effect that } S(X, Y) \\ \text{Not:} \quad \text{Y has versus X an immunity to the effect that not-}S(X, Y) \end{cases}$$

$$\begin{cases} \quad\quad \text{X has versus Y an immunity to the effect that } S(X, Y) \\ \text{Not:} \quad \text{Y has versus X a power to the effect that not-}S(X, Y) \end{cases}$$

Another consequence of the principles I–V and the explication is that certain rights-propositions of the kinds (1a)–(1d) are logical consequences of others of these kinds. In order to exhibit these relationships of logical strength in a simple diagram, we introduce some abbreviations. We shall write:

Cl(X, Y, S) for X has versus Y a claim to the effect that S(X, Y)

Fr(X, Y, S) for X has versus Y a freedom to the effect that S(X, Y)

Po(X, Y, S) for X has versus Y a power to the effect that S(X, Y)

Im(X, Y, S) for X has versus Y an immunity to the effect that S(X, Y)

Cl(Y, X, S̃) for Y has versus X a claim to the effect that S(X, Y)

Fr(Y, X, S̃) for Y has versus X a freedom to the effect that S(X, Y)

Po(Y, X, S̃) for Y has versus X a power to the effect that S(X, Y)

Im(Y, X, S̃) for Y has versus X an immunity to the effect that S(X, Y)

Note the difference between Cl(Y, X, S̃) and Cl(Y, X, S). The latter expression means: Y has versus X a claim to the effect that S(Y, X).

We now have the following strength diagram:

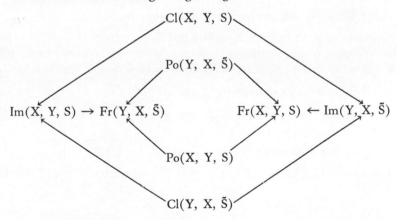

4. *Atomic Types of Rights*

A right which a party X has versus a party Y and which concerns a given state of affairs S between X and Y is not completely characterized by merely saying, e.g., that X has versus Y a power that S(X, Y). In order to illustrate this, let us return to the second example of § 1:

X has versus the Swedish state a right to the effect that a manuscript written by X be published in Sweden.

The right we are considering here is the so-called freedom of the press, and what we wish to say in the example is not only what was stated in § 1, viz.:

X has versus the Swedish state a power to the effect that a manuscript written by X be published in Sweden (i.e., X may see to it that the manuscript is published in Sweden),

but also that:

X has versus the Swedish state an immunity to the effect that a manuscript written by X be published in Sweden (i.e., the state may not see to it that the manuscript is not published in Sweden),

and, naturally, also that:

X has versus the Swedish state a counterpower to the effect that a manuscript written by X be published in Sweden (i.e., X may see to it that the manuscript is not published in Sweden),

and

X has versus the Swedish state a counterimmunity to the effect that a manuscript written by X be published in Sweden (i.e., the state may not see to it that the manuscript is published in Sweden).

The type of right in this example can thus be more closely stated not only as power, but as:

Power, immunity, counterpower, counterimmunity,

and we can restate the example by saying that X has versus the Swedish state a right of the type: power, immunity, counterpower, counterimmunity to the effect that a manuscript written by X be published in Sweden.

If we go back to the first example of § 1:

X has versus Y a right to the effect that X receive from Y what X has lent to Y,

we may assert that it states two things:

X has versus Y a claim to the effect that X receive from Y what X has lent to Y,

and

Not: X has versus Y a power to the effect that X receive from Y what X has lent to Y.

The type of right here is:

Claim, not power,

and we may restate the example by saying that X has versus Y a right of the type: 'claim, not power' to the effect that X receive from Y what X has lent to Y.

Both the type: power, immunity, counterpower, counterimmunity, and the type: claim, not power, are complete in a certain sense: any additional specification of them with the help of simple types of rights or negated simple types is either unnecessary or inconsistent.

We shall now list all the types of rights which are complete in this way. We call them the *atomic types* of rights. Our method is as follows: We start with the list:

Cl(X, Y, S)
Fr(X, Y, S)
Po(X, Y, S)
Im(X, Y, S)
Counter-Cl(X, Y, S)
Counter-Fr(X, Y, S)
Counter-Po(X, Y, S)
Counter-Im (X, Y, S)

and every list we can obtain from the above by negating one or more lines of it. There are 256 such lists, but some of them are inconsistent according to the strength diagram. A list which contains, e.g., the lines:

not Fr(X, Y, S)
not Counter-Po(X, Y, S)

is inconsistent, since the negation of the last line, i.e. Counter-Po(X, Y, S), is synonymous with: not Im(Y, X, S̃), which follows from: not Fr(X, Y, S), by the strength diagram.

We omit the inconsistent lists and then go through every one of the remaining 26 consistent lists and reduce them by striking out each unnecessary line, i.e. each line of the list which, according to the strength diagram, is a logical consequence of another line of the list. In a list where the lines:

Cl(X, Y, S)
not Counter-Po(X, Y, S)

appear, we thus cross out the latter line since it is synonymous with Im(Y, X, S̃), which, according to the diagram, follows from Cl(X, Y, S).

Each reduced list now indicates exactly one atomic type of right, and each atomic type of right is indicated by exactly one reduced list.

The 26 atomic types of rights are the following:

1. Power, not immunity, counterpower, not counterimmunity.
2. Not power, immunity, not counterpower, counterimmunity.
3. Claim, not counterfreedom.
4. Not claim, power, immunity, counterfreedom, not counterpower, not counterimmunity.
5. Power, immunity, counterpower, counterimmunity.
6. Claim, power, counterfreedom.
7. Claim, not power.

8. Power, immunity, counterfreedom, not counter power, counterimmunity.
9. Power, immunity, counterpower, not counter immunity.
10. Power, not immunity, not counterpower, counterimmunity.
11. Not freedom, counterclaim.
12. Freedom, not power, not immunity, not counterclaim, counterpower, counter immunity.
13. Freedom, counterclaim, counterpower.
14. Counterclaim, not counterpower.
15. Freedom, not power, immunity, counterpower, counterimmunity.
16. Power, not immunity, counterpower, counterimmunity.
17. Not power, immunity, counterpower, not counterimmunity.
18. Not power, not immunity, not counterpower, not counterimmunity.
19. Not claim, not counterfreedom, not counterimmunity.
20. Not counterfreedom, counterimmunity.
21. Not claim, not power, immunity, not counterpower, not counterimmunity.
22. Power, not immunity, not counterpower, not counterimmunity.
23. Not freedom, not immunity, not counterclaim.
24. Not freedom, immunity.
25. Not power, not immunity, not counterclaim, not counterpower, counterimmunity.
26. Not power, not immunity, counterpower, not counterimmunity.

These 26 types of rights can be displayed together as in the following diagram:

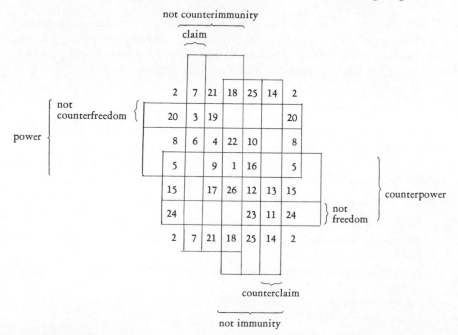

We see that we have here three atomic types of rights which come under the simple type of claim, namely, nos. 3, 6, and 7. We see also that we have 23 atomic types which come under freedom, namely, all the atomic types except 11, 23, and 24. To say that X has versus Y a freedom that S(X, Y) is, therefore, to say something which, in a certain sense, is very indefinite.

5. *Inversion, Conversion, and Co-ordination*

We say that a type of right, T_1, is the *inverse* of a type T_2, if it is always the case that:

X has versus Y a right of type T_1 that S(X, Y) if and only if
Y has versus X a right of type T_2 that S(X, Y).

We say that a type of right, T_1, is the *converse* of a type T_2 if it is always the case that:

X has versus Y a right of type T_1 that S(X, Y) if and only if
X has versus Y a right of type T_2 that not-S(X, Y).

We may now ascertain for ourselves that the atomic types 18 to 26 are inverses of 5 to 9 and 13 to 16, respectively. We can also establish that 11 to 17 are the converses of 3, 4, and 6 to 10, respectively. From the first 10 atomic types of rights, we can thus obtain all the others by conversion and inversion. Instead of saying, e.g., that:

X has versus Y a right of type no. 24 to the effect that S(X, Y),

we may as well say that:

Y has versus X a right of type no. 14 (i.e., the inverse of 24) to the effect that S(X, Y),

and instead of saying this, we could as well say:

Y has versus X a right of type no. 7 (i.e., the converse of 14) to the effect that not-S(X, Y).

We see in the diagram of the types of rights that the square for the inverse of an atomic type T is the mirror image of the square for T with respect to the line of symmetry: 2, 3, 4, 1, 12, 11, 2. Thus, 20 is the inverse of 7, 3 is the inverse of 3, etc. We see also that the square of the converse of T is the square we reach from T by rotating 180° about the central square 1. Thus, 14 is the converse of 7, 11 is the converse of 3, 1 is the converse of 1, etc.

We say that an atomic type of right T is *symmetric* if it is its own inverse, and we say that T is *neutral* if it is its own converse. The symmetric atomic types are nos. 1, 2, 3, 4, 11, and 12, and the neutral atomic types are nos. 1, 2, 5 and 18.

We say that a type of right T is the *co-ordinate* of a type T_1 paired with a type T_2 if it is always the case that:

X has versus Y a right to type T to the effect that S(X, Y)

if and only if

X has versus X a right of type T_1 to the effect that S(X, Y) and
Y has versus Y a right of type T_2 to the effect that S(X, Y).

Each atomic type of right T can be constructed as the coordinate of a symmetric atomic type T_1 paired with a symmetric atomic type T_2. In the diagram, the square for the co-ordinate of T_1 paired with T_2 then lies in the same row as T_1 and in the same column as T_2. We see, for example, that 7 is the co-ordinate of 2 paired with 3 and that 20 is the co-ordinate of 3 paired with 2. Note that some types are incompatible in the sense of not having a co-ordinate. Types 3 and 1, for instance, have no co-ordinates.

6. *The Concepts of Rights-Type and Right*

We can now make precise the concept of a type of right and the concept of a right, which we used above. In order to define the concept of a type of right, or rights-type, as we shall call it henceforth, we return to the 26 consistent reduced lists of § 5. We now think of a rights-type as a relation of three variables: a party X, a party Y, and a state of affairs S. We say that such a relation T is an *atomic rights-type* if there is a consistent list L which defines T, i.e. if there is a consistent list L such that T is the relation of all X, Y, and S which satisfy L. We have, for instance, the following reduced list:

Cl(X, Y, S)
not: Po(X, Y, S)

If T is the relation of all X, Y, and S which satisfy this list (i.e. the relation of all X, Y, S such that Cl(X, Y, S) and not: Po(X, Y, S)), then T is an atomic rights-type. More precisely, T is the atomic rights-type no. 7.

It can be shown for each X, Y, and S that X, Y, S occur in exactly one atomic rights-type. In other words, given X, Y, and S, it is always the case that X has versus Y a right of some atomic type to the effect that S(X, Y), but it is never the case that X has versus Y rights of two different atomic types that S(X, Y). It can also be shown with the help of examples that no atomic rights-type T is empty, i.e., there are always parties X and Y and a state of affairs S such that X, Y, and S stand in the relation T—in other words, there are X, Y, and S such that X has versus Y a right of type T to the effect that S(X, Y).

By a *rights-type* (which need not be atomic), we shall understand a relation T which is defined by a disjunction of one or more consistent lists. We can, in other words, say that a rights-type is a union of one or more atomic rights-types.

Among the rights-types, there are the simple rights-types: Claim, for example, is the union of the atomic rights-types nos. 3, 6, and 7. Cf. the diagram of rights-types.

We have defined a rights-type as a relation of three variables: a party X, a party Y and a state of affairs S. On the other hand, we have thought of a right as a relation of two variables: a party X and a party Y. We say now that such a relation R is a *right* if there is a specified consistent list L which defines R, i.e. if there is a specified consistent list L such that R is the relation of all X and Y which satisfy L. By a *specified consistent list,* we mean a list which can be obtained by taking one of the 26 consistent lists and in some way specifying S in it. S can, e.g., be so specified that S(X, Y) becomes: X receives from Y what X has lent to Y.

It follows from this definition that each right is uniquely determined by an atomic rights-type T and a state of affairs S, and the right determined by T and S is identical with the relation of all X and Y such that X, Y, and S stand in the relation T, i.e., the relation of all X and Y such that X has versus Y a right of atomic type T to the effect that S(X, Y).

By *the scope of a right R,* we shall understand the set of all ordered pairs (X, Y) of parties such that X has the right R versus Y. If each pair (X, Y) belongs to the scope of a right R (i.e. if each party X has R versus each party Y), then we say that R is a *universal* right. If no pair (X, Y) belongs to the scope of R, we say that R is an *empty right.* The right of atomic type 3 to the effect that a person be tortured is an example of an empty right.

7. Rules of Rights

By a *rule of rights* we may often understand a proposition which says that each pair of parties which satisfies a certain condition belongs to the scope of a certain right. A rule of right very often can take the form:

For every party X and every party Y such that F(X, Y), it is the case that X has versus Y a right of atomic type T to the effect that S(X, Y),

where F(X, Y) is a condition characterizing X, Y. The proposition:

For every X and Y such that X is a pedestrian and Y is a motorist who encounters X, it is the case that X has versus Y a right of atomic type: claim, power, counterfreedom, to the effect that Y does not run into X.

is an example of a rule of rights of this form.

We say that a party Z *breaks* a rule of rights if either of the following alternatives holds: (1) according to the rule, it shall be that Z sees to it that . . ., but actually it is not so that Z sees to it that . . ., (2) according to the rule, it shall be that Z does not see to it that . . ., but actually it is so that Z sees to it that . . . .

According to our example of a rule of rights the following holds for each pedestrian X and each motorist Y who encounters X:

it shall be that Y sees to it that Y not run into X,

and hence also by the strength diagram:

it shall be that X does not see to it that Y run into X.

Thus, if Y is a motorist who does not see to it that Y not run into an encountered pedestrian, then Y breaks the rule. And if X is a pedestrian who sees to it that an approaching motorist runs into X, then X breaks the rule.

We can seldom say that a rule of rights is unconditionally valid or true, but we can often say that it is valid according to, for example, a certain political or legal ideology, doctrine or practice; and we say this if the rule follows in a certain sense from an authoritative codification K of the political or legal ideology, doctrine or practice. We obtain examples of this conditional validity if we let K be Swedish law. We call a rule of rights which follows from the law a legal rule of rights.

When we speak here of a rule of rights following from K, we mean that the rule is a consequence of an *elucidation* K′ of some parts of K. An elucidation of a part of K can be obtained by making precise and completing that part of K in a way which admits applications of logic and which is reasonable and in line with the spirit and purpose of K. And when we say that the rule is a consequence of K′, we mean that it follows from K′ by ordinary logic extended in a suitable way with logical principles for concepts such as 'shall' and 'seeing to it.' An example of an elucidation will be given in § 11.

8. *Background and References*

In analytical jurisprudence there are some interesting analyses, or attempts at analyses, of the concept of a right along the lines of the analysis we have set forth in this essay. John Austin (the founder of the analytical school of jurisprudence) emphasized in his *Lectures on Jurisprudence* (1861) that a right is a relation of a certain kind between two parties:

All rights reside in persons, and are rights to acts or forbearances on the part of other persons.

By a right, Austin usually meant a claim or a claim which followed from the law:

A party has a right, when another or others are bound or obliged by the law, to do or to forbear, towards or in regard of him.

Austin also distinguished the inverse of this type of right and called it a relative duty:

The term "right" and the term "relative duty" are correlating expressions. They signify the same notions, considered from different aspects, or taken in different series. The acts or forbearances which are expressly or tacitly enjoined, are the objects of the right as well as of the corresponding duty. But with reference to the person or persons commanded to do or forbear, a duty is imposed. With reference to the opposite party, a right is conferred.

Along with right and relative duty, Austin also distinguished a type of right which he called:

Political or Civil Liberty: . . . a term which, not infrequently, is synonymous with right; but which often denotes simply exemption from obligation, conferred in a peculiar manner: namely by the indirect or circuitous process which is styled "permission".

These distinctions between different types of rights were further developed in H. T. Terry, *Some Leading Principles of Anglo-American Law* (1884) and J. Salmond, *Jurisprudence* (1902).[4] The development was completed by W. N. Hohfeld. In the article, "Some Fundamental Legal Conceptions as Applied in Judicial Reasoning" (*Yale Law Journal*, 1913 and 1917),[5] Hohfeld distinguished the following types: (at the right is given our rights-type which most closely corresponds):

Claim, Right	Claim
Duty	Inverse of claim
Privilege	Freedom
No-right	Inverse of freedom
Power	Power
Liability	Inverse of power
Immunity	Immunity
Disability	Inverse of immunity

Hohfeld gave rigor to the distinctions among these eight types by establishing the following logical relations between them: (1) Duty, No-right, Liability, and Disability are to be correlatives of, i.e., identical with the inverse of, Claim, Privilege, Power, and Immunity, respectively. (2) No-right, Duty, Disability, and Liability are to be opposites of, i.e., identical with the negations of the converses of, Claim, Privilege, Power, and Immunity, respectively.

To say, e.g., that X has a Duty versus Y to the effect that S(X, Y) is thus according to (1) the same as to say that Y has a Claim versus X to the effect that S(X, Y), and according to (2) the same as to say that X does not have a Privilege versus Y to the effect that not-S(X, Y).

These logical relations are Hohfeld's most important contribution to the analysis of the concept of a right. They imply that each of the concepts Claim, Duty, No-right, and Privilege can be defined in terms of any other of these concepts. They imply also that each of the concepts Power, Liability, Immunity, and Disability can be defined in terms of any other of them. Thus, in order to

---

[4] A summary of these authors' distinctions is given in J. Hall, ed., *Readings in Jurisprudence* (1938).

[5] Reprinted in W. N. Hohfeld, *Fundamental Legal Conceptions as Applied in Judicial Reasoning, and Other Legal Essays* (1923), ed. by W. H. Cook.

give explications of Hohfeld's concepts we need explicate only one concept of each of the two groups—e.g. the concepts Claim and Immunity.

Hohfeld did not provide any such explications, except in an indirect way by giving examples and discussions of court cases. So much, however, is clear from Hohfeld's text—that what he calls Claim and Immunity cannot without further ado be interpreted as what we have called claim and immunity. Hohfeld's concept Claim can more accurately be interpreted in a way such that X is said to have a Claim versus Y to the effect that S(X, Y), if it follows from the law that it shall be that Y sees to it that S(X, Y). Hohfeld's concept Immunity can in certain cases be approximately interpreted by saying that X has an Immunity versus Y if it follows from the law that it shall be that Y does not see to it that not-S(X, Y). The cases in question are those in which S(X, Y) is a state of affairs which concerns X's rights versus Y or versus a third party. Other cases are not discussed by Hohfeld.

Hohfeld's distinctions have had great influence. They have, for instance, been adopted in *The American Restatement of Law*, which is published by the American Law Institute. They have also been adopted in subsequent jurisprudence, especially by the so-called American analytical school. Early expositions and applications of Hohfeld's system may be found, for instance, in A. L. Corbin, "Legal Analysis and Terminology" (*Yale Law Journal*, 1919), J. R. Commons, *Legal Foundations of Capitalism* (1924), and A. Kocourek, *Jural Relations* (1927).[6] Among later, more logical, approaches to Hohfeld's distinctions there is A. R. Anderson, "Logic, Norms and Roles" (*Ratio*, 1962).

In Scandinavian jurisprudence, accounts of Hohfeld's system are given in T. Eckhoff, *Rettsvesen og Rettsvitenskap i USA* (1953), and in A. Ross, *Om Ret og Retfaerdighed* (1953). A more thorough exposition is M. Moritz, *Ueber Hohfelds System der juridischen Grundbegriffe* (1960).

The logical core of Hohfeld's distinctions has created some difficulties for analytical jurists. Hohfeld says, for example, that Privilege is the opposite of Duty or the negation of Duty. But he emphasizes that:

> Some caution is necessary at this point: for, always when it is said that the given privilege is the mere negation of a duty, what is meant, of course, is a duty having a content or tenor precisely opposite to that of the privilege in question.

To say that X has a privilege versus Y that S(X, Y) can therefore be interpreted as: X does not have a Duty versus Y to the effect that not-S(X, Y), but not as: X does not have a Duty versus Y to the effect that S(X, Y). This point has not, as a rule, been perceived by jurists. One reason is that jurists seldom take the trouble to put the various notions of rights into a proper context. Sweeping formulations like: Privilege = the negation of Duty, are too elliptic to exhibit the Hohfeld distinctions. Another reason is that many jurists wanted to explain what Claim, Duty, Privilege, etc. really mean without being able to uphold the logic of the

---

[6] A summary of Corbin's and Kocourek's ideas may be found in J. Hall, ed., *Readings in Jurisprudence* (1938).

distinctions in their explanations. All this has caused the logical rigour of Hohfeld's distinctions to be partly lost sight of in jurisprudence.

This concludes our discussion of the notion of a right. We now turn to some applications.

PART II. GOVERNMENT POSITION STRUCTURE AND PARLIAMENTARISM

9. *The Notion of Government Position Structure*

In the study of a political system there is often good reason for distinguishing the following *single parties*:

H   the head of state
P   the prime minister
M   member of the government other than P
G   the government as a whole
C   the congress or parliament

and the *joint parties* that consist of two or more of the parties H, P, M, C or the parties H, G, C in union, as, for instance, the union HG of H and G or the union HPC of H, P and C. Unions of the type PG or MG are, of course, redundant; they do not differ from G. Thus, we get 19 parties: M, P, PM, G, H, HM, HP, HPM, HG, C, CM, CP, CPM, CG, CH, CHM, CHP, CHPM, CHG.

By the *position structure* in a government, we mean (in this part of the essay) the system of rights to appoint and to dismiss members of the government and to dissolve the congress which these 19 parties have versus each other. The position structure can be given in tabular form, one table for each of the following five states of affairs:

S_1 that C is dissolved
S_2 that P resigns as prime minister
S_3 that M resigns as member of the government
S_4 that the candidate X for the prime ministerial appointment is appointed
S_5 that the candidate Y for a ministerial appointment is appointed

Each table has the following form:

	M	P	P M	G	H	.	.	.	.	C H G
M										
P										
PM										
G										
H										
.										
.										
.										
CHG										

in which atomic types of rights are indicated by number. If in the table for S_2 we have number 4 in the row for C and the column for HG, we may read:

The congress C has versus HG (i.e. the head of state in union with the government) a right of atomic type no. to the effect that P resign as prime minister.

Thus, each table may be interpreted as a set of 19×19 rules of rights of this kind.

10. *Some Methodological Simplifications*

To construct one of the five tables which determine the position structure, we only need find the diagonal from the left downwards (i.e., the types of rights which the parties have versus themselves—note that these types must be compatible). When we have the diagonal, we get the rest of the table by means of co-ordination. For instance, if we have the atomic type no. 2 in the diagonal at M and no. 4 at C, then we have the co-ordinate of 2 paired with 4 (i.e., no. 21) in the row M at the column C.

We shall note also that the atomic types in the diagonal are uniquely determined by atomic types outside the diagonal. For instance, if we have no. 18 (i.e., the co-ordinate of 2 paired with 1) in row H at column CG, we have 2 in the diagonal at H and 1 at CG. Thus, to construct a table we only need to determine 10 of its 361 places, but these 10 places must, of course, be chosen in a suitable way.

The construction of the table can be further simplified if we add the following logical principle to the principles I–V in § 2:

VI   (a)   X sees to it that F $\longrightarrow$ XY sees to it that F
(b)   X sees to it that F $\longrightarrow$ YX sees to it that F
(c)   XY sees to it that F $\longrightarrow$ XZY sees to it that F

We call this principle the *principle of joint parties*.

By means of the principle of joint parties (added to I–V) we may prove facts like:

If X has versus Y a right of atomic type no. 1 to the effect that S, then so has every party that includes X.

Clearly, facts of this kind may further reduce the number of places we must determine to acquire the whole table.

11. *An Example: The Position Structure in West German Government*

As an example of a position structure we shall now describe the position structure of the present West German government. To do this it is sufficient to give the diagonals of the tables for the five states of affairs S_1–S_5. An asterisk is put at those places in the diagonal which we determined by means of the

German constitution. These places then yield the rest of the diagonal by logic, i.e., the principles I–VI.

The diagonals are these:

	S_1	S_2	S_3	S_4	S_5
M	2	2	4*	2	2
P	2	4*	4*	2	1*
PM	2	4	4	2	1
G	2*	4	4	2	1
H	12*	2	2*	2	2
HM	12	2*	4	2	2
HP	12	4	4	2	1
HPM	12	4	4	2	1
HG	12*	4*	4*	2*	1
C	12*	4*	4*	1*	2
CM	12	4	4	1	2
CP	12	1*	4	1	1
CPM	12	1	1*	1	1
CG	12*	1	1	1	1
CH	1*	4	4	1	2
CHM	1	4*	4*	1	2*
CHP	1	1	4*	1	1
CHPM	1	1	1	1	1
CHG	1	1	1	1	1

The numbers with an asterisk can be justified by references to the following articles of the German constitution: 58, 62, 63, 64:1, 67:1, 68:1, and 69:2. To demonstrate the method, we shall carry through the justification in case of S_2 (i.e., the fact that P resigns as prime minister). The articles we shall rely on in this case are these:

Art. 58 Anordnungen und Verfügungen des Bundespräsident bedürfen zu ihrer Gültigkeit der Gegenzeichnung durch den Bundeskanzler oder durch den zuständigen Bundesminister. Dies gilt nicht für die Ernennung und Entlassung des Bundeskanzlers, die Auflösung des Bundestages gemäss Art. 63 und das Ersuchen gemäss Art. 69:3.

Art. 67 1. Der Bundestag kann dem Bundeskanzler das Misstrauen nur dadurch aussprechen, dass er mit der Mehrheit seiner Mitglieder einen Nachfolger wählt und den Bundespräsidenten ersucht, den Bundeskanzler zu entlassen. Der Bundespräsident muss dem Ersuchen entsprechen und den Gewählten ernennen.

The method of justification is that of an elucidation (in the sense of § 7) of these articles. The elucidation will involve three kinds of data:

(i)   Facts that are explicitly or almost explicitly stated in the articles of the constitution. We shall be free to formulate these facts in a language suitable for applications of logic.

(ii) Political principles which hold in every feasible position structure of the type here in question. These principles are in most cases too obvious to be worth explicit statement in a document like the constitution, but they are often implicitly assumed in interpretations of the constitution.

(iii)   Hypotheses to fill in lacunas of the constitution which cannot be filled in with consequences of data of kinds (i) and (ii). These hypotheses shall be in line with the spirit and purpose of the constitution and with the actual political life.

The facts of kind (i) that are relevant for S_2 are these:

(1)   C may see to it that S_2.
(2)   HG may not see to it that not-S_2.

These facts are almost explicitly stated in art. 67:1 combined with art. 58. We need four principles of kind (ii):

(3)   P may see to it that S_2.
(4)   If X and Y are two parties in the position structure without any common member and if X may see to it that S_2, then Y may not see to it that not-S_2.
(5)   If every party of the position structure which may see to it that S_2 is identical with or contains one of the parties X and Y, then XY may see to it that not-S_2.
(6)   CHG may see to it that not-S_2.

We need one hypothesis of kind (iii):

(7)   HM may not see to it that S_2.

Now, from the elucidation (1)–(7) we can obtain all the facts necessary to determine the numbers with an asterisk. The only means we need is logic involving the five logical principles of § 2 and the principle of joint parties.

According to (1) and (3), C and P may see to it that S_2; it follows logically that every party that includes C or P may see to it that S_2.

Thus we get:

(8)   HG may see to it that S_2.
(9)   CP may see to it that S_2.
(10) CHM may see to it that S_2.

We note also that neither H nor M may see to it that S_2 since according to (7), HM may not see to it that S_2. Hence, C or P must occur in every party that may see to it that S_2. Then according to (5), we get:

(11) CP may see to it that not-S_2.

Next, according to (3) and (4), we get:

(12)   CHM may not see to it that not-S_2.

(13)   C may not see to it that not-S_2.

We also derive logically from (2):

(14)   HM may not see to it that not-S_2.

(15)   P may not see to it that not-S_2.

Since, according to (6), CHG may see to it that not-S_2, it is not the case that CHG shall see to it that S_2. Hence, no party included in CHG shall see to it that S_2. Thus we have:

(16)   It is not the case that CHM shall see to it that S_2.

(17)   It is not the case that C shall see to it that S_2.

(18)   It is not the case that HG shall see to it that S_2.

(19)   It is not the case that P shall see to it that S_2.

Now (3), (15), and (19) jointly state:

P has versus P a right of atomic type no. 4 to the effect that P resign as prime minister.

Further, (7) and (14) state:

HM has versus HM a right of atomic type no. 2 to the effect that P resign as prime minister.

(8), (2), and (18) state:

HG has versus HG a right of atomic type no. 4 to the effect that P resign as prime minister.

(1), (13), and (17) state:

C has versus C a right of atomic type no. 4 to the effect that P resign as prime minister.

(9) and (11) state:

CP has versus CP a right of atomic type no. 1 to the effect that P resign as prime minister.

Finally, (10), (12), and (16) state:

CHM has versus CHM a right of atomic type no. 4 to the effect that P resign as prime minister.

Thus we have determined all the asterisked numbers in the diagonal for S_2. We can easily derive the rest of the diagonal from these numbers by means of logic.

12. Some Main Types of Parliamentarism

The main characteristic of a parliamentary political system is the fact that its government position structure is of a certain kind, which we shall call parliamentary position structures. In this section we shall make some preparatory comments on these structures and we shall distinguish some main types or levels of parliamentarism.

First, a distinction is made between what may be called control parliamentarism and delegation parliamentarism.

Control parliamentarism is characterized by the fact that the parliament can dismiss the government, but not necessarily by the fact that the parliament has an influence on the appointment of the government members. Control parliamentarism is compatible with a strong position for the head of state with authority to appoint the government. The political system of the fifth French republic is a good example of this kind of parliamentarism.

Delegation parliamentarism is a control parliamentarism in which the parliament also has a decisive influence on the formation of the government. The government will then be a kind of delegate of the parliament. A good example of delegation parliamentarism is found in the political system of West Germany. Here the Bundeskanzler is elected by the Bundestag.

Next, we distinguish what we may call minister parliamentarism from government parliamentarism.

Minister parliamentarism is characterized by the fact that the parliament can dismiss single members of the government. Denmark provides an example of this kind of parliamentarism. In a system with *government parliamentarism*, on the other hand, the parliament can dismiss the government as a whole only. This is often done by a vote of censure on the prime minister. Example: West Germany.

Parliamentary political systems are characterized mainly by the fact that the parliament can dismiss the government. Besides these political systems there is a category of possible systems which are parliamentary in a wider sense—we may call them *pseudo-parliamentary*. As an example, we may take a system where the parliament appoints the members of the government for a period of, say, four years. During this period they cannot be dismissed, but every fourth year the parliament can dismiss a minister simply by refusing to reappoint him. Switzerland has a pseudo-parliamentarism of this kind.

In most parliamentary systems the government or the head of state may dissolve the parliament. In political science this right is usually considered a necessary feature of parliamentarism. But the agreement is not complete. There are also adherents of an opposite opinion.[7]

---

[7] For instance R. Fusilier in *Les Monarchies Parlementaires* (1960); "Le caractère non fondamental du droit de dissolution dans le fonctionnement du régime parlementaire est démontré non seulement par l'usage généralement de moins en moins fréquent de la dissolution dans les pays considérés, mais encore par la pratique norvégienne, qui l'ignore, et de l'étude de laquelle il ressort nettement que la dissolution ne constitue pas un facteur nécessaire du régime parlementaire" (p. 32). The standard view is maintained by D. V. Verney in *The Analysis of Political Systems* (1959): "The power of the Government to request a dissolution is a distinctive characteristic of parliamentarism.... Certain States generally regarded as parliamentary severely

In this essay, we shall hold the view that the question whether or not a position structure is parliamentary is independent of the question whether or not the parliament can be dissolved. We shall also disregard pseudo-parliamentarism and minister parliamentarism. Hence, in our study of parliamentarism, we may confine ourselves to a simplified kind of position structure where the parties P and M are not distinguished from G, and where the dissolution of parliament is left out of account.

These position structures—we shall call them *reduced position structures*—can be given by one table for each of the following two state of affairs:

R   that the government G resigns
S   that the candidate K for government is appointed government.[8]

Each table has the form:

	H	G	C	H G	H C	G C	H G C
H							
G							
C							
HG							
HC							
GC							
HGC							

in which, just as before, atomic types of rights are indicated by number. And, as before, we only need to establish the diagonals in order to determine the tables.

13. *Feasible Reduced Position Structures*

The number of logically possible reduced position structures is very large.[9] But most of them are politically unfeasible. In order to define those that are feasible we shall set forth some principles or axioms of political feasibility. The feasible structures will then be defined as those which fulfill the principles.

---

restrict the right of the Executive to dissolve the Assembly. In Norway the Storting dissolves itself, the Head of State being allowed to dissolve only special sessions, but this is a departure from parliamentarism inspired by the convention theory of the French Revolution" (pp. 31–32).

[8] The somewhat odd formulation of S should not cause confusion. We note that S is not synonymous with: Some government is appointed. It might very well happen that H may see to it that K not be appointed, but H may not see to it that no government be appointed at all.

[9] If we take into consideration the logical principles I–V of § 2 and the principle of joint parties given in § 10 we get 619 different tables for each of R and S. Hence, the number of logically possible reduced position structures is $619 \times 619 = 383161$. As a curiosity we may mention that the number would have been larger than 430 millions—$(4^7 + 3^7 + 3^7)^2$ to be precise—if we had not taken into account the principle of joint parties. And if we also had kept the unreduced structures with 19 parties and 5 states of affairs, the number would have been astronomical: $(4^{19} + 3^{19} + 3^{19})^5$.

The principles are these:[10]

(1) The principle of joint sovereignty:
     (a) HGC may see to it that R, and HGC may see to it that not-R.
     (b) HGC may see to it that S, and HGC may see to it that not-S.
(2) The principle of non-obstruction:
     (a) If X and Y are disjoint parties and if X may see to it that R,
         then it is not the case that Y may see to it that not-R.
     (b) If X and Y are disjoint parties and if X may see to it that S, then
         it is not the case that Y may see to it that not-S.
(3) The principle of non-compulsion:
     (a) If every party that may see to it that R is identical with or con-
         tains one of the parties X and Y, then XY may see to it that not-R.
     (b) If every party that may see to it that S is identical with or con-
         tains one of the parties X and Y, then XY may see to it that not-S.
(4) The principle of non-competition:
     If X and Y are disjoint parties and if X may see to it that S, then it
     is not the case that Y may see to it that S.
(5) The principle of resignation:
     G may see to it that R.
(6) The principle of preservation:
     If a party X may see to it that not-R, then X may see to it that not-S.
(7) The principle of elimination:
     If HC may see to it that R, then HC may see to it that S.

When we refer to parties in these principles, we always mean parties involved in
the reduced position structures.

Among the tables for R and S that are consistent with the logical principles
I–VI, there are 324 tables for each of R and S that contain No. 1 in the diagonal
at HGC. These tables are consistent with the principle of joint sovereignty. We
may easily examine these 324 tables one by one and omit those which are inconsistent with the principles (2)–(5). As a result, we get 5 tables for R and 11
tables for S. Thus, we have 55 combinations of a table for R with a table for S.
But we do not get 55 position structures, since only 25 of the combinations are
consistent with the principles (6) and (7). These 25 combinations are displayed
in the table on page 235:

----

[10] Note that principles corresponding to the principles 1, 2, 3 and 5 were applied in our
elucidation of some parts of the West German constitution. In principles 2 and 4 we say that X
and Y are disjoint parties if X and Y have no member in common.

	a	b	c	d	e
H	2	2	4	2	4
G	1	4	4	4	4
C	2	2	2	4	4
HG	1	1	1	4	4
HC	2	4	4	4	4
GC	1	1	4	1	4
HGC	1	1	1	1	1

	H	G	C	HG	HC	GC	HGC	a	b	c	d	e
A	1,	2,	2,	1,	1,	2,	1	—	—	Ac	—	Ae
B	2,	2,	1,	2,	1,	1,	1	—	—	—	Bd	Be
C	2,	1,	2,	1,	2,	1,	1	Ca	—	—	—	—
D	12,	2,	2,	1,	1,	12,	1	—	Db	Dc	Dd	De
E	2,	12,	2,	1,	12,	1,	1	Ea	—	—	—	—
F	2,	2,	12,	12,	1,	1,	1	—	Fb	Fc	Fd	Fe
G	12,	12,	2,	1,	12,	12,	1	Ga	—	—	—	—
H	12,	2,	12,	12,	1,	12,	1	—	Hb	Hc	Hd	He
I	2,	12,	12,	12,	12,	1,	1	Ia	—	—	—	—
J	2,	2,	2,	1,	1,	1,	1	—	Jb	Jc	Jd	Je
K	12,	12,	12,	12,	12,	12,	1	Ka	—	—	—	—

In the table, a, b, c, d, e are the 5 diagonals for R, and A, B, C, . . ., K are the 11 diagonals for S. The table shows that diagonal A can be combined only with diagonal c and diagonal e. We call the position structures determined by these combinations Ac and Ae, respectively.

Thus, we have exactly 25 feasible reduced position structures. Of these, 11 are parliamentary, namely those indicated in the d- and e-columns. Ae is purely control parliamentary without delegation parliamentarism, while Bd is completely delegation parliamentary. To see the delegation parliamentarism of Bd, we note that diagonal B has no. 1 at C and no. 2 at HG. Hence C has versus HG a right of atomic type no. 5 (i.e., the co-ordinate of 1 with 2) to the effect that S. In other words, the parliament has versus the head of state joined by the government a power, counterpower, immunity, and counterimmunity to appoint a new government. We note also that diagonal D has no. 4 at C and at HG. Hence C has versus HG a right of atomic type 4 to the effect that R. This implies that C has versus HG a power and an immunity to dismiss G.

14. *Some Concluding Remarks*

So far we have considered two types of position structures: the unreduced and the reduced type. Of course, there are also other possible types. There are, for instance, types of extended position structures involving new single parties like the supreme court, the central committee of the communist party, the army, etc.

In the study of a political system, the position structure is a main topic. But, of course, the type of the structure must be adequate in the sense that it permits the structure to mirror the political life of the system. The type of structure suggested in § 9 with 19 parties and 5 states of affairs is fairly adequate in the case of many western political systems. But it is clearly inadequate in the case of the

Soviet system, for instance, where the central committee of the communist party has a decisive influence on the appointment and dismissal of the government.

We shall note also that the validity of the principles of political feasibility depends on the adequacy of the position structure. For instance, the principle of joint sovereignty is clearly false in the case of political systems where the army can dismiss the government.

Finally, we shall note that not all the 25 feasible reduced position structures we have defined above are politically attractive. The structure Ca, for example, is certainly not attractive from a democratic point of view. But the problem of indicating those that are attractive is a problem of political ideology and not a problem of political science.

Anders Wedberg

Some Problems in the
Logical Analysis of Legal Science[1]

SECTION I

1. *Legal science and legal rules.* Any study which is concerned with the Law and phenomena closely connected with the Law may be included in legal science, in the widest sense of that term. In a narrower sense, legal science is the endeavor to give a systematic exposition and a logical analysis of the Law (of a given country, at a given time). German authors have coined the convenient term *Rechtsdogmatik* to cover this narrower sense. In what follows, whenever I use the phrase "legal science," the phrase will be synonymous with the German term.

The Law itself—in the sense of that which legal science endeavors to analyze and systematize—is a class of legal rules (laws, rulings, stipulations, 'norms').

This understanding of the phrase "the Law" must be carefully distinguished from certain other connotations of which the phrase is likewise capable. To state that "law prevails" in a society is to say that the life of the society is characterized by a smooth running legal organization. To say that "the law has caught up with" a criminal, is to say that the legal authorities have caught him. Both these connotations are entirely distinct from that sense in which the phrase "the Law" will be understood in the sequel of this paper.

There are some possible ambiguities in the term "legal rule" which entail corresponding ambiguities in the preceding explanation of the term "Law." A legal rule is usually thought of as a legal proposition that possesses a certain essential generality. The proposition, "All thieves shall be hanged," has the generality commonly required of a legal rule. The proposition, "Smith shall be hanged,"

Professor Wedberg, of the University of Stockholm, is a native of Sweden.

Reprinted, with slight changes, from *Theoria*, vol. 17, pp. 246–75 (1951), with permission of the author and the editor.

[1] The present paper is a revised version of some chapters in a manuscript on the logical analysis of legal science, the first version of which was composed in 1944.

lacks that generality. Are we then to deny the title "legal rule" to the latter proposition? The question is obviously only a matter of terminological choice. Here I am going to use the term "legal rule" in somewhat the same sense in which Hans Kelsen is using the term "legal norm."[2] Thus, also, particular propositions such as "Smith shall be hanged" may be legal rules and, therefore, parts of the Law.

When speaking of a legal rule, we may have in mind either a certain form of words or the proposition expressed by such a form. In what follows I shall exclusively use the phrase "legal rule" in the latter sense. Thus, the Law in the present sense is a class of legal propositions, not a class of linguistic expressions.

Even if the proposition, "All bicyclists shall be hanged," will never become a part of any system of positive law, it is obviously similar in meaning to propositions which are parts of systems of positive law, and, hence, we may say that it is qualified to become a part of such a system. The proposition, "2 + 2 = 4," is not qualified to become such a part. When I say that a proposition is a rule, I shall mean only that it is qualified to become a part of a system of positive law. When I say that a proposition is a legal rule or a positive legal rule, I shall mean that it actually is a part of some such system.

2. *The factual basis and its legal interpretation.* Insofar as the study of law has the qualities of an objective science, its statements and procedures must submit to the test of observations of facts and logical reasoning on the basis of such observations. As a collective name for the observable facts which are of direct relevance to legal science, I shall here use the phrase "the factual basis of legal science." An essential part of the factual basis consists of certain (oral or written) utterances to which a specific legal authority is accorded. Such utterances are codified laws or statutes, court decisions, formal contracts, etc. Another part of the factual basis is formed by certain habits, customs, or practices, which likewise are recognized as possessing a specific legal authority. These facts can be considered from infinitely many points of view. The point of view of the legal scientist is a very particular one. To him the facts are the starting point of a logical process, the outcome of which is the statement of such rules as "All thieves shall be hanged" or "Smith shall be hanged." Along with Hans Kelsen, we shall call this process the legal (or juristic) interpretation of the facts.

3. *Some methods of legal interpretation.* The methods of interpretation can, of course, vary from one legal system to another. However, some or all of the following methods are encountered in connection with most well developed systems.

(i) Given an authoritative utterance U, the jurist asks the question: "What proposition P is expressed by U?" The authority accorded to U means that if P is expressed by U, then P is accepted by the jurist as an element of the Law, as a member of that body of legal rules which it is his task to systematize.

[2] Cf. no. IX, p. 38 et passim.

(ii) Given, e.g., a set of court decisions $U_1, \ldots, U_n$, the jurist may also apply a somewhat more complicated type of reasoning. Having established that $U_1, \ldots, U_n$ express the propositions $P_1, \ldots, P_n$, he may go on and ask: "Which is the general proposition P of which $P_1, \ldots, P_n$ are special applications?" If $P_1, \ldots, P_n$ are found to be special applications of P, the jurist may then accept P as an element of the Law.

(iii) Having established that a rule P, concerned with a type of situation C, is an element of the Law, the jurist may ask: "What rule P' is related to the type of situation C' in a manner analogous to that in which P is related to C?" This rule P' may then be accepted as an element of the Law.

(iv) Similar to the preceding method is the following: If the rules $P_1, \ldots, P_n$ are parts of the Law, the jurist may try to ascertain the 'spirit' or 'purpose' exhibited by those rules. If, then, a further rule P is seen to be in line with that spirit or purpose, the jurist may also accept P as an element of the Law.[3]

(v) Customs or practices may also belong to the factual basis of legal science. Suppose, e.g., that since time immemorial the inhabitants of a farm A have walked across the territory of a neighboring farm B. In view of such a practice the jurist may accept the rule, "The inhabitants of A have the right to cross the territory of B," as an element of the Law.

(vi) Suppose that a rule P has already been accepted as an element of the Law and that another rule Q is found to be logically derivable either from P alone, or from P in conjunction with certain verified factual propositions F. Then, Q, too, is accepted as an element of the Law. When speaking of rules, let us use the sentence, "P entails Q," as shorthand for the more complicated phrase, "Q is logically derivable either from P alone or from P in conjunction with certain true factual propositions F." Legal interpretation seems to involve the postulate that any rule which is entailed by rules belonging to the Law itself belongs to the Law.[4]

4. *The practical nature of legal science.* The peculiar method of legal science —in the present sense of *Rechtsdogmatik*—is dictated by its predominantly practical aim. The activity of the legal scientist is seldom, I think, guided merely by the speculative interest of seeing what rules are arrived at when such and such

---

[3] In these juristic reasonings the relations connoted by the following phrases are seen to play a crucial role:
  (i) "The utterance U *expresses* the rule P."
  (ii) "The rules $P_1, \ldots, P_n$ are special *applications* of the rule P."
  (iii) "The rule P for the type of situation C is *analogous* to the rule P' for the type of situation C'."
  (iv) "The *spirit* or purpose A is *exhibited* by the rules $P_1, \ldots, P_n'$."
  To a great extent the significance of these relations is supposed to be sufficiently defined by common sense. To some extent their significance is defined by (largely tacit) conventions, peculiar to legal interpretation.
  [4] This type of juristic reasoning presupposes the relation expressed by the phrase:
  (vi) "The rule Q is *entailed* by the rule P."
  The logic of this relationship is tacitly borrowed from common sense.

methods of reasoning are applied to the factual basis. The rules of the Law are directives, enjoining certain patterns of behavior. By its moral authority the Law is a power determining the behavior of men. The legal scientist is usually himself a member of the society whose Law he studies, and he is interested in maintaining, changing, or exploiting the power of the Law. Although, in the present essay, I shall say little or nothing about this practical aspect, it is something which must always be borne in mind, unless we shall obtain a falsely intellectualized picture of legal science.

5. *The logical analysis of legal science.* An outside observer may study legal science from many different angles. To psychology and sociology the legal phenomena offer a rich and varied field of investigation. However there is also another, perhaps more artificial, but still legitimate and important point of view from which an outsider may consider legal science. I shall here endeavor to explain this point of view, which perhaps may be called that of *logical analysis* or *rational reconstruction.*[5]

Let D_n be some doctrine (scientific, ethical, religious, etc.) in a 'naive' formulation. Rationally to reconstrue the doctrine D_n is to replace it by another formulation D_r which is more exact than D_n but still somehow expresses the same set of ideas as D_n. There are several directions in which such a rational reconstruction may take place:

(i) It may happen that in D_n the same term expresses several distinct ideas on different occasions. Since ambiguity is a possible source of error, in D_r we make each term carry a unique connotation.

(ii) Usually D_n does not clearly indicate which terms are *undefined* (primitive) and which terms are *defined*, nor are the definitions of the defined terms explicitly stated. In D_r we list the undefined terms and then we introduce the defined terms by a series of formal definitions.

(iii) The sentences of D_n will usually be of many different kinds. If D_n possesses a certain minimum of complication, D_n will contain *definitions* that introduce new terms as shorthand for combinations of old terms. All sentences which are not definitions we may call statements. Some statements will be *analytic* in the sense that they are true on purely logical grounds, given the meaning of the terms involved. Other statements will be *synthetic* in the sense that the question of their validity cannot be decided on logical grounds alone. It is often very difficult to decide to what category a given sentence of D_n belongs. It is a desideratum that the sentences of D_r should clearly announce their character in this respect.

(iv) Of specific importance for the analysis of legal science is the distinction between factual and normative sentences. By a normative sentence I mean a sentence which—explicitly or implicitly—involves a normative idea. Normative ideas are the ideas of prescription, prohibition, and permission. The first is often

---

[5] An interesting exposition of this point of view is found in no. XI.

expressed by such words as "shall," "ought," "must," the second by "shall not," "ought not," "must not," and the third by "may." A normative idea is explicitly involved in a sentence, if the sentence contains some phrase which directly expresses prescription, prohibition, or permission. A normative idea is implicitly present in a sentence, if it does not occur explicitly, but the sentence is synonymous with another sentence in which it does occur explicitly. In a rational reconstruction of legal science, it is desirable to make the division of sentences into factual and normative clearly discernible.

(v) Between the sentences of D_r there will exist certain reations of a logical nature. In particular, it will often be possible logically to derive one sentence from certain other sentences. Although such possibilities of derivation exist, they are frequently not explicitly indicated. In D_r we may first list the sentences which are supposed to be accepted without derivation, and then indicate in what order the other sentences can be derived from them.

(vi) Finally, it may be desirable to make the methods of derivation themselves explicit. Whereas D_n is satisfied to take a certain understood logic for granted, D_r may explicitly state its own logic.

It is this problem of a rational reconstruction of legal science in which I am interested here. Let D_n be legal science in a 'naive' state. I wish to indicate certain lines along which this naive formulation D_n may be developed by rational reconstruction into a more clarified formulation D_r. The same legal system L which is presented with a lower degree of logical clarity by D_n, will be presented with a higher degree by D_r.

The rational reconstruction of legal science is a very comprehensive task. In the two subsequent sections of this paper I shall consider only two limited problems, namely, the distinction between external and internal sentences (Section II) and the concept of 'property' or 'ownership' (Section III).

SECTION II

6. *Internal and external sentences of legal science.* Consider any textbook on law—what does it say? It states a number of rules which, either explicitly or implicitly, separately or jointly, have normative contents. Explicitly or implicitly, the textbook adds: "These rules are in force in such and such a society at such and such a time," or: "These rules belong to such and such a system of positive law." If it is a textbook on ancient Roman law, it asserts that the rules explained were in force in ancient Rome at some time in its history. If it is a textbook on, say, contemporary Swedish law, it states that the rules enumerated are in force in Sweden now. Accordingly, we have to distinguish between two types of juristic sentences, namely, (i) sentences stating the rules themselves, and (ii) sentences stating that a given rule is (or is not) in force in a given society at a given time. Let us say that to state a rule pertaining to a given system of law is to make a statement that is *internal* relative to that system. Let us say that to state that a

rule belongs (or does not belong) to a given system of law, is to make a statement that is *external* relative to that system. From the point of view of legal science, the statement of a rule *P* is always somehow incomplete unless it is accompanied by an external statement to the effect that *P* is (or is not) in force in a society *S* at a time *t*.

There are several types of external statement and several distinct external concepts, i.e., concepts that are characteristic of such statements. Let us here consider a few. With respect to a rule *P*, a society *S* and a moment (period) in time *t*, we may state:

(1) *P is in force in S at t*.

We can also form the notion of a system of law by collecting into one class all the rules that are in force in the same *S* at the same *t*. Let us call such a system:

(2) *The legal system of S at t (The Law of S at t)*.

History offers us a large number of classes of rules that are the legal systems of given societies at given times. All the rules of these classes have the common property of being legal rules, and all the classes have the common property of being just such legal systems. Of a given rule *P* we may thus state:

(3) *P is a legal rule,*

and of a given class of rules *C* we can say:

(4) *C is a legal system.*

These examples of external statements and external concepts could easily be multiplied.[6]

A primary task of the logical analysis of legal science is to clarify the role and significance of these external statements.

7. *The definition of a given legal system.* As long as we are interested only in a particular legal system, say, contemporary Swedish law and its legal science, obviously, we may disregard the problem of defining the general notion of a legal system which occurs in statement (4) (heading 6). Although we shall be presupposing that contemporary Swedish law is a legal system—in the same general sense in which history offers us a multitude of legal systems—the general notion of a legal system is only of a subsidiary interest. Likewise, we do not really need to define, in general, what is meant by saying that something is a legal rule or that (any rule) *P* is in force in (any society) *S* at (any time) *t*. It is enough for us to know what we mean by saying:

(5) *P is in force in Sweden now,*

and what connotation we attach to the expression:

---

[6] For our present purpose, a more exact definition of the terms "external statement" and "external concept (term)" does not seem to be necessary. In a more exact definition we should have first to define what is meant by "external concepts (terms)." Such external concepts may occur also in internal sentences, stating legal rules pertaining to a given system of law. The 'external statements' in the present sense are, thus, a subclass of all those sentences which involve external concepts.

(6) *Contemporary Swedish Law.*

It is a logical commonplace that there is not, in general, only one definition of a given term. In this context it is of interest to observe that a definition is 'adequate' or 'acceptable' if some designated relationship holds between its definiens and its definiendum, and that there are a number of distinct such relations between which we must make a choice. What demand in this respect shall we, then, make upon an adequate or acceptable definition of (5) and of (6)?

Some will suggest that, in an adequate definition of (5), the definiens should express "what jurists think when stating the definiendum." However, I think that to look for such a definition would be rather unprofitable. Of course, it may be of great psychological interest to ascertain what such and such a jurist 'thinks' ('imagines,' 'has in mind') when he asserts about a rule *P* that (5). It is likely, however, that what is thus thought varies from one jurist to another. Quite possibly, too, what some jurists think is false or unreasonable, and some jurists may think very little. The thoughts which jurists associate with phrase (5), therefore, can hardly be our guide in the search for a definition of (5) which will be scientifically useful.

Although the thoughts associated with (5) are probably fluctuating and partially false or absurd, the manner in which (5) is actually used seems to be rather stable. Concerning a very large body of rules *P*, most contemporary Swedish jurists agree when it comes to deciding whether (5) can be truthfully stated or not. Therefore, we shall be wise in taking this use of the phrase (5) as our starting point. Accordingly, we agree to accept a definition of (5) as adequate if and only if the definiens is a 'necessary and sufficient condition' for the definiendum: i.e., if the definiens can be truthfully stated of any rule *P* of which the definiendum can be truthfully stated, and conversely; or if definiens and definiendum delimit exactly the same set of rules. The same remarks apply to the definition of (6).

Clearly, there may be many distinct definitions of (5) and of (6) which are all in this sense adequate. What adequate definitions are available will naturally depend upon the actual characteristics of contemporary Swedish law. In view of what was said under headings 2–3, it should, e.g., be possible to construe an adequate definition of (5) as follows. By a study of contemporary Swedish law we find that its factual basis consists of a set of facts *F* and that the legal interpretation of *F* consists in a certain method of reasoning *M*. We could then lay down the definition:

$D_1(5)$ *P is in force in Sweden now* = def   *P is obtainable by applying M to F.*

Another approach has been suggested by Hans Kelsen in his 'pure theory of law.' It may be that contemporary Swedish law can be exhibited as a system of rules which are all entailed by an easily definable set of basic rules *B*. If such is the case, we can lay down the definition:

$D_2(5)$ *P is in force in Sweden now* = def *P is entailed by B.*[7]

And—of course—there may be still other adequate definitions of (5).

8. *The vagueness of (5) and (6).* The notions expressed by the phrases (5) and (6) are obviously vague. Concerning many rules *P*, we can with great assurance affirm (5), and concerning many others, we can with equally great assurance deny (5). But then there are a large number of borderline cases, rules concerning which neither affirmation nor denial is clearly justified. A logical analyst, who desires to remain on safe ground, therefore, will not be able to lay down very exact definitions of (5) and (6). He will have to make the definiens about as vague as the definiendum—and salve his logical conscience by describing as exactly as possible the amount of vagueness involved. More exact definitions of (5) and (6) are, of course, desiderata. But the exactification can hardly be achieved except as a consequence of the development of legal science itself. Perhaps, also, the logician's desire for exactness here comes in conflict with the practical needs to which legal science is subservient.

9. *The definition of the general external concepts.* If our interest is not restricted to the study of one given system of law but is essentially comparative, we may also find it obligatory to define the general notions expressed by the phrases (1)–(4). Adequately to define these notions is obviously a much more difficult task than to define (5) and (6). In order to find adequate definitions of the general notions we shall have to survey all the various rules of all the various legal systems and to elicit some very general features that constantly recur. Whereas (5) and (6) are employed daily by the entire legal profession in Sweden, the more abstract notions (1)–(4) are mainly found in somewhat abstruse books on general jurisprudence. Even if we stick to what may be considered the best current usage of the terms, we shall find that they are extremely vague. Some authors refuse to grant the title of "legal system" to a set of rules which does not conform to certain standards of justice, while others deny that there is any essential connection between being a 'legal system' and exhibiting such conformity.[8] Some assert that only a 'sovereign' state can possess a legal system, in the proper sense of the term, while others also speak of legal systems in connection with social organizations that do not enjoy 'sovereignty.' Whether international law is really a system of positive law or merely some kind of moral or political ideology, is a question over which innumerable books and articles have been written. Since the facts about international law are well-known or easily ascertained, the debate is obviously possible only because the very term

---

[7] Cf. no. IX, p. 124 et passim. Actually Kelsen maintains that every legal system contains one single basic rule (*Grundnorm*) by which all the remaining rules of the system are entailed. Both the meaning of this assertion and Kelsen's reasons for it are very obscure. (If we have a finite set of rules, $P_1, \ldots, P_n$, we can always combine them into the single conjunctive rule, $P_1 \& \ldots \& P_n$. When stressing that each legal system is entailed by a single basic rule, does Kelsen wish to state that each such system is entailed by a basic rule which is not equivalent to a conjunction of several rules?)

[8] A similar divergence is analyzed in no. X.

"legal system" or "system of positive law" is here confronted with a borderline case. As long as we restrict our attention to the present-day societies that have reached a relatively high degree of civilization, the agreement as to what is and what is not a legal system will, nevertheless, be fairly large. But the agreement ceases when we ask ourselves the question of at what stage legal systems first make their appearance in the development of human society from a more primitive to a more civilized state. In deciding that question we cannot fall back upon any well-established usage of the phrase "legal systems." If we dare or bother to decide the question, our decision will be a proposal as to how *we* intend to use the term, not an explanation of a pre-existing usage.

Seeking a fairly exact definition of the notions under discussion may, therefore, seem about as unprofitable as seeking exact definitions of such words as "poetry," "religion," "chair" or "table."[9]

10. *The roles of internal and external statements.* In their attitude to the two classes of sentences—the internal and the external ones—the practical jurist (the judge, the lawyer, the businessman, the calculating criminal, etc.) and the legal scientist (the theorizing professor of law) frequently differ, I think, in a characteristic manner. In a given situation the practical jurist is interested in finding and analyzing the legal rule that is applicable to the situation. Of course, he cares only about such rules as belong to the Law of his country at the time. But his interest is centered around the contents of the rule itself, not around the fact that the rule is an element of the Law. The motive which prompts him to study the Law is not the purely theoretical desire to know what rules possess the property of being in force. If he is a good judge or a lawful citizen, the Law will to him be a moral authority which is to be obeyed. If he is a man calculating a prudent and profitable course of action, the Law is to him a social power which he has to take into account. In any case, the practical jurist is mainly interested in what I have called the internal sentences. The legal scientist, on the other hand, has a theoretical interest in ascertaining what rules belong to the Law, and if he is studying comparative jurisprudence, he may embrace with an impartial eye both the rules that are in force in S_1 at t_1 and the rules that are in force in S_2 at t_2. Thus, what I have called the external sentences are in the focus of the legal scientist's attention.

---

[9] John Austin was probably the first to attempt to give a careful definition of the external concepts of legal science. Having explained what he means by "sovereign person or body" and "independent political society" in terms of habits of obedience, he states the following definition of (3): "Every positive law, or every law simply and strictly so called, is set, directly or circuitously, by a sovereign person or body, to a member or members of the independent political society wherein that person or body is sovereign or supreme." (no. II, p. 225.)

Although Kelsen never gives any formal definitions, the following definition of (4) could, I think, be extracted from his writings: A class C of rules (Kelsen: "norms") is a system of positive law, if and only if C fulfills two separate conditions: (i) C has a certain specified internal logical character (a basic norm, consistency, dynamic nature, coerciveness, etc.), and (ii) C is on the whole effective (in the sense that people's behavior on the whole conforms with the rules of C). (Cf. no. IX, passim.)

The difference here described is about the same as that between a believing Christian and a detached theologian in their attitude toward the sayings of the Bible. While the former is interested in the doctrine of the Bible as a guide in life, the theologian may be mainly preoccupied with deciding the theoretical question as to what dogmas or prescripts are truly biblical.

However, most legal scientists are also good citizens acknowledging the moral authority of the Law, just as most Christian theologians are convinced Christians, recognizing the authority of the Bible. The 'naive' legal scientist does not stop at asserting: "P is in force in S at t." Especially when S is his own society and t is his own time, he goes on to assert P itself. In so doing he, consciously or unconsciously, presupposes what may be called *The Axiom of Naive Jurisprudence*: "For all P, if P is in force in S at t, then P"—at least for the special case when S and t are his country and his time. (There is a similar Axiom of Naive Theology which could be stated thus: "For all P, if P is biblical, then P.")[10]

11. *Is legal science a genuine science?* The answer to this common question[11] seems to be rather simple. The question can be divided into two separate questions:

(i) What is the scientific status of the external sentences of legal science?

(ii) What is the scientific status of the internal sentences of legal science (those sentences which state the legal rules)? Let us consider them in this order.

(i) We have already seen that the external terms of legal science are rather vague. But so, in varying degree, are most terms outside of pure mathematics. We have also seen that the external sentence, "P is in force in Sweden now," can be adequately defined in several distinct ways. To what type of scientific study such a sentence belongs will naturally depend upon what definition we choose. Under heading 7 we suggested a definition by reference to the factual basis of legal science and the method of legal interpretation. If such a definition is adopted, the external sentences become sociological, in a broad sense of the term. They are comparable to such a sentence as, "P is an official doctrine of the Swedish state church." Under heading 7 we mentioned also a definition by reference to a set of basic rules. If we adopt this definition (which seems to be Kelsen's), the external sentences acquire a slightly different meaning. The sentence, "P is in force in Sweden now," will mean the same as the sentence, "P is entailed by the set of basic rules B" or "There are true factual propositions which in conjunction with B logically imply P." Such a sentence bears a strong resemblance to, e.g., the sentence, "The laws of Newtonian mechanics entail that the earth will pursue an elliptical orbit" or "There are certain true propositions which in con-

---

[10] The jurist who proceeds on the assumption of The Axiom of Naive Jurisprudence is usually influenced also by other moral and political ideals. A large part of the traditional philosophy of law is comprehensible only if it is seen as a confused attempt to reconcile these other ideals with the axiom. (A similar situation seems to exist in theology.)

[11] Recently raised in no. I.

junction with the Newtonian laws logically imply that the earth will pursue an elliptical orbit."

Insofar as vagueness does not interfere, we can decide, by a combination of logical and empirical methods, whether a given rule is in force in S at t. In this sense, the external sentences of legal science undoubtedly possess a scientific quality. If a legal scientist *asserts* only external sentences, all of what he asserts may very well be true, and his aims and methods are not essentially different from those of many other scientific activities. The scientific status of the external sentences is entirely independent of the scientific status of the internal sentences, i.e., the legal rules themselves.

(ii) If, in conformity with The Axiom of Naive Jurisprudence, the legal scientist also asserts the internal sentences, the situation changes. The scientific status of such sentences then becomes an important question.

If we consider the unbiased search for truths as essential to any scientific activity, we must, I think, deny that that part of legal science which consists in asserting internal sentences is scientific. It is no more a genuine science than is an intellectual activity which proceeds on the assumption of the Axiom of Naive Biblical Theology.

An even more fundamental objection to that jurisprudence which asserts internal sentences is raised by those philosophers who maintain that normative sentences are the expressions of emotional attitudes rather than statements of theoretical assumptions or beliefs.[12] In the naive formulation D_n of legal science the internal sentences are undoubtedly of many different kinds: some but not all of them have a normative character. What a rational reconstruction D_r of legal science will look like in detail remains an open question. However, in any adequate rational reconstruction, there will likewise have to occur normative internal sentences. I am inclined to think that the interpretation of normative sentences in terms of emotional attitudes is correct.

For these reasons I think that the assertions of a rationally reconstructed legal science should mainly be assertions of external sentences. Internal sentences, expressing legal rules, should be asserted not wholesale in virtue of any principle like The Axiom of Naive Jurisprudence but only when (i) they are factual and (ii) their truth can be empirically ascertained.[13]

SECTION III

12. *The internal concept of 'ownership' or 'property.'* In this section I shall consider the question as to how certain terms occurring in the internal sentences should be introduced in a rational reconstruction of legal science. As an example

---

[12] Cf., e. g., no. XIV.

[13] The above remarks are not invalidated by an interesting observation that has been made by Ingemar Hedenius. When a legal scientist asserts a sentence which literally and ostensibly expresses a legal rule, he is, it seems, frequently using an elliptical mode of speech. Although the sentence asserted literally expresses the rule P, what the legal scientist actually wants to state is often, not P itself, but merely the fact that P is in force (here and now). Cf. no. VI.

of the type of terms with which we shall be concerned, we may take the term "ownership" or "property." Although our discussion will be explicitly concerned only with the particular example chosen, the premises for our analysis will be so general that they apply to a very large number of internal terms. Hence, the present mode of analysis, if applicable to the term "ownership," will be applicable also to those other terms.

The problem that the term "ownership" presents to the analytic study of law is—formally stated—the problem of explaining the significance of the sentence form:

(7) *O is the property of P at t,*

where *O* is a certain object, *P* a person (or group of persons) and *t* a moment (or period) in time. Synonymous with (7) is the sentence form:

(7′) *P owns O at t.*

The sentence form (7) is one occurring in the internal sentences that state legal rules. We are looking for a definition:

D(7) (7) = def . . .

which should be such that, if (7) is everywhere replaced by ". . .," the significance of the internal sentences remains 'unchanged,' in a sense that will soon be made more precise.

Before we embark upon the attempt to find such a definition, it may be wise to state exactly what requirements we do and what requirements we do not expect the definition to fulfill.

(i) We wish our definition to render the meaning of the sentence form (7) as it occurs in the internal sentences of a legal science, concerned with a given system of positive law *L*. Hence, the definition which we are going to indicate must not be expected to render the meaning of the same sentence form as it occurs, e.g., in sociological discourse. If the sociologist means the same by (7) as the legal science in question, then our definition will apply also to his use of the term. But most probably he does not mean the same thing. The Law is not a description of sociological facts, and only in exceptional cases do the terms of the internal legal statements coincide with sociological terms.

(ii) The sentence form (7)—or its equivalents in languages other than English—occurs in connection with many distinct systems of positive law. *A priori* it is by no means certain that (7) when used in the formulation of one system *L* will mean the same as (7) when used in the formulation of a different system *L′*. In the subsequent discussion we shall be concerned with giving a general method for defining (7) as used in each of a large number of formulations of legal systems. Because of the practical difficulties involved we shall not give any actual definition conforming to the method. The same method, it is assumed, applies to very many systems of positive law, but it is not presumed that the resulting definitions will be the same for the different systems. The presumption is, in fact, on the contrary, that the definitions for the different systems will not coincide.

(iii) It would be an interesting task to elicit what (7) as used in connection with a system L has in common with (7) as used in connection with a different system L', and thus to explain how the same terminology has come to be employed for different concepts. But that is a task which we shall not attempt to tackle here. It lies beyond the scope of our investigation, and it would, besides, require a detailed comparative acquaintance with the historically given systems of positive law—something that the present writer entirely lacks.

(iv) An equally interesting, but probably even more difficult, problem is to determine those general features that (7) as used in connection with the various systems of positive law has in common with certain other forms of internal sentences, and that account for the fact that all these forms of sentences are regarded as stating 'legal rights.' That problem is even farther beyond the modest aim of our inquiry.

13. *Adequate definitions of (7).*

(i) A definition of a given expression is always in terms of certain other expressions. The same expression may be defined in terms of several distinct sets of other expressions. To make definite the aim at which we are striving, therefore, we have to state the expressions in terms of which we intend to couch the definition of (7). The method which we are going to explain will lead, if actually applied to a system of positive law L, to a definition of (7) as used in the formulation of L in terms of other expressions which either already occur in the formulation of L or are easily explained in terms of expressions which do.

(ii) Finally, it remains to state what relationship we require to hold between definiendum and definiens in order that the definition of (7) shall be 'adequate' or 'acceptable.' *A priori* many distinct requirements are possible, and the rather weak requirement that will here be stipulated is the result of a deliberate choice.

Some will no doubt be inclined to require of $D(7)$ that its definiens shall express the same 'idea' or 'thought' that is expressed by (7) when used in existing legal science, or—in other words—that the definiens shall express what legal scientists commonly 'think' (have in mind, imagine) when using (7). The reasons which forced us to reject this requirement in connection with the definition of the external terms of legal science, however, possess an equal or even greater weight in this connection. What 'thoughts' accompany the use of (7), probably varies from one jurist to another, and even, in the same jurist, from one occasion to the next. The thoughts of some jurists are probably highly inarticulate. The Swedish legal philosopher Axel Hägerström maintains that, in ancient Roman law, certain curious magical ideas were associated with the Roman equivalents of (7), and that the magic of the Romans can still be traced in many, if not in most, modern legal conceptions.[14] If Hägerström is even partially right—a question upon which I am incompetent to pass any judgment—that would constitute an additional reason why our definition, which is intended to be incorporated in

14 Cf. no. VIII.

a rational reconstruction of legal science, can not aim at reproducing what jurists actually have in mind when using (7).

(iii) When discussing the external concepts of legal science, we decided to judge the adequacy of proposed definitions by a purely extensional criterion. A definition of an external concept, we agreed, is adequate provided that the definiens is true (false) if and only if the definiendum is true (false). It might be suggested that the same criterion of adequacy be adopted here. However, the criterion is reasonable only if the definiendum is a phrase which is capable of truth or falsehood. (If the definiendum is never true and never false, the criterion amounts only to a prohibition against choosing a definiens that is ever true or ever false. The criterion gives us complete liberty to define any expression which is never true and never false by any other expression of the same kind. This result is obviously contrary to what we expect of a sound definition.) I have accepted the common view that normative sentences are incapable of truth and falsehood. Since some legal phrases have an essentially normative connotation, there are legal phrases to whose definition the suggested extensional criterion can not, reasonably, be applied. We do not yet know whether the present definiendum is to be considered as a normative or a factual phrase; hence, we do not yet know whether proposed definitions thereof can, reasonably, be tested by the extensional standard.

An additional reason for rejecting the extensional criterion is that we are considering the phrase (7) only as an arbitrarily chosen example of a large class of legal conceptions and that we wish our discussion to apply not merely to this particular example but to the entire class. Hence, in view of the possible normative nature of some of these conceptions, we must not choose an extensional criterion of adequacy.

(iv) The criterion which I have chosen is this: A definition, "(7) = def . . .," will be recognized as adequate provided that the rules of L logically imply that (7) if and only if . . ., i.e., provided that the equivalence of definiens and definiendum is logically implied by the rules of L themselves.[15]

14. *A first method of definition.* In order to find a definition of the desired kind we have to consider what rules concerning 'ownership' are contained in the system L under discussion. If the system L is sufficiently developed, it will contain a set of rules which regulate the generation of ownership and another set of rules which regulate the extinction thereof. Let us assume that the former set of rules is expressed by the two sets of sentences:

(8) *If A_i then O becomes the property of P at t ($i = 1, \ldots, m$).*

(9) *If B_i then O becomes the property of P at t ($i = 1, \ldots, n$).*

The antecedents A_i and B_i state that, prior to the moment t, a certain specified situation obtains. The difference between the antecedents A_i and B_i is that the former do not but the latter do involve some phrase of the type (7). Let

---

[15] Similar ideas are expressed and discussed in nos. I, III–V, XIII, XV, and XVI.

us likewise assume that the latter set of rules is expressed by the two sets of sentences:

(10) *If C_i then O ceases to be the property of P at t $(i = 1, \ldots, p)$.*
(11) *If D_i then O ceases to be the property of P at t $(i = 1, \ldots, q)$.*

Here, too, the antecedents state that, prior to the moment t, some specified situation obtains. The difference between C_i and D_i is the same as that between A_i and B_i.[16]

David Hume suggested that phrase (7) might be defined in terms of the rules under discussion: ". . . when a definition of property is required, that relation is found to resolve itself into any possession acquired by occupation, by prescription, by inheritance, by contract, etc."[17] If we presuppose the formulation (8)–(11) of the relevant rules, Hume's idea could be expressed in the form of the following definition: $D_1(7)$: (7) = def *There is a moment t' preceding t such that A_1 or A_2 or . . . or A_m or B_1 or B_2 or . . . or B_n holds for t', and there is no moment t'' intermediate between t' and t such that C_1 or C_2 or . . . or C_p or D_1 or D_2 or . . . or D_q holds for t''.*

Is this an adequate definition of (7) in the previously agreed sense? A first objection to the definition $D_1(7)$ is that it is beset by a vicious circle, unless the two sets of sentences (9) and (11) are empty. If these sets are not empty—and for most systems of positive law L they would not be empty—the definiens will contain phrases of the very same type to which the definiendum belongs. The definition could, of course, be rendered non-circular by simply dropping the conditions B_i and D_i from the definiens.[18] But, clearly, that operation would render the definition inadequate. However, it is easily seen, I think, that the circle can be eschewed by using a more subtle logical technique. The direction in time, so to speak, points from the situations stated by the antecedents to the situations stated by the consequents in the sentences (8)–(11). In view of this fact, it should be possible to eliminate the circle by using what mathematicians call a 'recursive' procedure. Carrying this out in detail would no doubt involve the solution of many technical logical problems, but still it should be possible.

Here I shall only indicate in gross outline the general idea of such a recursive definition. Let us say that the fact that O is the property of P at t constitutes an

---

[16] If all rules entailed by rules of L themselves belong to L, we can, by considering hypothetical situations of any degree of complexity, construct an unlimited number of rules that belong to L. But all these rules, which are unlimited in number, are entailed by a limited number of rules of L. The sentences (8)–(11) are supposed to express, not all the constructible rules of L of the indicated types, but a set of such rules which is sufficiently comprehensive to entail all such rules.

[17] Cf. no. VII, pp. 201–2.

[18] The Danish legal philosopher Alf Ross says: "Evidently the rules governing the changing of rights are distinct from the rights themselves, and hence the definition of right is best obtained if we disregard the dynamic phenomena" (no. XII, pp. 185–86, my translation). It seems possible to interpret this statement as implying a recommendation to disregard the sentences (9) and (11) in the definition of (7). If that interpretation is correct, I think, for the reason stated in the text, that the statement involves a mistake.

'ownership situation.' Let us assume that an ownership situation S_n exists at the moment t_n. In order to establish the existence of S_n we may find it necessary to establish the existence of certain ownership situations S'_{n-1}, S''_{n-1}, . . . at a previous moment t_{n-1}. Let us then say that S_n is a 'descendant' of S'_{n-1}, S''_{n-1}, ... Some of these latter situations may themselves turn out to be the descendants of other still earlier ownership situations. We then continue to trace their line of descent, and we obtain a genealogical table:

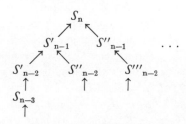

This table contains a number of lines of descent: $(S_n, S'_{n-1}, S'_{n-2}, S_{n3-}, \ldots)$, $(S_n, S'_{n-1}, S''_{n-2}, \ldots)$, $(S_n, S''_{n-1}, S'''_{n-2}, \ldots)$. Sooner or later each such line of descent will come to an end: as its last member it will contain an ownership situation whose existence can be established independently of the existence of any previous ownership situations. Let us say that in such an ultimate ownership situation there is firsthand ownership. Firsthand ownership can be defined in terms of its generation, without any circularity. We can then define secondhand ownership as ownership whose generating conditions involve only firsthand ownerships, thirdhand ownership as ownership whose generating conditions involve only first- and secondhand ownerships, and so on. None of these definitions will involve any circularity. Finally, we can define ownership, in general, as ownership which is either first- or second- or third- or . . . hand. This is only a very rough explanation of how a non-circular recursive definition $D_2(7)$ can be reached. In actual fact, the definition would probably be even more complicated, but still the general pattern of its construction will be the same.

Let us then assume that we have replaced the preliminary definition $D_1(7)$ which is circular by a recursively constructed definition $D_2(7)$ which is non-circular. The question still remains of whether that definition $D_2(7)$ is adequate, in the previously stated sense. Do the sentences which express the rules of L logically imply that (7) holds if and only if the definiens of $D_2(7)$ holds? Let us first ask the question of whether the four sets of sentences (8)–(11) by themselves logically imply that such is the case. The answer is obviously in the negative. The set of sentences (8)–(11) is 'logically open,' in the sense that it can be enlarged by the addition of further such sentences, which are not logically implied by the set itself, without incurring any contradiction. The changes which a system of law L undergoes from time to time, through legislation or otherwise, sometimes consist, I think, only in such additions. However, if to the set of sentences (8)–(11) we add a further condition to the effect that the set is 'logically closed,' the set with that extra condition guarantees the adequacy of the definition $D_2(7)$. To say that the set is 'logically closed' is to say that no ownership is created or extinguished except in conformity with the rules expressed by the set. In actual fact, at each separate moment in the historical development of a legal system, this assumption of the logically closed character of the set $(8)-(11)$ seems to be tacitly presupposed by legal scientists. In a rational reconstruction of legal science, we would, I think, be entitled to render this assumption explicit. If this is correct, the definition $D_2(7)$ is an adequate definition of (7).

If we introduce the phrase (7) in our rationally reconstrued legal science by the definition $D_2(7)$, the phrase (7) will not, I think, express any essentially normative idea. The question of whether or not (7) holds for given O, P, and t, becomes a question of matters of fact, of recursively tracing certain lines of descent. Thus, also, the sentences $(8)-(11)$, upon the present analysis, will not express any normative propositions. We may consider them either as parts of the recursive definition of (7) or as analytic statements derived from that definition.

The introduction of (7) through $D_2(7)$ entails a consequence which has a certain air of paradox. The meaning of (7) becomes radically relative to the rules governing the generation and extinction of ownership. Whenever these rules are changed, the very meaning of the phrase (7) will also change; the phrase will not mean the same in connection with any two systems of law which differ in these rules. This air of paradox is not, in my opinion, any serious objection to the present mode of analysis.

15. *A second method of definition?* The method of definition outlined under heading 14 makes use of those conditions which, according to a system of positive law L, generate and extinguish ownership. But a system L does not merely determine the generation and extinction of ownership. It also determines that existing ownership has certain 'legal consequences.' If O is the property of P at t, then, if such and such an event should happen, the consequence would be such and such. We can assume that the rules of this kind, which belong to L, are expressed through the sentences:

(12) *If (7), then if F_i, then G_i (i = 1, ..., r)*.
(13) *If (7), then if H_i, then J_i (i = 1, ..., s)*.
(14) *If (7), then if K_i, then L_i (i = 1, ..., t)*.
(15) *If (7), then if M_i, then N_i (i = 1, ..., u)*.

Here, the constituents J_i, K_i, M_i, and N_i involve some phrase of the type (7), while the remaining constituents do not involve any such phrase.[19]

It has often been suggested that a phrase like (7) should be defined in terms of 'legal consequences.' Thus, e.g., Östen Undén says: "Like a large category of juristic concepts, the notion of ownership has been framed as an expression and

---

[19] A remark analogous to that which was made in footnote 16 above concerning sentences $(8)-(11)$ applies also to these sentences $(12)-(15)$.

a comprehension of a complex of legal consequences."[20] In conformity with this idea, one might try to define (7) in the following manner:

$D_3(7)$ (7) = def *(if F_1 then G_1) and . . . and (if F_r then G_r) and (if H_1 then J_1) and . . . and (if H_s then J_s) and (if K_1 then L_1) and . . . and (if K_t then L_t) and (if M_1 then N_1) and . . . and (if M_u then N_u).*

As it stands, this definition will involve a logical circle, unless the sets of sentences (13), (14), and (15) are all empty. The circle could, I believe, be eliminated by transforming $D_3(7)$ into a recursively framed definition $D_4(7)$, although the recursive construction will be even more complicated in this case than in the case of the definition $D_2(7)$.

Assuming that such a non-circular recursive definition $D_4(7)$ can be construed, will it be an adequate definition of (7), in the previously stipulated sense? To answer this question in the affirmative is to say that the set of internal sentences which express the rules of L logically implies that there is no legal relationship holding between an object O and a person P at a time t, which has exactly the same consequences as ownership and is yet distinct from ownership. I do not know if such is in general the case. For some systems of law it probably is, but I can see no reason why it always should be. It will be the case for a given system of law L, if the following two conditions are fulfilled:

(i) Consider the sentence form:

(16) *The legal relationship R holds between O and P at t.*

Let $(8')-(15')$ be the sentences which express the rules of L concerning R just as (8)–(15) express the rules of L concerning ownership. Let us finally say that a sentence involving (16) is a 'transformation' of a sentence involving (7), if the former results from the latter when we replace each expression of form (7) by the corresponding expression of form (16). The *first* condition can then be stated thus: The system L countenances no relationship R for which the sentences $(12')-(15')$ are exactly the transformations of (12)–(15), whereas the sentences $(8')-(11')$ fail to be exactly the transformations of (8)–(11).

(ii) The *second* condition is this: The system L (tacitly) claims its own 'completeness' in the sense, roughly speaking, that there are no legal relationships save those which obtain in consequence of the rules of L.

If we introduce phrase (7) into our rationally reconstructed legal science by a definition $D_4(7)$, the phrase will express an essentially normative idea. Among the 'legal consequences' of ownership are, e.g., that thieves *shall* be punished in such and such a manner. Such normative consequences will enter as constituents into the definiens of $D_4(7)$. Thus, all sentences involving (7) will express normative propositions. The sentences (12)–(15) will become either parts of the definition of (7) or analytic statements derived from the definition. A definition $D_4(7)$ renders the meaning of (7) relative to the rules governing the legal consequences of ownership in the same way that the definition $D_2(7)$ makes it relative to the rules governing the generation and extinction of ownership.

---

[20] Cf. no. XVII, p. 83 (my translation).

17. *A third method of introducing (7).* The concept of property or owner-ship is, in a certain sense, merely auxiliary. To establish that such and such an object O is the property of a person P at a time t, seems to be of interest only as a step toward concluding that, therefore, such and such legal consequences ensue. By employing the general sentences (8)–(15) as our premises, we can, in a greater or less number of steps, derive from a given condition which does not involve the concept of property a certain consequence which likewise does not involve that concept. To make possible such logical transitions appears to be the essential function of the statement form (7) and of those sentences in which it occurs.

If this is correct, in our rational reconstruction D_r of a given legal theory D_n we may choose to treat the phrase (7) in a manner entirely different from that which has been indicated in the preceding paragraphs. We may regard the phrase (7) as a linguistic symbol whose sole function in legal reasoning is to facilitate inference from statements not involving that phrase to other statements not involving it. The definition of an expression within a given context usually has two aspects. (i) If we define an expression A in terms of other expressions $B, C \ldots$, occurring within the same context, we open the possibility of eliminat-ing A in favor of $B, C \ldots$ within that context. (ii) Provided that we have already attached interpretations or meanings to $B, C \ldots$, A will indirectly receive a certain corresponding interpretation or meaning in virtue of the defini-tion. If we wish to leave an expression uninterpreted, 'meaningless,' hence, we must not define it in terms of expressions already interpreted. Accordingly, we now refuse to state any definition whatsoever of (7), and, in addition, we refuse to attach any independent interpretation to (7). The first refusal implies making (7) a basic expression of legal discourse. The second refusal implies regarding this basic expression as a 'meaningless' linguistic vehicle of inference.

It may be shocking to unsophisticated common sense to admit such 'mean-ingless' expressions in the serious discourse of legal scientists. But, as a matter of fact, there is no reason why all expressions employed in a discourse, which as a whole is highly 'meaningful,' should themselves have a 'meaning.' It appears likely that many expressions employed by other sciences, especially by the so-called exact sciences, lack interpretation and function solely as vehicles of sys-tematization and deduction. Why should not the situation be the same within legal science?

It may perhaps be objected that it can never be 'necessary' to introduce meaningless expressions in order to make possible the deduction of meaningful sentences from other meaningful sentences. The objection is certainly true, if 'necessary' is taken in a sufficiently strict sense. But the introduction of meaning-less expressions can be very advantageous, almost 'necessary,' from a practical point of view. Suppose that we have m sentences A_i and n sentences B_j and that, for every i and j, we wish to state: "*if A_i then B_j*." The number of such hypo-thetical sentences that we would have to write down is $m \cdot n$. This number rapidly increases as m and n increase, and if m and n are sufficiently large, their product may become so large that it is practically almost impossible to write down all the $m \cdot n$ hypothetical sentences. In this situation it is very helpful to introduce a meaningless symbol, say Z, and state merely the two sets of hypothetical sentences: '*If A_i then Z*' and '*If Z then B_j.*' The number of these sentences is only $m + n$, a number which, for large m and n, is very much smaller than $m \cdot n$, and still from these sentences all the $m \cdot n$ sentences which we wish to assert, can be logically derived. The analogy between the use of the symbol Z in this extremely simple case and the use of the phrase (7) in legal science is, I think, obvious.

BIBLIOGRAPHY

I. Ahlander, B. *Ar juridiken en vetenskap?* [Is jurisprudence a science?] (Stockholm, 1950).

II. Austin, J. *Lectures on Jurisprudence*, vol. I (London, 1861).

III. Ekelöf, P. O. "Juridisk slutledning och terminologi." [Juristic inference and terminology]. *Tidskrift for Retsvidenskab* 58: 211–70 (1945).

IV. ———. "Till frågan om rättighetsbegreppet" [On the concept of right]. *Tidskrift for Retsvidenskab* 59: 309–13 (1946).

V. ———. "Om begagnandet av termen rättighet inom juridiken" [On the use of the term right in jurisprudence]. *Svensk Juristtidnings Festskrift för Birger Ekeberg* (Stockholm, 1950), pp. 151–77.

VI. Hedenius, I. *Om rätt och moral* [On law and morals] (Stockholm, 1941).

VII. Hume, D. *An Enquiry concerning the Principles of Morals*, ed. L. A. Selby-Bigge, ed. 2, (Oxford, 1946).

VIII. Hägerström, A. *Der römische Obligationsbegriff*, vols. 1–2 (Uppsala, 1927–1941).

IX. Kelsen, H. *General Theory of Law and State*. Twentieth Century Legal Philosophy Series, vol. 1 (Cambridge, Mass., 1945).

X. Ofstad, H. "The Descriptive Definition of the Concept 'Legal Norm' Proposed by Hans Kelsen." *Theoria* 16: 118–51 (1950).

XI. Oppenheim, F. "Outline of a Logical Analysis of Laws." *Philosophy of Science* 11: 142–60 (1944).

XII. Ross, A. *Virkelighed och Gyldighed i Retslæren* [Reality and validity in legal science] (Copenhagen, 1934).

XIII. ———. "Tu-tu, eller en ny og underbar beretning om Noit-kif-folkets sprog etc." [Tu-tu, or a new and marvellous account of the language of the Noitkif-people, etc.]. Stencilled outline of a lecture given in the Law Club of Uppsala in the spring of 1951.

XIV. Stevenson, C. *Ethics and Language* (New Haven, 1945).

XV. Strahl, I. "Till frågan om rättighetsbegreppet" [On the notion of right]. *Tidskrift for Retsvidenskab* 59: 204–10 (1946).

XVI. ———. "Till frågan om rättighetsbegreppet" [On the notion of legal right]. *Tidskrift for Retsvidenskab* 60: 481–514 (1947).

XVII. Undén, Ö. *Svensk sakrätt, I. Lös egendom* [Swedish law of things, I. Personal property] (Lund, 1927).

B

Legal and Moral Philosophy
Philosophical Ideology

Ingemar Hedenius

The Criminal Law and Morals

The statutes of the criminal law usually say that he who does this or that shall be sentenced to this or that punishment. In other words, its statutes are commands to prosecutors and judges. The criminal law thus addresses itself immediately to a relatively small minority in the community. Its addressees are certain people whose profession it is to bring those who commit crimes to account. There can be little doubt that these officials to a great extent follow the bidding of the criminal law. In a civilized society, there is no reason to expect that they would exhibit any significant resistance to what the criminal law ordains.

The officials in question are, in the sense just indicated, the primary proponents of the doctrine of what should be done or forborne (hereafter referred to as "legal doctrine") that finds expression in the criminal law. No one has reason to take legal doctrine with greater seriousness than they. This group has been specially trained to know the commands of criminal law and to enforce them. Also, because of the mutual scrutiny that is usually found within an official organization, the risk of discovery and the unpleasant consequences of disobedience are great. To depart from regulations would be to court danger. If anyone can be expected to really adhere to legal doctrine, it is those charged with applying criminal law. What they adhere to may be called "the first part of legal doctrine."

In accordance with the dictates of the criminal law, no one *can* be prosecuted, sentenced, or punished by the rest of us. Hence we do not violate criminal law even though we consistently omit to do all that it prescribes. We cannot be either obedient to or in violation of what it commands, inasmuch as it is not addressed to us.

On the other hand, it is manifest that the criminal law does have a certain

Professor Hedenius, of the University of Uppsala, is a native of Sweden.
Translated from the Swedish by Raymond E. Olson.

interest for us and that in *this* sense it does also address itself to us. We may interpret its directives to certain authorities as a kind of plain threat directed to the public—including, of course, the officials who in part are more than just officials and can easily enough find themselves on the other side of the bar. Hence, we may read the statutes in a subjective way, and so say to ourselves: If *I* do this or that, *I* shall evidently be punished in this or that way. On the basis of this, we may also reinterpret the commands to punish as so many prohibitions against our behaving such that prosecution, sentencing, and punishment shall follow. The criminal law contains no direct command to us to take note of its threats; nevertheless, our own prudential concern and perhaps our morals can impel us to do so.

For many of us, it is natural to take yet another step. We may come to regard it as our moral duty to refrain steadfastly from punishable acts, and may conceive the same mode of behavior as a moral obligation for everyone. A variety of reasons can be advanced for this view. Some may feel that it is morally indefensible to render oneself miserable by subjecting oneself to punishment. One may also feel that morality exacts 'good citizenship' from each and every person. The individual may also believe that every punishable act is in itself morally reprehensible. The last-mentioned idea may be said to embrace 'the second part of legal doctrine.'

How generally is it adhered to? While infractions of the first part of legal doctrine certainly are uncommon, those of the second part are much more common. We must not forget that many people occasionally do what they themselves consider wrong. But the enormous spread of crime in every civilized society (*how* widespread it is no one knows) makes it impossible to believe that the second part of legal doctrine is just as strongly adhered to as the first.

Here it is relevant to note that certain investigations disclose great discrepancies between ordinary people's ideas about right and wrong and those of legal doctrine. Most people will admit that murder is the worst sort of crime. But many are of the opinion that homosexuality between adults and failure to pay for the support of one's children are almost equally odious, although, according to the criminal law in civilized societies, these modes of behavior are not in themselves crimes. To pilfer forty farthings is a trivial crime, one supposes, and to falsify for forty farthings—for example, by erasing the ink mark on a stamp and using it again—is little worse. But legal doctrine judges these actions completely differently, and is especially severe against the latter. Prevaricating slightly in order to help a friend, however blameless one may take this to be, is a dreadful thing according to legal doctrine and can bring on unconditional punishment if it involves perjury. But many are convinced that this sort of thing, even if inconsiderate, is something to be excused and, moreover, they would be inclined to be sympathetic to it. Ignorance that an act is a crime is usually no excuse according to legal doctrine, but it is often so according to the common moral point of view.

One often sees legal doctrine and ordinary moral consciousness at odds over what comprises a serious offense; that is, legal doctrine sometimes acquits what public morals condemn and vice versa.

Furthermore, people are so far removed from legal doctrine as scarcely to know what it contains. The afore-mentioned officials and others close to their sphere no doubt have a good (if not always perfect) comprehension of the law. If there are any perfect followers of legal doctrine they must be in this group. Among them, also, since earliest times, there has existed the idea that criminal law and its application must agree with public moral consciousness in order for criminal justice to be able to function, or—a still more bizarre notion—in order for it to be called "right" at all. Moreover, this idea has fostered the extreme attitude that legal rights originate in public moral consciousness, which is then represented as having been awakened to articulation and clarity through the activity of legislators and jurists. That all of these ideas are erroneous would seem obvious.

It is true that certain elements of the common moral consciousness have to be repeated in legal doctrine. But when we think of the great extent to which people in the fortunate countries conform to standards of good behavior, and then of the extent to which governments in the unfortunate ones are able to achieve the same result through terror, we find that from the standpoint of functional efficiency the fact that so great a part of criminal law has no correspondence with popular conceptions of right and wrong is much less significant than many believe.

It would be unfortunate if criminal justice were always shaped in accordance with the public's moral consciousness, if indeed such a thing were possible at all. This would make the regulation of large areas regarded by the public as morally indifferent impossible, while in other areas the state would be bound to support the development of the prejudices that appear frequently in the common moral consciousness.

Administration of criminal justice is not just one of the methods for dealing with willfully criminal behavior. It is also a means for educating the public. An example of this is provided by the legal mode of proceeding against even slightly intoxicated drivers. But the idea that legal doctrine on the whole coincides with the so-called moral consciousness is an illusion. In times past, this illusion was a source of satisfaction for certain officials and others of the ruling class, but it is now retreating in the face of the great swelling of crimes as defined by legal doctrine.

Public apathy toward legal doctrine is illustrated by a phenomenon often discussed by social workers. People at large not only often tolerate persons who do things that are offenses in the eyes of the criminal law, they also refrain from warning or instructing the offenders, when they certainly would have done so had the offense been failure to take precautions against a cold or unconventionality in dress or behavior at a party (for example, going barefoot). But, as perhaps could have been foreseen, once such a person is discovered, sentenced, and punished, *then* he becomes the object of the greatest moral disapproval, ostracism. This attitude is contrary to legal doctrine, which insists that all crime, including the as yet undiscovered, should be disapproved, but, reasonably, does not continue to press sanctions once punishment has taken place.

The attitude under consideration points out a much more primitive viewpoint than that of legal doctrine, namely, the tendency to disapprove, condemn, or ostracize those who through their own fault meet with misfortune or, as one says, "don't take care of themselves." Moreover, this reaction it to be understood as one of the numerous manifestations of a double standard without which our society certainly would never be what it is. Crime is not so abominable when only a few people know about it, but once it is discovered and becomes widely known it becomes inordinately despicable.

This double morality may not extend to those who adhere to the first part of legal doctrine—officials and others like them. Rather, it is no doubt more at home in lower-level circles. Some of the legal elite have a kind of double morality in their philosophies of criminal law. This has its basis in the following factors.

Everyone knows which acts are the gravest crimes according to the law: murder, rape, assault and battery, arson, robbery, the worst property crimes, and so forth. These kinds of behavior are also regarded as morally wrong to a high degree. They become objects of strong disapproval from the ordinary man, whose tolerance of them is quite limited and never leaves room for any double morality. Further, the severe legal sanctions are generally regarded as an expression of society's moral condemnation of these modes of behavior. Here, punishment appears not merely to be motivated by a preventive purpose but also to be just and well-deserved, that is to say, to be a morally necessary retribution.

Apart from the more serious crimes, it may be natural to regard punishment as being merely a way of correcting through discomfort, a kind of 'social surgery.' The thinking behind such punishment may be something like this: in order to lessen the frequency of this kind of behavior, we shall make it expensive to be caught so behaving. But this view does not predominate in the case of truly grave crime. In such cases, the suffering of punishment is also a means to satisfying the public's need to feel indignation toward the morally inferior.

But among the officials and those closely associated with them, there is an enlightened, philosophical faction. It dissociates itself from regarding criminal legislation as a manifestation of moral disapproval or retributive intent, and is firmly convinced that anything of that sort is absent, especially from the criminal law of the Scandinavian countries. At the same time, this philosophical faction is convinced that punishment for serious crime needs to be thought of *by the public* as 'well-deserved' and that society for the present cannot avoid resorting to this more primitive attitude. This is actually a part of the 'morality-building' function of criminal law administration and, in fact, contributes in no small degree to abstention from the grossest offenses. Even so, the philosophical faction, for its own part, wants to regard criminal justice merely as an unfortunately indispensable method of controlling by means of discomfort. The no doubt necessary but (it is felt) dirty job of moralizing is to be left to the broad mass of the people.

Thus, in this situation, there is the double morality that while the criminal law and its administration in fact nourish the retributive attitude, this attitude is at the same time regarded as antiquated and as having been replaced in enlightened circles by a more rational outlook. It may be that the philosophical faction comprehends well the first part of the legal doctrine, but it by no means fully shares what for the ordinary man is a principal element of its second part.[1]

The philosophical faction's position would certainly be thought cynical if it become widely known. It has, in brief, the following import. Of the different methods of combating major crimes, punishment is the cruelest. Punishment very seldom improves those who commit the offenses. It torments and degrades them, with the result that they are fixed more firmly in an existence of confirmed criminality and deep misery. Dealing with grave breaches of behavior the way the criminal law does results largely in an irreparable degradation of human beings in order to satisfy the interests of the law-abiding part of the population. The aim is to frighten and to uphold the social morality by interventions intended to brand criminal behavior as shameful. Not least among the effects produced is that the family of the offender and others who are dependent on him are also degraded. What is intended is that inhibitions be placed on quite a large number of people who might have ventured into crime had a more humane system prevailed.

On the other hand this system is generally less effective than might be imagined from observing its cruelty. Therefore, the philosophical faction is also in favor of its humanization. But to completely abolish the repressive method is evidently not possible in the foreseeable future. According to the philosophical

---

[1] This calls to mind the arrangement of parts in a play where some characters represent a primitive outlook and others a more developed one, and where both points of view, although incompatible, must be represented for the drama as a whole to proceed. Society provides further examples of this. One is the role-playing of opinion-makers on the occasion of visits by foreign despots. Government leaders and those associated with them must then display the more primitive stance: the people of Sweden feel themselves honored; there is a strong sense of fellowship; hopes of cooperation in mutual understanding and friendship are expressed; and so on. Certain intellectuals take a position informed by a higher culture: that words are words and a tyrant is a tyrant, even if he controls Europe's mightiest military power and is now being entertained at the expense of the Swedish state, that no person of honor can ever forget what has happened, etc. Then double morality is present on the side of these intellectuals, since they probably understand the opinion-makers' role too. There is outward condemnation of an attitude that secretly is admitted to be one that has to be tolerated and that is even in its way prudent. But the government and its supporters are just as guilty of double morality, for their complaining about irresponsible intellectuals is combined with their insight that it would be a shame if the intellectuals' attitude were not *also* to be proclaimed as the only right one. In such a case we may have a good deal of mere tilting with pens. That a situation like this should sometimes arise is to be expected within the framework of the double standards of morality here being discussed. *Here* the double morality cannot be reciprocal.

faction, this method is justified by the still greater harm that would result if it were now abandoned. Specifically, it is thought that crimes of violence would then increase to an unmanageable extent.

The philosophical faction's view of the punishment of innocent persons is also interesting. According to the popular way of thinking it can never be just to punish the innocent. But the philosophical faction notes that in reality no proof has 100 percent certainty, although jurists often express themselves as if this were the case. The best that can be attained is a very high probability. Now, since even the improbable does sometimes occur, there must be a certain number (hopefully, a very small one) of guilty verdicts, based on only probable proof, that fall upon innocent people. From this it follows that there is only one way to avoid judicial murder and that is to stop judging. But it is necessary to judge, and thus the occurrence of judicial murder is justified.

Without doubt, the question of what strength of proof is necessary for the administration of justice to serve the two different purposes—convicting criminals and minimizing the number of judicial murders—is a difficult one. Solutions to this problem must always have the character of a compromise between two actually incompatible demands of justice. It is not only by prosecuting criminals that we try to protect life and property, but also by permitting judicial murder. Both aspects are justified by social utility, that is, utility for the majority, those who are not oppressed. Naturally, this way of thinking is abhorrent in the extreme for the moral consciousness.

The illusion of the moral consciousness that judicial murder cannot be justified has perhaps a certain practical value in inclining courts of law to exhibit caution with regard to the testing of evidence in criminal cases. Another important moral illusion is the idea that each and every one who is guilty of a crime ought to suffer the punishment that is stipulated for the crime. This illusion can inhibit people who feel themselves tempted to commit a crime, and, indeed, it certainly does so.

It is nonetheless an illusion. A multitude of crimes are never prosecuted, due, among other reasons, to the inadequate resources of the police. To prosecute all criminals would prove catastrophically embarrassing for the operation of prisons. But a still graver probability would be the harmful effects of an enlarged scope of suppression. It can be assumed that the majority of the Swedish people in their youth commit at least one serious offense, but, by far, most of these youthful crimes are never prosecuted. This may be just as well, for the majority of these undetected lawbreakers are likely to be one-time offenders, among other reasons, precisely because they are never subjected to prosecution. In contrast, many of the young who have the bad luck to get caught and actually be punished develop into confirmed criminals.

However, we must reject the seemingly reasonable idea that *all* young people who commit a crime for the first time should escape prosecution and punishment. This would probably have the consequence of youthful crime's becoming intolerably extensive. The threat of punishment and its general deterrent effect would doubtless be removed entirely for a large segment of the population to the extent that the *risk* of prosecution would have disappeared. The fact that only a minority of these first-time offenders are subjected to any discomfort or are eventually punished, and that this minority is chosen at random, conflicts with the popular demand for justice. But, according to the philosophical faction, under present circumstances this is the best arrangement.

What is consequently recommended is a system that, for reasons of social utility, will allow innocent persons to be punished while guilty ones escape.

The points just developed show discrepancies between the common moral consciousness and a so-to-speak rationalistically fashioned legal doctrine. But whether we think in terms of the formal legal doctrine or interpret it more informally, the distance between legal doctrine and the ordinary man's way of thinking is so great that it may be doubted that legal doctrine has any popular support.

But we may reduce what is required for being an 'adherent' of legal doctrine. If so, the picture changes.

Legal doctrine seems to possess enormous authority, which may be compared with that of science or religion. No one has anything like a detailed knowledge of all of the propositions of science. But one may have faith in science nonetheless, in the sense that as soon as one has become aware of a scientific result one accepts it simply because science has arrived at it. At any rate, one does not object if some of the assertions of science appear strange or inconceivable. To a large extent, this is the educated man's attitude toward science. The Christian church, with its often intricate dogmas, assumes a similar position in certain circles, perhaps especially among Catholics. One may believe what the Church teaches but have little clear conception of the meaning of those teachings. The faith itself signifies just this, that if one becomes aware that something is maintained by one's religion, one accepts or at least does not oppose it. This attitude is called "implicit faith" and is considered sufficient for salvation.

No doubt, for the great majority of the public, a similar 'fundamental' loyalty toward legal doctrine exists. This is not altered by the double morality that may arise from conflicts between legal doctrine and actual life situations or underlying attitudes toward it. To regard a form of behavior as unlawful or punishable is to express condemnation of it. Conversely, to regard an act as not subject to prosecution is to grant its permissibility, and even halfway to recommend it. We find, then, that legal doctrine possesses unquestionable authority even among those who know but little of what it contains.

Is a loyalty of this type morally approvable? Of course not. One cannot escape responsibility by allowing others to dictate one's decisions. Responsibility is by no means reduced if a person subjects himself to the dictates of another before knowing what the dictates contain. It makes no difference whether the decision concerns method or goal. These self-evident maxims conflict with full acceptance of legal doctrine, whether it be knowledgeable or implicit acceptance. No doubt there are many circumstances in which obedience is a good rule. But obedience cannot be valid without exception since it can never be right to do wrong, and it always lies within the bounds of possibility that it would be wrong to obey.

In every conflict between a dictate of the criminal law and one of morality, the moral must be followed and that of criminal law disregarded, for by "moral" we mean just those dictates that should prevail when in conflict with other considerations. Legal rules can have moral authority and deserve our allegiance only if they agree or at least do not conflict with our moral convictions.

But which moral convictions? I propose the maxim that it is always wrong to make the world worse than it would otherwise have been. What is meant by "worse" or "better," "poor" or "good," and the like must in this connection be left open. The only relevant question is how human life is affected, and humanity alone can decide what is better or worse.

Let us assume that the criminal law contains only reasonable statutes and that no wrong commands issue from them. This means that *in the long run*, at least, obeying the regulations of the criminal law would not make the world worse than it would be if, instead, other rules or none at all were obeyed. It is, then, a good maxim to obey the criminal law, even in those cases in which we are not able beforehand to determine what effects for good or evil will result from our obedience. Analogously, a doctor treats a patient by a method that has 'the best statistics,' although the doctor may not know if certain factors are present in a given case that will make the patient worse than he would have been if the doctor had chosen another treatment or no treatment at all. Let us assume that the law is altogether reasonable. It follows that we must obey it even in those cases in which we can foresee no good effects from doing so. In unusual circumstances, where we plainly see that obedience will make the world worse than it otherwise would have been, however, we must of course not obey.

Opposed to this is the idea that one must often obey even when obedience would produce worse consequences than disobedience. Some maintain that certain 'absolute rules' (that is, rules to be upheld without exception for as long as possible) have such valuable consequences that they ought not to be given up for the sake of the short-term benefits from one or another exception. What is meant by this is not always clear. One often-expressed concern is for the authority that a good rule always ought to have, but which, it is thought, is diminished or undermined every time the rule is set aside. There are two different matters to take into consideration here.

The first of these is the fact that a rule can be lessened in authority only if it becomes known that an exception was made. Hence, if the disobedience can be kept secret, that inconvenience does not arise.

The other matter is that even if departures from the rules are kept secret, the offender himself loses respect for them. His successful bending of a rule tends to habituate him to an undesirable attitude. We have also to reckon with other bad effects on the secret rule-breaker, for instance, pangs of conscience or long-lasting fear of detection, possibly culminating in his so regretting his deed as to vitiate whatever benefits it initially entailed. But these risks also may be practically nonexistent.

In support of the proposition that there are rules that have to be honored more or less without exception, observers of the law sometimes offer the following illustration. A wealthy American, S, wills his fortune to medical research at Yale University. On his deathbed, however, S becomes angry for some inconsequential reason with the people at Yale. As a means of venting his anger, S secretly summons his friend V and dictates a new will to him in which he directs that the fortune be used instead for the establishment of a dog cemetery. S makes V promise to see to the execution of this new will, but when S is dead, V takes it home and burns it. Is it right to deviate from legal doctrine in this way?

In commenting on this and similar stories, which aim at being morally shocking, it is usual to say that V acted wrongly, because it would be unfortunate if dying persons could not rely upon the promises made to them or because either V must suffer for the questionable thing he did or else he must be a person of a bad moral character in order to have been able to do such a thing. But nothing prevents us from construing the example in such a way that no undesirable consequences follow. Let us suppose that V's offense cannot be discovered and, further, that he has a conscience reinforced by philosophy. In that case, he made the world better by his action than it would otherwise have been. Consequently, according to our moral presupposition, he did nothing wrong. But if V had acted correctly according to legal doctrine, he would have acted wrongly. In fact, V did his duty.

That it not be found out is often necessary for a transgression of the law to be justified. Sometimes the authorities must work together in certain ways to quiet a matter. A departure from the second part of legal doctrine is then combined with a departure from the first part.

The following example, which I have found myself, may serve as an illustration of this point. Two military flyers who are out on a reconnaissance mission crash-land. One of the participants is unhurt, but the other catches on fire, is hopelessly burned, suffers horribly, and begs his comrade to shoot him. The comrade does just this. According to the criminal law this is a very grave crime. In order to quiet the matter juridically, the prosecutor turns to a doctor who, inspired by the prosecutor, certifies that in the light of present knowledge it can by no means be strictly or even probably inferred that the burned flyer was alive when shot. People who have just died of severe burns often show certain bodily movements which laymen usually misunderstand as signs of life and severe pain. With the support of this expression of opinion, which removes the risk of consequences to himself, the prosecutor decides not to proceed in this matter. In this way a conscientious and courageous youth escapes being tried for murder and thereby having his career ruined. At the same time he himself is relieved of brooding over whether he had actually killed his comrade, which is a matter of comparable importance. By definition, it is impossible to kill, or even to try to kill, a corpse.

This example could be described as a realistic fantasy. But the frequent euthanasia that many doctors practice is real. According to the criminal law, this activity is murder. Police and prosecutor alike shut their eyes to this, perhaps because the scandal would be too great otherwise, perhaps from a feeling that euthanasia is necessary for humanitarian reasons. If measures against it were begun in accordance with the criminal law, doctors would have to restrict themselves to such euthanasia as would incur no risk of discovery or else desist completely from this part of their activity. Either alternative would be most unfortunate.

There are also many other cases, more or less, of compassion. Thus, for example, a certain impoverished artist may decide to evade his taxes. The tax authorities have large possibilities for winking at such things and in this way making *their* small contribution to the advancement of the country's esthetic culture.

With the help of another realistic fantasy, a case can be shown in which both breaking *and* championing the law would be right.

The king of a certain country is being blackmailed by a man with whom he had a sexual relationship. In his loyal eagerness to protect the king, a high-level official commits a disagreeable transgression of the law: with the cooperation of Hitler's secret police, the blackmailer is sent to Germany. On his return, he is unjustifiably confined in an insane asylum, along with other similarly absurd measures. However, it turns out to be impossible to keep this affair completely secret. A rumor not wholly lacking in evidence threatens to discredit not only the court but also some of the country's highest officials. (And for just this reason the deviation on their part from legal doctrine must be regarded as especially indefensible.) Only after the king has died and the statute of limitations has run on the various official misconducts is prosecution of the blackmailer permitted. But the legal proceedings against him are to take place behind locked doors. At this point rumors begin to spread rampantly.

A novelist makes the scandal public by revealing some officially embarrassing documents of the case which he has obtained by falsely representing himself. Since consequently there is little reason for further concealment in this matter, the proper authorities decide to divulge essential parts of the legal proceedings in the blackmail trial. The air is cleared, and confidence in the authorities returns after they have been chastised for their behavior in the popular press. The novelist is brought to court for his high-handed actions. But it is noteworthy that his sentence is a fine of six thousand pounds rather than imprisonment. The amount is immediately collected and turned over to him by exasperated and grateful citizens.

This man's act of lawbreaking was particularly meritorious. Nevertheless, "out of regard for general obedience to the law," it was probably right that he was punished—although it was also gratifying that his punishment could be mitigated through the intervention of private parties. So curious can the relationship sometimes be between criminal law and morals.

But usually there is nothing strange about justifiable lawbreaking, for example, such acts as helping offenders to avoid discovery, destroying evidence, and the like—in short, anything that to some extent reduces the ill effects of crushing the human spirit. To be justifiable, this sort of crime must be committed only if the risk of discovery is minimal. Otherwise the result may be worse than if the law had been completely enforced.

There is a principle that has been so often proclaimed that many people probably believe it to be correct—namely, that with regard to the present matter there is a great difference between dictatorships and democracies. Thus, in a dictatorship the citizens are not duty-bound to obey the laws if obedience appears repugnant to a conscience that is at all enlightened. On the contrary, in such a case a person is morally obligated not to obey, despite the fact that disobedience may bring on torture, slow hanging, or some other horrible consequence. In a democracy, however, where the citizens themselves—through their freely chosen representatives—decide what the laws shall be, everyone is morally obligated to obey the law until it is repealed by the democratic process. If the application of the law in some individual case is repugnant to one's conscience, then one must work by democratic means to have it modified. (With what prospect of success can this be done?) But one may not violate it, not even if it would be fairly safe for one to do so.

This principle is indeed a fine specimen of democratic self-deception.

Manfred Moritz

Indeterminism, Determinism, and Definitions of Freedom

I

1. At least five different views are comprehended by "indeterminism." I will first list these five views, and then comment on them:

a. Ontological indeterminism (section 2)
b. Normative indeterminism (section 3)
c. Ontological-normative indeterminism (as a combination of a and b) (section 12)
d. Indeterministic definition of freedom (section 13)
e. Complete indeterminism (section 15)

2. Ontological indeterminism, as I understand it, is a view as to whether events in the world ('ontological') are causally determined or not. There is an ontological-indeterministic view which maintains that some occurrences in the world are not causally determined. There are several 'ontological indeterminisms.' I shall state a few of them.

  i. All events in the world are causally undetermined (i.e., no events in the world are causally determined).
  ii. Some (but not all) events in the world are causally undetermined (i.e., some events in the world are determined).
  iii. All/some events in the world could be undetermined.

(Further forms of ontological indeterminism could be found, for example, if the

Professor Moritz, of the University of Lund in Sweden, is a citizen of Sweden.
Translated from the German by Mrs. Ramona Griffiths. An earlier version, "Om definitioner av frihet" [Definitions of freedom] appeared in Swedish in *Sanning Dikt Tro. Till Ingemar Hedenius* [Truth fiction belief: In honor of Ingemar Hedenius], edited by Ann-Mari Henschen-Dahlquist, Anders Wedberg, *et al.* (Stockholm: Albert Bonniers, 1968), pp. 233–42.

various ontological indeterminisms under i to iii were restricted to the past or future, etc.)

3. By "normative indeterminism" I understand a normative view that appears in various forms. One variant is as follows: "If a person P has performed a wrong act, and if he has not acted indeterminedly, do not hold him responsible for this action!"[1]

The norm in question has two characteristics: It is concerned with a conditional prohibition—under the stated condition that person P should *not* be held responsible; and the condition is formulated in the negative—"If the person has *not* acted indeterminedly. . . ."[2]

4. I shall express this norm symbolically: Indet $(p)//c$-Com $\sim R(p)$. "$\sim$" is to be read as a negation sign; "Indet(p)" means "P has acted indeterminedly"; "c-Com" is to be read as "conditionally commanded"; and "to be conditionally commanded" means "to be commanded by a conditional command." "$R(p)$" means "P is held responsible." I put the oblique lines "$//$" between the condition of the conditional command and the description of the imperative part of the conditional command ("It is c-commanded not to hold person P responsible"). A prohibition against carrying out action A can be interpreted as a command not to carry out action A. Prohibitions, therefore, may be expressed with the help of commands and negation. The sentence "$\sim$Indet$//c$-Com $\sim R(p)$" is not itself an imperative, but it describes an imperative. We are concerned with a descriptive sentence.

Let me add still another remark about the use of symbols. "Indet$(p)//c$-Com $\sim R(p)$" is not an imperative, but a judgment about an imperative. In some cases symbolic expressions for names of imperatives are used. I have indicated the names of imperatives by placing an exclamation mark in front of the descriptive sentence: "!Indet$(p)//c$-Com $\sim R(p)$." Hence, "!If person P has acted indeterminedly, do not hold P responsible," is the name of the corresponding imperative.

5. With respect to a conditional imperative (or a conditional norm), one can always ask which norm is valid in the case of the opposite conditional (or

---

[1] In the following account I omit one condition in the formulation of normative indeterminism, namely, "If person P has carried out a wrong act." The reason for this is as follows. When it is said that a person is to be held 'responsible' for an act, the implication is that the act is wrong. As far as I can see, to say that "A person should be held responsible for carrying out a right (good) act" is not a normal way of speaking. Right and wrong actions can be 'ascribed' to persons. One cannot be held responsible for right actions; only where wrong actions are concerned can it be said that a person is to be held 'responsible' for them. I have not made empirical investigations into the use of "responsible" and "to ascribe." Rather, my impression is based on my intuitive linguistic sense. If what has been said is correct, it is superfluous to add "If the person has carried out a wrong act" as a special condition. Consequently, I will omit this condition in what follows. This applies not only to the formulation of normative indeterminism but also to normative determinism and to other similar formulations.

[2] That the condition is negative means only that linguistically it is negatively formulated ("not"). Relative to this negative condition the opposite condition is then "positive."

whether a norm exists). The formulation of normative indeterminism holds for the negative condition (that person P has *not* acted indeterminedly). What is the situation for the case in which the opposite positive condition exists? Is something commanded for the cases in which the person is undetermined? And what is commanded? Three cases are possible:

(a) If P has acted indeterminedly, it is commanded that person P be held responsible.

(b) If P has acted indeterminedly, it is forbidden that person P be held responsible.

(c) If P has acted indeterminedly, it is neither commanded nor forbidden that person P be held responsible.

6. In the case of a conditional imperative with a negative condition ("P has not acted indeterminedly"), how is the imperative situation constituted if the accompanying positive condition exists ("P has acted indeterminedly")? There are three possibilities, cases (a), (b), and (c) of section 5. The conditional prohibition ("!If P has not acted indeterminedly, do not hold P responsible") can accordingly be combined with (a), (b), or (c). (In the following I shall abbreviate the conditional prohibition that I have just mentioned as "the prohibition.")

I shall now take up and comment on the three combinations.

(i) Prohibition and case (a):
$$[\sim\text{Indet }(p)//c\text{-Com }\sim R(p)] \text{ \& } [\text{Indet}(p)//c\text{-Com }R(p)].$$

I am not sure that such a normative view has ever been held. That is, I am not sure that a view has ever been maintained according to which it is (positively) commanded to hold a person responsible whenever he has acted indeterminedly. Rather, it appears to me, the view that is or has been maintained is that it is *permitted* (but not directly commanded) in such a case to hold a person responsible. Compare this with combination (ii). On the other hand, I am not sure that view (i) has not been held.

(ii) Prohibition and case (b):
$$[\sim\text{Indet}(p)//c\text{-Com }\sim R(p)] \text{ \& } [\text{Indet}(p)//c\text{-Com }\sim R(p)].$$

Such a combination is peculiar. It states that holding a person responsible is forbidden irrespective of whether he has acted indeterminedly or not indeterminedly. In other words, holding people responsible is always forbidden. To my knowledge, such a view is not on record. But irrespective of whether it has existed or not, and irrespective of whether it is peculiar or not, such a theory is surely not (normative) indeterminism. That holding people responsible whenever they have acted indeterminedly is forbidden surely is no part of a (normative) indeterministic view. For the present discussion, where we are dealing with normative indeterminism, combination (ii) is without interest.

(iii) Prohibition and case (c):
$[\sim\text{Indet}(p)//c\text{-Com} \sim R(p)]$ & $\{\text{Indet}(p)//[\sim c\text{-Com} \ R(p)]$ &
$\sim c\text{-Com} \sim R(p)\}.$

In this case, only the prohibition is in question. For in the case in which the positive condition exists ("*P* has acted indeterminedly"), nothing is either commanded or forbidden. "One may act as one wishes."

As far as I can see, both variants (i) and (iii) can be characterized as "normative indeterminism." The formulation of normative indeterminism given above (in section 3: "If a person *P* has performed a wrong act *A*, and if *P* has not acted indeterminedly, do not hold *P* responsible") cannot without further ado be regarded as an adequate formulation of normative indeterminism. It can at most be regarded as synonymous with variant (iii). This itself, however, is only justifiable if a definite assumption is made. The assumption is that the description presented by the prohibition (for the negative condition) is a *complete* description of the imperative situation. Or: since an imperative (for the positive condition) is not mentioned; therefore, no such imperative exists. Nothing is either commanded or forbidden for the positive condition.

If this assumption is not made, then the formulation in section 3 is not identical with variant (iii). It can then only be viewed as a partial formulation of normative indeterminism. The prohibition must be completed with a statement as to whether there is a norm for the case of the positive condition, and, if so, what it is.

7. In section 5, I introduced three imperatives (a) through (c), with which the following prohibition can be combined: "If *P* has not acted indeterminedly, do not hold *P* responsible." That produced variants (i) through (iii). I shall now discuss three further combinations.

(iv) $[\sim\text{Indet}(p)//c\text{-Com} \sim R(p)]$ & $[\text{Indet}(p)// \sim c\text{-Com} \sim R(p)].$

That is to say: for the negative condition a prohibition exists, and as to the positive condition, holding person *P* responsible if the condition exists is not prohibited.

This variant is more general and comprehensive in its form than variants (i) and (iii). It is compatible with both, but it is not on an equal basis with them; rather, it is of a higher degree.

The first part of this variant is identical with the prohibition expressed in both other variants: "If a person has not acted indeterminedly, holding him responsible is conditionally forbidden."

The second statement ("If a person has acted indeterminedly, holding him responsible is not conditionally forbidden") is compatible (a) with the partial statement of variant (i), "If a person has acted indeterminedly, holding him responsible is conditionally commanded," and (b) with the partial statement of variant (iii), "If a person has acted indeterminedly, holding him responsible is neither commanded nor forbidden."

I need not delve further into case (b). That holding a person responsible is not conditionally commanded, therefore, is identical with a part of the partial statement last mentioned. Hence, it is shown that variant (iv) is compatible with variant (iii).

I shall now discuss case (a) of section 6. Variant (iv) is compatible with variant (i). This variant (i) states that holding a person responsible is conditionally commanded. If at the same time a norm existed to the effect that (under the same circumstances) holding the person responsible is conditionally prohibited, then two norms would exist that are not coexecutable.

8. Instead of saying that an act that is commanded in a coexecutable[3] command is *not forbidden*, it is sometimes said, "If an act is commanded, it is also permitted." I shall make two comments on this formulation.

(a) "To be permitted" is used in several different senses.[4] I shall give two meanings (there are still others):

> (i) "Not to be prohibited." If "to be permitted" is used with this meaning, then I shall say that "to be permitted" is being used in the "non-prohibitive sense." I shall make clear that this sense is the one intended by "to be permitted$_{np}$."

> (ii) "Not to be prohibited and not to be commanded." Here I would say that "to be permitted" is being used in its "complete sense." Correspondingly, I shall then write "to be permitted$_c$."

9. (b) The second comment concerns the word "is" in the sentence "If an act is commanded, it *is* also permitted." Whether this statement is correct or not depends on the meaning of "is." As is well known, it can happen that one and the same act is commanded as well as forbidden (by one and the same person). Then it 'is' therefore completely possible that one and the same act is commanded as well as forbidden (by one and the same person). Therefore, it 'is' certainly *not* the case that an act is necessarily not forbidden when it is commanded. A commanded act is not forbidden only if a 'consistent' person has commanded the act. And a person is 'consistent' only if he observes the prohibition against issuing commands that are not coexecutable. If an order is issued and the rule against issuing non-coexecutable imperatives is observed, then an act that has been commanded is not forbidden. If the prohibition against issuing non-coexecutable imperatives has been observed, it is naturally correct that an act that is commanded is not forbidden.

10. In the following considerations, variant (iv) may serve as the 'minimal formulation' of normative indeterminism. Hence, when no other indication is

---

[3] That a command is coexecutable should be taken as including that no command is given which is non-coexecutable.

[4] Compare with my article, "Permissive Sätze, Erlaubnissätze und deontische Logik [Permissive sentences, permission sentences, and deontic logic], in *Philosophical Essays Dedicated to Gunnar Aspelin*, edited by Helge Bratt, Sten Duner, Manfred Moritz, and Hans Regnell (Lund: C. W. K. Gleerup, 1963), pp. 108–21.

given, when I speak simply of 'the' (doctrine of) normative indeterminism, I shall mean this variant (iv) of normative indeterminism.

The two variants (i) and (iii) can be regarded as special cases of variant (iv). Variant (i) arises when variant (iv), "If a person has not acted indeterminedly, holding him responsible is *c*-forbidden," and "If he has acted indeterminedly, holding him responsible is not *c*-forbidden," has been accomplished by adding to it: "And if he has acted indeterminedly, holding him responsible is *c*-commanded."

Variant (iii) arises from changing variant (iv) by means of the sentence, "If a person has acted indeterminedly, holding him responsible is not *c*-commanded." The complete wording is thus: "If a person has not acted indeterminedly, holding him responsible is *c*-forbidden, and if he has acted indeterminedly, holding him responsible is neither *c*-forbidden nor *c*-commanded." This is precisely the formulation of variant (iii).

11. If it is accepted that at least some acts are undetermined, and if normative indeterminism is accepted, then it is possible to hold people responsible. Whether the act in question was undetermined or not must be decided from case to case. In any case, the possibility that people may be held responsible cannot be generally excluded. On the other hand, if it should be denied that ontological indeterminism is true in any form, then it would be 'impossible' (i.e., it is forbidden) to hold people responsible at any time for their actions.

12. Sometimes a view that accepts normative indeterminism as well as ontological indeterminism is designated as "indeterminism." In this case, "indeterminism" means neither "normative indeterminism" nor "ontological indeterminism." Rather, it is used then in a third meaning, a view that combines normative with ontological indeterminism ("ontological-normative indeterminism").

13. It seems to me that "indeterminism" is used in yet a fourth meaning. "Indeterminism" also designates a view the result of which is that "to be free" means the same as "to be causally undetermined." Then, being an adherent of indeterminism means approximately that one is an adherent of an 'indeterministic definition of freedom.' Adherents of indeterminism in the first three senses are often also indeterminists in the fourth sense. Many philosophers (and others as well) accept a sentence such as: "If a person has not acted *freely*, he should not be held responsible, and if a person has acted *freely*, holding him responsible is not forbidden" (responsibility norm).

If we define "to be free" as "to be undetermined," we have normative indeterminism. In other words, the indeterministic definition of freedom leads to normative indeterminism if "to be free" is defined indeterministically and this definition is inserted into the responsibility norm.

14. I can be brief about the relationship of the indeterministic definitions of freedom to ontological indeterminism. The question as to whether 'there is freedom,' i.e., whether there are actions (and possible events) that are 'free,' is put in terms of the indeterministic definition of freedom as "Are there causally

undetermined actions?" The answer, "Free actions exist," is ontological indeterminism, if the indeterministic definition of freedom is applied.

15. Many philosophers who accept normative indeterminism and ontological indeterminism also accept the indeterministic definition of freedom. If, as adherents of indeterminism, these philosophers are called indeterminists, then what we are saying is that they accept these three indeterminisms, and, therefore, "indeterminism" is being applied in another (fifth) sense.

II

16. The term "determinism" is equally ambiguous. Here five different meanings can be distinguished. They are:

a. Ontological determinism (section 18)
b. Normative determinism (section 22)
c. Complete determinism
d. 'Determinism' (ontological-normative determinism (section 26 (a))
e. Deterministic definition of freedom (section 18)

In the following I shall explain what is to be understood under these terms. I begin with point (e).

17. The indeterministic definition of freedom is not the only one. There are also deterministic definitions of freedom. Deterministic definitions of freedom are so constructed as to permit formulation of the sentence, "Action A is free and action A is causally determined," without resulting in a contradiction. In the present article I shall say more about such deterministic definitions of freedom, and shall propose a method by which an entire series of deterministic definitions of freedom can be formulated.

18. By ontological determinism (section 16 (a)), I understand the theory according to which all events and all acts are causally determined.

19. A philosopher who accepts normative indeterminism but at the same time also accepts ontological determinism arrives at the familiar consequence: people can never (must not) be held responsible for their actions. Holding them responsible is always forbidden.

One arrives at that consequence after the following consideration: normative indeterminism includes the conditional norm, "If a person has not acted indeterminedly, do not hold him responsible for his actions!" Ontological determinism maintains that this condition exists; actions are never undetermined. If a person were to be held responsible, this conditional norm would have been disobeyed. This is often expressed in this way: a person may never be held responsible for his actions.

Such an interpretation is often found in literary naturalism. Its adherents are often referred to as "determinists." And this they are. They are *ontological* determinists. At the same time they are indeterminists; they accept normative indeterminism. If they were not adherents of *normative* indeterminism at the same time, ontological determinism alone could not induce them to say that people may never be held responsible.

20. A deterministic definition of freedom is obtained in the following manner. One can say approximately, "Action A is free (freely carried out), if action A is causally determined, but if among the causes of action A cause C_1 is not to be found." Whether a certain action A is then 'free' depends on whether or not cause C_1 occurs among the causes of action A. If it does occur, then action A cannot be characterized as free; the person P who has carried it out may not be held responsible. However, if cause C_1 is not present, then the action is characterized as free. The person P who carried it out may be held responsible.

A second deterministic definition of freedom is obtained if another cause, C_2, besides C_1, is "removed." Then "Action A is free$_2$": means "Action A is causally determined, but neither C_1 nor C_2 occurs among the causes."

Obviously, one can employ this procedure and "eliminate" further causes. "Action A is free$_3$," for example, means "Action A is causally determined, but neither C_1 nor C_2 nor C_3 occurs among the causes." In this way more and more causes are 'eliminated.' Additional definitions of freedom are obtained.

21. I should like to call attention to two borderline cases. One borderline case is that in which *all* causes are eliminated. Action A is free if it is not determined by any causes. This is obviously the case with respect to the indeterministic definition of freedom. The indeterministic definition of freedom is a borderline case of the deterministic.

The other borderline case is the one in which *no* causes are eliminated. "The action is free" would then mean "The action is determined." But whether "to be free" can be thus defined is more than questionable. There would then be no difference between "to be free" and "to be determined." As far as I can see, "to be free" is never used in this sense. At least—so it appears—one cause must be eliminated from the causal conditions of the action in order that it may be said that the action is free. (I have not attempted an empirical investigation of this. What I am saying rests on my 'linguistic sense.' I shall return to this point [see section 25].)

22. The different definitions of freedom lead to a series of different 'normative determinisms.' If different definitions of "to be free" are used in the sentence, "If a person P has not acted freely, do not hold him responsible for this action," then a series of different norms result from it. They are different in that they lay down different conditions as to when a person may be held responsible. If "to be free" is defined as "to be free$_1$," and in turn "to be free$_1$" means "to be causally brought about, and cause C_1 does *not* occur among the determining causes," then the cited norm is formulated as follows: "If a person has acted and his action was caused, among others, by cause C_1, do not hold this person responsible for performing the action!"

There are corresponding definitions for the other condition: "If a person has acted freely, holding him responsible for the performance of the action is not permitted (i.e., it is permitted$_{np}$)." The corresponding insertion receives the following formulation: "If a person has performed the action, and if cause C_1 does not appear among the causes of the action, then holding person P responsible for this action is not forbidden."[5]

23. The same can be done with other definitions of "to be free"—"to be free$_2$," "to be free$_3$," etc. The following formulations are then obtained: (a) "If a person has performed action A and if one of causes C_1 or C_2 has occurred, do not hold the person responsible for the action"; and (b) "If a person has carried out action A and if neither cause C_1 nor cause C_2 occurred among the causes, then holding the agent responsible is permitted$_{np}$."

24. The case in which *all* causes are eliminated is normative indeterminism: "If a person has performed action A and if this action has been brought about by a cause, do not hold him responsible for performing this action"; and "If a person has carried out action A and if no causes have brought about the action, holding the person responsible is permitted$_{np}$." Normative determinism turns into normative indeterminism.

25. What of the case in which no causes are eliminated? In this case, "to be free" is defined as "to be determined." The responsibility norm receives a formulation that could be labeled "total normative determinism." In the attitude toward normative determinism there are two different points of view to be differentiated:

a. According to what was said above (in section 21), it would be incorrect to define "to be free" as "to be determined." If one wants to express oneself in accordance with ordinary speech, the responsibility norm cannot be worded as: "If a person has not acted in a causally determined manner, holding him responsible is forbidden, and if a person has acted in a causally determined manner, holding him responsible is permitted."

b. To say that it would not be in accordance with ordinary language to so formulate the responsibility norm means nothing more than that it is not in accordance with ordinary language to express oneself in this manner.

---

[5] I shall call the sentence, "If a person has not acted freely, do not hold him responsible for the action," the "prohibition norm" (for the negative condition). Whenever there can be no misunderstanding I shall simply say "prohibition norm." I shall call the sentence, "If a person P has acted freely, holding him responsible for his action is permitted$_{np}$," simply a "permissive norm" (for the positive condition). Sometimes I shall simply say "permissive norm." Prohibition norm and permissive norm together will be referred to as "responsibility norm." The responsibility norm, therefore, has the following wording: "If a person has not acted freely, holding him responsible is forbidden," and "If a person has acted freely, holding him responsible is permitted$_{np}$." Only this combination will be called the responsibility norm. This concerns the formulation that results when variation (iv) of normative indeterminism is transformed. The transformation consists in that "to be indeterminate" (undetermined) is replaced by "to be free."

One can no longer object that the sentences, "If a person has not acted in a causally determined manner, holding him responsible is *c*-forbidden," and "If a person has performed an act that is causally determined, holding the person responsible is permitted," are not in accordance with ordinary language. The objection collapses if it is no longer maintained that this is a formulation of the responsibility norm. Then it is not maintained that "to be free" can be translated as "to be determined." But other objections can be raised. It can be objected that it is immoral and impractical to hold (respectively, not to hold) persons responsible under such conditions. Further objections are conceivable. These are normative-ethical (moral) objections. They may be morally justified or unjustified. But I am not going to express my opinion here on normative-ethical objections. This is not a normative-ethical paper.

26. I shall also characterize as deterministic those definitions of freedom in which "to be free" and "to be causally determined" are taken to be synonymous. I have explained above (sections 21, 25) that this is not completely correct, but I shall express myself in this way for the sake of simplicity. Normative indeterminism can be combined with various ontological views—with ontological indeterminism and with ontological determinism. If normative indeterminism is combined with ontological determinism, then it is 'impossible' to hold persons responsible. If it is combined with an ontological indeterminism, then holding persons responsible is possible.

Also, normative determinism (the total determinism) can be combined with both ontological points of view.

a. If one combines normative determinism with ontological determinism, then it is possible to hold people responsible. (This may seem paradoxical. But one of the partial norms of normative determinism reads: "If a person has acted determinedly, holding the person responsible is permitted$_{np}$.") This combination would be a form of normative-ontological determination.

b. If normative determinism is combined with an ontological indeterminism, then it is impossible to hold people responsible. For the requirement of the permission sentence (that the person has acted determinedly) is not fulfilled in consequence of ontological indeterminism. On the contrary, the condition of the prohibition ("If a person has not acted determinedly, do not hold him responsible") is fulfilled. The conditional prohibition would be violated if a person were held responsible. (If partial ontological indeterminism is accepted, whether or not action A was causally undetermined must be decided from case to case.)

27. The possible combinations of 'normative indeterminism' and 'normative (total) determinism' on the one hand, and 'ontological indeterminism' and 'ontological determinism' on the other, can be represented in a diagram:

	A Normative indeterminism	B Normative (total) determinism
I. Ontological indeterminism		
II. Ontological determinism		

By "normative indeterminism," I even here mean the combination of the two sentences (a), "If the action is undetermined, holding person P responsible is permitted$_{np}$," and (b), "If a person has not acted indeterminedly, holding him responsible is forbidden," should also be understood here. By "normative (total) determinism," I understand the extreme position which can be characterized by the following two sentences:

(a) If a person has acted determinedly, holding him responsible is permitted.
(b) If a person has not acted determinedly, holding him responsible is forbidden.

Combinations I.A and II.B allow persons to be held responsible. Neither combination II.A nor I.B allows persons to be held responsible.

28. The diagram can be expanded to cover the combinations of normative positions and ontological views that I set forth in section 27. It can also be expanded in such a way as to include the other normative determinisms in addition to normative (total) determinism. The diagram would appear approximately as follows:

	A Normative indeterminism	B . Normative	. M Determinisms	N Normative total determinism
I. Ontological indeterminism				
II. Partial ontological indeterminism				
III. Ontological determinism				

Everything that is important for cases I.A and III.N has already been said. For cases I.B . . . I.M, responsibility becomes impossible. The same is true for case III.A: responsibility (i.e., holding responsible) turns out to be 'impossible.' On the other hand, for cases II.B...II.N, whether or not the ascription of responsibility is possible must be decided from case to case.

The ontological intermediate form states that some actions are undetermined, some are determined (respectively, some could be undetermined).

29. Let us assume that two different normative deterministic positions are in question. They differ from each other in that different conditions are stipulated. Within the condition of the one formulation, causes C_1, C_2, and C_3 are eliminated; within the condition of the other, cause C_4 is also eliminated. The result of this is that in the two formulations different severe conditions are stipulated for the cases in which persons may be held responsible. That this is the case can readily be seen if one agrees with that proposition which states under which conditions holding the person responsible is forbidden if at least one of causes C_1, C_2, or C_3 occurs. In the other formulation, cause C_4 is also eliminated. That is, it is forbidden to hold the person responsible if at least one of the four named causes had determined his action. It happens then—probably—more often that a person may not be held responsible.

30. The different deterministic definitions of freedom—when inserted into the responsibility norm—constitute different conditions as to when a person may be held responsible. Different normative determinisms are differentiated, among other things, by their liberality or severity, respectively. If no causes are eliminated, then in any combination of causes, holding the person responsible is permitted. Contrariwise, if a normative indeterminism is considered, then every combination of causes you like leads to the conclusion that the person may not be held responsible.

31. The method of constructing definitions of "to be free" with which I have dealt up to this point is not the only one. There are others. I want to note a few briefly. For instance, it could be required that one cause from a group of causes be eliminated, that from the group C_1, C_2, C_3, one cause, at most, be eliminated, etc. If none of the causes is present, the action is not 'free.' Two of the causes must be present. The group can be larger; the number of necessary causes can be larger or smaller, etc. If none of the causes in question is present, then the action is not free, and if more than the necessary number are present, then in like manner the action is not free, and so on.

'Concepts of freedom' do not have to be formed in terms of causes being eliminated. On the contrary, concepts of freedom can also be formed which require that certain causes be present. If an action is carried out determinedly, but causes C_1 or C_2 of the determining causes do not occur, then (for example) the action can be characterized as non-free. It can also be required here that groups of causes occur, that it is not enough that one of the causes which belongs to the group occurs, etc.

32. I should like to mention another method of constructing concepts of freedom. In a definition of "to be free," one can take the consequences of the action into consideration. Thus it can perhaps be said that if the performance of an action can only be carried out under great (foreseeable) suffering, then the action is not free.

Such a view is not unusual. Thus it can perhaps be said that a person 'can' not carry out action *A* because performance of the action is connected with great suffering (for the agent). If "can" here is replaced by "to be free" (which is certainly possible), then one has an example of "to be free" and "to be non-free"'s being defined with the aid of the consequences of the action. That a person is not free to carry out action *A* would then mean that the accomplishment of the action entails (for the agent) suffering that is 'too great.'

I wanted to point out a few of these further possibilities of defining "to be free." I shall not go into further detail about them.

III

33. In the manner given above, the result is a whole series of different concepts of freedom. Which is the correct one?

This question is ambiguous. I shall state two meanings of it:

a. Is "to be free" de facto used in the described manner in 1971 (in Germany, Sweden, France, etc.)?
b. Is the definition of "to be free" (i.e., the 'definition' of the conditions for holding a person responsible) *morally* correct?

Let us assume that an unambiguous answer to question a is obtained. Are we then forced to use "to be free" in this sense? As far as I can see this is not the case. This negative answer is not based on the trivial circumstance that every word can be used in a way that deviates from the customary use in a 'Pickwickian' sense. The negative answer has another basis—every definition of "to be free" is at the same time the determination of the conditions under which a person may be held responsible and when not. To accept the conventional definition of "to be free" is to accept something *more* than a linguistic use.

A "*moral* usage" is accepted. A definite condition for when a person may be held responsible, and when he may not, is accepted.

The position taken for or against the conventional use of "to be free" is at the same time a position taken for or against the conditions that are customarily and morally laid down for when a person may be held responsible.

34. The responsibility norm is a conditional norm, and as a norm it is not a sentence that can be true or false. If different definitions of freedom (to be free) are inserted into it, then the result is a series of different norms. Different conditions are thereby stipulated for when people may be held responsible. The choice between different definitions of freedom is a choice between different conditions

of responsibility. The position taken for or against a certain condition of responsibility is not a theoretical position. The choice itself is not to be made in a theoretical manner. As in every choice, theoretical considerations can play a part. However, when one is faced with all of these theoretical considerations, it is necessary to make a choice.

The theoretical considerations involved in that choice concern the *consequences* that the different definitions of freedom and the corresponding responsibility norms have. The question that requires to be answered is: which are the consequences that (probably) ensue if a person (or group of persons) may be held responsible under the condition that is expressed in the corresponding definition of freedom? What one must finally take a stand on, are the consequences of such a condition of responsibility. Whether the consequences of a condition or responsibility are acceptable or not, whether other consequences are more acceptable, can no longer be decided only by theoretical considerations. The position taken is a practical position; it is a moral choice. The question as to how "to be free" is to be defined, is itself a moral question. The question as to what freedom means (or is supposed to mean) is thereby not set above or set before other moral questions. The question as to the meaning of freedom is a moral question among other moral questions.

Philosophers, moralists, and jurists have often asked themselves the question, what does freedom mean? They presupposed in that question that "freedom" has only one sense and that it would all depend on ascertaining 'the' meaning of freedom (to be free). If the meaning of freedom were ('really') known, then the problem of freedom would be solved. But that is not the problem. The problem is not what freedom means, but what freedom should mean. Perhaps it would be best if the question of how freedom is to be defined were no longer asked at all, and if instead the question of under what conditions we should hold people responsible were asked.

This appears to me to be the real problem. The discussion would improve if this were recognized as the problem and if attentions were directed to this real moral problem.

Harald Ofstad

Responsibility and Freedom

The Free Will Issue and Moral Systems

Solving the so-called free will issue requires solving three different kinds of problems: (1) In what sense (or senses) of "moral responsibility," if any, is it correct to assert that we may be morally responsible? (2) In what sense (or senses) of "freedom," if any, is freedom a condition of moral responsibility as clarified in (1)? (3) Under what conditions, if any, are we free in the senses clarified in (2)? The issue cannot be solved by investigating whether or not our decisions and actions are caused, nor by studying our use of such sentences as "He could have decided [acted] otherwise," for it is not at all certain that "uncaused" is the correct answer to question (2), and it is not at all certain that the responsibility-relevant sense (or senses) of "freedom" happens to be expressed by our actual use of "could have decided or acted otherwise" sentences. The solution involves the clarification not only of scientific and analytic problems, but of moral problems as well.

Given that the crucial question is to discover whether or not we are free in the sense required by moral responsibility, the next step must be to admit that this sense may vary with the nature of the moral system within which the concept of responsibility is defined. Within system E_1, for example, "moral responsibility" is defined in terms of moral guilt and an agent is considered guilty of a certain wrongdoing only if he acted freely in sense x; whereas according to E_2, defining "responsibility" in terms of modifiability, an agent is responsible only if he acted freely in sense y. And if we now suppose that we are free in sense y but not in sense x, do we then have a free will? That depends upon whether system E_2 is 'more correct than' system E_1. Hence, there is an important

Professor Ofstad, of the University of Stockholm, is a native of Norway.

The present paper, to a large degree, is based upon my works *An Inquiry into the Freedom of Decision* and "Recent Work on the Free-Will Problem."

sense in which a solution of the free will issue presupposes a clarification and solution of certain basic problems within the philosophy of justification of moral systems.

In this paper I shall not try to decide which concept of responsibility is ethically[1] correct. The most reasonable procedure seems to be to focus attention on some of the prevailing interpretations of "morally responsible," concentrating on the most important ones and leaving the discovery of responsibility in the morally correct sense to the future.

Different Interpretations of "Responsible"

Let us assume that on May 1, 1968, a certain Mr. Smith shot his wife Olga to death, and that someone says the Smith is responsible for her death. By this he may mean only (1) that a certain activity of Smith's was a causal factor in the series of events that led to her death. The statement that Smith is responsible in this sense is empirically true or false, and there is no plausible sense of "freedom" in which freedom is a condition of responsibility in this sense. Next, he may mean (2) that her death was due to something Smith did, where "doing something" at least implies that Smith was sufficiently conscious to understand that his behavior was dangerous. In relation to this sense, it seems appropriate to ask whether freedom in any sense is a condition of responsibility. Furthermore, he may mean (3) to give a negative moral evaluation of Smith as the producer of Olga's death, or, as we can also say, he may mean that Smith is morally guilty of her death—to this or that degree. To analyze the respect, if any, in which freedom is a condition of moral guilt in this sense is a crucial task within the free will debate. He may also mean (4) that Smith is morally blameworthy, which may be interpreted to mean that Smith is morally guilty to some degree, and that we consequently have a reason for blaming him. I have already mentioned the relation between freedom and guilt, and the only new question raised by (4) concerns the relation between freedom and blame, a problem that can be more adequately dealt with by turning to our final interpretation: (5) someone (but not necessarily *you* or *I*) ought to express moral disapproval of Smith.

My discussion must be limited to some of these senses of "responsible," and by concentrating on sense (3), moral guilt, and sense (5), moral blame, we seem to have the best chance of reaching the most important issues. My problem, therefore, can be formulated thus: In what sense, if any, of the term "freedom" is freedom a condition of moral guilt, and in what sense, if any, is it a condition of moral blame? And under what conditions, if any, are we free in these senses?

Moral Guilt and Freedom

In order to clarify in what sense freedom is a condition of moral guilt, we may raise the following question: "It there any sense of 'freedom' in which the

---

[1] The terms "moral" and "ethical" are used interchangeably in this paper.

lack of freedom is an acceptable excuse in relation to a charge of moral guilt?" This question cannot be answered solely by a linguistic analysis of the term "freedom," but must be answered in relation to the moral system within which the concept of moral guilt is defined. An answer involves an interpretation of the system, or—if it is undetermined on the point in question—an addition to it. Since no formulated and accepted system of this kind exists, the best procedure seems to be to try to clarify one's own ideas, hoping to be somewhat representative.

Suppose that Smith defends himself by saying that "to act freely" means to act as one ought to act, and that his action was not free in this sense. Far from accepting this as an excuse, we acknowledge that lack of freedom in this sense is a condition of guilt. Let us next suppose that he says that "a free action" means a rational action, and that his action was not rational. If by this he means that he did not understand the nature of his act and its probable consequences, this, if true, may reduce, or perhaps even eliminate, his guilt. On the other hand, this is not the kind of excuse we usually have in mind when we say that an agent may excuse himself by proving that he did not act freely. But suppose he means that his action was irrational in the sense that it was caused by passions over which he had no control? What he is then saying is not only relevant as an excuse, but closer to what we seem to have in mind when we maintain—in contexts of moral responsibility—that a person did not act freely. The same holds true if Smith maintains that his action did not express his self or character in a sense implying that his action was determined by factors over which he had no control. Another typical excuse is to contend that one was subjected to physical or psychical compulsion. This, again, is relevant only to the degree that the compulsion reduced the agent's power to act otherwise.

Suppose that Smith meant that his decision was not uncaused. Is the lack of freedom in this sense sufficient to exclude moral guilt? The answer, it seems to me, is in the negative. The statement that Smith's decision was caused is not in itself an acceptable excuse. It is morally relevant only insofar as it implies that Smith for this reason could not act otherwise than he did, or, at least, not as easily as if his decision had been uncaused. The crucial question—from the point of view of moral guilt—is therefore whether or not the agent had it in his power to abstain from that for which he is held guilty, or, more correctly, whether he had it in his power to do something else which would have been ethically better ("ethically better" = "less bad") than what he did. If boiling Olga in oil was Smith's only alternative, the fact that he had it in his power to do this does not suffice to fulfill the requirement of freedom.[2]

---

[2] If a person is considered guilty of having *decided* in a certain way, then, of course, moral guilt does not presuppose that he had it in his power to *act* otherwise, only that he had it in his power to *decide* otherwise (see below, p. 291). Since Mr. Smith, in our example, is considered guilty of having killed his wife, we shall primarily be concerned with the question of his power to *act* otherwise.

The task before us now is to clarify what should be meant by saying that a person had it in his power to act otherwise than he in fact did, and to discuss under which conditions, if any, we have such power—to this or that degree. But let me first clarify in what sense, if any, freedom is a condition of moral blame.

Moral Blame and Freedom

By "being subjected to moral blame," I mean being subjected to moral disapproval, whether verbal or non-verbal, the former being expressed, for example, by such sentences as "You ought to have decided (acted) otherwise." The question is: "In what sense, if any, of the term 'freely' must a person have decided or acted freely if blaming him in this sense shall be justified?" The answer depends upon the nature of the moral system in relation to which the question is raised. Let us limit our analysis to two types of systems: the retributive and the preventive.

According to the retributive view, it is ethically right (good) to blame a person if, and only if, he is morally guilty of a certain wrongdoing. Hence, moral blame, according to this view, presupposes freedom in the same sense as moral guilt presupposes freedom. This sense has been indicated above, and will be analyzed further later in this paper.

The preventive principle may be formulated thus: It is ethically right to blame an offender if, and only if, this is a more efficient means of motivating him, or someone else, to behave better in the future, than any other action we have in our power to do. It may be maintained as an underived ethical statement but is usually derived from certain premises within teleological or deontological systems. Let us first suppose that it is part of a deontological system. Several forms of such systems exist. In accordance with one type, the system permits of no exceptions to the rule that it is forbidden to blame an innocent person. In other words, the person to be blamed must be guilty of a certain wrongdoing. If the preventive principle is part of a system of this kind, it first of all presupposes freedom in the same sense of "freedom" as we found with regard to the retributive principle, namely, that the agent must have had it in his power to act in an ethically better way than he in fact did. Secondly, it presupposes that the agent is free in the sense that blame will have some modifying effect on his future behavior (see below).

Usually, however, the rule that it is forbidden to blame an innocent person is—even within deontological systems—not absolute, but rather, is based on a prima facie obligation not to blame in such cases. In accordance with this way of thinking, it will be our duty to blame an innocent person if this best fulfills our total set of prima facie obligations. Hence, power to act otherwise is not a necessary requirement.

Let us finally suppose that the preventive principle is derived from a teleological criterion of right action and certain empirical means-end statements. (It should be emphasized, however, that a teleological system very well may imply a non-preventive principle. This depends upon the empirical premises in question). The question now is: "In what sense is freedom a condition of preventive blame based on teleological premises?"

In order to answer this question, we must introduce certain suppositions with regard to the contents of the underived statements of the system that imply the preventive principle, since it must be interpreted in view of them.

Suppose that the moral system includes only one underived moral statement, namely:

Premise 1:   We ought to choose that course of action which will result in a higher balance of pleasure over pain, over any other action in our power.

According to this norm, blame is justified only as a means to the production of pleasure, and this is not the same as saying that it is justified only as a means to the prevention of future wrongdoings. Perhaps the members of a certain society would become most happy by practicing retributive blame. Hence, we must also postulate the following empirical premise, which is as yet unclear in meaning and far from validated:

Premise 2:   In a given society S, in the time interval t_1–t_2, the balance of pleasure over pain will be greater if blame is applied only to the extent that it will motivate the agent, or other persons, to abstain from wrongdoings in the future, than if it is applied according to another principle.

The crucial question is whether we can also establish:

Premise 3:   In society S, in the time interval t_1–t_2, the motivating function of blame, and thereby the production of pleasure over pain (cf. premise 2), is realized more effectively if we blame only persons who acted freely in the following sense . . ., than if we blame persons who did not.

Hence, it is in part an empirical question to find the possible sense in which a person must have acted freely if blame is to be justified, for the tenability of a statement in accordance with the scheme in premise 3 will, among other things, depend upon the attitudes and expectations of the members of the relevant society. Consequently, those advocating the preventive view on teleological grounds may have to presuppose freedom in the same sense as those who accept the retributive view.

Let us suppose that we can neglect the attitudes and expectations of the members of the society. Then the question (applied to our example) would be: "In what sense of "free," if any, must we presuppose that Smith's action was free in order that blame shall influence him in such a way that the probability of similar or, ethically speaking, worse actions is thereby decreased?"

The answer, it seems to me, is that we do not have to presuppose that his action was free in any plausible sense of this term, since the only question is whether blame will modify his future behavior. Smith's past life is of interest only insofar as it can tell us under what conditions this or that kind of blame will be most effective. The possibility of future modifications is independent of whether or not Smith had it in his power to act otherwise than he did; nor does it depend upon his beliefs about this. For even if he lacked this power and believed that he did, our judgment about his action may influence his motivation in such a way that he will be able to act otherwise in a future situation. We must only presuppose that his preference for killing wives is not rooted in such a strong and stable motivation that it will resist all kinds of cognitive or emotive attacks.

According to a rather common view, preventive blame, as justified within a teleological system, presupposes that the agent would have acted otherwise if he had chosen to, or decided otherwise if he had tried to. If my reasoning is correct, this requirement is not a consequence of the preventive principle. It is rather a requirement pertaining to moral guilt, obtaining in addition to this principle. The defenders of the preventive principle are quite often more guilt-oriented than they seem to be.

Let us focus our attention, not on the situation in which Smith acted (the *original* situation), but on the situation in which he is to be blamed. Is there some sense in which he must be free in *this* situation in order for blame to fulfill a preventive function? If by "blaming" Smith we mean expressing a negative emotional reaction toward him, then he does not have to be free in any other sense than the sense in which a dog must be free in order to be able to adjust to negative sanctions from his master's voice. But if by "blaming" Smith we mean expressing a judgment about his action ("Your action was morally wrong"), we must presuppose, first of all, that he is able to understand the meaning of the sentence. And some, perhaps, would add that we must also assume that he has it in his power to accept or reject the judgment, not only react to it as a stimulus. Let us note, however, that it is not the preventive principle that necessitates this requirement, but the idea of how a rational man ought to behave. From the point of view of preventive blame, the important thing is only that the modification take place. The nature of the psychological processes involved in the modification is, from that point of view, irrelevant.

CONCLUSION

We have reached the following conclusions: If blame is administered according to teleological principles and the demands and expectations of the members of the relevant society concerning the policy of blame are neglected, then there is no sense in which the agent necessarily must have acted freely in order to be blamed.[3] As a matter of fact, he may not have acted at all, for according to certain versions of this view, it may be justifiable to blame an innocent person. The only requirement is that his behavior must be modifiable by the use of blame. If we claim that his behavior ought to be modified in a rational way, we may add that he must have it in his power to accept or reject the negative judgment about his behavior and act on the basis of his judgment. On the other hand, if we pay attention to the demands and expectations of the members of society concerning the policy of blame, then it is possible that preventive blame will presuppose moral guilt. The same holds true if the preventive principle is derived from a deontological system that includes as a prima facie obligation that only persons guilty of a certain wrongdoing ought to be blamed, and if the system includes this condition as an absolute requirement, it is not only possible but necessary that preventive blame will presuppose moral guilt.

As I have tried to show, moral guilt can be attributed only to a person who had it in his power to act in an ethically better way than he did.[4] Therefore, our main task now is to clarify the ethically relevant meaning of saying that an agent had it in his power to act otherwise than he did, and to discuss whether or not such power is compatible with the so-called principle of causality and with the empirical factors operating. Obviously, interesting questions pertaining to modifiability can also be asked, for example, under what conditions, if any, this or that kind of blame will have this or that kind of modifying effect on such and such persons, but I shall not take up such questions in this paper.

POWER TO ACT OTHERWISE

Let us try to formulate an interpretation of "having something in one's power," which is such that if the agent had it in his power to act otherwise in this sense, then he cannot excuse himself by maintaining that he was powerless when he acted wrongly. Hence, the interpretation must be such that it can refer to the power of the agent in what I have called the original situation, for, obviously, the conditions of guilt must be fulfilled with reference to that situation. Moreover, the power required will vary with what he is considered guilty of. If Smith is considered guilty of his wife's death, he must have had it in his power to prevent her death. If he is considered guilty of deciding to kill her or of not trying to save her, he must have had it in his power to decide not to kill her or to try to save her. Hence, in relation to certain types of responsibilities, the agent must have had control not only over himself but also over certain aspects of his surroundings. In relation to other claims of responsibility, it suffices that he had it in his power to try to do certain things or to decide in a certain way.

---

[3] If an agent is blamed for having *decided* in a certain way, then, analogously, there is no sense in which he necessarily must have decided freely in order to be blamed.
[4] But see n. 2.

If we concentrate on the example chosen previously, the relevant question is whether Smith had it in his power to refrain from shooting Olga, and not whether he had it in his power to prevent her death in the situation in question. Moreover, that Smith had it in his power to refrain from shooting her must be interpreted, as mentioned above, as meaning that he had it in his power to do something that would have been ethically better than shooting her.

Suppose Smith says that he thought it was wrong to kill her, that he tried not to kill her, that he made an effort not to kill her, decided not to kill her, and so on—and let us grant that what he says is true—then we would begin to wonder whether he really had it in his power not to kill her. On the other hand, if he did nothing of this sort, and we knew that if he had, he would not have killed her, we seem to have evidence for saying that he had it in his power to refrain from killing her. This suggests that "Smith, in S, had it in his power to do A_2 instead of A_1," in contexts of moral guilt, may be equivalent to "If Smith, in S, had tried to do A_2 instead of A_1, then he would have done A_2 instead of A_1." The objection that these two sentences are not equivalent in so-called ordinary language, is irrelevant, for the crucial question is not whether they are, but whether they ought to be, given that our interpretation is to be ethically relevant.

Power To Try

The above equivalence seems acceptable from the point of view of moral guilt insofar as it implies that Smith can excuse himself as being powerless if it is false that he would have done A_2 instead of A_1 if he had tried to do so. On the other hand, the truth of "If Smith had tried to do A_2 instead of A_1, then he would have done A_2 instead of A_1" does not imply that he had it in his power to do A_2 instead of A_1, for we cannot *a priori* assume that Smith had it in his power to try to do A_2. And if he did not have it in his power to try, then he did not have it in his power to do A_2 instead of A_1, even if he would have done A_2 instead of A_1 *if* he had tried to do so. Hence, it is necessary to improve the equivalence in the following way:

Smith, in S, had it in his power to do A_2 instead of A_1 = If Smith, in S, had tried to do A_2 instead of A_1, then he would have done A_2 instead of A_1, and he had it in his power to try to do A_2 instead of A_1.

This seems better. On the other hand, the term "power" reappears in the second conjunct, and the question is how to interpret it. Different possibilities may be suggested: "Smith had it in his power to try to do A_2" must be analyzed (1) indeterministically, namely, as "Smith's trying as well as his not-trying to do A_2 in S is [or would be] uncaused"; (2) [it must be analyzed] by the use of an if-analysis, e.g., as "Smith would have tried to do A_2, if he had tried to try or decided to try to do so"; or (3) [it must be analyzed] as a categorical statement, implying that one can always try.

(1) does not work, because saying that Smith's not-trying was not caused does not imply that he had it in his power to try. (2) does not work, because it leads to an endless regression. Both defects have often been pointed out, and I shall say nothing more about them, but turn to the third suggestion.

According to Hampshire, Smith can excuse himself by saying that he tried with all his power and failed, or that he abstained from trying because he knew that he would fail, but he cannot excuse himself by saying that he did not have it in his power to try, for

There is no sense in which it is impossible for him to intend to do something, provided that he knows what would be involved in doing it. He can always set out on the course of action, even if he knows that he will encounter difficulties at the very first stage of effective action, and even if he believes that he will in fact fail before any effective action has been taken.[5]

Whether or not we accept that one can always try depends upon what is meant by "trying." If we are willing to say that Smith tried not to kill Olga if he whispered certain words of inhibition to himself, then we may assert, on empirical grounds, that we always have it in our power to try, for those who cannot whisper certain words to themselves are not rational animals. But if we take "trying" in this sense, we at the same time reduce the likelihood that the statement "If he had tried to do A_2 instead of A_1, then he would have done A_2" will be true, except in very unimportant cases. On the other hand, if we interpret "trying" in a stronger sense, referring to making an effort, perhaps even a strong and energetic effort such as thinking about the consequences, studying the case quite closely, etc., then it is probably false that one can always try.

Concretely speaking, to try not to kill Olga (in a strong sense of "try") involves that Smith reconsider the issue, think about the consequences of killing her, of the misery and suffering he will produce, think about the fact that he will break moral rules that he may be interested in having others obey toward him, and so on. And he must not only be able to think about these things, but to react emotionally to his cognitive expectations. He must be able to react toward Olga, and other persons involved, not as dead things but as living creatures whose suffering would be analogous to what his own suffering would be.

Society expects that we in a strong sense of "try" have it in our power to try to follow its moral rules, for example, to refrain from killing persons. And this expectation is not ungrounded, for our power to try is correlated with our ability to function normally in other respects: to be able to buy milk and bread, to look after our house and fire. Certainly, psychological and other factors may break us down, making us more or less powerless for a shorter or longer period of time. But in such cases the symptoms tend to be rather visible. The important thing, from the point of view of moral responsibility, is that we cannot exclude the possibility that a person functioning quite normally in a specific situation did

[5] See Hampshire, *Thought and Action*, pp. 182–83.

not have it in his power to try in this sense. Perhaps he was mentally disturbed at the crucial moment. He was unable to think about the consequences of killing his wife, holding this cognitive picture before his mind for the amount of time required to react emotionally to it, or he was unable to experience her as a living creature in analogy with himself, seeing her only as a tasty chicken or a paper tiger. Hence, we can never be certain that a person who did not try to do A really had it in his power to try to do A.[6] Even if everything looked quite normal, something might have prevented him. And if we know that he was mentally disturbed, we can, at least in some cases, be certain that he was power-less to try.

Even if we assume that Smith had it in his power to try not to kill Olga, it does not follow that he had it in his power not to kill her, for the first conjunct in our proposed analysis may be false, that is, it may be false that if he had tried to do A_2 instead of A_1, he would have done A_2 instead of A_1. Hence, the first conjunct also presents us with an empirical problem: was Smith, in the original situation, mentally in such a state that if he had tried to do A_2 he would have succeeded in doing A_2? The answer will depend upon the psychological forces operating in the situation. Hence, the evidence relevant to both the first and the second conjuncts must be based upon studies of Smith's psychological condition in the original situation. If we could have a sort of psychological X-ray giving us a picture of all of the forces operating during his deliberation, and, if we knew how to interpret the picture, we could, by looking at it, decide whether or not Smith had it in his power to refrain from killing Olga.

Power versus Beliefs about Power

If God went mad, he might start to believe that he were a powerless sparrow, forgetting that he could create universes by his bare words. If an ordinary mortal went mad, he might start to believe that he could create solar systems by a smile or a pointed finger, forgetting that he could not even if he worked hard for an entire year. Thus a discrepancy may exist between the power that we actually have and the power that we believe we have. Returning to our example, suppose that Smith has been taught, from his childhood on, that there is no point in his trying to resist evil impulses because he is a powerless creature. Then even if Smith had it in his power to refrain from killing Olga in the sense indicated above, he might not be fully responsible, or perhaps not responsible at all, because he believes what he has been taught. In some cases we could perhaps main-

---

[6] It is often maintained that "P did A at t" implies "P at t had it in his power to do A," and, similarly, "P at t tried to do A" implies "P at t had it in his power to try to do A." How-ever, this way of presenting the implications hides the fact that our power to act or try varies in degrees. The statement that P did A should perhaps be considered incompatible with the statement that P was powerless to do A, but it is compatible with the statement that it cost him an enormous amount of effort to do A, or, in other words, that he was *nearly* powerless to do A.

tain that he had it in his power to understand that he accepted a false belief about himself. But in other cases we could not, and even when we could, this would not change the fact that an agent like this is, ethically speaking, different from a person who was aware of his own power. A person who believes himself to be powerless in a sense *is* powerless. Hence, in order to be guilty of a certain wrongdoing, the agent must not only have had it in his power to do something that would have been ethically better, it must also be true that he did not believe that he lacked this power.[7]

THE SELF

In order for Smith to be declared morally guilty, *he* must have committed the wrong act, and *he* must have had the power to act otherwise. How shall we conceive of this relation between power and the self?

Evidence provided by abnormal psychology makes it useful to distinguish between "efforts to do A_2 instead of A_1 occurred in Smith" and "Smith made an effort to do A_2 instead of A_1." In order for the trying to have been Smith's trying, it seems reasonable to require that it in some way corresponded to his norm and value system. I shall not, however, go into this question here, because the decisive thing, from the point of view of moral responsibility, is the agent's control over the relevant activities. For example, suppose that we had asked Eichmann whether or not he had it in his power to refrain from sending the Jews to the gas chambers and that he had answered: "If I had tried to stop the transportations, I would have succeeded, but such a trying would not have been a trying of the good and obedient, but of the bad and disobedient Eichmann. Hence it would not really have been *my* trying at all." This would not be a relevant excuse. (But "I was *unable* to be disobedient" would have been a relevant excuse).

Suppose that it was not Smith's deliberation, but certain electric impulses transmitted to his brain that led to A_1 and would have led to A_2. How would this affect his responsibility? Whether or not we can attribute the action to Smith will depend upon his amount of control over these electric impulses. For instance, if he knew that if he decided not to kill Olga, then electric impulses would be transmitted to him in such a way that he would succeed in refraining from killing her, then he cannot excuse himself by saying that *he* did not have it in his power to refrain. He can excuse himself only if he had reasons to believe that he was so completely powerless that there was no point in trying, and then he can excuse himself even if he actually would have succeeded if he had tried.

But suppose Smith's deliberation, conceived as mental activity, does not influence his decisions and actions; suppose his mental activity was an epiphenom-

[7] In order to be maximally guilty (see p. 303), it must be true not only that the agent did not believe that he lacked the required power. He must have been convinced that he had this power.

enon only. Then, one might say, Smith has no self, and any power to act otherwise, located in his body, cannot be referred to as *his* power and provide a basis
for moral guilt. But let us note that even if we assume that Smith's deliberation,
conceived as mental activity, was caused by certain neurophysiological processes
which were caused by some previous neurophysiological processes and related by
a law of nature to his action, this does not imply that his mental activity did not
influence his action. In order to prove that his mental activity was superfluous,
one would have to prove that the correlations between the act and the neurophysiological processes in question would remain the same regardless of the
characteristics of the agent's mental activity.

In conclusion, power to act otherwise—in the sense relevant to ascriptions of
moral guilt—contains four components: (a) that the mental activity would not
have been epiphenomenal; (b) that the agent had it in his power to try; (c) that
his trying would have led to an ethically better action; (d) that he believed that
(b) and (c) were fulfilled.

Degrees of Power

Components (b) and (c) of the above analysis suggest that it may be more
fruitful to talk about power in comparative than in dichotomous terms. Let us
try to indicate some of the factors determining our degree of power, limiting
ourselves to our power to *decide* (rather than to *act*) otherwise.

P's power in S, to decide D_2 instead of D_1 (his actual decision) was greater:
the less the effort he had to make in order to decide D_2 instead of D_1, and
this effort would be less:

1. the less the difference in value between D_2 and D_1 as interpreted by P in
    view of his ethical system (the less the value-distance between D_2 and D_1).
    For example, between deciding to give a child a Norwegian or a Swedish
    crown, equally strongly desired, there is, for P, no difference in value. The
    situation is an indifference situation. There is great difference in value be-
    tween giving him a crown or taking a crown away from him;

2. the stronger his motivation toward D_2 as compared with his motivation
    toward D_1;

3. the stronger his conviction that he ought to decide D_2 as compared with his
    conviction that he ought to decide D_1;

4. the stronger the cognitive support of his belief that he ought to decide D_2
    as compared with the support of his belief that he ought to decide D_1;

5. the more conscious he was of the possibility of deciding D_2;

6. the more he knew about how to proceed in order to make himself prefer
    D_2 to D_1.

This list, which is not meant to be exhaustive, indicates some of the difficulties involved in determining to what degree a certain agent had it in his power to decide otherwise than he in fact did and, thereby, also some of the difficulties involved in ascribing a certain degree of moral guilt to an agent. Moralistically inclined persons may want to overlook these difficulties. In order to do so, they may depart from empirical interpretations of "having something in one's power," moving toward some standardized conception according to which all so-called normal persons always have it in their power to do the ethically right thing. Actually, however, power to decide and act otherwise is not something that we have either in full or not at all. It is a matter of degrees and individual variations. What one man can do is not necessarily what another can do, and what we can accomplish in one situation may be different from what we can accomplish in another.

CAUSALITY, MODIFIABILITY, AND POWER

We have seen that if moral blame is administered according to teleological principles, then the only requirement that with any plausibility can be said to be a requirement of freedom is that the agent's future behavior must be modifiable by the use of blame. If we also claim that his behavior should be modified in a rational way, the requirement may be added that he must have it in his power to accept or reject the negative judgment about his behavior and act according to his decision.

The principle of causality, according to any plausible interpretation, is not incompatible with assertions to the effect that future behavior may be influenced by the use of blame. On the contrary, if such influence is conceived of as a causal process, the possibility of such influence presupposes that at least certain instances of human behavior are connected with causal factors. The interesting question is whether the principle of causality is compatible with asserting that the agent had it in his power to accept or reject the negative judgment about his behavior. And this is part of the broader question regarding the relation between causality and our power to decide and act otherwise—the requirement presupposed by moral guilt. This is the crucial question. Let us start by formulating the problem in the following way:

Given the two statements:

(1) Smith's killing Olga (A_1), in S, was caused, and
(2) Smith, in S, had it in his power to do A_2 (something which would have been ethically better than A_1) instead of A_1.

Does (1) imply that (2) is false?

I have argued that (2) can be taken as equivalent to:

(3) (a) the mental activity that would be involved in Smith's trying to do A_2, in S, would not have been epiphenomenal;

    (b) Smith, in S, had it in his power to try to do A_2;

    (c) if Smith, in S, had tried to do A_2 instead of A_1, then he would have done A_2;

    (d) Smith, in S, believed that conditions (b) and (c) were fulfilled.

Obviously, (1) does not imply that (c) and (d) are false, and since neither (1) nor the so-called principle of causality must be interpreted as stipulating any limitations with regard to the nature of the causal factors—they may be mental, behavioral, neurophysiological, or what not—(1) does not imply that (a) is false. Hence, the important question is whether (1) implies the falsity of (b): Smith, in S, had it in his power to try to do A_2.

In order to make this problem as explicit as possible, let us assume that Smith did not try to do A_2, and that his not-trying was caused. (1) may then be thus reformulated: Smith, in S, killed Olga (A_1), and did not try to do A_2 (NTA_2), and both A_1 and NTA_2 were caused.

For the purpose of discussing the relation to (b), we can shorten this re-formulation to:

(4) Smith's NTA_2 in S was caused.

The standard argument for showing that (4) implies that (b) is false is this: If NTA_2 was caused, then certain conditions C, in S, were causally suffici-ent for NTA_2. If C were causally sufficient for NTA_2, then it was causally im-possible for Smith, in S, to try to do A_2. If it was causally impossible for Smith to try to do A_2, then he could not try to do A_2. And if he could not try to do A_2, then he did not have it in his power to try to do A_2.

Let us grant that if NTA_2 was caused, then certain conditions C, were causally sufficient for NTA_2. The crucial question is whether or not this ad-mission implies that it was causally impossible for Smith, in S, to try to do A_2 in such a sense of "causally impossible for Smith" that it follows that Smith did not have it in his power to try to do A_2. If we choose to interpret "It was causally impossible for Smith, in S, to try to do A_2" in such a way that what it asserts follows from what we have admitted, namely, that C was causally sufficient for NTA_2, then it must be formulated in, e.g., one of the following ways:

    (4.1)   It would be inconsistent with certain laws of nature to assert that C was the case in S and Smith's NTA_2 did not occur in S, or

    (4.2)   It could not have been the case that C occured in S and Smith, in S, tried to do A_2.

Let us choose (4.1) as a convenient formulation. Does (4.1) imply that it is false that Smith, in S, had it in his power to try to do A_2(b)? The answer, it seems to me, is in the negative. (b) does not assert that given C and the laws of nature, it nevertheless was empirically possible (or probable to this or that degree) that Smith's trying to do A_2 would occur in S. (b) talks about Smith's power to try. It attributes a certain potentiality to him. (4.1), on the other hand, asserts that C and Smith's trying to do A_2 in S add up to an empirically impossible totality, but does not talk about Smith's power. For instance, it does not assert that Smith would have had to overcome strong inner resistance in order to try to do A_2 in S. In relation to (4.1), it might have been just as easy for Smith to try to do A_2 as to whisper certain words. In other words, (4.1) asserts that a certain logically possible state of affairs (C and Smith's trying to do A_2) would be contrary to the laws of nature, but does not deny the existence of potentialities in Smith. (b), on the other hand, attributes a certain potentiality to Smith, but does not assert that the state of affairs mentioned would be in agreement with the laws of nature. Hence, since (4.1) and (b) talk about different things in this sense, (4.1) can imply neither that (b) is false nor that it is true.

CAUSALITY AND TRANSEMPIRICAL POWER

How can we explain the fact that so many philosophers maintain that the principle of causality is incompatible with our power to decide and act otherwise? One possible explanation can be exemplified in the following way: suppose that a philosopher is dissatisfied with all empirical interpretations of "power to decide and act otherwise," because such interpretations cannot guarantee that every wrongdoer had it in his power to act rightly. In order to obtain this guarantee, he then expands his conception of power beyond the limits set by empirical evidence. He says that the alcoholic who repeatedly tries to stop, and fails, really is able to stop drinking; there is within him a transempirical power center able to overcome any degree of inner resistance. Taking this position, it becomes understandable that he sees a conflict between power and causality, for suppose that a scientist objects to his postulation of a transempirical power center and says: "I don't know whether we have a transempirical power center or not. I don't even understand what that expression means. I only know that I don't have to worry about such things. I can predict the characteristics of decisions and actions without paying attention to the operation of any such entity. And I must be permitted to say, therefore, that this power center seems to live a rather quiet life." My hypothesis is that our libertarian philosopher will try to meet this objection by denying that the scientist can give perfect predictions. He may maintain that such predictions are impossible, because the transempirical power center manifests itself in the empirical domain in a way that for the scientist must appear as partly random.

The primary thing is the transempirical expansion of our power. The belief in indeterminacy is secondary, intended as a wall of defense around the belief in such power.

POWER AND EMPIRICAL CONDITIONS

The fact that the principle of causality does not annihilate or reduce our power to decide or act otherwise does not imply that we have it in our power to decide and act otherwise. Our power may be limited by empirical conditions, for example, by our lack of imagination and knowledge, or by our inner conflicts and ethical convictions. Hence, we must raise the following question: To what degree do we, from an empirical point of view, have it in our power to decide and act? The comments below will be limited to our power to decide, since I consider this the most fundamental question.

The answer depends, *inter alia*, on the conditions we require in order to say that a decision has been made. If by "decision" we refer to lowly integrated decisions, our power is rather unlimited.[8] Even the most aggressive person can say the sentence, "I ought to be friendly towards all people," and even the most benevolent person can say, "All people ought to be tortured to death." Hence, if by "decision" we mean just forming the words "I ought to do so and so," then all who can think have the power to make any decision whatsoever. The statement, "Every person has it in his power to make any decision," may even become analytically true, since "person" may be so defined that the ability to form sentences is one of the necessary conceptual characteristics. This interpretation, though seldom made explicit, may be one source of the strength of the conviction that we have a completely free will. We believe that we are free because we can think.

Let us turn to the question of our power to make stable decisions that are highly integrated. Even such decisions can easily be made if they encounter no inner resistance. The crucial question, therefore, concerns our power to make decisions that are stable even though they meet with strong inner resistance. We may formulate the question thusly: to what degree does a person who in a certain situation decided in an ethically wrong way, and felt a strong resistance against deciding as he ought to, have it in his power to make a stable and ethically right decision? And, conversely, to what extent does a person have it in his power to decide in an ethically wrong instead of in an ethically right way?

I cannot here and now create within myself a stable decision to exterminate humanity. The conditions of such a decision do not exist. The decision would presuppose a change in my personality. And I cannot here and now form my own personality just as I form a piece of clay. I have it in my power—as unconditionally as I have anything in my power—to say the words, "I ought to exterminate humanity." I may even envisage some good consequences of this action, but there is nothing I can do, no instructions I can give myself, no process of reasoning I can carry out, by the use of which I can get myself to make a stable decision to this effect.

---

[8] I distinguish between lowly and highly integrated decisions, and between more or less well-integrated decisions. A decision D_1, made by P_1, is more well-integrated than D_2, made by P_2, if, and only if, D_1 more than D_2 is supported by the agent's motivational, ethical, and cognitive orientations. A highly integrated decision is deeply rooted in the agent's ethical system, supported by arguments and deep lying traits of his personality, whereas a lowly integrated decision has a minimum of such support. See Ofstad, *An Inquiry into the Freedom of Decision*, pp. 17–18. See also Augustine, *The Confessions of St. Augustine* (New York: Cardinal edition, 1952), pp. 141–42.

To give another example: suppose that a person has been brooding over the pacifist problem for many years, and slowly his decision to refuse to perform military service has emerged. His decision is highly integrated with other attitudes and is deeply bound up with his self-evaluation. If someone asks him to decide to become a soldier, he might answer, "I can *say*: 'I ought to become a soldier.' I can even stimulate some desire to do so, but it is very unlikely that I, in this situation, can make a highly integrated decision in favor of doing so. In order to do so, I would have to change important parts of my value system and personality. Whereas such changes sometimes can be accomplished over years, they cannot always be made in five minutes. We cannot make important decisions as easily as we make grimaces."

Festina Lente

Even decisions over which we have no immediate power may be brought about eventually, for our power is neither an innate ability nor a product finished once and for all. Just as we acquire the ability to make use of symbols, we acquire the ability to use symbols for building and strengthening motivational and cognitive orientations toward certain goals.

Suppose that a man is engaged to Miss *C* and partly wants and partly does not want to break the engagement, being unable to make a highly integrated and stable decision to break it. Seeking advice from his philosophical friend, he is told that he should not force himself to make the decision, but rather find a more indirect approach. Instead of aiming at the break directly, he should try to find out what is holding him back. Although he has great trouble in making a stable decision to break the engagement, he may have less trouble in trying to find out *why* this is so, and still less, for example, in noticing changes in his behavior in certain situations, in increase and decrease of his tensions, etc. By a procedure of this kind the person may find a point from which he can direct his attacks toward the further goal. As a first program, he may try to keep some records of his own verbal and non-verbal responses to a number of cues related to his problem, and to notice what Sullivan called his "marginal thoughts."[9] When responding to this flow of information, he may be able to label some of his suppressed action tendencies, and to develop, on the symbolic level, more adequate forms of discrimination and generalization.[10] Furthermore, he may try to notice what kind of verbal and non-verbal responses are most strongly associated with anxiety. Through this the person gradually changes. His perceptions, cognitions, and valuations of his environment and self become different. A person who, after an interval of this kind, returns to a more direct consideration of arguments

[9] See H. S. Sullivan, *Conceptions of Modern Psychiatry* (Washington, D.C.: W. A. White Foundation, 1947), p. 99 ff.
[10] Cf. J. Dollard and N. E. Miller, *Personality and Psychotherapy* (New York: McGraw-Hill Book Co., 1950).

for and against his planned decision may find that he does not have to *make* a decision at all. It has developed as a by-product of his thinking and analysis.

I do not believe that an approach of the kind indicated, what we might call the *festina lente* approach, always will be successful. I do not believe, for example, that most people would ever be able to make highly integrated decisions in favor of sadistic behavior. But some decisions which could not have been made by a direct attempt may develop as the result of a more indirect procedure. The point is to arrange the agent's abilities in a series, first making him do what he can do with no further stimulation than being asked to do it, or by trying to do it. Among the kinds of activities that he has in his power to this degree, he selects the one that is the best means for increasing his power to perform the next activity in the series, and so on.

The Moralistic View

Common thinking about our power to decide and act tends to be dichotomous in its conception of this power as something that we either have in full or not at all. Both so-called determinists and indeterminists tend to accept a dichotomous conceptualization. What we may call the *moralistic view* is an example of this way of thinking. According to this view, every normal mature person has the power necessary for acting in an ethically right way. If anybody says that he lacks this power, he is only trying to excuse himself in order to escape his duty or responsibility. The view implies a standardized conception that makes a quick and easy application to individual cases possible:

Are you an idiot?

No.

Are you insane?

No.

Are you a child?

No.

Well, then you are in possession of the power to decide and act otherwise.

As is no doubt clear from the above discussion. I regard this view as untenable. In order to determine the degree to which a certain wrongdoer had it in his power to decide or act otherwise in a certain situation, his individual case must be studied in detail. General statements can be made only on the basis of inductive research.

Moral Guilt and Power

Power to act otherwise is not the only condition of moral guilt[11]—knowledge of facts and the acceptance of moral norms are necessary too—but it is the only condition that interests us in this paper.

[11] Cf. n. 2.

Moral guilt, like criminal guilt, should be conceived of in such a way that it can vary in degree. An agent may be guilty to a high degree if he intentionally did evil and had a high degree of power to act otherwise. He may be guilty to a low degree if he either did not expect any harmful consequences of his behavior or had a very low degree of power to act otherwise. A maximum of guilt presupposes power to act otherwise in its highest possible degree, but seldom, if ever, do we have this amount of power, especially in situations where we acted wrongly. It may be emotionally convenient to believe that the great evildoers are maximally guilty, but usually they are closer to evil things than evil agents, petrified by their limited power to act otherwise as well as by their limited knowledge and moral understanding.

Power to act otherwise is a condition of moral guilt because a wrongdoer who is unable to act rightly is not a morally bad man. If he acted wrongly in spite of the fact that he tried with all his energy to act rightly, he may be a morally good person. The same holds for a wrongdoer who on sufficiently good grounds held the false opinion that he was so completely powerless to act rightly that he had no reason to try. But what should we say about a wrongdoer who did not have it in his power to act otherwise, who, though believing that he did, nevertheless refrained from even trying to do so? It seems to me that such a person may be just as morally bad as one who actually had the power in question. However, it would be misleading to say that he is morally guilty of the wrongdoing, though he may be guilty of not having tried to act rightly.

MORAL BLAME, POWER, AND MODIFIABILITY

Just as we may have to catch a tiger and lock it up, we may have to catch a man running wild. And just as we may blame a dog, we may blame a man just because it is useful. But in such cases we should talk about non-moral, rather than moral, blame.

According to my own ethical position (which I cannot try to formulate and defend in this paper), moral blame presupposes moral guilt in the sense developed in this paper, but guilt is not a sufficient condition.[12] To blame a person is to act toward him in a certain way, and an act is unjustified if it makes the world worse than if one had acted otherwise. Hence, moral blame presupposes utility as well as guilt. We must ask: Is blame a more useful instrument of reformation, prevention, deterrence, or moral education than other instruments of which we could make use? We do not know, but a large number of studies on the effects of punishment suggest that the use of blame is an ineffective way of modifying people's behavior.[13] Perhaps blaming primarily fulfills a function for the moral judge, whereas argumentation, knowledge, or a nicer wife are more

---

[12] See my *An Inquiry into the Freedom of Decision*, chap. 10.

[13] See, e.g., W. K. Estes, "An Experimental Study of Punishment," *Psychological Monographs*, vol. 57 (1944).

effective instruments of change. Hence, though it is not logically contradictory to assert that a wrongdoer ought to be morally blamed, it is seldom that our imperfect world satisfies those conditions of guilt and utility which give us the right to engage in this noble practice.

POWER AND UNCERTAINTY

I have tried to defend the view that the crucial question within the free will debate concerns our power to decide and act otherwise, that these powers vary in degrees, and that the degree depends upon the agent's personality and the situation. In order to know to what degree a certain Mr. Smith had it in his power to act otherwise, we must know how his 'heart' and 'kidneys' (and perhaps something else too) functioned at the crucial moment. But our evidence on such matters is indirect and inconclusive, to say the least. Hence, in most cases we cannot know to what degree he had it in his power to decide or act otherwise. We can only have a more or less well-grounded opinion. Consequently, since moral blame and guilt presuppose power, we can neither be certain that our wrongdoer is morally guilty, nor that he ought to be blamed. And this is not a bad reason for being rather careful in matters of guilt and blame.

BIBLIOGRAPHY

Aune, B. "Abilities, Modalities, and Free Will." *Philosophy and Phenomenological Research* 23: 397–413 (1962–63).

Austin, J. L. "Ifs and Cans." *Proceedings of the British Academy* 42: 109–32 (1956); reprinted in *Philosophical Papers*, edited by J. O. Urmson and G. F. Warnock. London: Oxford University Press, 1961.

——. "A Plea for Excuses." *Proceedings of the Aristotelian Society*, n.s., 57: 1–30 (1956–57); reprinted in *Philosophical Papers*, edited by J. O. Urmson and G. F. Warnock. London: Oxford University Press, 1961.

Beardsley, E. L. "Determinism and Moral Perspectives." *Philosophy and Phenomenological Research* 21: 1–20 (1960–61).

Broad, C. D. "Determinism, Indeterminism and Libertarianism." In *Ethics and the History of Philosophy*. London: Routledge & Kegan Paul, 1952; 1st ed., 1934.

Campbell, C. A. *In Defence of Free Will*. London: Allen & Unwin, 1967.

Danto, A. C. "Basic Actions." *American Philosophical Quarterly* 2: 144–48 (1965).

Ebersole, F. B. "Free-Choice and the Demands of Morals." *Mind* 61: 234–57 (1952).

Ewing, A. C. "May Can-Statements Be Analysed Deterministically?" *Proceedings of the Aristotelian Society*, n.s., 64: 157–76 (1963–64).

Feinberg, J. "Action and Responsibility." In *Philosophy in America*, edited by Max Black. Ithaca, N.Y.: Cornell University Press, 1965.

Hampshire, S. *Freedom of the Individual*. London: Chatto and Windus, 1965.

——. *Thought and Action*. London: Chatto and Windus, 1959.

——, and Hart, H. L. A. "Decision, Intention and Certainty." *Mind* 67: 1–12 (1958).

Hart, H. L. A. *Punishment and Responsibility: Essays in the Philosophy of Law*. Oxford: Clarendon Press, 1968.

Hook, S., ed. *Determinism and Freedom in the Age of Modern Science*. New York: Collier Books, 1958.

Kaufman, A. S. "Moral Responsibility and the Use of 'Could Have.'" *Philosophical Quarterly* 12: 120–28 (1962).

Lehrer, K., ed. *Freedom and Determinism*. New York: Random House, 1966.

Moore, G. E. *Ethics*. London: Oxford University Press, 1912.

Nowell-Smith, P. H. *Ethics*, chaps. 19–20. London: Penguin Books, 1954.

———. "Ifs and Cans." *Theoria* 26: 85–101 (1960).

Ofstad, H. "Analyses of 'P Could Have Decided Differently in the Situation S.'" *Actes du XIème Congrès International de Philosophie,* vol. 24. Brussels, 1953.

———. "Broad on Ought and Can." *Theoria* 21: 105–16 (1955).

———. "Can We Produce Decisions?" *Journal of Philosophy* 56: 89–94 (1959).

———. "Frankena on Ought and Can." *Mind* 68: 73–79 (1959).

———. *An Inquiry into the Freedom of Decision*. Oslo: Norwegian Universities Press; London: Allen & Unwin, 1961.

———. "Libertarianism and the Belief in Transempirical Entities: L. J. Russell on Causation and Agency." In *Philosophical Essays Dedicated to Gunnar Aspelin*. Lund: C.W.K. Gleerup Bokförlag, 1963.

———. "Recent Work on the Free-Will Problem." *American Philosophical Quarterly* 4: 1–29 (1967).

Pears, D. F., ed. *Freedom and the Will*. London: MacMillan & Co., 1963.

Raab, F. V. "Free Will and the Ambiguity of 'Could.'" *Philosophical Review* 64: 60–77 (1955).

———. "The Relevance of Morals to Our Denials of Responsibility." In *Morality and the Language of Conduct*, edited by H. Castañeda and C. Nakhnikian. Detroit: Wayne State University Press, 1963.

Smart, J. J. C. "Free-Will, Praise and Blame." *Mind* 70: 291–306 (1961).

Taylor, R. *Metaphysics*, chaps. 4–5. Englewood Cliffs, N.J.: Prentice-Hall, 1963.

Windelband, W. *Über Willensfreiheit*. Tübingen and Leipzig: I. C. B. Mohr, 1904.

Anfinn Stigen

Philosophy as World View and Philosophy as Discipline

To be able to state the principles of one's procedure, we are told, is the highest of one's professional attainments. A man who can talk method earns the respect of his colleagues; and if, in addition to that, he can defend his own methods by appealing to scientific principles, he has shown himself to be a master in his field. True, a blind hen may also find the grain, but the blind hen must not be allowed to rule the roost!

1. Is There a Philosophical Method?

Can one speak of a *philosophical* method? This is not one but many questions: Are philosophical investigations in general of such a kind that one can speak of a *method*; that is, are they systematic enough and do they proceed according to plan, so that one can set up rules according to which one does, or should, proceed? Has philosophy a *special* method—in the way in which one of the methods in the natural sciences can be said to consist in the testing of hypotheses by experiments, or in the way in which mathematicians operate by conjoining theorems in order to discover contradictions or necessary relationships between them? Is there *one* method in philosophy—one method which is best, whether in the sense of being the most fruitful, or easiest to apply, or perhaps which emerges from the very nature of philosophy itself?

According to Plato and Hegel, there was one method peculiar to philosophy, and although they disagreed as to what it consisted in, they both called it "dialectic." Bergson thought that all genuine philosophy made use of intuition, a kind of 'intellectual sympathy.' For Wittgenstein, the only strictly correct philosophical method consisted in the pointing out of meaninglessness; for

Professor Stigen, of the University of Oslo, is a native of Norway.
Translated by A. Hannay.

Schlick, it was the elucidation and explication of given propositions, and for Husserl, phenomenological description. Hume, on the contrary, thought that the philosopher had no special method at all, and that in the main he should proceed experimentally. Spinoza adopted the 'geometrical' method as his form of presentation.

Any view as to what method or methods the philosopher should use must of course be based on a definite conception of what philosophy is. Because there has not been, and fortunately is not now, agreement as to the nature of philosophy, there cannot be agreement as to method—in characteristic opposition to such disciplines as physics and mathematics. There doesn't even seem to be much accord between the method a philosopher professes and the method he actually employs in his writings. Descartes' doubt is anything but 'universal,' Hume proceeds mainly *non*-experimentally, and Wittgenstein's work is much more than a demonstration of meaninglessness.

What is worse, to profess one definite method presupposes a definite conception of philosophy—a presupposition, however, that has not itself been arrived at by the recommended method. Husserl's phenomenological description and his 'bracketing' method rest upon the distinction between the given and its interpretation, and it is only when this distinction has been established that the method can be employed. The young Wittgenstein's dividing up and analysis of propositions assumes, as a matter of course, that the propositions consist of elements that cannot be further divided.

2. THE METHOD DEPENDS UPON ONE'S CONCEPTION OF WHAT PHILOSOPHY IS

Why this long introduction? To make it clear that the following discussion of certain procedures that I have found serviceable in my work with philosophical problems is made in full consciousness of, and should be understood with clear recognition of, the considerations that have been pointed out above: that all talk of method in philosophy is a kind of idealizing of the modes of procedure one actually employs, and that in philosophical practice one always departs from the rules of method one sets up, that every philosopher with respect for his profession speaks not of "the only correct method," but of *his* method or methods, that he emphasizes his methods, not to the neglect or disparagement of the methods of others, but only because he has found his own methods fruitful in his treatment of the philosophical problems that he considers essential, and—perhaps most important of all—that each recommendation of a definite method, each and every choice of a definite procedure, rests on a definite conception of philosophy.

The two last points in fact merge into one, for it is through the choice one makes of the philosophical problems one finds interesting and significant enough to be concerned with that one's conception of what philosophy is becomes apparent. Not, of course, that a simple enumeration of problems will express one's philosophy; rather, it is the principle that lies behind the selection—the principle that indicates one's understanding of the *peculiarity of philosophical problems*—that is the determining factor. It is a source of surprise to many that there can be relatively wide agreement as to which problems are genuinely philosophical ones, even among people of widely differing views as to the nature of philosophy. Most philosophers are agreed, for example, that freedom of the will and the relationship of soul and body, or thing and property (substance and attribute), are philosophical problems. But this should not be surprising, for in the first instance it is in the *treatment* of the problems that the difference in philosophical views makes itself apparent; it is only here that one's grounds for recognizing certain problems as philosophical appear, that one's conception of the peculiarity of philosophical problems becomes evident.

Nevertheless, an enumeration of the philosophical problems one regards as especially interesting is a good first step toward clarifying one's own conception of philosophy. Accordingly, such a listing will provide my own point of departure in the clarification of what I understand philosophy to be. But let me first say a few words about this way of presenting one's conception of philosophy. It should be clear that what I present in this way is my conception of philosophy as a *discipline*, and not *my* philosophy, as differentiated from the philosophy of, for example, Plato or Kant.

3. Philosophy as a View of the World and Philosophy as a Discipline

There is an interesting, but generally overlooked ambiguity in the question "What is philosophy?" It is this ambiguity that allows one, on the one hand, to talk of philosophy in the following way: "There is in all philosophy a unity, which no single person is in possession of, but which all serious efforts have always sought to attain: the single eternal philosophy—which manifests itself in the works of the great philosophers and which is echoed in the works of the minor philosophers";[1] and, on the other hand, to define philosophy by enumerating problems and suggesting one or more ways of dealing with them. In the former case, philosophy is spoken of as something one "is in possession of," as something one *has*—namely (if one should attempt a definition, however vague and obscure) one's conception of the connection among the various aspects of life and the relatedness of things, one's view of the meaning of existence and of man's place in the universe—one's *view of the world* and *conception of life*. When we speak of a 'genuine philosopher,' we usually mean one who possesses such a definite viewpoint or conception. In the second case, contrary to the first, philosophy is regarded as a *discipline*. By stating what kinds of problems are philosophical and how one tries to solve such problems, one states one's conception of the *profession* of philosophy. One who works with such problems is a philosopher by profession, whether he has a definite conception of the world or

---

[1] Karl Jaspers, *Einführung in die Philosophie* (Zurich: Artemis Verlag, 1953), p. 17.

not. It is worth noting that when we contrast philosophy with biology or mathematics, for example, we are thinking of philosophy as a *discipline*. One cannot speak of *my* biology as opposed to another's. Neither can one speak of *my* or *your* mathematics. And this is not because of the circumstance that there is no more than one biology or mathematics. There is simply no sense in saying that I *have* or *am in possession of* a definite biology or mathematics.

But one must not assume, either, that these two meanings of "philosophy" have nothing in common. On the contrary, I believe they are intimately connected. I will attempt to show that certain problems have traditionally been viewed as philosophical precisely because the treatment and clarification of them have been regarded as significant for the views that form one's philosophy. The *discipline* of philosophy is therefore connected with the views and conceptions that form a part of *one person's* philosophy—his view of the world and his conception of life. A more precise account of the nature of this relationship must be postponed until we have reached a better understanding of what makes a problem philosophical.

4. PHILOSOPHICAL PROBLEMS

Let us begin by listing some topics and problems that I believe most philosophers would regard as characteristically philosophical: abstract and concrete; action; belief and knowledge; cause and effect; concept; consciousness; doubt and certainty; duty; existence (being); freedom and determinism; good and evil; language and reality; matter and form; morality and justice; nature; person; phenomenon and reality; the potential and the actual; purpose and motive; responsibility and blame; sensation and notion; sense and meaning; the simple and the complex; solipsism (I and others); soul and body; thing and property (substance and attribute); thought; truth; value; the will and its freedom. I have excluded from this list such problems as analysis and synthesis; definition; identity and difference; stating and evaluating; necessity and contingency— that is, problems of a logical nature—because one may claim that these are problems that arise only in the course of the philosopher's work and are therefore of a metaphilosophical character rather than 'genuine' philosophical problems of the first order.

As we have said, such a list does not tell us very much, but perhaps it may indicate the principle behind the formation of such a list. This is precisely the question we must now seek to answer: what gives these problems their philosophical character? I feel that this question can best be answered by examining a particular philosophical problem, for example, the problem of free will.

Of course, only *certain* features in the treatment of this problem are of interest here, namely, the features that characterize the problem as *philosophical*, and not the features peculiar to *this* philosophical problem. However, we must examine the problem itself deeply enough to understand it; we must have some idea of what the problem is about, what the issue is.

5. An Example: The Problem of Free Will

The problem of free will presupposes that one recognizes, or accepts as a fact, that human beings, and perhaps higher forms of life, possess something that we call "will"—"will," then, not in the sense in which, for example, an ant is assumed to have a will when we say that it *wills* to go in the direction of the anthill, or a cat when we say that it *wills* to kill birds, but "will" understood as a capacity to reach decisions in accordance with which one acts. The assumption that human beings are able to assess various possible courses of action, to decide upon one of them, and to act accordingly, generates a host of questions which severally are objects of philosophical investigation and yet seem to radiate from this assumption in the same general direction. For instance, the fact that man, as distinct from other living beings, bears *responsibility* for what he does and says depends on this assumption, for it is first and foremost what a man does and says deliberately and by design for which he is held responsible. Furthermore, the assumption that man is capable of choice provides the basis for our ideas about actions and utterances as conscious expressions of meanings and attitudes; for unless one assumes that a person has the ability to choose his action and utterances, these will be reduced to movements and sounds and must be placed in a class with reactions, facial twitches, and shrieks of pain.

What is it about these matters, then, that creates problems? And above all, what is it about them that makes them *philosophically* important, that gives rise to *philosophical* problems?

Of the many problems raised by the notion that man has the ability to decide for himself, I will mention only one here—perhaps the most central issue because it questions the assumption itself: Is it the case that man is special in this respect? Does he have an ability that other living beings lack to evaluate possibilities, to select one—at least apparently on his own initiative and according to his own wishes—and to act in accordance with this choice?

6. Can the Question of Whether Human Beings Have a Free Will Be Decided Empirically?

But why, we should first ask, is this not a question for biology or psychology? Certainly the question of what abilities a living being has—as, for example, whether a certain animal has the ability to see in the dark or to determine the distance to the nearest wall by means other than the usual senses—is one for biologists and zoologists to answer. Why then is it not left to experimental scientists to determine whether or not human beings have this faculty we call the free will?

The crucial thing is: Can the question of man's free will be resolved in the same way as, for example, a zoologist determines which senses an animal has? Is it an *empirical* question? That is, can we resolve it by a more precise observation of the behavior and reactions of human beings, or by attempting to find an organ analogous to the sense organs which could be the seat of the free will's activity?

It would be dogmatic—even misleading—to answer that question definitely with a "yes" or "no." If one maintains that the problem of free will can be resolved empirically, one shows that one does not consider it a characteristically philosophical problem. On the other hand, if one denies that the question of whether or not man has free will can be resolved within biology or zoology or some other empirical science, then one has classified the question as philosophical—and one's argument for saying that it cannot be treated empirically will have to indicate the philosophical nature of the problem, that is, what gives it its philosophical character.

Most people will probably claim that the assumption that man has the capacity to form decisions is so central to our conception of ourselves and other human beings as persons, and that it is so intimately connected with other fundamental human concepts—for example, responsibility and morality—that the denial of this assumption is quite straightforwardly unacceptable. After all, rightly or wrongly, we do consider human beings as essentially different from other beings in this respect. It is part of our conception of man and therefore part of our conception of the peculiar position of man, that we sometimes act by design and that we sometimes act freely. It is essential to our conception of man's place in the universe and of our relationship to other beings and other things—and thereby an essential part of our view of the world. We take it for granted that man alone (aside from God and, possibly, other higher beings) has a *consciousness* of what he does, that man alone has an *intention*, a *conscious purpose* in his actions, that therefore man alone among all beings can distinguish between right and wrong and take full responsibility for the actions he freely performs.

This is not to say that empirical discoveries cannot have significance for our conception of man and our view of man's place in nature. They can, of course— as long as they do not attack the very notion of man as a free being, a being with the capacity for conscious decisions. For example, if, through a behavioral study, zoologists found that it was highly probable that the dolphin had as highly developed a consciousness as man with respect to what it does and to right and wrong, this would mean that the dolphin, too, must be accorded free will. At the same time, we would have also to apply to the dolphin the associated concepts that are connected with our idea of free will, for example, the concept of responsibility.

7. The Peculiarity of Philosophical Problems

The reason we can consider such a modification of our world picture and yet be unwilling to deny man the capacity for conscious decisions seems to be the following: To deny man this capacity would be tantamount to destroying the distinction between two types of beings. It would be an attack on the conceptual division that forms, on the one side of this distinction, the idea of man's consciousness and will, and, at the same time, all the ideas that are logically dependent on this: intention, action, responsibility, and the like. A recognition of the dolphin's free will, however, would not affect the conceptual distinction itself or the system of classification that rests on it. We would still have beings with and without free will; the dolphin would simply be transferred from one side of the dividing line to the other, that is, from one class to the other—a zoological event, certainly, but no philosophical revolution. The ideas that lie behind our view of what constitutes the most significant lines of division in nature would remain unchallenged.

The problem of free will, then, concerns principal features of our conception of man, his place in the universe, his relationship to his environment, and his existence. In my opinion, this is what makes the problem a genuinely philosophical one. My theory is that the philosophical character of a problem arises precisely from its concerns with ideas and conceptual distinctions that are regarded as crucial to our conception of man's place in the universe, and of his relationship with other beings and with other things. It is no coincidence that most philosophical problems can advantageously be formulated as oppositions between two concepts—for example, belief and knowledge, nature and convention, appearance and reality.

To return to the problem of free will: There is little doubt that our conviction that only man has this capacity crucially determines our relationship to other living beings. Our whole approach, our whole attitude toward a living being is determined in a decisive way by whether we regard this being as we regard ourselves—as a being with ideas and aims, conscious of what it does and responsible for its actions.

8. The Connection between the Discipline of Philosophy and Philosophy as a View of the World

We should now be able to see how the problem of free will as a problem for treatment within the discipline of philosophy is related to a person's philosophy— a person's conception of "the connection among the various aspects of life and the relatedness of things, one's view of the meaning of existence and of man's place in the universe."[2] For we can now see how the idea of man as a being with free will is linked to our conception of the basic distinction between man and non-man—however one formulates this idea of man: that being which has self-consciousness, ideas, thoughts, opinions, language, and so forth. And of a person who would deny man this capacity, one would have to say that his view of man differed decisively from that of most people and that he has quite another philosophy—in the sense of 'conception of man's place in the universe'—from that of most people. One must say the same of a person who would attribute to most

[2] *Ibid.*, p. 5.

or all living beings the capacity of deliberation and decision. Such a conception would have significant consequences in the person's relationships to other living beings.

I believe that a closer investigation of each of the problems that have traditionally been regarded as philosophical will confirm this conception of the peculiarity of philosophical problems. I shall mention here just one more traditional philosophical problem: the relationship between body and soul. This is a very diffuse problem mainly because of the many, widely different, meanings of the word "soul." For example, Aristotle uses the word in a sense very close to our word "life." In his philosophy, all living things, not only animals and man, but plants as well, have soul. Others attribute soul only to animals and man, while still others regard the soul as something so elevated and rare that it can be attributed only to human beings. To ask in general what the distinction between soul and body is, is not a precise question, then, and the major part of philosophical treatment of the problem therefore aims precisely at clarifying just where the distinction is drawn in each case and how one should decide what falls on each side of the conceptual division.

But here, too, we are concerned with altogether basic distinctions. If one gives to the word "soul" a meaning such that all living things must be said to have a soul, the relationship between soul and body then concerns the distinction between living and non-living nature. On the other hand, if one gives "soul" a meaning such that man and animals, but not plants, can be said to have soul, the problem concerns the distinction between animals and man on the one hand and plant life on the other; one then naturally becomes involved, for instance, in questions about the nature of sensation and perception, since according to the prevailing belief it is just by these faculties that the animal kingdom is distinguished from the plant world. Again, if "soul" is given a meaning such that it is reasonable to attribute soul only to man, the distinction between soul and body approaches the distinction applied in differentiating between a person's 'inner' and 'outer' life, that is, between, on the one hand, his life of emotion and thought, and, on the other, that about him which others can perceive with their senses: the 'tangible' aspects of a person, including what he does and says, whether or not it is meant and understood as the expression of his inner self.

We cannot go further into this question here, but it should be clear enough that the soul-body problem, too, concerns ideas that result from distinctions that are of extraordinary significance not only for professional philosophers but for everyone. The distinction between soul and body—whether we conceive of it as distinguishing between man's inner and outer life, between the animal kingdom and the plant world, or between the living and the non-living—concerns basic classifications. A change in the classifications formed with the aid of these concepts, for example, by attributing feeling and sensation to plants, would profoundly affect our view of nature; we would avoid treading on flowers not only to preserve their beauty but also to avoid inflicting pain on them.

But just as in the question of free will, what is philosophically revolutionary first occurs when the idea of soul, the idea of an inner life—or, for that matter, on the other side of the distinction, the concept of anything bodily—is subjected to attack. An attack on the conceptual division itself is tantamount to the introduction of another philosophy, another view of the world. An attack on the legitimacy of the idea of a soul can take—and has taken—many forms, resulting in various versions of 'materialism' and radical behaviorism. An attack upon the legitimacy of our idea of anything bodily can result in various forms of 'idealism.' A consistent and sustained materialism or idealism must, so far as I can see, have drastic consequences for one's view of existence in general, and for one's relationship to other beings in particular.

I believe that an examination of other recognized philosophical problems will point to the same conclusion: that they rest upon or arise from the most crucial distinctions and classifications that are of significance for our conception of the universe and our place in it. Some philosophical problems are less central than others; these are of philosophical significance only to the degree that they can be connected with a distinction that is important to us. The problem of good and evil is a philosophical one, I believe, insofar as our ideas of good and evil are related to the essential distinction that exists between pleasure and suffering, between satisfaction and dissatisfaction, between that which promotes good and that which promotes evil.

In summary, philosophical problems concern the most basic ideas or concepts to be found in that whole system of ideas, in that *conceptual system*, within which we think and with the aid of which we arrange all things—the system into which we place, and in which we evaluate, ourselves, other beings, other things, and life as a whole.

9. Philosophy's First Task: The Clarification of Basic Ideas and Conceptual Distinctions

What follows, then, about the philosopher's task and the philosopher's method from such a view of philosophy? If it is correct that we have certain ideas and conceptual distinctions that are of crucial importance for our view of life and the universe, the philosopher's first task must be to clarify these ideas and conceptual distinctions as far as possible. This *conceptual clarification* seems to be a necessary first step whether one is exclusively interested in getting a better understanding of our conceptual system or whether one aims to attack or modify it. If one wants to show that there is no basis for the distinction an idea is based upon, or that other difficulties are encountered by accepting the idea, one must first be clear about the idea itself.

But how should one set about this task? How should one actually proceed to acquire a survey of those parts—parts of an enormously complicated conceptual system—that one feels one should master before being able to handle the philosophical problem (or, as often is the case, the constellation of problems) that one is interested in at the moment? As I have said, I do not believe in simple formulas in philosophy. Sometimes one follows one procedure, at other times one proceeds in quite another way. Even though the account one finally gives of one's treatment of the problem very often exhibits features in common with accounts of other approaches, one must not assume that the accounts provide the true picture of how one actually proceeded—of all the blind alleys encountered, of all the inspirations abandoned, of all the modifications introduced into the original working hypothesis before one finally rejected it. It is the goal not the method that remains constant: the acquisition of a perspective on that constellation of concepts which the problem in question concerns. Gilbert Ryle says that in his philosophy he tries to "determine the logical geography of concepts"—a very appropriate metaphor for me as well.[3] If, as I maintain, philosophical problems concern our most basic conceptual distinctions, it is natural to present the philosophical clarification of concepts as the study of borders, a closer investigation of the lines of demarcation, a "taking stock in the field" of the often unclear and imprecise picture we have of our logical landscape.

10. LOGOGRAPHY: CONCEPTUAL CLARIFICATION BY PRESENTING THE STRUCTURE OF ONE'S CONCEPTUAL SYSTEM

What does such a structural map look like? And how is it to be prepared? To avoid generalizations, let us take an example. Suppose the philosopher is working with the problem of responsibility. Perhaps the question has been posed in connection with the distinction between moral and legal responsibility, or perhaps the problem has arisen as a question of which parts of a person's behavior he can be held responsible for. Is a person responsible equally for all that he does and says, or, if not, how is the degree of responsibility fixed?

The first thing we must do is to orientate ourselves, to try to arrive at some clarity about where we are in the conceptual landscape; that is, we must determine which concepts regularly appear together with the concept of responsibility, or, to use another metaphor, which cogwheels are interlocked with and move with the cogwheel of responsibility. At this stage in the inquiry, I often make use of a form of linguistic investigation: I make extensive use of comprehensive dictionaries, among other things. With the aid of quotations and examples in which the word "responsibility" and its synonyms are used, I try to track down the concepts to which the concept of responsibility seems to be connected. In my opinion, this is a more satisfactory way of revealing that part of the conceptual network in which we are interested than the intuitive method usually adopted. The intuitive method assumes—and correctly, I think—that we have the conceptual network within ourselves, and that therefore we need not go elsewhere to acquire it. However, the conceptual network is enormously complicated, it turns out, and what we see of it at any one time depends upon the situation and the interests involved. A dictionary with its collection of occurrences of the word

---

[3] Gilbert Ryle, *The Concept of Mind* (New York: Barnes and Noble, 1949), p. 8.

brings out the interplay of these factors; the method assures that the problem is illuminated from many sides.

The very registering of associated concepts goes hand in hand with organization of these concepts into a system; the concepts find their places in relation to each other rather than being placed by the philosopher, for they should interlock with one another and constitute a whole, as do the pieces of a jigsaw puzzle. At this stage, the investigation really is very much like a jigsaw puzzle— sometimes successfully solved, sometimes not. I do not think that rules can be laid down for arranging the concepts into a system; what is required is a certain acumen and a sense of the finer nuances. Often the arranging occurs first in distinguishing vertically between main and subordinate concepts, and then horizontally between concepts on the same level, in a manner similar to the classical method—namely, the method we use, for instance, in dividing all things first into natural and 'artificial,' next dividing nature into living and non-living things, then living things into those things without sensation, i.e., plant life, and those things with sensation, then again this last group into living beings lacking the ability to think, i.e., animals, and beings having this ability, and the animal kingdom further into the different animal species.

To mark clearly the difference between this way of handling concepts and other prevalent ways of clarifying concepts, for example, the usual analysis by definition, I will introduce the term "logography." By "logography" or a logographical treatment I mean the clarification of (parts of) one's conceptual system by indicating the relationship among the individual concepts or ideas. I shall give an example of the logographical treatment of a philosophical conceptual complex below.

Before proceeding further, an important point should be mentioned. Philosophical problems, as we have seen, concern in one way or another the interrelationship of concepts; philosophical problems essentially concern how the concepts are coordinated or should be coordinated in relation to each other. In other words, any account of the mutual relationship among the concepts gives not only a picture of the framework within which the philosophical problem in question arises, but also a definite presentation of the problem complex itself—a presentation, moreover, which is not neutral with regard to the solution of the problem. Where the relationships are complicated—as they always are with philosophical problems—no such arrangement of concepts is uncontroversial. It never has the last word in philosophical debate; on the contrary, this is where the debate usually begins.

11. An Example of Logographical Treatment and Arranging of a Logogram

To continue with our example of the problem of responsibility, we want first to locate our idea of responsibility in relation to other ideas. On the basis of the occurrences of "responsibility"—and words of similar meaning, for example, "answer for," "account for," "obligation," "blame," "punishment"--which we have at hand, we try to specify for which kinds of things a person can in principle be considered to be held responsible. It will be fairly easy to establish that a person must, as a rule, have done or said something—or in certain instances neglected to do or say something—before responsibility can come into play. The person is not responsible for what merely happens if it is clear that he himself has not been contributory. To be sure, one may have to assume full responsibility, for instance, for being run down, but responsibility in such cases is ascribed not for the being run down itself, but for one's carelessness in crossing the street without looking—again, for something one has done.

The next stage in the investigation, naturally, is the question: Can one be held responsible for *all* one does and says? For simplicity's sake, we will confine ourselves here to what one 'does.' And there is much that one does! One looks out of the window, one lets one's thoughts wander, one sneezes, one reaches for a book on the shelf, one looks for it, one accuses one's assistant of having taken it, one sneaks into one's colleague's office and takes his copy.

Most of what I do involves no question of responsibility. I am not responsible for what I 'can't help.' Nor am I responsible for what I do inadvertently or accidentally, what I merely 'happen' to do; I happen to smash a saucer in washing up, I step inadvertently on a snail, but each of these is 'one of those things' that can happen to anyone, and it is not relevant to speak of responsibility in these cases unless I have displayed negligence or the like. What I can be held responsible for is what I do *intentionally*, what I do *on purpose*, in brief: for my *actions*. For all my actions I bear a certain responsibility.

But am I responsible for all my actions to the same degree? Common sense, represented by our linguistic material, tells us that we make an important distinction—significant for the question of responsibility—between the actions we carry out under pressure or duress and the actions we credit to our 'own free will.' I am not held responsible to the same degree for the letter of extortion I write with the gang leader standing over me as for the letter I write later after seeing how easily things went with the first. I am indeed responsible for the former action, too, to the degree that the letter was written in full consciousness of what I was doing, but responsibility can be distributed and blame shared both by persons and by circumstances. Compulsion and pressure can vary from physical violence, to the influencing of another's will by threat or persuasion, to the subtle 'moral pressure' that can be said to exist when one feels bound by one's obligations, by law and justice, or by tradition. But if one has performed an action of one's own free will, willingly, perhaps even gladly, then responsibility cannot be placed outside the agent. For one's fully voluntary actions, one must assume full responsibility.

If we now arrange the conceptual system revealed by this investigation with a view to the principal lines of demarcation, we arrive at the following scheme or *logogram*:

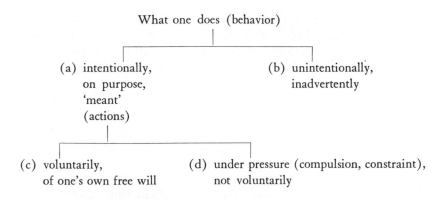

12. THE APPLICABILITY OF CONCEPTUAL SCHEMES IN WORKING WITH
PHILOSOPHICAL PROBLEMS

What has one achieved, then, with this scheme, assuming that it has been devised correctly? Not much per se; such a scheme places the concept of responsibility in only one dimension. If we are interested in elucidating this concept in relation to others than those introduced here—in relation to blame and punishment, for example—we must draw up another scheme and work with other coordinates. The logical space in which a concept is located has many dimensions.

But neither should one underestimate the clarity that such a scheme can bring to a region that, perhaps more than anything else, craves the conceptual cartographer's art. Whatever philosophical significance the mapping of the mutual relationship among our principal ideas has, naturally, can only be determined by investigating the degree to which logograms are actually able to elucidate, or even resolve, philosophical problems.

Here, of course, we have room only for suggestions. Nevertheless, it should be clear enough that the conceptual scheme we have sketched on the basis of our notion of responsibility does throw light on, for example, the problem of free will. From the scheme we may see directly that what is usually meant (according to our linguistic material) by someone's doing something voluntarily, or of his own free will is, first, that he does it intentionally or on purpose (this is implied by its being a voluntary *action*), and second, that he does not feel compelled to perform the act, but does what he does because and only because he so wishes (this is implied by the act's being performed *voluntarily*). If 'free will' is to be referred to as a capacity—an interpretation which, however, finds little support in non-philosophical uses of language—this must mean, according to our scheme, the capacity to (or, simply, being able to) act without pressure, that is, of one's own accord. The idea of man as presumably the only being possessing free will should thus suggest that only with regard to man is there any sense in distinguishing between what is done under pressure and what is done of one's free will. On the basis of our linguistic material, we should be able to verify whether this is the case and whether this applies also to some of the other distinctions that we have made, for instance, the distinction between what is done intentionally (actions) and what is done inadvertently. For example, has this distinction any significance for the behavior of *cats*? If not, why not?

The devising of a conceptual scheme on the basis of linguistic material can also lead to unexpected by-products of no little significance. A study of the material will show, for example, that the contrary of an act performed voluntarily is not, as most philosophers seem to have assumed, an *involuntary* act, but a *not-voluntary* act. The word "involuntary" is of course to be found in our vocabulary, but it is not commonly used to characterize a special kind of action. It occurs naturally, for example, in "an involuntary bath" and "I was an involuntary witness," that is, in cases where the subject is passive, not active, where something which he does not desire happens to, or befalls, him. Has this elucidation any philosophical significance? A study of the reasoning of certain philosophers on the problem of the will shows that because of their tendency to speak of 'involuntary acts' instead of 'not-voluntary acts' they easily confuse the meanings of "involuntary" and "not-voluntary" as used in everyday language—where these expressions have distinct meanings, as has just been pointed out. The confusion generally occurs in the following way: Actions are classified into voluntary and involuntary ones, but there is something odd about the latter group. On the one hand, these are indeed actions and as such call for an agent, that is, an acting person; but on the other hand, these actions have the peculiarity (actually a logical inconsistency) that the agent (as a person) is in fact passive. This peculiarity—the feeling that in this case there is something which acts upon the person rather than the person himself acting—involves a transference of meaning from the everyday use of the word "involuntary." In this way difficult philosophical problems are *created*, for example: How can it ever be correct to hold a person responsible for what he does 'involuntarily' (remembering that according to the conceptual schemes adopted by these philosophers, this category covers all that a person does not do voluntarily) if he is actually passive? How can it be correct to say that a person acts 'involuntarily,' for example, out of a feeling of obligation, and at the same time claim, as we do, that he acts on purpose, intentionally? These are pseudoproblems which are resolved by an understanding of the conceptual relationships indicated by the logogram.

The same applies to a problem such as: How can one and the same action be performed with will, or intentionally, and still not be a freely willed act—if my will according to human nature is free? Aristotle gives an example of such an action: A ship encounters bad weather, the crew jettisons the cargo to save the ship and themselves; they did not throw the cargo overboard *of their own free will*, but they acted with will or intentionally. The conceptual scheme gives the answer: That the crew threw the cargo overboard with will, means that they did so with a definite purpose, namely, with the aim of saving what could be saved. But they threw the cargo overboard in a forced situation, that is, it was not done voluntarily; the action was willed, but not freely willed. That human beings have free will, according to the scheme, cannot mean that they can act freely, that is, in an uncompelled way, regardless of the conditions, but that under certain circumstances they may act on their own accord, only because they themselves wish to, without pressure of any kind's being present.

13. THREE KINDS OF OBJECTIONS TO A GIVEN LOGOGRAM: TERMINOLOGICAL, LOGOGRAPHICAL, AND LOGONOMICAL

But what if someone objects to the scheme as it is drawn up? I will distinguish here between three types of objections. First, one may attack the scheme by maintaining that the linguistic material used as a basis does not agree with one's own and several others' linguistic usage, and that therefore the distinctions made do not apply for these linguistic deviates. I call such an objection a *terminological* one. Secondly, one may object that the conceptual scheme as presented is not justified by the material, that it does not reflect the actual relationship between our concepts. Such an objection concerns the correctness of the logogram as drawn up, and I shall call an objection of this kind *logographical*. Thirdly, one may admit that the logogram on the whole gives a correct picture of the conceptual system we actually use and mirrors correctly the main distinctions of everyday language, but that this system suffers from certain inherent weaknesses or actually gives a wrong view, an incorrect picture of the world, and that it should therefore be revised. Such an objection does not assume that the logogram depicts the actual conceptual relationships incorrectly, but attacks the validity of the prevailing conceptual system. We may therefore call such an objection a *logonomical* one. These three types of objections may all be advanced by one and the same person; in fact, in one and the same argument against a proposed conceptual scheme, the objector may act as *terminologist, logographist,* and *logonomist.* Nevertheless, it is an advantage to be able to consider the three separately, as more or less 'pure' types.

14. OBJECTIONS CONCERNING TERMINOLOGY AND LINGUISTIC USAGE

A terminological objection may take the following form (in connection with the logogram in section 11, above): "Suppose that I take the sugar bowl down from the shelf and happen to knock down the creamer. I would then say that I involuntarily broke the creamer. But that does not agree with your scheme, for you say that 'involuntary'—or in your terminology, 'not-voluntary'—is used for acts that are in the first place intended and in the second place performed under duress. But in this case the act was neither intended nor subject to compulsion." This objection is ostensibly of a logographical nature, but actually involves only terminology.

Such an objection is best answered by refraining from insisting on a definite linguistic usage and instead emphasizing the fact that, regardless of the designations one applies to the various concepts, the scheme is just as valid if only one accepts the correctness of the conceptual distinctions. The answer really consists of a reminder that a logogram represents relationships between *concepts* or ideas, not between linguistic designations or expressions. The linguistic designations are only the labels of the concepts, labels that can be changed or may come off. The conceptual distinctions themselves can be made clear by examples, without the use of labels. Let us hope, then, that it will be clear that the misfortune with the creamer falls under class (b) in our scheme (see section 11, above), whatever its label, and the objection is disposed of in this way.

But one may go a step further and ask the objector to consider the use of the designation "involuntary" in the case in question. One can point out that it is unfortunate to use "involuntary" in two senses: (1) with reference to accidents of the kind in which the creamer was broken, where the person indeed does something, but not on purpose, and (2) in cases such as an involuntary bath, where the person is subjected to something unwanted. One can then recommend that "involuntary" be used only in cases of the latter type, whereas cases of the former type should rather be characterized as "inadvertent," "accidental," or the like—a suggestion of a linguistic nature that can surely be defended by reference to the linguistic material.

15. Logographical Objections Concerning the Correctness of the Representation

Logographical objections, that is, objections to the effect that the proposed scheme gives an incorrect picture of the relevant conceptual interrelationships, are of a more serious nature. They are of course raised also by the logographer himself while he is working with the logogram, in the same way as a cartographer must always be alert to possible discrepancies between map and terrain when he is preparing his map. The map can never be as detailed as the terrain, for the value of the general survey would then be lost. And in the same way a logogram neither can nor will ever represent the conceptual relationships in all their amazing complexity. The logogram, like a map, is a representation of main features, and all we can and should demand is that the relationship among the features included be correctly represented. We can demand completeness neither from a map nor from a logogram, but only that they not be misleading. We must be aware, moreover, that while our concepts are placed in a logical space—a conceptual space—with many dimensions, our representation is very limited in dimension. In the logogram in section 11 the concept of action is placed in what can be called a will and responsibility dimension, while it is actually related to a host of other ideas as well; that is, it can be located in a number of other dimensions, and each of the conceptual structures we clarify in this way must be represented in its own logogram. In my book *Betydning og mening, handling og ytring*, I have proposed one logogram in which action is related, among other things, to meaning in various senses, and also another logogram in which action as a conscious expression is related to our inner life (our sensations, experiences, thoughts, etc.) and to movements, reactions, and other spontaneous expressions;[4] and we may easily imagine a scheme which attempts to clarify how our idea of an action is related to our ideas of motive, desire, intention, and purpose. By taking various viewpoints one brings out different aspects of the relationships between our concepts.

Many objections apparently directed at the correctness of the proposed scheme are in reality demands for elucidation of the relationship from another angle. But of course a logogram may easily give a misleading picture. Clearly, one may often discover or others may point out mistakes in it. This is not a weakness of logography as a philosophical method. On the contrary, the only thing one must demand is that the corrections gradually become fewer and fewer.

16. WHAT PRESUPPOSITIONS ABOUT THINKING AND LANGUAGE UNDERLIE LOGOGRAPHY?

But are our ideas at all of the nature, of the solidity, that is needed for setting up such conceptual schemes? Does this firm structure which the method seems to assume really exist? This is a problem that concerns our conception of the nature of our thinking and our language, a conception that is basic to the method—and is much too large a question to treat here. I will only guard here against certain likely misunderstandings. One may perhaps believe that the method is based on the assumption that we all think and speak alike, but this is not so. It would be more correct, in any case, to say that we think in the same basic concepts and speak the same language. But not even this is essential for the method to be fruitful. A conceptual scheme of the type illustrated will be illuminating only to the degree that, and within the circle in which, it is accepted. Even for just two persons who disagree about certain problems concerning action and free will, but who can agree that a given scheme gives a correct representation of concepts important to their problems, the scheme will, as a rule, give their discussion quite another, more solid character than would otherwise have been possible—and the danger of verbal disagreement will be considerably lessened.

In practice, the possibilities for coming to agreement about a scheme are much greater than we have just suggested. In the first place, many of the objections would prove to be of a terminological nature—for example, if one maintains that one cannot distinguish between "intentionally" and "voluntarily." In the second place, apparently real disagreements, for example, about what is implied

---

[4] Anfinn Stigen, *Betydning og mening, handling og ytring* [Significance and meaning, action and utterance] (Oslo: University of Oslo Press, 1967), pp. 81, 110.

by the distinction between 'voluntary' and 'not voluntary,' are really no more than questions of the way in which the conceptual distinction is formulated. Thus, Benson Mates points out that while Ryle in his *Concept of Mind* maintains that "voluntary" and "involuntary" in their ordinary use are applied only to actions that ought not to be done, J. L. Austin says that "We may join the army or make a gift voluntarily . . ." Mates adds: "If agreement about usage cannot be reached within so restricted a sample as the class of Oxford Professors of Philosophy, what are the prospects when the sample is enlarged?"[5] It can be seen that our logogram (see section 11), which is relevant here, agrees with Austin, whereas it does not seem to support Ryle. However, the disagreement Mates thinks he has found between Ryle and Austin is not a real one. What our scheme shows, and what Austin is talking about, are the relationships between the concepts, that is, the conceptual content or significance of words such as "voluntary," and this is what is meant by "without pressure." It is clear that if I enlist in the army or give a gift to someone just because I wish to, I do so voluntarily. Ryle, on the other hand, is speaking of the circumstances under which I will *use* the expression "voluntarily," that is, the circumstances under which I will *say* that I do something voluntarily; he is not saying what the content of the concept of "voluntary" is. In this case it is indeed reasonable to reply that I use it when someone thinks I have done something that ought not to have been done. I then have a motive for making it clear either that I acted under duress or that I acted of my own initiative, that is, according to my wish. But this implies no disagreement over the meaning of the concept of 'voluntary.' One calls attention to the *use*, the other to the *content* of the concept.

It must be made quite clear that it is not the *use of language* that interests us most, but the relationships between *concepts*—even if it is language that puts us on the track of conceptual distinctions. If, still in keeping with the above scheme, we can agree on the importance of distinguishing between what we do intentionally and what we do, for instance, gratuitously, or between what we do knowingly but under pressure, and what we do readily; and if, given a case and all the information we need, we can reach agreement as to which category in our scheme the given case belongs, then the question of designation is not of such great interest. If we agree about the jars and about which pills are to go into which jars, then the labels are of less interest.

But the labels cannot be ignored completely. Serious misunderstandings arise when labels are exchanged, if, for example, the label "voluntary" is placed on all actions performed intentionally and on purpose. This label leads others, who understand "voluntary" to mean "without compulsion," to assume that no action performed under duress will be found in this jar. But in the present case the jar will actually contain such actions as the incident above referred to by

[5] Ryle, *Concept of Mind*, pp. 66 ff.; J. L. Austin, "A Plea for Excuses," *Proceedings of the Aristotelian Society* (1956–57), p. 17; Benson Mates, "On the Verification of Statements about Ordinary Language," *Inquiry* 1:165, 10 (1958).

Aristotle in which the seamen had to jettison their cargo because of bad weather —an action of which the label gives a quite mistaken impression by suggesting that the seamen were not forced to do what they did.

Furthermore, it is, after all, with the aid of language that we become acquainted with these important conceptual distinctions. This is certainly to put it very cautiously; one may perhaps claim that even the *need* for these conceptual distinctions and ideas first arises in a linguistic context. But even if we stop at the claim that the conceptual system is *learned* through language, we must, for that reason, suppose that agreement as to labels can be reached among persons who can speak of the things that their conceptual system concerns without often misunderstanding each other.

As to the validity of a conceptual system beyond this given circle, the question immediately becomes much more difficult. A claim that the validity of a given conceptual system extends beyond a definite period of time (to maintain, for example, that the same conceptual system is, by and large, valid both for ourselves and the ancient Greeks) would be even more dubious. We all know that new concepts arise and old ones disappear; not only technical and scientific concepts, but also concepts that form part of the common man's system of thought. There is reason to believe that for the Greeks the idea of *hubris*, for example, was fundamental precisely in questions of actions and man's will. On the other hand, it has been claimed that the concept of a *person* was unknown to the Greeks.

However, it is not easy to decide, apart from purely technical and scientific concepts, whether a given concept has disappeared and whether a new one has been created; nor is it easy to say how this could be established. Clearly it is not enough to ascertain that the Greeks had a word for it and we don't—or the converse—even if this may be a useful indication. In one sense, we still have a concept if and to the degree that we can have any understanding of it at all. With regard to the most fundamental ideas—which are philosophy's main interest—it does not appear that great changes in the conceptual structure have occurred since the time of Aristotle. The logogram in section 11, for example, is just as valid for Aristotle's discussion of actions in the *Nicomachean Ethics* as it is for us.

In practice, I think that this question of the extent—historically, geographically, socially—to which a conceptual system is relevant is of minor significance. My reason for preparing these logograms and for attempting to acquire a general view of the interrelationships of our concepts is the existence of certain philosophical problems. What I require of the logogram is that it be convincing for a person who is occupied with the problem that caused me to take up just these concepts for treatment. This form of conceptual clarification can be elucidating for a person only to the degree that he recognizes that this is a conceptual system for *him*. This person may be myself, another philosopher, a group of philosophers, the man in the street, a theologian, etc.

17. Logonomical Objections, Suggestions for Revising Our
Conceptual System

And so we come to the type of objections that are of greatest philosophical interest: those in which not only the correctness or the faithfulness of a given representation of a conceptual structure is contested, but the conceptual structure itself. The purpose of *logonomers,* first and foremost, is not clarification of the rules that determine the relationship between our concepts; rather, they desire to change them, to decide the rules, to be the lawgivers.

However, it is not always so easy to distinguish, among all the objections directed at a logogram, between those that raise logographical and those that raise logonomical issues. Even among philosophers, it is not often that one meets someone whose avowed intention is the revision of our most fundamental ideas about ourselves, things, and the world. Usually the revisionist proposals take the following form: Our understanding and our possible representation of our conceptual system suffer from certain weaknesses; for example, under closer investigation, our assumptions appear inconsistent. A thorough consideration and genuine understanding will unveil these weaknesses and lead to necessary revisions and modifications in our original understanding and representation. Only this revised version can serve as the authoritative logogram.

An example of this is to be found in one of the greatest philosophical revisionists, George Berkeley. He attacks the distinction between soul and body, or, in his own terminology, between "mind with its contents of consciousness" and "material substances without the mind," by maintaining that only the former group exists; our belief in the existence of anything material and bodily is mistaken. But he does not advance his theory as an attack on peoples' general ideas or as a revision of our view of existence, though he himself is aware that it will be taken as such. He presents his philosophy as a necessary conceptual tidying up:

It is indeed an opinion strangely prevailing amongst men, that houses, mountains, rivers, and in a word all sensible objects, have an existence, natural or real, distinct from their being perceived by the understanding. But, with how great an assurance and acquiescence soever this principle may be entertained in the world, yet whoever shall find in his heart to call it in question may, if I mistake not, perceive it to involve a manifest contradiction. For, what are the forementioned objects but the things we perceive by sense, and what do we perceive besides our own ideas or sensations; and is it not plainly repugnant that any one of these, or any combination of them, should exist unperceived?[6]

We note the form of the attack. Let us set aside for the moment the question of how the logographer will react to it. First we shall consider another revisionist attack in a region where we may be gradually beginning to feel at home—that of the concepts represented in the above logogram (section 11).

---

[6] George Berkeley, *The Works of George Berkeley,* 2:42 (London, 1967).

18. Logonomic Objections Illustrated by a Determinist's Attack on
Our Notion of Voluntary Action

As we know, there are certain thinkers—let us call them determinists—who use various arguments to attack the distinction between groups (c) and (d) in our logogram. They argue that class (c), i.e., 'what one does intentionally and of one's own free will,' or, more briefly, 'voluntary actions,' is empty. For the sake of clarity, we will take as our starting point one of the more precise accounts of the determinist's thesis in recent literature:

> The question of the freedom of the will, reduced to its barest essentials, is simply this: *Are all human acts of will causally produced by antecedent conditions or are at least some volitional actions exempt from causal determination?* The determinist insists that all actions, even the most carefully planned and deliberate, can be causally explained and that if we knew enough about a man's hereditary traits and the environmental influences which have moulded his character, we could predict just how he would behave under any specified set of circumstances.[7]

It is important to recognize that the determinist will not deny that people are justified in characterizing certain acts as voluntary or free. In view of their conception of the situation and their ignorance of the causal conditions, it is reasonable and proper that they should claim that they act voluntarily or freely. The determinist will claim, however, that closer investigation will show that every act is in fact determined causally by antecedent conditions. Since, according to the determinist, it is exactly this that is denied when one characterizes one's action as voluntary or free, such a characterization will never accord with reality. In other words, there are really no voluntary actions.

At first glance, the determinist's reasoning seems difficult to refute; the result, at best, seems destined to be undecided, for one must admit, it seems, that *if* it can be demonstrated that all our acts are causally determined, *then* none of our acts are free or voluntary, and even if this cannot be positively demonstrated, we still cannot be *sure* that we do at any time act freely.

But this is just where an explicit conceptual scheme—a scheme that clearly shows what is implied by the distinctions—is of value. And this is a case where extensive linguistic material proves of use—material that clearly shows the criteria we actually employ in determining whether a given case falls under one class or another. The determinist's attack affects our idea of voluntary action only if it actually *is* this distinction—that between voluntary and not-voluntary, actions, between classes (c) and (d) in our conceptual scheme—of which he contests the validity. And *this* has to be determined by investigating whether he has correctly understood the meaning of the distinction between voluntary and not-voluntary, whether he has understood what most people *mean* when they characterize an action as voluntary or not-voluntary.

---

[7] Ledger Wood, "The Free-Will Controversy," *Philosophy* 16:386–87 (1941); italics in the original.

The determinist's attack on free will is based upon the following identifications:

voluntary   = not causally determined
not-voluntary = causally determined

At first glance this seems plausible, for is not the criterion of what one does voluntarily that one acts without being compelled, and of what one does not do voluntarily that one acts under pressure? Our material, it seems, establishes that this is correct. But now we must ask the next question. Let us consider concrete examples: When we say of the cashier of the bank that he handed over the money to the robber under pressure, do we *mean* that his action was "causally produced by antecedent conditions"? And when a man maintains that he voluntarily offered his resignation, does he mean to say that his resignation was "not causally produced"? Can one reasonably claim that in these two instances the matter of 'cause' is relevant at all? Is it not reasonable to imagine even that— for evidence that the man resigned voluntarily—he will point precisely to all the reasons and grounds that made him offer his resignation?

When exposed in the light of the conceptual distinction in question, and under the pressure exerted by a number of examples, the determinist's attack will not only falter, but, I think, completely break down. The examples will show clearly that what is regarded as compulsion is in fact never what we would actually call cause. (Another group of examples will show what *cause* is.) To be sure, occasionally there might be reference to what one might specify as a *physical* or *mechanical* constraint (for example, the rack, glowing cigarettes), but even in these cases such things are not referred to as *causes*, that is, as something that has a definite effect as its necessary consequence; rather, the instruments of compulsion are cited as *excuses*. When a sailor says that the storm forced his ship into port, he is not emphasizing the causal conditions (as perhaps would be the case if he said "The storm washed the ship aground"). What he means is rather that the storm got him to do something, got him, against his wishes, to carry out a definite act—an act that otherwise he would have been unwilling to do. The *meaning* of "forced" or "compelled" in such a case—a typical one—is to be construed not as "causally produced by antecedent conditions" or the like, but as "got one to do something that one did not want to do or was unwilling to do," or something close to that.

This is seen even more clearly in the majority of cases of compulsion, where what compels one is not of a physical or mechanical nature, but what might be called *moral* pressure—influencing by threats, appeal to authority, reference to law and justice, or reference to social conditions (e.g., traditions of social intercourse). None of the above factors is cited in these instances as part of a causal explanation. That the husband cannot force his wife to love him means, not that her love does not have its grounds and reasons, or that it cannot be evoked, but that it cannot be evoked by such means as, for example, threat, persuasion, or a sense of obligation—as long as these are in conflict with his wife's wishes.

But it is not our task to resolve the conflict between the 'advocate of free will' and the determinist. Perhaps enough has been said to suggest how a logogram can help us to direct the spotlight upon central issues and how a comprehensive collection of examples, upon which such a scheme should always be based, can serve as a magnifying glass through which to gain a sharper view of our conceptual distinctions and notions.

Berkeley's attack on the distinction between mind and matter could be treated similarly. The main point in Berkeley's reasoning, as many have emphasized, is the premise that what we 'perceive' is nothing but "our own ideas or sensations." At this point, we must try to draw up a scheme representing the relationships among such activities as perceiving, sensing, experiencing, imagining, conceiving, and the like. Our exposition would give examples of what it is that one says one perceives. The important question, naturally, is whether one can be said to perceive one's own ideas or sensations, or what this would mean if, like Berkeley, one nevertheless chose to express oneself in such a way. I can well understand what a person means if he says that he perceives *my* idea, but *his own* . . . ? The searchlight would then be directed toward a central point, and a concrete treatment would be assured.

19. The Possibilities for Revision of Our Conceptual System

In general, one may say of a proposal to revise our conceptual structure (if it deals with central concepts, as indeed it does in philosophy) that all experience indicates that such proposals have little chance of being accepted; very seldom do they have any effect, which, again, seems to show that these concepts and this system *are* basic. In particular, attempts like Berkeley's and the determinists' to *nullify* the distinction between principal concepts, are of little avail. The argument for erasing the distinction in question may well be convincing, but this does not eradicate the practical need we have for it. The distinction may be driven out the front door, but it comes in again through the back. Whatever Berkeley says, there is a great difference between being hit by a dagger and being hit by a withering remark. And whatever the determinist says, there will always be an important difference between those of my acts that I seek to excuse and those that I wish to defend.

A proposal to *introduce* new conceptual distinctions, on the other hand, has a much better chance of acceptance. But here it is a matter of refinements rather than revisions, of expanding rather than rebuilding. One might even say that an essential aspect of the development of the individual sciences consists just in the fact that the conceptual system that is basic to everyday speech is refined and expanded. At the same time scientific terms characteristically seem less susceptible of nuance than the words we use in everyday life. Scientific concepts, such as temperature, are not placed in so many dimensions as those we use in everyday life, such as warmth (glow, enthusiasm, feeling). A scientific conceptual system can be said to arise through the development of one plane through the multidimensioned logical space of everyday speech.

The view of philosophy and philosophical method outlined here does not of course imply any dismissal of such reformatory proposals as Berkeley's or any devaluation of the sciences. It does, however, imply the belief that on a more general level than that of Berkeley's philosophy and the sciences, a conceptual structure that is more or less clearly visible in our everyday language exists, and it is here that both Berkeley and the sciences have their conceptual basis. As a practical consequence of this view, it is possible to test both Berkeley's philosophy and scientific concepts in terms of this conceptual system. Thus, it is my view that this conceptual system is logically basic. Accordingly, it must also have the first word in philosophical discussion. First, we must be clear about this system. We must be prepared for the possibility that the philosophy, the world view, that lies hidden in our everyday notions and distinctions is more fundamental and perhaps also more consistent than the philosophy any single person can fashion by sitting in his armchair 'philosophizing.'

The danger here, as always in philosophy, is that a view that has proved fruitful may crystallize into a doctrine. The temptation is great in this case, for the conceptual system that a person has will appear to him as *a priori*—something the validity of which cannot be shaken by his experiences, because it serves as the system within which his experiences are to be accommodated. And the sentences that can be read from the conceptual scheme (e.g., "What one does voluntarily is what one does intentionally and moreover not under pressure") have an analytical character. To say, for instance, to a child that plants do not have sensation, is not to impart information in the usual way, as when one says that the plant is in bloom, or that it needs water. It is to convey to the child the adults' conceptual scheme.

But this very example shows that such sentences are not analytical and uncontroversial, at least not in the same way as logical sentences, which cannot be *thought* otherwise. We *can* think contrary to even the most fundamental conceptual structures—all we need is imagination. We *can* imagine that plants have feeling and perception. In the world of fairy tales and make-believe, trees and animals can even speak. Are these, then, new conceptual systems that we experiment with—or, perhaps, old conceptual systems that turn up again? If in his mental development the child repeats in abbreviated form the whole history of culture, then the latter possibility may not be such a wild theory. Here we are faced with some fascinating prospects!

Knut Erik Tranöy

The Ideology of Scientific and Scholarly Conduct

Denn nichts ist für den Menschen als Menschen etwas wert,
was er nicht mit Leidenschaft *tun* kann.—Max Weber*

1. INTRODUCTION

Heart transplantation and the destructive potential of atomic weapons present moral problems which seem, in some ways, to be new. The questions of whether or not such problems *ought* to affect the behavior of scientists and scholars, and to what extent and how, have become issues.

There has also been a growing interest lately, in Europe as well as in the United States, in what I shall call the ideology of scientific and scholarly conduct. It is my impression that in the United States these problems have been pursued mainly by people in the physical and biological sciences. In Europe they have attracted the attention of, or have been articulated by, scholars working in the borderland between philosophy and the social sciences. To the best of my knowledge, few moral philosophers, properly speaking, have so far discovered that problems concerning the ideology of science and "the morality of scholarship," to quote a recent book title, invite or require precisely the attentive interest of moral philosophers.[1]

Professor Tranöy, of the University of Bergen, is a native of Norway.

The present paper is of the nature of a preliminary survey. It is in part the result of a series of interdisciplinary seminars which I organized at the University of Bergen Institute of Philosophy during the spring term of 1968. Participants came from the humanities as well as from the medical, natural, and social sciences.

I was motivated to write such a survey by the feeling that there is an urgent need for clarification of the extent and nature of the responsibilities, commitments, and functions of scientists and scholars, a clarification which will surely not come unless we ourselves initiate and sustain a reflective discussion of problems that are central to the issue of our identity as members of the community of academic researchers and teachers.

* *Vom inneren Beruf zur Wissenschaft* (1919), p. 312 of Kröner edition (see n. 3, below). Italics are Weber's.

[1] Max Black, ed., *The Morality of Scholarship* (Ithaca, N.Y.: Cornell University Press, 1967), is an important contribution, not least because it articulates some of the problems of

In what follows, I shall attempt to clarify, from the point of view of a moral philosopher, the genesis and the structure of some of the ethical problems that arise in connection with modern science and scholarship. I want to include in my considerations the humanities as well as the natural, the biological, and the social sciences. In our educational institutions humanistic scholars work alongside scholars in all the other fields. The influence and importance of teachers in fields such as language, literature, art, and history are indubitable.

Awareness of the magnitude and urgency, though not necessarily the complexity, of problems on the 'moral fringe' of science has been growing within as well as outside of the academic world. From the outside, scientists and scholars are admonished to accept responsibility, morally speaking, for what they are doing. Many have felt for quite some time that the problem of the moral responsibility of scientists is indeed a disturbing one. Early evidence of such concern is found in the Pugwash movement and the *Bulletin of the Atomic Scientists*. For a while, in fact, problems connected with nuclear science and technology predominated. More recently, transplantation surgery has enjoyed or suffered a similar vogue. However, other areas of research have their own share of moral or morally relevant problems. The following (not at all exhaustive) list serves to remind us of what we all know.

Where we do not deplete our natural resources, we pollute them. Pesticides make us worry about silent springs. Social and behavioral scientists encounter accusations ranging from alleged infringements of the right to privacy to allegations of manipulative social engineering. Rapid advances in transplantation surgery and resuscitation techniques have brought the medical sciences face to face with acute problems in which the general public is also beginning to take an active and inquisitive interest. The thalidomide tragedy accentuated the problem of the responsibilities of pharmaceutical research, technology, and salesmanship. Genetic manipulation in consequence of advances in molecular biology may still be in the science fiction stage, although the practice of 'eugenics' by other methods has been shown to be more than a mere possibility. Representatives of the humanities seem by and large to be bewildered about their own place and

---

humanities in this context. Three titles demonstrating the contribution of natural scientists are: J. Bronowski, *Science and Human Values* (New York: Harper & Row, Harper Torchbooks, 1965); John R. Baker, *Science and the Planned State* (New York: Macmillan Co., 1945), with an excellent bibliography; and Bentley Glass, *Science and Ethical Values* (Chapel Hill, N.C.: University of North Carolina Press, 1966).

The reactions of some American philosophers are recorded by Noam Chomsky in "Philosophers and Public Philosophy" and in the contributions of his co-symposiasts in *Ethics* 79: 1–23 (October, 1968). Other references will be given below.

On the European continent, Jürgen Habermas is a name worth noting. See, for example, his "Demokratisierung der Hochschule—Politisierung der Wissenschaft?" *Merker: Deutsche Zeitschrift für Europäisches Denken*, vol. 7 (1969), and "Knowledge and Interest," *Inquiry* 9: 285–300 (1966).

The medical profession has done more than most others to open a systematic inquiry into the nature and scope of its moral problems. See, for instance, G. E. W. Wolstenholme and Maeve O'Connor, eds., *Ethics in Medical Progress: With Special Reference to Transplantation*, Ciba Foundation Symposium Volumes (London: J. & A. Churchill Ltd., 1966).

role in the picture. But they tend to insist that they are more important than ever.[2]

It is a truism that the world of learning, research, and technology is one of the major formative influences in the present world. It might then appear all the more striking that there should be so much uncertainty and disagreement about the extent and nature of the moral commitments of science and scholarship in a world which is so much the product of the scientific and technical advances of the last three hundred years.

2. THE 'MORAL NEUTRALITY' OF SCIENCE

Contemporary scientists and scholars tend to accept a principle with I shall provisionally give the following formulation: "The scientist-scholar qua scientist-scholar should be morally [politically, religiously, etc.] neutral." This formulation I shall call "Weber's Principle" (WP).[3]

As I formulated it, Weber's principle is ambiguous. If it is taken as saying that (a) for the scholar as scholar, for the scientist qua scientist it is not legitimate to engage in evaluative and normative moral (and political, etc.) activity, the practical consequences of the principle are weighty and the acceptability or validity of the principle becomes dubious. On the other hand, it seems very difficult not to accept WP if it is taken as saying that (b) a scientist or scholar is under an obligation to distinguish as clearly as he can between moral (and other) evaluations, on the one hand, and statements of empirical fact on the other. The latter interpretation seems, incidentally, to be closer to what Weber himself had in mind.[4]

---

[2] The beginnings, at least, of a good discussion of the humanities is found in Black, *Morality of Scholarship.*

[3] I refer in the first place to the following three works by Max Weber: *Die "Objektivität" Sozialwissenschaftlicher Erkenntnis* (first published, 1904); *Der Sinn der "Wertfreiheit" der Sozialwissenschaften* (1917); *Vom inneren Beruf zur Wissenschaft* (1919). All three can be found in Max Weber, *Soziologie, Weltgeschichtliche Analysen, Politik*, Kröners Taschenausgabe, vol. 229 (Stuttgart: Albert Kröner, 1956; henceforth cited as Kröner edition).

No officially or generally accepted statement of the principle exists. Quite a few scientists may have heard of Max Weber and his doctrine of the '*Wertfreiheit*' of the social sciences. Few have read Weber, and Weber's own formulations can be neither 'official' nor generally accepted since most of us are ignorant of them. Nevertheless, it is hard to avoid the impression that scientists today give to Weber's principle an interpretation that Max Weber himself would have rejected.

[4] In *Der Sinn der "Wertfreiheit,"* Weber complains that his doctrine has been misunderstood in various ways, explaining: "Aber es handelt sich doch ausschiesslich um die an sich hochst triviale Forderung, dass der Forscher und Darsteller die Feststellung empirischer Tatsachen ... und *seine* praktisch wertende ... Stellungnahme unbedingt *auseinanderhalten* solle ..." (Kröner edition, p. 263; italics are Weber's).

The expressions "scientist qua scientist" and "scholar as scholar" are not very satisfactory; nor have I found it better to speak of the scholar/scientist's *role*. The difficulty is to keep this role or function separate from other roles or functions. I am focusing on the values and the norms that define or determine the scientist's conduct insofar as it is at all possible to separate his scientific from his non-scientific conduct. This *is* possible to some extent in spite of the fact that one or more roles or functions often intertwine.

It is difficult or impossible to accept (a)—the strict version of WP—without also accepting (b); but one can very well accept (b) without therefore accepting (a) as well.

Today most (Western) scientists and scholars in most fields of inquiry— certainly not only in the social sciences, and not even excluding branches of theology—*do* feel conscience-bound by some rather strict version of Weber's principle. For many, WP is part of, or presupposed in, the very concept of science and scholarship.

Now, a scientist who accepts a strict version of WP places himself under a certain kind of moral restriction,[5] for the principle authorizes and demands passivity or non-interference in situations that are morally (politically, religiously) 'charged'—*even though the situation itself is in part a product of, or has only been made possible by, activities in which the scientist has participated.* (If illustration is required: the problems of population and birth control consequent upon inadequate food production, and explosive population growth due to the introduction of modern medicine, hygiene, and maternity care, raise moral as well as political and religious issues. A scientist who accepts the strict version of WP would literally be forbidden to deal with such issues, qua scientist.)

Naturally, conflict of an unpleasant kind is likely to arise if and when one who feels bound by a strict version of WP comes under pressure to abandon his attitude of moral neutrality. There is little doubt that the world of scientists and scholars is under such pressure today. And there may be reason to fear that, viewed from the outside, this world appears to be in a state of confusion precisely over this conflict and how to resolve it.[6]

3. Scientific and Scholarly Activities Viewed as Human Conduct

How tenable is the belief, still apparently widely held, that scientists and scholars are in fact 'value-free' and 'morally neutral' in their conduct as scientists or scholars? Such a belief, I shall argue, is not tenable at all.

It may be useful, again as a reminder, to survey some of the actions and activities with which scientists and scholars find themselves professionally concerned, or concerned qua scientists and scholars.

In addition to experimentation, theory construction, and the like—which loom so large in the philosophy of science picture of science—there is also the formulation and writing down of results and theories; publication of same in books and journals; criticism, acceptance, and rejection of the results of experi-

---

[5] In section 4 below, I shall return to the problem of whether and in what form we should accept Weber's principle.

[6] I suggest that Noam Chomsky's book, *American Power and the New Mandarins* (New York: Pantheon, 1969) is a case in point. See, for instance, the reviews in the *New York Times Book Review* (by Jan E. Deutsch, 16 March 1969) and in *The Washington Post Book World* (by Arthur Schlesinger, 23 March 1969). The unrest and upheavals at our universities are other cases in point, cases not sufficiently well understood by either outsiders or insiders.

ment and investigation; argumentation, reasoning, and debate with colleagues; criticism and judgment of the work of others; attempts—written and spoken—to influence the views of others on a professional and a popular level, through lecturing and direct instruction as well as in other ways; selection of personnel for projects and jobs; passing and failing students on examinations; advising students at all levels; functioning as an expert or consultant for private or public employers (the 'mandarin function');[7] applying for and using grants, physical facilities, and other resources in scientific work; revising, reforming, initiating, and planning curricula and courses of study; proposing or deciding on what courses or degrees will qualify for various professions or functions—in brief, participating in the formation of scientific and educational policies.

The list is, of course, not complete, and I shall not try to complete it. Instead, let me state another trivial truth the consequences of which sometimes seem to be overlooked.

One of the most important and consequential activities in which a person can engage in a modern society is scientific-scholarly activity. It would be remarkable, indeed, if the separate acts and kinds of action which make up this activity, were not guided by moral—and other—norms and valuations. For if they are not so guided they are beyond conscious and rational control.

4. THE IDEOLOGY OF SCIENCE AND SCHOLARSHIP

I shall use the term "ideology of science and scholarship" (or "academic ideology") to refer to the total set of values and norms, moral on non-moral, that serve to guide and direct scientific and scholarly conduct. This ideology is made up of at least five distinguishable components.

(a) The principle ascribed to Max Weber, requiring the scientist to be 'morally neutral' (or 'value neutral').

(b) The norms, values, and virtues embedded in a general scientific methodology (directives for scientific research and scholarship), defining what we might call "the scientific attitude."

(c) The doctrine, first formulated by Francis Bacon, that science should be for the benefit of mankind.

(d) The idea that knowledge and pursuit of truth are valuable in themselves (the Platonic-Aristotelian tradition).

(e) The idea that scientists and scholars have a rightful claim to 'freedom of inquiry.'

I shall consider each of these points in turn, and I shall show how norm or value conflict is likely to arise if one tries to accept this five-fold ideology uncritically and *in toto*.

---

[7] The term is inspired, of course, by Chomsky's terminology in *American Power and the New Mandarins*.

(a) It should be noted and emphasized that *Weber's principle* is itself a norm. It enjoins or recommends the observance in speech and in writing of a distinction between valuations and statements of fact; or it forbids a certain type of participation in the political or moral life of one's society.

What reasons are there for accepting Weber's principle? By what evidence or argument or proof should a scientist qua scientist accept as valid a norm which possibly is neither true nor false?

There are at least two different ways of arguing for any version of WP. (i) It might be shown to be the consequence of other, more fundamental norms and valuations. Or (ii) one can argue from the *usefulness* or *harmfulness* for scientific research respectively of obeying or disobeying it.

(i) It is possible to argue that there is a connection between WP and the thesis that norms and valuations are not logically derivable from factual statements. However, although "Hume's principle"—i.e., the principle that norms and valuations can be neither true nor false—might be logically necessary, it is not sufficient for the derivation of Weber's principle. We should also need premises of a normative kind—e.g., "It is not legitimate to accept unsupported statements"—plus a principle that normative statements cannot (logically) be supported by descriptive statements,[8] or that there are certain ('direct') ways in which they cannot be thus supported.

Weber himself does refer to the impossibility of deriving norms and valuations from facts.[9] But this is not his only argument.

(ii) Arguments of a more utilitarian nature are also available. But, again, a norm (or a valuation) is presupposed. If a scholar-scientist's first concern (primary duty, basic value, or ultimate goal) is to produce as much and as pure truth as possible, to 'optimize' the truth output of his scientific activity, so to speak, then one can plausibly argue that it is harmful to let other goals (or norms, or values) take precedence. The reason for accepting Weber's principle is then its instrumental value.

Weber himself makes extensive use of arguments of this utilitarian kind.[10]

---

[8] Given a norm to the effect that a scientist qua scientist is authorized to deal with scientific statements only, *and* a definition that excludes norms or valuations from the class of scientific statements, WP might be seen to follow, trivially. But this is an obvious *petitio principii.*

What is sometimes called "scientific methodology" does, of course, contain a complex set of norms and rules governing precisely the acceptance and rejection, etc. (briefly, the *use*), of empirical statements (descriptions, observation, statements, hypotheses, theories, etc.). I shall say more about this in section 5 below.

[9] "Wertideen, die ihrerseits zwar empirisch als Elemente alles sinnvollen menschlichen Handelns konstatierbar und erlebbar, *nicht* aber aus dem empirischen Stoff als geltend begundbar sind." This very characteristic statement is found in *Die "Objektivität" Sozialwissenschaftlicher Erkenntnis* (Kröner edition, p. 260; italics are Weber's).

[10] One quotation only: "Die stete Vermischung wissenschaftlicher Erörterung der Tatsachen und wertender Raisonnements ist eine der . . . schädlichsten Eigenarten von Arbeiten unseres Faches" (*Die "Objektivität" Sozialwissenschaftlicher Erkenntnis* [Kröner edition, p. 197]).

It is worth emphasizing that Weber's own basic concern in writing about objectivity is the relationship between the *social* or *cultural* sciences on the one hand, and practical politics

Arguments of types (i) and (ii) do not exclude each other.

Regardless of the 'logical status' of WP, it is in any case a conspicuous fact about the contemporary scene that Weber's principle has won almost universal acceptance, not only among social scientists, but also—and perhaps even more so—among natural scientists as well as among representatives of the humanities. It is equally noteworthy that it is a strict version of the principle that seems to have gained the widest currency. For many of us, it seems to be part of, or pre-supposed in, our very concepts of science and scholarship. I have not come across any systematic attempt to question or criticize its validity or acceptability: it appears to be (or to have been) regarded as being almost axiomatic or self-evident.[11] There are, indeed, social scientists who insist upon the social, political, and moral *relevance* of their sciences. In fact, there is probably no branch of academic inquiry that does not consider itself as having, actually or potentially, *some* kind of importance or relevance for our ways of life. But, as I shall point out below (section 8), scientists and scholars tend to regard themselves as not being responsible for *the use* of the goods they produce and deliver, for the ways in which the practical relevance of their insights and theories are translated into social, moral, and political actuality. Refusal to accept such responsibility can be held to be justified precisely by appeal to Weber's principle.

A peculiar 'split personality' attitude is therefore not uncommon among contemporary scientists: qua scientist, one has no moral or political concerns; as a 'private citizen,' when one has removed the lab coat or the gown, one is on a par with anybody else with the same right and duty to participate in the political and moral life of his community—no more, no less.[12]

This, apparently, is one way in which one may persuade oneself that one is obeying Weber's principle. But such an attitude is not self-justifying. Nor is it practiced with consistency, as I shall also observe below (section 7).

What some are now beginning to suspect is that even if it were possible for a scientist to be two separate persons in this way, it would be immoral. Consequently, to the extent that such 'schizophrenic' conduct can be traced back to WP, the principle itself comes into question. The unobtrusive plausibility of

---

and economics on the other. The latter deal with, and must necessarily presuppose, values and valuations which in their turn are among the objects studied by the social sciences. This is precisely why Weber is so much concerned with the distinction between fact and value, i.e., with the importance of not confounding the two. Such confusion (*Vermischung*) is damaging to the scientist *as well as to the politician*. Politics and social science were both of great importance to Weber. He did not deny their interdependence. Indeed, it might be said that for him their fruitful interdependence in practice required precisely their separation in theory.

[11] This passage was first formulated in June, 1968. I still (November, 1969) do not know of any really *systematic* attempt to criticize WP, although it is now clear that it no longer finds such undoubting or unqualified and universal acceptance as before. Titles cited in notes 1 and 6 bear evidence to this. In *Ethics*, vol. 79 (October 1968), under the title of "Philosophers and Public Philosophy," Noam Chomsky gives a candid account of his own development from a devout believer to a harsh critic of WP (especially pp. 5, 6).

[12] In the article referred to in the preceding footnote, Chomsky also uses terms such as "split personality" and "schizophrenic" to describe the predicament of the scientist/scholar who tries to accept a strict version of WP.

the vague and general formulation of Weber's principle—the scientist qua scientist should be morally, politically, and religiously, neutral—is thus deceptive. The principle is open to widely divergent interpretations. The interpretation chosen may be decisive for one's view of the role and function of the scholar-scientist in contemporary society—and for the moral problems in which he finds himself embroiled. For it is clear that in the present state of the world a scholar or scientist who accepts an injunction to the effect that qua scientist he is not permitted to have moral problems is already caught in a very special kind of moral quandary. If he is also, qua scientist, under norms which authorize or command him to *be* concerned with moral and other value problems, a conflict is generated that is not easily resolved.

5. Norms of Scientific Methodology

"Scientific methodology" is a loose term of rather indefinite extension. I take it to cover—*inter alia*—a set of directives generally accepted as valid for scientific inquiry and scholarship. These norms are rarely formulated with any degree of precision. They are nowhere codified,[13] and thus resemble moral rather than legal rules. About their normative character—their action-guiding or regulative or directive purpose and force—there can be no doubt.

Basic among these directives seems to be a norm to the effect that the scholar-scientist should seek to discover and to accept as much truth as possible—to use plain language. It follows that he should seek to avoid accepting false statements. These two norms are obviously not equivalent: the latter is a necessary but insufficient condition of the former. The former might be said to follow, or be derivable, from a value statement to the effect that the supreme value of the scholar-scientist qua scholar-scientist is (knowledge and/or pursuit of) truth, or perhaps rather, its 'optimization'. I shall refer to this value, the realization of which is in that case the basic goal of scientific and scholarly activity, as the 'optimization' of the truth output.[14]

---

[13] Attempts at 'private' codification have been made; see, for instance, Glass, *Science and Ethical Values*. But such collections of rules are partial and unofficial. It is worth remarking that scholars and scientists (research workers) do not form a group or a profession (like the physicians) that has found it possible or necessary to enact and approve a code of professional ethics officially.

[14] Bronowski formulates a 'social axiom' that he regards as valid for and accepted by the society he calls "the body of scientists": "*We* OUGHT *to act in such a way that what* IS *true can be verified to be so*" (*Science and Human Values*, p. 74; italics and capitalization are Bronowski's). In chapter 3, "The Sense of Human Dignity," especially sections 3–5, he discusses several of the issues which I here consider in section 5 below. See Baker: "The primary duty of the research scientist, as such, is to make the greatest possible contribution to demonstrable knowledge" ("The Value of Science," chap. 2 in *Science and the Planned State*, pp. 84–85); and Glass, "The Ethical Basis of Science," chap. 3 in *Science and Ethical Values*. I may add that in my dissertation "On the Logic of Normative Systems" (Cambridge, 1953), I attempted to analyze the structure and the validation procedures of general scientific methodology viewed as a normative system.

Ignorance, confusion, and false beliefs are clearly not conducive to the realization of this goal.

Superimposed on this valuational and normative foundation of scientific methodology, there is a set of other norms requiring, for instance, honesty, sincerity, and truthfulness; intersubjective testability; objectivity and what the Germans call "*Sachlichkeit*" (professional integrity?); accuracy and completeness; simplicity; consistency, coherence, and system. (I shall not attempt to make the list exhaustive.) There are, furthermore, what one might describe as special norms for scientific *research* and *publications*, requiring or recommending or idealizing independence and originality and, on a 'higher level,' creativity, meaningfulness, fruitfulness, and relevance.

Most or all of the terms occurring in this list of scientific and scholarly virtues are vague and unclear, some of them notoriously so ("simplicity," "objectivity"). Although clarification is indeed desirable, I shall restrict myself to comments that appear to me to be pertinent in the present context.

(i) These methodological norms (*m*-norms) are incumbent upon *all* scientists and scholars from those in mathematics and physics to those in philosophy and the humanities. They should be distinguished from the more specific methodological rules of separate and delimited fields of inquiry, such as physics, medicine, or history. But they are presupposed in, or prior to, the various specific methodological rules and practices of the separate disciplines. Thus they might be taken to define a *general* scientific or scholarly attitude.

(ii) The *m*-norms are related to norms (and values and virtues) that are current among us as non-scientist citizens. Some of the former norms have their 'non-academic' counterparts, perhaps the most conspicuous example being the demand for honesty, sincerity, and truthfulness: "Thou shalt not lie."[15] But in our non-academic lives we also (sometimes) frown upon slovenliness and untidiness as against accuracy and order, for instance. Nor is it difficult to see that the requests for independence and originality in research are related to the more commonly accepted ban on theft and our failure to value blind imitation: the academic equivalents are plagiarism and some of its minor brethren such as 'quoting' without giving the source or the reference. (There is a complex, but largely uncodified set of rules concerning the rights of ownership of scientific ideas.[16]) But there are also norms here that appear to be more specifically 'scientific' such as the ideal, however problematic, of simplicity and the demand for intersubjective testability. However, not even these are without their distant relatives in the non-scientific world: there is a limit to the unnecessary complications we are willing to tolerate—and we cannot *always* simply take each others' word for it.

---

[15] The interesting and important differences among an injunction to 'optimize' the truth output, a duty to tell the truth, and a ban on lying ought to be noted in this context.

[16] "Thou shalt neither covet thy neighbor's ideas nor steal his experiments" (Glass, *Science and Ethical Values*, p. 90).

(iii) In this light, the norms and virtues of methodology may be viewed as specialized varieties of more general moral norms and virtues. But while the similarities may be too striking to be overlooked, the differences are too interesting to be neglected.

It is clear that the *m*-norms require an atmosphere of general trust and confidence among the practitioners. It is a noteworthy fact that by and large there exists among scholars and scientists trust and confidence that transcend both disciplinary and geographical borders. The community of scientists and scholars is—and not only in times of peace—essentially, though certainly not invariably, an international community. It might be an interesting task for moral philosophy to find out precisely *why* this is so. Part of the answer seems rather obvious: shared *values* and a comparatively simple value structure. The norms have for the most part, a clearly *instrumental* function in relation to these values, and above all to the basic value—'optimization' of the truth output.

A further striking difference: the *m*-norms tend to be more rigorous than their non-academic counterparts. In the courts we may be required to speak the truth, the whole truth, and nothing but the truth. Ordinarily we are under no compulsion to speak all the important truths we know—we are sure to give offense if we do. A scientist or scholar who fails to include data or material unfavorable to his own hypothesis is severely critized if he has shown negligence; if the exclusion is willful, discovery of this might mean the end of a career. In our everyday lives the ban on lying is in principle overridden by other norms; in certain situations it is not only permitted but actually praiseworthy to be a convincing liar. In the conduct of research and scholarship, there are not even white lies. It seems difficult to imagine a situation in which deliberate lying about—e.g., research procedures or results—could be at all forgivable, except perhaps where one feels or fears a spying colleague or competitor at work.[17]

Attempts to lie to, steal from, deceive, or cheat a colleague—in general, negligent or willful infringements of these norms—meet with very strong disapproval. The anger and indignation which such breaches call forth may be taken to show that these norms are firmly internalized among scholars and

[17] From a theoretical point of view, it is interesting to note that in such a case breach of one norm—the ban on lying—is justified insofar as it may prevent breach of another norm—the ban on theft, the 'property rights' of the research worker. Compare paradigmatic illustration from non-scientific conduct: lying to the would-be murderer to conceal the whereabouts of a victim. In ordinary life, we hold that a one-time criminal should be allowed and encouraged to return to the 'good' society. It is difficult to envisage the reintegration into the scientific community of one who is known to have wilfully broken the norms of methodology. The seriousness with which we view attempts to cheat at examinations becomes understandable and reasonable when viewed in this perspective. We have here a marginal illustration of the Socratic problem, "Can virtue be taught?" One who is not prepared, or cannot be taught, to accept these norms is not fit to be a scientist or scholar, no matter what his or her other talents may be. On the strictness of the norms of academic conduct, see Bronowski: "A scientist who breaks this rule [of truthfulness—see n. 14 above], as Lysenko has done, is ignored. A scientist who finds that the rule has been broken in his laboratory, as Kammerer found, kills himself" (*Science and Human Values*, p. 76).

scientists. A case of conflict between these norms and other well-established norms would be very difficult to resolve.

Such conflict is conceivable if you were to be told to put the interests of your own country/firm/race ahead of *any* other interest.

(iv) The ideal of objectivity is of particular interest from the point of view of Weber's principle. To the extent that it is not simply equivalent to a ban on subjectivity or sheer arbitrariness, it is not easy to say what a demand for objectivity really means. It could—but need not—be taken to be more or less equivalent to Weber's principle. Indeed, Weber first formulated his doctrine of 'value freedom' in an attempt to explicate the notion of '*Objectivität.*'[18]

Weber's principle and the general methodological norms are not likely to be incompatible. There is a close link-up between the notion of objectivity and the notions of honesty, accuracy, completeness, and the like. We might think of the latter as rules designed to protect us from accepting and propagating falsehoods. WP may also be held to be a useful or even necessary means for attaining the basic goal of scientific and scholarly activity (see n. 10, above).

The tenability of such a view would then depend on whether, and in what version, the principle is in fact useful or indispensable, given agreement on the basic goal to be attained.

How is the optimization of the truth output—here assumed to be the basic goal and value of science and scholarship—related to other 'non-academic' human goals and values? When comparing the *m*-norms with the norms and values of general morality, it is obvious that the former set is not as rich as the latter. General morality contains norms which have *no* counterpart among the methodological norms so far discussed—most notably, perhaps, norms (and values) centered around the 'love thy neighbor' morality.

And, naturally, the values of love and compassion are not the nearest substitutes for truth value. In the wider context of human life, however, both types of values appear to be necessary.

6. THE VIEWS OF BACON AND ARISTOTLE

I now turn to problems concerned with the ultimate end in view, or purpose and justification of scientific and scholarly activity.

In a society where research and education demand a substantial percentage of the gross national product, the systematic pursuit of knowledge is hardly a self-justifying undertaking.

---

[18] Note, however, that the ideal of objectivity is applicable not only in empirical inquiry and teaching but also in moral and political discourse and argument. Neither the politician nor the scientist should try to represent concealed valuations as "facts speaking for themselves" (Weber, *Vom inneren Beruf zur Wissenschaft* [Kröner edition, p. 326]); neither should he be too quick to say on the basis of one firm fact that (given a commonly accepted goal) we must now do such and such. There might be other relevant facts.

In our Western culture, the pursuit of knowledge has been, and still is, justified and legitimated by at least two types of argument. One type can be identified as the (Platonic-)Aristotelian tradition: knowledge and science are necessary for the betterment and perfection of the *individual*. Knowledge—contemplation—is intimately connected with that type of virtue and/or happiness which is characteristic of and proper to human beings. One might refer to this as the project of human self-realization. Those who stress the importance of this view come close to regarding the possession of knowledge and insight as a value in itself. To Augustine as well as to Aquinas, the essence of the supernatural perfection of man, the fulfillment of his highest potentiality in the beatific vision of God, was *gaudium de veritate*—joy in (the possession of) truth.

Around the year 1600, this tradition was supplemented—if not replaced— by a more mundane and utilitarian view of the purpose of science. The first and classical spokesman of the new tradition which finds the justification of science primarily in its usefulness for human projects and purposes in this world is Francis Bacon. This tradition is not only still alive; it predominates among representatives of the natural, biological, and social sciences. A resolution adopted by the Pugwash conference in Vienna, September 14–20, 1958, gives characteristic and eloquent expression to this view when it describes the 'true purpose' of science as being "to increase human knowledge, and to promote man's mastery over the forces of nature for the benefit of all."[19]

There is little doubt that the justification of science is today sought and achieved largely by explicit or implicit reference to Bacon's gospel. To what extent is this justification a *sufficient* or a *necessary* justification? Will it do equally well for all branches of science and scholarship?

(i) The Baconian view tends to regard the value of science as *instrumental* in relation to a goal or a set of goals that surely are presupposed or taken for granted by Bacon, and perhaps even by ourselves. But we are certainly not very clear about the contents and the ordering of this set. We are probably not willing to say that our ultimate goal is simply a steadily growing gross national product. But, at least among some of us, it is not considered quite well-mannered to press the question: if and when a society has attained a reasonably decent average standard of living, should it still strive to increase its gross national product?[20] And if it should not, would the 'optimization' of the truth output still retain its value?

(ii) One reason why some are hesitant to press for a further detailed answer may be linked with Weber's principle, taken in the strict sense. The

---

[19] From the "Vienna Declaration" of the conference on "The Dangers of the Atomic Age and What Scientists Can Do about Them" (Third Pugwash Conference, Kitzbühel, September 14–19; and Vienna, September 20, 1958, *Bulletin of the Atomic Scientist* 24:344 [1958]). I have assumed that Bacon's main ideas as expressed in his *Instauratio Magna* and *Novum Organum* are so well known that a general reference to them is sufficient.

[20] There certainly are exceptions. Baker's central thesis is that "science does not exist solely to serve man's material wants" (*Science and the Planned State*, p. 109).

scholar-scientist is not, qua scholar or scientist, allowed to be concerned with such questions, because they would necessarily involve him in issues concerning moral and other values. Weber's principle then functions as the angel with the flaming sword, though not precisely at the post to which *Genesis* assigns him. Even a scholar-scientist who feels bound by the strict version of Weber's principle may be eating of *some* tree of knowledge; but he is still forbidden to eat of 'the tree of the knowledge of good and evil.' Weber's principle is not necessarily compatible with Bacon's view; and yet we apparently want to accept both of them. Should we expect it to be unproblematic to believe *both* that science is 'value free' *and* that the ultimate justification of science is by reference to 'the benefit of all'?

(iii) If the Platonic-Aristotelian justification of the pursuit of knowledge can be linked with an ideal of individual self-realization, the Baconian view may be said to be related to the spirit of the 'love thy neighbor' morality. The scientist and scholar are now invited to see themselves as the benefactors *of others* in the first place; their own happiness or betterment comes second. As the critics of J. S. Mill have repeatedly emphasized, the problem of reconciling these two principles or points of view is a notoriously difficult one, although both principles may be acknowledged as necessary and legitimate. It should not surprise us if modern scholars and scientists, in trying to accommodate both concerns, do run into problems, especially if they are not particularly clear about the priorities of the two ideals—or about their interrelations. For, of course, the two ideals are also interdependent. It could hardly be a question of choosing one or the other; the problem rather is how to pursue both with as little conflict and confusion as possible.

There now are signs that the importance and legitimacy of the Aristotelian tradition is gaining renewed recognition.[21] Nor are we always blind to the fact that the two views are interrelated:

Nowadays we all give too much thought to the material blessings or evils that science has brought with it, and too little to its power to liberate us from the confinements of ignorance and superstition.[22]

Outside of the academic communities there certainly is an active and growing interest in problems concerning the uses, functions, value, and, thus, the justification of scientific and scholarly activity and its products. Universities in all parts of the world become objects of reform and centers of unrest. The question of why we maintain universities no longer answers itself. Education and knowl-

[21] See, for instance, T. R. Gerholm, "Experimenta lucifera och experimenta fructifera" (with an English summary), *Nordisk Forum*, Universitetsforlaget Oslo No. 5/6 (1967), pp. 383–91), where some of these problems are discussed against the background of Bacon's doctrines. See also articles by Joel Alan Snow, Don K. Price, J. Bronowski, and Polykarp Kusch, under the common heading "Science and the Human Condition," in *Bulletin of the Atomic Scientist* (October 1968), pp. 23–43.

[22] P. B. Medawar, *The Art of the Soluble* (London: Methuen & Co., 1967), p. 15.

edge are no longer simply 'good'; whether they are good or bad depends on the purposes they are made to serve.[23]

These concerns need not remain quite so general and vague. They will be broken down and answered in detail within the framework of scientific and educational policies. It would be odd if scientists—from mathematics to the humanities—were not to participate in the formation of such policies. Such participation must necessarily imply a concern with the preferential ordering of moral, social, cultural, economic, technological, and other values.

If Weber's principle or any other part of the ideology of science should appear to make such participation illegitimate, we probably ought to question our own understanding of that ideology.

(iv) There is one distinction, familiar to philosophers but often overlooked by others, that is important in this context. Any norm, morality, or ideology serves a double function. (1) It may justify or condemn—be available as a reason for or against—an action for which it is valid or relevant. (2) It may causally motivate the agent to do (or abstain from) an action for which it is valid or relevant. Kant insisted that these two functions ought always to coincide; most of us today find it impossible to agree with him.

I have been concerned throughout with the *justification* available for scientific and scholarly activity, not with the motives of scientists and scholars.[24] Thus what I have called Weber's principle is important because it can be—and is—invoked in justification of types of scholarly and scientific activity and non-

---

[23] Universities have had and still have two main functions: education and research. Education and research presuppose each other. All this probably is as plain as ever, but the ends and purposes of the education provided are no longer clear or uncontroversial. Much of the present student unrest is spurred by the absence of clear answers to questions such as the following: Should universities, as educational institutions, primarily cater to and seek to fill the practical needs of society—or should they primarily (at least in greater measure than at present) cater to the needs of the individuals? If they are to do both, what is the order of priority?

It is hardly farfetched to see a connection between issues such as these and the current confusion in science and scholarship over the problem of adjusting the two inherited views of the 'true' purpose of science to each other. Although the conflict has been potentially present for a long time, the greatly accelerating rate of change and growth in nearly all fields has brought the issues to a head in the period following World War II.

Critically and systematically, we must now inquire: What is the internal order of the uses, functions, and values of scientific and scholarly activity, research, technology, and education; and how is this set of values to be placed within a wider set of human needs, goals, and values? What is the place and task of the humanities in this picture—a question that representatives of the humanities appear afraid to ask and unable to answer. Reference must be made at this point to Black, *Morality of Scholarship*.

[24] It seems to me that in *Science and the Planned State* (especially p. 26 ff.) Baker provides a striking illustration of the confusion to which one may fall prey by failing to distinguish between the justifying and the motivating forces and functions of norms and valuations. To say, with P. W. Bridgman, whom Baker castigates, that science must have ends-in-view beyond the abolition of want is not to insist that the research worker should be motivated in his research activity mainly or exclusively by these ends. I know of no better example than scientific activity to lay bare the fallacy involved in the Kantian position.

activity. And the two versions of the principle clearly will not have the same range of justification.

7. Scientists as Norm-Authorities

In the preceding section I suggested that the norms of methodology, or some of them, could be viewed as the counterparts of norms found in ordinary 'non scientific' morality. I shall now briefly touch on some of the ways in which norms which are shared by the scientist and his society may justify or legitimate certain types of normative activity on the part of scientists.

Consider the following two norms:

(a) If a person X is aware of a danger, risk, or harm threatening another person Y, of which Y is ignorant, then X has a duty (and, *a fortiori*, a right) to inform, aid, and/or protect Y.

(b) If X is informed of something that is necessary (indispensable) for Y, of which Y is ignorant and which Y would not obtain without the intervention of X, then X has a right and/or a duty to inform and/or aid Y.

The two norms (a) and (b) are not equivalent or synonymous.

To the extent that they are valid, these norms seem to hold for scientists and non-scientists alike. In our type of civilization, the scientist is a person who is professionally equipped to foresee certain risks and dangers as well as benefits and blessings. Illustrations of scientific conduct in conformity with these norms are easy to find. The *right* of scientists to warn against risks and to proclaim benefits is hardly in doubt,[25] nor is the likelihood of their thereby coming into conflict with various types of vested interests.

Basically the same argument can be stated in a slightly different form. We have one (normative) premise P_1N and one descriptive premise P_2D.

P_1N: We ought to reduce the frequency of cardiac disease.

P_2D: Reduced intake of animal fats is likely to reduce the frequency of cardiac disease.[26]

Two such premises make acceptable the conclusion $C(N)$: We ought to reduce the animal fat content of our diet.

The acceptability of the conclusion depends upon the *truth* of the second premise as much as on the *acceptability* of the first, normative premise. For determining the truth value or the probability of empirical propositions such as the one in the second premise, scientists are in a special position. If, then, they share

[25] Glass (*Science and Ethical Values,* p. 98 ff.) discusses the "social and ethical responsibilities of scientists" under the three headings of "proclamation of benefits, warning of risks, and discussion of quandaries." By the latter, he means roughly the responsibility to give and demand information about the consequences of possible alternative choices of ends of action. A related problem is that raised by the demand for 'informed consent' from persons subject to surgery or experimentation. See, for instance, W. Wolfensberger, "Ethical Issues in Research with Human Subjects" (with references), *Science* 155: 47–51 (1967).

[26] One may object that "disease" is not a descriptive term. My answer to this kind of objection will be found in section 7 where I discuss the concept of a *vital or legitimate need.*

with society at large the normative premise P_1N, they are permitted—and expected—to proclaim $C(N)$, which is a normative statement. And, of course, many of our more fundamental norms and valuations are translated into concrete practical action through the interpolation of some empirical premise (like P_2D) which scientists are well equipped to supply.

Under this model, scientists are permitted and even expected to act as 'norm-administrators'—to the extent that they share the general morality of their society. When a scientist assumes a normative function in this way, he acts in the spirit of Bacon's tradition. Neither Weber's principle nor any other part of the scientific ideology is held to constitute a hindrance.

But scientists, like other people, do not always share the morality of their culture on all points. However, I believe there is at least one pattern of argumentation, commonly accepted, under which a scientist is justified in attempting to change even the more fundamental norms and valuations of his society.

This 'norm-generating' argument goes by way of the concept of a *vital or legitimate need*. Let "a vital or legitimate need" be defined as a need the permanent or prolonged frustration of which brings death or disability to the individual; and let the criteria of disability be determined, in part at least, by various sciences. In this case, we can assume that (in our type of culture) most of us would be prepared to admit that the individual has a right to (seek) satisfaction of vital or legitimate needs. This, of course, is a normative principle, but one that —though certainly not self-evident—has today acquired an undeniably imperative force.[27] One important function which the sciences have in a modern society, is to investigate and disclose the contents, order, and structure of the set of human needs. This applies to the needs of the individual (trivial examples: special food for babies; extra insulin for diabetics) as well as to common, or public, needs (e.g., the supply of reasonably unpolluted air and water). When the (physiological) need for vitamin C (and other vitamins) was first discovered, scientists— as a matter of course—began to use normative language about it. When the psychological need for love was officially given scientific recognition—which was not so long ago—psychologists soon made us agree that, consequently, children have a right and a claim to love and attention. Today very strong emotions are at play, guarding this right against infringements. As new needs are thus recognized, new human rights are also recognized.

Nobody seems to think that it might be morally improper for scientists to engage actively in the generation and recognition of new 'need-based' rights and norms. Such activity is, on the contrary, regarded as both legitimate and praiseworthy. It is, of course, fully in accord with the Aristotelian as well as the Baconian view of the purpose of science. It does not seem to be so easily reconciled with a strict version of Weber's principle.

---

[27] This is no more than a sketchy outline of an argument that needs to be stated in much greater detail. I have tried to do so in a forthcoming paper, " 'Ought' implies 'Can': A Bridge from Fact to Norm?"

However, even a scientist who tries to adopt the 'split personality' solution is not likely to feel that in deriving human rights from vital human needs the scientific part of his personality is invading the territory of his moral and non-scientist alter ego. But, of course, it is, as I believe the preceding arguments suffice to show.

8. CONCLUSION

Scientific, scholarly, and educational activities demand an increasing share of our total resources, in money and in manpower. The allocation and use of resources for such purposes has to be *justified*, and the demand for justification naturally comes from those who feel they possess the right to distribute and allocate these resources—the general public, the politicians, the departments of government.

Scientists and scholars, on the other hand, make two demands on society in general. First, they demand the money, the manpower, and the other resources needed to carry on their activities. Second, they claim the right to make certain decisions about the use of the resources allocated without 'undue' public, political, or ministerial interference. What I am now referring to is the doctrine known variously as 'academic freedom' or 'freedom of inquiry.'[28]

There is, of course, a connection here with other aspects of the ideology discussed above. According to the Baconian view, the more we know about something, the greater is our power over it—that is, the greater the truth output of the total scientific endeavor, the greater its utility value. Therefore, scientists might feel that they are entitled—perhaps even, have a duty, precisely as benefactors of mankind—to concentrate on the truth output, that is, on the fundamental goal and value of scientific activity, to the exclusion of other interests and concerns. What this amounts to, of course, is a more or less categorical insistence on the right of a scientist or scholar to be bound in his conduct by nothing but the ideology of science and scholarship itself, the norms of methodology in the first place.[29] In other words, the doctrine of the freedom of inquiry can be understood as involving the claim that the (set of) norms and values of the academic ideology are not only necessary but even sufficient to guide the conduct of scientists qua scientists.

Three points can now be made. First, the doctrine of the freedom of science thus understood—that is, as being a *sufficient* ideology—may turn out to be a very close relative of Weber's principle in its strict version. It can therefore be a very practical doctrine for one who wants to be left in peace. Second, the assump-

---

[28] This topic has attracted considerable attention already, which is one reason why I do not discuss it more fully. See Glass, "Science and Intellectual Freedom," in *Science and Ethical Values*, pp. 89 ff; Baker, "Freedom of Inquiry," in *Science and the Planned State*, pp. 41 ff; or Bronowski, *Science and Human Values*, for instance, p. 80: "Independence and originality, dissent and freedom and tolerance, such are the first needs of science . . ."

[29] See section 5, above.

tion tacitly made in the classical plea for freedom of inquiry seems to be the following: increases in knowledge more or less automatically lead to over-all betterment, to better living conditions and better lives. Third, *why* should society at large be willing to grant to scientists and scholars this kind of autonomy if the soundness, the usefulness, the morality of some of (the implications of) their acts—and their abstentions—must appear problematic, that is, if the assumption just mentioned does not hold?

Obviously, if a growing truth output increases our ability to do good it equally increases our ability to do harm; and perhaps the latter ability actually grows more rapidly than the former.[30]

There is a growing feeling among scientists and students of all kinds that an attitude toward society that demands freedom while refusing to assume or to share responsibility for the implications of this freedom is inadequate, from a practical as well as from a moral point of view. It could be the signpost directing you into the ivory tower.

It is generally felt, I think, that scientists and scholars—and not only the 'new mandarins' of Chomsky—have, actually and potentially, more power and influence today than ever before. This power can be used essentially for two purposes: (1) in the service of 'the establishment,' that is, to perpetuate the kind of world we have today; or (2) to change the less desirable aspects of today's world so that the world of tomorrow might be a better one. At this point one observation seems to me to be crucial. The power of scientists to change the world rests on a trust vested in them. Scientists and scholars have the confidence of the general public as well as of government, industry, and other identifiable groups only as long as they are identified as bona fide scientists and scholars. That is, only as long as they are believed to be devoted to certain ideals of objectivity, integrity, disinterested search for truth—*and* to the ideal of promoting "man's mastery over the forces of nature for the benefit of all." It is conceivable that scientists and scholars might lose the general trust now placed on them, which is a presupposition of their having, and continuing to have, the influence they now have. In that case they might also lose their power to change the world for the better. The public is quick to reproach scientists for 'non-scientific' conduct, that is, for violating the ideology of academic conduct. This aspect of the problem may also be worth serious consideration.

Scientists and scholars do have a special 'academic ideology'; and this ideology is necessary for them. As an 'in-group' ideology, by and large, it functions quite well. But academic communities are not the only communities in the world. In the areas of interaction with the surrounding society, problems are generated, some of them of a clearly moral nature. I understand the previous arguments as having shown that the main difficulty here is not a sacred doctrine to the effect that it is fundamentally immoral for a scholar-scientist qua scholar

[30] The latter problem I have discussed in "Asymmetries in Ethics," *Inquiry* 10: 351–72 (1967).

or scientist to have moral concerns and problems. The difficulties lie in working out the theoretical as well as the practical solutions to a set of ethicoscientific problems of ever increasing complexity, magnitude, and urgency.

It seems to me, however, that we may have made these tasks unnecessarily difficult by persuading ourselves of the existence and validity of a sacred doctrine that probably will not survive the kind of scrutiny that we are normally so willing to apply to anything except—with a final glance at Bacon—the idols of our own tribe.[31]

[31] *Novum Organum*, aphorism 52.

III

Philosophy of History
Historical and Interpretive Studies

A

Philosophy and
Methodology of History

Gunnar Aspelin

On the Selection of Facts in History

1

In his effort to reconstruct past events and to explain their connections, the historian meets with an inexhaustible multitude of facts. Some of them will be passed over as uninteresting and of small use for his task; others must be regarded as highly important. Hence, we can ask for the points of view from which he judges facts to be relevant or irrelevant.

This question was raised in an essay by the German philosopher Wilhelm Windelband, and his ideas were pursued in a strictly systematic manner in Heinrich Rickert's famous work *Die Grenzen der naturwissenschaftlichen Begriffsbildung*.[1] Like Windelband, Rickert considered the generally accepted values of culture (*"die allgemein erkannten Kulturwerte"*) as the principles of selection in historical research. As to the historian of science, he finds his point of departure in theoretical value or the value of truth. The historical investigations of art, of religion, and of law proceed, respectively, from the esthetic and religious values and from the value of social order and security. The history of technology is concerned with events of importance for satisfaction of material wants, likewise belonging to the realm of cultural values.

But, Rickert emphatically states, this does not imply that a historian has to evaluate his objects, as by awarding moral certificates to kings and statesmen, expressing his approval or disapproval of political and religious movements, or rendering verdicts concerning style and content of artistic works. To evaluate in those ways and to refer creations of human activity to general values are two wholly different operations. The scholar may hold any opinion whatever about

Professor Aspelin, of the University of Lund in Sweden, is a native of Sweden.
[1] Heinrich Rickert, *Die Grenzen der naturwissenschaftlichen Begriffsbildung*, ed. 3 (Tübingen: J. C. B. Moor-Paul Siebeck, 1912).

the beauty of Goethe's poems, or about the religious value of the revelations in the Koran. Irrespective of his appreciations he cannot but award to Goethe a central place in the history of poetry, nor can he contest the role of Mohammed in the history of religious beliefs.

It is, I think, well advised to start from Rickert's discourse, if we wish to discuss the question of selection in historical inquiries. To begin with, it must be ascertained that we are dealing with a legitimate question, not with a spurious problem (*'Scheinproblem'*), devoid of foundation in real research situations. Perhaps you would reply that the historian, in his choice between 'relevant' and 'irrelevant' facts, is in no need of any established criterion. Much like an artist, he is free to select and reject at will. He occupies himself with those individuals, events, and situations in which he takes interest in a positive or negative manner. However, no scholar would accept such a license for unrestrained arbitrariness. Imagine a young graduate student, defending his doctoral thesis. His dissertation is a study in the social philosophy of Karl Marx. Let us make the improbable presumption that the author summarily mentions the influence of Hegel in a footnote, giving no information at all. In defense of his neglect, he says only that Hegel's philosophy appears to him a blind alley in the history of learning, an uninteresting, unsympathetic, and sterile offspring of an ivory-towered scholar's speculations, removed from the world of realities. Certainly, the opponents and the members of the faculty would reject such reasons for his astonishing omission. If we make a selection, if we pass over the fact A and lay stress upon the fact B, we are obliged to adduce some generally acceptable argument for our procedure. Thus we see that Rickert's basic problem is just and legitimate. It must be solved either in his way or in some other.

2

Let us regard Rickert's theory as a serious candidate for answering the question at issue. Then we may ask if its supposed validity is universal or particular. Can it be applied to all situations in the field of historical research? Or are there cases to which it seems hardly applicable? I think there are such difficulties. Georg Brandes, the Danish scholar and man of letters, once published monographs on Benjamin Disraeli and Ferdinand Lassalle, two prominent figures in the political history of the nineteenth century.[2] Of course, we find in these books much information about their political activity. But with Brandes they are not essentially considered in their relation to a general value. The choice of his subjects was determined primarily by the vivid interest for him of the individuality of these men of genius, and only secondarily by their contributions to the formation of the British Empire or the Social Democratic movement in

---

[2] Georg Brandes, *Benjamin Disraeli* (Copenhagen: Gyldendalske Boghandels Forlag, 1878); Brandes, *Ferdinand Lassalle* (Copenhagen: Gyldendalske Boghandels Forlag, 1881).

Germany. He was attracted to unique individuals quite apart from their importance from any general viewpoint. As he once confessed in the poem "Proteus":

Han ynder de Maistre, den reaktionaere,
beundrer Lassalle og vrager hans Laere.

[He likes de Maistre, the reactionary,
admires Lassalle and rejects his doctrine.]

A scholar of this temper wants to understand a peculiar individuality from
its reactions to the environment. Thereby his principle of selection is given: the
historical facts are relevant according to their capacity for widening and deepen-
ing our knowledge of the man behind his work. History, declares Georg Brandes
in his essay "Om Laesning," "can and may well be the most amusing of all
subjects. I think it is bound to be more interesting to find out something about
real men than about fictitious ones, even if the latter had their models in the
real world. But historians take their responsibilities at times too lightly; they
describe men entirely outwardly without first having experienced them as they
were within themselves."[3] Brandes and other historical writers akin to him start
from a vague and incomplete image of the personage who has stimulated their
interest. Through continued study of available sources the image will be made
more clear and distinct, and at the same time it will be corrected on essential
points. Here the details assume their value as integral moments of a totality.
The alternative is seen as a soulless enumeration of disparate facts which would
be quite idle and sterile. Hence such a historian's goal, typically, is to construct
the living picture of an individual manifesting his peculiar character and playing
his unique role in varying situations.

Another historian may be curious about the conditions of commonplace men
from a past period. His point of departure is more a sociological than a psychological one, if by "psychology" we understand what the Germans call
Persönlichkeitspsychologie. His aim is to study typical situations in a limited
social field at a certain time. The point is to become acquainted with the external
relations of men, with their chief means of support, habits of thought, and
prevalent opinions in moral, political, and religious matters. The Danish historian
of civilization, Troels-Lund may exemplify this type of scholarship. I refer to his
classical work *Dagligt Liv i Norden i det 16. Aarhundrede*.[4]

In the interpretation of this sort of history, Rickert's concepts can be applied
only with difficulty. With Brandes, the selection of facts is not directed by any
general value—e.g., an ideal end of political activity—but by his endeavors to
know the predominant features of admirable, uncommon men. In the work of
Troels-Lund, the time-related features of social life are illustrated by an immense
manifold of details, often trivial in and of themselves but important in connection

3 Georg Brandes, "Om Laesning" [On lecturing], in *Studentföreningen Verdandis
småshrifter 120* (Stockholm: Albert Bonniers Förlag, 1909).

4 Troels Frederik Troels-Lund, *Dagligt Liv i Norden i det 16. Aarhundrede* [Daily life
in the northern countries in the 16th century], ed. 8 (Copenhagen, 1908–10).

with a social totality. A dogmatic disciple of Rickert could possibly dispute consideration of the right of *Daily Life* as a genuine historical presentation. Perhaps he would be inclined to regard it as sociology rather than as history, on the ground that it has to do with *einmalige Ereignisse* and not with general traits repeating themselves at various times. I suppose, however, that the famous line of demarcation between 'history' and 'sociology' is of very questionable use for an empirical explanation of historical science. In fact, it is applied in a more modulated manner by Rickert himself than by his vulgarizing repeaters.[5]

As to Rickert's argumentation, he has in view the successive development of historical events and states of affairs, as regarded from some general aspect. The working concern is one of distinguishing between various manifestations of cultural activity. These differ from one another as to the kinds of products which they produce, e.g., household furniture and industrial tools, buildings, paintings, and sculptures, political institutions and laws, scientific theories, religious rites and creeds. Different values of culture (*Kulturwerte*)—satisfaction of elementary wants, embellishment of life, insight into the real world, social security, and the incomparable experience of everlasting rest in a painful and instable world—are actualized by these forms of activity. Rickert distinguished between values and value objects (*Wertgegenstände*). His philosophy posited two realms, the factual world with its ever-changing things, and the world of eternally valid values. He was a follower of the idealistic tradition in Germany with its basis in the Platonic system of ideas, interpreted by Lotze as a system of values. In the dialogues of Plato prior to the *Parmenides*, the ideas or paradigms are present in the sensible things, and the things participate in the ideas. In Rickert's philosophy, the valid but (in a sense) unreal values are manifested in concrete *Wertgegenstände*, as, for instance, works of art, religious symbols, social institutions, functioning as warrants of justice and security. History is a process in which objects of value are created, or, in other words, the timeless principles enter the world of temporal and spatial relations.

Now we may ask if this Platonized conception of eternal values is necessarily connected with Rickert's theory about the problem of selection in historical research. But before proceeding to that we must discuss some questions brought forward by Rickert's opponents:

(1)   Now and then critics have raised the objection that the statement, "The importance of any historical event can be measured by and only by its relation to general values," must imply a valuation of the event at issue.

(2)   Is there any sense in the conception of 'values' as standards of our selection, if we should refuse to admit their validity for us?

[5] In an inquiry concerning some historiographical problems, which will soon be published, I give an analysis of the conceptions *"individualisierender und generalisierender Wissenschaftstypus"* in Rickert's epistemology.

It seems to me that the first objection can be refuted without difficulty. Martin Luther is very generally regarded as one of the most important personages in ecclesiastical history, i.e., in a branch of study concentrated upon facts in relation to religious value. Consequently, one is obliged to admit that every investigator of religious movements in the sixteenth century must pay special attention to the lifework of the Saxon reformer. But this acknowledgment does not necessarily imply a positive evaluation of the man's creed or actions. Perhaps a person is an ardent partisan of orthodox Catholicism, inclined to condemn Lutheranism as one of the most mischievous heresies in the Christian world. Nevertheless, he can agree with any convinced Protestant in judging any account to be incomplete and unsatisfactory if it fails to give due place to the great religious figure of Wittenberg.

To measure the weight of facts in relation to some general value and to grade them as value objects of higher or lower degree are two wholly different operations. The statement, "In relation to the general value of religion, the contributions of Luther are more important [have produced more far-reaching effects] than the efforts of the South German reformer Martin Buber," evidently differs from such grading judgments of value as, e.g.,

(1) Catholic Christianity signifies, at any rate till now, the highest stage in the history of religions.

(2) From the esthetic point of view, French classical tragedy must be preferred to the drama of the Spanish renaissance.

(3) The ethical ideal of Buddha is higher than that of Confucius.

(4) In relation to the value of justice, a democratic government is better than a dictatorship.

The second objection deserves to be treated more seriously. To select historical dates with regard to a general *Kulturwert,* and yet refuse to accept the validity of this standard, seems to be a very odd practice. Suppose that some hard-boiled 'materialist' summarily dismisses all religious beliefs as irrational atavisms or as infantile daydreams. Why should he then make such phantoms the principle of his selection? Another person professes—at any rate in theory—an extreme moral nihilism, perhaps inspired by Stirner's cultus of the Sovereign Ego. A third extremist may ruthlessly condemn esthetic 'illusions' from an ascetic, or possibly utilitarian, point of view. Reply might be made that even in such cases the dismissed values can function as criteria, because history evidently shows that they have been generally acknowledged and that their role in the development cannot be overrated. But then an appeal is being made to historical science as an already established fact, while the very point at issue concerns the legitimacy of its claims on citizenship in the *Universitas scientiarum.* To what principle of selection can one refer when adducing the important role of these values in the course of history? If, on the other hand, you refer to their objective

validity, the question will be submitted to the tribunal of philosophy. Unfortunately, our philosophers are at variance on this problem. There are objectivists who
assure us that judgments of value can be true or false, quite as are statements of
physical facts. But there are also adherents of an emotive theory, who regard
talk of objective values as a play with words, devoid of real content.

Obviously, we have come upon a rather awkward situation. The problem of
selection seems to be a quite legitimate question. Is there any acceptable alternative to the proposal of Rickert? Perhaps we can find it in the concept of 'grade
of action' ('*Wirkungsgrad*'). Historians, we have been told, select their facts
according to the facts' capacity for influencing subsequent chains of occurrences.
The argument is just, but incomplete. Rickert was in the right when he objected
to the historian Eduard Meyer that all discourse about various grades of action
must involve a general point of view to which we can refer the contributions of
individuals and groups.[6] As far as I know, no one has been able to show any
tenable alternative to his theory.

On the other hand, Rickert's solution of the problem seems to involve certain difficulties with regard to the function of values as *Masstäbe* for the selection
of facts. The worries are such that we need to ask: Is it possible to modify his
conception so that it can be accepted independently of any controversial philosophy of values?

3

To consider this matter thoroughly, we must subject the so-called problem
of selection to a closer analysis. To this end I think we have mainly to concern
ourselves with two questions:

(1)   A problem of classification: From which points of view does historical
      research organize its heterogeneous material?

(2)   A problem of selection in the strict sense of the word: From which
      points of view can facts before us be judged as more or less important
      within a region, ordered by some determining principle (a general
      value or some other concept)?

The first question is weightier than the second. We will now attempt to deal
with it.

Let us start from the presumably undisputed statement that most historical
facts are human actions and effects of actions, allowing that these may be intentional or unintentional. (The historian must also, of course, consider physical
factors such as climate and soil, but they are regarded as conditions and, to some
degree, as effects of human activity.) Now, all historical facts can be subject to
positive or negative valuations. In relation to a moral measure, an action can be

---

[6] Eduard Meyer, Introduction, in *Geschichte des Altertums*, vol. 1: *Elemente der Anthro-
pologie* (Stuttgart and Berlin: J. G. Cotta'sche Buchhandlung, 1921).

judged as good or evil; from a utilitarian point of view, we make use of such expressions as "prudent and well-advised" or "rash and unguarded." A material artifact is appreciated as suitable for some practical end, or rejected as a thing of no use. We employ such comparative words as "better"-"worse," "superior"- "inferior," thus placing actions and products of actions on a scale of positive and negative values. Every one of us plays the role of a critic, whether as a simple layman or a highly learned expert.

We can hardly doubt that our critic, Mr. Everyman, must operate from some point of view of general principles. Of course, as soon as he sets himself to judging actions and objects of culture, his basis for conducting criticism can be either vague and unreflective or well-digested and well-defined. And substantively it may vary as between an economic, moral, theoretical, or religious criterion. These starting points correspond to Rickert's *allgemeine Kulturwerte*, but for my part I prefer the neutral phrase "principles of valuation."

In agreement with Rickert, but avoiding his terms, *"Werte"* and *"Wertgegenstände,"* we will introduce two basic concepts, namely, 'principle of valuation' and 'valued object.' The former concept is abstract and formal; the latter refers in a contrastingly material way to concrete things and modes of behavior in "the world of action and business." Each principle of valuation corresponds to a certain field of application, i.e., we normally are able to decide whether correct language permits us significantly to assess a given object from a certain general point of view. We don't ask for the esthetic value of the purchase of a Renault, or of the receiving of a sum lent against a mortgage on real estate. But we can esthetically appreciate the elegance of a car or the beauty of an old manor.

The significance of this last point can be indicated more fully by noting the difference between the two statements that make up each of the following pairs:

(1) Semantics is no art.
     Haymarket art is no art.[7]

(2) Boxing is no science.
     Phrenology is no science.

Semantics is outside the field of esthetic criticism, and the noble art of self-defense is similarly outside of scientific scrutiny. Haymarket art can be judged from an artistic point of view, and phrenology with regard to the scientific standard. But in both cases, the verdict will be a negative one. Such things have nothing to do with true art or with true science.

Above, I alluded to the valuation of concrete cultural facts from a general principle accepted by the scrutinizer himself. But these principles can in turn be subjects of critical examination. Criticism of religion can constitute either an

---

[7] *Hötorgskonst* (haymarket art) is a Swedish word for unanimated pictures according to set patterns.

inspection of existing creeds in relation to an ideal concept of its essence, or a scrutiny of religion as a whole. In the latter case, the critic assumes another principle of valuation, for instance, of a theoretical or a moral type. Perhaps he regards all religion as an illusion, inconsistent with rational thought (Freud), as an antagonist to the ethical demand of loyalty to 'the Earth' (Nietzsche), or as a reactionary phenomenon in the struggle for better social conditions (Marx). Another critic may be inclined to accept religion under certain conditions, e.g., if it gives up its positive content and appears as an undogmatic veneration of 'the Unknowable' (Spencer), or as a belief in the duration of values in the cosmic process (Høffding). The value of art has been disputed with regard to the ideal of truth. It was regarded by Plato as a bewitching illusion, "a shadow of a shadow." In his poem *"Sömngångarnätter"* [Nights of a sleep-walker], Strindberg bids farewell to the world of the fine arts; he cannot but feel the attraction of its charms, yet it is nothing but vanity. Severe moralists (e.g., Plato, Rousseau, and Tolstoy), have rejected many forms of art. Social reformers take the idea of general happiness as their principle of valuation, but a rugged individualist objects to this as a spurious ideal and glorifies natural selection. An equally extreme admirer of Rousseau will perhaps condemn our entire civilization as inimical to a life of innocence and happiness.

But even if one disputes the validity of a given principle of valuation, he must recognize a certain class of objects to which the principle can be applied. The general concepts, functioning as starting points of positive or negative criticism, can also function as starting points for an entirely theoretical procedure, namely, the organizing of facts in various fields of research. Thus we get a manifold of special branches such as economic history, political history, history of the arts, of the sciences and of religions. The choice of these principles has evidently nothing to do with individual or generally prevalent valuations. It is only determined by the necessity of an applicable classification. We distinguish between fields of criticism and fields of historical research, although each possible member of one field is also a possible member of the other. The principles of valuation work as principles by which a heterogeneous subject matter is divided into well-determined classes.

By such a modification of Rickert's leading ideas, it seems possible to free the theory from its dependence on controversial presuppositions, which arise from the tradition of Platonic idealism.

The second question, the problem of selection within an organized historical world, does not seem to present any really serious difficulty. We must, indeed, attempt to formulate the concepts as precisely as possible.

As a beginning, we can say that the selection of facts is dependent on their degree of importance in relation to the chosen principle of classification. This statement may be rather vague, and we must seek for a more precise formulation. Under which conditions will a fact appear as of more or of less importance from some general point of view?

With Riehl and Meyer, we could perhaps refer to its 'degree of action,' its power of influencing the future course of events by causing more or less extensive changes in given situations. From that point of view, a political historian must give preference to Mirabeau and Robespierre over Hébert and Chaumette, to William Pitt the Younger above Sidmouth and Eldon, to Lenin and Trotsky above Radek and Bucharin. No historian of science could pass over the contributions of Boyle, Newton, and Lavoisier, or give prominence to the last repeaters of Aristotelianism in comparison to Galileo and Kepler. But the rule is applicable if, and only if, he intends to study the progress of scientific ideas. If, on the other hand, his object is to describe the intellectual state of affairs in general, traditional discourses in physics and metaphysics could quite possibly be more suited to his intention than the *Sidereus Nuncius* or the *Discours de la méthode*. In like manner, he might well pay more attention to the arguments of conservative biologists in the nineteenth century than to the views of revolutionaries such as Darwin, Huxley, and Haeckel. It is the same with political and literary history; under certain conditions mediocre parliamentarians and commonplace writers are more suitable objects of study than men of genius.

In summation, the selection of facts within the field of a general principle of classification will be determined by the intention of the investigator. He may take wide liberty in his choice of theme, but once this is decided upon the question of 'essential' and 'unessential' facts will be easily answered. The historian is confined by unwritten laws, which, while not written in the stars, are nevertheless of a sort which makes them compellingly present to his *esprit de finesse*.

Herman Tennessen

On What There Was:
Toward an Empirical, Experimentally Oriented
Behavioral Science of History

"It is preposterous, absurd! It just can't be done!"[1] When it comes to judging general approaches to history, this and similar statements are not infrequently heard among metahistorians. Other metahistorians, however, may gleefully confront their colleagues with contrary cases—to wit, actually existing historiog-

---

Professor Tennessen, of the University of Alberta in Canada, is a native of Norway.

[1] This is again most typically exemplified by reactions to historians' attempts at employing 'grand,' 'historical laws' (Ernest Nagel, *The Structure of Science* [New York: Harcourt, Brace & World, 1961], pp. 350 ff.), 'covering laws' (Alan Donagan and Barbara Donagan, eds., *Philosophy of History*, Sources in Philosophy Series [New York: Macmillan Company, 1965], pp. 106–12; William Dray, *Laws and Explanation in History* [London: Oxford University Press, 1957]); Dray, *Philosophy of History*, Foundations of Philosophy Series [Englewood Cliffs, N.J.: Prentice-Hall, 1964]; Carl G. Hempel, "Explanations in Science and in History," in *Frontiers of Science and Philosophy*, Philosophy of Science Series, vol. 1, chap. 1 [Pittsburgh: University of Pittsburgh Press, 1962], or these 'magnificent cyclical theories' (Pitirim A. Sorokin, Foreword to Grace E. Cairns, *Philosophies of History* [New York: Philosophical Library, 1962], p. v), but is as frequently found in overzealous attempts to keep history free of social sciences and psychology (R. G. Collingwood, *The Idea of History* [London: Oxford University Press, 1946], p. 29). For examples of history that "couldn't be done," see, e.g., Gordon Allport, *Pattern and Growth in Personality* (New York: Holt, Rinehart and Winston, 1961), pp. 179–98; Gunnar Aspelin, *Historiens problem, utvecklingsfilosofiska studier* [The problem of history: Studies in evolutionary philosophy] (Stockholm: Geber, 1926), p. 343 ff.; Cairns, *Philosophies of History*; Collingwood, *Idea of History*; Collingwood, *Essays in the Philosophy of History* (Austin: University of Texas Press, 1965); Richard Dietrich, ed., *Historische Theorie u. Geschichtsforschung der Gegenwart* (Berlin, 1964); Edward T. Gargan, ed., *The Intent of Toynbee's History* (Chicago: Loyola University Press, 1961); B. Mazlish, *The Riddle of History* (New York: Harper & Row, 1966). For 'great speculators in history,' see J. Vogt, *Wege zum historischen Universum, von Ranke bis Toynbee* (Stuttgart: W. Kohlhammer Verlag, 1961); W. H. Walsh, *Philosophy of History* (New York: Harper & Row, Harper Torchbooks, 1960), pp. 119–55). For equally unenlightening approaches, see Marc Bloch, *Apologie pour l'Histoire*, English translation by Peter Putnam, *The Historian's Craft* (Toronto: Vintage Books, 1953), p. 3; also, J. R. Strayer's Introduction in *ibid.*, p. viii.

raphers who do in fact employ those very approaches which outraged their colleagues and were deemed in principle impossible by them. *Their* reaction to this confrontation is again equally predictable: "That isn't history."[2] What is it then? It may be religion, metaphysics, Spenglerism, Toynbeeism, or, worse still, social science, even psychology!

In other words, there cannot be much doubt that the question "What is history?" is in an important respect on a par with "What is art?" Perhaps art ('art,' "art") is somewhat more notorious than history ('history,' or "history," respectively). Perhaps one is more readily inclined to resign vis-à-vis any attempt at 'finding out'—either empirically by conceptual, logical, linguistic analysis, or the like, or by dialectical method—"what art is," and, *pari passu*, more inclined to settle for suggestions as to what art *ought* to be. It shall be my contention in the present paper, however, that it is an almost equally hopeless task to try to determine "what history (or 'history' *is*—or how "history" is used—by observing what so-called "historians" do. Trying to seek orientation here in a search for *the* nature, *the* concept, *the* Platonic form, *the* idea of 'history,' I find it more than safe to say, is just as futile with regard to 'history' as it is with regard to 'art.' Consequently, we have equally valid reasons for giving up any descriptive task of determining what 'history' is, and settling for a slightly different assignment: deciding what we would wish to see history developed into.

Fortunately, we shall not have to bother about the (pseudo-)distinction between 'art' and 'science,' as the extreme impreciseness of "art" and "science" makes for an entirely unenlightening distinction. The exotic impreciseness of "history," moreover, allows us free rein if we should want to switch from an indicative constative to an optative mood. No option is precluded by the notion ('nature,' 'idea,' 'concept,' 'use') of 'history,' as there is nothing so even remotely precise or specific inherent in that notion as to lead to anything like contradictions, 'logical oddities,' or anything as 'interesting' as that, come what may.

THE SO-CALLED "AUTONOMY" OF HISTORY

It has been maintained that at least the *problem area* pertinent to historical enterprise, may—even if only tentatively and roughly—still be to some extent delimited. To Cicero this area was *res gestae*. To German metahistorians, *"Geschichte ist was geschehen ist."*[3] "History," claimed James Harvey Robinson, "is

---

[2] See, e.g., A. J. P. Taylor's comment ("this is not history") on Toynbee's work in M. F. Ashley Montagu, ed., *Toynbee and History*, p. 115, quoted from Nagel, *Structure of Science*, p. 551; and Collingwood, *Idea of History*, pp. 29, 30. Needless to say, this and the following remarks should not be construed as attempts to support the general position of Spengler, Toynbee, and other 'great speculators' (Mazlish, *Riddle of History*). I fully subscribe to Karl Popper's ridicule of 'holistic' approaches in general (see his *The Poverty of Historicism* [London: Routledge and Kegan Paul, 1957], section 23; and his *Of Clouds and Clocks* (St. Louis: Washington University Press, 1966), p. 3.

[3] See Louis Gottschalk, *Understanding History* (New York: Alfred A. Knopf, 1950),

all we know about everything man has ever done, or thought, or hoped, or felt."
And the "prime duty of the historian," according to Collingwood, is *"a willing-
ness to bestow infinite pains on discovering what actually happened."*[4] However,
needless to say (it has been commonplace for centuries), it takes even more pain
to discover and sort out, in any tenable or justifiable way, from all that actually
happened, that which is worthwhile reporting.[5] In this paper I shall not deal
directly with this insufferably trite and trivial truism, but shall assume that any
event or sequence of events mentioned below is for some reason or other historically remarkable. Needless to say, it is in any event not a problem unique to
history. All inquiries are unquestionably selective, as Dray somewhat redundantly
emphasized.[6]

The answer to the question of what history ought to be is obvious; it should
be good. Less obvious are the specific difficulties or obstacles that are alleged to
hamper the achievement of this objective. In point of fact, I don't believe there
are any difficulties whatsoever that apply to history, *sui generis*. Problems of
preciseness and objectivity, for instance, are more or less painfully felt within any
branch of any 'hard' or 'soft' scientific discipline. True enough, there was a time
when philosophers and scientists dreamt of 'incorrigible sentences.'[7] But, for one

---

p. 41; *Das Fischer Lexikon: Geschichte* (Frankfurt-am-Main: W. Besson, 1961). Note the
use of "history" (*Geschichte*) as a label for the facts and phenomena 'themselves,' rather than
for 'written history' (*Geschichtsschreibung*, 'historiography')!

[4] James Harvey Robinson, *The New History* (1911), cited by H. E. Barnes, "History,
Its Rise and Development," *Encyclopedia Americana* (Canadian edition), 14: 205–63; Collingwood, *Idea of History*, p. 55 (italics are those of present author); or in Ranke's famous
words: *"zu endecken wie es eigentlich gewesen."*

[5] The problem rose to some prominence around and shortly after the turn of the century,
during the debate between Heinrich Rickert (see his *Science and History*, a translation of
Die Grenzen der Naturwissenschaftlichen Begriffsbildung, 1902 [Tübingen: J. C. B. Mohr,
1929; The Hague: Mouton & Co., 1962], and Aloys Reihl (see Aspelin, *Historiens problem*,
pp. 132–33; and Aspelin, *Tankelinjer och trosformer, Vår egen tids historia* [Lines of thought
and forms of faith: The history of our own time] [Stockholm: Geber, 1955], 6: 334,
377–42). Rickert strictly maintained the distinction between the *'nomothetische'* methods of
the *'Naturwissenschaften,'* and the *'ideographische'* methods of the *'Kulturwissenschaften'*
(Wilhelm Windelband, "Geschichte und Naturwissenschaft," in *Präludien* [Tübingen: J. C. B.
Mohr, 1903], 2: 136–60), and maintained, as did Windelband, that *value judgments* serve
the same function as *laws* within the natural sciences. Riehl, on the other hand, was satisfied
that historically significant facts could be selected by ascertaining their relative importance for
a satisfactory explanation of the status quo. The 'disagreement' may well have been a pseudo-
disagreement.

[6] William Dray, "The Historian's Problem of Selection," in *Logic, Methodology and
Philosophy of Science: Proceedings of the 1960 International Congress* (Stanford, Calif.:
Stanford University Press, 1962).

[7] Moritz Schlick used words such as *"Konstatierungen"* and *"Beobachtungssätze"*
(*Erkenntnis*, 1934), while Otto Neurath and others used *"Protokollsätze"* (*Erkenntnis*,
1932–33). English renditions of Schlick's notion(s) are "reports" (by Wilfrid Sellars, *The
Foundations of Science and the Concepts of Psychology and Psychoanalysis*, edited by H.
Feigl and M. Scriven, vol. 1 [Minneapolis: University of Minnesota Press, 1956]), and
"confirmations" (by David Rynin, in *Logical Positivism*, edited by A. J. Ayer [Glencoe, Ill.:
The Free Press, 1959]). Perhaps "constatives" would be a less misleading expression.

thing, such sentences were not, at any time, or by anyone, considered incorrigible with regard to level of preciseness. They were rather expected—or, more likely, invented—to fully satisfy any reasonable, or even possible, demand for truth or tenability. They were meant to constitute the terra firma of all ampliative, non-demonstrative, non-tautological, synthetic, empirical knowledge. Unfortunately, these 'confirmations' or 'reports' were either *acognitive*, and *eo ipso* totally un-equipped to serve as the basis for any segment of (cognitive) knowledge, or they were to be conceived as *cognitive* statements or sentences, in which case they would, unknowingly perhaps, *presuppose* or imply a conceptual orientation—in fact, a total view, a (coordinate) system, *"eine komplette, vollständige Weltan-schauung,"* the tenability of which would, to say the least, be quite contentious. More generally speaking, it is not at all easy to make sense of any observer's or narrator's claim to "merely report what actually happened," or "just give the facts and data themselves."[8] However, as I have pointed out, these are all problems that are encountered within any rigorous or moldable discipline. They obviously do *not* reflect difficulties specifically faced by historians. It is indeed more than doubtful whether any fundamental methodological problems peculiar to 'the craft of historians' as such could even be invented without resorting to utter arbitrariness.

The most frequently indicated 'historical problem' is 'the problem of the autonomy of history.' I suppose there should be no reason for more dreary repetition on this topic (references here are innumerable), as the explosion-like expansion and differentiation of *all* disciplines in the last few centuries have rendered the very notion of 'autonomous discipline' so obsolete that it has only, as it were, historical interest.

In his Cambridge inaugural lecture in 1895, Lord Acton "said very truly that historical studies had entered upon a new era. . . . It would be an under-statement to say that since 1800 history has passed through a Copernican revolution. Looking back from the present day one sees that a much greater revolution has been accomplished here than that associated with the name of Copernicus."[9]

As James Harvey Robinson has claimed:

The "New History" is escaping from the limitations formerly imposed upon a study of the past. . . . *It will avail itself of all those discoveries that are being made*

[8] Cf. Skinner's example: " 'She slammed the door and walked off without a word.' Our report is a small bit of history. History itself is nothing more than a similar reporting on a broad scale" (B. F. Skinner, *Science and Human Behavior* (New York: Macmillan Company, 1953), p. 15. As Arne Naess points out: "Other witnesses might have reported the 'same' event in a number of different ways. What is indeed difficult, is to make a report of the event 'itself' which can be used as a *common basis* for various interpretations. . . ." (Arne Naess, "Science as Behaviour," in *Scientific Psychology*, edited by B. B. Wolman [New York: Basic Books, 1965], p. 57 [italics are Naess's]).

[9] According to Collingwood, *An Autobiography* (London: Oxford University Press, 1939), p. 79; reprinted in Donagan and Donagan, eds., *Philosophy of History*, p. 98. In the same autobiography, Collingwood contends that something similar to the "suddenly and enormously increased velocity of the progress" of the sciences was happening to history at "about the end of the 19th century."

about mankind by anthropologists, economists, psychologists and sociologists,... discoveries which during the last fifty years have served to revolutionize our ideas of the origin, progress and prospect of our race.... History must not be regarded as a narrow, stationary subject which can only progress by refining its methods and accumulating, criticizing, and assimilating new material, *but it is bound to alter its aims with the general progress of the social sciences, and it will ultimately play an infinitely important role in our intellectual life....*[10]

In the final analysis this 'super-Copernican revolution'—if one wants to go overboard with Lord Acton and Mr. Collingwood—does not amount to more than the practical elimination of the notion of 'autonomous disciplines' in the traditional sense of "discipline." This has made itself felt, particularly in the last forty to fifty years, within all fields of human inquiry. It is simply a result of the banal fact that few clear-cut classifications are apt to survive the sudden, spectacular increase of information within their relevant fields of knowledge without rendering the relevant distinctions entirely arbitrary. The snails of Celebes would probably not have presented a problem to the zoological systematist had the cousins Sarasin not taken their task quite so seriously.[11] Their enormous material revealed "an unbroken series of varieties where the extremes were as different as those of different species (*verschiedene Arten*)."[12] Similarly, the venerable distinction 'organic'/'inorganic' was initially destroyed when Friedrich Wöhler (1828) converted ammonium cyanate (NH_4OCN) to urea $CO(NH_2)_2$.[13] Indeed, presumably the most fundamental borderline intended to divide 'living organisms' and 'inanimate objects' really became a problem only when the electron microscope and the ultracentrifuge isolated the viruses of the mosaic diseases, and radioscopy revealed their crystalline nature.[14] The effect of the kinetic gas theory on the barrier between 'mechanics' and 'theory of heat' is also well known. Other examples may be borrowed from acoustics and mechanics, from optics and electrodynamics, and so forth *ad infinitum, ad nauseam usque*. More recently, difficulties have arisen in connection with the increasingly arbitrary discrimination between physics and chemistry, due to some peculiar characteristic details of the whole explanatory system originally designed to deal with problems concerning black body radiation. Finally, Darwin could still permit himself some optimism with regard to deciding at what particular point in the series of hominidic fossils the application of the term "man" would be appropriate. He did not foresee skull finds (from the Second Interglacial Period—between Mindel

---

[10] According to H. E. Barnes, in "History: Its Rise and Development," p. 242 (italics are those of present author).

[11] See Paul Sarasin and Fritz Sarasin, *Materialen zur Naturgeschichte der Insel Celebes* (Wiesbaden: C. W. Kreidel, 1898–1906).

[12] Translated after W. Weismann, *Vorträge über Descendenztheorie* (Jena: Fisher Verlag, 1902), p. 13.

[13] "Organic" has long since been used more exactly, but less excitingly as a synonym for "carbon compound."

[14] The attempt, within so-called "organismic biology" (and "general system theory" in general) to introduce a dichotomy of 'open' versus 'closed' system does not add anything but verbiage to the difficulties.

and Riss) showing a rich variation of combined neanderthaloid and sapiens traits, thus rendering indefensible the common claim, presumably intended to boost feelings of human dignity, that "Man forms an entirely new dimension, fundamentally distinct from all other beings."[15]

However exciting such examples may seem, they all merely illustrate the trite but true saying that "Modern science is characterized by its ever-increasing specialization, necessitated by the enormous amount of data, the complexity of its techniques and of theoretical structures within every field. . . ." On the other hand, this does not seem "to lead to a breakdown of the science as an integrated realm." Quite the contrary, it leads to a breakdown of the border-lines between the various disciplines or 'sciences,' and a realization of "the structural uniformities of the various applied schemes" hitherto considered expressive of *the* "nature," "essence," "concept," or "character" of one or another particular discipline, by the rigid representatives of those so-called disciplines.[16] No wonder Toynbee feels that in his works he has been trespassing in a rich variety of 'disciplines,' that he incidentally finds to be "a curious piece of medieval sculpture," utterly obsolete, and maintained solely as a "self-defence against the fear of being overwhelmed by the sheer mass of information" in which the historian would seem to drown were he "to bestow infinite pains in discovering" (Collingwood) *"wie es eigentlich gewesen"* (Ranke), namely, "everything man has ever done or thought, or hoped, or felt" (J. H. Robinson). "People feel that the only hope of saving ourselves from being swamped by this, is to maintain water-tight compartments between one branch of knowledge and another—even if these compartments are arbitrary and out of date. . . ."[17] It seems absurd to Toynbee "that we should say we are now inhibited from asking the questions that are really of vital importance, . . . just because we have too much knowledge to cope with them." And he points to the necessity of finding "a means of studying human affairs as a whole, . . . which would not be superficial and at the same time, comprehensive."[18]

To tautologize a commonplace platitude, none of the issues aired above touches upon any problem unique to history, or even to the more general field of knowledge concerned with human affairs and human personalities. And, although everybody is yearning these days for a 'general practitioner' to synthesize smaller or larger chunks of information, there cannot be much doubt that one

[15] See, e.g., H. Prinzhorn, *Charakterkunde der Gegenwart* (Berlin: Junker & Dünnhaupt Verlag, 1931), p. 32. For a further discussion of this point, see H. Tennessen, *Typebegreper* [Concepts of type] (Oslo: Oslo University Press, 1949), 2: 207–10.

[16] Quoted from Ludwig von Bertalanffy, "General System Theory," *General System: Yearbook of the Society for the Advancement of General System Theory* (1956), 1: 1, 8.

[17] See R. Aron, ed., *L'Histoire et ses interpretations* (The Hague: Mouton & Co., 1961), p. 34: "C'est le sentiment que j'ai franchi les lignes de démarcation entre les différentes prétendues disciplines telles qu'on les définit pour l'enseignement scholaire. A cet égard je déclarerais voluntiers la guerre aux spécialistes et je dis que je ne crois pas du tout à la nation de 'discipline'. Je crois qu'il s'agit là d'une vieille sculpture médiévale, qui ne présente plus qu'une valeur de curiosité mais qui a eu la chance de se conserver jusqu'à nos jours."

[18] *Ibid.*

neither can, nor even ought to, halt (let alone reverse) the accelerating trend to ever-subtler specialization. No road leads back toward a unification of physics, astronomy, metallurgy, biology, psychology, history, or any other 'discipline.' We may as well face the fact that the name of an institution or department does not any longer offer any decisive clue as to what its researchers are doing. In the United Kingdom and North America, where it is more common to lump university faculty members together in departments with labels borrowed from the names of more or less traditional disciplines, we constantly see not only how departments overlap, but how they float over into different *faculties* as well. Particularly interesting are the cases where a growing college finds it necessary to divide so-called "arts" and so-called "sciences" into two independent faculties. If the college is fairly advanced, troublesome cases may well occur that lend themselves only to a most arbitrary decision, e.g., psychology, geography, etc. Some departments are divided right down the middle. I find these cases particularly interesting as they shed some rather revealing light on the naive, antiquated notion of 'the two cultures.'[19] No such dichotomy is to be found. There may be two thousand 'cultures,' but certainly not just two. Moreover, one apparent result of the gradual (although intensely accelerated) shift from a macro- to a micro-specialization is the proportional degree to which this development seems to interfere with the researcher's psychological ability to rest comfortably within any narrow intellectual confinement. Another effect is the researcher's discovery of related methodological problems, similar conceptions and approaches appearing in the most diverse fields of scientific inquiry and other types of intellectual endeavor. Thus the long dreaded 'overspecialization' takes an unexpected turn! Dead is the feudal organization of disciplines and clear-cut dichotomies; a profound wholeness of human research in general is emerging.

The historians should therefore, as I see it, not only "*avail* themselves of all these discoveries that are being made," but *make* them, if necessary. I foresee future historians undertaking (historically relevant) pioneer studies in pollen and fluorpartite analysis, in radiocarbon dating, as well as in climatology (or, at least, in the *effects* of climatic fluctuations). The principal concern, however, should naturally lie with those *behavioral* sciences that J. H. Robinson mentions such as psychology and sociology. On the other hand, this coagency is not to be compared—as is often done—with the relationship between geology and physics. Geology, so the argument goes, admittedly *avails* itself of what are commonly referred to as "laws of physics," but without any geologist's ever attempting to

[19] See F. R. Leavis, *Two Cultures?*, with an essay on "Sir Ch. Snow's Rede Lecture" by Michael Yudkin (London: Pantheon, 1962), and C. P. Snow, *The Two Cultures: And a Second Look* (Cambridge: Cambridge University Press, 1964). It may be convincingly argued (see e.g., Helen Liebel, "History and the Limitations of Scientific Method," *Toronto Quarterly* 34: 16, 17 [October, 1964] that the division science/art, *Naturwissenschaften/Geisteswissenschaften*, nomothetic/ideographic (Windelband, "Geschichte und Naturwissenschaft," pp. 136–60), etc., is rather more pronounced the further back in the history of man we delve. Maybe the real conflict is to be found fifty thousand years ago, namely, between, on the one hand, poets and musicians, and, on the other hand, toolmakers and men of outstanding dexterity.

establish such laws. That would be absurd! True enough. However, it is a *contingent* truth, a function simply of the fact that physics is relatively rigorous—particularly when compared to the 'soft' sciences with which it is suggested that history seek some sort of symbiotic existence. In order to make the partnership mutually profitable, the craft of historians will undoubtedly and rapidly be transformed beyond recognition. Not only will historians exploit, for instance, 'latent attribute-' and 'reason-analyses'[20] *à la* Lazarsfeld, but, by theoretical and experimental studies, they will attempt to measure the utility of such techniques. Mathematics and (at least certain branches of) physics constitute peculiar buildings where order, peace and rigor, and an almost complete unanimity prevail in a number of the 'middle floors,' as it were; whereas on the 'top floors' (i.e., 'the frontiers of knowledge') and in the 'basement' (*Grundlagenforschung*) the situation is exceedingly shaky, with perennial controversies and fierce fighting. As we move on to 'softer' sciences, we find the number of 'middle floors' steadily decreasing. The historian who intends to avail himself of the results of 'soft' scientific research should be prepared to find himself involved in altercations "as to what are matters of established fact, what are the reasonably satisfactory explanations for the assumed facts, and what are some of the valid procedures in sound enquiry." One can easily sympathize with the historians who shy away from such turbulent entanglement to keep their hands clean, even at the cost of ignorance in relevant matters.[21] However, I cannot imagine how the historians would plan to escape any such involvement were they to take to heart Collingwood's code, were they to shun no pain to find out what actually happened, what man has done, thought, hoped, or felt.

HISTORY AND PSYCHOLOGY

For example, the historically quite reliable (although, needless to say, its reliability is here irrelevant) *Egil's Saga* portrays the most versatile and original poet of Icelandic antiquity, Egil Skaldagrimson. To his contemporaries, Egil was even more celebrated as one of the most terrifying of the Norse *berserkr.*[22] The

[20] I.e., "a research technique for determining why people behave as they do on given occasions" (George Nadel, *Studies in the Philosophy of History: Selected Essays from History and Theory* [New York: Harper & Row, Harper Torchbooks, 1965], p. 554). See Paul Lazarsfeld and M. Rosenberg, eds., *The Language of Social Research* (Glencoe, Ill.: The Free Press, 1955), section 5, and, particularly with regard to the relationship between socioscientific and philosophically relevant normative judgments, W. P. McEwan, *The Problem of Social Scientific Knowledge* (Englewood Cliffs, N.J.: Prentice-Hall, 1963), pp. 29–31, 36–47, 48–54, 481–83, 527–46.

[21] It seems most charitable to see in this light W. B. Gallie's absurd persistence in conceiving history as 'purely narrative'—whatever is meant by that (*Philosophy and the Historical Understanding* [New York: Schocken Books, 1964]).

[22] I.e., those wild Norse warriors who led Viking attacks with a frenzied fury (allegedly caused by the consumption of amanitine, the active narcotic principle of poisonous fungi, particularly of "flybane" or *amaita muscaria*).

following incident is reported to have taken place after Egil's final settling as a fierce but highly respected autocrat on his paternal estate in Iceland. As Egil was passing by one of his men who was bending to arrange his footwear, Egil drew his sword and swiftly beheaded the man. Egil's excuse (or explanation) is famous: "He posed so conveniently for a blow." If we assume the veracity of the narrative, to what extent are we entitled to say that we have, in the above brief narrative, presented *what actually happened*, let alone what the people involved thought, hoped, or felt? The *Saga* makes it clear that Egil had no particular grudge against his victim. Perhaps he just 'took his aggressions out on him,' an aggression caused by some unrelated, recent frustration to which Egil happened to have been exposed—so interested historians may conjecture. But the mere contemplation of this hypothesis plunges the historian headlong into the meta-psychological dispute between the proponents of (1) the 'learning model' and (2) the 'frustration-aggression model' for aggression. According to the former, a perfectly adequate explanation of the decapitation is offered in Egil's fervent devotion to the *berserkr* profession—namely, that he had *learned* to react ag-gressively on a minimum of provocation. According to the latter model, however, Egil's long career as a *berserkr* should have prevented any accumulation of ag-gression, because of the frequent 'discharge' in numerous battles.[23] It would clearly be preposterous for any historian to endeavor to give an account of Egil's behavior in terms of either of the indicated models. It is commonly admitted that this general area of research does not readily lend itself to rigorously controlled experiments. But it is equally obvious that nothing is accomplished by putting experiments aside as impossible. "Experiments in history" (or, for that matter, in any other empirically oriented field of behavioral research) is not a locution that entails a logical contradiction. The onerous task of carrying out such experiments consequently is not inherently insuperable. One may initially have to lower (drastically) the level of ambition with regard to rigor and controllability, but surely the most reliable road to methodological improvement is through a tireless employment of the available methods in full awareness of all their potential shortcomings and general inadequacy. Historians have wondered whether Antony fled from the battle of Actium blinded by an all-devouring adoration (or insati-able desire) for Cleopatra—who, he was informed, had already withdrawn her support and pulled out—*or* whether he simply realized that the battle was lost anyway.[24] Somehow it seems as though historians have resigned; they rest in the riddle, waiting for the earth to erupt with some miraculous 'historical' evidence. It is hard to understand why any pertinent evidence whatsoever should be inad-missible to the historians if it has the slightest bearing on a historical conjecture. There is no reason why history should remain psychology (or whatever it may

---

[23] For further discussion of the two aggression models, see H. Tennessen, *Language Analysis and Empirical Semantics* (Alberta: University of Alberta Bookstore, 1964), pp. 269, 270.

[24] See Nadel, *Studies in the Philosophy of History*, pp. 549, 550, 555.

be) *in the past tense*. It is perfectly possible to do *something* to find out, for instance, how subjects of Antony's general description are inclined to react under external stress, and when engaged (in the extreme) in some kind of hetero-sexual relationship. Results of such 'experiments in history' may admittedly not appear to be so frightfully enlightening, at first. The important thing here is to establish a precedent to a practice, to break the spell of 'an autonomous discipline' and open doors of potential insights and improvement of knowledge, which, with hard work and a little bit of luck, might one day contribute to establishing *"wie es eigentlich gewesen."*

Resistance against Scientification

Needless to say, there is nothing new or exciting in the above argumentation. "Es entspricht nur der fortschreitenden Scientifizierung, welche die Historie im 19. Jahrhundert erfahren hat, indem sie mehr und mehr aus dem Bereich der schönen Literatur in das der wissenschaftlichen Forschung hinübergezogen wurde."[25] Qualms about accepting this 'scientification' of history may most plaus-ibly be ascribed to a combination of the following two rather recalcitrant miscon-jectures: (1) that "scientific" *must* be used in a way so as to properly designate only certain particularly exact and rigorous branches of physics; (2) that "history" *must* be defined in terms of what historians pro tempore, e.g., anno 1971, actually do. One may deplore the increasing dilution of the venerable notions of 'science' and 'scientific'; it is nevertheless precisely this wide or diluted sense that cur-rently has come to conceptually characterize 'scientification of history.' With reference to point (2), it is sufficient to note the utter fatuity of any attempt to demarcate at any given time the ultimate cincture of any branch or field of any variety of research. For instance, were the genetics of a century ago to be de-limited according to what Mendel at that time was doing, most of the work of modern geneticists should have to be subsumed under some other heading (than "genetics"). There is no reason to believe that future scientists would find it less preposterous if "history" were restricted to specify 'the craft' of our contemporary historians. Chances are, moreover, that some metahistorians' numerous pretexts for renouncing 'a science of history'—or declining to recognize it as a possibility —will (prospectively) sound equally absurd. The mere idea that all history, or a substantial part of professional historiography, ought to have (or actually has) the general character of scientific research (even in the above wide or diluted sense of "scientific") is undoubtedly the most valuable feature of the whole historical tradition, from Ashurbanipal, Hecataios, and Hesiod through Herodo-tus and Thucydides to von Ranke, Lamprecht, Richert, and Riehl. That such an idea is now 'in,' now 'out' is obviously irrelevant. What is important is only that

---

[25] See Windelband, "Geschichte und Naturwissenschaft," pp. 136–60. See also Rickert's "Geschichtsphilosophie," in *Festschrift für Kuno Fischer: Die Philosophie im Beginn des 20. Jahrhunderts* (Heidelberg: C. Winter, 1904–5).

any attempts, systematic or not, to avoid a 'history' that *resembles* scientific research, are clearly without foundation.[26]

'HISTORY' AND 'PERSONALITY'

Finally, and curiously enough, there appears to be a notion of *personality* which on occasions seems to afford a last refuge to those who are most hesitant in accepting a 'science of history.' After a careful examination of a great number of definitions of "personality,"[27] I think it is safe to say that the most common notions of 'personality' offer no intrinsic or insuperable difficulties for a science dealing with *decisions* or *actions* carried out by *personalities*. Certainly nothing important hinges upon the fact that such actions or decisions are commonly said to be understood, explained, or predicted only on grounds of *reasons* or *norms*, etc. (accepted by the person, or characterizing the personality in question), rather than in terms of *causes*. Let us say (1) that Arne Naess has given an adequate reconstruction of Gandhi's norm system; (2) that, in conflict situations, Gandhi was always aware of his norms; and (3) that Gandhi was self-consistent and resolute. It is hard to imagine a sense of "understand," "explain," or "pre-

---

[26] Although distinctions like nomothetic/ideographic (Walsh, *Philosopohy of History*) have long since disappeared, as have intentionality/casuality, *questio juris/questio facti, vérités de raisonnement/vérités de fait*, etc. (H. Tennessen, "On Worthwhile Hypotheses," *Inquiry* 2: 197 [1959]), a contrast is occasionally sought between the scientific laws of certain branches of physics and the not-so-scientific laws employed elsewhere, for instance, in the behavioral sciences (see, e.g., Carl G. Hempel's *Philosophy of Natural Science* [Englewood Cliffs, N.J.: Prentice-Hall, 1966], pp. 54–69, and Richard Rudner's *Philosophy of Social Sciences* [Englewood Cliffs, N.J.: Prentice-Hall, 1967], sections 5, 14. See also Nagel, *Structure of Science*, chaps. 2–5, 12–15). But, again, the difference is plainly one of degree. In the most typical cases, a law is a universal or general statement—and even if singular in form, it should be able to support so-called "counterfactuals," "subjunctive conditionals" (see, e.g., Nelson Goodman, *Fact, Fiction and Forecast* [Indianapolis: Bobbs-Merrill Co., 1965], ed. 2, chap. 1). When a statement is pronounced a "law" within an explanatory system, it implies that its verity (and that of its entailments) is not to be questioned, even in the face of quite a bit of apparent evidence to the contrary. The less rigorous the system, the more susceptible the laws to evidential influence. Conversely, laws 'on the middle floors' of, e.g., physics, take on a near analytic chracter, as though physics were a purely deductive system.

[27] I.e., of more or less definoform statements about 'personality.' I am indebted to my colleague in the Department of Psychology, William Blanchard, for furnishing quite a few of the examples. See, e.g., Gordon Allport, *Personality* (New York: Holt, Rinehart and Winston, 1937); Allport, *Pattern and Growth in Personality*; Allport, *Becoming* (New Haven: Yale University Press, 1955); R. Brandt, "Personality Traits as Casual Explanations in Historiography," in *Philosophy and History: A Symposium*, edited by Raymond Klibanski and H. J. Paton (New York: New York University Press, 1963); R. B. Cattell, *Personality and Social Psychology* (San Diego, Calif.: Robert R. Knappel, 1964), sections 1, 2; Yehudi A. Cohen, ed., *Social Structure and Personality* (New York: Holt, Rinehart and Winston, 1961), especially sections iii–v; Robert H. Dalton, *Personality and Social Interaction* (Boston: Houghton Mifflin Co., 1961), chaps. 11, 12; F. E. Emery and A. O. Oeser, *Information, Decision and Action* (Cambridge: Cambridge University Press, 1958); J. Gould and W. L. Kolb, *UNESCO Dictionary of the Social Sciences 1964* (Glencoe, Ill.: The Free Press, 1964), p. 493; Louis Z. Hammer, *Value and Man* (New York: McGraw-Hill, 1966); Richard M. Martin, *Intention and Decision*, Philosophy Series (Englewood Cliffs, N.J.: Prentice-Hall, 1963).

dict" such that if the three above conditions were met we wouldn't be abundantly well equipped to understand, explain, and predict any historically significant decision ever made by Gandhi. True, Gandhi may be a particularly fortunate case, but again it is only a matter of degree between Gandhi's case and that of, for instance, a scatterbrain or even a mentally deranged person. And the interesting thing in this connection is to note that most typically (or maybe only) in the Gandhi type of case would particularly enthusiastic users of this 'personality' notion be inclined to admit that "the *personality* was active in making the decision." Oddly enough, it seems as though, according to this apparently ponderous notion of 'personality,' often labeled "integrated," the personality, P, *must make* the decision, D_i, *but in such a way as to insure that D_i cannot be said to be caused by P*. The rationale behind this clause is unclear. It is probably connected with scruples against accepting roughly the following reasoning: if D_i *is caused* by P, P could not have been able to make any *other* decision than D_i, e.g., D_j, thereby excluding P's being considered 'an integrated personality,' namely, a master in his own house, determining which dispositions will be enacted and how and when they will become overt—or words to that effect.

One would certainly be well advised not to accept this peculiar piece of argumentative discourse, but not for any more interesting reason than the difficulty of making sense of it. To say that Gandhi's decisions were *caused* by Gandhi's *norms* may admittedly sound a bit exotic, at first. On second thought, however, it doesn't sound half as exotic as the claim that there were no connections whatsoever between Gandhi's decisions and his norm system. Such a claim could only be based on new information, revealing, for instance, that Gandhi did not consider his norms at all when making historically significant decisions. However, if he *did* consider his norms when deciding (which it so happens we know that he did), then certainly Gandhi's norms—together with tenable assessment of his self-consistency, resoluteness, etc.—give us a most valuable key to understanding, explaining, and predicting Gandhi's decisions and actions. Whether the connections are to be seen as 'causal,' 'intentional,' 'rational,' 'motivational,' or whatever, is inconsequential. It is sufficient to realize that in no sense of "understanding"—e.g., *Begreifen* or *Verstehen*—are we to attempt to understand Gandhi's choice of 'enacted dispositions' without having acquainted ourselves with his system of ethical norms. And in no sense of "causal," "caused," or "causality" does it make any difference to a person P's *degree of power* to choose D_j rather than D_i, that there *is* causality, or that D_j or D_i *is* caused, or *has causal connections* with something inside (or outside of) P. In the case of Gandhi, it is certainly true that *if* Arne Naess's reconstruction of Gandhi's norm system were correct, and *if* we could foresee which norms would apply and *how* in each choice situation (as conceived by Gandhi), then *Gandhi could not have decided otherwise*, that is, in the sense that the probability was 100 percent that Gandhi would decide as he either actually decided or was predicted to decide (say, D_i). In other words, we have constructed a case such that there was *by definition* no probability left for the choice of D_j. But we have impoverished Gandhi's capacity *neither* for decision-making nor for moral effort, endurance, consistency, resoluteness, or anything of the sort. On the contrary, we are indeed *counting* on the fact that we have—at least in Gandhi's case—subtracted nothing from (and added nothing to) what may be called "P's pre-decisional activity" eventually leading up to the decision, D_i. D_i is here not itself to be seen as an activity (or an action), but as an *achievement* accomplished through the pre-decisional activity, the deliberation, the more or less laborious efforts to 'make up one's mind,' attempting to 'arrive at' either D_i or D_j. In any case of decision-making, P then either *pronounces* D_i or in any other way conveys his predilection for D_j. Hence, since P always (except in peculiar cases) would have it in his power to utter any other constellation of phrases than those intended to convey D_i (i.e., those meant to express D_i), P is always, it might be argued, completely 'free' to make any decision whatsoever.[28] It goes without saying that this sense of "P (freely) deciding D_i (D_j, D_k, . . .)" should be ignored as nothing but an example of a primitive linguistic pitfall—a pitfall, which, under particularly unfavorable circumstances, may become a fatal trap, namely, an 'argument' for man's 'unlimited freedom of the will.' Students of decision-making do in most, but not in all cases, use "decision" in a way that renders 'decision' cognitively somewhat similar to 'judgment,' 'verdict,' 'assessment,' 'determination,' 'estimate,' 'appraisal,' and the like (all of which logically precludes the attribute of 'duration').[29]

Our concern here is most typically with the general kind of cases such as those in which subjects are asked to 'decide' (less misleadingly, 'conjecture' or 'bet') whether, in a deck of cards with positive and negative numbers, the mean will be above or below zero. It seems reasonable to assume that such practice is likely to pave the road for the aforementioned fatuous use of "decision." Be that as it may, in everyday use, if P decides (on) D_i, he also *commits* himself *ipso facto* to *post-decisional activity* A_i. In point of fact, if P does not make some manifest and serious attempts to carry out A_i, we should hardly consider D_j a decision (or we should say that P had reconsidered his decision). If P decides to marry Miss S, the implication is that he eventually takes steps to marry her. This is clearly different from P's 'deciding' ('finding out') whether he is in love

---

[28] See Harald Ofstad, "Can We Produce Decision?" *Journal of Philosophy* 56: 84–94 (January, 1959). I am also more generally indebted to Ofstad for his whole analysis of 'decision(-making)' in *An Enquiry into the Freedom of Decision* (Oslo: Norwegian University Press, 1961).

[29] See, e.g., Emery and Oeser, *Information, Decision and Action*; Martin, *Intention and Decision*; and Irving M. Copi, "Deciding and Predicting," *Philosophy of Science* 28: 47–51 (January, 1961). This seems to be the case regardless of whether the student's approach is theoretical (logicians, mathematicians) or experimental (psychologists).

Some students group D_i and the pre-decisional activity together under the heading "decision," and talk about 'post-decisional activity' as "consequences of a decision." See, e.g., M. A. Wallach and N. Kogan, *Risk-Taking: A Study in Cognition and Personality* (New York: Holt, Rinehart and Winston, 1964), p. 70.

with Miss *S*, although, again, an unlimited number of difficult borderline cases may be found. At any rate, insofar as post-decisional activity is conceptually included in the notion of 'decision,'[30] the question as to what a personality, *P*, at any time had it in his power to decide becomes a straightforward empirical problem—a problem, if *P* is a historically significant person, for an empirical, experimentally oriented behavioral science: *history*.

[30] That is to say: D_i is a decision if and only if it is not too unlikely (i.e., possible) that *P*, at least according to *P*, is capable of carrying out A_i. For instance, *P may* decide to take the world championship in tiddlywinks, but (probably) *not* to become ten thousand years old, or a hippopotamus, or an imaginary number. The problem of assessing whether *P* could— mistakenly—have *believed* that he could possibly become, say, a hippo, does not raise any principle difficulties. *More* problematic: How *definite* were *P*'s intentions, when embarking upon decision-making . . . ?

B

History of Philosophy

Egil A. Wyller

The Architectonic of Plato's Later Dialogues

By the term Architectonic *I mean the art of constructing a system . . . By a system I mean the unity of various cognitions under one idea.*—Immanuel Kant*

In this paper[1] I wish to offer some main results of an investigation of mine into the interrelatedness of Plato's later dialogues.[2] The theme is, of course, a much debated one among philologists and philosophers, quick and dead. The neo-Platonists of late antiquity (Iamblichus/Proclus) and of the Renaissance (Ficino), and the Plato scholars of German Romanticism (Schleiermacher) and later, have all tackled the question in their own ways. I hope, however, that the *hubris* of my own attempt in this field will be somewhat alleviated by a 21-year study of the works of Plato. Such an apprenticeship gives one the courage to transcend mere deference to established authority and to state a case of one's own.

1

From a Scandinavian point of view it is natural to start a discussion of the 'Platonic question' with Hans Raeder's standard work, *Platons philosophische Entwickelung* (Copenhagen, 1905). By a careful examination of the internal and external references of the dialogues, together with a judicious use of criteria of language and style, Raeder succeeded in bringing an elementary order to the chaos bequeathed by the Platonists of the preceding century. As we know, it was not until the end of that century that objective criteria were established for determining the internal order and interconnection, as well as the authenticity of

Professor Wyller, of the University of Oslo, is a native of Norway.

Reprinted, with changes, from *Classica et Mediaevalia*, vol. 27 (Copenhagen, Librairie Gyldendal, 1960), pp. 101–14, with permission of the author and editor.

*From *Critique of Pure Reason*, "Transcendental Doctrine of Method," chap. III, "The Architectonic of Pure Reason," trans. Meiklejohn.

[1] Read to the Linguistic-Historical Society, Copenhagen, November, 1966.

[2] For the details of my case I must refer the reader to my book *Der späte Platon: Tübinger Vorlesungen 1965* (Hamburg: Felix Meiner Verlag, 1970).

the dialogues; and it was due to such broad, synoptical works as that of Raeder (as well as those of C. Ritter, U. von Wilamowitz-Moellendorff, and others) that a chronology was arrived at which, at least in its broader outlines, later became generally accepted. Today this generation of Plato scholars, with its positivistic inclination toward matters of fact, has to some extent faded into oblivion; but the results of their research still form the basis for any genuinely scientific interpretation of the dialogues.[3]

From the 1930's on it was felt that those historical and contextual matters could be set aside as more or less settled and that the way lay open to an investigation into the meaning or content of the dialogues; the works were therefore subjected to literary and philosophical analysis. Here we should mention the major contribution of the German, so-called *"paideia"* school (Friedländer, Stenzel, Jaeger), which expressly claimed to extend its approach beyond that of von Wilamowitz. On the assumption that every literary text has an 'inner form' (an idea which can be traced back to Plato's analyses of *'logos'* in the second part of the *Phaedrus*), this school was able to arrive at a deeper understanding both of the content of a series of individual dialogues (such as the *Symposium* and the *Phaedrus*) and of certain larger units into which the dialogues can be seen to fall. Its analyses of the works of Plato's youth and prime were especially convincing. Thus the *Republic* was shown (particularly by Jaeger) to be the 'lake' into which flowed the widely separated tributaries of the earlier dialogues. Correspondingly, there was the attempt to make the basic idea of the *Republic*, the Good, the main one for all of Plato's work.

But when we ask these scholars where the 'river' which—if we are to maintain the metaphor—must inevitably flow from the great lake of the *Republic* goes, the answer we receive is: to Aristotle. Thus for Werner Jaeger the middle part of the *Theaetetus*, the 'episode,' where Socrates refers to the absent-mindedness of the 'theoretical' philosopher Thales, forms a caesura so complete that not only Plato, but, *nolens volens*, the entire course of ancient Greek *paideia* nearly divides in two. First, there is the period from Homer to the 'episode' in the *Theaetetus* (the Sophistic and/or Socratic practice in managing the city-state); then the period from the 'episode' up to and including Aristotle (the theoretical life [ὁ θεωρητικὸς βίος] for the sake of research itself).[4] Plato becomes, accordingly, one-half the pupil of Socrates and one-half the teacher of Aristotle. Regarded from a literary point of view, however, the sum of two halves is never a whole. What, then, has become of Plato himself?

An answer to this last question, I believe, is to be found in the later dialogues. But to find the right answer we must approach these dialogues from

---

[3] Proof that even today there is reason to keep this generation's contribution to Plato research alive is provided by Gilbert Ryle's recently published *Plato's Progress* (Oxford, 1966), which ruthlessly subverts any recognized chronology, yet has little more than its author's wits to fall back on in support of its own.

[4] W. W. Jaeger, "On the Origin and Cycle of the Philosophic Ideal of Life," Appendix to *Aristotle* (Oxford, 1934).

the right direction, which is naturally the direction from which Plato himself approached them—from the dialogues of his youth through those of his prime. For this we must exchange the literary perspective of the *'paideia'* school for a more purely philosophical one. However, if we look at the technical way in which philosophers since 1945 have approached Plato, we find although the later dialogues here occupy the center of attention, they are considered either as isolated units, examined in the light of the special philosophical interests of the respective interpreters, or as a collected whole to be understood in the light of their 'fullfil-ment,' the works of Aristotle. This approach is particularly evident today among British and American scholars. In order to study 'the mid-fourth century,' one should direct one's gaze toward the year 350, letting the left eye fix upon the late Plato from the preceding decade and the right eye upon the early Aristotle from the succeeding decade. But from this wide-angle view there emerges at best a *Plato diminutivus*, at worst no Plato at all since the Aristotle one sees with the right eye, by virtue of his more 'scientific' procedure, becomes the normative thinker (Owen, Düring). The break in the middle of the *Theaetetus* has become —even without Jaeger's help—the tacitly agreed upon dividing line that segre-gates the literati and the humanists captivated by the Plato of the Beautiful and the Good, from the professional philosophers fascinated by Plato the epistemolo-gist and/or ontologist, etc. Few have seriously tried to bridge the gap.

One very relevant attempt at bridge-building should be mentioned, the so-called "esoteric" school of H. J. Krämer and K. Gaiser, which followed in the footsteps of Julius Stenzel and dates from the 1960's. These energetic scholars from Tübingen, whose work is causing quite a stir among contemporary German Platonists, have found a key to the understanding of all the dialogues, and particularly the late ones, in the doxographic tradition surrounding Plato's oral, esoteric teaching in the Academy, and especially in connection with his so-called lecture(s) *On the Good*. This has led to the gathering of much new material for the placing and understanding of a doctrine of principles (*'Prinzipienlehre'*) that transcends the doctrine of ideas in Plato. The progress of this school is to be watched with keen interest; it may also throw light on the question of the con-tinuity of Platonism in antiquity, from Plato through Speusippus and Xenocrates to the neo-Platonists of late antiquity.[5] Nevertheless, an unkind critic might say, with some justification, that the basic principles of Unity and Unlimited Duality stressed by this school appear in its treatment of them to differ from the Platonic ideas only insofar as they have become *fixed* ideas. And despite all assurances on the part of these scholars, their approach has not yet done full justice to the dialogues themselves, which lose their integrity as works "with limbs and joints which suit each other and the whole" (*Phaedrus* 264 C).

No, the way toward a Platonic understanding of the late Plato has in my opinion been exemplarily shown by the form-analysts of the *paideia* school, and

---

[5] Cf. Hans Joachim Krämer, *Über den Ursprung der Geistmetaphysik* (Amsterdam, 1964).

especially by Friedländer and Jaeger. On a closer scrutiny, the dialogues preceding the *Theaetetus* should be arranged in an ellipse, that is, with two focal points, the *Republic* and the *Symposium*, rather than in a circle with just one center, the *Republic*. The *Symposium*'s doctrine of the Beautiful forms the focus for the aesthetic interests of Plato in the man Socrates and his religious background. The *Republic's* doctrine of the Good forms the focus for the ethicopolitical development of Socrates' seminal thought. The main ideas of these two dialogues, respectively, the Beautiful and the Good, combine the perspectives of the early and the middle dialogues on the basis of the Greek educational idea of *kalokagathia*. It is essential to keep this ideal in mind, and its philosophical implications are brought to bear on everyday affairs and practice nowhere more than in the works of Plato's earlier and middle period. But this makes the problem of finding a way of transition from the 'paideutic' point of departure to the philosopher's purely speculative later works all the more pressing.

We cannot here take up for discussion the question of transition ($\mu\epsilon\tau\alpha\beta o\lambda\acute\eta$) as such. But let us recall that for Plato the leap—referred to as the 'spark' in the *Seventh Letter*, or the 'sudden' in the third hypothesis of the *Parmenides*—can, under certain conditions, be a meaningful mediatory category: *saltus datur*. One who would bridge the Jaegerian gap need not, therefore—in order to understand Plato Platonically—establish a continuity (as Stenzel himself has attempted to do, and following him, Krämer and Gaiser); a Platonic transition can just as well consist in the 'sudden' introduction of something quite new—as when Alcibiades turns up quite unexpectedly after the Diotima speech in the *Symposium*. Only that reader who on his way "from the beginning, through the middle, to the end," can take this suddenness into account, will be capable of recognizing whatever it is that nonetheless unites a Diotima with an Alcibiades—that Platonic unit, namely, which *transcends* the whole made up of the gradual growth and maturing of a continuum.

The 'sudden' marked by the 'episode' in the *Theaetetus* (and consequently by the dialogue itself) is, as Jaeger quite rightly suggested, a *theoretical* moment in Plato's philosophical profile. But the path up to this point has indicated two other moments in his thinking, namely, the productive (concerning the Beautiful) and the practical (concerning the Good). The 'break' is thus quite simply located within the triad of the productive, the practical, and the theoretical, which, according to Plato's own pupil, Aristotle, constitutes the whole of philosophy! Why not, therefore, adopt this very 'theoretical' way of thinking, follow it up "from the beginning, through the middle, to the end" and see whether or not it, too, has one or more focal centers which let it stand on its own. Thus, far from setting ourselves unduly apart from the early Plato, we would be making our theoretical approach precisely in continuation of Plato's productive and practical thinking. And at the same time, far from having to keep a firm grasp of the Beautiful and the Good with a view, simply, to throwing a new, 'theoretical,' light on them, we would have every chance of finding in the later dialogues, and in conformity with Plato's principle of the 'sudden,' a new basic idea standing in a meaningful relation to the two earlier ones, but not necessarily being absorbed by them.

From this point of departure my research has obtained the following results:

The theoretical, later dialogues—not only the productive and practical dialogues of Plato's youth and prime—form in themselves a total, even if not complete, universe of thought with its center in one dialogue and its basis in one idea. This central dialogue is the *Parmenides*, and the basic idea, 'principle,' or whatever one should call it, is the One. Plato's *'philosophische Entwickelung'* from youth through maturity to old age can be seen as a development from the productive stage of the Beautiful, through the practical stage of the Good, to the theoretical stage of the One. The Beautiful, the Good, and the One thus constitute, on this interpretation, the three Platonic manifestations of the absolute ('God'), these three, neither more nor less.

It should be stressed, however, that this talk of stages is not meant to suggest compartments completely shut off from one another. On the contrary, the supreme task of the interpreter of Plato is to arrive at a unified view of these three stages, perhaps on the basis of the neo-Platonic dictum "Everything is in everything, but each in its own way"; thus the Good and the One may be in the stage of the Beautiful, and the Beautiful and the Good in the stage of the One, but each in its own way. And this indeed seems to be the case, for fundamental features of the doctrine of the One appear already *aesthetically veiled* in the *Ion*, in the account of the divine magnet whose power of attraction draws everything in motion toward it; and conversely, the Beautiful and the Good are clearly indicated as themes in the later dialogues, for example, in the *Philebus* and the *Timaeus*, but then *under the conditions of the One*. Just what these conditions amount to can only be understood if we scrutinize Plato's doctrine of the One as such. The following attempt at an explanation of the architectonic of Plato's later dialogues is intended to assist such an inquiry.

2

First we must state what works are implied by the term "Plato's later dialogues." We also have to clarify their order of sequence—be this the order in which they were actually written or in which Plato meant us to read them—and give them an elementary grouping.

Except for the *Epinomis*, all the works I shall be concerned with are unquestionably authentic. Conversely, there is no unquestionably authentic work from the late period which I do not take into account.

Our chronology in the main follows traditional Raederian lines, and is as follows: *Theaetetus, Sophist, Politicus, Parmenides, Philebus, Phaedrus, Timaeus/ Critias, Laws/Epinomis.* There are reasons for placing the lecture(s) *On the Good* between the *Parmenides* and the *Philebus*, and for placing the *Seventh*

Letter between the *Timaeus/Critias* and the *Laws/Epinomis.* The only problematic dialogue is the *Phaedrus,* whose definite place in the corpus is not yet established. Our juxtaposition of that dialogue and the *Philebus* has been excellently argued for in a recent study.[6] While the *Philebus* studies the passions of the soul, the *Phaedrus* studies that special passion which is 'eros.' The *Cratylus,* the linguistic dialogue, I would consider as a prelude to the later dialogues as a whole. This inquiry into the nature of the name (ὄνομα) is naturally to be seen as introducing the investigation into the nature of knowledge (ἐπιστήμη) that begins with the *Theaetetus.* Thus, I should like to look upon it, even if it should have been written at some earlier time, as one of the 'later' dialogues.

Within this rich multiplicity of individually substantial works there are certain compositional units of a higher order. We have the incomplete *Timaeus* trilogy, which was probably intended to comprise the *Timaeus, Critias,* and *Hermocrates,* but which is broken off shortly after the opening of the middle dialogue, *Critias.* At the beginning of the *Timaeus* the following plan is set forth: Timaeus himself is to expound the birth of Man as a natural being within the framework of the perceptible cosmos, this being understood on Pythagorean premises. Then Critias has to take over Man, thus constituted, and place him in a historical context, a setting which, in turn, would enable the *Republic's* static model of society to be set in motion. The *Critias* itself opens, accordingly, with the pre-historical stage in the form of the legendary meeting between Poseidon's Atlantis and Athene's Athens. Finally the theme was to have been taken over by Hermocrates, who would probably have brought the actual course of history into view, following it up to Plato's own time and focusing upon the events at Syracuse that are associated with Hermocrates' name. This assumption would allow us to see in the *Seventh Letter* an explanation not only of Plato's final failure at Syracuse, but also of why he was unable to complete his *Timaeus* trilogy. "Creation, Man and Messiah" is the title of a great Christian visionary poem by the Norwegian poet Henrik Wergeland. The *Timaeus* trilogy would presumably have given us the Platonic version of the same theme: "Creation, Man and—Plato." Thus the *Timaeus* represents Plato's triumph as a (mathematical) philosopher of nature; the unfinished *Timaeus* trilogy reveals him as the frustrated philosopher of history.

Then we have what we may term the *Sophist* trilogy—the *Sophist, Politicus,* and *Parmenides*—a trilogy which *expressis verbis* is introduced through the epistemological discussion of the *Theaetetus.* At the close of this discussion Socrates expresses a wish to renew acquaintance on the next day with his mathematical friends Theodorus and Theaetetus, and at the opening of the *Sophist* they arrive, bringing with them the Eleatic Stranger, who then takes charge of the discussion. Urged to elucidate the threefold theme: what is a Sophist? what is a statesman? and what is a philosopher? the Stranger immedi-

---

[6] Otto Regenbogen, *Bemerkungen zur Deutung des platonischen Phaidros* (1950) (Munich: Kleine Schriften, 1961), p. 269 ff.

ately takes up the first of them, and the next dialogue, the *Politicus*, proceeds to the second. Then the *Parmenides* follows, with a 'sudden' change of scene in which we no longer have the anonymous representative of the Eleatic school but the master himself, Parmenides, who explains what a philosopher is. The reason for this sudden transition, as Stallbaum has most brilliantly indicated (1841), is that although one can speak philosophically about what a Sophist or a statesman is, one can speak only doxographically, and not philosophically, about what a *philosopher* is. The question calls for a kind of philosophic *self*-reference, which is why in the *Parmenides* Plato—in the mask of Parmenides—*shows* himself as a philosopher (*"non quidem describit . . . ob oculos ponit"*).[7]

Further, the *Phaedrus* is to be grouped with the *Philebus* according to a common theme—the nature of the passions ($\pi\alpha\vartheta\acute{\eta}\mu\alpha\tau\alpha$) of the soul. The *Philebus* takes up the theme at its most basic and general level, in association with an examination of the 'false' infinity of sensual emotions, while the *Phaedrus* takes it up in connection with a specific passion, *eros*, which is combined with the 'true' infinity qua $\dot{\alpha}\vartheta\alpha\nu\alpha\sigma\acute{\iota}\alpha$ experienced in the inspired moment's $\vartheta\varepsilon\tilde{\iota}\alpha$ $\mu\alpha\nu\acute{\iota}\alpha$.

Finally, the *Epinomis*, if genuine, has to be regarded as an Appendix to the *Laws*.

This quite elementary survey serves to reduce what at first glance appears a confusing multiplicity of dialogues to four structural units, namely:

(1) The complete surviving, Eleatically based *Sophist* trilogy, introduced by the *Theaetetus* (which is, in its turn, anticipated in the *Cratylus*).

(2) The incomplete surviving Pythagorean *Timaeus* trilogy, in whose context the *Seventh Letter* belongs.

(3) The complementary dialogues, *Philebus* and *Phaedrus*.

(4) The concluding work, *Laws* (whose twelve books comprise about one-fifth of the collected corpus), with possibly the *Epinomis* as an appended thirteenth book.

Plato's late dialogues thus can be collected into a number of larger systems (by "system" I mean Kant's "unity of various cognitions under one idea"). The idea behind the 'logical' system (1) is not easily discernible; but that behind system (2) is patently the World, that behind system (3) equally clearly the Soul, and that behind system (4), as will be shown, God.

---

[7] When Stallbaum's thorough argumentation for the placing of the *Parmenides* as the latest dialogue within this group fell into oblivion among the following generations of Plato scholars, this was due not so much to the discovering of new facts as to a reinterpretation and re-evaluation of the dialogue itself, through which it was reduced from the status of what Plotinus calls "higher" to that of "lower" dialectics (cf. Plotinus I, 3). For a detailed argumentation on this point I will refer to my paper "The *Parmenides* is the *Philosopher*," forthcoming in *Classica et Mediaevalia*, as well as to my book *Platons Parmenides in seinem Zusammenhang mit Symposion und Politeia* (Oslo, 1960), a synopsis of which is given in "Plato's *Parmenides*: Another Interpretation," *Metaphysical Review* (1962).

However, this question of Platonic 'systems' is not our ultimate concern. Our thesis is that these systematic units can themselves be seen to form *a single architectonic whole*, such that, comprehending the Eleatic and Pythagorean, the 'logical' and cosmological, the psychological and theological subject matters in the later Plato, we can trace a consistently Platonic design which integrates the elements into one basic unitary vision.

The possibility of such a unitary conception in the case of a diversity as conspicuous as that which we have here should not be in question. It is shown by the unity in the multiplicity underlying such great literary works as Dante's *Commedia* and—better—both parts of Goethe's *Faust*. If Goethe could, indeed, had to, take sixty years to write one single work which nonetheless displays notable structural unity, there is no reason why we should not expect Plato to have been capable of a similar achievement, with the difference that in his case the basic vision had to be materialized in several mutually related works.

3

The outstanding works within Plato's later dialogues are, from our 'architectonic' viewpoint, the *Parmenides* (alias the *Philosopher*) and the *Laws*, the former dialogue lying in the middle, the latter at the end of the series.

A. The *Parmenides*, as we have interpreted it, is to be regarded as the final cause (οὗ ἕνεκα) of all the preceding later dialogues. As an introduction we have the *Cratylus*, with its inquiry into the name (ὄνομα). Then follows the *Theaetetus* with its examination of knowledge (ἐπιστήμη), an examination which stops halfway and has therefore to be continued in the *Sophist*. The *Theaetetus* examines *episteme* as *aesthesis* (sense perception) and as *doxa* (opinion), while every reader of Plato up to this point knows, notably from the instructive 'divided line' in book VI of the *Republic*, that he sets *dianoia* (understanding) and *noesis* (intelligence) above these forms of knowledge. The *Sophist* then makes the first thrust into the sphere of higher knowledge, initially with the help of its dianoetically based methodology (the diairetic method), then through a noetically based study of some of thought's highest 'genera,' namely, Being, Identity, Difference, Motion, and Rest. The *Sophist's* investigation of these genera is still, however, confined by the narrow limits of the subject matter of the dialogue as such: the 'Sophist' and his illusionary form of being. Thus the *Politicus* brings us a step higher on the ladder. This dialogue investigates the knowledge of the statesman, that is *episteme* as a superior spiritual authority (ἐπιτακτικόν), which receives its guidance, not from a relative level of being, but from an absolute measure (μέτρον). The investigation within this dialogue culminates in the middle part with its demonstration of the necessity of such an absolute *metron* as the norm for all higher spiritual activity. And finally, the *Parmenides* provides us with the requisite measure—*ob oculos ponit*—in the form of a doctrine of the One. The first hypothesis investigates the One as such;

the remaining eight hypotheses investigate the One's and the Other's relationship to, respectively, Being (2nd to 5th hypotheses) and Non-Being (6th to 9th hypotheses). Not the *Parmenides* as a whole, but precisely the first hypothesis of this work is what gives us the final cause of the progress hitherto. Here the absolute *metron* at the top of the ladder of knowledge comes into view, for anyone "related to the thing itself," as the Unnamable 'One' above (ἐπέκεινα) all Being and Non-Being.

This path from ὄνομα over αἴσθησις, δόξα, διάνοια, and νόησις, aiming at a confrontation with the absolute ἕν, we will call the *way to the Philosopher*. The problems connected with it are predominantly epistemological; its task is to give a transcendental foundation for the possibility of knowledge, and the question it asks is not what things are, but what are the conditions for the possibility of our knowledge of things. The path itself culminates in that *silentium* which Proclus later rightly found to be expressed at the end of the first hypothesis of the *Parmenides*.

B. How different are the dialogues that end in the *Laws*! Already within the *Parmenides*, from the second hypothesis on, we have a change of objective. Now it is no longer the One, but that which is *Other* to the One, that figures as the basic concept of the dialectic. And after the *Parmenides* the drift of thought within the later writings reaches a decisive turning point. The *Philebus*, although methodically closely related to the *Sophist* group, thematically deviates from it insofar as it is concerned with a definite thing, a natural phenomenon, namely, the Soul in its characteristic emotionality. That which is Other to the One turns out here to be Nature (φύσις), which is defined as a "growth (γένεσις) toward substance (οὐσία)" (26D), and this then constitutes the framework for the 'physiologia' of all the following works. Thus in the *Phaedrus* the passion ἔρως is seen from its physiological aspect, and when the *Timaeus* trilogy subjects the World to scrutiny, it places History, that is, the aspect of γένεσις, in the center. The dialogue *Timaeus* itself works out the principles for natural philosophy in the famous middle part where Plato develops his anti-Empedoclean as well as anti-Democritean theory of physical elements, according to which nothing *is* earth or fire, etc., but earth and fire, etc., are in a state of becoming, generated constantly anew every time the elementary schemata of intelligible space collect a suitable substantial substrate under their 'yoke.'

And so, finally, we arrive at the massive *Laws* in which the aging Plato appears as the lawgiver of an imaginary state. In the *Politicus* we are told that the true lawgiver is like the true physician. When personally present, he makes decrees ad hoc, but should he depart, he must leave written instructions to be put into effect by others. Now it is Plato himself who is preparing for his final journey. The instructions he leaves behind are to be considered in a purely realistic way, as directed toward a state to be founded by his own Academy (cf. the conclusion of the work in Book XII). The elderly Plato is far from becoming infatuated with the ideal, his soul climbing up to the *flammantia moenia mundi*; on the contrary, he turns his mind to the nearest environment, and its immediate future, with the intention of founding a society for the protection of ideals already achieved. It is true that the *Laws* are built around a fiction, a Cnossian 'colony' (ἀποικία), and it is only to this that the laws are supposed to apply. But the fiction breaks down in the very last pages of the work, Plato himself here throwing away the mask of the Athenian Stranger in order to command the members of the Academy to go out and found this state *in natura*. Thus in the *Laws*, the supposed way within the *Timaeus* trilogy from the Creation through man and history to the Plato of Syracuse is provided with a continuation into the future on earth beyond the death of Plato. Here, too, 'nature' appears as a growth (γένεσις) toward substance.

With respect to this concrete termination, I should like to call the whole of this pathway within Otherness, beginning with the second hypothesis in the *Parmenides*, the *way to the Academy state*; its purport is ontological not epistemological, and the type of 'natural' problems to which it gives rise are those that call not for the conceptual dialectic of the Eleatics, but for the mathematical nomothetic of the Pythagoreans.

The *Parmenides* and the *Laws*—these two works indicate the scope of the later dialogues of Plato: the one an exalted and purely abstract dialogue in which the transcendental 'way to the Philosopher' culminates, the other a concretely legislative dialogue which carries to its conclusion the physiological 'way to the Academy State'; the former aiming at foundation and seeking for the absolute as it is, the latter aiming to clarify, constitute, 'save' the appearances as they continually are coming into being.

And what is the view, the vision which supports the whole? It is quite simply the vision from the Allegory of the Cave, with its two paths: from the darkness (of the senses) up toward the intelligible light with its beautiful, good, and unitary source, the sun (this is the way to the Philosopher)—a journey which is motivated exclusively by the will to know and understand—and from the light back toward the darkness, or, more correctly, toward the 'cave's' *clair-obscure*, now with the purpose of propagating the new understanding by forming and reforming what apparently exists (this is the way to the Academy state). Always faithful to his basic vision, which can be metaphorically recognized in the three similes in the central books of the *Republic*, Plato in these last dialogues has tried to think through its theoretical implications—not *in abstracto*, and certainly not from doxographical considerations, but in such a way as to lay his own thought out in the full breadth of his basic vision and expose it to the philosophical experiences presented to it in each of its stages.

We may conclude with a concrete example in order to show how consciously Plato must have had the whole of his vision in mind in the working out of the individual stages, and also in the hope of showing the possible fruitfulness of our total view for detailed interpretation. Let us try to state the problem of God in Plato's later dialogues.

If we take a look at our two 'paths' we see immediately how the phenomenon of 'God' is kept in the background during the ascent toward the Philosopher, while the same phenomenon gradually increases in strength and power during the descent toward the Academy state, the climax being reached in the *Laws*. This is no accident. 'God,' and particularly the divinity as grasped by the Greeks, does not appear as an object for a thinking that focuses itself upon the transcendental foundations of its own possibility; in this context it is Oneness which constitutes the basic phenomenon. We can even indicate the precise point at which 'God' withdraws from the 'upward' discussion, namely, at a certain place in the *Theaetetus*. The Sophist Protagoras has just made his *homo mensura* contribution and, accordingly, lets us understand that he will not listen to anything about the 'gods' in this context. Perhaps gods exist, perhaps they do not—the question is one that has its place in debates on views on life, but not, as here, in contexts of strict philosophical and epistemological argumentation (*Theaetetus* 162D). It is true that Plato himself lets 'God' be invoked in the ensuing 'episode,' but that is precisely a debate upon views on life in the manner of his earlier periods. Otherwise, during the entire progress toward the Philosopher, Plato remains largely true to this Protagorean principle.

How different, however, on his returning "genesis toward substance"! For now the naturally given phenomena are to be described and promoted in accordance with their ideal structure—centered first upon the soul, then upon the World and finally, in the *Laws*, upon God and the gods. The *Laws* from their very first words on, are imbued with thoughts upon 'God,' the cultic god, the mythical god, the notional god, in short upon 'God' as revealed to Greek imagination (cf. the anti-Protagorean *deus mensura* dictum in Book IV). It is characteristic that the first *theologia* in our spiritual history attempting to give a proof of divine existence (Book X of the *Laws*) occurs, not in the course of a philosopher's search for fundamental knowledge, but in connection with a lawgiver's desire to secure the states 'anchorage' (ἄγχυρα; *Laws* 961C). It is followed, as we know, by rigorous rules for the punishment of the unbeliever.

Thus, not only each individual trilogy or larger complex of dialogues, nor only each individual late dialogue itself, but also every major theme within the context of these dialogues must be read in the light of the all-pervasive basic vision of Plato, must be understood from its place within an articulated, architectonic whole. The One is the all-prevailing Ground (ἀρχή). Toward the One, thought seeks to find a foundation for itself; away from the One, thought seeks to describe as well as to transform the nature of things—the One which, in as much as it is, "never is one, but constantly in process of becoming two" (*Parmenides* 143A).

Understood in this way, Plato's later dialogues bear significant relationships not only to the *kalokagathia* of the earlier periods, the topic we took as our point of departure, but also to the succeeding Aristotle and Speusippus. For precisely in the central dialogue, the *Parmenides*, that '*Prinzipienlehre*' enters vitally into consideration which in the later tradition becomes established textbook material. And precisely against Plato's doctrine of the One 'above' Being, a doctrine which Speusippus took over and sought to expand,[8] Aristotle launched his attack in the form of a theory of that which *is,* in as much as it is (ὄν ᾗ ὄν, *Metaphysics* V).

Which is, however, another story.

[8] See Konrad Gaiser, *Testimonia platonica* no. 50 (Appendix to *Platons ungeschriebene Lehre* (Stuttgart, 1963).

Arne Naess

Pyrrhonism Revisited

THE OCCASIONAL AND THE ESSENTIAL SEEKER

Investigators are likely either to find what they seek or to reject discoverability, asserting incomprehensibility, or to persist investigating. This is perhaps why also in regard to what is sought in philosophy, some have claimed to have found truth, others asserted that it is impossible, but others go on inquiring. Those who are called dogmatics believe they have found it, thus Aristotle, Epicurus, the Stoics and some others. The incomprehensivity was argued by Cleitomachus, Carneades and other Academics; but the skeptics keep on searching.[1] (Sextus Empiricus)

Some of my fellow beings are researchers or, simply, searchers. When asked what they are and what they are doing, they honestly tell about what they are trying to find, but have not found. When asked about what they implicitly seem already to presuppose having found, they eagerly try to answer my question straightforwardly and with assurance. They try also to describe *exactly* or in *exact* outline or abstract form what they know for certain that they are honestly trying to find (what they 'are' looking for). But they fail in this or they tend to think they fail, or they at least discuss the aspect of possible failure in complete seriousness, using the technique of *pro et contra dicere*. It is as if their findings, even as regards their own intentions, are essentially, and not only *pro tempore*, conceived as tentative, ad hoc, or as hypothetical findings good only as starting points for more systematic and better focused search. If I ask for their exact intentions, they might raise their arms, saying, "Ah, you are a phenomenologist! I wish I had time to do research on my intentions!"

Professor Naess, of the University of Oslo, is a native of Norway.

[1] I follow, in the main, the terminology of Sextus Empiricus in his *Outlines of Pyrrhonism*. This quotation, from the opening of the work, is translated rather freely. *Tois zetousi* is translated as "investigators" rather than as "searchers" or "seekers" in order to make it more plausible that a person can be an *all-around* 'zetetic.' He is a permanent searcher relative to all *systematic* investigations, not relative to all everyday searchings. He does not find his socks less often than others (but perhaps they never were his).

This seemingly evasive behavior is frustrating to me when trying to grasp exactly *where they stand*: I wish to find out what they tacitly, but steadily, assume to be definitively true when asking their questions—in short, their presuppositions. For, of course, they *stand*. But just *where*? Or perhaps 'standing somewhere' is just one possibility among several? *Must* we always stand?

A Dialogue Exemplifying a Pyrrhonian Who Does Not Admit His Pyrrhonism

"Surely you presuppose that this stuff here will not explode," I said to my contemporary, Boyle, the 'skeptical chemist,' in his laboratory.

"I am completely convinced," he answered, "Don't be afraid, there is nothing I hold for more certain than this. There will be no explosion."

"So, in this experiment you *presuppose* that the stuff will not explode?"

"Of course," he answered.

"But then you also presuppose the truth of a variety of chemical propositions —all of those needed to derive the non-explosiveness."

"Do not make me laugh," he answered, "I am, as you ought to know, contributing to the downfall of several of those 'truths.' They have too long been taken for granted. Any of them may tumble and fall, at any time."

I was completely taken aback. "You are completely convinced that an explosion will not take place as that stuff is mixed, but you nevertheless see no decisive arguments for the truth of any of the premises!"

"No decisive argument for the *truth*. But more than enough for my *trust*, my confidence, insofar as it rests on premises."

"So you only have probabilities!"

"Probabilities? What are they? Perhaps only a pseudoscientific way of reporting about past regularities."

He was still smiling, unaware of the serious attack on his character that I now found inevitable. "Robert," I said, "not a single time in any of our discussions have you found *decisive* arguments for or against the truth of any proposition. *You* are a *Pyrrhonian* or zetetic *skeptic! A seeker!*"

My friend's face darkened. "What nonsense. In research matters I have not found instances of decisive verification or falsification, but there are innumerable truths I *might* believe in. Pyrrhonism as described by Sextus Empiricus is dead. Short, conclusive refutations abound."

"Forgive me, if my memory fails me, but you seem always to have regard for human fallibility—including your own—stressing the difference between firm convictions and truth, between life and philosophy."

"I firmly believe that this is *my laboratory*."

"*Is* it *true* that it is yours?"

"I have absolutely no reason to doubt it."

"From *that* you infer the truth?"

"Of course not. Truth does not depend on *my* reasons, or anybody else's. Why should I make that inference? What need is there for infallibility?"

"Could you not admit that if pressed you switch from truth claims to claims that you are convinced, that you do not have reasons or spare time to doubt, that you do not see why you should be in error in the present case, etc.? Pyrrhonism does not oppose conviction if conviction is defined as an implicit attitude of trust."

"Anyhow, Pyrrhonism is not my *philosophy*. If I have never found decisive arguments for or against the *truth* of a proposition, this fact is only of biographical interest. From a diary of such failures no philosophy can be inferred."

"Perhaps not, but could the failures *prevent* you from having a philosophy?"

"Perhaps you trust your philosophy, but do not affirm its truth?"[2]

Here I shall leave my imaginary debate with a skeptical friend. It exemplifies a frequent kind of debate with the not very numerous persons whom I would class as 'Pyrrhonian in their life and philosophy' but who resent and resist this label. This resistance I find laudable ("why labels?"), but perhaps the resentment is only a reflection of the low quality of descriptions of Pyrrhonism in textbooks. The arguments of the resistors, if carried far enough in long discussions, sometimes only strengthen my belief that I have found Pyrrhonians in the sense of seekers—zetetics. *There are consistent Pyrrhonians.* Looking back, I would tentatively class myself as one, approximately between 1952 and 1962. Now I find it difficult to decide what I am, or to rediscover the question.

THE PYRRHONIAN MAY BE STRONGLY ATTRACTED TO CERTAIN (DOGMATIC) PHILOSOPHIES

The arguments so far published against Pyrrhonism as a philosophy are weak. My motivation in writing this article is simple: there are Pyrrhonians, and they had better come out into the open. The refutations are rather conventional, and for the most part do not reach Pyrrhonism as described by Sextus Empiricus. In no instance are they decisive. Furthermore, being a Pyrrhonian does not exclude having strong philosophical affiliations of other kinds. In antiquity, Pyrrhonians were *close to* Heraclitus. Pyrrhonians are 'seekers,' and in philosophy this implies prolonged working, however tentatively, within definite conceptual frames.

Within this short article, I shall introduce some definitions and postulates for the sake of argument:

DEFINITIONS AND POSTULATES OF PYRRHONISM

(1) Pyrrhonian philosophy, maximally condensed: Decisive arguments are worth looking for, but there seems to be no decisive argument *pro* or *contra* the truth of any proposition!

---

[2] See *Outlines of Pyrrhonism*, book I, chap. 29.

(2) A philosophy does not need to contain any truth claim.

(3) True means 'that it is so.'

(4) I only know that p, if "p" is true, that is, if it *is* such that p. "I know that p, but p may be false" is not an acceptable position; the claim to know excludes the admission of the *possibility* of failure.[3]

Some of these sentences admit rather different interpretations. The selection of different definite sets of interpretations forms somewhat different systems.

"No Decisive Arguments," the Core of Pyrrhonism, Is an Exclamation, not a Proposition

Sentence (1), expressing the core of Pyrrhonian philosophy, has the form of a pronouncement, not an assertion. In this, Pyrrhonism may resemble the philosophy of Socrates, Kierkegaard, and the early Wittgenstein, and differ from that of Spinoza or any other philosopher who takes a set of propositions with a truth claim to adequately and basically express his philosophy. In this respect, Pyrrhonian philosophy, together with certain forms of Buddhist and Western philosophies, is to be classified as non-propositional.

The term "pronouncement" is used in adherence to the terminology of Sextus Empiricus, when characterizing 'skeptical utterances.' The term "exclamations" also might be used.[4] They signify primarily the state of mind of the Pyrrhonian when confronting the dogmatic in debate.[5] Secondarily, they signify a basic existential attitude toward conceptual thinking. It is an attitude that cannot adequately be expressed by a set of propositions with truth claim.[6] But this does not imply that the Pyrrhonians cannot find each other and communicate. Everyday use of language does only marginally *require* pure conceptual thinking and those engaged in conceptual thinking may have a variety of different attitudes toward their own activity. In the long run, the attitudes interfere with the activity, transforming it into something it was not before. This takes place in the maturing skeptic according to Sextus.

---

[3] The exclusion of the admitted possibility of error in knowledge claims goes back to Plato and Aristotle. See my *Scepticism* (London: Routledge & Kegan Paul, 1968), p. 77n.

[4] For affirmation of truth, Sextus mainly uses the term *apophasis*; for utterances such as exclamations, he uses *phoné*, "sound." It is an uncommitted word that largely leaves open the *kind* of meaning, whether propositional or performatory.

[5] See *Outlines of Pyrrhonism*, book I, chap. 23, and my *Scepticism*, p. 10. The skeptic is said to report things 'as a chronicler,' to report what strikes him at the moment without reflecting upon truth or falsity. This way of characterization is misleading today because a chronicler *is* generally supposed to tell what is true. The Greek expression is *historikos apangellomen*. The latter term may be interpreted in the direction of uttering something as indicative of one's mind, giving vent to a feeling or attitude or unreflective belief.

[6] The skeptic deliberately 'talks loosely,' according to Sextus, because otherwise the dogmatist misunderstands his pretensions. The skeptic does not pretend to have a definite conceptual framework within which he conceives his own skepticism. See my *Scepticism*, p. 10.

The skeptical exclamations in the terminology of Sextus are utterances indicative of something quasi-permanent, a disposition acquired through prolonged development. At this point Pyrrhonian biographies are relevant: one can begin to understand the historical background of the Pyrrhonian existential attitude. To the biographies belong the seeking and not finding, the frustrated primary need of a total view or at least a life philosophy with evidently true premises. Then comes the peace of mind in spite of not finding and, characteristically, linked to a continuing search. The peace is already there. *But human beings (like rats and some other mammals) seem also to engage in seeking as an autotelic engagement.*

As a classification unit in philosophy, Pyrrhonism is an ideal-typical construction which includes systematized attitudes toward every position in logic, methodology, ontology, epistemology, and other branches of philosophy; and one of ad hoc *epoché* as regards truth, reflecting a more or less complicated *pro et contra* argumentation, depending upon the current beliefs of dogmatists.

Superficial critics have charged Sextus Empiricus with repetitiousness and unnecessary argumentation, such as against p when p implies q, and he has already argued against q. But, clearly, Sextus does not adhere to any definite organon of inference and implication, and, in principle, he has to visit every corner of every dogmatic philosophy. He cannot eliminate any of them with generalities as a dogmatic skeptic or 'academician.' And just as clearly, a systematic Pyrrhonian exposition contains arguments in favor of each dogmatic philosophy. To every dogmatic con-argument, at least one Pyrrhonic pro-argument will correspond. Only at a distance has Pyrrhonism a negativist coloration.

According to the Pyrrhonian, adequate expositions of arguments do not add up to a decision of "true" or a decision of "false." But because new arguments appear from time to time among dogmatists as well as among Pyrrhonian seekers, and because memory is fallible, no exposition can be classified as 'authorized.'

The exposition of argumentations on all philosophical subjects *and* the pronouncement of a general lack of decisive arguments *and*, perhaps, the pronouncement of the 'skeptical way' (*agogé*) as one that leads to happiness, characterize Pyrrhonism. I say "perhaps" because one might wish to take the latter pronouncement as part of an inducement to learn about Pyrrhonism rather than as part of it. Sextus tends to the latter view in his famous genetic definition.

If we exclude Pyrrhonism as a philosophy we shall have to exclude a long list of philosophies that traditionally are conceived to be such, and that fail only to satisfy the arbitrary postulate that a philosophy must contain at least one proposition claimed to be definitely and definitively true.

But even if we exclude Pyrrhonism as a philosophy, that does not imply that the Pyrrhonian is not a philosopher. A philosopher may be always 'on the way' (emergent, *geworfen*), and may therefore transcend any classification. The Pyrrhonian is always on the way when working out and testing positions, looking for one that will satisfy the criteria of truth, or criteria of these criteria, or

questions of still higher metalevels. The way in which he is 'on the way' characterizes him just as deeply and consistently as Kantianism may characterize a
non-skeptical personality.

Pyrrhonians Incline toward Absolutistic Concepts of Truth, but not toward Absolutistic Requirements of Grounds for Action

From the point of view of ordinary language, it may be asked whether the
Pyrrhonian does not make *pointless* requirements of decisiveness. Does he
really have any idea of what he requires? Could he specify kinds of evidence that,
if at hand, would show the truth of a proposition? If the requirements he poses
never are realized, why pose them anyway?

The answer to this seems to be that there are different kinds of decisiveness.
If I have a choice between *A* and *B*, I may *decide* to choose *A* on grounds different from those of believing in certain truths. The Pyrrhonian may be a rapid
chooser, known for his trusting and benevolent attitude. But he *does* have ideas
about truth that are such that no one is *guaranteed* to find it even after a long,
laborious search or series of deep intuitions. The idea of truth is important for
him, and he does not give it up easily. He does not say: "Well, I did not find a
single argument decisive all last year, so why not just take at least 5 percent
probability to be decisive next year?" Nor does he predict with certainty that the
requirements will *never* be realized. Nor does he pretend that his idea of truth
amounts to a definite concept of truth.[7]

One crucial point is this: he finds arguments *not good enough* so far.
Charged with the contention that he poses extravagant requirements, he neither
denies or admits the charge but listens to the arguments for the contention. They
have so far been vaguely circular: the requirements 'must' somehow be too severe
since they are satisfied by hardly any arguments. But if one eats five cakes and
finds that *all* taste bad, this does not make the decision "bad" pointless. Even if
one cannot define clearly what is lacking in flavor, it makes sense to refuse to eat
them and to wait for cake no. 6—as long as one is not overly hungry. If no. 6
tastes bad, but one eats it, one has not lowered the requirements of goodness but
of acceptance. The skeptic feels that he might accept an argument as pragmati-
cally conclusive, deciding to act upon it, but not necessarily as decisive for *truth*.

Does the Pyrrhonian really retain an absolutistic concept of truth which is

---

[7] In defending Sextus' way (*agoge*-way, not doctrine), it is important to use a distinction
such as that between an idea or notion and a (fairly precise) concept. The arguments used by
Sextus against holding evident or trivial sentences such as "There are men" rely heavily on
requests for definitions of "man" or other crucial terms in the proposed 'truths.' He may be
said to ask for a conceptualization of "There are men" such that it is made into a theoretical
proposition constituted (*konstituiert*) within a definite conceptual frame. Sextus tends not to
hold back positive reaction to what 'seems so,' what 'seems evident,' but starts reflecting when
utterances are taken to express true or false propositions.

artificially separated from concepts of validity, evidence, verification, reasonableness, and tenability?

There are certain reasons to suppose this is the case. According to Sextus Empiricus, Pyrrhonism does not exclude trust and confidence. But is this not to believe in truths, at least in an unsophisticated way?

To believe strongly and consistently that so and so, to be confident and trust that so and so, seems somehow to be consistent, according to Pyrrhonism, with an attitude of *epoché* toward the truth of so and so.

The exclamation "There are no decisive arguments for or against the truth of any proposition!" refers also to propositions of the kind "*A* is more probable than non-*A*." Otherwise it would be probabilism, not Pyrrhonism. The attitude of trust and confidence cannot therefore be due to the attribution of higher probability to *A* than to non-*A*, or vice versa.

One would expect that lack of decisive arguments for or against truth would diminish decisive action and increase mistrust, lack of confidence, vaccilation, and doubt. According to Pyrrhonism, this is not necessary; and I think it *is* a removal of the notion of truth from certain other notions that makes decisiveness in action compatible with *isosthenia*.

First, "*X* is true" is taken in Pyrrhonism to be synonymous with "It is the case that *x*"—an ontological notion in principle separated from any process of verification or falsification. Second, the claim "to know that *x*" is emphatically identified with a certain kind of claim of incorrigibility: "I know that *x*, but possibly *x* is false" and "It is known that *x*, but possibly it is not the case that *x*" are rejected. "*X* is possibly false, therefore I do not know that *x*" is accepted. The Pyrrhonian trusts that the claim "*X* is true" is made with consciousness of its implied postulate of incorrigibility.[8]

This *awareness* of incorrigibility separates Pyrrhonian use (and absence of use) of the term "true" from that of everyday life. It makes it understandable that terms with explicit reference to belief attitudes are preferred: "I believe that *x* is true," "I believe that *x* is the case," "I feel confident that *x*," "I trust that *x*."

Even the following expressions might well be used: "I trust that *x* is true," "I am confident that *x* is true," "I am convinced that *x* is true." These expressions would be used *angelikos*, expressive of one's mind. Thus one would not blindly accept inferences of these kinds:

Premise: I am confident that *x* is true

Conclusion: *x* is true

Premise: I am convinced that *x* is the case

Conclusion: *x* is the case.

[8] Detailed discussion of incorrigibility is to be found in my *Scepticism*, pp. 136–51.

The Pyrrhonian's Openness in Debates about His Own Presuppositions

According to Aristotle, true statements are statements which say about that which is the case (*esti*) that it is the case, and false statements are those which say about that which is not the case that it is the case. If it is the case that *p*, it *cannot* also be the case that not-*p*.

Suppose a person who is considered a Pyrrhonian is entangled in a discussion on the notion of truth and ends up adhering to a definitely absolutist, non-pragmatic, non-voluntaristic concept of truth such as that introduced by Aristotle. His stand may then be expressed by propositions with truth claim, and he would presumably accept as decisive certain pro-arguments for the truth of propositions, of the following kind for instance, "What follows is an adequate definition of truth . . ."

However, such a development from the Pyrrhonian to the dogmatic posture is most surprising, considering the confusing controversies about truth among dogmatists. What a blind will to believe must be required for someone to settle down with any *definitive* conclusions in this foggy field!

In the middle nineteen thirties there was a strong belief that Alfred Tarski[9] had given an adequate definition of truth and solved an old problem, but subsequent discussion has left the matter in the air. Exactly *what* does Tarski solve? No clear answer has been given. His definition is said to be adequate, but it is admitted that one requirement of adequacy is some sort of agreement with ordinary use. There is, however, no agreement as to how one decides which use is ordinary. Even if the Pyrrhonian must be expected to interest himself vividly in the possibility that he somehow presupposes a non-pragmatic, absolutist notion of truth, his very openness to various approaches in contemporary discussion has so far frustrated his efforts to find decisive arguments.

In general, the Pyrrhonian today, perhaps more than at the time of Sextus Empiricus, will stress an argument against dogmatists who say that the very attitudes and the questions involved in ordinary debate *presuppose* the acceptance of certain propositions *as true* and therefore presuppose at least one decisive argument. The trend of increased belief in transcendental philosophy has made the maxim "There *must* be fundamental presuppositions!" more influential. But when concrete instances are offered, they seem to be dependent on specific approaches in the philosophy of language and epistemology that are controversial, since they lack decisive empirical and intuitive support. At best, they are research programs. Therefore, I do not see how the Pyrrhonian could easily be converted into a dogmatist by prolonged discussions of epistemological presuppositions. Quite on the contrary. Discussions of such presuppositions tend to promote skepticism.

---

[9] In his first publications, Tarski proclaims that his conceptual construction is adequate in relation to what "true" ordinarily means, that it is '*sachlich richtig.*' But no empirical investigation had been made. The data I gathered in the nineteen thirties confirmed his hypotheses in only about 70 percent of the cases, and then only when adopting several non-intuitive auxiliary hypotheses.

Furthermore, the way from the discovery and clarification of a presupposition to its acceptance in the form of a true proposition is long. The form of rule, postulate, norm, or the like is more likely to be adequate. But the Pyrrhonian is still without truth claims.

A Whole Doctrine or Philosophy Is Postulational if There Is at least One Postulate at Its Foundation

In general, if the verification of a body of beliefs presupposes the acceptance of at least one rule or postulate among a group of conflicting ones, the whole body of propositions corresponding to the beliefs acquires postulational or regulative status. At best, our conclusion will be of the form "The propositions are true if the postulate or rule is accepted." From this alone, "The propositions are true" does not follow.

No Proposition Is Neutral toward a System. Is Grass Really Green?

This brings us to the crucial point of this article: the relevance of systems to Pyrrhonism. Among professional philosophers today there are of course many attitudes toward philosophical systems. My own point of view (stated elsewhere) is highly positive, because I consider the autonomy of the sciences and that of so-called common sense to be an illusion. I understand a full systematic philosophy to be a synthesis of a logic, a methodology, an ontology, an epistemology, a philosophy of history, an axiology and (normative) ethics. To *publish* in all these fields is of course a hazardous undertaking, but I take it to be normal among philosophers to have or *seek* such a synthesis. A philosophy in this sense interacts with one's way of seeing and experiencing life, the universe, and oneself.

The distinction between 'in itself' and 'in something else' (*in se, in alio*) is fundamental in Spinoza's system.[10] Substance, cause, freedom, wisdom, joy, passion, goodness, perfection, slavery, democracy—all are conceived in terms of distinction. It colors the perception of everything and therefore makes an impact upon the meaning of any proposition in the system. A follower of Spinoza is therefore more easily exposed to skepticism: it is enough to doubt the meaningfulness of the fundamental distinction. Belief in systems favors the emergence of skepticism.

Let us for a moment return to the opening quotation from Sextus Empiricus. Skeptics and dogmatists are there defined *only* in relation to "what is sought in philosophy." If questions of science or common sense were independent of philosophical questions, therefore, Pyrrhonism would be a partial skepticism, on

[10] For some detailed arguments, see my "Freedom, Emotion, and Self-Subsistence," *Inquiry*, vol. 12, no. 1 (1969).

a par with religious or historical skepticism. The idea of systems in which every question is placed in a conceptual framework, and of the explicitness of fundamental assumptions and postulates which therefore are required, enlarges partial skepticism into total.

I do not see that *any proposition whatsoever* can be completely neutral toward differences in systems, and this makes a genuine seeker of a system normally indecisive with regard to the truth value of any proposition.

Exceptions are vulgarities such as "grass is green"—expressive, perhaps, of the kind of dumbness, sluggishness, or conventionality of perception of which painters and other artists try more or less in vain to cure us. If taken seriously as propositions, such formulas become non-neutral toward conceptual frameworks and therefore toward differences in philosophical systems.

Sextus' stock example is not "grass is green" but "honey is sweet." It is his contention, as I understand him, that efforts to conceptualize this utterance soon meet the formidable question of whether the sweetness is in the honey or not.[11] The problem area of secondary and tertiary qualities is relevant, and here evidence is scarce and meaning obscure.

When a person affirms that he is a logical empiricist, a liberal, and an admirer of Beckett, he does not mean to say that in his mind there is every second a recognizable manifestation of logical empiricism, liberalism, and admiration of Beckett. Most people would agree to this. But if somebody tentatively affirms that he might be a philosophic skeptic, there tends to be an immediate outcry: insincere! pointless! inconsistent!, or the requirement is laid down that he must then doubt *everything at once*—not assume, presume, trust, or believe anything even for a split second. (Cf.: "Now you are just eating fish. But if, as you say, you are an admirer of Beckett's, *turn on immediately* and stop doing anything else!") What is characteristic of a Pyrrhonian, however, is a disposition, a structure of traits that manifests itself in the long run, not a split-second reaction. This colors, for example, his assumptions; these acquire the character of posits, not assertions with truth claim. In order to assess a truth claim that involves a whole system, the Pyrrhonian must let himself sink deeply into it. This requires time and an openness that is inconsistent with a continuous flow of doubt, vaccilation, and counterargumentation running through his mind. One may hear a dogmatist say, "He is supposed to be a skeptic, but he has been arguing enthusiastically in favor of Heraclitus all year!" It is of course suspicious to act like this for a whole year. The long time it takes to manifest a skeptical pattern of thought makes it always relevant to ask, as colleagues of skeptics have done since Pyrrho: Is he not really a Heraclitean, or an empiricist or . . . ? But trying to balance argument *pro et con* every minute is bad research heuristic. Nothing decisive can be inferred from temporary imbalances.

---

[11] See, for instance, *Outlines of Pyrrhonism*, book I, chap. 7 and 10.

Tentative Conclusions

1. Pyrrhonism as a personal philosophy is neither inconsistent nor psychologically impossible.

2. A Pyrrhonian undertaking a systematic inquiry assumes, presupposes, and uses postulates, but he does not assume the truth of any proposition. He posits, takes for granted until further notice, and acts upon 'natural, spontaneous beliefs,' but does not affirm, or feel inclined to affirm, any truths. Among his spontaneous beliefs there are some on the metalevel concerning notions of truth.

3. He does not 'resist' what seems obvious at the moment, but finds it difficult to decide for or against as soon as an utterance is made more precise by means of a set of conceptual distinctions.

4. One may speak of a Pyrrhonian attitude in a psychological sense, but it is not to be identified with doubt. There is also a searching *Einstellung*, way of being, of existential import, and which as a personal philosophy transcends the mere psychological, just as Kantianism or any other philosophy that a person 'has.'

5. A philosophy, insofar as it tends toward a total view, colors everything. Therefore, indecision with regard to its truth is an indecision as to truth value in general. One kind of genesis of a Pyrrhonian may therefore be that of a seeker who, after having delved deeply into two different possibilities of total views, finds arguments for or against in part indecisive, in part irrelevant.

Jan Berg

Bolzano's Theory of an Ideal Language

1. INTRODUCTION

In his logical inquiries Bolzano employed a partly formalized language embracing an ordinary language extended by constants, variables, and certain technical expressions. In the second volume of the *Wissenschaftslehre*[1] he investigated the relations of this semiformalized philosophical language to colloquial language (*WL*, sections 127–46, 169–84). He believed that all sentences of colloquial language were 'reducible' to sentences of certain canonical forms expressed in the philosophical language. These canonical sentences were said to mirror their corresponding propositions in the sharpest way.

Had Bolzano's theory of reduction been completely developed it might have resulted in the construction of an ideal language for philosophical analysis. In this ideal language, however, sentences of canonical form would not play quite the same role as the atomic sentence forms on the basis of which more complex forms are built up in modern quantification theory. It seems, on the contrary, that Bolzano intended even the most complicated sentences to have canonical forms or to be reducible to sentences having such form.

This paper attempts a reconstruction of an extensional Bolzanian ideal language on the level of elementary logic. After some preliminary explanations of fundamental notions in Bolzano's logic, the main points of his theory of reduction of sentences are described. Two principles that determine the construction of an elementary Bolzanian ideal language emerge from the exposition. We then move toward building such a language and begin by modifying the standard representation of elementary logic, replacing the universal and existential quantifiers by Hilbert's ϵ-operator. By further modi-

---

Professor Berg, of the Munich Institute of Technology, is a native of Sweden.
[1] B. Bolzano, *Wissenschaftslehre,* vols. 1–4 (Sulzbach: Seidel, 1837; hereafter cited as *WL*).

fications of both the syntax and the underlying semantics, a logical language satisfying the two principles is obtained.

2. Concepts and Attributes

The notion of abstract non-linguistic proposition (*Satz an sich*) is central in Bolzano's philosophy. A proposition in Bolzano's sense is a structure of concepts; hence a concept (*Vorstellung an sich*) is a part of a proposition but is not itself a proposition. To enable the generation of propositions, however, concepts have to be characterizable independently of propositions. This stipulation is to be found implicitly in Bolzano. He worked extensively with a relation—let us symbolize it here by "Σ"—which corresponds to the relation of being a member of the extension of a concept. In terms of this relation Σ, taken as a primitive by Bolzano, certain implicit postulates concerning the existence and general properties of concepts can be extracted from his writings.[2]

Bolzano elaborated a special theory for a large set of cases where a concept comes under another, second-order concept. For example, according to Bolzano, the sentence obtained by inserting an expression for a particular concept A in place of "X" in

(1)   "X is omniscient,"

would, under a reduction to canonical form, be an elliptical formulation of a sentence of the following form:

(2)   "X is something which has omniscience."

The concept of being something which has omniscience is a so-called concrete concept (*concrete Vorstellung; WL*, section 60). From this concept one can derive a corresponding 'abstract' concept (*abstracte Vorstellung*) of omniscience, thereby obtaining the sentence form:

(3)   "X has omniscience,"

and the corresponding proposition:

(4)   A has omniscience.

The concept expressed by the word "omniscience" is a singular concept of a certain attribute (*Beschaffenheit; WL*, section 80) of being omniscient which has the relation Σ to the second-order concept of omniscience. This attribute, in turn, could usually be analyzed into other attributes. Now, to every 'abstract' concept b of an attribute B' such that B'Σb, there is a 'concrete' concept B with respect to b which is coextensive with B'. The situation could be schematized as follows:

---

[2] J. Berg, *Bolzano's Logic* (Stockholm: Almquist & Wiksell, 1962); "Bolzano als Logiker," *Sitzungsberichte der Österreichischen Akademie der Wissenschaften,* Philosophisch-historische Klasse, vol. 252, essay 5 (1967), pp. 95–120.

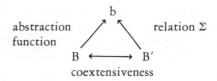

coextensiveness

In Bolzano's theory, logical constants such as 'something' and 'nothing' fall outside of this scheme. For example: on the one hand, the concept of 'something' cannot be analyzed as the concept of being identical with something that has a certain attribute, and, on the other hand, it is not an 'abstract' concept since no attribute comes under it. Bolzano even considered individual concepts, such as the concept of Socrates, as being neither 'abstract' nor 'concrete.'

Incidentally, it appears that Bolzano's attributes correspond uniquely to concepts of classes and relations. Theoretically, then, Bolzano's notion of attribute is a redundant part of his ontology.

3. The Reduction of Sentences

When Bolzano speaks of reducibility, he uses phrases such as "*auf einen Ausdruck zurückführen*" (cf. *WL*, 2: 56) or "*heisst wesentlich nichts Anderes als*" (*WL*, 2: 214). The criterion of adequacy of such reductions would seem to be that the sentences be synonymous in the sense of expressing the same proposition (*WL*, 2: 9).

In Bolzano's theory of an ideal language, all sentences of ordinary language are reducible to sentences obtained by inserting expressions for particular (singular or general) concepts for "A" and expressions of particular 'abstract' concepts having an attribute as the sole member of their extensions for "b" in one of the following two expressions:

(i) "A has b,"
(ii) "A has lack-of-b"

(*WL*, sections 127, 136). Here the substituend of "b" is also correlated with another, 'concrete' concept B (cf. *WL*, section 2).

In a formalization of Bolzano's ideal language, the vocabulary would include as predicates both substituends of "b" and corresponding instances of "lack-of-b" in (i) and (ii), respectively. Hence the contradictory of a sentence of the form of (i) is not a sentence of the form of (ii) but another sentence of the form of (i), namely

(iii) "Prop(i) has falsity,"

where Prop(i) is the concept of the proposition expressed by the particular instance of (i) (*WL*, 2: 269).

We shall give a few examples of Bolzano's application of his theory of reduction to ordinary language.[3] Sentences obtained by inserting a particular

---

[3] Berg, *Bolzano's Logic*, pp. 55–56.

expression of a concept for "A" in "There is an A" and "Nothing is an A" are reducible to sentences of the canonical forms of "A has non-emptiness" and "A has emptiness," respectively (*WL*, sections 137, 170). A sentence of the form of "All A are B" is reducible to a canonical sentence of the form of (i), where the substituend of "b" indicates the 'abstract' concept correlated to the substituend of "B" (*Anmerkung; WL*, section 225).

As pointed out in the introduction, Bolzano apparently intended all sentences to have canonical forms or to be reducible to such sentences. Hence, as the *first principle* for the construction of an elementary Bolzanian ideal language, we propose the requirement:

(R 1)   to construct a language $\mathcal{L}^*$ of elementary logic in which all expressions are of the form of an application of an *n*-ary function symbol to *n* arguments ($n = 0, 1, 2, \ldots$).

4. EMPTY TERMS AND PROPOSITIONS

The notion of truth is defined by Bolzano for propositions corresponding to sentences of the canonical forms of (i) and (ii) of the preceding section substantially as follows (*WL*, 1: 108 ff.):

(i$^+$)   Prop(i) is true if and only if each member of the extension of A is a member of the extension of b's extension,

(ii$^+$)   Prop(ii) is true if and only if each member of the extension of A is a member of the complement of the extension of b's extension,

where *A* and *b* are indicated by the substituends of "A" and "b," respectively. Bolzano apparently presupposes that the set of sentences of colloquial language and of his own philosophical language could be mapped into the set of propositions, so that an indirect definition of truth for these sentences would be forthcoming.

Bolzano elaborates his theory of reduction by imposing a necessary condition for the truth of sentences of the forms of (i) and (ii) in section 2. If A is non-empty (*gegenständlich; WL*, 1: 297–98), i.e., if there is at least one member of the extension of A, then Prop(i) and Prop(ii) are also said to be non-empty; and if A is empty (*gegenstandlos*), i.e., if there is no member of the extension of A, then Prop(i) and Prop(ii) are said to be empty (*WL*, section 146). Now, if Prop(i) is true or Prop(ii) is-true, then A is non-empty (*WL*, section 225.4). Hence if A is empty, both Prop(i) and Prop(ii) are false (*WL*, section 234.3). Since the entity indicated by the substituend of "A" in (i) and (ii) can be a class concept, Bolzano's condition implies the existential interpretation of classical syllogistic. Curious as it may seem, the very same condition shows that Bolzano was heading substantially for a philosophical language without existence assumptions (cf. section 6).

Thus all propositions are true or false. Furthermore, the following form of the law of contradiction:

Prop(i) and Prop(ii) are not both false,

is valid even for empty propositions (cf. (iii) of section 3). In the case of certain propositions ascribing properties such as emptiness or simplicity to concepts, the adaptation to the law of contradiction is made along other lines.[4]

As *second principle* for the construction of an elementary Bolzanian ideal language we therefore propose the requirement:

(R 2)   to construct a language $\mathcal{L}^*$, satisfying (R 1) of section 3, such that if f is a predicative function symbol of $\mathcal{L}^*$ and the term t_i of $\mathcal{L}^*$ is empty under an interpretation J of $\mathcal{L}^*$ for a particular $i = 1, \ldots, n$, then $f(t_1, \ldots, t_n)$ is false under J. (f is a predicative function symbol of $\mathcal{L}^*$ if f corresponds to a predicate of L* under a suitable mapping; cf. section 8.)

5. Elementary Logic with ϵ-Operator

As a preliminary step toward the formulation of an elementary Bolzanian ideal language, we now construct a language L of two-valued first-order predicate logic with identity and ϵ-operator. The vocabulary of L consists of the following symbol shapes: "(," ")," "$\neg$," (denial), "$\wedge$" (conjunction), "$\equiv$" (identity), "ϵ" (choice), and a denumerable number of n-ary function variables and predicates ($n = 0, 1, 2, \ldots$). Nullary function variables are also called *individual variables*. In the metalanguage we shall use "$=$" for identity, "$\in$" for membership, "$\subset$" for inclusion, "$\sim$" for difference, and "$\emptyset$" for the empty set.

The set of *terms* of L embraces all individual variables and all symbol combinations of the following two forms:

(1) $f(t_1, \ldots, t_n)$, where $t_1, \ldots, t_n$ are terms of L and f is an n-ary function variable;
(2) $\epsilon x(F)$, where x is a (bound) individual variable and F is a formula of L (to be defined shortly).

No other symbol combinations are terms of L.

The *atomic formulas* of L are of the following form:

$$P(t_1, \ldots, t_n),$$

where $t_1, \ldots, t_n$ are terms of L and P is an n-ary predicate. In particular, an atomic formula containing the identity symbol is of the form:

$$\equiv (t_1, t_2).$$

The set of *formulas* of L is the intersection of all sets Φ containing all atomic formulas of L and containing $\neg(F)$ and $\wedge(F, G)$ if $F, G \in \Phi$.

A term of the form $\epsilon x(F)$ may be expressed in ordinary language as "a representative object x such that F holds." We shall assume that substitution

[4] *Ibid.*, p. 54.

of *t* for free occurrences of *x* in *F*, yielding $F(t/x)$, will always be possible (by rewriting bound variables). The usual existential and universal quantifiers can then be introduced into L by definition:[5]

$$\exists x F = \text{def. } F[\epsilon x(F)/x],$$
$$\forall x F = \text{def. } F\{\epsilon x[\neg (F)]/x\}.$$

We take a *domain* D of individuals as a non-empty set. We shall need a *choice operator* σ over D such that $\sigma(K) \in K$ for non-empty $K \subset D$ (moreover, $\sigma(\varnothing) = \sigma(D)$). In general, the notation "D^K" will be employed to denote the set of functions from the set K into the domain *D*. In particular, if N is the initial *n*-member segment of the natural numbers, "D^N" denotes the set of ordered *n*-tuples $\langle x_1, \ldots, x_n \rangle$ such that $x_i \in D$ ($i = 1, \ldots, n$).

An (extensional) *interpretation* of L over a domain D with respect to a choice operator σ is a unary operator J, defined for terms *t* and *n*-ary function variables *f* and predicates *P* of L, such that:

$$J(x) \in D, \text{ where } x \text{ is an individual variable;}$$
$$J(f) \in D^{D^N}, \text{ i.e., a function from } D^N \text{ into D;}$$
$$J(f(t_1, \ldots, t_n)) = J(f)(J(t_1), \ldots, J(t_n)); \text{ and}$$
$$J(P) \subset D^N.$$

(The value of $J[\epsilon x(F)]$ will be provided after the statement of some intermediate definitions.)

By a *realization* of L we understand an ordered triple $\langle D, J, \sigma \rangle$ such that D is a domain and J is an interpretation over D with respect to σ, which is a choice operator over D. The notion of *satisfaction* ("Sat") is that binary relation between formulas of L and realizations R = $\langle D, J, \sigma \rangle$ of L which always fulfills the following recursive conditions (hereafter "iff" means if and only if):

$$\text{Sat } [\equiv (t_1, t_2), R] \text{ iff } J(t_1) = J(t_2);$$
$$\text{Sat } [P(t_1, \ldots, t_n), R] \text{ iff } \langle J(t_1), \ldots, J(t_n) \rangle \in J(P);$$
$$\text{Sat } [\neg (F), R] \text{ iff not Sat } (F, R);$$
$$\text{Sat } (\wedge (F, G), R) \text{ iff Sat } (F, R) \text{ and Sat } (G, R).$$

We shall employ the notation "$J' = {}_x J$" to indicate that $J'(P) = J(P)$, $J'(f) = J(f)$, and $J'(y) = J(y)$ for all individual variables $y \neq x$. We can now complete the description of the operator J by stating that:

$$J[\epsilon x(F)] = \sigma(\{w : J'(x) = w \text{ and Sat } (F, \langle D, J', \sigma \rangle), \text{ for some } J' = {}_x J\}).$$

(The first semantic interpretation of the ϵ-operator appeared in Asser.)[6]

If Γ is a set of formulas of L, then Sat (Γ, R) holds iff Sat (F, R) holds for all $F \in \Gamma$. We then say that F is a *logical consequence* of Γ or *follows from* Γ ('$\Gamma \Rightarrow F$') if Sat (F, R) whenever Sat (Γ, R), for all realizations R of L. If $\varnothing \Rightarrow F$, then F is said to be *valid*.

    [5] D. Hilbert and P. Bernays, *Grundlagen der Mathematik*, vol. 2 (Berlin: Springer, 1939).
    [6] G. Asser, "Theorie der logischen Auswahlfunktionen," *Zeitschrift für mathematische Logik und Grundlagen der Mathematik* 3: 30–68 (1957).

6. A LANGUAGE L* WITH EXISTENCE PREDICATE

In L the formula:

$$\equiv \{\epsilon y[\equiv (y,\, t)],\, t\}$$

is valid. Hence incorporating an existence predicate "e" into L would be pointless, since "e" would be applicable to all terms. If we want to be able to interpret a language similar to L in the empty set, however, we can take a domain D as a non-empty set always including some objects, the existence of which is not guaranteed. Within D the set D_e of *existing* individuals is delimited, and in distinction to the domains of L, the domain D_e may be empty.

As an intermediate step toward the construction of a Bolzanian ideal language, we shall consider a modified language L* of elementary logic with ϵ-operator and a non-trivial existence predicate. The vocabulary of L* embraces that of L and, moreover, the unary predicate "e" (as an abbreviation for "exists"). Hence an atomic formula of L* containing the existence predicate is of the form: $e(t)$.

Now, various ways are open for constructing logics without existence assumptions. Elegant syntactic-semantic systems of this kind, building on an elementary logic with ordinary quantifiers, have been propounded by Cocchiarella and Scott.[7] In order to fulfill the second principle for the construction of an elementary Bolzanian ideal language, however, the semantics of L* will be set up in such a manner that the following two formulas are valid $(i = 1, \ldots, n)$:

(1) $P(t_1, \ldots, t_n) \rightarrow e(t_i)$,

(2) $e[f(t_1, \ldots, t_n)] \rightarrow e(t_i)$,

where $F \rightarrow G$ abbreviates $\neg \{ \wedge [F, \neg (G)] \}$. Deduction rules corresponding to these formulas are introduced and treated systematically in connection with soundness and completeness proofs by Schock.[8] As far as I know, Bolzano was the first philosopher to propound explicitly a rule corresponding to (1) (cf. section 4). Considerations similar in part to Bolzano's emerge (independently, it seems) in Katz.[9] Katz essentially adds to (1), though, the assumption:

(3) $\neg [P(t_1, \ldots, t_n)] \rightarrow e(t_i)$,

with the consequence that all empty terms are excluded from a "genuine synthetic sentence."

[7] N. Cocchiarella, "A Logic of Actual and Possible Objects" [abstract], *Journal of Symbolic Logic* 31: 688–89 (1966); D. Scott, "Existence and Description in Formal Logic," in *Bertrand Russell, Philosopher of the Century*, ed. R. Schoenmann (London: Allen & Unwin, 1967), pp. 181–200.

[8] R. Schock, "Contributions to Syntax, Semantics, and the Philosophy of Science," *Notre Dame Journal of Formal Logic* 5: 241–89 (1964).

[9] J. Katz, *The Philosophy of Language* (New York: Harper & Row, 1966), p. 214.

An *interpretation* of L* over $\langle D, D_e \rangle$ with respect to a choice operator σ is a unary operator J, defined for terms t and n-ary function variables f and predicates P of L*, such that:

$J(x) \in D_e$, where $D_e \neq \varnothing$;

$J(f) \in D^{D^N}$, where the cardinality of $N \geq 1$;

$J(f) \in D_e^K$ only if $K \subset D_e^N$;

$J[f(t_1, \ldots, t_n)] = J(f)[J(t_1), \ldots, J(t_n)]$;

$J(P) \subset D^N$, in particular

$J(\text{'e'}) = D_e$.

(The value of $J[\epsilon x(F)]$ will be given shortly.)

By a *realization* of L* we shall understand an ordered quadruple $\langle D, D_e, J, \sigma \rangle$ such that D_e is a proper subset of the domain D and J is an interpretation over D_e with respect to σ, which is a *choice operator* over $\langle D, D_e \rangle$ such that $\sigma(K) \in K$ for non-empty $K \subset D$ (moreover, $\sigma(\varnothing) = \sigma(D \sim D_e)$). The notion of *satisfaction* is then redefined with respect to the modified concept of realization and supplemented by the following clause:

Sat $[P(t_1, \ldots, t_n), \langle D, D_e, J, \sigma \rangle]$ only if $J(t_1), \ldots, J(t_n) \in D_e$.

Finally, the description of J is completed as follows:

$J[\epsilon x(F)]$

$\qquad = \sigma(\{w : J'(x) = w \text{ and Sat } (F, \langle D, D_e, J', \sigma \rangle), \text{ for some } J' = {}_{e,x}J\})$,

where "$J' = {}_{e,x}J$" means that $J'(P) = J(P), J'(f) = J(f)$ for n-ary f ($n = 1, 2, \ldots$), $J'(y) = J(y)$ for all $y \neq x$, and $J'(x) \in D_e$. Hence in L* the quantifier ranges over D_e only.

The passage from L to L* involves a modified notion of quantification. As a consequence, analogues of the existential and universal quantifiers of standard elementary logic are no longer available in L* along the lines described in section 5. For if $P(x)$, for instance, is satisfied for all existing values of the individual variable x under suitable interpretations of L*, then the term $\epsilon x\{\neg [P(x)]\}$ under those interpretations denotes a non-existent which cannot be mapped onto the value truth by the denotation of P. The fact that all members of D_e satisfy $P(x)$, however, can be construed in L* by saying that the representative of $\neg [P(x)]$ does not exist.

7. A LANGUAGE $\mathcal{L}^*$ FOR A LOGIC OF TERMS

We now complete the construction of an elementary Bolzanian ideal language by modifying L* into the language $\mathcal{L}^*$ of an elementary logic of terms. Under an interpretation J of L*, an n-ary predicate P of L* may be viewed as denoting a function that maps the sequence of denotations under J of the argument terms of P onto a truth value. First of all, then, the non-logical predicates are dropped from the vocabulary.[10] Furthermore, the

[10] Cf. H. Hermes, "Eine Termlogik mit Auswahloperator," in *Lecture Notes in Mathematics*, ed. A. Dold and B. Eckmann, vol. 6 (Berlin: Springer, 1965).

logical symbols "e" and "¬" are considered as unary function constants and the logical symbols "≡" and "∧" as binary function constants. As before, the individual variables are nullary function variables, and the context "ϵx" operates on terms. Among the function symbols, we shall distinguish between the predicative and the non-predicative; the two kinds will be referred to by the variables "ψ" and "φ," respectively.

The *terms* of $\mathcal{L}^*$ are of one of the following two forms:

(1) $f(t_1, \ldots, t_n)$, where $t_1, \ldots, t_n$ are terms of $\mathcal{L}^*$ and f is an n-ary function symbol $(n = 0, 1, 2, \ldots)$;

(2) $\epsilon x(t)$, where x is an individual variable and t is a term of $\mathcal{L}^*$.

By a *domain* we now understand a non-empty set D containing a proper subset D_e of *existents*. The set D_e in turn includes the set T, which is intended to represent the truth value *truth* and which is non-empty if D_e is non-empty.

An *interpretation* of $\mathcal{L}^*$ over $\langle D, D_e \rangle$ with respect to a choice operator σ is a unary operator J, defined for terms t and n-ary function symbols f, such that:

$J(x) \in D_e$, where $D_e \neq \varnothing$;

$J(f) \in D^{D^N}$, where the cardinality of N ≥ 1;

$J(\psi) \in T^K$ only if K $\subset D_e^N$, where ψ is a
    predicative function symbol of $\mathcal{L}^*$,

in particular,

(α) J("e") is a unary function over D, and J("e")(x) $\in$ T iff x $\in D_e$,

(β) J("≡") is a binary function over D, and J("≡")(x, y) $\in$ T iff
    x, y $\in D_e$ and x = y;

and furthermore,

(γ) J("¬") is a unary function over D, and J("¬")(x) $\in$ Y iff x $\notin$ T,

(δ) J("∧") is a binary function over D, and J("∧")(x, y) $\in$ T iff
    both x $\in$ T and y $\in$ T;

$J(\varphi) \in D_e^K$ only if K $\subset D_e^N$, where φ is a non-predicative function symbol of L*;

$J[f(t_1, \ldots, t_n)] = J(f)[J(t_1), \ldots, J(t_n)]$;

$J(\epsilon x(t)) = \sigma(\{w: J'(x) = w \text{ and } J'(t) \in T, \text{ for some } J' = {}_{e,x}J\})$.

By a *realization* of $\mathcal{L}^*$ we shall understand an ordered quintuple $\langle D, D_e, T, J, \sigma \rangle$ such that D is domain, D_e is a proper subset of D of existents, T is a subset of D_e, and J is an interpretation over $\langle D, D_e \rangle$ with respect to σ, which is a choice operator over $\langle D, D_e \rangle$. If Γ is a set of terms of $\mathcal{L}^*$, then $J(\Gamma) \in$ T iff $J(t) \in$ T for all $t \in \Gamma$. We then say that $\Gamma \Rightarrow t$, if $J(t) \in$ T whenever $J(\Gamma) \in$ T, for all realizations $\langle D, D_e, T, J, \sigma \rangle$ of $\mathcal{L}^*$. Finally, the term t is said to be valid if $\varnothing \Rightarrow t$.

8. The Relations between L* and $\mathcal{L}^*$

To study the relations between the two languages L* and $\mathcal{L}^*$ of elementary logic with a non-trivial existence predicate, we consider a one–one mapping $^\circ$ such that:

(1) f in L* corresponds to f^o in $\mathcal{L}^*$, where f and f^o are n-ary function variables and there is no f in L* such that f^o is "e," "¬," "≡," or "∧;"

(2) P in L* corresponds to P^o in $\mathcal{L}^*$, where P is an n-ary predicate and P^o is an n-ary function variable.

The mapping of formulas and terms can be defined recursively as follows:

(3) x^o is a nullary function variable;

(4) $[f(t_1, \ldots, t_n)]^o = f^o(t_1^o, \ldots, {}_n^o t)$;

(5) $[P(t_1, \ldots, t_n)]^o = P^o(t_1^o, \ldots, t_n^o)$,

in particular,

(6) $[e(t)]^o = e(t^o)$,

(7) $[\equiv(t_1, t_2)]^o = \equiv(t_1^o, t_2^o)$;

and furthermore:

(8) $[\neg(F)]^o = \neg(F^o)$;

(9) $[\wedge(F, G)]^o = \wedge(F^o, G^o)$;

(10) $[\epsilon x(F)]^o = \epsilon x^o(F^o)$.

Now suppose that we have the two realizations:

$$R = \langle D, D_e, J, \sigma \rangle \text{ of L*, and}$$
$$R^o = \langle D, D_e, T, J^o, \sigma \rangle \text{ of } \mathcal{L}^*.$$

Suppose further for all function symbols f and all predicates P that:

(11) $J^o(f^o) = J(f)$,

(12) $J^o(P^o)(x_1, \ldots, x_n) \in T$ iff $\langle x_1, \ldots, x_n \rangle \in J(P)$, for all $x_1, \ldots, x_n \in D$.

It can be shown by induction on the length of the terms and formulas of L* that:

(i) $J(t) = J^o(t^o)$, for all terms t of L*,

(ii) Sat (F, R) iff $J^o(F^o) \in T$, for all formulas F of L*.

The proof will be sketched only for formulas of L involving the logical constants "e" and "ε":

(a) Sat $[e(t), R]$ iff $J(t) \in D_e$

iff $J^o(t^o) \in D_e$, by the hypothesis of induction,

iff $J(\text{"e"})[J^o(t^o)] \in T$, by ($\alpha$) of section 6,

iff $J^o(\text{"e"})[J^o(t^o)] \in T$, by (11),

iff $J^o[e(t^o)] \in T$

iff $J^o\{[e(t)]^o\} \in T$, by (6).

(b) $J[\epsilon x(F)] = \sigma(\{w : J'(x) = w \text{ and Sat } (F, \langle D, D_e, J', \sigma \rangle))$, for some $J' = {}_{e,x}J\})$

$= \sigma(\{w : J'^o(x^o) = w \text{ and } J'^o(F^o) \in T$, for some $J'^o = {}_{e,x^o} J\})$, by the hypothesis of induction,

$$= \sigma(\{w : J\circ'(x^\circ) = w \text{ and } J\circ'(F^\circ) \in T, \text{ for some }$$
$$J\circ' =_{e,x^\circ} J\})$$
$$= J\circ[ex^\circ(F^\circ)]$$
$$= J\circ\{[ex(F)]^\circ\}, \text{ by (10)}.$$

Moreover, it can be shown that:

(iii) $\Gamma \Rightarrow F$ iff $\Gamma^\circ \Rightarrow F^\circ$.

To prove the implication from right to left, we assume Sat (Γ, R) for an arbitrary realization $R = \langle D, D_e, J, \sigma \rangle$ of L^*. Let $T \subset D_e$. Then there are functions $J("e")$, $J("\equiv")$, $J("\wedge")$, and $J("\neg")$ fulfilling (α) through (δ) of section 6. Put $J\circ("\equiv") = J("\equiv")$, $J\circ("e") = J("e")$, $J\circ("\wedge") = J("\wedge")$, and $J\circ("\neg") = J("\neg")$, and let (11) and (12) hold. $J\circ$ is chosen so that $\langle D, D_e, T, J\circ, \sigma \rangle$ is a realization of $\mathcal{L}^*$. Now $J\circ(\Gamma^\circ) \in T$ by (ii), and hence $J\circ(F^\circ) \in T$ under the assumption of $\Gamma^\circ \Rightarrow F^\circ$. Then Sat (F, R), and therefore $\Gamma \Rightarrow F$.

9. CONCLUDING REMARKS

It is possible to axiomatize the set of valid terms of $\mathcal{L}^*$ by constructing a calculus C with the soundness property (1) that all applications of the rules of C yield valid results and with the completeness property (2) that all valid terms of $\mathcal{L}^*$ are obtainable by applications of the rules of C.

The language $\mathcal{L}^*$ is our reconstruction of an elementary Bolzanian ideal language. We now have to explain the relations between $\mathcal{L}^*$ and the corresponding part of Bolzano's philosophical language.

A relation B, holding between the entities $A_1, \ldots, A_n$, is considered by Bolzano as an attribute of the sequence $\langle A_1, \ldots, A_n \rangle$, which therefore 'has' the 'abstract' concept b corresponding to B (*WL*, section 80). Now if the substituend of "A" in (i) of section 3 represents the sequence $\langle A_1, \ldots, A_n \rangle$ ($n = 1, 2, \ldots$), and if "A_1," $\ldots$, "A_n" and the substituend of "b" are translated into the terms $t_1, \ldots, t_n$ and the function symbol f of $\mathcal{L}^*$, respectively, then a sentence of the form of (i) of section 3 corresponds to the term $f(t_1, \ldots, t_n)$ in $\mathcal{L}^*$.

As suggested in section 3, predicates in Bolzano's language of the form of "lack-of-b" correspond to predicative function symbols in the basic vocabulary of $\mathcal{L}^*$. Furthermore, the particular predicates "non-emptiness" and "falsity" in Bolzano's language are rendered by the function constants "e" and "$\neg$" in $\mathcal{L}^*$, respectively. Regarding semantics, the truth of sentences in Bolzano's theory corresponds to membership in the set T of the realizations of $\mathcal{L}^*$.

Dagfinn Føllesdal

An Introduction to Phenomenology
for Analytic Philosophers

While philosophy in the English-speaking countries and in Scandinavia is largely analytic, phenomenology and existentialism prevail on the continent.

Phenomenologists and existentialists do not form sharply separated camps; one may find philosophers taking a variety of intermediate positions between phenomenology and existentialism, and both Heidegger and Sartre, to mention only two prominent existentialists, started out from phenomenology. Yet there appears to be a chasm between these philosophers and those of the analytic schools in England and the United States.

Phenomenology and existentialism have only very seldom managed to arouse the interest of analytic philosophers. And, conversely, analytic philosophy has been an almost closed world to phenomenologists and existentialists.

Though we should certainly not ignore the differences between the two camps, it would be a mistake to despair of communication altogether. Especially between analytic philosophy and *phenomenology*, mutual understandings, and perhaps even fruitful exchange, seems to be possible. And once this connection is established, phenomenology may in turn serve as a link of communication between analytic philosophy and existentialism.

In this paper, I shall try to present phenomenology in such a way as to clarify its connection with analytic philosophy on the one side and with existentialism on the other.

The very background of the man who created phenomenology, Edmund Husserl, leads one to suspect that phenomenology should demand some of the

Professor Føllesdal, of the University of Oslo, is a native of Norway.

This paper, in slightly different form, was read at the third in a series of five lectures on the varieties of contemporary philosophy at Harvard University in July, 1962. It was preceded by a lecture on linguistic philosophy by Professor Rogers Albritton and succeeded by a lecture on existentialism by Professor Asher Moore. I am grateful to Professor Henry D. Aiken and Dr. Alastair Hannay for several helpful comments.

qualities of precision and logical rigor that analytic philosophers tend to look for and relish.

Husserl, who was born in 1859 in Czechoslovakia and died in Freiburg, Germany, in 1938, began as a mathematician. He earned a Ph.D. in this subject and then worked for a short time as an assistant to his teacher Weierstrass, who was one of the foremost mathematicians of his time and a man whose discoveries in the foundations of mathematics led him to stress the importance of making one's terminology precise and one's presuppositions explicit. Even after Husserl turned to philosophy at the age of twenty-five, at the prompting of the scholastic-inspired Franz Brentano, it was by Bolzano and Frege, the two most important forerunners of analytic philosophy in the nineteenth century, that he was most decisively influenced.

Both Bolzano (1781–1848) and Frege (1848–1925) did their most important work in the foundations of logic and mathematics. Frege, probably the most important figure in logic since Aristotle, contributed much to the thought of Russell and Wittgenstein, who, together with G. E. Moore, are the founders of modern analytic philosophy in England. Husserl never met Frege, nor of course Bolzano, but he studied all that they published, and Frege wrote a critical review of Husserl's first book, *Philosophy of Arithmetic*.

Franz Brentano (1838–1917), under whom Husserl studied philosophy in Vienna after he had left mathematics, is important for phenomenology mainly because of his theory of 'intentionality.'

Characteristic of all mental activity, according to Brentano, is that it is directed toward something, intends something.

> Every mental phenomenon is characterized by what the scholastics in the Middle Ages called the intentional (and also mental) inexistence of an object, and what we could call, although in not entirely unambiguous terms, the reference to a content, a direction upon an object . . .[1]

Just as when we love, there is something that we love, so there is something that we sense when we sense, something we think of when we think, and so on. This may sound commonplace, but difficulties arise when we try to apply this principle to a person who has hallucinations, or a person who thinks of a centaur. Brentano held that even in these cases our mental activity, our thinking or our sensing, is directed towards some object. The directedness has nothing to do with the reality of the object, Brentano held. The object is itself contained in our mental activity, 'intentionally' contained in it. And Brentano defined mental phenomena as "phenomena which contain an object intentionally."

---

[1] Franz Brentano, *Psychologie vom empirischen Standpunkt*, vol. I, bk. 2, chap I (Leipzig: Duncker und Humblot, 1874), p. 85, reprinted in *Philosophische Bibliothek* (Hamburg: Felix Meiner, 1955, 1st ed., 1924). The quoted passage occurs on p. 85 of the first edition and on p. 124 of the *Philosophische Bibliothek* editions. It is here quoted from D. B. Terrell's English translation of this chapter in Roderick M. Chisholm, ed., *Realism and the Background of Phenomenology* (Glencoe, Ill.: The Free Press, 1960), p. 50.

Many of Brentano's students, among them Husserl, felt that the problems of intentionality were important. But they were dissatisfied with Brentano's proposed solution, which I have just sketched, namely, Brentano's principle that for every act there is an object toward which it is directed. They found it unclear, partly because it leads to the following dilemma: Let us consider a man who sees a tree. If we say that the object toward which his act of seeing is directed is the real tree in front of him, we shall have difficulties in explaining hallucinations. And if we modify our concept of what the object of an act is in such a way that we can say that hallucinating is also directed toward an object, we risk having to say that what we see when we see a tree is not the real tree in front of us, but something else that we would also have seen if we had had an hallucination.

These difficulties led one of Brentano's students, Meinong, to his *Gegenstandstheorie*, which, mainly through a series of reviews by Bertrand Russell, became influential for the so-called realist movement in England and the United States in the first twenty years of our century.

Husserl's way out of the difficulties, which shortly after the turn of the century led him to phenomenology, was to deny Brentano's principle that for every act there is an object toward which it is directed. But he nevertheless retained the basic intentionalist view that acts are directed.

In order to see how he did so, it will be helpful first to consider an idea that Frege set forth in his article "On Meaning and Reference" in 1892.[2] In this article, Frege introduced a distinction between a linguistic expression's *meaning* and its *reference*. Though this distinction is by no means the most important of Frege's many ideas, it is quite helpful in explaining what phenomenology is all about.

We shall approach the distinction by making use of one of Frege's own examples: The morning star is a bright star sometimes visible in the morning sky. The evening star sometimes appears in the evening sky. The astronomers of antiquity had already discovered that the morning star and the evening star are identical. "The morning star" and "the evening star," then, are two different names for a single celestial body, the planet Venus. The ancients had discovered that the two names had the same *reference*, in Frege's terminology. This was an astronomical discovery based on observation, not something that could be concluded from the two names "the morning star" and "the evening star," for these two names evidently have different *meanings*, illuminating different aspects of their common reference. The name "the morning star" indicates that its reference is a star visible in the morning, the name "the evening star" indicates that

---

2 "Über Sinn und Bedeutung," *Zeitschrift für Philosophie and philosophische Kritik* 100: 25–50 (1892). English translation: ("On Sense and Reference," in Frege, *Philosophical Writings*, ed. Peter Geach and Max Black (Oxford: Blackwell, 1952); and also as "On Sense and Nominatum," in Herbert Feigl and Wilfred Sellars, eds., *Readings in Philosophical Analysis* (New York: Appleton-Century-Crofts, 1949).

its reference is a star which can be seen in the evening. If we had complete knowledge of a reference, we could immediately decide whether a given meaning belonged to it. But, according to Frege, we shall never obtain such a complete knowledge of a reference, since we can never know an object in all its aspects.

Frege thus operated with a trichotomy of name, meaning, and reference. He found that this trichotomy shed light upon a difficulty which turns up in connection with the following central principle in logic, the so-called principle of substitutivity of identity:

> (P) If two names are names of the same object, they can be substituted for each other in every sentence in which they occur without any change in the sentence's truth value (i.e. without the sentence's changing from a true expression to a false one, or vice versa).

An example which illustrates this principle is the sentence:

> (1) The morning star is a planet.

Here the name "the morning star" can be replaced by the name "the evening star," because the two names, as shown above, have the same reference. But there are apparent exceptions to this rule. If we substitute "the evening star" for "the morning star" in the sentence,

> (2) Tom believes that the morning star is a planet.

we risk finding that the new sentence has truth value different from that of (2), because Tom may not know that the morning star and the evening star are identical, believing instead that one is a planet, the other a fixed star. Likewise, if Mr. Smith reads in the newspaper that a man in a gray hat is wanted for murder, but does not know this man to be his nearest neighbor, Mr. Smith may be afraid of the man in a gray hat yet not afraid of his neighbor.

In these and other contexts, where a name follows an expression like "believes that," "knows that," "thinks that," "likes that," "hopes that," "fears that," "is afraid that," the name cannot be replaced by just any name having the same reference, but only by a name of the same meaning, Frege observed. Thus, in (2) although we could not replace "the morning star" with "the evening star," we could replace it by something like "the bright star which sometimes can be seen in the morning sky to the east." (Eager to preserve the principle of substitutivity, Frege maintained that names are used in two different ways. Ordinarily, as in (1), a name is used as a name of its reference, but in some contexts, as in (2), it is used as a name of its meaning. However, this part of his theory need not concern us here.)

Contexts which do not obey the principle of substitutivity, or, as Frege would have said, make a name function as a name of its meaning, we may call (referentially) "opaque," because they blur the connection between the name and its reference. (This term was introduced by Whitehead and Russell. Frege did not have a special name for these contexts, but said that names in such contexts are used 'obliquely' and have 'oblique reference.')

Frege held that a name's reference is a function of its meaning. Two names may have different meanings but the same reference, as we have just seen in the example above. But the converse does not hold true. If two names have the same meaning, they also have the same reference. And there are name-like expressions having a meaning but no reference: "Pegasus" is an example. It has a meaning: "winged horse," etc., but it has no reference, since there is no object having an aspect that is illuminated by this meaning. Some philosophers have had difficulties in explaining how we can meaningfully use a name like "Pegasus," that has no reference. They have tried to solve the problem by saying that we talk about our mental idea, or conception, of Pegasus. Frege did not approve of this solution. The name "Pegasus" has a meaning, he said, and we can use it in meaningful sentences. But it does not have a reference; there is nothing we talk about when we use it.

Frege extended his theory of meaning and reference to include much that is not mentioned here. For example, he simplified logical theory by conceiving whole sentences as names. What has already been said about the meaning-reference distinction is, however, all we need for our study of the structure of Husserl's philosophy. Frege's distinction is rather natural, and the same, or similar, distinctions have been clarified by other philosophers. There are indications of such distinctions even in Plato and Aristotle, and the Stoics made use of a distinction very similar to that of Frege. Husserl was aware of a related distinction from John Stuart Mill, and he had found similar ideas in Bolzano. The reason why I have chosen Frege's presentation here is that it is simple and clear. Also, it—together with Brentano's theory of intentionality, described above—is well suited to clarifying the main features of Husserl's phenomenology.

Let us now see how a distinction similar to that between meaning and reference enabled Husserl to overcome Brentano's difficulty.

Just as we solved the problems connected with the term "Pegasus" by introducing a trichotomy,

name-meaning-reference

instead of the dichotomy,

name-object

so Husserl attempted to overcome the problem of hallucinations and centaurs in Brentano's theory of intentionality. Instead of Brentano's dichotomy between the activity of the mind, or the human *act*, and its intentional *object,*

act-object

Husserl introduced a trichotomy, distinguishing an *act*[3] from its 'meaning', which he called its *noema*, and from its *object*:

act-noema-object.

Each act has a noema. By this noema it is directed towards its object, if it has any. Not every act has an object; when we think of a centaur, our act of thinking has a noema, but it has no object; there exists no object of which we think. Because of its noema, however, even such an act is directed. To be *directed* simply is to have a noema.

What Husserl did, therefore, was, in effect, to combine the theory of intentionality with the theory of name-meaning-reference. About the distinction between

act-noema-object

he says that "The noema is nothing but a generalization of the idea of meaning to the field of all acts."[4] On this simple and natural generalization, phenomenology is based. (Of course Husserl did not simply read Brentano and Frege and then put them together; the story of his contribution is far more complicated than that. But I have chosen this step-by-step procedure in order to facilitate our approach.)

ACT CONTEXTS ARE 'OPAQUE'

Much of what Frege said about a name's meaning and its reference can be applied directly to the theory of an act's noema and its object: To every act there belongs a particular noema, and to the noema a particular object (if the act has an object; the noema of an act may be such that the act does not have an object). But to a particular object may belong several different noemata and acts. When we are to describe an act, therefore, it is not sufficient to indicate its object; we have to indicate its noema. If Mr. Smith became afraid of the man in the gray hat, it would have been wrong to describe this by saying that Mr. Smith became afraid of his neighbor. Likewise, if Tom believes that the morning star is a planet, we cannot describe this by saying that Tom believes that the evening star is a planet.

This holds for all acts. Frege had pointed out that a number of contexts are opaque—they do not obey the law of substitutivity of identity. All of the contexts of this type which Frege mentions are what we could call 'act contexts': "believes that," "knows that," "thinks that," "is pleased that," "hopes that," "is afraid that." If the phenomenologists are right we can add a series of contexts to

---

[3] The notion of an act is notoriously obscure. What is an act? What is to count as one act and what as two? Rather than starting with an attempt to answer these questions, Husserl first seeks to clarify his notion of a noema. Then, with the help of it, he can illuminate what is meant by an act; for the noemata 'individualize' the acts, in the sense that each act has one and only one noema.

[4] *Ideen*, 3 (The Hague: Martinus Nijhoff, 1952), p. 89.

this list, so that it will comprise *all* act contexts. Because, for example, to see is an act for Husserl, the sentence: "Tom *sees* the morning star," when regarded as a phenomenological description of an act, may happen to change its truth value if we replace the name "the morning star" with another name having the same reference. So we must demand that the new name have not only the same reference but also the same meaning as the original.

We should expect the same peculiarity in connection with expressions like 'hear,' 'feel,' etc.—in short, with all expressions relating to sense impressions—since to hear, feel, or sense something is, for Husserl, an act. The principle that act contexts possess this peculiarity of being 'opaque' is fundamental to the phenomenological theory of perception.

The Noema and Its 'Filling'

When we see a tree we do not see a collection of colored spots, for example, brown and green distributed in a certain way: we see a tree, a material object with top, back, sides, and so forth. Parts of it, for example, the back, we cannot presently see, but we see a thing which has a back. We may also keep our eyes directed toward the tree and see some spot of green color, but then it is the colored spots we see, not the tree. The impressions our senses receive when we see a tree are only a small portion of the sense impression we expect to receive from the tree if we move a little, walk around it, for example. A series of such expectations corresponds to the noema in our act. Some of them are already filled by the sense impressions we have received from the tree. These expectations, and some others which are intimately connected with them, are completely determined and correspond to a sort of 'noematical nucleus' in our act's noema. For example, we expect the tree to have a side presently hidden from view. If we go around the tree and find no such side, or if others of these completely determined expectations are not filled, we no longer say that we see a tree, but perhaps that we see a stage prop or have a hallucination. The noema then becomes a different one, with a different pattern of expectations. Husserl uses the following example. We may walk toward an object believing that it is a human being. When we draw nearer we may see that it neither moves nor breathes, but only stands there. Our pattern of expectations is destroyed, and we perhaps begin to believe that it is a doll. Our act's noema becomes a different one with new possibilities for sensing, mistakes, and so forth.

Other expectations are not completely determined, only their general tendency is given. We expect to receive color impressions when we look at the tree from the other side, but are perhaps not quite sure whether the color will be green or yellowish. Our act's noema also contains expectations to the effect that we will receive impressions of touch when we move closer to the tree and make contact with it; we also possibly expect impressions of smell, taste, or sound. We expect to see the tree again after we have turned away from it for a moment, and so forth. Some of these expectations are determined, others are open. By moving around and using our senses, we may see to it that more and more of our expectations become fulfilled and determined. Our experience of the tree, which in the beginning was one-sided, in this way becomes richer. But we can never reach any end. There will always be infinitely many expectations left which are not fulfilled and not determined. The tree is a material object and therefore *transcends* our experience, Husserl maintains. That the thing transcends our experience does not mean that what we see, hear, smell, and so forth is something different from the thing itself. The object transcends the sense impressions—i.e., the act's noema can never be completely filled—but the object is not therefore unrecognizable. It is, on the contrary, what is recognized in the act.

Phenomenology Is a Science of Noemata

An *object*, for Husserl, is anything toward which an act can be directed. Not all objects are material; there are also immaterial objects, for example, numbers and the other ideal objects of mathematics.

Mathematics and all natural sciences, including psychology, are sciences about the objects of our acts. But we have just noticed that in addition to possibly having an object, every act also has a *noema*. And what Husserl wanted to create with his phenomenology was a new science, a science of noemata.

Noemata are objects, too. In an act of reflection the noema of one act can be made the object of another act.

Mathematicians and scientists explore what we experience, the world of nature around us. In the phenomenological reduction we disregard this nature, this world of objects toward which our acts are directed. We do not deny that it is there, as if we were sophists, nor do we doubt that it is there, as if we were sceptics, but we, as it were, put it in brackets. We perform an *epoché*, Husserl said, borrowing a word which the skeptics of antiquity used to denote abstinence from any judgment.

The phenomenologist does not worry about what is or is not in the real world around him. He is not disturbed by the fact that some of our acts have objects, others not, but turns to the noemata of our acts. These are the *phenomena* he considers. The real world is reduced to a correlative of our acts, which constitute it, bring it forth. All that is transcendent is put in brackets together with the other objects of our acts. What is left, purified of all that is transcendent, Husserl called *transcendental*. The phenomenological reduction hence leads us from the transcendent to the transcendental.

Phenomenological Analysis

The phenomenologist analyzes the noemata of his acts in order to clarify how the world is 'constituted' by his consciousness. He observes that he expects a tree to have a back, to continue to be there if he turns away from it for a moment, and so forth. He studies the structure of the noemata of his acts. He elucidates how his expectations are arranged in patterns, how new sense impressions can change his expectations and sometimes lead to an 'explosion' of the noemata and make him reject his original supposition about the direction of his act. According to Husserl, phenomenology thereby becomes an analysis of something similar to what Kant called the *a priori*. If one were to describe phenomenology in brief, it would therefore be this: an investigation of the *a priori*, the necessary. Its *aim* is similar to that of many other philosophies from antiquity onward. But its methods, and the general framework of acts, noemata, and objects within which it tries to make sense of this aim, are different.

It is also not difficult to see the close connection between *analytic philosophy* and phenomenology here. For just as analytic philosophers, especially those of the so-called linguistic variety, analyze *meaning*, meanings of linguistic expressions, so the phenomenologist analyzes *noemata,* or meanings of acts in general.

THE TRANSCENDENTAL EGO

All acts are directed. They are often directed toward something, and always directed *from* something. That toward which they are directed, their object, is put in brackets by the phenomenologist. But what they are directed from—his ego—remains within the phenomenological sphere. His body, everything which is in time and space, and all other real objects are put in brackets. But an ego remains, which gives his acts meaning and thereby 'constitutes' the world in which he lives. This remaining ego Husserl called 'the transcendental ego,' because it, like everything else within the phenomenological sphere, is transcendental, purified of all that is transcendent.

According to Husserl, the transcendental ego constitutes not only the objects around us—those which we 'bracket' during the phenomenological reduction—it also constitutes itself. In Husserl's own words, the transcendental ego "is continuously constituting itself as existing."[5]

The question of how this can happen leads us to the *existentialist* aspect of phenomenology. We have noticed how phenomenology as *noematic* analysis has much in common with linguistic philosophy. Let us now observe how the phenomenological theory of the ego-constitution leads us into existentialism. To clarify the manner in which the transcendental ego constitutes itself, Husserl starts out with this example: If, in an act of judgment, I decide for the first time in favor of a being and a being-thus, the fleeting act passes; but from now on *I am abidingly the ego who is thus and so decided*; "I am of this conviction."

[5] *Cartesianische Meditationen* (The Hague: Martinus Nijhoff, 1950). Here quoted from Dorion Cairn's translation (The Hague: Martinus Nijhoff, 1960).

That, however, does not signify merely that I remember the act or can remember it later. This I can do, even if meanwhile I have "given up" my conviction. After cancellation it is no longer my conviction; but it has remained abidingly my conviction up to then. As long as it is accepted by me, I can "return" to it repeatedly, and repeatedly find it as mine, habitually my own opinion, or, correlatively, find myself as the Ego who *is* convinced, who as the persisting Ego, is determined by this abiding *habitus* or state.[6]

There is thus a close correlation between the ego and the world in which it lives. As the ego constitutes the world, it thereby constitutes itself.

This point is followed by an important, though fairly obvious, step: The same holds for decisions of every other kind; Husserl mentions *value* decisions and *volitional* decisions. I decide; the *act process* vanishes, but the decision persists; whether I become passive and sink into heavy sleep or live in other acts, the decision continues to be accepted, and *correlatively*, I am so decided from now on, as long as I do not reject the decision. So not just the facts of the world, but also the values of the world are constituted by me.

If the decision aims at a terminating deed, it is *not* 'revoked' by the deed that fulfills it; in the mode characteristic of fulfilled decision, it continues to be accepted: "I continue to stand by my deed."

The next step is most important: "I myself, who am persisting in my abiding volition, become changed if I 'cancel' my decisions or repudiate my deeds."[7]

This point deserves emphasis, for it is one of the clues to the relationship between phenomenology and existentialism. This same element recurs in all existentialists, for example in Kierkegaard, in Marcel, and in Sartre. They disagree as to the manner in which they think that our acts determine, or constitute, our ego: for Kierkegaard there are some important acts which determine it irrevocably, while for Sartre the determination almost passes away with the termination of the act itself. Thus, for Kierkegaard, the ego-determining effects of our acts appear to be *more* abiding than for Husserl; for Sartre, they appear to be *less* abiding. But they all agree that our acts determine, or constitute, our ego.

THE 'LIFE-WORLD'

Toward the end of his life Husserl became more and more concerned with the problems of intersubjectivity and objectivity. He tried to solve them by a theory of how we all live in a 'life-world' which is constituted by everyone in community. The term "life-world" (*"Lebenswelt"*) first appeared in an unpublished article on Kant which he wrote in 1924, and the life-world became the main theme of his last major work, *The Crisis of the European Sciences* (1936).

The phenomenologist is surrounded by other human beings. These human

[6] *Ibid.*, pp. 100–101.
[7] *Ibid.*, p. 101.

beings have bodies and perform acts as does he himself. These men and their acts can be the objects of the phenomenologist's own acts. By a kind of empathy (*Einfühlung*) he acknowledges that these men also have egos which stand behind their acts and constitute the world in which they live. His own acts and constitution of the world in which he lives are colored by this. Even from his own isolated experience, he knows that the sense impressions he receives from, for example, a tree, depend upon his position and vary when he walks around it, moves toward it or away from it, and so forth. The tree, the object toward which his act is directed, remains identical during this incessant variation of sense impressions. In the same way, his life amidst other human beings, makes him aware of more points of view. His own ego becomes one among many others. The world in which he lives becomes an intersubjective world, a life-world, "constituted by harmonious interplay and reciprocal adjustments between the individuals who live in it." The I which constitutes this world becomes in a way no longer his personal, isolated ego, but an intersubjective ego. His acts are directed toward intersubjective objects through intersubjective noemata, and the I to which they refer back has the character of a neutral I. Husserl said that the difference between the personal pronouns disappears within the phenomenological sphere.[8]

The natural sciences and all other sciences build on this life-world. Scientific expressions and sentences have meaning for us only insofar as they state something about the life-world. An investigation of the life-world is therefore important for all sciences and is the foremost task of phenomenology. Through phenomenological analysis we must try to uncover the structures of the life-world, Husserl held, and get a clear understanding of how our patterns of expectation are characterized by general laws that are products of reciprocal adjustment among all members in a society.

The analyses of such structures given by Husserl in the *Crisis* and in many of his earlier works resemble the analyses of many analytic philosophers. And no wonder, for remember that just as analytic philosophers analyze *meaning*, the meanings of linguistic expressions, so the phenomenologist analyzes *noemata*, or meanings of acts in general.

CONTINENTAL AND ANGLO-AMERICAN PHILOSOPHY

To conclude this paper, I would like to say something more about the relationship between continental and Anglo-American philosophy.

If there is ever to be communication and contact between these varieties of contemporary philosophy, I think it will be by way of phenomenology; for as I have tried to point out in this essay, phenomenology is unique in having—

---

[8] *Die Krisis der europäischen Wissenschaften und die transzendentale Phänomenologie* (The Hague: Martinus Nijhoff, 1954), p. 188.

through the analysis of meaning, or noemata—much in common with analytic philosophy, and on the other hand—through its theory of the ego constitution—central ideas in common with existentialism.

Now, although both phenomenologists and analytic philosophers analyze meanings, the notion of meaning has turned out to be a difficult notion to clarify, and it has become a major concern of many analytic philosophers, some of whom even hold that meaning analysis as practiced by many analytic philosophers and as presupposed in many contemporary views on, for example, linguistic truth versus factual truth, is without a satisfactory philosophic foundation.

A few years ago, an analytic philosopher, W. V. Quine, in *Word and Object*,[9] stated that he agrees with Brentano and, hence, as we have seen, also with Husserl, that there is something peculiar about opaque contexts, i.e., statements of the form "Tom believes that the morning star is a planet" or "Mr. Smith is afraid of the man in a gray hat," which makes them irreducible to statements of a nonintentional kind, such as statements about physical objects or about people's behavior. Quine finds evidence for this irreducibility of intentional idioms in the failure of the many attempts to perform such a reduction, and in several difficulties in the way of such a reduction which seem insuperable. But unlike Brentano, and, we may add, Husserl, who interpreted this irreducibility as showing the indispensability of the intentionalist idioms and the *importance of an autonomous science of intention* (in Husserl's case, *phenomenology*), Quine accepts the irreducibility as showing the baselessness of intentional idioms and the *emptiness of a science of intention*.

Quine substantiates his position by working out a philosophy of language which from simple beginnings leads up to this view of intentionality and its baselessness. This view is fatal to phenomenology and also to much of modern and contemporary analytic philosophy, concerned as they have been with *meaning* in some *irreducible* sense.

Now, who is right, Quine or Husserl? In order to defend themselves against Quine's criticism, phenomenologists would have to come up with a theory of meaning as good as or better than that of Quine.

They would probably have to do so without accepting Quine's starting point that in exploring language (and, I think, implicitly, man in general, in all his acts) any realistic theory of evidence must be inseparable from the psychology of stimulus and response. For if one accepts this view of evidence, then Quine's drastic conclusions seem to follow inevitably. But is there another basis for claiming that there are other ways of access to man, his acts, and his language? Phenomenology claims to open such a way, that of phenomenological analysis, through reflection on noemata. But is all this pure postulation, empty talk? Surely the vernacular of semantics and intention in which meanings and transla-

    9 W. V. Quine, *Word and Object* (Cambridge: Massachusetts Institute of Technology Press, and New York: Wiley & Sons, 1960).

tion relations are talked about as if they were objective and not indeterminate as Quine claims them to be, might be pointed to as evidence for phenomenology and against Quine's view. But what kind of evidence is this? And what does it signify if not that we have all been led astray and that our illusions about the nature of language have left their sediments in language itself?

But what kind of evidence could we then hope for to decide the issue? The pursuit of this problem will, I believe, give us fundamental insight into both language and philosophy. And such a pursuit can and should also lead to greater understanding and closer collaboration between phenomenologists and existentialists on the one hand and analytic philosophers on the other.

Guttorm Fløistad

On Understanding Heidegger: Some Difficulties

Heidegger's writings are no exception to the remarkable rule that influential works of philosophy are often very difficult to understand. The reasons are notorious: the subject matter is complicated; the method and the corresponding way of thinking are difficult to follow; the terminology is unfamiliar. These considerations apply in full to Heidegger's chief work from his early period, *Being and Time*,[1] to which the following remarks are devoted. In this work Heidegger purports to analyze the human way of being as preliminary to clarifying the meaning of Being in general. He employs a kind of descriptive-intuitive method and he introduces a number of terms either not previously occurring in philosophical discourse or previously used in a different sense.

In this paper I shall disregard the background question concerning the meaning of Being in general. The book, which is limited to the analysis of man, is interesting and also intelligible of itself.[2] I shall not comment upon the terminology. Instead I shall simply try to avoid the most unusual terms and present the essay in more familiar language. This may in some cases involve the risk of not doing full justice to Heidegger's intentions. Nevertheless, I think it justified since the choice of terminology in *Being and Time* is no doubt to a great extent determined by the background question.

Guttorm Fløistad, Research Fellow at the University of Oslo, is a native of Norway.
[1] The references will be given to the German edition of *Sein und Zeit* (hereafter abbreviated as *SuZ*), 8th ed. (Tübingen: Max Niemeyer, 1957). The references are easily found in the English translation by John Macquarrie and Edward Robinson (London: SCM Press Ltd., 1962).
[2] See *SuZ*, p. 45: "In our introduction we have already intimated that in the existential analytic of *Dasein* we also make headway with a task which is hardly less pressing than that of the question of Being itself—the task of laying bare that *a priori* basis which must be visible before the question of "what is man" can be discussed philosophically." See also section 1.A, below.

What I want to do is to focus on two distinctions which are basic to the whole analysis in *Being and Time*. These are the distinction between man's actual existence[3] and the ontological structures or 'existentialia'[4] of this existence, and the distinction between so-called inauthentic and authentic existence. I shall first briefly characterize the methodological burden carried by these distinctions, then discuss certain points in Heidegger's use of them in his analysis. The first task presupposes some further remarks on the goal of the analysis. In dealing with the second task I shall draw on the theory of understanding put forward in *Being and Time*. Certain aspects of this theory may, I think, be used to explain why it is difficult to understand the two distinctions and consequently the whole analysis in *Being and Time*.

1. THE METHODOLOGICAL SIGNIFICANCE OF THE TWO DISTINCTIONS

A. In *Being and Time* Heidegger purports to point out and describe the ontological structures constituting man's existence in general. His enterprise is similar to Kant's: The ontological structures are the categories of man's existence. A description of these structures is a description of the *a priori* categories which make this kind of existence possible.[5] Hence Heidegger is not concerned with analyzing particular forms of human existence. He does not want to recommend specific ways of being or behaving. He warrants no partial or total world view. Concerns such as these fall outside the scope of his inquiry. On the other hand, his contentions in working toward a structural analysis of man do not make descriptions of various forms of existence or ways of being irrelevant. On the contrary, descriptions of how this existence actually is or occurs are, in a sense, the basis for the structural analysis. It is via such descriptions that the structures may be pointed out and described. The actual existence, it may be said, serves as a kind of verificatory basis for the structural analysis. Without such a basis, as Heidegger says, the structural analysis is groundless (see *SuZ*, pp. 44–45, 312).

Accordingly, the analysis in *Being and Time* proceeds on two levels— the level of actual existence on the one hand and the structural level on the other. The former is auxiliary to the latter.

B. The analysis is complicated by the distinction between *inauthentic* and *authentic existence* (see *SuZ*, section 9). The distinction is admittedly difficult to

---

[3] In the following I shall use this term interchangeably with terms such as "being," "way of being," and "behavior." The justification for this, I hope, will emerge in the course of the analysis. In addition, I shall sometimes be using the terms in a general sense (applying to man as opposed to nonhuman entities) and sometimes in a specific sense (applying to a specific type of human behavior as opposed to other types). The sense in which the terms are used should in each case be clear from the context.

[4] The term "structure" seems to be used just as frequently as "existentiale" (plural: "existentialia"). I shall adhere to the former throughout the essay. See n. 19.

[5] See n. 2, above. The relation between Heidegger's structures and the Kantian categories is a delicate problem. Heidegger proposes to discuss it (*SuZ*, p. 45), yet he never does, the reason presumably being that the question of the meaning of Being in general is left undetermined in his philosophy.

explain, however the idea behind it is fairly clear. Heidegger holds that not all ways of being or behaving are equally apt to disclose man's structural constitution.[6] He begins his analysis with a description of how man ordinarily behaves, of man's existence in its "average everydayness," as he puts it. It turns out, in the main, to be a description of various practical attitudes, particularly of that which is ordinarily involved in handling and understanding the use of tools (*Werkzeuge*) or implements (*Zeug*) (see *SuZ*, section 15).[7] This is a description of the inauthentic way of being. It serves as a basis of a *preliminary* structural interpretation of man (see *SuZ*, pp. 41, 231). This is important enough: it helps to bring out structures such as 'world' (*Welt*), 'spatiality' (*Räumlichkeit*), 'being with (others)' (*Mitsein*), 'state of mind' (*Befindlichkeit*), 'facticity' (*Faktizität*), 'understanding' (*Verstehen*), 'discourse' (*Rede*), 'falling' (*Verfallen*), and 'care' (*Sorge*). This interpretation is preliminary in the sense that it gives no answer to the question of what it is that makes the human way of being possible. The structures brought out are rather those in respect of which this question may be meaningfully asked. Heidegger sets out, therefore, in part 2 of *Being and Time*, to find a sufficient way of being, that is, one which allows for a complete structural interpretation. He finds this way of being, as is well-known and much criticized, in the anxiety arising in man's attitude toward death. This specific state of mind enables man to exist authentically and shows, if we are to believe Heidegger, the complete structural constitution of man.

More specifically, the account of anxiety serves a twofold purpose. It is first used to group the manifold structures worked out in the analysis of the inauthentic way of being. Care, which is man's concern with his being, is shown to have a basic position. The other structures turn out to be substructures of care (see *SuZ*, sections 40, 41).[8]

The account of anxiety or of authentic existence is then, in a second step, used to show the basic structure of man's being. This structure is time, or rather, temporality, with its three anthropocentric dimensions of future, past, and present. That is to say, temporality, with its three dimensions, is that which makes the specifically *human* way of being possible. It makes it possible for man to be concerned with his own being 'in the world.'

Hence, the interpretation of man's being in terms of temporality is Heidegger's concern in *Being and Time*. Thus the analysis in *Being and Time* pro-

---

[6] See the methodological discussion in *SuZ*, section 7, particularly p. 28ff.

[7] "Implement" is rightly, I think, advanced as the best translation of German *Zeug* by Vincent Vycinas, in *Earth and Gods: An Introduction to the Philosophy of Martin Heidegger* (The Hague: Martinus Nijhoff, 1962). "Equipment" is the term used in the English translation of *Being and Time*. However, Heidegger often uses *Zeug* in the narrow sense of *Werkzeuge* (tools) to make his points. See section 2.A, below. The meaning of the various terms is briefly discussed in an article by Robert A. Goff, "Wittgenstein's Tools and Heidegger's Implements," *Man and World*, vol. 1, no. 3 (1968).

[8] In fact, Heidegger defines man in terms of care at the beginning of his inquiry (see *SuZ*, pp. 41–42). This initial definition may be regarded as a hypothetical one, the fruitfulness of which is shown in the course of the analysis.

ceeds in two steps, from an analysis of the inauthentic existence to an analysis of the authentic one, and in each step on two levels, the auxiliary and the structural level.

C. The two distinctions present a number of problems to the reader. *First* of all, we have the problem of distinguishing properly between the two levels of description, the auxiliary and the structural, a task which is not always easy since the analysis frequently changes from one level to the other, often within the same paragraph.

The *second* problem consists in seeing how Heidegger is justified in his choice of the particular sort of existence or way of being to be described in the two steps on the auxiliary level. The two steps present problems which are partly the same and partly different. Concerning the first step, we may ask: What is the justification for describing practical attitudes? In what sense, if any, are these attitudes representative for the human way of being in general? And also, what does it mean to say that the description of this attitude suffices only for a preliminary structural interpretation? With regard to the second step, we may ask: What is the justification for describing anxiety in the face of death? Is this rather specific state of mind at all capable of bearing the methodological weight put upon it within Heidegger's analysis? What, strictly speaking, is this authentic being as brought about by anxiety? And what is the relation, if any, between the inauthentic and the authentic way of being?

A *third* problem is implicit in the first, yet it may be mentioned explicitly. This is the problem of keeping constantly in mind the fact that descriptions belonging to the first level are only auxiliary to descriptions on the structural level. Although intelligible and, no doubt to many readers, also interesting in themselves, none of the descriptions belonging to the auxiliary level expresses Heidegger's formal structural concern. If this is overlooked, Heidegger is likely to be misinterpreted as a phenomenologist in the Husserlian sense,[9] or an existentialist on a par with or even directly descended from Kierkegaard.[10]

The *fourth* problem—perhaps the most difficult one—consists in properly understanding the auxiliary function of the first level description. This is the problem of pointing out and describing the structures on the basis of the first level description. The structures and the description of them cannot simply be derived from the first level description in any sense of "derive." Rather, a kind of intuitive effort is required, or in Heidegger's terms: the structures must be grasped on the basis of the first level description in such a way as they "show themselves in themselves" to be.[11] This is, of course, in no way revolutionary. It

---

[9] What I particularly have in mind are Husserl's own remarks on Heidegger's description of the practical attitudes, that is, of how we ordinarily see 'the world.' See Alvin Diemer, *Edmund Husserl* (Meisenheim am Glan: Anton Hain K.G., 1056), pp. 30–31.

[10] Due to a common interest in phenomena such as anxiety and death.

[11] See *SuZ*, p. 34. That the structures must be described on the basis of the first level description is not mentioned by Heidegger in his methodological discussion (section 7) but is an addition from later sections, particularly section 9. That the method is in a sense intuitive, is clear from a remark on pp. 36–37.

merely says that the alleged structures of the human way of being must themselves, via the first level description, 'tell' the observer in which way they are to
be described. Or, roughly put, the human way of being must itself reveal its
structural constitution.[12]

In this essay I shall discuss some of these problems with a view toward
elucidating the two distinctions. However, since the discussion requires an outline of substantial parts of *Being and Time*, the essay, I am afraid, is bound now
and then to be rather sketchy.

2. HEIDEGGER'S CHOICE OF THE ORDINARY WAY OF BEING AS A BASIS FOR THE PRELIMINARY STRUCTURAL ANALYSIS

A. No great effort is required to see the significance of the first step in the
structural analysis—the choice of the way of being or behaving to be described
as a basis for pointing out and describing the structures of man's being.[13] The
structures are, or are meant to be, general, covering all ways of being, all kinds
of behavior. Is there, however, a way of being which may justly be characterized
as general, that is, common to man; or is any description of human existence
bound to be a description of a specific, limited kind of being or behaving? If
the latter is the case, one is of course immediately confronted with the problem
of the general validity of the structures thus disclosed.

Heidegger's solution to this problem is suggested above. He claims to offer
a description of how man commonly behaves, of man's existence in its 'average
everydayness.' In this way he tries to avoid giving the impression of deliberately
construing a theory of man (see *SuZ*, p. 43). It would seem, then, that Heidegger
escapes the problem of basing a general structural analysis on description of a
specific way of being. But this is not obvious in view of the 'practical' way of
being or behavior he actually describes (see section 1.B, above). This would seem
to restrict Heidegger's view on common behavior, so as to make it invalid for a
general structural analysis of man. The so-called theoretical attitude, for instance,
seems to fall outside the range of his analysis. And since his own procedure in
Being and Time no doubt is theoretical, this would mean that he is what we
call self-referentially inconsistent.

However, it would be presumptuous to say this before knowing more pre
cisely what Heidegger has in mind when talking about how man commonly
behaves. His main idea is mentioned above. Man is to be conceived of in terms

---

[12] That no inferences from description of other non-human beings is permitted is undoubtedly involved in the view that man's being has itself to disclose its structural constitution. Any such inference, for instance, from description of animals or physical objects, Heidegger would say, is bound to miss the specific character of man's being. Presumably the same
holds true if the distinction between mind and body is taken as a starting point for the
analysis (see *SuZ*, sections 9, 10).

[13] "The right way of presenting it [that is, its actual existence] is so far from self-
evident that to determine what form it shall take is itself an essential part of the ontological
analytic of this entity" (*SuZ*, p. 43).

of care, that is to say, man is such that he is continuously concerned with his being. This concern is shown to involve a concern with things (other entities). It is in being concerned with things that he is concerned with his being. This is what "being in the world," according to Heidegger, means (see section 3.A, below). At present it is man's concern with things that matters.

To say that man is generally concerned with something comes to much the same as saying that man is generally doing something and also using something for some purpose or other. And that concepts such as 'being concerned with something' or 'doing something' or 'using something'[14] have at least a very wide application to man's way of being is intuitively clear. The use of tools or implements is but a limited case. One is equally doing or using something when one's praxis is of a theoretical kind. And that it makes perfectly good sense to say that one is doing something with language, or using language, needs no further argument.

This being so, the question arises as to why Heidegger mainly describes the use of tools (such as hammer, nails, traffic signs), and its implications for our understanding, in order to make his points. Could he, for instance, have employed the use of language or the theoretical attitude to the same effect? The answer to the latter question seems to be a qualified "yes." He could have used them, but it would, presumably, have been far more difficult to elucidate the structures of man's being, that is, of his concern with something, or of his doing or using something, as involved in the use of language or in the theoretical attitude. The use of tools, I think, shows most immediately and clearly what is involved in doing something or using something. In other words, what Heidegger is maintaining, if I am right, is that man is commonly characterized by being concerned with something, or doing something, or using something, and that the structural meaning of this way of being may best be brought out by describing attitudes which are most typically practical. And this it just what common, average, everyday behavior is.

If this is so, the following procedure seems appropriate: first, briefly to account for Heidegger's description of how man commonly exists or behaves, then, to point out one of the most elementary structures of this behavior, and, third, to show that and how this structure applies to, or is operative in, other ways of being. The purpose is a twofold one—to argue for Heidegger's choice of a starting point for the structural analysis, and to prepare for the presentation of further difficulties connected with this analysis.

B. One of Heidegger's main points in his description of man's everyday behavior, of his use of things, is that a thing used never occurs alone or in isolation from other things (*SuZ*, p. 68). A thing used points, by virtue of its use, toward other things. A hammer, for instance, is used to drive in a nail. The nail

---

[14] To decide whether these concepts have the same meaning is not necessary for present purposes. See below.

is driven in with a view to fastening a plank, and so forth. A hammer points to a nail by way of hammering. Thus each thing used enters into a connection with other things. The connection between such things is determined by the specific use or function of each thing. Which thing and which use or function is relevant on a certain occasion is determined by an overall purpose (for instance, building a house). It is the understanding of this overall purpose which picks out, and guides the understanding of, the relevant things in their relevant use or function. The overall purpose is, as it were, distributed in a number of subpurposes (sub-uses, subfunctions). The understanding of the overall purpose is clearly prior to the understanding of particular things in their use. It is logically or, rather, phenomenologically impossible first to use the hammer and then to arrive at the point in doing so *post hoc*.

C. It is this fairly simple state of affairs that Heidegger uses to point out some preliminary structures. A most elementary one has already indirectly been mentioned, namely the 'in order to' (*um zu*). It is a structure of the use of things in general (they are used 'in order to . . .'), and hence also of the connection between things used. In accordance with the above description, we may talk of an overall 'in order to' underlying and being distributed in various sub-structures (sub-'in order to's'). Moving to the individual auxiliary level again, for purposes of illustration, we may say, "A hammer is used in order to drive in a nail in order to build a house," and, similarly, "a nail is used in order to fasten a plank in order to build a house," and so forth.

That a structure such as the 'in order to' is fairly easily developed on the basis of a description of tool-using behavior is fairly obvious. That the structure is not so easily developed, for instance, by using the use of language, particularly as occurring in a case of 'theoretical' behavior, is equally obvious. Given a certain string of propositions (for example, the preceding ones), it is hard, if indeed possible at all, to detect an 'in order to' (i.e., a specific use) that is characteristic of the various propositions. It is probably of little help to take a 'closer look' at the content of the proposition since we then tend to loose sight of its functional aspect, that is, its specific use in a certain context. However, it makes perfectly good sense to say that each proposition is used, and more specifically that it is used, for instance, as part of an argument (as in the present case, to evaluate a certain distinction in *Being and Time*). This means that each proposition is characterized by having a particular use (a particular 'in order to . . .') within an overall purpose (an overall 'in order to . . .').

D. This being said, it is of course immediately necessary at this point to ask whether the structure hinted at in the analysis of tool-using behavior is representative for the human way of being in general, including the use of language. In other words, it is necessary to ask whether, structurally speaking, we are dealing with one and the same concept of using something in each case.

Two arguments may, I think, be found in *Being and Time* in support of this view—indirectly, in the theory of language (*SuZ*, section 34), and, directly, in the attempts to show how the stating of a theoretical proposition (more precisely, the act of predication) is generated from a 'practical' context (*SuZ*, section 33). The latter argument may also be used as an argument showing why it is more difficult to use theoretical statements in developing man's structural constitution. However, to examine these arguments in any detail is beyond the scope of this essay. I shall therefore merely outline Heidegger's procedure in the two cases and then suggest a simpler way of arguing the case.

Language in the form of discourse is a structure, that is, a given necessary feature of the human way of being. This not particularly revolutionary statement implies that we do not do anything or use anything for any purpose without involving language. No uttering of words is necessary for this to be the case. The 'essence' of language is meanings (see *SuZ*, p. 161). Meanings are generated from the understanding of (the use of) something within a context (see *ibid*. and pp. 87, 151). To use something 'in order to . . .' involves the understanding of this particular something in its particular usage. 'In order to' may be said to be a structure of understanding and meaning and hence of the use of language in general. From this we may infer that a structural analysis of doing something or using something is implicitly an analysis of the use of language.[15]

The concept of using language is differentiated in the second argument. Heidegger remarks that a man actually pursuing his work is hardly ever 'lost for words' (*SuZ*, p. 157). If he says something, his statements are usually of a specific practical kind (such as "The hammer is too heavy"). Distinct from this type are theoretical propositions, for instance, in the form of simple predication (such as "The hammer is heavy") (see *ibid*.). The main difference between these two extreme ways[16] of using language is that a practical statement explicitly involves a reference to its context ("too heavy in order to . . ."), whereas the theoretical proposition, although its meaning primarily derives from its context, does not. On the contrary, a theoretical proposition often tends to draw one's attention away from the contextual dependence of its meaning in that it is taken to point explicitly to the state of affairs to which it refers. Thus its particular use on a certain occasion (one occasion, of course, being its use in the discussion of its relation to 'reality') is, as it were, suppressed. In this case, it may be said, the distinction between a proposition and the state of affairs to which it refers

---

[15] Heidegger does not himself discuss this implication. A proper understanding of it no doubt requires a discussion of its possible application to the various ways of using language. Its application to the use of theoretical propositions is given below. The general view that the analysis of the use of tools or implements in Heidegger (and in Wittgenstein) is also an analysis of the use of language is advanced by Robert A. Goff in his interesting article mentioned above (n. 7), which I, by the way, came across after having finished this essay. Goff, however, makes no attempt to show the application of the structural analysis in *Being and Time* to an analysis of language.

[16] This is not quite precise. The extreme in the 'practical' case, according to Heidegger, is not a proposition of the kind just mentioned. The 'practical' extreme is to be found in the non-verbal use of things. But this does not matter for the point I want to make.

is taken as prior to the distinction between the proposition and its context, whereas with a practical proposition the converse is the case.

Heidegger does not explicitly say this, but I think it is clearly involved in his view on how the uses of the two types of statements are generated from a contextual understanding. The two ways of saying that something is the case, according to him, are due to two ways of articulating what is contextually understood beforehand. The two ways are two ways of seeing or understanding *something as something*. In the practical case we are seeing or understanding something as something 'in order to . . .' In the theoretical case we are merely seeing or understanding something as something, that is, as something which 'has' such and such a property.

Heidegger's contention now is that the sense of the latter way of seeing or understanding things is derivative as compared with the former. And it is derivative in the way suggested. The 'theoretical' understanding of something derives just as much from a contextual understanding (that is, the understanding of an overall 'in order to . . .') as does the 'practical' understanding of something. The difference is merely that the latter, expressed in a practical statement, clearly displays this dependence relation, whereas the former, being expressed in a theoretical proposition, does not.

E. Instead of following Heidegger's rather complicated argument on this point, I shall suggest a much simpler way of showing that the structure 'in order to' applies to the understanding of a theoretical proposition. More precisely, understanding such a proposition is only possible given the condition that the proposition has a use or is something 'in order to,' and that the understanding of its use or 'in order to . . .' derives from the understanding of an overall 'in order to.' What is needed is merely to regard a theoretical proposition in one of its most proper environments, namely as part of a hypothetical deductive system.

The propositions in such a system have the form of axioms, theorems, and predictions. The system as a whole has an explanatory use or function—that is, it is (usually) advanced 'in order to' explain certain observations. This overall 'in order to . . .' is at work within the system in various ways. Axioms are used in order to derive theorems, which in turn are used in order to set forth predictions. And predictions are statements to be verified or falsified in order to confirm or falsify the theory.

As is apparent, the structure 'in order to . . .' both in its overall meaning and 'submeanings' falls naturally into place in a hypothetical deductive system. Although a very elementary structure, it sheds some light on how our understanding operates within such a system. The explanatory use of the system as a whole underlies and is involved in the various particular acts of understanding, such as deduction, verification, confirmation, and falsification. In performing one of these acts, the others are present as possibilities in the understanding of the context—that is, of the overall explanatory use of the theory. The particular performances are evidently not explainable in terms of the content of the various propositions involved. The performances all stem from the explanatory use of the theory as a whole. If we ask for the source of the explanatory use, there seems to be but one, so far not very illuminating, answer. It stems from one peculiar human concern with things (see section 3, below).

Propositions are of course used in a number of other ways as well. They are used, for instance, in the development of an argument and to illustrate what a theoretical proposition looks like (see above). In the latter case the particular 'in order to . . .' of the proposition is one of illustrating, a use which stems from the overall context in question.

F. It would seem then that the structure of use, the 'in order to . . .,' in its overall and particular sense, can generally be detected in our understanding of something. With respect to this structure, all kinds of things, including scientific theories and tools, seem to be of the same value, or to belong to the same class. As objects of our understanding they are used for some purpose, that is to say, they are either used for some purpose, or they do not occur as objects of our understanding at all. It would, moreover, seem that the practical tool-using behavior is the kind of behavior which lends itself best to a structural analysis.

Naturally, the arguments brought forth are not conclusive with respect to these general conclusions. In addition, some of the arguments and conclusions are not particularly interesting. In the following I shall try to remedy this state of affairs by pointing to some further steps in the structural analysis. I shall deal particularly with understanding. This structure has already frequently been mentioned, but it has not yet been described structurally.

The discussion of understanding serves several purposes. It shows how a major structure of man's being is described on the basis of his ordinary practical behavior. It may also be regarded as a further elucidation of what it means to use something. An account of understanding is moreover a minimum requirement for a discussion of the distinction between inauthentic and authentic existence.

3. ORDINARY BEHAVIOR AS AN AUXILIARY TO THE STRUCTURAL ANALYSIS

A. An instance of a structural analysis in connection with the structure 'in order to . . .' has already been given. In further developing the structural analysis we may refer to this preliminary structure of using something in connection with an argument in *Being and Time* (p. 84).

The argument is as follows: Given a certain use of certain things within an overall 'in order to,' we may, with respect to each thing used, ask the question, "To what purpose is it being used?" The answer is usually easily provided. We know it because we ourselves have put the thing into use. However, arriving at the 'end' of such a connection, that is, at the thing or work to be achieved or completed, we soon run into difficulties. If we ask to what purpose a house is built (an observation is explained, a proposition is analyzed and clarified), we are in all cases ultimately referred back to ourselves, to a need characteristic of the human way of being. We do it for the sake of ourselves, for the sake of (*umwillen*) our own 'being in the world.'[17]

This argument points to a close connection between man's concern with things and his concern with his own being. The concern with things ultimately stems from a concern with his own being, the latter being the source of the overall 'in order to . . .,' the former being its manifold 'distributions' in the use of things. Man conceived of in terms of care, or concern with his being, may hence be said to be somehow present *in* the use of things. Man is *in* the (i.e., his) world, as Heidegger puts it, the world being, roughly, constituted by our understanding of our use of things.[18] The concept of using something appears moreover to be the concept of a kind of interaction between man and things.

In order to clarify this 'interactive' force of using something, two further steps are required. I shall briefly first apply the concepts of 'assigning' and 'assignment' and then point to understanding as one of the major structures making the use of things possible.

B. A thing used is said to be assigned to its use (a hammer to hammering) (see *SuZ*, section 18). The thing thereby acquires the character of being assigned or of assignment. This merely means, I take it, that a thing used is encountered in its use and not as a thing having such and such physical properties. The use is the essential character of the thing (a hammer, when actually used, is solely to be conceived in terms of hammering). The source of this assignment is man's concern with something. It is this concern which assigns the thing to a particular use.

This is fairly straightforward. The next step, however, is more problematic. That which is assigned to a certain use is primarily man himself. He assigns himself to the use of certain things in a certain way, whereby the things are assigned to their use. The use of something may hence be conceived as a kind of double assignment, as man's self-assignment in the assignment of things.

For a proper understanding of this it is of course essential to keep in mind

---

[17] Of course, the concern with one's being often involves a concern with the being of other people, for the reason that they in various ways enter into and constitute one's being. I shall not, however, delve into Heidegger's analysis of how this is possible. For the purpose of the present discussion it is sufficient to accept Heidegger's view that the primary source of our concerns, whatever they are, is the concern with one's own being.

[18] It should perhaps be noted that the question of the meaning of "being in the world" is the starting point for the structural analysis in *Being in Time*. The analysis of the use of something is an analysis of the world *in* which man may meaningfully be said to be. The structures constituting the *being in* are state of mind, understanding, discourse, and falling. The 'Self' which is thus said to be in the world is in turn shown to be constituted by certain states of mind and certain ways of understanding things, oneself, and other people. That Heidegger begins his analysis of man by analyzing the world may at first seem surprising to many readers yet should be intelligible in view of his concept of world. Without a clarification of "world" (in terms of how we ordinarily encounter things, namely, by using them), the analysis of the 'being in' and the 'Self' cannot even get off the ground. That man is thus to be conceived in terms of 'being in the world' is of course one of the many presuppositions in *Being and Time*.

Heidegger's definition of man in terms of care or concern. It is man's concern with his own being that assigns itself to the use of, or concern with, things. And it is this 'self-concern' which consequently may be said to be *in* the use of, or concern with, things.[19]

An examination of Heidegger's account of understanding would be illuminating at this point.

C. An individual's use of things is guided by his understanding. In other words, this means that it is the understanding that assigns the things to their use and thus structuralizes the connection between them. This means, however, that the understanding produces the structure 'in order to,' both in its overall and particular sense. And the question is, how is the understanding to be conceived if it is to have such a structuring function?

Heidegger's reply is that our understanding has the character of being a *projection* (*Entwurf*). If we ask how he knows this, the only answer seems to be that it shows itself in the way man commonly behaves. In other words, structurally speaking, that the understanding is a projection can be seen from man's use of things by means of intuition (see n. 11).

True, at the beginning of his analysis (*SuZ*, section 31) he emphasizes the *possible* character of understanding which the idea of projection is meant to explain. This possible character is obvious from most human behavior. To use something, in general, is to use it in one possible way among many. Which way is determined by the context or the overall 'in order to' in question. And, similarly, a scientific explanation of something is usually an explanation of this something from a certain possible point of view, depending on the science in question. It is this possible character, the aspect-character of understanding, so to speak, that Heidegger tries to account for by describing understanding structurally as a projection. In the projection of an overall 'in order to . . . ,' it may be said, the understanding determines for itself which things are to be used (explained, etc.) in which way.

These remarks on the possible character of understanding may certainly be of some help in trying to comprehend its projective structure. However, they offer no clear-cut explanation of this structure, and I very much doubt whether it can be explained lucidly at all. One has in the end, I think, to regard oneself as being in a situation where one is actually using something for some purpose, preferably some kinds of tools or implements, and then try to grasp what is going on. (The various kinds of propositions which one is using or trying to use at present are presumably less suitable, although they should fall entirely within the scope of the structural analysis. That is to say, the structural analysis is meant to be valid also for the propositions in which this theory is set forth [see section 2.A, above]).

The adoption of a practical attitude and at the same time a theoretical one in which one reflects upon one's practical attitude is, I think, quite necessary in

---

[19] As to the 'self' in question here, see n. 18, above, and section 4, below.

order to understand the next step in the interpretation of a projection. To say that our understanding has the structural character of a projection in that it structures a possible connection between things used is only part of the truth. It merely accounts for the assignment of things to a certain use. The source of this assignment, that is, man's self-assignment, is not covered. In other words, that understanding is a main substructure of man's concern with his own 'being in the world' is left aside. What then is a projection when regarded from this basic point of view?

The intuitive answer would be that a projection of a possible connection between things used is basically a projection of a possible way of being. Thus, a projection, as is suggested by the word itself, has to do with the continuation of one's existence through time. It is by way of such projections that man continues to be. The being with which he is thereby concerned is not 'free-floating.' It is always tied up with a concern with things, a concern which in everyday behavior often (see section 4.D, below) takes the form of a firmly structured connection between things. Thus a projective concern with things is a projective concern with one's own being in the world as it is in the concern with things. In a projection, one is, in other words, concerned with things in a certain possible way *as* a certain possible way of being.

It should perhaps be remarked that as a structure the projective character of our understanding is a necessary, not a contingent, feature of the human way of being. The projective character of understanding is continuously at work. Consequently, it is determined for us as long as we exist and is not a matter of choice. One may certainly choose to use, that is, to assign oneself to the use of certain things in certain ways, rather than to the same things in other ways or to the use of other things. But one cannot decide whether this choice or assignment is to have the structural character of a projection of one's way of being. To put it roughly, as long as one exists, one is necessarily concerned with how one is going to exist.

Before leaving the difficulties involved here to the reader I shall make a few summary remarks and thereby suggest how the distinction between the inauthentic and authentic existence enters the structural analysis.

D. The distinction between actual existence and the structures of this existence should by now have become fairly clear. It is perhaps best illustrated by the distinction between the projective character of understanding in general (being the structure of understanding) and the 'existential' materialization of this character in an individual's understanding and use of things in a certain way. The materializations differ more or less from individual to individual and, within each individual's behavior, from one situation to another, whereas all materializations share the common property of being projections.

Heidegger's concept of a structure, moreover, is evidently a complex one. The complexity may perhaps best be accounted for by pointing to the different ways in which the structures are interrelated. First, there are some structures deriving directly from others. Thus the 'in order to' structuring of the use of things derives from the projective character of understanding. The projective character of understanding derives in turn from, and is a substructure of, care or the concern with one's own being. In both cases we have presumably to do with the same derivative kind of relation.

A second kind of relation is that between understanding and the other substructures of care, namely 'state of mind' and 'falling.' What this relation is, is a problem which goes beyond the scope of the present essay. I merely want to remark that the relation is not of a derivative kind, at least not in the same sense as the first one. It is moreover doubtful whether 'state of mind' and 'falling' are substructures of, and related to, care in the same sense as understanding is. (A few remarks on the two other substructures will be given below.)

Distinct from the derivative relation between structures is the relation between care (with all its substructures) and temporality. Temporality with its three dimensions (future, past, and present) is said to be the basic or 'deepest' structure of man's being in the sense that it makes man's being, conceived as care, possible. The relation of temporality to care is one of making possible. To illustrate: The projective character of understanding[20] as one of the main substructures of care involves the understanding's being anticipatory, and its being anticipatory in two senses: first, in the sense that the understanding of something in virtue of its contextual character involves an anticipation of what one is going to understand (often called foreknowledge); and secondly, in the sense of thereby being an anticipation of one's own way of being. In other words, due to the projective (context-creating) character of understanding, it is impossible to understand something without anticipating its continuation, and this impossibility is primarily an impossibility of existing without anticipating how one is going to exist.

The temporal character of this anticipation lies intuitively at hand. It is the occurrence of future which makes the projective, anticipatory character of man's understanding (and being) possible. It is also, I think, intuitively fairly clear that this projective, anticipatory character of understanding cannot be derived from the concept of future, at least not in the same sense as 'in order to . . .' may be derived from understanding. At present we may rest content with saying, as above, that the relation between future and projection or anticipation is one of making possible.

To explicate this relation requires an extensive analysis both of the concept of future and of anticipation as applied to the human way of being. Heidegger

---

[20] In his summary of the preliminary structures, Heidegger calls understanding and the structures deriving from it the existentiality of man's being (*SuZ*, section 41) in contradistinction to state of mind or facticity and falling as the two other substructures of care. It would seem then that Heidegger at this stage restricts the meaning of "existentiale" to a certain group of structures only. This is one reason for using the general term "structure" instead of "existentiale." See n. 5, above.

devotes himself to this task in the second part of *Being and Time*. The basis for this analysis is a description of the authentic way of being, that is, of anxiety in the face of death (see section 1.B, above). In the following I shall try to elucidate the distinction between the inauthentic and authentic ways of being, and in particular point to certain difficulties connected with a proper understanding of the latter.

4. THE DISTINCTION BETWEEN INAUTHENTIC AND AUTHENTIC EXISTENCE

A. The significance of this distinction in Heidegger's analysis was indicated earlier. On the basis of the preceding account of understanding we are now in a position to explain, at least roughly, the meaning of the two ways of being, particularly the inauthentic one (from which the structural character of understanding is 'derived').

In view of Heidegger's initial definition of man as one who is concerned with his own being, we may say that to exist inauthentically and authentically are, respectively, to be concerned in an inauthentic and authentic manner with one's own being. Since man's concern with his being, according to Heidegger, involves and is only possible in connection with a concern with other entities, we may also say that to exist inauthentically and authentically is to be concerned with things 'in the world' (that is, as they occur in a connection structured by their use) in an inauthentic and authentic manner, respectively.

A main structure of man's concern with himself in his concern with other entities is shown to be understanding. We are hence entitled to say that the inauthentic and authentic ways of being are or involve an inauthentic and authentic understanding, respectively, of oneself and other entities (i.e., of oneself in one's concern with other entities and of other entities in one's concern with them). To rephrase roughly, by existing inauthentically one has but an inauthentic understanding of what it means to exist as a human being and hence also of what it means to understand other entities. And, similarly, in existing authentically, one has an authentic understanding of what it means to exist (see *SuZ*, p. 146).

B. The ordinary way of being is inauthentic. And the question is, what does this mean? To say as above that it is inauthentic because it does not disclose the full structural constitution of man, is, within the context of *Being and Time*, a significant negative characterization to which I shall return in a moment. The inauthentic existence, however, is just as much a human way of being as the authentic one, and has its own positive characteristics. As far as it goes, the account of understanding is, of course, a positive account of this existence. Yet the account is purely formal and applies (with some qualification) equally to the authentic existence (see *SuZ*, p. 44). The account of understanding is useful in that it suggests a question relevant to the present problem—namely: In which way do we understand ourselves and other entities when existing inauthentically?

Heidegger's answer to this question is contained in his analysis of the Self and its relation to other people as occurring in everyday behavior (*SuZ*, sections 25–27) and, above all, in the analysis of 'falling' as one of the main substructures of care (*SuZ*, section 38). For present purposes it suffices to exhibit just a few features.

The general starting point for the analysis in the two cases is the presumably valid observation that man in everyday behavior, or usually, is *absorbed* in what he is doing, in his 'world' (see *SuZ*, p. 175). With regard to his self-knowledge this means that he understands himself in terms of what he is doing (see *SuZ*, p. 120). He *is* what he is doing (see *SuZ*, p. 126). This phrase, familiar also from analytical philosophy, means, with respect to the inauthentic way of being, that things encountered by an individual in his use of them are in command of that individual's self-knowledge. The individual, to use well-known terms, is not free to determine himself in his concern with other entities. Rather, he is determined by them, that is, by some usage to which the thing lends itself. He is certainly the one who puts the thing into use. The point is merely that he does not do this, does not assign himself to their use, freely.

Much the same holds true for an individual's knowledge of other people and his self-knowledge in relation to them. They enter into his doings (his 'world') in various ways by what they themselves are doing. They are understood as people who are doing or are concerned with certain things. They are understood in terms of, and hence as being determined by, what they are doing (see *SuZ*, sections 26, 27).

Insofar as other people thus enter into an individual's 'world,' he is absorbed in what they are doing. In effect, they act as determinators of his concern with things, of his own way of being, and, consequently, of his self-knowledge. One is under the command of each other's way of being, of one's understanding of things, and of oneself. No one is admitted as ranking 'higher' than others, or as having opinions about something that differ from everyone else's, and so forth. Heidegger's analysis of the Self and its relation to others in everyday life relies upon a structural analysis of this state of affairs.

C. The discussion of 'falling' is a further account of the inauthentic way of being—of the specific state of mind, understanding, ways of talking about or interpreting things and statements. All are characteristic of inauthentic existence. Above all, however, it is an attempt to explain why man gets absorbed in his own and other people's use of things—their opinions, and so forth—and thus looses the freedom to decide for himself.

Heidegger naturally maintains that the reason is to be found within the human way of being itself. Roughly speaking, to be given in such a way as to have to be concerned with one's own way of being is to be given with a responsibility for oneself (and for other people insofar as they enter into one's 'world' [see n. 17, above]). This is what Heidegger calls 'facticity of responsibility'

(*Faktizität der Überantwortung*),[21] the cognitive source of which is one's "state of mind" (see *SuZ*, p. 134). This is to say that one *is* or finds or feels oneself in a certain state of mind involving a (more or less explicit) feeling of having to *be* or to do something (cf. the questions "How are you?" and "How do you do?"). To be continuously responsible for one's own way of being is a burden. One way, and the easiest way, of solving this problem is to escape it. And this, according to Heidegger, is just what has happened in the inauthentic way of being. Following a tendency to 'take it easy' (which is one way of putting it [see *SuZ*, pp. 127–28]), which, due to the burden of responsibility, is inherent in this being itself, one has exempted oneself from determining one's own course of life, from exercising responsibility. Others have taken over, to the effect that everyone acquires much the same behavior and thus virtually turns himself into "no one in particular" (see the 'they,' *das Man, SuZ*, p. 128).

The term "falling" signifies this process of being and becoming inauthentic. One 'falls away' from oneself, that is, from a self which, conscious of its responsibility toward itself (and thereby toward others), is in command of itself, its decisions, and its actions, *to* a Self which has virtually given up its individuality in favor of an easygoing and standardized behavior. In inauthentic being the Self is thus no longer itself. It is 'alienated' from itself, alienation being one of the (sub)structures revealed in the analysis of falling.

These are some highlights of Heidegger's views on inauthentic being. They are certainly not sufficient for a proper understanding of this being and its significance in the structural analysis as a whole. But they are sufficient, I think, to help point out some major difficulties connected with the understanding of it. The difficulties, it will be shown, are in the end mainly due to the notion of authentic being.

D. As is apparent from the above, we have so far dealt with Heidegger's account of the inauthentic way of being as if it were for the most part conducted on the auxiliary level. The corresponding structural analysis has only occasionally been touched upon in the mention of structures such as 'the they' (*das Man*, 'no one in particular'), and 'falling.' The ontological description of these structures, of which the pointing out of a number of substructures is a main part, is merely suggested. The meaning of the structures is therefore in no way clear. What is clear, however, is that Heidegger's procedure in his analysis at this point is the same as previously; the structures are pointed out and described on the basis of auxiliary descriptions.

The auxiliary description used by Heidegger in these analyses presents problems, however. The reader is no doubt familiar with the parts of it that either refer directly to the previous description of the use of things or to extensions of such descriptions (for instance, when saying that other people are usually encountered as users of things). Other parts of the auxiliary description may yet be

[21] The usual translation of *Überantwortung* is "being delivered over (to oneself)." "Responsibility" designates rather the effect of this.

disturbing in that they apparently have little or nothing to do with the use of things (for instance, when the self in everyday inauthentic behavior is said to be commanded by standard opinions about things.) This naturally raises anew the problems of justification, as well as the no less important problems of compatibility between the various auxiliary descriptions. In this essay I shall merely suggest what I take to be a reasonable solution to these problems.

The starting point is the view that not all ways of being or behaving are equally apt to disclose the structures of man's inauthentic being. The use of things is a general feature of it. This feature, however, is not general in the sense that the various things used, due to some 'well-defined' purpose, are always used in a systematic manner. The everyday behavior is perhaps just as much characterized by proceeding in an unsystematic manner or by clinging to certain fixed views about things. A structural interpretation of these ways of being, that is, an explanation of what it is that makes them possible, requires an auxiliary description of them. Such a description need not be incompatible with the initial description of man's everyday behavior conceived in terms of a systematic use of things. The additional description merely counts for cases when things, opinions, and the like are used unsystematically or arbitrarily. One has, in any case, to deal with some use of things and, therefore, for instance, with (unsystematic or arbitrary) projections of one's being.

Hence, the analysis of these additional ways of using things may be regarded as a contribution to the structural analysis of the ordinary way of being in general. The account of man as being 'no one in particular' and of 'falling' thus explains the tendency in the human way of being to become absorbed in the things used (in opinions, etc.) and the consequences thereof.

E. Other aspects of the analysis of inauthenticity present difficulties of a different kind. These are difficulties connected with the very characterization of the inauthentic being as inauthentic. This suggests that the understanding performing the analysis of the inauthentic being is different from that involved in this being itself. Someone whose being, from Heidegger's point of view, is inauthentic (that is, is thus absorbed in the things he uses, is under the command of others, is alienated from himself, etc.), and who knows no other way of being, is likely not to understand what is meant by the description of his existence as inauthentic. He is not in a position to have the concept of being inauthentic. For to have this concept presupposes knowledge of some other way of being, from the viewpoint of which man's existence in its average everydayness appears as inauthentic. This means, in the Heideggerian context, that knowledge of what it means to be authentic is presupposed.

The use of notions such as 'inauthenticity' and 'falling' is not the only evidence that the structural analysis, from the outset, is performed from the viewpoint of authentic being. True enough, the initial auxiliary description of the use of things is for the most part fairly straightforward and, presumably, in principle if not in practice, accessible to everyone irrespective of authenticity or inauthenticity in his being. The same holds true, I think, for at least major parts of the preliminary structural analysis, for instance, of the interpretation of using things in terms of a two-level 'in order to . . .' (whole-part) and of the understanding involved in the use of things in terms of a projection. The structures are formal and apply, or are meant to apply, to the human way of being in general. Hence, though disclosed more clearly in certain ways of being than in others, the structures should be intersubjectively intelligible.

There remains a problem, however, as to whether a structure thus understood separately or in connection with some other structure (or substructures) can be said to be truly or completely understood. The answer must be no. For to a true or complete understanding of a structure, no doubt, belongs the understanding of its significance within the structural analysis as a whole. And at this point difficulties appear. Understanding a structure within the structural analysis as a whole is no longer a matter of an inauthentic or authentic being. Only the latter is sufficient here. This is shown at the end of part 1 of *Being and Time* (sections 39–41), where Heidegger summarizes the preliminary structural analysis. The summary is not merely a restatement of what has been said earlier. It is an attempt to show that and how the various structures are closely interconnected as substructures of care (see section 1.B and n. 20, above). To show this, a description of inauthentic ways of being is insufficient, presumably because man's concern with his own being does not show itself properly in everyday concern with things. Due to the tendency to become absorbed in the use of things, it rather covers up the interplay of the underlying structural constitution (see *SuZ*, p. 130).[22] The way of being having a sufficient structure-disclosing force is the authentic one. The authentic being is above all brought about by anxiety in the face of death. Anxiety shows the full impact of what it means to be given in such a way as to have to be concerned with one's 'being in the world' (see section 1.B, above).

The outstanding methodological function thus given to anxiety (see *SuZ*, p. 190) presents considerable difficulties both to the understanding of the auxiliary descriptions themselves and to the structural analysis depending upon them. We may rightly ask, I think, whether any of these descriptions and analyses really are intelligible unless one virtually is in the particular state of mind in question, that is, exists authentically. In other words, is it at all possible to understand descriptions of authentic existence and the structures and structural interconnections disclosed in them unless one already exists authentically? If not, major parts of the philosophy of *Being and Time* seem, intersubjectively speaking, to fall into an insecure position.

In the final paragraphs I shall briefly deal with these and other problems connected with the distinction between authentic and inauthentic existence.

---

[22] That is why Heidegger remarks that this constitution has to be brought forth against a tendency in itself (see *SuZ*, p. 311).

The starting point must obviously be an outline of authentic existence and of understanding as characteristic of it.

F. Anxiety is the state of mind enabling man to exist authentically. Being in this state of mind, he is liberated *from* his absorption in the things he uses and in the behavior (opinions, etc.) of other people, and is thus liberated *from* his being commanded by them. He becomes free *to* choose for himself his own way of being. He becomes, to paraphrase Heidegger, free to 'choose his own choices,' (see *SuZ*, p. 268). Why? Because of a salient feature of anxiety. Anxiety is a state of mind occurring in man's attitude toward death. In anxiety, death is anticipated. This is anticipation of the possibility not to be. In the light of the possibility not to be, one's being as a whole is disclosed. Thus, in anxiety one is concerned with one's being in the world as a whole.

What then does this mean and in what way does it explain the authentic way of being?

A first thing to be noticed is that, on the level of concrete existence, nothing at all can be said about the whole. The concern with the whole of one's being is a wholly indefinite concern (see *SuZ*, p. 186). To say this, from Heidegger's point of view, is perfectly reasonable in that there is no being to be concerned about apart from that consisting *in* the use of or concern with other entities (see section 2.A, above). For instance, in his view there is no definite kind of 'substantial ego' lying behind the concern with one's being in the concern with things. Care or concern, if anything, is the substantial or essential character of man (see *SuZ*, pp. 41–42, 98–99, sections 25, 64).

To say that the concern with one's being in the world as a whole is indefinite if separated from the concern with other entities does not mean that this concern (i.e., anxiety in the face of death) is *structurally* indefinite. On the contrary and as suggested above, this concern is structurally very definite in that it discloses the complete structural constitution of man, both in helping to summarize the preliminary structural analysis and subsequently in interpreting this summary in terms of temporality (see section 1.B, above). In other words, the concern with the whole of one's being, called forth along with anxiety in the face of death, helps to clarify the structural constitution of one's concern with or use of something. And how is this possible?

The answer has already been suggested and, at least to some extent, it should be intelligible without knowing details of the structural analysis: It is possible because it is in being concerned with, or using, or engaging in doing something that one is concerned with the whole of one's being. The projection of one's being as it occurs in the use of something is a projection of it as a whole. Or, in other words, we exist and continue to exist by doing something, that is, by being engaged in some *particular* action. It is, however, the *whole* of one's existence that thus exists and continues to exist. To say anything else would seem senseless. It would be tantamount to saying that a part of one's body continues to exist, while the rest is left behind.

It is this state of affairs, usually concealed, that anxiety in the face of death makes explicit. In anticipating the possibility not to be, one is explicitly concerned with the whole of one's being in the world; while being engaged in some particular action, and one understands that this is so.[23] One understands, as it were, the basic point in doing something, or one knows what one is doing in doing something. It is this understanding that characterizes the authentic existence and enables man to be free and in command of himself. Thus he can carry out the given responsibility toward his own way of being and toward the being of others as well.

G. As it appears, the distinction between the authentic and the inauthentic existence is in no way absolute. Following Heidegger, one is in both cases concerned with something (doing or using something or engaging in some particular action) and one is thereby concerned with one's being in the world. And insofar as "falling" is defined in terms of "being alongside the world of one's concern" (*SuZ*, p. 175), or in terms of adhering to the things with which we are concerned (think or talk about etc.), the term also applies to the authentic way of being. The difference is that in existing inauthentically, one's understanding or way of being is dominated by these things, whereas in existing authentically, one is able, due to an explicit understanding of what one's concern with things is about, to "take oneself back," as Heidegger says. One is able to take oneself back from one's absorption in them, or from one's absorbing self-assignment to them, and hence liberate oneself from one's concern with them.

For these and similar reasons, authentic existence is to be regarded merely as a modification of the inauthentic forms (see *SuZ*, p. 146). We should add that, for Heidegger, descriptions of the two ways of being are merely auxiliary to the structural analysis. It is as auxiliaries that the descriptions of them acquire their significance. And it is as an auxiliary that the distinction between the two ways of being is most apparent. The structure-disclosing force of inauthentic being is to some extent made clear in the analysis of the use of things and of understanding in terms of projection. The structure-disclosing force of the authentic being, on the other hand, is merely suggested, for which reason the description of this way of being may appear trivial.

Even if this is so, the description of authentic being and of authentic understanding may suffice to provide at least a tentative answer to the question of whether this description is generally intelligible. The answer may in turn be used to bring out an interesting distinction within authentic understanding.

H. First, the question is whether the description of actual authentic existence

---

[23] Compare this with an observation made by Hampshire: "When the uncertainty about the future is painful to me, it is painful usually because it is an uncertainty about my fate rather than about my action" (*Thought and Action* [London: Chatto and Windus, 1960], p. 110). The distinction between "my fate" and "my action" seems to be similar to Heidegger's distinction between "concern with one's being as a whole" and "particular action." Their analyses of this distinction are, however, different.

is generally intelligible. Particularly in view of the systematic character of the description, I think the answer must be in the affirmative. But the answer must at once be qualified, since the description may be understood in two relatively different ways. One's understanding of it may have implications for one's own actual existence, or it may not. That is to say, studying the description of authentic existence may bring about a change in one's own actual existence; it may itself become (if it were not already) authentic. Or no such change may be brought about. For instance, in studying the description of anxiety in the face of death, one may explicitly become concerned with the whole of one's being in one's concern with particular things, and then become free to determine one's own thoughts, actions, etc.; or the description may merely be viewed impersonally, or formally, as description of the human way of being in general with no personal existential implication.

In the former case one's understanding of the description is presumably what Heidegger calls *genuinely* authentic (see *SuZ*, p. 146). In the latter case one's understanding is presumably not inauthentic, since inauthentic understanding has, for instance, no regard for the idea of the whole of one's existence's being projected in concern with particular things. The merely impersonal or formal understanding of the description of authentic existence is, if I am interpreting Heidegger correctly, *not genuinely* authentic (*ibid.*).

A similar distinction may be drawn as to inauthentic understanding. The understanding is *genuinely* inauthentic, if I am right, when one, in an absorbed manner, is actually concerned with something or is engaged in doing something within a more or less systematically structured connection among things. And it is presumably *not genuine* if one is merely regarding something or someone from 'outside' in an absorbed manner (see *ibid.*). One may, for instance, be regarding someone who is absorbedly engaged in doing something from 'outside' in the sense of not sharing his concern.[24]

Just as in the case of authentic understanding, this distinction within inauthentic understanding is relative, not absolute. The absorbed 'onlooker' is also concerned with something. In general, we may say that the distinction between genuineness and non-genuineness in one's understanding (be it authentic or inauthentic) is a distinction in degree of actual existential involvement. Genuineness in one's understanding may hence be regarded merely as a modification of non-genuineness, presumably analogous to authenticity as a modification of inauthenticity (see above).

I. Again, however, the significance of the distinction between genuineness

---

[24] Heidegger's analysis of various ways in which someone's tool-using behavior is disturbed (*SuZ*, section 16) may, I think, be taken as an illustration of how an individual's inauthentic understanding changes from being genuine to non-genuine. If this is so, the two ways of seeing something as something (see section 2.D, above) may clearly be used in a further evaluation of the distinction between genuineness and non-genuineness of understanding (see n. 25).

and non-genuineness of understanding is most obvious within *Being and Time* from the structural analysis.[25]

The authentic understanding here offers the best example since it has the most significant methodical function and also is more unfamiliar than the inauthentic. If it is true, as Heidegger maintains, that anxiety in the face of death is an outstanding state of mind that discloses the temporal structure of man's being (see section 1.B, above), the question is whether the structure thus disclosed, despite the alleged formality and general applicability, is intelligible unless one is in that particular state of mind oneself, that is, unless one's understanding is *genuinely* authentic.

Heidegger's position is given in his methodological views: The basis for the structural analysis is actual human existence. No structures are pointed out and described unless they are disclosed in this existence, that is, in the understanding characteristic of it (see *SuZ*, p. 185). If one is not actually concerned with the whole of one's being in one's understanding, that is, if one does not exist (genuinely) authentically, the corresponding structural analysis is groundless (*bodenlos*) (see *SuZ*, p. 312).

The question here concerns the meaning of "groundless." There is no doubt, I think, that the statements concerning the temporal structures of man's being said to be disclosed in his authentic being and understanding, genetically speaking, require that one's understanding of the human way of being must be genuinely authentic. Moreover, I think there can be no doubt that a proper understanding of the temporal-structural analysis equally requires a genuinely authentic existence and understanding on the part of the reader. If this is so, the question of whether the structural analysis of the authentic being is intelligible from a non-genuine authentic point of view, that is, impersonally or formally, is less interesting. If thus intelligible, the structures brought out would presumably appear wholly trivial, since their significance would not be backed by one's actual existence.

Therefore, the conclusion seems to be that major parts of the structural analysis in *Being and Time*, due to the two distinctions dealt with in this essay, require that a specific state of mind or way of being be accessible. Thus, the intersubjectivity of these parts of the analysis with respect to a proper understanding of them is, in other words, conditional.

Finally, the truism remains that this and other difficulties pointed out in

[25] Although the theory of actual understanding in *Being and Time* is primarily developed with a view to serving the structural interpretation of man, the theory is no doubt meant to be generally applicable. This means *inter alia* that a statement (of whatever kind) may be understood in four different ways: in a genuine or non-genuine inauthentic way, and in a genuine or non-genuine authentic way. Normative statements are presumably more 'sensitive' to the distinctions than, for instance, purely descriptive ones. That the distinctions, moreover, are sociologically significant is at least intuitively clear. However, to show more precisely whether and how Heidegger's theory of actual understanding is generally applicable is a task that has yet to be attempted.

this essay may have at least two sources. They may be due to Heidegger's specific way of analyzing the human way of being. For example, because of some of his presuppositions concerning this being, he may artificially create the difficulties. Or they may be due to the human way of being itself, which may be such that it presents these and similar difficulties to anyone who attempts to explain what it is that makes it possible, that is, categorically. I do not think there is any straightforward decision-procedure in this problem of sources. We have, after all, no access to our way of being unless through understanding, which itself belongs to this being.

C

Scandinavian Philosophy

Johannes Sløk

Kierkegaard as Existentialist

Kierkegaard lived in Copenhagen from 1813 to 1854. Thus he worked in a period dominated by the late romantic, but which toward the end was more and more affected by the attitudes of realism. In philosophy and theology Danish circles were also much influenced by idealistic views; Hegel especially played an important role. In this connection one speaks of the "Danish Hegelians"—people such as Heiberg and Martensen, who took a prominent position in Danish spiritual life.

All of these currents affected Kierkegaard very strongly. It is not difficult to find romantic, realistic, and idealistic tendencies in his thought. Even so, one cannot identify him with any of these. This is because something new and special arose in his consciousness from this conglomerate, a conception for which he tried strenuously to find parallels in the past (Socrates, Hamann, Lessing), but which in reality was his own original creation. The conception pointed not backward but forward—as he himself guessed—and today we can give it a name. Kierkegaard was Europe's first existentialist.

Let us first investigate how the above tendencies affected him, and in what ways he broke with them. Characteristic romantic traits are to be found throughout Kierkegaard's writings. To begin with, he had a marked partiality for romantic mystification. This shows itself in the very construction of his works. Most were not even published in Kierkegaard's own name. They were either published under well-thought-out pseudonyms or appeared anonymously. The author was then supposed to be a very mysterious and completely unknow person, the manuscript of whose book was found under particularly romantic circumstances—in a secret drawer of an antique escritoire, or in a locked box fished up from the bottom of a secluded lake.

Professor Sløk, of the University of Aarhus in Denmark, is a native of Denmark. Translated by B. H. Mayoh.

This mystification is itself typically romantic—and in this respect Kierkegaard did not limit himself. For example we may consider the special section of *Either-Or* called "Diary of the Seducer." The diary is purportedly that of an unknown person. By chance one of his friends has found it and with great timidity has made a copy. This copy is found by a third person who hides it in the drawer mentioned above. Here it is found by a fourth person who eventually publishes it but with grave doubts. The setting could hardly be more mysterious.

Secondly, Kierkegaard favors the most intimate kinds of literature: diaries and letters. Thus there is no talk of books intended for publication. We have intimate revelations that after later vicissitudes are at last presented for publication. We have the impression of overhearing a person when he believes himself to be alone.

Thirdly, Kierkegaard has a marked predilection for typically romantic characters. His figures are almost always lonely and tragic people: people who are deeply troubled, lovers who cannot reach one another, the poet who writes from the suffering of his own lonely heart, the old man who looks back over a tragic and unsuccessful life, and many others of the same nature. If one is led by these and many other obviously romantic traits to believe that Kierkegaard is a romanticist, however, then one has misunderstood everything. The entire romantic setting is there merely to illustrate the situations in which one fails in really being a person. The romantic personages in his authorship are not presented as ideal but as exactly what they are: persons who could not solve the problem of being a person.

Thus the romantic magic is constantly penetrated by something that completely resembles a realistic outlook. Kierkegaard's real heroes are utterly unromantic figures. This is already noticeable in the second part of *Either-Or*, where, in contrast to the extremely romantic characters of the first part, Kierkegaard presents a character who from a romantic viewpoint is completely hopeless. To begin with, he has a very prosaic occupation; he is a judge in the lower court. (The romantic figures in Volume I have, of course, absolutely no bourgeois profession.) Secondly, he is married; even worse, happily married; this fact alone makes him quite impossible from a romantic point of view. On the other hand he has—and this is more profound than one at first thinks—a name; he is called William. This is not just a chance naming, but rather a deeper assertion that only by acquiring a name can one become a person.

The same kind of contrast is more marked still in *Fear and Trembling*. The purpose of this work is to discover what it is to be a religious individual. To this end Kierkegaard analyzes a large number of romantic types, who in this connection are referred to as "tragic heroes" and "knights of the infinite." However none of these can truly be said to be religious, and in the midst of them the author tries to evoke the picture of the truly religious man. What is he like? He exactly resembles the figure who stands farthest from romanticism: the archbourgeois. The solid citizen, employed as a tax collector, tending to develop a paunch because his wife—with whom, of course, he lives a happy life—knows nothing better than to fuss over him. He stands firmly on the ground and he quite belongs to the here and now. For a Dane the sketch of this individual unavoidably prompts certain associations. The great romantic poet in Denmark, Oehlenschläger, had just sketched such a good citizen, who takes to the woods with his family on a summer's day. Naturally he is made ridiculous by Oehlenschläger, because he is stupid, limited, and prosaic, without feelings for everything that only romantic characters—lovers, a child, an old man—understand, from a sense of the infinite and a togetherness with nature. When Kierkegaard deliberately urges a figure of just this kind as the ideal, he is expressing an antiromantic outlook on life, without of course thereby supporting the mundane. In this dialectic interplay his precise concerns are revealed: how is it possible to live one's life—not some artificial and calculated life but the average, everyday, concrete, and real life—in such a way that it does not become thoughtless and philistine but rather a true and ideal life?

To the bitter end, Kierkegaard retains the intention of pursuing this question. In the last major work he published, *Training in Christianity*, he unfolds with pitiless correctness the Christian ideal: abandonment of material goods, patiently facing persecution, suffering, and execution. But amidst all of this is inserted a little section, in his eyes of the utmost importance, under the title "Morals"—what does all of this mean, the author asks here. He answers himself: it means everyone must admit to himself that, strictly speaking, he is not a Christian, and thereupon need do no more—other than live his life, pleased with his work, his wife and his children, really pleased, because at length everything is given back to him as the situation in which he now has the God-given right to be. The meaning is thus: to be true and valid, living in this manner—average, bourgeois, common, and banal—is now transformed by the intervention of Christianity into the ideal life.

What Kierkegaard wishes to emphasize does not therefore emerge in a simple contrast between romanticism and realism. The presentation of the problem is quite different, as will become clearer if we dwell for a moment on his relationship to idealism. In Kierkegaard's work philosophic idealism is primarily represented by the two great thinkers, Plato and Hegel; he returns to them again and again. At first glance it appears that he has quite different attitudes toward the two. For Plato he has the deepest respect, and when Kierkegaard respects a man there are no limits to the eulogies he will shed upon him. In contrast, Hegel appears as the great opponent who must be conquered at any cost, and in such a case Kierkegaard's disgust and irony are equally without limits. Nevertheless his basic attitude is the same with respect to both figures, as is his main criticism of them. This criticism of Plato appears especially in two places: in *The Concept of Dread*, where he examines Plato's concept of 'moment' in the dialogue *Parmenides*, and in *Concluding Unscientific Postscript*, where he makes a fundamental separation between Socrates and Plato. On the other hand, the criticism is leveled against Hegel throughout his works; again and again he takes it up, sharpens and reformulates it, and makes it a degree more poisonous. His tone toward Hegel is quite different from that toward Plato, but the content of what he says is basically the same.

The criticism is that in the system of idealistic philosophy one incorrectly assumes that the primary philosophical difficulties are solely of a speculative kind. Therefore one exerts the keenest efforts to *think* existence, one constructs a system of concepts with which to help one grasp the nature of existence, understand its structure, and shed light on the relation of the separate parts to one another. Considered as a speculative system, the result is admirable, and for this at any rate it is possible to respect Hegel. But the speculative difficulty is really of minor importance. It is easy to solve insofar as one has the necessary speculative ability; if one does not have this ability one can calmly ignore the difficulty, because it is not on it and its solution that one's life as an individual depends. The real difficulty comes first when the system as such is compared with the individual who has to live in accordance with it. This is because the difficulty arises in passing from the speculative system of concepts to its realization in actual existence.

Therefore Kierkegaard does not see his problem as attacking the speculative system as such. When it does not present itself as something other than it is, a speculative system has its own right and must be judged solely by its consequences and its coherence. For this reason Kierkegaard can accept Plato because this philosopher, qua the essential Plato, can be seen as one who consciously intends only to be a metaphysician. For the same reason he must sharply reject Hegel, because the Hegelian system—as Kierkegaard understands it—also pretends to have solved the difficulty of application, in a sense, by adopting this difficulty within the system itself. But of course in Kierkegaard's view this rests on a misunderstanding. Conceptually the passage from the system to reality can not itself be a part of the system.

We see then that Kierkegaard in his relation to both romantic and idealistic philosophy stops with the same problem that neither romanticism nor idealism has felt. This is the actual individual's chance of realizing romantic beauty or idealistic truth. The problem is concentrated on the category that Kierkegaard wishes at this point to make basic, the single individual, and this category unfolds itself in all its forms throughout the analyses Kierkegaard sets up in order to illuminate the problem of application.

One can now ask whether this is a real problem at all. What does it mean to make something real, and what problems can be connected with this? Of course an individual throughout his life is placed in all kinds of concrete situations where he has the task of making something or other real. We all meet commands, orders, demands, and requests time and time again, and the question is then whether we will carry out, realize, that which we are commanded to do. This can raise psychological and ethical problems. Perhaps we have no desire to do so; perhaps we would rather do something else; perhaps we feel that it actually goes against our principles. We then find ourselves in conflict and have to see how the problem can be resolved. Nevertheless it is not of these problems, which we all unfortunately know so well, that Kierkegaard is thinking. Of course, he too knows them and has carefully analyzed them, both in the form of a conflict between duties and in the form of a conflict between desire and duty. But the curious feature of these analyses is that they constantly abstract from the actual conflict, because its resolution, the decision one finally takes, can, in Kierkegaard's opinion, only be understood on the basis of a decision that lies deeper. It is this deeper-lying decision that is of interest.

The point is that the single concrete situation in which I find myself, a conflict situation or, more straightforwardly, a choice situation, sometimes arises because of, and is always normalized by, the project to which I am subjected in advance. At every moment I am doing something. If at any time I momentarily become aware of myself, I will find myself engrossed in a project. It is this project that shapes the world around me in a certain way. Things are colored by the project; they are thereby qualified as important or not, relevant or not. Only in the light of my project can I interpret my surroundings.

We are, in other words, led back from the concrete choice situation to the project we have already formulated, and on which basis alone the concrete situation can become a choice situation. It is the structure of the formulated project that needs to be analyzed, and it is, as such, a project that an idealistic system can be for a person. The problem of the speculative system is to indicate and motivate the projects into which an individual can venture; therefore the passage from system to reality takes place not in the concrete decision but rather in the formulation of the project, on which basis alone is it at all possible to make concrete decisions.

However, if we try to be clear about the nature of the formulated project, we find that it in turn is related to something else, a project formulated earlier. If we trace these presuppositions sufficiently far back we will end with a fundamental project, the project an individual has basically with himself. What I essentially want of myself determines what other kinds of problems I can care about, and what choices therefore it is possible for me to make. The decisive point in the entire process of realization must therefore be an individual's project with himself. This dialectic interplay between choice and project expresses itself in the way Kierkegaard treats all of those concepts which in ordinary thought are combined with choice: guilt, responsibility, freedom, conscience, and the like. We may take as an example the concept of guilt. Usually we would say that a person is guilty in the sense of being guilt-burdened, if he himself is guilty in respect of not doing that which he ought to do. Thus one must first *be* guilty in one's 'guilt'; if a person is forced into being remiss, or the otherwise blamable thing happened by chance, then he is acquitted of guilt. Secondly, one ought to have done something else; only when there is some other kind of duty—a command, an order, an agreement—can there be question of guilt. If, however, one is oneself guilty in respect of not having done what one ought, then one (more generally speaking) is a guilty person. In Kierkegaard's opinion this usual concept of guilt cannot stand by itself. To begin with, one can question its validity in an actual instance. One can question whether one really was guilty in the action; one can easily produce so many arguments that this becomes doubtful. Then, one can always question whether one ought to have done so; here also one can produce a flock of arguments and thereby escape guilt.

But even if one ignores these escapes, even if one imagines that an individual admits his guilt, then the guilt still consists in nothing but an isolated event. In this single and determined matter perhaps I am guilty, but otherwise, generally speaking, I am not. Guilt never becomes a total category that fundamentally determines who I am, but rather a purely accidental verdict, from which many lines of escape lie open to me. After all, I can regret it, make up the damage, or repair the error in some other way. For Kierkegaard this really means that the guilt does not exist. It remains a transitory phenomenon, against which one must protest, and whose validity one must reject. The entire essay *Repetition* treats this preliminary concept of guilt, and in *The Concept of Dread* we find (in a typical Kierkegaardean turn of speech): "If one can only be guilty in terms of police regulations, then basically one is never guilty" (pp. 471–72).

This preliminary concept of guilt must therefore be based upon a guilt concept of a more fundamental nature, and if this cannot be done, then it must be dropped. The basic guilt concept is then an individual's fundamental project with himself; and an individual cannot avoid formulating such a project. Because an individual can only express his existence, choose his problems, and choose the manner of solution of these problems on the basis of this fundamental project with himself, an individual is, essentially and in all simplicity, guilty in himself. He is guilty in who he is, and thereby—in advance—is guilty in that which he does. In other words: by being guilty in himself, he is guilty in all he otherwise does, and at the same time he is guilty in that there are certain things he ought to do. Now all arguments are removed. He can no longer question his guilt, and every isolated guilt he takes upon himself thereby is transformed to an absolute guilt, because it does not reveal a merely minor detail, but rather that which an individual has done to himself because of his project.

In this way every decision will in the last instance be fastened to an individual's fundamental project with himself. What are the conditions for this project? Kierkegaard first infers the fact that none can avoid it but very few are aware of it. Man has a tendency to just live—to never come to grips with his own existence, but rather to leave it to develop in accord with convention. His opinions, views, and actions acquire their purpose from outside himself, namely, in all the opinions, views, and actions he meets in his milieu. But this in reality means that an individual has embarked on a project not to be himself; he will be 'another,' the average, the one who happens to be prevailing. He takes upon himself the responsibility of not taking upon himself any responsibility; he is guilty of not being guilty in himself; he uses his freedom to reject his freedom. In other words: even not to formulate a project with oneself or to be at all aware of the importance of this fundamental matter is also to formulate a project with oneself, namely, the project not to be, strictly speaking, an individual.

The ethical question then tries to recall an individual to the point where he can be aware of the formulation of a project. But if it succeeds, it immediately opens another way out. An individual, who after a time feels the importance of this project, can now want to formulate a fantastic project. He can suffer from the illusion that his freedom to formulate his project carries the freedom to decide what the content shall be. In other words, the individual will be, not himself but someone else. Kierkegaard is untiring in tracking down the ethical and psychological stuntedness that can arise in this way, and it is here that an existentialist-oriented psychotherapy enters.

The point then is that an individual first becomes genuine when he himself formulates his own project. Therefore, he need not search for the contents of the project; they are at hand, because they are none other than that which the individual is at the start. But by making this his project, the individual transforms it from the chance circumstances in which he now happens to find himself (interest, talents, given culture, education, and experiences) to the concrete subject matter to which he himself desires and agrees. He becomes himself by making himself the center of his existence, or he becomes subject to his own life development by freely and on his own responsibility having accepted that which he actually is, or—to put it in Kierkegaard's terms—for the first time in that process the individual becomes that which an individual is intended to be: a single person.

The extensive analyses of what resolution, decision, choice (and the related concepts: freedom, responsibility, guilt) are, now show the radical break with the romantic-realistic dichotomy and with idealism's trust in the speculative solution. Kierkegaard is himself conscious of what is decisive in this new orientation, and concerned with finding a term that can express it. He then fixes upon the word "existence." In his use of the word it acquires for the first time a new meaning.

"To exist" is not now identical with "to be." Animals, plants, and things are insofar as they actually are present; for none of these groups is it true that just being is a problem or resolution that can be made dialectic. For man, on the other hand, it is true that he, alone among all creatures, is not; he exists, and that he exists is for man himself the fundamental problem on whose solution the solutions of all other problems depend. It is this basic attitude within which an existentialist understanding of man originated, and it is by fastening onto this that an existential treatment of all other problems—ethical, political, psychological, pedagogical, etc.—acquires its quite special nature. This one could prove, for example, by a careful analysis of Kierkegaard's writings.

Mogens Blegvad

The Philosophy of Value of Harald Høffding

Søren Kierkegaard was unquestionably the most influential Danish thinker. His influence on contemporary philosophy throughout the world may make people wonder how his work was received in his own time and place. Often a great man is misunderstood or neglected by those closest to him, and it is left for posterity to recognize his greatness; as the saying goes, no one is a prophet in his own country. Kierkegaard was in many ways misunderstood, but certainly not neglected; his greatness was recognized very early and his influence on the intellectual life in Denmark around and after the middle of the nineteenth century was immense. Even within the department of philosophy at the University—a body to which he himself never belonged—he was admired. One of the professors, Rasmus Nielsen (1809–84), actually considered himself a pupil of Kierkegaard and sought his authority for his own doctrine that belief and knowledge (i.e., religion and science) are two spheres of thought so utterly different that they cannot really come into conflict with each other. When Nielsen presented this doctrine as a consequence of Kierkegaard's teaching, Kierkegaard was horrified and disowned Nielson. After Kierkegaard's death, however, a great debate on Nielsen's doctrine broke out in which many of the younger intellectuals took part. Among these was Georg Brandes (1842–1926), who attacked the doctrine from the radical anti-Christian point of view which came to dominate the movement he later led in Scandinavian literary and cultural life. Also, Nielsen's colleague and Brandes' teacher, Hans Brøchner (1820–75), contributed to the debate with a book published in 1868. Before that, quite a young man who had just passed his degree in divinity, and who had also studied with Nielsen and Brøchner, had published a small book, entitled *Philosophy and Theology,* in which he supported Nielsen's doctrine. His name was Harald Høffding. When

Professor Blegvad, of the University of Copenhagen, is a native of Denmark.

the book was published in 1866, Høffding was only 23 years old, and he did not for long maintain the position expressed in that book. As early as 1867 he wrote to his fiancée:

A change which has taken place within me this autumn consists in that I can no longer agree with Rasmus Nielsen. . . . It is partly his own vacillation, partly professor Brøchner's stringent criticism, partly, and above all, a renewed examination of the problem itself . . . . which have shown me the unsoundness of his view. However, this has not brought me any closer to the Church . . . . on the contrary, it has occurred to me that on several points I have held opinions which were not truly rooted in me but rather adhered to me as something external or secondhand. Christianity will—of this I am fully convinced—always be to me the highest truth, the only one in which I may find the solution to the mystery of life. But only that which I personally can experience and make my own can be the truth to me . . .[1]

The religious doubt which had been stirred up by the reading of Kierkegaard's works and which had caused him not to seek ordination but instead to earn his living as a teacher of Latin and Greek, could only for a time be neutralized by the Nielson dualism; not many years were to pass before he completely rejected Christianity. Through studies of philosophy in his spare time he tried to clarify his position and work out a personal viewpoint, and he succeeded. In his autobiography he tells how he lectured at the University of Copenhagen in 1874 on the "Introduction to Philosophy" and that these lectures in fact contained the "basic elements of all that I later worked out in more or less detail."[2] He obtained his doctorate of philosophy as early as 1870 with a thesis on a subject from ancient philosophy, and in 1883 he succeeded Rasmus Nielsen as Professor of Philosophy.

Although Høffding, as mentioned previously, gradually worked himself away from Christianity and as an older man was even rather sharply opposed to the Church, he never actually became anti-Christian, as did Brandes and his radical movement. He claimed that there were religious values in Christianity which must be preserved, although orthodox Christianity was to be rejected.

There can be no doubt but that these religious problems, which occupied him so much in his youth, greatly influenced his entire philosophical development. This development was from an early date marked by a tendency to escape from the more speculative spirit in which these matters were normally treated; by diligent studies of a more scientific nature Høffding tried to acquire a firmer foundation for his attitudes. He plunged into psychology; he believed that it was first and foremost via a thorough study of human mental processes that such a foundation could be found. For many years he worked on the book which established his reputation, *Psychology in Outline Based on Experience*. This book was published in 1882 and relatively soon was translated into several languages. Today he is remembered abroad not so much as a psychologist but as a historian

---

[1] *Erindringer* [Memoires] (Copenhagen: Gyldendalske Boghandel-Nordisk, 1928), p. 67.
[2] *Ibid.*, p. 94.

of philosophy. His great work on the history of modern philosophy is used as a textbook in many countries; as recently as 1952 a new English edition came out. The recognition he received abroad also benefited him at home, where his word carried great weight in public debate; he reached a high position, became Rektor (approximately equivalent to the office of vice-chancellor) of the University, and dating from 1914 he was granted the honorary residence at Carlsberg. He died in 1932.

Yet as a philosopher, as a creative thinker, he is almost forgotten today, abroad and at home. Relatively little is written about him, compared to other philosophers who in their time reached a similar position. In fact, it is a difficult task to penetrate deeply into Høffding's philosophy. As a writer he is rather dry, very expansive, and more than somewhat obscure. He is fond of using vague, metaphorical expressions such as "based on" without explaining to the reader whether a real logical relation is meant or something more vague, i.e., a psychological relation. One might say that Høffding is very far from satisfying the demands for precision required of a philosophical writer today. Neither are grave inconsistencies hard to find in his works; in the following remarks I shall deal with some of them. Moreover, much of his philosophy is antiquated, hardly worth the trouble of closer examination.

However, I do feel that what Høffding has to say about valuation and values is of interest. At an early date he outlined the problems of the philosophy of value and tried to offer solutions. Although he wrote no single work which is actually called philosophy of value or which exclusively deals with problems of value philosophy, he is among those who took the first step towards establishing value philosophy as a special discipline within philosophy. The explanations of the content of philosophy which he gives in various places in his works all add up to the fact that there are four main problems in philosophy. One of these he calls the valuation problem; the other three are the problems of existence, of knowledge, and of consciousness; these correspond, respectively, to the disciplines of metaphysics, epistemology, and psychology. (At that time others besides Høffding considered psychology a branch of philosophy rather than a separate science). As early as the 1874 Introductory Lectures mentioned above, he presented these main problems and offered a program for dealing with them, a program which he actually pursued during the many years to come.[3] It is noteworthy that he uses the expressions "valuation problem" and "ethico-religious problem" synonymously, and that he deals almost exclusively with these two kinds of values, the ethical and the religious, while he practically nowhere deals with aesthetic values or, indeed, any other kinds of values.

Let us first consider his treatment of moral value. It probably seemed to him that, having rejected Christianity, he must find a new foundation for morals in human nature. This may have been an essential reason for his interest in

[3] *Ibid.*

psychology. An indication of this tendency is his use of the expression "human ethics" rather than "religious ethics" or "Christian ethics." His first treatise within this field, indeed one of his very first published works, was called *Concerning the Basis of Human Ethics* (1876). During the following years, however, he was mainly occupied with psychology. His great, comprehensive study of ethics (*Ethics: An Exposition of the Principles of Ethics and their Application to the Major Aspects of Life*) did not appear until 1887. The first chapter of this book had already been published a year earlier under the title, *The Principles of Philosophical Ethics*. In 1891 he published a small treatise, *Ethical Investigations,* consisting of three papers of which one is entitled "The Possibility of Philosophical Ethics." Both in the introduction to *Concerning the Basis of Human Ethics* and in the first chapter of *Ethics*, Høffding is occupied with the question of the relation of scientific or theoretical ethics to what he calls "the positive morality." In *Concerning the Basis of Human Ethics* he distinguishes between the practical ethicist (every human being is a practical ethicist), the prophetic ethicist (the person who has a formative effect on morals), and, finally, the theoretical ethicist (the philosopher who, in Høffding's words, "preserves an enquiring attitude toward what the practical and prophetic ethicists will always perceive only in immediate relation to practical action").[4] He compares them by analogy in this way: the practical ethicist is the sailor, the prophetic ethicist the navigator, and the theoretical ethicist the astronomer. But he attributes to the theoretical ethicist further authority than his comparison would have one believe. In the first place he regards theoretical ethics as an "empirical science based on psychology and history" which "starts from the observation of the actual given action and from this lays down general rules."[5] Furthermore, he demands that theoretical ethics must go beyond the empirical. Thus, he says: "All scientific cognition is an ideal structure comprising empirical elements exclusive of all disturbing and inessential circumstances."[6] Later he says: "In this way theoretical ethics also constitutes an ideal type, an expression of human action as it would be were it carried to its completion."[7] We find here on Høffding's part a confusion of the fact that science abstracts and idealizes (which is true of practically all science) and the fact that ethics tries to establish ideals or norms (which in his opinion is particularly true of ethics). Not only the introduction but the entire treatise is marked by this fundamental obscurity; transitions are incessantly made from comments of a psychological or historical nature to actual normative ethics.

In the *Ethics* matters have been somewhat cleared up, and Høffding has to a certain extent realized that direct inferences cannot be drawn from empirical data to ideal demands. In the first chapter of this work, entitled "Positive Moral-

---

[4] *Om Grundlaget for den humane Ethik* [Concerning the basis of human ethics] (Copenhagen: Andr. Fred. Høst & Søns, 1876), pp. 3–4.
[5] *Ibid.,* p. 4.
[6] *Ibid.*
[7] *Ibid.,* p. 5.

ity and Scientific Ethics," he distinguishes between two parts of scientific ethics. The first is historical or comparative ethics, which must seek "to represent the positive morality such as it appears in a given community at a given time and to show the development it undergoes under various conditions, and to compare the various forms it may assume to various individuals and at various times."[8] Contrasted with this is philosophical ethics, which aims at "no description or explanation of given ethical phenomena but at a valuation of these. It is a practical discipline and it presupposes that we have set ourselves aims, which are to be effected by means of human actions."[9] Shortly afterward he says: "Philosophical ethics is valuation which is systematically carried out according to a specific foundation in human nature and according to the criterion set by this foundation."[10]

The change in attitude which thus may be observed between 1876 and 1887 is accounted for by Høffding himself partly in his autobiography and partly in the book *Ethics*. In the autobiography he tells of writing a lecture he was to give in February of 1886 to the Royal Danish Academy of Science and Letters. The lecture apparently is identical to the published essay *The Principles of Philosophical Ethics* and to the first chapter in *Ethics*. It was during his work on this lecture in January, 1886, that, as the autobiography puts it: "throughout several days [I] incessantly worked at [my] desk," until the realization came

that when sufficiently strict demands are made upon arguments, no ethics can be found that may rationally be forced upon everyone, as maxims of logic, mathematics and science may be. Psychological observation and historical experience show that human actions are judged from very different bases indeed. Since marked typical differences in ways of thought manifest themselves, and since human nature and the conditions in which it develops undergo incessant shifting and change, we could not expect to find matters otherwise. Ethical judgments are passed, and must be passed, from very different bases which may lead to agreement in results but not always for the same reasons. Through logical analysis we might arrive back at the premises peculiar to a particular position, but these are related to psychological and historical circumstances which do not manifest themselves in the same way in other positions.[11]

Thus when Høffding actually does try to penetrate the problem, he is forced to confess that one cannot establish any generally valid normative ethics, and that one cannot pass directly from empirical description to the establishment of moral rules having general validity. There is always a gap which can only be bridged by the acceptance of a certain position; only by including this position as a premise can a logical inference be made. According to Høffding—and in a way he always held this view—ethical valuation, like all other valuation, stems from an emotive source. It is moreover characteristic of Høffding that he never sharply distinguishes between ethical value and value as a general concept; this

---

[8] *Etik* [Ethics] (Copenhagen: P. G. Philipsens, 1887), p. 8.
[9] *Ibid.*
[10] *Ibid.*, p. 9.
[11] *Erindringer*, pp. 150–51.

is a typical ambiguity and weakness in his theoretical writings. Then, since ethical values, as do all other values, depend upon emotions, and these, as opposed to cognition, are not subject to general rules of reason, a limit in principle is set to moral rationality. Emotive life is regarded by Høffding in the light of the classic pleasure-pain doctrine; he is, particularly in his early works, a psychological hedonist.

This is already apparent in *Concerning the Basis of Human Ethics*. There he describes how sensations of pleasure will occur if "our conscious mental life on the whole is encouraged and enhanced" and how displeasure and pain appear if "it is inhibited and weakened."[12] In this same work he formulates the close connection between pleasure-pain and valuation as follows: "To all that promotes an elevation of our mental condition, hence a feeling of pleasure, we ascribe a certain value."[13] In *Ethics* he says that "all valuation of actions presupposes a subject with the ability to feel pleasure or pain. Valuation presupposes that a demand is made of the actions, which these are more or less able to meet, but such a demand will seem completely unmotivated when the action is not capable of provoking pleasure or pain."[14] And, finally, in the essay on "The Possibility of Philosophical Ethics" he says that "the nature of an action or an institution can only provoke an ethical judgment, a judgment of good or evil, when the action or institution in question provokes a feeling of pleasure or pain in us. If we were mere perceiving, sensing and comparing beings without the ability to feel pleasure or pain, such judgments would not arise."[15]

But emotive life is not isolated from or uninfluenced by other aspects of conscious mental life. It is above all developed under the influence of cognition. One may imagine a very primitive stage where the emotive life is unaffected by cognition such that no heed is paid to past or future but life is lived in the present; about such a stage Høffding has this to say in *Ethics*: "In this position— and only in this—good is completely merged with the feeling of pleasure, evil with that of pain."[16] But as soon as our memory and our expectations are involved, feeling, and hence valuation, will not be dependent exclusively upon the immediate situation but will be decided by these memories and these expectations of the future.

We find a particularly important connection between emotion, valuation, and cognition where we know of a causal relation and where, consequently, something may be valued according to its ability to serve as the means and the cause of producing a desired goal. Høffding touches on this question in *Concerning the Basis of Human Ethics*, where he says "But when certain ideas and

---

[12] *Om Grundlaget for den humane Ethik*, p. 7.

[13] *Ibid.*, p. 8.

[14] *Etik.*, 1' udg. [1st ed.], pp. 21–22.

[15] *Etiske Undersøgelser* [Ethical investigations] (Copenhagen: P. G. Philipsens, 1891), p. 7.

[16] *Etik.*, 1' udg., p. 23.

actions turn out to be closely related to each other, since one leads to another, as cause to effect, or there exists a close similarity or affinity between them, then gradually emotion will be extended to all such related ideas."[17] It will clearly be seen from this that to Høffding these are problems which may be explained according to the doctrine of association, and it is characteristic of his work of this early period that he firmly adheres to associationist psychology.

Later he describes in more detail how this emotive, and hence valuational, transition from goal to means and from means to goal may be explained by the principles of associationist psychology, and he here introduces the concepts of 'motive transfer' and 'value transfer.' Motive transfer occurs where something which was originally valued as a means of obtaining something else, because of this gradually acquires independent value, i.e., pleasure is associated with it through an association with the goal-connected pleasure. Value transfer works in the opposite direction; here something which originally was valued as an independent goal gradually takes on the character of a means of reaching a more distant goal, which itself acquires value.

But these concepts of motive and value transfer do not make their appearance until about 1890, that is to say, not until comparatively late in the development of Høffding's terminology.[18]

In *Ethics* Høffding constructs a course of development beginning with a pure 'ethics of the present moment,' where value is determined only by immediately occuring pleasure or pain, regardless of past or future. The development next leads to an 'ethics of the individual,' where past or future may be considered but only that of the particular individual in question. The basic law of individualistic ethics deals with the relationship between the separate moment and the total life of the individual: "It will consist of two main commandments, a negative one and a positive one: (1) the separate moment must not take on more independence than is compatible with its significance within the whole life; (2) but on the other hand each moment should be lived out as fully and richly as is consistent with the preservation of existence."[19]

Owing to the psychological mechanisms already mentioned, the development may further progress to the point where not only will the separate individual be considered but also other human beings, and ideally all other human beings. We here reach what Høffding calls "human ethics" or "welfare ethics." It is this position Høffding decides to develop throughout the entire remainder of the book. To reach this stage the most important factor is sympathy, the ability to feel pleasure or pain when others experience these feelings. The basic law of human ethics is "that actions should lead to as much welfare and progress for as many conscious beings as possible."[20] Between the individualistic stage and

[17] *Om Grundlaget for den humane Ethik*, pp. 8–9.
[18] See *Etiske Undersøgelser*, p. 5.
[19] *Etik*, p. 25.
[20] *Etik.*, 1' udg., p. 31.

the stage of human ethics lies a long series of intermediate stages where the relevant totality does not as yet include all conscious beings, but where, on the other hand, more is encompassed than the single individual himself. Here one may find systems of ethics which rest on consideration for the family, the nation, or some other social unit.

These intermediary stages do not particularly interest Høffding. He is mainly concerned with developing what is implied by the basic principle of human ethics in its application to various aspects of personal and social life. In addition he wants to show how it is psychologically possible for a human being to reach this position. As has been emphasized, he does not believe it possible to prove the truth of this ethical system; on the other hand he feels that the ethics put forward must be shown to be humanly possible, that it should be proved to correspond to motives actually belonging to human nature. It is essentially a question of demonstrating those psychological mechanisms which may result in consideration for others rather than oneself when valuations are made.

In *Concerning the Basis of Human Ethics*, it is primarily sympathy, secondly the motive-transfer mechanism, and thirdly the role of authority—be it educative, punitive, or rewarding—which are emphasized. In this connection it should be mentioned that Høffding, in *The Principles of Philosophical Ethics*, had already clearly rejected the common error that ethics on a hedonist basis will automatically result in pure egoism. His comments on this are sound, that is, his distinction between egoism and what he calls individualism is clear and to the point.

As for the role of sympathy, an important development in his thought occurs between *Concerning the Basis of Human Ethics* and *Ethics*, a development which Høffding himself repeatedly alludes to and emphasizes.[21] In the first works, he had not sharply distinguished between the motives that lie behind moral action and, on the other hand, moral valuation. However, he realized in the course of writing the second work that such a distinction must be made and is of great significance. He then assigns to universal sympathy the role of general psychological basis of valuation within the human ethics, but emphasizes that it may well be possible for an action to be morally praiseworthy as seen in the light of this ethics while not in itself arising from any feeling of sympathy.

Here, without doubt, we may speak of an improvement. It is one of the great weaknesses of the earlier ethical works, including *Concerning the Basis of Human Ethics*, that insufficient distinction is made between the moral action and its motivation on the one hand and the ethical valuation and its psychological basis on the other.

The fundamental position reached by Høffding in *Ethics* regarding the question of the possibility of a universally valid normative ethics is what might be called a relativistic one. Such a universally valid ethics does not exist, for

[21] See *Erindringer*, p. 152.

human beings hold different ethical positions; the transition from one position to another may be psychologically explained but not logically proved or required.

Logic only enters the scene in inferring the consequences of the position chosen, and here in particular the relation between means and ends plays a part. If one's end is general welfare, then a great many consequences follow concerning the means one must use: the question as to which actions will actually constitute the most suitable means for obtaining this end will be an empirical question. And the same will be the case with nationalistic or individualistic ethics.

In the essay "Philosophical Problems," which Høffding published in the University Annual of 1902, he introduced a concept which was to play an important part in his entire philosophy of values, the concept of 'basic value.' The separate ethical positions may be described by indicating a certain value which functions as the basic value for each position, a value in the light of which everything else is evaluated. "If a comparison is to be made between different values, and every conscious valuation consists of such a comparison, then a basic value must be presumed, according to which the order of precedence of the various values may be laid down."[22] In the editions of *Ethics* which came out after 1902 Høffding made certain alterations, since he found that by introducing this new concept of basic value he was able to express his thoughts more clearly than before.

The previous year he had published his *Philosophy of Religion*. Here again the concept of value is a central idea. This clearly appears from his famous definition of religion as a belief in the conservation of value. What are considered the central or highest values may vary from religion to religion, but it is the characteristic of religion as such that it arises from "the desire to hold fast to the conservation of the highest values beyond the limits which experience exhibits and in spite of all the transformations which experience reveals."[23] The value which then lies in religion itself, the religious value as such, must, according to this definition, have the character of a derivative or secondary value. This Høffding realizes and formulates thus: "Since all religion presupposes experience of values, the religious values in themselves must to a certain extent be derived, i. e., conditioned by the interest in the primary values which our experience of life has taught us to know and to maintain."[24] However, he does not consistently maintain this position. On the very same page he says, "Primary values often arise in a religious form from the outset, so that the two kinds of experience are had simultaneously." Further on he says: "And even when the difference be-

---

[22] "Filosofiske Problemer" [Philosophical problems], in *Indbydelsesskrift til Kjøbenhavns Universitets Aarsfest til Erindring om Kirkens Reformation* [University of Copenhagen annual in memory of the church reformation] (Copenhagen: J. H. Schultz, 1902), p. 71.

[23] *Religionsfilosofi.*, 1' udg. [Philosophy of religion, 1st ed.], (Copenhagen: Nordiske, 1901), p. 194.

[24] *Ibid.*, p. 196.

tween primary and religious values makes itself felt, the religious value may still retain its immediacy and independence." On the whole, his further treatment of religious values as secondary ones contains much that is obscure and inconsisent. Thus, in the *Philosophy of Religion* Høffding touches upon the question of pessimism and claims: "And yet even in pessimism there must be an underlying faith in the conservation of value, for were all value to disappear, the relation between value and reality must necessarily disappear also."[25] It is obvious, however, that a belief in the conservation of value presupposes that this value remains as part of reality, not only as a fictive value to be compared to reality, and I cannot conclude otherwise than that Høffding is here guilty of a real inconsistency.

The inconsistency becomes even more serious when he proceeds to say that it is not necessary for this primary value related to religion to be the same all the time, that "it is not any particular definite value which is preserved. If a value is to maintain itself it must suffer change."[26] This amounts to saying that religious belief only involves the idea that in a given situation something will always exist which will be perceived as valuable, but not the idea that it will continue to exist and continue to have value. It is obvious, however, that if religion is to be no more than this, then everyone must *eo ipso* be religious, insofar as he has values at all, which everyone must, even according to Høffding's psychology.

Having considered Høffding's treatment of ethical value in the ethical works and of religious value in the *Philosophy of Religion*, let us now proceed to what might be called his general philosophy of value. This in particular is worked out in his later writings, which are more concerned with epistemological questions—first in the 1902 essay, "Philosophical Problems," mentioned above, later in the major work, *Human Thought*, published in 1910, and finally in the 1917 essay, "Totality as a Category," the last being of special interest in this connection.

In these works the problems of ethics and religion are treated together with, and along the same lines as, those of epistemology, and here essentially new aspects of the problem appear. What might be termed Høffding's mature philosophy of value may be summed up in four main points, of which the first is this: that which satisfies a need and causes pleasure or wards off pain is of value.[27] The need as such does not have to be immediately sensed but may be postulated when pleasure or pain is felt and, therefore, something is thus valued. It is worth noting that this definition of value, for it is a definition, concerns only positive value; in fact it should have included negative value as well. It should also be mentioned that Høffding here introduces an abstruse distinction between potential and actual value.[28] The point of this seems to be that when a person has some kind of need but does not know what may satisfy this need, that which might satisfy it would have a sort of potential value even though the idea of it

[25] *Ibid.*, p. 202.
[26] *Ibid.*, p. 228.
[27] *Den menneskelige Tanke* [Human thought] (Copenhagen: Gyldendalske Boghandel-Nordisk, 1910), p. 238.
[28] *Ibid.*, p. 243.

may not evoke any pleasure. Thus, for something to be of actual value, a direct relation between the idea of the thing and the need through which the feeling of pleasure can occur is required.

The second main point is concerned with the relation between ends and means and the concept of basic value. This may be formulated in the following way: If the object of value is not immediately obtainable, then it is made into an end and means are sought to obtain it; the means then acquires mediate value, while values that are unfounded or underived from others are immediate. A norm is a rule concerning the means required in order to reach a certain goal.[29] This point may be illustrated by a quotation from "Philosophical Problems": "When the valuable object does not immediately fall to us, we make it into an end and seek the means with which to reach it. That which appears as a means of reaching something of immediate value, acquires mediate value to us."[30] It is here noteworthy that Høffding subordinates the concept of norm to that of value, thus placing himself in opposition to Kant, for example, who in an important section of *Kritik der praktischen Vernunft*, entitled "Von dem Begriff eines Gegenstandes der reinen praktischen Vernunft," takes the opposite direction altogether and traces the concepts of goal and value back to the concept of norm or law. Both Høffding and Kant probably took too one-sided a view of the problem. The relation between the concept of value and that of norm is more complicated than it appears from either of these two theories; it is probably not a question of defining one concept directly in terms of the other, but of a more complicated relation.

The third point involves an extremely important connection between the concept of value and that of totality. This connection may be briefly formulated as follows: A need presupposes a totality which tends to assert itself, and the feeling of pleasure indicates that the striving of this totality to exist and develop has succeeded.[31] In fact, one can only talk of value where such a totality is present.[32] The question of what is of value to such a totality may be decided objectively, since the conditions of its existence and development may be rationally examined. "Value can only be measured by means of value";[33] if values are to be compared, a basic value must be presumed, i.e., the growth of a certain value in relation to which the others are evaluated as mediate values.

In Høffding's theory of knowledge the concept of totality holds a central position; this is bound up with his theory of truth which is a kind of coherence theory. I shall now proceed to demonstrate that the concept of totality plays an extremely important part in his philosophy of value.

---

[29] *Ibid.*, pp. 242–43.

[30] "Filosofiske Problemer," p. 71.

[31] *Den menneskelige Tanke*, p. 238.

[32] *Totalitet som Kategori* [Totality as a category], Royal Danish Scientific Society Publications, series 7, Historical and Philosophical Division, vol. 3, no. 2 (Copenhagen: Andr. Fred. Høst & Søn, 1917), p. 69.

[33] *Den menneskelige Tanke*, p. 240.

First a few quotations from *Human Thought*: "We may only speak of values according to the given definitions, when a creation of totality has taken place,"[34] "Valuation, the value quality changes according to the totality on which it is based. Within this totality it may be the way in which various parts or qualities develop which particularly determines the value quality. Each separate series of values must therefore be founded on a certain value, determined by that totality, and within this yet again by that part or quality whose *sine qua non* is under discussion. All valuation rests on a basic value."[35] The position here is still relativistic, but it is not a subjectivistic one. For the totality from which the valuation is made in no way has to be the valuing agent itself. One can see that a certain development in relation to Høffding's earlier views in *Concerning the Basis of Human Ethics* has taken place; in that work he held that the feelings of the valuing subject sufficed as a basis for all evaluation. Moreover there lies in the whole of Høffding's concept of totality and its effect on value a tendency away from the relativistic towards a more absolutistic-objectivistic position. This appears when Høffding begins to speak of higher and lower totalities. Before embarking upon this question, we may ask what Høffding has in mind when he speaks of totalities.

As examples of totalities he mentions solar systems, planets, organisms, individuals, and communities. In *Human Thought* he claims that, strictly speaking, only the latter three determine valuation. He goes on to say: "There may be a biological, an individual and a social valuation. However we might well employ, analogically, a valuating process of thought with respect to all totalities; we might ask about the conditions of the existence and growth of a mountain, a planet, an astronomical system."[36] In *Totality as a Category* he says, however, "And in the strictest sense we may only speak of values from the point of view of individual beings, because only in individuals are the tendency and its conflict with conditions sensed and felt. The concept of value is transmitted to other totalities (communities, organisms, inorganic totalities) only through analogy; we already have an analogy when an individual being tries to acquaint itself with that which may be of value to other individual beings."[37] We may here accuse Høffding of a certain vacillation between the position that pleasure-pain is fundamental and the position that totality is fundamental. Perhaps what he meant is that each of us develops a general concept of value on the basis of his own feelings of pleasure and pain, and gains the insight that these feelings are produced by the changing fate of the totality which is himself. This concept of value can and will then be applied to other totalities. A more consistent position for Høffding to take would be to connect the concept of value only to totalities which tend to assert themselves against their environment in the way living beings and social groups do, and then disregard the question of feelings.

[34] *Ibid.*, p. 239.
[35] *Ibid.*, p. 240.
[36] *Ibid.*, p. 239.
[37] *Totalitet som Kategori*, p. 67.

With this I have reached the fourth main point, the question of how to distinguish between higher and lower totalities. I shall quote a long passage from *Human Thought* where a criterion is presented and justified:

If the various totalities are compared *inter se* they may be arranged in series according to viewpoints that are comprised in the concept of totality itself. A relation between unity and plurality will assert itself in all totalities. It is the interaction of various causal chains that condition totality. Thus is given a relation between the plurality of these chains on one side and the degree of unity and concentration presented by the totality on the other side. The richer a plurality assembled into unity and the more marked this unity, the higher the totality may be said to be . . . . we would then, according to this standard, be able to arrange those totalities that are presented by experience. And it is also such a standard that is used within the special fields, i.e. when comparing one planet with another, one organism with another, one individual with another and one community with another. Comparison becomes more difficult when the different types of totality are to be compared. Here a conflict between two points of view, that of degree or intensity and that of extension, enters. According to the former, the organism ranges above the planet, the individual, the community, and according to the latter the order is reversed.[38]

The train of thought with which we are here confronted is a very central one in Høffding; we might, in the words of Edgar Rubin, speak of it as a basic theme in his philosophy. We shall come across it several times in what follows, and Høffding himself emphasizes its central influence on his philosophy in his 1902 account of the problems of philosophy and also in *Human Thought*. In these works he claims that it is a common feature of the four main problems of philosophy that ultimately they all deal with the relation between unity and plurality, or, as he also puts it, between continuity and discontinuity. Moreover, in both his autobiography and *Human Thought*, he explains how this thought occurred to him. He refers here to Kierkegaard, among others. Through a closer study of Kierkegaard, he was struck by the idea that the "formal particularity of spiritual life lies in that unity, that concentration with which the life contents are held together, and that the measure of the value of spiritual life is found in the relation between the wealth of its contents and the energy of its concentration. This idea, which has been seen before Kierkegaard in the history of philosophy, is the basis of Kierkegaard's philosophical characterization of the various stages or types of life."[39]

Høffding probably here attributes more to Kierkegaard than the latter would acknowledge; what he has in mind must be Kierkegaard's emphasis on the fact that the higher the stage at which we live, the higher is the tension under which we live. This tension then, according to Høffding's interpretation, should be due to the fact that a plurality must be held together to form such a degree of unity that a certain stage may be said to have been reached.

Here we touch upon something which played a very important part in Høffding's own development as a person. His interest in the relation between

[38] *Den menneskelige Tanke*, pp. 222–23.
[39] *Erindringer*, p. 51.

unity and plurality probably dates back to the crisis of his youth. At that time he felt within himself a strong conflict between various tendencies, partly the Christian-religious tendency and partly more wordly ones, and he longed for harmony—however, preferably one which was not attained by eliminating and rejecting any tendencies, but by incorporating as much variety as possible within the same totality.

This is also something which strongly influenced his psychology, i.e., in the idea that mental disease consists in a lack of harmony.

Among possible 'philosophical' sources of Høffding's doctrine of value Herbert Spencer must be mentioned: the concept of totality is treated in *Human Thought* in close connection with the concept of evolution. Also, in the thought of Spinoza, the philosopher Høffding most admired, he may have found ideas leading in the direction of a connection between value and totality. Currents in contemporary English idealistic philosophy, as represented by Bernard Bosanquet and Høffding's friend W. R. Sorley, may also have been influential.

It seems to me that this talk of higher and lower totalities, where one is partly concerned with how rich a variety is contained within the totality and partly to what extent this forms a harmonious whole, makes good sense when considered from a personal point of view regarding conflict or harmony in the life and attitudes of the individual. It is, however, questionable how meaningful it is when presented as a metaphysical principle of values. If the principle is applied to those totalities which are selected as basic values for various ethical positions it may easily be thought to imply that one ethical position is better and truer than another if its basic value ranges higher in the order of totalities. This applied, it entails an objectivistic line of thought. Certainly Høffding emphasizes in the above quotation from *Human Thought* that the two points of view, of degree and of extension, respectively, will very often lead to the opposite result when two totalities are compared. But in saying so Høffding in a way has admitted that if the two points of view lead to the same result, that is, if there are two totalities of which one holds greater variety as well as more harmony than the other, then one ought to choose the first as a basic value rather than the other. But apparently he did not appreciate this consequence since doing so would have resulted in his abandoning relativistic ethics.

Thus we see that while Høffding in his works before the turn of the century developed a relativistic position in ethics based on a psychological theory of value, he later moved toward an absolutistic one based on a metaphysical theory of value. The key to this theory is the concept of totality, a concept which also plays a central part in his conception of consciousness and his theory of knowledge. The vagueness of his concept, as used by Høffding, makes it hard to see how much is gained by trying to explain not only beauty—as did Aristotle— but also truth and goodness as 'unity in plurality.' On the face of it, this idea may seem attractive, but could one not with some justification inquire: Why in fact should a closer connection between a greater number of elements be better?

Konrad Marc-Wogau

Axel Hägerström's Ontology

A philosopher's ontology—his answer to the question "What is real?"—can often throw light on many of his more special theories. In this study of Hägerström's ontology I intend to investigate his view about what kinds of entities are real and in what sense they are real. To begin with I shall present a summary of Hägerström's theory of reality.

The theory consists of three main theses:

(1) "Reality" means the same as "determinedness."

(2) There is one and only one determined context—the *in toto* real—in which all other determined (real) entities are elements and besides which no other is thinkable; every determined entity belongs to this total context of the real, either as the content of apprehension (consciousness) only or as something that is real apart from the apprehension of it, i.e., as something that may be but is not necessarily an object of apprehension.

(3) This, the 'all-real' context, is the context of our experience in time and space.

If we disregard the context itself, which of course is something determined, the three expressions "x is determined," "x belongs to the *in toto* real," and "x belongs to the context of our experience in time and space," can be considered as equivalent for all x. In other words, everything that is determined (with the exception of the context itself) belongs to the *in toto* real and thus also to the context of our experience in time and space, and everything that belongs to our experience in time and space belongs also to the *in toto* real (all-real context) and is by virtue of that determined.

Professor Marc-Wogau, of the University of Uppsala in Sweden, is a native of Sweden.

The first thesis, "*x* is real if and only if it is determined," or, as Hägerström also says, is "self-identical and free from contradiction," is obviously directed against every assumption of the contradictory nature of reality. Hägerström maintains, "This, *to be something*, would dissolve into pure nonentity, did not self-identity belong to reality as such. The real could then be anything whatever."[1] The same idea is worded as follows in *Religionsfilosofi*:

The real is as such something fixed that cannot be in more than *one* way. Take away this supposition and the nerve of life will be cut off. The question "Does God exist?" will then be the same question as "Does the devil exist?" or "Does a cat exist?" Were the real not [real] in *one* way only, we should have God as the devil and the devil as a cat.[2]

The second thesis, that all definite entities make up *one total context* and belong to it either as the content of an apprehension only or as something that is also real apart from the apprehension of it, is opposed to every assumption of two separate worlds of reality.

The third thesis, finally, that the context of all real entities is identical with the spatiotemporal context of experience, is in opposition to every idealistic theory, according to which reality is spiritual and consequently something beyond time and space.

In the essay "Selbstdarstellung" Hägerström adduces arguments for the second and the third theses.[3] He gives us to understand that the second thesis can be deduced from certain premises, one of which is the first thesis, and that the third thesis can be deduced from certain premises, one of which is the second thesis. But even if he considered these arguments as conclusive, it is very probable that he was also persuaded of the validity of the third thesis quite independently of them. This is the thesis which naturally became a stumbling block for all adherents of idealistic metaphysics.

That all determined entities must belong to the spatiotemporal context of our experience does not, of course, mean that they must be spatially extended, i.e., have length, breadth, and depth. Only some determined entities are such spatial elements. These elements belong to the context *directly*, or independently of other elements. All other determined entities belong to the context *indirectly*: they are qualities of the spatial elements or qualities of something that is a quality of a spatial element.

We are now prepared to illustrate Hägerström's ontology by the following schema.

---

[1] *Till analysen av det empiriska självmedvetandet* [Analysis of the empirical self-consciousness] (Uppsala, 1910), p. 30.

[2] *Religionsfilosofi* [Philosophy of religion] (Stockholm: Natur och kultur, 1949; hereafter cited as *Rf.*), p. 233.

[3] "Selbstdarstellung," in *Philosophie der Gegenwart in Selbstdarstellungen*, ed. Raymund Schmidt, vol. 7 (Leipzig: Felix Meiner, 1929; hereafter cited as *Sd.*).

SCHEMA 1

The Ontological Schema

The real

(1) x is real = x is determined
(2) x is real = x belongs to the all-real context

(3) x is real = x belongs to the spatiotemporal context of our experience

The unreal	as content of apprehension only	not only as content of an apprehension	
		directly (as independent elements)	indirectly (not as independent elements)
Round Squares God as spirit Ego as something internal and spiritual	**A**	**C** Physical objects Conscious or unconscious organisms Events	
Self-consciousness Values Proprietary rights	**B** Products of imagination, e.g., characters in fiction, centaurs; also the property of being a centaur Objects of hallucinations and illusions Contents of feelings		**D** All kinds of consciousness: e.g., sensations, perceptions, ideas, judgments, feelings Universals, e.g., qualities of bodies

We may note at once that there are three senses of the words "real" and "reality" in Hägerström's ontology, as shown by schema 1.

(1) $real_1$ = determined,
(2) $real_2$ = belonging to the all-real context, i.e., $real_1$, not only as content of an apprehension ("not only as apprehended"), and
(3) $real_3$ = belonging directly to the spatiotemporal context of our experience.

Let us now comment on the schema presented here.

Square A is empty. No entity which is only a content of an apprehension belongs directly to the spatiotemporal context of our experience. It can only belong to it indirectly, namely, as a content of an apprehension, which in its turn is an attribute of an organism ('physical person') directly belonging to the spatiotemporal context.

The contents of square B are only $real_1$: they are determined, but belong to the all-real context only as contents of consciousness, and they are only indirectly elements of the spatiotemporal context.

The contents of square C are real in all three senses: they are determined, they belong to the all-real context not only as contents of consciousness, and they are directly elements of the spatiotemporal context.

The contents of square D, finally, are both $real_1$ and $real_2$. They are (1) determined and (2) belong to the all-real context not only as contents of an apprehension. But they lack $reality_3$ in that they belong to the spatiotemporal context only indirectly through being a quality of something that belongs to the context directly.

In "Selbstdarstellung" (pp. 121 ff.) Hägerström explains the meaning of the statement that something is a quality of something else. That *solubility in aqua regia* (S) is said to be a quality of gold (G) does not mean that being *gold* is determined by that quality. Gold is as such determined, and this determinedness cannot be modified or limited by anything else. The statement under consideration means only that *solubility in aqua regia* (S) can be distinguished in the whole SG as a characteristic of this whole quite apart from the characteristic golden or being *gold* (G). The two characteristics S and G do not determine each other; rather they constitute the whole SG. According to Hägerström, the relation between S and G, expressed in the statement "G is S," is not a third element in addition to S and G. If applied to an act of consciousness (C) and the organism (O) which is said to have this consciousness, this means that there is a whole CO in which one can distinguish the two elements C and O, and which does not contain a relation between C and O as a third element. Also in the case of an apprehension of something, e.g., a body (B), Hägerström reckons only with two elements, the apprehension and B. The content (B) of the apprehension is an element of the whole 'apprehension of B' and is said to be a characteristic of the whole. If the apprehension were an illusion, its content (*B*) would belong to the spatiotemporal context of the real only indirectly, indeed as being a characteristic of the whole 'apprehension of *B*,' but where this in its turn is a characteristic of a conscious organism which alone belongs directly to the spatiotemporal context.

The rest of the schema (the rectangle on the left side) contains all that Hägerström considers unreal, contradictory, or senseless. There is nothing real that corresponds to the expression "round square." The qualities *round* and *square* are both real (at least in the sense "real$_1$") but they cannot compose a complex unit; they cannot, unlike the qualities *red* and *square*, be thought of in *one* thought. According to Hägerström, in trying to realize such a thought one oscillates between two incompatible thoughts, *round* and *square*. The expression "round square" cannot be predicated of anything; it does not connote anything unambiguous or determined. It lacks both denotation and connotation. Also, the word "God," as name for an omnipotent spirit and not for something material (as in some primitive religions), is senseless. The main characteristic of the usual concept of spirit is, according to Hägerström, self-consciousness, i.e., a consciousness which is identical with its object (see below). But such a concept, he maintains, is a pure contradiction. "God" does not connote anything; it is only an emotive expression. The same is true of the word "I," when used not to designate one's body but something that is supposed to be internal and spiritual—an entitative self-consciousness.

Value words like "good," "right," "beautiful," belong also to the same rectangle, although the situation with respect to them is in some ways different. Within a community, a social unit with commonly shared words such as "good," "right," and so on can predicate them of the same objects, properties, or actions. They seem to have a more or less definite denotation. What Hägerström nevertheless emphasizes is that they lack connotation, i.e., that they do not refer to qualities of the denoted objects, although one may believe that they do so. That values are unreal means, according to Hägerström's emotive theory of value, at least in many contexts, that value words only express the speaker's feelings and do not connote any quality of the real.

Many other words belong to the same column. Hägerström says, for instance, that there is nothing in the realm of reality that corresponds to the word "fatherland," i.e., "fatherland" in the sense not of native country but as uttered with trembling voice as an expression of patriotism. Used in this way, the word "fatherland" does not connote any characteristic of the native country; it lacks connotation and is only an emotive expression.

Hägerström's assertion that there are no rights, e.g., no proprietary rights, means something different. In his view there is nothing real that corresponds to "proprietary right," if this word-complex is used to refer to a metaphysical power in respect to the acquired thing, as is often the case in jurisprudence. "There is no proprietary right" means that there is no such metaphysical power. Insofar as it supposed to involve anything of the kind, 'proprietary right' belongs to the column for the unreal.

Schema 1 can throw light upon several other points in Hägerström's philosophy, among them Hägerström's *materialism*. His view is that only material objects and organisms (which, of course, may have mental characteristics) belong to the spatiotemporal world of our experience directly, i.e., as independent elements. But Hägerström does not deny the reality of mental acts or different kinds of consciousness. Only those spiritual entities which are not spatial and not characteristics of something spatial have no place in Hägerström's realm of reality. Mental acts as such lack length, breadth, and other qualities which characterize spatial entities. But the fact that they as such are not in space does not, according to Hägerström, preclude their "belonging to organisms that are in space," i.e., belonging to the spatiotemporal context indirectly (as characteristics of conscious organisms). All kinds of mental acts have their place in square D of the schema (see *Sd.*, p. 132; *Rf.*, p. 243).

This way of picturing the ontology can also help us to understand Hägerström's view of universals. We see that universals lack reality$_3$, so that while they do not, as the forms of Plato, exist in some place beyond the heavens, neither do they belong directly to the spatiotemporal context of our experience. But they are real not only in the sense that they are determined. At least some of them—namely, those universals which are not only products of imagination—have reality$_2$; as qualities of objects which are real in the sense of "real$_3$" they have reality not only as contents of consciousness. According to Hägerström's *Botanisten och filosofen*, it is a necessary condition of experience as knowledge—knowing, or coming to know—that "the sensible reality is determinable by universals and that the universals really exist in the individual objects."[4] Universals as abstract qualities are like mental acts in that they lack length, breadth, and other spatial characteristics. But this does not preclude their being in space (indirectly belonging to the spatiotemporal context) as characteristics of spatial objects (see *Sd.*, p. 132; *Rf.*, p. 243). They also belong in square D.

Schema 1 as presented does not, however, exhaust Hägerström's ontology. There are many entities not indicated in it of which the ontological status is not quite clear.

The ontology of Hägerström, unlike the ontology of Wittgenstein in the *Tractatus*, lays stress upon things, not upon facts. His real world consists of things and events, not of facts. The red rose is real$_3$, but the fact that the rose is red is not. And events like the ringing of bells at a certain time t belong to our world of experience, but hardly the fact that the bells rang at t. On the other hand, Hägerström does sometimes speak of facts in such a way as to suggest

---

[4] *Botanisten och filosofen* [The botanist and the philosopher] (Stockholm: Bonniers, 1910), p. 59; cf. p. 61 ff.

that he ascribes some positive ontological status to them. He says, in particular, that sentences describe facts. But if *facts* are to be considered as special kinds of entities, it is not easy to know where their place in the schema is. It is also difficult to decide what view Hägerström held as to the ontological status of *propositions*. By "propositions" I mean such things as, for instance, the Pythagorean theorem or the laws of Galileo. Propositions in this sense are obviously something determined; they have reality$_1$, but do they have reality$_2$? Does a proposition belong to the context of the real not only as content of a thought? As to the nature of *numbers*, there are, so far as I know, no statements in Hägerström's works to give us a hint concerning their place in the schema.

Neither is Hägerström's view concerning the reality of *sense data* quite clear. In the manuscript "Relativitetsteori och kunskapsfilosofi" unambiguous answers are given to the questions of the reality of the rainbow and the apparently bent shape of a stick immersed in water.[5] Hägerström adduces two criteria of perception in contradistinction to imagination: (1) we conceive the object of perception but not the object of imagination to be real, in that we refer the former to the spatiotemporal context, not only as a content of consciousness; and (2) we are passive in perception but not in imagination, i.e., the object of perception appears to us to be the cause of the perception of it, which is not the case with an object of imagination (*FoV.*, p. 216 ff.). A hallucination is like a perception insofar as its object at the moment of its apprehension appears to us as something real which also is the cause of the apprehension; not until we reflect on the hallucination do we become aware that its object is not real. In this connection, Hägerström emphasizes the special role of the tactual sense for our belief in the reality of the perceived object. "If an educated person sees in his visual field a figure which, according to his knowledge, cannot be touched, it is for him something unreal, even if it—as e.g., the rainbow—presupposes something real" (*FoV.*, p. 194). We decide that the apparently bent shape of a stick immersed in water is an illusion by virtue of "the primacy of the tactual sense in relation to the sight" (*FoV.*, p. 193). The stick looks bent but feels straight, and thus as a matter of fact is straight. Hence, although the aggregate of raindrops and the straight stick belong to square C of schema 1, the rainbow and the bent stick belong to square B, although as objects of illusions they differ from mere products of imagination. But what is the nature of a flash of lightning which we perceive as a streak of light in the sky? Does it belong to square C or square B? Here it is not clear how any evidence of the tactual sense can be appealed to. How Hägerström would answer these and similar questions can probably never be decided, simply because he did not reflect upon them or, at least as far as I know, treat them in his works.

---

[5] *Filosofi och vetenskap* [Philosophy and science], ed. M. Fries (Stockholm: Ehlins, 1957; hereafter cited as *FoV.*). This book contains *inter alia* the posthumous edition of Hägerström's essay "Relativitetsteori och kunskapsfilosofi" [Theory of relativity and epistemology].

There is, however, one kind of entity which Hägerström mentions often but whose ontological status is nevertheless disputed. I mean the *contents of feelings or emotions.*

In his theory of feeling Hägerström repeatedly emphasizes the distinction between the act of feeling and its content. Feeling is, he says, "an experience of something" (*Rf.*, p. 157), "a kind of consciousness" (*Sd.*, p. 141). In this consciousness we experience a quality—pleasure, pain, or the like—which is the content of the feeling. For instance, when feeling joy I experience the quality of joy (*Rf.*, p. 129). Unlike knowledge, feeling is not an apprehension of an object, but it is nevertheless consciousness of something, and it belongs to the "stream of the manifestations of an organism's consciousness."[6] Like other kinds of mental acts feeling can be considered as a characteristic of an organism. Feeling is not a cognitive act, not an apprehension of the reality of an object. But this does not, Hägerström holds, preclude the fact "that a feeling itself can be an object of observation and then also be conceived as something real" (*ibid.*, p. 147). "Real," here, has the meaning of our "real$_2$." When reflecting upon a feeling experience we conceive of it as an object, i.e., as something that belongs to the all-real context not only as a content of a mental act. It is clear that experiences such as having specific feelings or being in one or another emotional state are real in the sense of the entities in square D of schema 1. On the other hand, according to Hägerström, the distinctive content of any such experience lacks 'objective reality,' i.e., reality$_2$. It cannot be assigned to square D. If it has a place in our schema, it must be in square B.

But this is disputed. Hägerström characterizes the relation between act and content in an emotive experience in a rather confusing way. Many of his interpreters have held the opinion that such experiences, according to Hägerström, are characterized by what Hägerström's followers in Uppsala have called "subject objectivity," i.e., identity of the act of experiencing and what is experienced. The term "subject objectivity," however, is not unambiguous; on the contrary it has two quite different senses. In the case of feelings, it is natural to distinguish between the object and the content of a feeling. For example, I feel glad at the arrival of a friend; the arrival of my friend is the object of my feeling, but the content is something quite different, namely, the pleasure I feel. Both the identification of the act of feeling with its object and that with its content have been called "subject objectivity." The idea that there are feeling experiences in which— as in Spinoza's *amor dei intellectualis*—the act of feeling coincides with its object is totally foreign to Hägerström. The situation is different with regard to the relation between the feeling and its content. In an early (1907) lecture Hägerström characterizes this relation as "immediate self-consciousness." The feeling of pleasure is itself pleasure, he says, and "the experience which is given in a feel-

---

[6] *Socialfilosofiska uppsatser* [Essays in social philosophy] (Stockholm: Bonniers, 1939; hereafter cited as *Su.*)., p. 148.

ing is totally its own object. . . . I feel glad; here the feeling of pleasure is a feeling in which I experience the feeling itself."[7]

Even this identification of the feeling experience with its content has been called "subject objectivity." Some interpreters of Hägerström's theory have inferred that the relation between the act and the content of feeling, according to his theory, has the character of 'subject objectivity' in this sense. For instance, Tegen writes:

. . . we have here in Hägerström the old concept of feeling as a state of mind or of consciousness where the content and the experience of this content have been confused and united in such a way that it is impossible to distinguish between them. Only with such a concept of feeling can Hägerström maintain the exclusive character of subjectivity he attributes to feeling.[8]

It is, however, very difficult to believe that after *Das Prinzip der Wissenschaft* where he criticizes all kinds of idealism ('subjectivism'), Hägerström could ever have maintained such a theory of feeling.[9] Feeling is a fundamental notion in his philosophy, and it seems incredible that he could have embraced a theory of feeling which on the least reflection must appear incompatible with other theses of that philosophy. According to Hägerström's refutation of idealism, no consciousness whatever has the character which Tegen thinks Hägerström attributes to feelings. "I refuted subjectivism"—Hägerström says in "Selbstdarstellung"—"by showing that there is no consciousness in which it itself is given; what is apprehended is always different from the apprehension" (*Sd.*, p. 116). There is, according to Hägerström, an important difference between feeling and knowledge, but nevertheless in both it is necessary to distinguish the mental act from the content. If we let them coincide, the result will be nonsensical: "The consciousness would be the same as the thing itself" (*Rf.*, p. 155). Feeling would become a self-contradictory notion like the notion of self-consciousness. It would lack determinedness; neither the content nor the mental act could then be said to be real.

This consequence, however, is discouraging. It is also obviously inconsistent with Hägerström's opinion that feelings are real experiences, that they are caused by and can be associated with ideas or thoughts. The given interpretation can thus be dismissed as absurd. The question then is how to avoid the above-mentioned consequence in the face of some of Hägerström's other declarations about the nature of feelings.

Many of the statements seem compatible with locating the content of feelings in square B. Among them are the following: "Feelings are not experiences of an object"; "They are not experiences of something real"; "Feeling as experience is such that its content cannot possibly be separated from the experience of it" (*Rf.*,

---

[7] *Jesus. En karaktärsanalys* [Jesus: An analysis of his character], ed. M. Fries (Stockholm: Natur och kultur, 1968), p. 87.

[8] Einar Tegen, "The Basic Problem in the Theory of Value," *Theoria*, vol. 10 (1944).

[9] *Das Prinzip der Wissenschaft*, vol. 1: *Die Realität* (Uppsala, 1908).

pp. 157, 130, 164); feelings are experiences in which "the content is not temporalized or localized" (Sd., p. 142; Su., pp. 127, 148; Rf., p. 18); "The reality of a feeling's content is the reality of the emotional act itself."[10] All statements of this order amount to saying that the content of a feeling lacks reality$_2$, i.e., that it belongs to the all-real context only as content of a feeling experience.

There are, however, other statements which seem to conflict with placing the content of feeling in square B. Hägerström uses the expression "the form of feeling" in a way that seems to suggest that he thinks of the relation between act and content of a feeling as one of subject objectivity. "The only way in which something can be given so that it becomes one with the consciousness of it is in the form of feeling" (Rf., p. 128; cf. p. 164). However, these statements also make sense, as far as I can see—sense which is compatible with location of all feeling content in square B of schema 1.

It is important to distinguish between two different questions which Hägerström has in mind when analyzing a concept, and to keep his answers to the two questions clearly separated. The following observations may serve to highlight the distinction:

(1) Some of the relevant statements have primarily to do with providing a correct analysis of a concept. In these Hägerström is concerned to settle the facts which the concept or the corresponding word denotes.

(2) Other statements are concerned with how—as to meaning—common sense or philosophers can understand given concepts. The interpretation given by common sense and by many philosophers is, according to Hägerström, very often erroneous and inconsistent. He undertakes to account for some of these interpretations by psychological explanations of their origins.

A look at Hägerström's *analysis of the concept of the ego* or self-consciousness may now illuminate the relation between the two questions mentioned. His answer to the question pertaining to (1), i.e., what is present in my mind, when I use "I" in the normal way of saying something about myself, is this: the real nature of the ego is characterized by (a) an idea, (b) a feeling, and (c) an association between them. The idea in question is described by Hägerström as a prehension of a continuous organism (my body), and the feeling as a specific 'life feeling' in connection with certain more contingent experiences (sensations of tension, volitions, and so on). The association between the idea and the feeling—a point of great importance in Hägerström's theory but one which has been analyzed very little—is sometimes said to be such that the idea and the feeling come before the mind simultaneously, but other times is said to be such that there can be an oscillation between the idea of the organism and the feeling.

When answering the other question (2)—how common sense and some philosophers regard the nature of the ego—Hägerström gives special attention to

[10] *Till frågan om den objektiva rättens begrepp* [On the question of the notion of law] (Uppsala, 1917).

the idea that the ego is something internal and spiritual. From thinking of the ego as spiritual, people come to think of it as self-consciousness (i.e., a consciousness of itself). When one says "I am sitting," or "I am going," etc., the word "I" is intended by the speaker as referring primarily to his own body. But when a person says such things as "I am sorry," or "I am glad" he tends to believe that the word "I" refers to something internal and spiritual (*Rf.*, p. 18). And the spirit is thought to be "essentially self-consciousness" (*Rf.*, p. 163).

According to Hägerström, this view is absurd. He proposes an ingenious explanation of its origin. Every feeling, including the life feeling which is an important element in the ego, is characterized by the fact that the content of the feeling is dependent on the experience of it. Apart from this experience the content has no reality. Because of the intimate association of the feeling with the idea of the organism, the content of the feeling (i.e., the experienced quality of pleasure or whatever), by means of a kind of projection toward the organism, is thought to be a quality of the organism itself. In one's life feeling—experiencing *it*—one imagines he is experiencing the organism. But since the content of the feeling cannot be considered as something real apart from the feeling itself, the alleged experience of the content of the feeling *as* a quality of the organism means at the same time a kind of introjection of the organism into the experience of feeling. The organism, so to speak, penetrates the feeling and melts together with it. The ego coincides with the consciousness of it. The idea of the self-consciousness and spirituality of the ego is a consequence of this development. Both the projection of the content of the feeling and the introjection of the conceived organism into the feeling are, in Hägerström's view, illusory. But they explain, according to him, the origin of the (in his view) absurd idea of the ego as something spiritual.

Sometimes Hägerström does not clearly mark his transition from trying to explain the idea of the ego as conceived by common sense and some philosophers to presenting his own theory. Consequently, one could be led to believe that self-consciousness in the aforementioned sense characterizes the ego according to his own view. This would certainly be a misunderstanding. Hägerström very often emphasizes that he finds the common sense idea of the ego as self-consciousness absurd. It is absurd because it identifies two different things, the act of consciousness and the object of consciousness. In *Religionsfilosofi*, for instance, Hägerström says that there is "a great philosophical difficulty" in the idea of the ego as self-consciousness.

As a matter of fact, it is an absurdity that the consciousness of an object should be the same as the object itself. That would mean that the object coincides with the consciousness. But then there would only be a consciousness which is not a consciousness of anything at all (*Rf.*, p. 155).

But does this remove the following objection? It is true that Hägerström regards self-consciousness and the form of subject objectivity according to which the object or content of consciousness coincides with consciousness itself as something which presents a "great philosophical difficulty"; but in explaining this identification of consciousness and its object or content, which according to him characterizes the common sense idea of the ego, he himself assumes a relationship between feeling and its content which is so intimate that the content can be said "to be one with" the consciousness of it. Does this not prove that he thinks of the relation involved as identity and consequently admits of a case of virtual self-consciousness himself, i.e., experience in which the act and the content coincide? I do not believe that this consequence has to be drawn.

Many things would have to hold true of the adduced concept of self-consciousness because of the identity of consciousness and object or content which is supposed to characterize it. Among other things this would mean that the object (content) of self-consciousness cannot possibly be separated from the experience of it and be supposed to exist apart from this experience. Further, it would mean that its reality is the same as the reality of self-consciousness, and that it cannot be localized within a place which is not the place of the experience of it. It would, in short, mean all the things which, according to Hägerström, hold true of the content of a feeling in its relation to the act of feeling. It is possible that Hägerström had this correspondence in mind when he maintained that the experience of feeling has "the form of self-consciousness." But there is no reason to interpret this assertion as meaning that feeling and its content are *identical*, i.e., are only two names for one and the same thing.

If this is correct, Hägerström's statements about the form of feeling are not an obstacle to placing the content of feeling in square B of schema 1. That the content of a feeling "is one with" the consciousness of it means that it has no reality apart from this consciousness. But consciousness and content need not, for all that, be identical.

Johannes Witt-Hansen

The Impact of Niels Bohr's Thought
on Danish Philosophy

Through Niels Bohr's and Werner Heisenberg's investigations of the foundations of quantum mechanics a new view of nature emerged.

Bohr's contributions to this development were presented in a set of lectures or papers, mostly originating in the twenties and thirties and published in the volumes *Atomic Theory and the Description of Nature* and *Atomic Physics and Human Knowledge*, the former with an introductory survey. Bohr gave a summary of his views concerning the relations between quantum physics and philosophy in a paper in *Philosophy in the Mid-Century*. This paper and later addresses or lectures were published in *Essays 1958/1962 on Atomic Physics and Human Knowledge*, prefaced by Aage Bohr.[1]

Outstanding expositions of Bohr's philosophy and its main ideas, complementarity, and correspondence, were given by L. Rosenfeld, K. M. Meyer-Abich, and Aage Petersen. In a book on the correspondence principle and its philosophical significance, I. V. Kuznecov gave an illuminating picture of the relationship between Bohr's principal methodological idea and Marxian dialectics.[2]

Professor Witt-Hansen, of the University of Copenhagen, is a native of Denmark.

[1] Niels Bohr, *Atomic Theory and the Description of Nature* (Cambridge: At the University Press, 1961, 1st ed. 1934); Bohr, *Atomic Physics and Human Knowledge* (London: John Wiley & Sons, 1958); Bohr, "Quantum Physics and Philosophy. Causality and Complementarity," in *Philosophy in the Mid-Century*, ed. R. Klibansky (Florence: La Nuova Italia Editrice, 1958), 1: 308–14; Bohr, *Essays 1958/1962 on Atomic Physics and Human Knowledge* (New York: Interscience Publishers, 1963).

[2] Léon Rosenfeld, *Niels Bohr: An Essay Dedicated to Him on the Occasion of His Sixtieth Birthday, October 7, 1945*, 2nd ed. corr. (Amsterdam: North Holland Publishing Co., 1961, 1st ed. 1945); Rosenfeld, "N. Bohr's Contribution to Epistemology," *Physics Today* 16: 47–54 (1963); Klaus Michael Meyer-Abich, *Korrespondenz, Individualität und Komplementarität* (Wiesbaden: Franz Steiner Verlag GMBH, 1965); Aage Petersen, "The Philosophy of Niels Bohr," *Bulletin of the Atomic Scientists* 19: 8–14 (1963); I. V. Kuznecov, *Princip sootvetstvija v sovremmenoj fizike i ego filosofskoje značenie.* [The correspondence principle in contemporary physics and its philosophical significance] (Moscow and Leningrad: OGIS. Gosudarstvennoe izdatel'stvo texnikoteoretičeskoj literatury, 1948).

Whereas Bohr in his philosophical writings and in his discussions of the epistemological problems raised by quantum mechanics concentrated mainly on the idea of complementarity, for which he discovered or suggested a wide field of application in psychology, anthropology, biology, and epistemology, Danish philosophers took greater interest in the idea of correspondence, which, in fact, was the guiding thread of Bohr's work from the beginning of his epoch-making discovery in 1913.[3]

For the physicist and philosopher Aage Petersen, who was in close contact with Bohr for ten years, the idea of correspondence served as an analytical tool for clarifying the relationships between quantum physics and the philosophical tradition encumbered by ontological concepts. Guided by the conviction that epistemologically the quantum development can be described as an articulation of the correspondence idea, he concluded that atomic physics, in entering its logical stage, not only broke away from its own ontological roots, but inaugurated a decisive break with ontological philosophy in general.

Consequently it became imperative to abandon the traditional attitude toward such concepts as 'nature,' 'reality,' 'objective world,' etc., and look for the features of physical description which confer on them a logical function. Aage Petersen's solution of the problem points toward a profound relationship between the philosophical problems of quantum physics and the problems discussed in connection with Gödel's Incompleteness Theorem.

In his analysis of the conditions for description, Peter Zinkernagel set forth definite rules of informal logic, stating certain general characteristics of ordinary language. He considered such rules indispensable for the description of empirical reality, whether given in scientific enquiry or in ordinary discourse.

This analysis was influenced by modern structural linguistics and by the so-called Oxford School analysis of ordinary language. Since Peter Zinkernagel has stated that his epistemological attitude is in accordance with the attitude expressed in the papers of Niels Bohr, one can venture to say that one of the pillars of his analysis is Bohr's contention, rooted in the correspondence principle, that classical mechanics is as indispensable for the description of physical experience as is ordinary language for the description of experimental apparatus and results.[4]

By reformulating the problem of objective reality and the problem of induction in terms of informal logic, Zinkernagel purported to deal a severe blow to scepticism.

A somewhat different line of investigation was pursued by J. Witt-Hansen, who attempted to clarify the relationships between the developmental aspects of

---

[3] Niels Bohr, "The Rutherford Memorial Lecture 1958," *Proceedings of the Physical Society* 78: 1083–115, especially p. 1092 (1961).

[4] Peter Zinkernagel, *Conditions for Description* (London: Routledge & Kegan Paul; New York: Humanities Press, 1962), p. 11; Bohr, *Atomic Theory and the Description of Nature*, pp. 8, 16.

the correspondence principle and Marxian dialectics. Whereas I. V. Kuznecov analyzed the correspondence principle from the standpoint of dialectical material-ism, J. Witt-Hansen's approach was just the opposite. Borne by the conviction that a serious study of Marxian dialectics must be based upon Marx's *Capital*, volumes 1–3, he set out, guided by the pattern furnished by Bohr's correspondence principle, to disclose the logical relationships among the social theories presented in *Capital*. According to this analysis the core of Marxian dialectics is essentially identical with the central idea of the correspondence principle, namely the idea of 'mathematical generalization.'[5]

This is not the place for a detailed exposition of the correspondence principle and its history or for a nuanced discussion of its different aspects and problems. It will suffice to state that the correspondence principle or the correspondence argument was introduced as the requirement of asymptotic coincidence of the predictions of quantum theory and classical electron theory. From the outset the correspondence argument was an analogical argument, emerging from the study of the formal analogy between classical theory and quantum theory. This analogy, which was already explicit in Bohr's theory of line spectra,[6] led him in 1918 to formulate the correspondence principle. This formulation involved the require-ment that a theory of the elementary quantum should emerge as a 'harmonious' or 'mathematical' generalization of classical mechanics.

This requirement was fulfilled by Heisenberg (1925), Born, and Jordan and, independently, by Dirac. They discovered that the quantum of action could be inserted into a formalism which had the character of a non-commutative algebra, in which Hamilton's classical equations of motion were preserved.

As Aage Petersen points out, the correspondence idea played a constructive role in more than the development of matrix mechanics. It had a central position in the subsequent discussion of the interpretation question as related to such concepts as 'nature,' 'reality,' and 'objective world.' In fact the chief aim of Bohr's work on the interpretation question was to show that quantum physics is "in every respect a generalization of the classical physical theories."[7]

However, Bohr concentrated more on the specific characteristic of the quantum generalization expressed in the idea of complementarity than on the very fact that the quantal description is a generalized mechanics, and con-sequently he made every effort to encompass complementary relationships within

---

[5] Johannes Witt-Hansen, *Historical Materialism: The Method, the Theories*, Book I: *The Method* (Copenhagen: Munksgaard; New York: Humanities Press, 1960), pp. 134–38; Witt-Hansen, *Generalisation og generalisationsproblemer i de matematiske og historiske videnskaber* [Generalization and problems of generalization in mathematical and historical sciences]. Københavns universitets festskrift i anledning af dets årsfest November 1963 (Copenhagen, 1963), pp. 104–11.

[6] Aage Petersen, "On the Genesis of the Correspondence Argument" (Paper delivered at the Annual Meeting of the History of Science Society, December 28, 1963).

[7] Aage Petersen, *Quantum Physics and the Philosophical Tradition* (New York: Belfer Graduate School of Science, Yeshiva University, 1968), p. 32; Bohr, *Atomic Theory and the Description of Nature*, p. 4.

the traditional philosophical framework rather than to see the core of the interpretation problem in the conflict between ontological philosophy and the idea of a generalized description of nature.

Aage Petersen's contribution to a philosophy of science, which he presented in *Quantum Physics and the Philosophical Tradition*, is permeated by the spirit of the Copenhagen School and bears the stamp of his thoroughgoing familiarity with Bohr's exoteric and esoteric philosophy, without being burdened by its dogmas or prejudices. His work gives evidence of unmistakable originality.

It is fair to say that he departed from a definite line of investigation pursued by Bohr because he realized that Bohr's efforts to establish a link between complementarity and the basic elements of traditional philosophy was a failure.

Since, consequently, the complementarity concept did not furnish the guide for the study of the relations between quantum physics and the idea of traditional metaphysics and epistemology, Aage Petersen looked for other characteristic elements of the theory more suitable for the purpose. An essential part of his philosophy is contained in the proposition that correspondence in a broad sense—and therefore a less specific characteristic of the quantal description than complementarity—is such an element.

This position was taken with the proviso that we do not adequately understand the description problem raised by a generalized mechanics[8] or the meaning of a generalized physical algorithm. On the other hand, this deficiency of our knowledge is properly outweighed by the fact that we have already mastered the problem raised by the conflict between ontology and the generalized conceptual schemes in number theory, algebra, and geometry.

It would seem that the applicability of the correspondence argument as an analytical tool and its epistemological significance is rooted in the fact that it rendered possible the establishment of a consistent mathematical formalism, containing the quantum of *action* as a characteristic element. Such a generalized scheme made ontological disquisitions concerning the indivisibility of the quantum superfluous or even misleading.

This situation contrasted strikingly with the deficient foundation of classical atomism whose basic idea, the indivisibility of *matter*, involved manifest logical contradictions, which ontological philosophy could not solve, and which still remain unsolved.

Since the logical difficulties of quantum physics turned out to be analogous to the logical problems solved by the construction of generalized conceptual schemes in mathematics, the character of the interpretation problem in quantum physics changed fundamentally.

Guided by the paradigms of mathematics, for instance the paradigm emerging from the Pythagorean discovery of incommensurable quantities,[9] Bohr

---

[8] Petersen, *Quantum Physics and the Philosophical Tradition*, p. 143; Petersen, "On the Genesis of the Correspondence Argument."

[9] Petersen, "Philosophy of Niels Bohr," p. 10.

abandoned the classical requirement of intuitive or pictorial understanding of physical phenomena in favor of the requirement of unambiguous conceptual communicability. To Bohr "objective" was synonymous with "unambiguous."

However, although Bohr, on the basis of analysis of Einstein's imaginary experiments, made the shift in physics from the ontological sphere to the sphere of conceptual frameworks and developed this viewpoint by the creation of the concept of quantum *phenomenon*,[10] he did not pursue in greater detail the line of investigation which he prescribed.

Assessing Bohr's dictum that the conceptual framework determines the possibilities of definition, Aage Petersen emphasized that this dictum would seem to apply not only to concepts like position and momentum but equally well to the concept of physical reality. "If the reality concept is fundamental, then presumably it refers to elements of the description that can be identified and interrelated.[11]

In his analysis of the meeting of quantum physics and ontological philosophy, this problem came into focus. In Bohr, the concept of reality did not play a prominent role, although he often stressed in discussions that "reality" is a word in our language and that this word is not different from other words in that we must learn to use it correctly.[12]

Taking the position that the various ontological formulations of the language-reality problem from Plato's idealism to modern materialism, in realism and empiricism, are misleading, Aage Petersen reached the conclusion, evidenced by the development of modern mathematics and physics, that the significance of the algorithm suggests that the language-reality problem has to do with subtle logical aspects of the frame itself. However, accepting the epistemological primacy of the conceptual framework in physical and philosophical disquisitions, he warned against an interpretation of this attitude in an idealistic sense—a warning not quite out of place, since Aage Petersen's standpoint should be understood as a rational evaluation of Bohr's famous aphorism: "Ultimately, we human beings depend on our words. We are hanging in language."[13]

Consequently, the core of the reality problem is quite different from what it was supposed to be in ontological philosophy. The point in question is not to identify 'being as such,' but to identify those features or characteristics of description which confer on the words "reality" and "nature" a logical function. According to Aage Petersen, the logical elements of the reality concept seem to be related to the elements of arbitrariness in physical description, i.e., to those elements of the description that are not fixed by the conceptual scheme but which must, at least at present, be specified without using an algorithm.

---

[10] Niels Bohr, "On the Notions of Causality and Complementarity," *Dialectica* 2: 312–19, especially p. 317 (1948).

[11] Petersen, *Quantum Physics and the Philosophical Tradition*, p. 172.

[12] *Ibid.*; Petersen, "Philosophy of Niels Bohr," p. 10.

[13] Petersen, *Quantum Physics and the Philosophical Tradition*, p. 188.

Viewed in the light of the development of physics and philosophy, it is not to be expected that these characteristics can be determined through analysis of common language, because the distinction between elements of arbitrariness and those elements of physical description that must be specified by using an algorithm was not made explicit until the emergence of classical mechanics.

Although this distinction is an elementary feature of mechanical description, "its epistemological significance has not been sufficiently stressed. It throws interesting light on the difficulties that the ontological viewpoint presents for the understanding of the role of the conceptual framework."[14]

Indeed, in mechanical philosophy it has typically been overlooked that a mechanical problem is well defined only when the *values* of various variables or parameters, including the initial position and velocity of the object, are specified, and that the conceptual frame contains no directives for such specification. It was overlooked that we must make a choice in order to specify a mechanical problem, and, in general, that the concept of choice in the sense of non-algorithmic decision, is not in conflict with the mechanical description, but rather an integral part of it.

In mechanical philosophy it was therefore too little understood that the arbitrariness of the mechanical parameters is as important, and perhaps more important, a feature of the mechanical description as the deterministic character of the equations of motion.[15] The fact that in classical physics choice of parameters and system behavior are mutually exclusive was therefore often apprehended as an intolerable paradox or even as the crux of philosophy.

However, like several other paradoxes or apparently unsolvable problems in mathematical sciences, this paradox was solved by the procedure of mathematical generalization. The obstacle to understanding its character was consequently removed by the emergence of generalized mechanics.

Since classical mechanics is not *the* mechanics but only a *special case* of a mechanical description, the relation between the arbitrary and the deterministic elements of physical description appeared in a new light, to the effect that a seemingly dominant feature of the description, namely its deterministic character, turned out to hold only under exceptional conditions. Conversely, in generalized mechanics the significance of the concept of arbitrariness has become more conspicuous as an element of mechanical description.

Hence, if it is assumed that the concepts of reality or nature are related to the concept of arbitrariness, quantum mechanics undoubtedly provides a more suitable basis for illuminating the logical function of these concepts than does classical mechanics, not to speak of the language in which ontological views are expressed: ordinary language.

In particular, the typical quantal aspects of the formalism gave clues to the question of why classical mechanics apparently could be ontologized while

---

[14] *Ibid.*, p. 149.
[15] *Ibid.*, p. 150.

quantum mechanics cannot. The failure of attempts to interpret quantum mechanics in ontological terms became manifest in questions like: Which onto logical status can one give an entity like an electron that appears to be an elementary particle of matter and yet is able to interfere with itself like a wave? What kind of jump is a quantum jump? Are the quantum probability waves subjective or objective, or do they perhaps possess an intermediate degree of reality? etc., etc.

Referring to Leibniz' famous ontological description of $\sqrt{-1}$, Aage Petersen suggests that "a quantum object like a photon appears indeed to be an amphibian between Being and non-Being."[16]

The assumption that the concept of reality or nature is related to the elements of arbitrariness in physical description is evidenced by the fact that the necessity of fixing these elements prior to the algorithmic generation of specific predictions requires conceptual reference to something 'outside' the algorithm. It might therefore be part of the logical function of the words "nature" or "experimenter" to contain such a reference.

Of course, the occurrence of free parameters in classical mechanics necessitates the performance of experiments or of asking nature questions. Although the questions are defined by the conceptual framework, the answers are not furnished by the frame.

However, in generalized mechanics the situation is somewhat different, for whereas the word "nature" in classical mechanics is needed only in connection with the specification of initial conditions and other free parameters like material constants, this word is connected in quantum mechanics with *additional* arbitrary elements, rooted in the fact that the quantal algorithm together with initial and boundary conditions specifies only the *probability* of each classical describable outcome.

Since, consequently, the range of arbitrariness is wider in the quantum domain, the word "nature" has here a wider applicability. "Part of its logical function is to express the fact that on the basis of the quantal algorithm the outcome is undecidable but that a decision is, nevertheless, made."[17]

As Aage Petersen points out, the new arbitrary elements in quantum physics have strongly emphasized the epistemological significance of non-algorithmic specification in the description of nature, and they point therefore toward a profound relationship between the problems raised by quantum physics and problems concerning the intrinsic limitations of deductive reasoning discussed in modern logic and metamathematics.

This relationship is not specified, but it may be connected with the surprising properties of elementary number theory expressed in Gödel's Incompleteness Theorem. For since in the arithmetic of natural numbers there are sentences

[16] *Ibid.*, p. 136.
[17] *Ibid.*, p. 189.

which cannot be specified algorithmically (or are not provable) although they are *true* interpreted as number theoretical statements, they refer obviously to something 'outside' the algorithm.

It would seem that Aage Petersen succeeded in indicating the logical function of the words "nature" or "reality" in the same way as Gödel and Tarski succeeded in determining the logical function of the words "true" and "false." An analogy is therefore suggested between the relationship of arbitrary and algorithmic elements in physical description and the relationship between elements of truth and provability, semantics and syntax, in logic and mathematics.

In both cases the analysis was performed, not as an ontological analysis, but as an analysis of conceptual frames.

Aage Petersen does not overlook the fact that a deeper insight into the epistemological significance of the undecided or free components of the algorithm is required and that it is likely to come from a more rigorous formulation of the situation in quantum physics.[18]

One of the crucial points in the discussion of the correspondence principle, and consequently of the foundations of quantum mechanics, concerns the role of classical concepts and 'plain language' in the quantum domain. It has been suggested that classical concepts might be superfluous in this domain or that they might at least be supplemented by new physical concepts that were less directly connected with the structure of classical theories and more adapted to the typical quantal parts of quantum mechanics. Bohr rejected such possibilities in a remarkably categorical way. Denying that we can dispense with our customary ideas or their direct verbal expressions when reducing our sense impressions to order, he said that "No more is it likely that the fundamental concepts of the classical theories will ever become superfluous for the description of physical experience." "It continues to be the application of the classical concepts alone that makes it possible to relate the symbolism of the quantum theory to the data of experience."[19]

Having discussed the problem of interaction between atomic objects and the measuring instruments necessary for the definition of the experimental arrangements, he gave a more nuanced illustration of the subject in the remark that "the aim of every physical experiment—to gain knowledge under reproducible and communicable conditions—leaves us no choice but to use everyday concepts, perhaps refined by the terminology of classical physics, not only in all accounts of the construction and manipulation of the measuring instruments but also in the description of the actual experimental results."[20]

The role of 'plain language' was stressed in a paper on "The Unity of Knowledge," where he said:

[18] *Ibid.*
[19] Bohr, *Atomic Theory and the Description of Nature*, p. 16.
[20] Niels Bohr, "Natural Philosophy and Human Cultures," *Nature* 143: 269 (1939).

Even when the phenomena transcend the scope of classical physical theories, the account of the experimental arrangement and the recording of observations must be given in plain language, suitably supplemented by technical physical terminology. This is a clear logical demand, since the very word "experiment" refers to a situation where we can tell others what we have done and what we have learned.[21]

In a comment on these remarks Aage Petersen observed that they are based on Bohr's general attitude toward the epistemological status of language and the meaning of unambiguous conceptual communication. Emphasizing that Bohr's remarks should be interpreted against that background, Aage Petersen pursued a line of investigation based on a clear-cut distinction between those elements of physical description that must be specified by using an algorithm and those elements that must be otherwise specified, namely, the elements of arbitrariness.

In the philosophy of language which Peter Zinkernagel set forth in *Conditions for Description*, such a distinction has no central place, perhaps because, after all, his line of thought is closer to the Oxford School of ordinary language analysis than to the thinking of Niels Bohr. Nevertheless, referring to Bohr's epistemological views in general,[22] and to his remarks concerning 'plain language' in *The Unity of Knowledge* in particular, Peter Zinkernagel attempted "to give a precise formulation of Bohr's demand, by pointing at such characteristics of everyday language as must at least be presupposed in descriptions of physical experiments."[23]

Since algorithms are characteristics of logical, mathematical, and physical theories, whereas they are no part of everyday or ordinary language, it is plain that the rules which Peter Zinkernagel derives from his analysis of the characteristics of everyday language must have conceptual reference to the elements of arbitrariness of physical description or to something 'outside' the algorithm.

Consequently his three 'rules of language' are rules of 'informal logic,' which impose definite restrictions on the use of words, for instance "thing," "action," "possibility of action," and "experience," which are required for the description of physical experiments and the outcome of such experiments. Since "it is simply necessary to face the fact that there are certain word-uses or concept relations which we can understand, and others which we cannot understand; that certain conceptual formations are qualified for description, others are not,"[24] it seems appropriate to look for definite general rules for formation of permissible conceptual relationships or for a sort of semantic rules of wide generality.

It is surprising to learn that Peter Zinkernagel has ventured to formulate such rules, which, at first sight, seem to be of unrivaled triviality. However, in Zinkernagel's view such triviality is comparable to that of the rules of formal logic, the law of contradiction in particular.

[21] Bohr, *Atomic Physics and Human Knowledge*, p. 72.
[22] Zinkernagel, *Conditions for Description*, p. 11.
[23] *Ibid.*, p. 120.
[24] *Ibid.*, p. 129.

"The law of contradiction is like a rule in a game, in so far as it states certain things that we may do, and others which are not allowed. It is different from such a rule in that we cannot modify it in the same way as we can modify the rules of a game." In other words, "we cannot alter or abolish the law of contradiction if we want to use language for unambiguous and well-defined description."[25]

The three rules of language are analogous to the laws of formal logic in both respects, for although there is no reason to regard them as definitive, they cannot be abolished or circumvented. They can only be modified or made less ambiguous.[26] On the other hand, non-observation or 'denial' of these rules will lead to absurd or unintelligible statements. Examples of such absurd or unintelligible statements are easily discovered in the doctrines of classical philosophy, for instance in Descartes, Berkeley, and Hume. The implication seems to be that classical philosophers put forward their unwarranted doctrines because they failed to observe definite simple rules of language.

The rules are: (1) We must not use names of ordinary things and expressions for possibilities of action independently of each other; (2) we must not use psychological expressions independently of the personal pronouns; (3) we must not use the personal pronouns independently of designations of bodies and, in consequence, of names of ordinary things.[27]

On the basis of this conception of language, Zinkernagel developed a non-traditional view of two classical problems, the problem of objective reality and the problem of induction.

In the first place, he does not make any attempt to 'prove' the existence of things independently of our consciousness of things. He simply insists that ordinary language implies such existence because we cannot use the word "see" at all without presupposing the objective existence of things.[28]

Whereas Berkeley "rightly points out that we cannot apply the verbs of perception except in connection with the personal pronouns. . . . , he. . . . still fails to see the significance of the fact that we cannot apply the personal pronouns unless we speak about our body by means of the language of ordinary things."[29] Obviously Berkeley violated the third rule of language.

David Hume was no better off, for since he used the words "impression" and "idea" without explaining that these words cannot be applied independently of the personal pronouns, the language of ordinary things, and designations of what we can do and what we cannot do, he violated the second and third rules. "Consequently his use of the words "ideas" and "impressions" was meaningless and unintelligible."[30]

Since Hume formulated the problem of induction in terms of impressions

[25] *Ibid.*, p. 31.
[26] *Ibid.*, pp. 154–55.
[27] *Ibid.*, p. 103.
[28] *Ibid.*, p. 173.
[29] *Ibid.*
[30] *Ibid.*, p. 231.

and ideas, the problem of induction thus formulated was unintelligible. However, even in its traditional form as a problem regarding the validity of empirical generalizations of the type: "All observed swans have been white; therefore all swans are white," the problem of induction was erroneously conceived. In Zinkernagel's view, it is a problem concerning the validity of classical physics in the future.[31]

The interesting consequence of such a position is "that there does not, and cannot, exist any problem of induction."[32] This is supposed to be obvious because the validity of classical physics is uncontestable. "If we understand that the use of classical physical concepts constitutes our only possibility of giving a precise description of fundamental physical experiences, we also understand the unconditional validity of this view."[33]

As remarked above, Bohr was remarkably insistent concerning the indispensability of classical physics for the description of the behavior of physical systems, but his arguments in favor of this position were different from those advanced by Peter Zinkernagel; and even such remarks as, "The language of Newton and Maxwell will remain the language of physicists for all time,"[34] were set forth with a certain proviso.

According to Peter Zinkernagel, "We can think of no situation in which we are able to describe physical reality correctly without applying classical physics. The sentence 'We describe physical reality correctly without applying, or presupposing the use of, classical physics,' is a simple contradiction, which, therefore, has no content."[35]

This is so because the fundamental concepts of classical physics, namely, 'momentum,' 'time,' 'mass,' 'force,' etc., are attached to each other by "implicit definitions,"[36] as are the fundamental concepts of Euclidean geometry. Consequently, we cannot use the physical concepts in question independently of each other. "If we want to apply one of the concepts of classical physics in accordance with classical physics, we shall have to apply all of them in accordance with classical physics."[37]

This applies to 'Hume's problem,' for apart from his use of psychological terms in the description of the behavior of physical systems, he tried to entertain doubts concerning the future while using the term 'future' independently of all other physical concepts. Hence his failure to see that there is no problem of induction.

The difficulty of assessing such a position concerning classical physics is due partly to the fact that the term "implicit definition" is used in a rather loose way. For although Zinkernagel in his emphasis on implicit definitions refers to

[31] *Ibid.*, p. 217.
[32] *Ibid.*
[33] *Ibid.*, p. 228.
[34] Niels Bohr, "Maxwell and Modern Theoretical Physics," *Nature* 128: 692 (1931).
[35] Zinkernagel, *Conditions for Description*, p. 229.
[36] *Ibid.*, pp. 218, 221.
[37] *Ibid.*, pp. 218–19.

"the fundamental concepts of geometry,"[38] his use of the term is not, as is the case in modern geometry (for instance in Hilbert's version) related to strictly *formal* systems and consequently to the question of *interpretation* of such terms as "point," "straight line," "between," "congruent with," etc. Its meaning therefore remains doubtful.

Another difficulty, related to the former, is connected with the conception that "classical physics must of necessity be regarded as a precise formulation of the language of ordinary things." This conception is based on the assumption that "the objects described in classical physics and those described in the language of ordinary things are the same,"[39] or on the assumption that (macroscopic) physical reality can be described in a twofold way: in classical physics and in "the language of ordinary things," i.e., in a precise and in a less precise way.

It was Zinkernagel's droll ambition "to write a book on epistemology in which everything, even the conclusions, was trivial,"[40] and therefore it is hardly possible to reproach him for not having considered definite non-trivial aspects of classical physics.

However, it is hard to believe that the relations between theoretical systems, like classical physics and natural languages, for instance English, are trivial. The subtlety of the relations is apparent in the fact that Zinkernagel's three rules of language have conceptual reference only to the elements of *arbitrariness* of physical description, namely, to the mechanical parameters or the *values* of mechanical variables. These can be determined only by asking nature questions, whereas the laws or equations of motion of classical physics have a *deterministic* character because they are the backbone of the algorithm of physics.

Since Zinkernagel's three rules of language refer to something 'outside' of the algorithm they have a logical status or function different from the laws of classical physics, even if the latter are called 'rules of language' or conditions for description.[41] Or, since the specification of the behavior of a physical system requires completion of the algorithm 'from without,' it would seem that ordinary language has a role in physical description essentially different from that of the algorithm.

As indicated above, the problem seems to be connected with a non-trivial aspect of the theory of natural numbers discovered by Gödel and presented in his Theorem of Incompleteness. In recognition of the far-reaching consequences of this theorem for the understanding of the respective roles of algorithms and facts in the process of cognition, Stafford Beer introduced a new principle, 'Completion from Without,'[42] for which he discovered or suggested a wide field of application in technology and management.

[38] *Ibid.*, p. 218.
[39] *Ibid.*, p. 224.
[40] *Ibid.*, p. 259.
[41] *Ibid.*, pp. 223–24.
[42] Stafford Beer, *Cybernetics and Management* (New York: John Wiley & Sons, 1964, 1st ed. 1959), p. 76.

It is that according to the Incompleteness Theorem of Gödel any control language is in an ultimate sense inadequate to its task, but that this deficiency can be remedied by the technique of inserting a black Box in the control circuitry. . . . I call it *Completion from Without*, because it expresses a practical method of protecting from the Incompleteness Theorem. The undecidable language is to be "keyed in" to the real life it seeks to describe by an inherently indefinable black Box.[43]

'Real life' is undoubtedly described in ordinary language.

The correspondence principle in a broad sense is a proposition according to which the laws of a definite (elementary or classical) theory appear as a special case of more general laws, discovered in attempts to submit a wider field of observational and experimental data to ordering. An asymptotic passing of the laws of the 'new' theory into the laws of the 'old' theory takes place when the value of a parameter, absent in the old but characterizing the new theory, approaches the limit where the laws of the old theory are sufficient.

The correspondence principle bears witness to the conception that theories in physics, and in geometry as well, do not change in a disorderly way, but develop according to rules similar to those governing the emergence of number systems. Although scientific concepts and laws in these fields change fundamentally under the pressure of paradoxes or new experimental data, every new stage of development of this process presupposes the preceding stage as an indispensable stepping-stone or model which furnishes the semantic rules for the new system or theory.

For the present, the theory of natural numbers, Euclidean geometry, and classical mechanics are, in their respective fields, such indispensable stepping-stones.

If it is understood that the central ideas of the correspondence principle are the idea of mathematical generalization (including the ideas of extension and restriction), the idea of balance between content and form of conceptual communication, and the idea of conceptual development by the discovery and solution of interesting paradoxes, it is no wonder that this argument has attracted the attention of dialectical materialists.

According to I. V. Kuznecov, the correspondence principle "can fairly be acknowledged as one of the most momentous achievements of physical-mathematical science of the 20th century." It has "furnished a most excellent confirmation of the dialectical-materialistic doctrine of absolute and relative truth."[44]

Nevertheless, dialectical materialism as presented in textbooks is hardly capable of illuminating Bohr's ideas. On the other hand, it is reasonable to assume that the correspondence idea might shed some light on dialectic, and relieve it of some of its aphorisms.

[43] *Ibid.*, p. 81.

[44] Kuznecov, *Princip sootvetstvija v sovremmenoj fizike i ego filosofskoje značenie*, pp. 9, 115; see also A. S. Arsen'ev, "O principe sootvetstvija v sovremmenoj fizike" [Concerning the principle of correspondence in contemporary physics], *Voprosy filosofii* 4: 88–97 (1958); S. V. Illarionov, "Princip ograničenii v fizike i ego svjaz' s principom sootvetstvija" [The principle of limitation in physics and its relation to the correspondence principle], *Voprosy filosofii* 3: 96–105 (1964).

On this assumption and by the study of the structure of *Capital*, volumes 1–3, J. Witt-Hansen discovered a striking analogy between the correspondence relation of 'old' and 'new' theories in physics and the relation between theoretical structures established according to the method of historical materialism. It is an oddity that dialectical materialists, interested in a possible connection between Bohr's correspondence idea and dialectic, did not choose Marx's *Capital* as an object of study and analysis, since *Capital* is the only place where such theoretical structures are presented.

However, in order to discover such connection it was necessary to abandon the current conception of historical materialism, according to which Marx established "a theory of historical materialism," which he specified in the famous "15 sentences" in the preface to *A Contribution to the Critique of Political Economy*.[45] In lieu of such conception and in conformity with Marx, the "15 sentences" were regarded as part of the method[46] of historical materialism or as "a guiding thread"[47] for the study of different social formations, which in fact are the subject matter of historical materialism.

As I. I. Kaufman wrote almost a hundred years ago: "The one thing which is of moment to Marx is to find the law of the [social] phenomena with whose investigation he is concerned," i.e., what Marx calls the "law of motion" of a definite social formation. Kaufman continues: "Not only of moment to him [Marx] is that law, which governs these [social] phenomena, in so far as they have a definite form and mutual connection within a given historical period. Of still greater moment to him is the law of their variation, of their development, i.e., of their transition from one form into another, from one series of connections into a different one," or from one social formation into another.[48]

Marx, who accepted this as a fair description of his dialectical method,[49] defined social formations in terms of relations of production. Since the criterion of recurrence is applicable to such relations, it is reasonable to look for laws governing definite social formations. Moreover, it becomes appropriate to investigate the possibility of discovering definite laws of transition from one social formation into another: the historical laws of development proper in Marx.

The methodological viewpoint underlying such a project was outlined in the introduction to *A Contribution to the Critique of Political Economy*, which was not published in Marx's lifetime.[50]

In *Capital*, volume 1, Marx gave a detailed description of the social formation of early capitalist commodity production. However, it is often overlooked

---

[45] Karl Marx and Friederich Engels, *Selected Works* (Moscow: Foreign Languages Publishing House, 1950), 1: 328–29.

[46] Karl Marx, *Capital* (New York: Charles Kerr & Company, 1906, 1st German ed. 1867), 1: 24.

[47] Marx and Engels, *Selected Works*, 1: 328.

[48] Marx, *Capital*, Preface to the second German edition (1873), 1: 22.

[49] Marx, *Capital*, 1: 24.

[50] Karl Marx/Friedrich Engels, *Werke* (Berlin: Dietz Verlag, 1969), 13: 615–42.

that the first volume of *Capital* also contains a succinct outline of the pre-capitalist social formation where simple commodity production is the dominant form of production. This outline is detailed enough to enable us to discern two theories in *Capital,* volume 1, one dealing with the pre-capitalist commodity-producing social formation, and the other with early capitalist society. The suggestion was made to call these theory I and theory II, respectively.[51]

It is noteworthy that theory I, describing the commodity-producing social formation historically preceding early capitalist society, is logically related to theory II in a way well known from the mathematical sciences. As it turns out, the key concepts of theory II (surplus value, capital) are the generalized key concepts of theory I (value, money).

The idea that 'real' historical development can be depicted in a series of conceptual systems or theories, each of which refers to a definite stage of development or to a definite social formation, is perhaps the central idea of *Capital.* Every 'new' stage emerging in history requires for its description 'new' concepts and laws which in their *statu nascendi* tend to conflict with the concepts and laws adequate for the preceding stage. This conflict is resolved and logical harmony re-established through such definitions and formulations of the 'new' concepts and laws as leaves the 'old' concepts and laws unimpeached in their own domain.

Under the influence of Hegel, Marx laid stress upon the *contradictions* encountered when a definite conceptual system, adequate for the description of a definite domain of social phenomena, is applied to a domain of greater complexity. He paid little attention to the analysis of the logical relations between 'old' and 'new' concepts and laws, however.

In an outline of the transition from the social formation of simple commodity production to the social formation of non-competitive capitalist commodity production, Marx points out that "the form which circulation takes when money becomes capital, is opposed to [*widerspricht*] all the laws we have hitherto investigated bearing on the nature of commodities, value and money, and even of circulation itself."[52]

Marx refers to two laws, often summarized as 'the law of value,' pertaining to theory I: one governing the sphere of production, and one governing the sphere of exchange or circulation of the social formation of simple commodity production. (1) The value of any commodity is determined by the amount of abstract identical labor expended on its production or by the labor-time socially necessary for its production; (2) the exchange-ratios are equal to the labor-time ratios, or the exchange of commodities is an exchange of equivalents, i.e., of equal quantities of abstract identical labor.

Whereas the first part of the law of value of theory I remains valid for the

[51] Witt-Hansen, *Historical Materialism. The Method, the Theories*, Book I: *The Method*, pp. 116–18, 137–38.

[52] Marx, *Capital*, 1: 173.

social formation of non-competitive capitalist commodity production, insofar as it can be maintained without contradiction, it is impossible without important modifications to apply the second part, governing the sphere of exchange or circulation, to the more complex social formation; for if it is acknowledged that surplus value or capital *exists,* or that the owner of money, i.e., the capitalist commodity-producer, "must buy his commodities at their value, must sell them at their value, and yet at the end of the process must withdraw more value from circulation than he put into it at the start,"[53] then the contention that an exchange of commodities is an exchange of equivalents is invalidated.

Faced with the contradiction that "Capital . . . must have its origin both in circulation and yet not in circulation"[54] Marx suggested that the concepts of commodity and value be generalized so as to comprise a 'thing' not produced as a commodity, but offered for sale on the market: labor power.

Since labor power has the property in common with usual commodities of being exchangeable with any commodity, and the additional property of being a source of value, the generalization can be accomplished and the contradiction resolved. In the sphere of exchange or circulation, labor power is bought and sold at its value as are usual commodities. Through the insertion of an act of production into the sphere of circulation, an act not provided for in the social formation of simple commodity production, labor power becomes the source of surplus value. Hence, if labor power is added to the stock of commodities, and the concepts of commodity and value are generalized accordingly, the existence of surplus value or capital is compatible with the contention that all commodities are exchanged at their value. In such modified form the second part of the law of value remains valid also for the social formation of non-competitive capitalist commodity production, and is consequently a law of theory II.

According to the view here advanced, three theories are presented in *Capital*: theory I deals with the social formation of simple commodity production and theory II with the social formation of non-competitive capitalism, whereas the subject matter of theory III is the social formation of competitive capitalism or the stage of development of capitalism where the so-called average profit emerges. Theory III is presented in *Capital*, volume 3.

An interesting contribution to the discussion of Marx's magnum opus was furnished by the Austrian economist Eugen von Böhm-Bawerk who, shortly after the publication of volume 3 of *Capital* (1894), pointed out in his treatise *Karl Marx and the Close of his System* that Marx's 'system' contained a contradiction which would ruin the whole structure.[55]

Marx's "theory demands that capitals of equal amount, but of dissimilar

[53] *Ibid.*, p. 185.
[54] *Ibid.*, p. 184.
[55] Paul M. Sweezy, ed., *Karl Marx and the Close of His System by Eugen von Böhm-Bawerk & Böhm-Bawerk's Criticism of Marx by Rudolf Hilferding* (New York: Augustus M. Kelley, 1949).

organic composition, should exhibit different profits. The real world, however, most plainly shows that it is governed by the law that capitals of equal amount, without regard to possible differences of organic composition, yield equal profits."[56]

Marx's own commentary is:

We have thus demonstrated that different lines of industry have different rates of profit, which correspond to differences in the organic composition of their capitals and within indicated limits, also to their different periods of turnover; given the same time of turnover, the law [as a general tendency] that profits are related to one another as the magnitudes of the capitals, and that, consequently, capitals of equal magnitude yield equal profits in equal periods, applies only to capitals of the same organic composition even with the same rate of surplus value. These statements hold good on the assumption which has been the basis of all our analyses so far, namely that the commodities are sold at their values. There is no doubt, on the other hand, that aside from unessential, incidental and mutually compensating distinctions, differences in the average rate of profit in the various branches of industry do not exist in reality, and could not exist without abolishing the entire system of capitalist production. It would seem, therefore, that here the theory of value is incompatible with the actual process, incompatible with the real phenomena of production, and that for this reason any attempt to understand these phenomena should be given up.[57]

At this point in the discussion Böhm-Bawerk asks the interesting question: "How does Marx himself try to solve this contradiction?" The answer is: "His solution is obtained at the cost of the assumption from which Marx has hitherto started, *that commodities exchange according to their values.* This assumption Marx now simply drops."[58]

However, this is hardly so, for although the second part of the law of value of theory II is admittedly inapplicable to the social formation of competitive capitalism, it remains unimpeached in the domain of theory II. Therefore Marx solved the contradiction not by dropping the law of value but through a further generalization of the concept of value.

Such generalization must be guided by the viewpoint that the exchange of commodities in competitive capitalism is also an exchange of equivalents, and the new law of exchange or circulation should therefore contain a reference to the 'new' phenomenon which in a specific way distinguishes competitive capitalism from non-competitive capitalism. The 'new' phenomenon in question is 'average profit' or rate of average profit.

The 'new' generalized concept of value which contains such reference is the concept of 'price of production.' As Kenneth May observes: "The 'price of production' is with Marx a form of value derivable from value, and like it distinct from price."[59]

56 *Ibid.*, p. 20.
57 Karl Marx, *Capital* (Moscow: Foreign Languages Publishing House, 1959), 3: 151.
58 Sweezy, *Karl Marx*, p. 21.
59 K. May, "Value and Price of Production: A Note on Winternitz' Solution," *Economic Journal* 58: 597–99 (1948).

In the competitive phase of capitalism, commodities are consequently sold, not at their values, but at their *prices of production*, or, the equivalents exchanged in the domain of theory II are values, in the domain of theory III prices of production.

Although Marx did not furnish a detailed analysis of the relationships of the key concepts of the three theories, he arrived at the insight that the rational core of dialectic is contained in the assumption that the *historical* development or the transition from one social formation into another is expressed in the *logical* connections between the conceptual systems adequate for the description of the respective domains.

Applying this viewpoint to the relationship between theory II and theory III, and their respective domains, he says that "The exchange of commodities at their values, or approximately at their values, thus requires a much lower stage than their exchange at their prices of production, which requires a definite level of capitalist development." Therefore "it is quite appropriate to regard the values of commodities as not only theoretically but also historically *prius* to the prices of production."[60]

Of course, the analogies among the relationships among theories in the fields of number, geometry, physics, and social science do not involve the content of these disciplines but only similarities in the logical relationships between definite theoretical structures. A further analysis of the concepts of generalization, extension, and restriction of concepts and theories might shed some new light on the problem of dialectic, so intimately connected with the problem of describing a process of historical development.

[60] Marx, *Capital*, 3: 174.